Service–Driven Approaches to Architecture and Enterprise Integration

Raja Ramanathan
Independent Researcher, USA

Kirtana Raja
Independent Researcher, USA

A volume in the Advances in Systems
Analysis, Software Engineering, and High
Performance Computing (ASASEHPC)
Book Series

Information Science
REFERENCE
An Imprint of IGI Global

Managing Director:	Lindsay Johnston
Editorial Director:	Joel Gamon
Production Manager:	Jennifer Yoder
Publishing Systems Analyst:	Adrienne Freeland
Development Editor:	Monica Speca
Assistant Acquisitions Editor:	Kayla Wolfe
Typesetter:	Alyson Zerbe
Cover Design:	Jason Mull

Published in the United States of America by
Information Science Reference (an imprint of IGI Global)
701 E. Chocolate Avenue
Hershey PA 17033
Tel: 717-533-8845
Fax: 717-533-8661
E-mail: cust@igi-global.com
Web site: http://www.igi-global.com

Library of Congress Cataloging-in-Publication Data

Service-driven approaches to architecture and enterprise integration / Raja Ramanathan and Kirtana Raja, editors.
    pages cm
 Includes bibliographical references and index.
 Summary: "This book addresses the issues of integrating assorted software applications and systems by using a service driven approach, highlighting the tools, techniques, and governance aspects to design and implement cost effective enterprise integration solutions"-- Provided by publisher.
  ISBN 978-1-4666-4193-8 (hardcover) -- ISBN 978-1-4666-4195-2 (print & perpetual access) -- ISBN 978-1-4666-4194-5 (ebook) 1. Service-oriented architecture (Computer science) 2. Enterprise application integration (Computer systems) I. Ramanathan, Raja, 1958- editor of compilation. II. Raja, Kirtana, 1987- editor of compilation.
  TK5105.5828.S455 2013
  004.6'54--dc23
                                    2013010170

This book is published in the IGI Global book series Advances in Systems Analysis, Software Engineering, and High Performance Computing (ASASEHPC) Book Series (ISSN: 2327-3453; eISSN: 2327-3461)

British Cataloguing in Publication Data
A Cataloguing in Publication record for this book is available from the British Library.

Advances in Systems Analysis, Software Engineering, and High Performance Computing (ASASEHPC) Book Series

Vijayan Sugumaran
Oakland University, USA

ISSN: 2327-3453
EISSN: 2327-3461

MISSION

The theory and practice of computing applications and distributed systems has emerged as one of the key areas of research driving innovations in business, engineering, and science. The fields of software engineering, systems analysis, and high performance computing offer a wide range of applications and solutions in solving computational problems for any modern organization.

The **Advances in Systems Analysis, Software Engineering, and High Performance Computing (ASASEHPC) Book Series** brings together research in the areas of distributed computing, systems and software engineering, high performance computing, and service science. This collection of publications is useful for academics, researchers, and practitioners seeking the latest practices and knowledge in this field.

COVERAGE

- Computer Graphics
- Computer Networking
- Computer System Analysis
- Distributed Cloud Computing
- Enterprise Information Systems
- Metadata and Semantic Web
- Parallel Architectures
- Performance Modeling
- Software Engineering
- Virtual Data Systems

IGI Global is currently accepting manuscripts for publication within this series. To submit a proposal for a volume in this series, please contact our Acquisition Editors at Acquisitions@igi-global.com or visit: http://www.igi-global.com/publish/.

Titles in this Series

For a list of additional titles in this series, please visit: www.igi-global.com

Service-Driven Approaches to Architecture and Enterprise Integration
Raja Ramanathan (Independent Researcher, USA) and Kirtana Raja (Independent Researcher, USA)
Information Science Reference • copyright 2013 • 367pp • H/C (ISBN: 9781466641938) • US $195.00 (our price)

Progressions and Innovations in Model-Driven Software Engineering
Vicente García Díaz (Universidad de Oviedo, Spain) Juan Manuel Cueva Lovelle (University of Oviedo, Spain) B. Cristina Pelayo García-Bustelo (University of Oviedo, Spain) and Oscar Sanjuan Martinez (University of Oviedo, Spain)
Engineering Science Reference • copyright 2013 • 352pp • H/C (ISBN: 9781466642171) • US $195.00 (our price)

Knowledge-Based Processes in Software Development
Saqib Saeed (Bahria University Islamabad, Pakistan) and Izzat Alsmadi (Yarmouk University, Jordan)
Information Science Reference • copyright 2013 • 318pp • H/C (ISBN: 9781466642294) • US $195.00 (our price)

Distributed Computing Innovations for Business, Engineering, and Science
Alfred Waising Loo (Lingnan University, Hong Kong)
Information Science Reference • copyright 2013 • 369pp • H/C (ISBN: 9781466625334) • US $195.00 (our price)

Data Intensive Distributed Computing Challenges and Solutions for Large-scale Information Management
Tevfik Kosar (University at Buffalo, USA)
Information Science Reference • copyright 2012 • 352pp • H/C (ISBN: 9781615209712) • US $180.00 (our price)

Achieving Real-Time in Distributed Computing From Grids to Clouds
Dimosthenis Kyriazis (National Technical University of Athens, Greece) Theodora Varvarigou (National Technical University of Athens, Greece) and Kleopatra G. Konstanteli (National Technical University of Athens, Greece)
Information Science Reference • copyright 2012 • 330pp • H/C (ISBN: 9781609608279) • US $195.00 (our price)

Principles and Applications of Distributed Event-Based Systems
Annika M. Hinze (University of Waikato, New Zealand) and Alejandro Buchmann (University of Waikato, New Zealand)
Information Science Reference • copyright 2010 • 538pp • H/C (ISBN: 9781605666976) • US $180.00 (our price)

Large-Scale Distributed Computing and Applications Models and Trends
Valentin Cristea (Politehnica University of Bucharest, Romania) Ciprian Dobre (Politehnica University of Bucharest, Romania) Corina Stratan (Politehnica University of Bucharest, Romania) Florin Pop (Politehnica University of Bucharest, Romania) and Alexandru Costan (Politehnica University of Bucharest, Romania)
Information Science Reference • copyright 2010 • 276pp • H/C (ISBN: 9781615207039) • US $180.00 (our price)

www.igi-global.com

701 E. Chocolate Ave., Hershey, PA 17033
Order online at www.igi-global.com or call 717-533-8845 x100
To place a standing order for titles released in this series, contact: cust@igi-global.com
Mon-Fri 8:00 am - 5:00 pm (est) or fax 24 hours a day 717-533-8661

This book is dedicated to my brilliant and loving wife, Sheela. To say that Sheela has "been there for me" is inadequate. She has been thoughtful, consistently supportive, and encouraging during almost three decades of marriage; and needless to say, inspired me to formulate the idea for this book, freed up time to help me write, patiently listened and offered valuable suggestions. Her sense of humor is the reason my daughters and I laugh so often. She also wanted to write this dedication herself!

I would also like to thank my sweet daughters Kirtana and Kanchana for their love and support, especially Kanchana, for understanding my inability to spend much time with her while I worked on this book project.

Table of Contents

Foreword xv

Preface xviii

Acknowledgment xxvi

Chapter 1
Service-Driven Approaches to Software Architecture: Principles and Methodology 1
    Raja Ramanathan, Independent Researcher, USA

Chapter 2
Enterprise Integration: Challenges and Solution Architecture 43
    Leo Shuster, Nationwide Insurance, USA

Chapter 3
Enterprise Integration: Architectural Approaches 67
    Venky Shankararaman, Singapore Management University, Singapore
    Alan Megargel, Singapore Management University, Singapore

Chapter 4
Mediating Message Heterogeneity in Service Compositions: A Design Model 85
    Prashant Doshi, University of Georgia, USA
    Nithya Vembu, University of Georgia, USA

Chapter 5
Improving the Quality and Cost-Effectiveness of Process-Oriented, Service-Driven Applications:
Techniques for Enriching Business Process Models 104
    Thomas Bauer, Neu-Ulm University of Applied Sciences, Germany
    Stephan Buchwald, T-Systems International GmbH, Germany
    Manfred Reichert, University of Ulm, Germany

Chapter 6
Maintaining Transactional Integrity in Long Running Workflow Services: A Policy-Driven
Framework 135
    Stephan Reiff-Marganiec, University of Leicester, UK
    Manar S. Ali, University of Leicester, UK

Chapter 7
Access Control in Service Compositions: Challenges and Solution Architecture............................ 165
    Aurélien Faravelon, Laboratoire d'Informatique de Grenoble, France
    Stéphanie Chollet, Laboratoire de Conception et d'Intégration des Systèmes, France

Chapter 8
Architectural Practices for Improving Fault Tolerance in a Service-Driven Environment 188
    Raja Ramanathan, Independent Researcher, USA

Chapter 9
Governing the Service-Driven Environment: Tools and Techniques 210
    Leo Shuster, Nationwide Insurance, USA

Chapter 10
Coordinating Enterprise Services and Data: A Framework and Maturity Model............................. 241
    Keith R. Worfolk, AvantLogix, USA

Chapter 11
Enabling Vendor Diversifiable Enterprise Integration: A Reference Architecture 275
    Lloyd Rebello, Independent Researcher, Canada

Chapter 12
Enterprise Mobile Service Architecture: Challenges and Approaches 295
    Longji Tang, FedEx, USA
    Wei-Tek Tsai, Arizona State University, USA & Tsinghua University, China
    Jing Dong, Hewlett-Packard, USA

Chapter 13
Extending Service-Driven Architectural Approaches to the Cloud 334
    Raja Ramanathan, Independent Researcher, USA

Compilation of References 360

About the Contributors 376

Index.. 380

Detailed Table of Contents

Foreword xv

Preface xviii

Acknowledgment xxvi

Chapter 1

Service-Driven Approaches to Software Architecture: Principles and Methodology 1
Raja Ramanathan, Independent Researcher, USA

Software Architecture has evolved from simple monolithic system designs to complex, multi-tiered, distributed, and componentized abstractions. Service-driven architectural approaches have been a major driver for enabling agile, cost-effective, flexible, and extensible software applications and integration solutions that support the business dynamics of today's fast-paced enterprises. SOA and the SCA model have been the typical Service-driven architectural approaches used in enterprises today, to tackle the challenges of developing and implementing agile and loosely coupled software and enterprise integration solutions. Recent trends involve the use of Web APIs and RESTful architecture in the enterprise for agile service development and application integration. The goal of this chapter is to explore, discuss, and recommend methodologies for Service-driven Computing in the enterprise. Service versioning is detailed as a primary architectural approach for accommodating modifications to services during their life cycle. Service Mediation, Enterprise Service Bus, and Composition mechanisms including Enterprise Mashups are explored. The chapter also presents the business value of APIs in the enterprise and investigates the value-add to Social Media and Cloud enterprise initiatives. The typical phases of a Service-driven development life cycle are explained and service design patterns to facilitate the engineering of flexible service-based applications are described. The chapter concludes with thoughts on future opportunities and challenges in the area of Service-driven computing.

Chapter 2

Enterprise Integration: Challenges and Solution Architecture 43
Leo Shuster, Nationwide Insurance, USA

The purpose of this chapter is to discuss the current state and associated challenges of Enterprise Integration (EI). The chapter will explore EI's past, present and future, examine its path towards the current practices, and contemplate its future evolution. Synergies between Service-driven and other modern architectural approaches will be investigated. Major challenges associated with EI strategy and execution will be explored in depth. This will include organizational, technology, process, methodology, and governance challenges. In addition to the current state concerns, future trends and directions will be investigated and specific challenges outlined. A major part of this chapter will be devoted to defining and discussing modern solution architectures associated with EI. This will include current architectural best practices, technology constructs employed, design patterns, governance mechanisms, and implementation considerations.

Chapter 3
Enterprise Integration: Architectural Approaches...67

Venky Shankararaman, Singapore Management University, Singapore
Alan Megargel, Singapore Management University, Singapore

Enterprise Integration enables the sharing of information and business processes among the various applications and data sources within and beyond an organization. Over the years, due to changes in business requirements and availability of sophisticated technology, the architectures for integrating applications and data sources have evolved from simple point-to-point integration technique to more comprehensive architectures leveraging Service Oriented Architecture (SOA) and Event Driven Architecture (EDA). In this chapter, the authors trace this evolution, and examine the architectures in terms of complexity versus business benefit. The architectures are presented in a logical progression starting with the simplest form.

Chapter 4
Mediating Message Heterogeneity in Service Compositions: A Design Model...................................85

Prashant Doshi, University of Georgia, USA
Nithya Vembu, University of Georgia, USA

Atomic Web Services (WS) may not always be sufficient for service requests. For such cases, several services may have to be assembled to create a new composite service of added functionality and value. Establishing message exchange between related but independently developed Web Services is a key challenge faced during WS composition which has hereto received inadequate attention. One of the challenges lies in resolving the differences in the schema of the messages that are input to and output from the Web Services involved. Data mediation is required to resolve these challenges. This chapter introduces a formal model for data mediation that considers the types and semantics of the message elements. Based on this model, it proposes methods for resolving different kinds of message-level heterogeneity. These methods are evaluated on synthetic and real-world pairs of Web Services, with the ultimate aim of integrating the data mediation techniques presented within WS composition tools.

Chapter 5
Improving the Quality and Cost-Effectiveness of Process-Oriented, Service-Driven Applications:
Techniques for Enriching Business Process Models 104

Thomas Bauer, Neu-Ulm University of Applied Sciences, Germany
Stephan Buchwald, T-Systems International GmbH, Germany
Manfred Reichert, University of Ulm, Germany

A key objective of any Service-driven architectural approach is to improve the alignment between business and information technology (IT). Business process management, service composition, and service orchestration, play major roles in achieving this goal. In particular, they allow for the process-aware integration of business actors, business data, and business services. To optimize business-IT alignment and to achieve high business value, the business processes implemented in process-aware information systems (PAISs) must be defined by domain experts, and not by members of the IT department. In current practice, however, the information relevant for process execution is usually not captured at the required level of detail in business process models. In turn, this requires costly interactions between

IT departments and domain experts during process implementation. To improve this situation, required execution information should be captured at a sufficient level of detail during business process design (front-loading). As another drawback, existing methods and tools for business process design do not consider available Service-oriented Architecture (SOA) artifacts such as technical service descriptions during process design (look-ahead). Both front-loading and look-ahead are not adequately supported by existing business process modeling tools. In particular, for many process aspects, appropriate techniques for specifying them at a sufficient level of detail during business process design are missing. This chapter presents techniques for enabling front-loading and look-ahead for selected process aspects and investigates how executable process models can be derived from business process models when enriched with additional information.

Chapter 6
Maintaining Transactional Integrity in Long Running Workflow Services: A Policy-Driven
Framework 135
    Stephan Reiff-Marganiec, University of Leicester, UK
    Manar S. Ali, University of Leicester, UK

This chapter presents a framework to provide autonomous handling of long running transactions based on dependencies which are derived from the workflow. Business Processes naturally involve long running activities and require transactional behaviour across them. This framework presents a solution for forward recovery from errors by automatic application of compensation to executing instances of workflows. The mechanism is based on propagation of failures through a recursive hierarchical structure of transaction components (nodes and execution paths). The authors discuss a transaction management system that is implemented as a reactive system controller, where system components change their states based on rules in response to triggering of events, such as activation, failure, force-fail, completion, or compensation events. One notable feature of the model is the distinction of vital and non-vital components, allowing the process designer to express the cruciality of activities in the workflow with respect to the business logic. Another novel feature is that in addition to dependencies arising from the structure of the workflow, the approach also permits the workflow designer to specify additional dependencies which will also be enforced. Thus, the authors introduce new techniques and architectures supporting enterprise integration solutions that cater to the dynamics of business needs. The approach is implemented through workflow actions executed by services and allows management of faults through a policy-driven framework.

Chapter 7
Access Control in Service Compositions: Challenges and Solution Architecture............................. 165
    Aurélien Faravelon, Laboratoire d'Informatique de Grenoble, France
    Stéphanie Chollet, Laboratoire de Conception et d'Intégration des Systèmes, France

Pervasive applications are entering the mainstream, but at the present time, exhibit significant security weaknesses. Service-driven architectural approaches facilitate the development of pervasive applications, however, security with respect to access control and data privacy of pervasive applications are currently not managed comprehensively from design time through run time. This chapter presents a use case emphasizing the security challenges for pervasive applications and proposes a novel, generative architectural approach, to include security in pervasive applications at design time. This is a model-driven approach based on models pertaining to access control management that respect the temporal constraints relating to pervasive applications. The approach is implemented with a design and runtime environment and the results of the validation applied to the pervasive use case are presented.

Chapter 8

Architectural Practices for Improving Fault Tolerance in a Service-Driven Environment 188
Raja Ramanathan, Independent Researcher, USA

Enterprises that implement Service-driven applications face challenges relating to unprecedented scale, high availability, and fault-tolerance. There is exponential growth with respect to request volume in Service-driven systems, requiring the ability to provide multipoint access to shared services and data while preserving a single system image. Maintaining fault-tolerance in business services is a significant challenge due to their compositional nature, which instills dependencies among the services in the composition. This causes the dependability of the business services to be based on the reliability of the individual services in the composition. This chapter explores the architectural approaches such as service redundancy and design diversity, scaling, clustering, distributed data caching, in-memory data grid, and asynchronous messaging, for improving the dependability of services. It also explores the data scaling bottleneck in data centralization paradigms and illustrates how that presents significant scalability and fault-tolerance challenges in service-driven environments. Prevalent strategies to handle failure recovery such as backward and forward recovery mechanisms as well as the built-in mechanisms in WS-BPEL for exception handling and transactional compensation are discussed.

Chapter 9

Governing the Service-Driven Environment: Tools and Techniques 210
Leo Shuster, Nationwide Insurance, USA

The purpose of this chapter is to discuss tools, technologies, and practices employed to govern the service lifecycle in a Service-driven environment. Aside from defining the complete service lifecycle, the discussion will concentrate on specific approaches to governing each stage in the lifecycle and best practices associated with it. SOA governance methodology will be covered in great detail. The topics discussed will include SOA Governance program structure, methodology, processes, funding, value demonstration, and adoption levers. These governance mechanisms will be aligned with each stage in the service lifecycle, and appropriate applications will be identified accordingly. Current and future state of governance tools and technologies will be explored. Some examples of existing tools will be provided to highlight and support the assertions made throughout the chapter. Connection between stages in the service lifecycle and the governance tools and technologies will be identified and best practices explored.

Chapter 10

Coordinating Enterprise Services and Data: A Framework and Maturity Model.............................. 241
Keith R. Worfolk, AvantLogix, USA

The critical inter-dependencies between Enterprise Services and Enterprise Data are often not given due consideration. With the advent of Cloud Computing, it is becoming increasingly important for organizations to understand the relationships between them, in order to formulate strategies to jointly manage and coordinate enterprise services and data to improve business value and reduce risk to the enterprise. Enterprise Services encompass Service-driven applications deployed on-premises in the enterprise data centers as well as in the Cloud for the "extended enterprise." Enterprise Data Management encompasses the cross-application enterprise-level perspective of data in an information-sharing enterprise, and the critical business data that is created, maintained, enriched, and shared outside the traditional enterprise firewall. This chapter discusses and proposes best practice strategies for coordinating the enterprise SOA & EDM approaches for mutual success. Primary coordination aspects discussed include: Service & Data Governance, Master Data Management, Service-driven & EDM Architecture Roadmaps, Service Portfolio Management, Enterprise Information Architecture, and the Enterprise Data Model. It recommends a facilitative Service-driven Data Architecture Framework & Capability Maturity Model to help enterprises evaluate and optimize overall effectiveness of their coordinated Service-driven & EDM strategies.

Chapter 11

Enabling Vendor Diversifiable Enterprise Integration: A Reference Architecture 275

Lloyd Rebello, Independent Researcher, Canada

Without effective architectural oversight, enterprises risk stifling their ability to innovate, because vendor products are too tightly woven into their key business processes, which impedes the evolution of their technology environment in support of business needs. Vendors gain negotiation leverage due to monopoly on the technology that supports key enterprise processes and capabilities. The goal of this chapter is to provide practical guidance on business flexibility advantages through carefully managed vendor diversification options for enterprises that are implementing Service-driven applications and integration solutions. The approach presented in this chapter recommends adherence to four basic principles, namely, owning the ability to control delivery channels and integration, compartmentalizing concepts into fulfillment roles in the Service-driven enterprise, using a vendor agnostic enterprise service interface, and owning the key data. The dual reinforcing concepts of ownership and control underpin the vendor diversification opportunities. A reference architecture is presented that distills these principles into a conceptual model that can be applied to any enterprise. A real world transportation and logistics business enterprise integration project is used as an example to illustrate the advantages of using vendor agnostic principles in a Service-driven environment.

Chapter 12

Enterprise Mobile Service Architecture: Challenges and Approaches 295

Longji Tang, FedEx, USA
Wei-Tek Tsai, Arizona State University, USA & Tsinghua University, China
Jing Dong, Hewlett-Packard, USA

Today, enterprise systems are integrated across wired and wireless networks. Enterprise Mobile Service Computing (EMSC) is a recent development style in distributed computing, and Enterprise Mobile Service Architecture (EMSA) is a new enterprise architectural style for mobile system integration. This chapter introduces the concepts of EMSC, discusses the opportunities, and addresses mobile constraints and challenges in EMSC. The mobile constraints include aspects relating to mobile hardware, software, networking, and mobility. Many issues such as availability, performance, and security are encountered due to these constraints. To address these challenges in EMSC, the chapter proposes seven architectural views: Enterprise Mobile Service, Enterprise Mobile Service Consumer, Enterprise Mobile Service Data, Enterprise Mobile Service Process, Enterprise Mobile Service Infrastructure, Enterprise Mobile Service Management, and Enterprise Mobile Service Quality. Each is described with principles, design constraints, and emerging technologies. In order to illustrate a practical implementation of EMSA, the chapter presents a major shipping and delivery services enterprise as a case study to describe the integration of Service-driven mobile systems in the enterprise.

Chapter 13

Extending Service-Driven Architectural Approaches to the Cloud 334

Raja Ramanathan, Independent Researcher, USA

Today, most enterprises own their IT infrastructures. In the future, it may well be more cost effective to use infrastructure and software provided by entities that are specialized in provisioning infrastructure and services on a need and usage basis. This is the Cloud Computing model. The Cloud enables ubiquitous, elastic, and on-demand network access, which can be rapidly self-provisioned. Information Technology is beginning to migrate to the Cloud, where dynamically scalable, virtualized resources, are provided as a service over the network. Currently, IT leaders focus on managing on-premises, centralized, and service-driven methodology, to deliver services and integration solutions for their businesses. In the future, they will be expected to deliver and manage a network of flexible services that are federated across on-premises and outsourced infrastructures. This chapter explores the capabilities and service models offered by the Cloud and the challenges of extending the Service-driven architectural approaches to that paradigm. It presents design principles and implementation guidelines to architect application services in the Cloud ecosystem. Finally, the chapter takes a look ahead at the future of Cloud Computing.

Compilation of References 360

About the Contributors 376

Index 380

Foreword

Service-Oriented Computing (SOC) is the computing paradigm that utilizes software services as fundamental elements for developing and deploying distributed software applications. Services are self-describing, platform-agnostic computational elements that support rapid, low-cost composition of distributed applications. They perform functions, which can be anything from simple requests to complicated business processes. Services allow organizations to expose their core competencies programmatically via a self-describing interface based on open standards over the network using standard languages (XML-based) and protocols.

A *Service System* is a system that depends on distributed control, cooperation, cascade effects, orchestration, and other emergent behaviors as primary compositional mechanisms to achieve its purpose. A service system's purpose, structure, and number of components are increasingly unbounded in their development, use, and evolution. Service systems support the development of Web-scale service-based applications that are characterised by unbounded numbers and combinations of software-intensive, geographically dispersed, and globally available services.

Service-driven Applications are qualitatively different from traditional large-scale applications. They are typically realized by creating alliances between service providers, each offering services to be used or syndicated within other external services. They usually comprise aggregations of services in the form of end-to-end processes that cross organizational boundaries and can deliver effective solutions to the daunting challenges of *Enterprise Integration*.

Service development is continuously in flux. The pace of development has accelerated greatly due to the advanced requirements of service systems and the increasing complexity of application architectures (e.g. heterogeneous, virtualized, and increasingly Cloud-based). The standardization of *Service-driven Architectural Approaches* in conjunction with the advent of Cloud technologies offers new possibilities for developing pervasive Service-driven applications due to their flexibility and on-demand nature.

As a result of the technological advances described above, we are gradually experiencing the rise of "smarter service systems," which become more versatile, flexible, mobile, dependable (i.e. continuously available, recoverable, and robust), energy-efficient, self-configurable, self-healing, and self-optimizing by adapting to changing operational contexts and environments.

As enterprises, governments, and non-profit organizations re-conceptualize their operations in terms of the Service-driven approaches and architectures, they will be well positioned for continuous efficiency improvements as well as capability expansions. The "double win" opportunity of both improved productivity and quality of service is for the first time feasible within this emerging computing paradigm.

Before software services can achieve their full potential and we can reap their benefits, the next generation of academia and professionals must master the fundamentals of Service-oriented Computing, and the technologies and Service-driven methodologies that underpin it. I am especially aware of the need to build this area on strong practical foundations. This book provides just such a foundation for software engineers, application developers, and enterprise architects.

The book covers an enormous wealth of important topics and technologies that mirror the evolution of software services. It provides an exhaustive overview of the challenges and solutions of major achievements pertaining to software services and architectures. Each chapter is an authoritative piece of work that synthesizes pertinent literature and highlights important accomplishments and advances in its subject matter. The content of this book is a testimonial of the leading role of its editors, authors, and reviewers and their highly influential work in the area of software services and architectures.

Chapter 1 overviews Service-driven architectural approaches which are a major driver for enabling agile, flexible, and extensible software applications and integration solutions that support today's complex, multi-faceted and fast paced enterprises. It also focuses on architectural practices for implementing enterprise APIs into the overall Service-driven strategy of the enterprise.

Chapter 2 explores Enterprise Integration and examines its transition towards the current software service practices, and contemplates its evolution. Chapter 3 overviews Enterprise Integration approaches and focuses in particular on evaluating service architectures (e.g. Service-oriented Architecture (SOA) and Event-driven Architecture) in terms of complexity versus business benefit.

Chapter 4 deals with the important subject of processes and service compositions and proposes methods for resolving different kinds of message-level heterogeneity. Chapter 5 presents a methodological approach that improves the quality and cost-effectiveness of process-oriented, service-based applications by suggesting techniques on how to enrich business process models. Chapter 6 presents a framework to provide autonomous handling of long running business process transactions based on dependencies derived from the workflow. This chapter presents a solution for forward recovery from errors by applying compensation techniques to workflow enactments.

On the topic of processes and service compositions, Chapter 7 presents a model-driven design-time approach for access control in applications that comprise composed services. Chapter 8 explores the architectural practices and approaches such as service redundancy and design diversity, scaling, clustering, distributed data caching, in-memory data grid, and asynchronous messaging, for improving the dependability of services.

Chapter 9 overviews the topic of SOA Governance, and discusses tools, technologies, and practices employed to govern the service lifecycle in a Service-driven environment. Chapter 10 surveys the critical interdependencies between enterprise services and enterprise data and proposes best practices and strategies for coordinating the enterprise SOA and Enterprise Data Management approaches for mutual benefit. Chapter 11 provides practical guidance on business flexibility advantages obtained by careful management of vendor diversification options for enterprises that are implementing service-based applications and integration solutions.

Chapter 12 presents the important topic of Enterprise Mobile Service Architecture (EMSA), discusses the opportunities, and addresses mobile constraints and challenges in EMSA, which include aspects relating to mobile hardware, software, networking and mobility. Finally, Chapter 13 explores the capabilities and service models offered by the Cloud and the challenges of extending the Service-driven approach to the Cloud paradigm. This chapter presents design principles and implementation guidelines to architect application services in a Cloud ecosystem.

It is pleasant to see that diverse and complex topics relating to software services and architectures are explained in an eloquent manner and include important references to help the interested reader find out more information about these interesting topics.

I commend the editors and the authors of this book on the breadth and depth of their work and for producing a well thought out and eminently readable book on such a complicated topic. All in all, this is an inspiring book and an invaluable source of knowledge for researchers and practitioners working on or wishing to know more about the exciting field of software services and enterprise architectures. It is well thought out and eminently readable!

Michael P. Papazoglou
European Research Institute in Service Science, The Netherlands

Michael P. Papazoglou *is a full Professor and the Director of the European Research Institute in Service Science and the Scientific Director of the European Network of Excellence in Software Services and Systems (S-Cube) at Tilburg University, The Netherlands. He also holds honorary professorial positions in Australia, France, Italy, Spain, and Cyprus. His research interests include Service Oriented Computing, Cloud Computing, business processes, and federated and distributed information systems. He is one of the most cited researchers and internationally recognized for his research contributions in Service-oriented Computing. He has published 22 books and well over 200 journal and conference papers.*

Preface

As a professional IT enterprise architect and SOA subject matter expert, I have provided enterprise architecture and development expertise and best practice recommendations to large enterprises in the oil and gas, energy and utilities, financial services, and software product development domains. In my experience, I have observed that most enterprises that venture into the Service-driven architectural methodology for designing and developing their enterprise solutions, do so in bits and pieces; without being guided by best practices in taking a comprehensive view of the service architecture within the overarching enterprise architecture framework, or without realizing the benefit of a structured governance approach right from the inception of the service development lifecycle. This results in the proliferation of "islands of services" that do not integrate with all mission critical applications in the enterprise; thus reducing the potential business benefit derived from implementing a Service-driven model and leading to vendor lock-in in strategic areas of the enterprise and an inflexible enterprise architecture.

There is a dearth of written material that clearly delineates the challenges and architectural best practices applicable to the Service-driven architectural practices for software architecture and enterprise integration. These challenges motivated me to write a book that can cater to a diverse audience of enterprise architects, integration architects, software engineers, technical managers, researchers, and developers, that captures the breadth of my experience and the experiences of brilliant researchers and practitioners from around the world.

The goal of this book is to explore and discuss the challenges of Service-driven architectural approaches that have been a major driver for enabling agile, cost-effective, flexible, and extensible software services and integration solutions; and present architectural approaches, implementation techniques, and best practice recommendations for designing and implementing effective architectural solutions that support the business dynamics of today's fast-paced enterprises.

The book first lays the groundwork by discussing the principles of Service-driven architectural practices and its application to software architecture and enterprise integration. Subsequently, architectural approaches to tackle the significant challenges of heterogeneous enterprise integration, autonomous mediation of services in a service composition, enrichment of business process models to enable cost-effective process design, policy-driven fault management in long-running business processes, comprehensive security architecture for pervasive service applications, improvement of service composite dependability, holistic governance of the service lifecycle, optimization of the coordination strategies of enterprise services and data, and avoidance of vendor lock-ins in enterprises, are presented. Finally, the book explores how Service-driven approaches can be effectively leveraged in the emerging areas of Mobile Computing and Cloud Computing to meet enterprise initiatives.

In Chapter 1, I have explored the principles of the Service-driven methodology for architecture of software components and services. A Service-driven approach typically uses Service-oriented Architecture (SOA) to design and implement enterprise applications and integration solutions; though more recently, RESTful Web APIs are driving easy to use, agile, and low cost techniques for Service-driven development in the enterprise. Service-driven architectural approaches enable the interaction and interoperability of services within and across enterprises. Well designed, standards-based, Service-driven approaches can provision a flexible infrastructure and processing environment for the enterprise and provide a robust and secure foundation for leveraging services for enterprise integration of data and business processes.

A common misconception is that, because services are defined through the interface and not the implementation, changes in the service implementation will not affect service consumers. This chapter attempts to clarify this misconception and presents a valid case for service versioning. This chapter also delves into Service Mediation which is an abstraction layer that decouples service consumers from service providers and incorporates protocol and message level transformations to enable connectivity between consumers and providers. The mediation layer can also handle cross cutting concerns such as authentication, encryption, and audit logging across all service requests, thereby relieving individual service providers from having to deal with these common concerns.

Enterprise business solutions are created by combining or composing individual fine-grained or coarse-grained application services into business services. Service Compositions can be implemented primarily using orchestration and choreography mechanisms. This chapter explores Service Composition in greater detail. Enterprises have to constantly modify and improve business processes to align with new business decisions, practices, and regulations which make business processes highly dynamic in nature. There is a widespread need for composition techniques that can transparently adapt to unforeseen changes and requirements in the business environment with minimal user intervention.

The Enterprise Service Bus (ESB) provides a Service-driven integration backbone with mediation and orchestration capability. This chapter provides an overview of the ESB. Furthermore, it also delineates Workflow services that can service-enable business processes to create a synergistic ecosystem.

Web Services implemented using APIs have been trending away from using SOAP messaging towards the faster and more direct REST architectural style. Enterprises have historically made use of proprietary APIs; however, in recent years, enterprises are utilizing more Web-based public APIs to enable functionality via the Internet. Mashups, which are novel applications created by aggregating API-specified functionality and data sources have impacted the way software is developed in the enterprise setting. RESTful Web APIs are also pertinent in the areas of Social Media and Cloud applications. This chapter explores the business value of APIs in the enterprise and investigates the value-add to Social Media and Cloud enterprise initiatives and delves into the architectural considerations in implementing Enterprise APIs and their incorporation into the overall Service-driven strategy of the enterprise.

In Chapter 2, Leo Shuster describes the challenges of enterprise integration. Spaghetti integration (or point-to-point integrations) presents one of the most typical integration problems in the enterprise. This chapter classifies integration challenges into organizational, technological, and process related challenges and attempts to provide practical best practice solutions. Various architectural approaches and design patterns have been created to address the integration challenges. They have evolved from simple, proprietary techniques to standards-based mechanisms. Today, Service-driven architectural approaches are the predominantly used integration methodology.

This chapter explores why many enterprise IT shops struggle to adequately integrate their systems. Integrations have to enable heterogeneous systems, processes, and platforms to be able to talk to each other and accommodate for continuously changing application interfaces and functionality. Enterprises that do not have well defined Service-driven integration approaches in place or address the integration requirement without a strategic plan to manage the integrations in the long term will face the issue of integration proliferation that leads to systems being dependent on each other and completely exposed to one another's internal changes. Change in one system results in cascading changes through multiple integrations and related systems causing an integration nightmare.

In Chapter 3, Venky Shankararaman and Alan Megargel explore the various architectural patterns for integrating enterprise applications, namely, hub-and-spoke messaging, SOA with ESB, SOA with ESB and BPM, and Event driven architectural styles. The integration patterns examined here vary in terms of complexity versus business benefit. With an ESB, services are developed once and then used by multiple consumers. The ROI (Return on Investment) on service development is quickly realized when two or more composite services reuse an existing service. Besides cost avoidance, another primary goal of an ESB solution is flexibility that enables changes to the services with little or no impact on service consumers. This is made possible by decoupling the front-end service consumers from the backend service providers through data abstraction.

Business processes can be optimized for reuse across an enterprise much like business services exposed via an ESB can be optimized for reuse. The benefit of reusable assets is amplified when BPM and ESB patterns are used together. While BPM and ESB patterns are effective and efficient in executing business processes, there is some limitation in the way processes can be started. They need to be initiated through events or human interaction. Event-driven Architecture is based on the concept that events drive business interactions. More recently, enterprises have become interested in proactively monitoring, analyzing, and acting upon business events in order to support decision making in real time. Event processing can help with detecting event patterns that satisfy constraints and enable enterprises to leverage current event streams in order to predict the future.

In Chapter 4, Prashant Doshi and Nithya Vembu describe establishment of message exchange between related but independently developed services as a key challenge faced during service composition. The challenge lies in resolving the differences in the message schema that are input to and output from the services involved. Data mediation is required to resolve these challenges. They introduce a model for autonomous data mediation that considers the types and semantics of the message elements. It has its roots in schema mapping techniques, but there has been a general scarcity in applying those techniques to the relatively new problem of mediating between services.

Standardized interfaces, platform transparency, and the Web-based loosely-coupled nature of services make their automated composition feasible. Considerable attention has been directed to the problem of automatically determining the flow of control in a service composition with the objective of satisfying the functional and non-functional objectives of the composition. Given that services are usually independently developed, their input and output message schemas are often heterogeneous with structural heterogeneity at the attribute-level, entity-level, and abstraction-level. This chapter introduces a mathematical model of the message-level mediation problem that captures the common types of heterogeneity in service messages and prescribes a translator function that defines the set of syntactic and semantic rules that govern the transformation of message schemas. Mediating message-level heterogeneity is a key step toward successful execution of service compositions.

In Chapter 5, Thomas Bauer, Stephan Buchwald, and Manfred Reichert introduce the concepts of front-loading and look-ahead to present two fundamental techniques for achieving the goal of capturing sufficient process details during the design phase itself. A key objective of Service-driven architectural approach is to improve the alignment between business and IT. Business process management (BPM), service composition through orchestration and choreography play major roles in achieving this goal. In particular, they enable process-aware integration of people, data, and services. Any Process-aware Information System (PAIS) should meet the needs of all stakeholders involved in the business processes it implements. To meet that requirement, the PAIS must capture all business process model aspects relevant for process automation in a sufficient level of detail during the design phase itself. Furthermore, existing service artifacts should be reused in this context if available. To optimize business-IT alignment and achieve high business value, the business processes implemented in PAIS must be defined by domain experts, and not by IT experts. However, in the current practice, many aspects required by process implementers are missing in the business process models or are only defined in a rather imprecise manner. Consequently, this results in significant delays during process implementation or in imprecise implementation of the business process model.

With contemporary business process modeling tools, front-loading and look-ahead can be realized to some degree for selected process aspects; however, existing process modeling tools do not provide an appropriate basis for business process implementation due to their restricted functionality as well as the incomplete and ambiguous specifications that they capture. This chapter presents appropriate techniques for enabling front-loading and look-ahead for selected process aspects and delves into how executable process models can be derived from business process models, if the latter are enriched with additional information.

In Chapter 6, Stephan Reiff-Marganiec and Manar Ali present a framework to provide autonomous handling of long running transactions based on dependencies which are derived from the workflow. Business processes involve long running activities and require transactional behavior across them. A significant requirement of Long Running Transactions (LRTs) is the preservation of the consistency of the systems being involved in the LRT. The database community has traditionally implemented transactional methodologies to ensure the integrity of data. It would seem appropriate to employ the same techniques to manage the integrity of long running business processes. However, there are a number of new challenges with respect to business processes that necessitates using new techniques. The two most significant challenges are the long running nature of business transactions and the delicate and complex nesting that naturally occurs. Database transactions usually complete within a matter of seconds and the most common solution for addressing the transactional integrity challenge in databases involves some form of resource locking. This is not possible with business transactions as these often span several days or weeks or even years.

This chapter presents a solution for forward recovery from errors by automatic application of compensation to executing instances of workflows. The mechanism is based on propagation of failures through a recursive hierarchical structure of transactional components. A notable feature of this model is the accountability of vital and non-vital components, allowing the process designer to express the cruciality of activities in the workflow with respect to the business logic. Another novel feature is that the approach also permits the workflow designer to specify additional dependencies which will also be enforced. The approach is implemented through workflow actions executed by services and allows management of faults through a policy-driven framework.

In Chapter 7, Aurélien Faravelon and Stéphanie Chollet outline the challenges in access control enforcement in service compositions. Service-driven architectural approaches are a major trend for developing pervasive applications. However, security with respect to access control and data privacy is not currently managed comprehensively from design time through run time. Dynamic service compositions are complex, especially when they have to enforce an access control policy defined at the application level. Challenges include the need to have policies that are easy to understand even for non-technical users who may be customizing the application security of these pervasive applications; and the need to have both fine-grained and contextual policies so that the privileges and contextual information of users can be managed at runtime and be able to support a highly heterogeneous and dynamic environment for application runtime. This chapter presents a generative approach to manage security in pervasive applications at design time using a model-driven architecture based on models pertaining to access control management that respect the temporal constraints of pervasive applications.

In Chapter 8, I explore the typical challenges faced by enterprises for implementing scalability and fault tolerance in a Service-driven environment and recommend architecture best practices to improve fault-tolerance for services. Service-driven environments are different from traditional user-centric application environments in terms of the magnitude of the rate of consumption requests generated. Consequently, the technologies that were capable of handling traditional user loads are unable to keep up with the increased load requirements associated with a service-driven environment. Service-driven approaches enable to distribute applications or services to multiple locations within an enterprise and off-premises. Enterprises implementing Service-driven solutions face challenges relating to unprecedented scale, high availability, and fault-tolerance. Service availability and fault-tolerance requires the elimination of all single points of failure within a given service and its dependents. Maintaining fault-tolerance in business services is a significant challenge due to their compositional nature, which instills dependencies among the services in the composition. This causes the dependability of the business services to be based on the reliability of the individual services in the composition.

This chapter delves into the architectural approaches, such as, service redundancy and design diversity, scaling, clustering, distributed data caching, in-memory data grid, and asynchronous messaging for improving the dependability of services. It also explores the data scaling bottleneck in data centralization paradigms and illustrates how that presents significant scalability and fault-tolerance challenges in Service-driven environments. Failure recovery such as backward and forward recovery mechanisms as well as exception handling and transactional compensation practices in business processes are also discussed.

In Chapter 9, Leo Shuster presents specific approaches to governing each stage in the lifecycle of a Service-driven environment and provides guidelines on best practices associated with them. A Service-driven approach manages the delivery and reuse of shared services. Since each service is managed independently, its evolution can be described as a well defined lifecycle. A service can pass through each of its lifecycle stages multiple times until it reaches retirement. The service versioning stage starts a new iteration of the entire lifecycle which results in a creation of a new service version. There may be multiple service versions running at the same time. Each of them can reach retirement at different times depending on company's policies and its ability to migrate consumers to the new version of the service. Different actors participate in different phases of the service lifecycle. These range from a service architect to a developer and support technician. While roles may be persistent across phases, their expected contributions and deliverables change from one phase to another.

Enterprise services are reused across organizational boundaries, while domain services are reused within a single organization, business unit, or functional domain. To pursue the enterprise goal of creating shared services and increasing their reuse requires effective governance of the Service-driven environment. Since services could be owned and consumed by various business units within an organization, all changes have to be carefully choreographed at the enterprise and business unit levels. SOA Governance tools help define, automate, and execute SOA governance processes. SOA governance is critical to the success of a Service-driven environment. Without its guidance, best efforts will quickly disintegrate in the face of political resistance, lack of cooperation, and unsustainable funding. This chapter delves into program, development, implementation, runtime, and change time governance methodologies, and explores funding models required for maintaining an effective SOA program in the enterprise. To be successful, the Service-driven initiative has to demonstrate value by collecting and communicating metrics to the stakeholders. The chapter attempts to provide guidelines on demonstrating value of the SOA program to enable increased adoption of the Service-driven approach. Current and future state of governance tools and technologies as well as service runtime management is also discussed.

In Chapter 10, Keith Worfolk describes how an organization's Service-driven and Enterprise Data Management (EDM) strategies can fall short of expectations and potential business value, if key aspects and interrelated components of each strategy are not taken into account in a coordinated manner. Strategies for Service-driven and EDM approaches have traditionally been treated as disparate programs and initiatives within organizations, both from a business requirements perspective as well as from an IT implementation perspective. However, there are critical overlapping and interdependent components, processes, and quality checkpoints of each strategy, for which coordination between them becomes necessary in order to ensure mutual success. Pursuing these initiatives as unrelated approaches and with disconnected objectives and measures of success, often risks the success of both strategies, and is likely to execute poorly and ultimately fail to deliver the expected business results.

This chapter delineates the Service-driven and EDM strategic coordination points, addressing their synergies, dependencies, and interrelated infrastructure and processes. This chapter also prescribes a facilitative Service-driven Data Architecture (SD/DA) framework and Capability Maturity Model (CMM) that can assist organizations in evaluating and optimizing the benefits of their coordinated strategies to improve the overall effectiveness and success of the Service-driven and EDM strategies for the enterprise.

In Chapter 11, Lloyd Rebello provides practical guidance on gaining business flexibility through carefully managed vendor diversification options to enterprises that are implementing Service-driven applications and integration solutions. Vendor dependencies that are not carefully managed can limit an organization's vendor diversification options that inhibit its business flexibility and put the organization at a negotiation disadvantage for contracts or system enhancements. When vendor products and solutions are tightly woven into key business processes of the enterprise, the organizations no longer have any leverage to negotiate with. The ideal solution starts with service orientation, and the application of a few key principles to maintain vendor boundaries in enterprise systems to build a highly flexible business solution platform. In order to enable flexible, vendor diversifiable enterprise integration, the organization should plan and govern the technology architecture and integration of vendor products in a thoughtful and deliberate manner.

The chapter delves into the dual reinforcing concepts of ownership and control that underpin the vendor diversification opportunities. By presenting a reference architecture that distills these principles into a conceptual model that can be applied to any enterprise, this chapter illustrates the advantages of using vendor diversifiable principles in a Service-driven environment.

In Chapter 12, Longji Tang, Wei-Tek Tsai, and Jing Dong introduce the concepts of Enterprise Mobile Service Computing (EMSC), discuss the opportunities, and address mobile constraints and challenges. Mobile computing is a distributed computing model that allows mobile devices and their applications to connect and interact with other mobile devices and applications in a wireless communication environment. The mobile computing model extends the traditional computing model which requires using stationary computing devices connected to the enterprise network through wires. Mobile devices are becoming the major interfaces for consuming services, such as, email, internet, entertainment, and social media. EMSC is a recent development in mobile computing, and Enterprise Mobile Service Architecture (EMSA) is a new enterprise architectural approach for mobile system integration in the enterprise.

Mobile devices utilize a broad variety of system and application software. Mobile constraints include aspects relating to mobile hardware, software, networking, and mobility. Many challenges, such as, availability, performance, and security are encountered due to these constraints. Furthermore, mobile operating system constraints greatly impact mobile application software design and the capacity for consuming enterprise mobile services. The ability of a mobile device to communicate with wired information systems and services, such as enterprise applications and services, and Cloud-based services is significant for mobile computing. The communication capabilities of mobile devices directly impact mobile application design. To address these challenges in EMSC, this chapter proposes an EMSA architectural style which provides design guidelines for enterprise mobile application integration.

In Chapter 13, I have focused on exploring the capabilities of the Cloud and the challenges of extending the Service-driven enterprise to the Cloud. Enterprises are constantly interested in improving business agility, growth, and profitability, while at the same time, reducing expenses, and implementing better management of risk and compliance. Today, most enterprises own their IT infrastructures. In the future, it may well be more cost effective to use infrastructure and software provided by entities that are specialized in provisioning infrastructure and services on a need and usage basis. By leveraging economies of scale, such providers will be able to supply the required processing power and software applications and platforms at a lower cost, than could be achieved by enterprises internally. This is the Cloud Computing model.

The Cloud enables ubiquitous, elastic, and on-demand network access, which can be rapidly self-provisioned. Information Technology is beginning to migrate to the Cloud, where dynamically scalable, virtualized resources are provided as a service over the Internet. Cloud Computing is making it possible for enterprises to access and create applications on virtual servers that scale dynamically to meet demand. Service-driven architectural approaches provide a foundation for moving to the Cloud. The Cloud can change the way enterprises think about data, collect data, and manage data. Cloud services are pervasive, thereby lending themselves to connecting across businesses, people, experiences and time. This encourages enterprises to combine data with context information and increase relevancy of the data. The Cloud also shifts the burden of application integration from users to the providers, thus enabling consumers to interact with one composite application rather than having to interact with each of the individual applications or services that comprise the workflow.

There are potentially significant business benefits to building applications in the Cloud. This chapter describes the Cloud ecosystem in terms of the business benefits, service model offerings, standards, deployment models, and challenges; and provides guidelines and best practices for architecting application services that leverage the capabilities of the Cloud. With Cloud Computing, businesses can reap the benefit of agility and cost-effectiveness of technology and enable IT to enhance alignment with the business.

While the Cloud will transform business capabilities and deliver a great deal of benefit to the enterprise, moving from a centralized on-premises IT architecture to a public infrastructure can present new risks to the enterprise. There are several challenges with Cloud Computing in terms of standardization, security, governance, and federation which need to be tackled effectively to make the Cloud a serious enterprise initiative. This chapter explores some of those risks and provides guidelines for mitigating them. Cloud will become essential to enterprises because of its capability to deal with rapid change in external markets. Adopting a service-driven architectural approach will enable IT leaders to address today's critical challenges, while at the same time provide for a solid foundation for the enterprise to adopt Cloud for tomorrow.

Service-driven architectural approaches have enabled the delivery of agile and easily maintainable applications and integration solutions to enterprises. With current research and practice focused on dynamic, autonomous, and context-aware service compositions and Mashups, and pervasiveness through the Cloud; Service-driven applications are expected to play a major role in the implementation of robust, adaptable, fault-tolerant, and dynamic enterprise applications that are closely aligned with the ever changing needs of the business.

Raja Ramanathan
Independent Researcher, USA

Acknowledgment

This reference book on "Service-Driven Approaches to Architecture and Enterprise Integration" has been a very interesting project for me, involving authors and experts from around the world. The success of this book project is due to the efforts of many people working together as a team.

I would like to thank my coeditor Kirtana Raja, for time spent brainstorming and her extensive help with editing, layout, proofreading, and finalizing the content for publication.

It has been tremendously insightful and a great pleasure to work with all my authors. I would like to acknowledge my deepest and most sincere appreciation for their cooperation, time, and effort. I strongly believe that the variety of topics they have contributed collectively present knowledge that is effective to a comprehensive study of Service-driven approaches. The authors were also very supportive of the review process and responded suitably.

I would like to thank each and every one of them as listed below (in alphabetical order): Manar Ali, Dr. Thomas Bauer, Dr. Stephan Buchwald, Dr. Stéphanie Chollet, Dr. Jing Dong, Dr. Prashant Doshi, Aurélien Faravelon, Alan Megargel, Lloyd Rebello, Dr. Manfred Reichert, Dr. Stephan Reiff-Marganiec, Dr. Venky Shankararaman, Leo Shuster, Dr. Longji Tang, Dr. Wei-Tek Tsai, Nithya Vembu, and Keith Worfolk.

As we all know, the editorial review process is fundamental to setting a standard for the academic value and integrity of publishing reference material. I am happy to note that my team of Editorial Advisory Board members and Editorial Review Board members provided extremely useful and detailed chapter reviews promptly. Their suggestions and recommendations have proved instrumental to revising and adapting the content in keeping with the theme of this book.

I would like to thank each and every one of them as listed below (in alphabetical order): Dr. Laura Bocchi, Dr. Christoph Bussler, Dr. Brian Cameron, Dr. Alfredo Capozucca, Dr. Hong-Mei Chen, Jeremy Deane, Dr. Prashant Doshi, John Falkl, Dr. Aditya Ghose, Dr. Rean Griffith, Rahul Gupta, Cregg Hardwick, Lothar Hinsche, Dr. Matjaz Juric, Dr. Pericles Loucopoulos, Dr. Flora Malamateniou, Dr. Chris Mattmann, Alan Megargel, Dr. Harry Perros, Dr. Manfred Reichert, Dr. Stephan Reiff-Marganiec, Dr. Marcello La Rosa, Dr. Michael Rosemann, Dr. Wilhelm Rossak, Dr. Marek Rychly, Dr. Venky Shankararaman, Dr. Amjad Umar, Dr. Jari Veijalainen, Dr. Francois Vernadat, Dr. Jianwu Wang, and Dr. Mathias Weske.

I feel very fortunate and deeply humbled by the elaborate and interesting foreword written by the distinguished Service Oriented Computing expert, Professor Michael Papazoglou.

Last but not least, I would like to thank the publisher IGI Global for giving me this fantastic opportunity. I am especially happy to thank Monica Speca, Jan Travers, and Kayla Wolfe of IGI Global for their kind, continuous, and prompt support.

Raja Ramanathan
Independent Researcher, USA

Chapter 1
Service–Driven Approaches to Software Architecture:
Principles and Methodology

Raja Ramanathan
Independent Researcher, USA

ABSTRACT

Software Architecture has evolved from simple monolithic system designs to complex, multi-tiered, distributed, and componentized abstractions. Service-driven architectural approaches have been a major driver for enabling agile, cost-effective, flexible, and extensible software applications and integration solutions that support the business dynamics of today's fast-paced enterprises. SOA and the SCA model have been the typical Service-driven architectural approaches used in enterprises today, to tackle the challenges of developing and implementing agile and loosely coupled software and enterprise integration solutions. Recent trends involve the use of Web APIs and RESTful architecture in the enterprise for agile service development and application integration. The goal of this chapter is to explore, discuss, and recommend methodologies for Service-driven Computing in the enterprise. Service versioning is detailed as a primary architectural approach for accommodating modifications to services during their life cycle. Service Mediation, Enterprise Service Bus, and Composition mechanisms including Enterprise Mashups are explored. The chapter also presents the business value of APIs in the enterprise and investigates the value-add to Social Media and Cloud enterprise initiatives. The typical phases of a Service-driven development life cycle are explained and service design patterns to facilitate the engineering of flexible service-based applications are described. The chapter concludes with thoughts on future opportunities and challenges in the area of Service-driven computing.

DOI: 10.4018/978-1-4666-4193-8.ch001

INTRODUCTION

Organizational agility and business process adaptability are key considerations for businesses looking to establish a competitive advantage in the marketplace. The ability of an organization to adapt itself very quickly to the changing needs of the business can make a positive impact on its growth and profitability.

Today's businesses are complex, multi-faceted entities that transcend geographical boundaries, utilize a multitude of diverse technology platforms and implementation techniques, and deal with enormous amounts of coordinated data to make effective business decisions. Isolated data in "Silos" are not acceptable anymore. Businesses are working towards seamless integration of data and processes within the enterprise and with their external business partners in order to build agile and adaptable business models.

Software Services are autonomous, platform-independent, computational entities. They implement business functions that can be dynamically assembled into distributable and interoperable business services (Alonso et al., 2004), and invoked to execute the use cases implemented by the business functions. They are exposed to clients (consumers of the service) as a formal interface that can be published and discovered.

Service Oriented Architecture (SOA) is the typical Service-driven architectural approach used in enterprises today to tackle the challenges of software development and enterprise integration, allowing application developers to overcome many distributed enterprise computing challenges (Georgakopoulos & Papazoglou, 2008). The promise of Service-oriented Computing is a world of cooperating services, where application components are assembled with little effort into a network of services that can be loosely coupled to create flexible and dynamic business processes and agile applications that may span organizations and computing platforms (Papazoglou, Traverso, Dust-

dar, & Leymann, 2008). REST (REpresentational State Transfer) (Fielding, 2000) is another popular architectural style that is gaining momentum in the realm of service architecture and focuses on development agility and simplicity.

A Service-driven approach primarily uses SOA and RESTful architectures to accomplish its goal of facilitating the development and implementation of enterprise applications and integration solutions that support the dynamics of the business. A well designed, standards-based, Service-driven methodology can provision a flexible infrastructure and processing environment for the enterprise and provide a robust and secure foundation for leveraging services for enterprise integration of data and business processes. Efficiencies in the design, implementation, and operation of service based systems will enable organizations to align their information technology with their agile business practices.

Services are generally built independently of the context in which they are used, thus enabling Loose Coupling between the service consumer and the service provider. Service providers can perform varied functions that range from simple queries to complex business processes that involve sophisticated message transformations, dynamic routing of messages to other services, orchestration (discussed later) among multiple application services, and choreography (discussed later) among multiple layers of service providers.

Web Services (Jini Service and UPnP Service are other examples of service technologies) are currently the most widely used technology for implementing Service-driven applications; and they provide the basis for the development of business processes and enterprise integration mechanisms, using components and services that are distributed across the network and accessible through standard interfaces and protocols. The idea is to promote a building blocks approach to developing business services with minimal effort by assembling application components into services that are loosely coupled to create dynamic business processes that span organizations and computing platforms of the enterprise.

Web APIs are Web-enabled APIs (Application Programming interfaces) (Kunze, 2009) that provide and expose an interface to the underlying functionality and data exposed by applications to enable application-to-application interaction over the network primarily using RESTful Web Services. Using Web APIs for enterprise application development and integration have shown to provide substantial cost savings and return on investment (Linthicum, 2010), because API-based approaches are often simpler to implement than traditional full-blown SOA service approaches. Web APIs utilize lightweight, Web-oriented architecture (WOA) concepts and protocols and enable end-user development to reduce the burdens of software creativity and testing.

Services enabled through Web APIs can be composed into Mashups (Hoyer et al., 2008) by combining the data and functionality from several services, resulting in a new application that provides novel functionality. Enterprise Mashups specifically enable data aggregation and service integration in the enterprise. For example, Yelp provides location-based information and reviews on restaurants, hotels, and shopping to end users. By utilizing the Google Maps API, Yelp can augment its functionality with destination mapping, to provide end users a better overall service – without having to spend time creating their own mapping functionality.

This chapter is focused on delineating Service-driven architectural approaches that utilizes "Software Services" and the properties and capabilities of those services, to build cost-effective, agile, and easily maintainable software applications and enterprise integration solutions. Service-driven approaches help to seamlessly integrate heterogeneous software systems within an enterprise and with external systems and facilitate alignment with the dynamic needs of the business.

The chapter starts out by briefly exploring the evolution of software architectures and comparing their characteristics. SOA and RESTful Web Services are defined and characterized. Anatomy of a Service Contract is discussed and Service Implementation methodology is examined. An overview of the mechanisms useful for designing and building modular, scalable, and reusable software components that can be aggregated using a building blocks approach is discussed. The Service Component Architecture (SCA) model (OASIS, 2011) is presented as a standard and portable methodology for SOA service component design and assembly. REST architecture is presented as a simpler and more agile architectural style for developing RESTful Services. The service versioning architectural approach for accommodating changes in the service contracts and service policies is highlighted. Key aspects of Service-driven Computing, including the mechanics of mediation and orchestration are covered.

Additionally, this chapter also covers an overview of RESTful Web APIs and their importance in a Service-driven environment in the enterprise. The business value of using Web APIs in the enterprise and its use in Social Media and Cloud Computing applications is discussed. Along the way, architectural practices for implementing API-driven service architecture are highlighted, such as, composition of Enterprise Mashup applications and non-functional aspects of Web API.

Finally, this chapter explores the typical Service-driven life cycle and presents popular service design patterns that facilitate effective design of service applications. The chapter concludes by examining future expectations and emerging trends in Service-driven computing, such as, semantically intelligent and dynamically self-configuring services, service federation, and data-centric Web APIs, among others.

BACKGROUND

Overview of Software Architectures

Software architecture has evolved from simple monolithic concepts to complex, multi-tiered, distributed, and componentized abstractions. In the last couple of decades, the most prevalent approaches to software design were client-server, web-based, component-based, object-oriented, message-driven, event-driven, service-oriented, and RESTful architectures.

A multi-tiered Client-Server architectural style partitions an application into stacked groups or layers based on application concerns or functionality and partitions the system into two applications; one on the client side that makes requests to the server, and the other on the server side that accepts and services those client requests.

An Object-Oriented Architecture (OOA) approach divides the responsibilities of an application or system into reusable and encapsulated objects, each containing the data and the behavior relevant to the object. In a similar manner, the Component-Based Architecture (CBA) focuses on decomposing an application into reusable and modular components that expose well defined interfaces.

Message and Event-driven approaches enable interacting applications to send and receive messages or events using one or more communication protocols, without needing to know specific details about each other.

Web-based architecture uses Web technologies such as HTTP, Web pages, and Servlets to enable invocation and servicing of application requests through the network.

A Service Oriented Architecture style enables applications to publish, discover, and invoke granular business services (services that fulfill a business functionality) using loosely coupled components, service contracts, messages, and events; and builds complex business services through orchestration of simpler application services that may be reusable.

A REST architectural style focuses on the Web resource as the key element of abstraction and emphasizes simplicity, scalability, and usability through the use of the standard HTTP model.

Architecture methodologies such as OOA and CBA do not support the primary elements of a Service-driven approach, namely services, service components, and service assembly. An "Object" is the primary entity in an OOA or a CBA, whereas a "Service" is the primary entity in a Service-driven methodology. While both OOA/CBA and Service-driven architectural approaches facilitate encapsulation, modularization, separation of concerns, reusability, composability, and flexibility, there are significant differences between the OOA/CBA and the Service-driven approaches.

Services and Objects are different in terms of data structure visibility. While Objects try to hide the structure of the data by encapsulating and privatizing them, services publicize the data structure. Service-driven architectural approaches permit any service anywhere to operate on the data, within the realm of the security constraints. It is important to note that object-orientation is based on the entities, namely, type, state, and identity. In other words, every object is of some type, carries relevant state information, and is identified by its instance and hierarchy. However, in service-orientation, only type is of significance.

In order to make Service-driven applications scalable and interchangeable, services don't maintain an identity or state. Each time a service is invoked, it starts out with a clean slate. Services and Objects are also different with regard to the verbosity of data. Services primarily use XML (eXtensible Markup Language) to exchange information, unlike Objects that exchange native data structures, thereby making service orientation less efficient due to the verbose nature of XML – trading-off some efficiency for better reusability, looser coupling, and agile extensibility.

Components and Services are also different along the lines of granularity, coupling, interface, and invocation. Components are generally built with finer granularity than Services. Components interact based on an interface and are tightly coupled with respect to the method of invocation of the component. On the other hand, SOA Service interactions are based on a *Service Contract* that de-couples the service operation from the communication protocol used to invoke the service.

They also differ fundamentally in the way they approach flexibility and reusability. Services are continuously improved in scope and performance and offered to more consumers without affecting the existing consumers. Service selection can happen dynamically based on a set of policies. Components do not allow for a similar reuse and dynamic behavior. Moreover, Components are generally built using object modeling techniques and therefore manifest the scalability and complexity issues associated with object-orientation in distributed and clustered environments and the extensibility issues across enterprise boundaries.

SOA uses SOAP (Simple Object Access Protocol) based Web Services, and in spite of the declining popularity of SOAP Services as compared to RESTful Services, it has a strong staying power due to its flexibility, standardization, service contract, and security capabilities, among other features. While SOA Services use the SOAP messaging protocol, Services exposed by Web APIs have been trending away from using SOAP towards the faster and more direct HTTP-based (Hypertext Transport Protocol) RESTful

messaging style (Benslimane et al., 2008). Today RESTful Web APIs are being utilized not only in the context of the Web, but also in important areas in the enterprise, such as in Social Media and Cloud applications.

On the one hand, RESTful Services use the standard HTTP transport protocol and HTTP methods (i.e. GET, POST, PUT, and DELETE, HEAD) and Resource URLs (Universal Resource Locators that contains the server information and the resource information). On the other hand, SOAP can use a generic transport protocol (i.e. HTTP, JMS Transport, etc) and is not restricted to HTTP and SOAP wraps the message data in an XML envelope. In RESTful Services, the data is usually formatted using JSON (Javascript Object Notation) or XML without an envelope, both standard formats for Web-based data.

Here is an example of a SOAP-based request for weather information – to retrieve Houston city weather from a Weather Service (Figure 1).

Comparing this SOAP request to a REST architectural style request for weather information as shown in Figure 2, it is clear that to acquire the same data, SOAP requests are more complicated to formulate and less readable than RESTful requests.

The inherent complexity of SOAP enables more variety in execution and flexibility of choice. While it can be more complicated to format SOAP as such, tools have been developed to automate

Figure 1. Weather SOAP request example

```
<SOAP-ENV:Envelope>
    xmlns:xsd="http://www.w3.org/2001/XMLSchema"
    xmlns:SOAP-ENV="http://schemas.xmlsoap.org/soap/envelope/
    xmlns:xsi="http://www.w3.org/2001/XMLSchema-instance">
    <SOAP-ENV:Body>
        <ns1:getCityWeather xmlns:ns1="Weather">
            <op1 xsi:type="xsd:string">Houston</op1>
        </ns1:getCityWeather>
    </SOAP-ENV:Body>

</SOAP-ENV:Envelope>
```

Figure 2. Weather RESTful request example

```
GET /restapp/weather/Houston HTTP/1.1
```

the code generation. While this automated code is not very elegant, it is able to provide the needed functionality.

The ability to provide enterprise integration through service contracts is a key benefit of SOA. This is accomplished through the publishing of functional and non-functional aspects of the service in a WSDL (Web Service Description Language) (W3C, 2001a; W3C, 2007a) file using an XML-based language to describe the Web Service. The service contract is the key to integration of heterogeneous applications and the enablement of autonomous service compositions. However, RESTful Services do not typically use service contracts and therefore is not ideal for enterprise integration of heterogeneous applications and for autonomous compositions.

In contrast, the key benefit of REST is its simplicity and ease of integration. REST boasts lightweight (Pautasso & Wilde, 2009) requests as compared to SOA. This is because SOA services typically use the SOAP protocol that requires an XML wrapper around each request and response, thus increasing the message size and complexity. REST messages are typically smaller in size and can be in the form of JSON or XML and do not need an XML wrapper envelope for messages.

A RESTful service call can be executed on a Web browser by using only standard HTTP methods; compared to SOAP, wherein RPC (Remote Procedure Call) is not well supported over browsers. Furthermore, the emphasis on utilizing HTTP model in REST means that there are benefits from the widespread HTTP support; for example, every HTTP stack has built-in behavior irrespective of the platform, leading to similar program logic that does not need to be programmed into the Web Services (e.g. a HTTP server return value

of 4xx indicates a client error; 5xx indicates a server error, etc).

In RESTful Web Services, the output from one service call can be fed as the input to another service request executed sequentially, by providing just a one-line URL; and thereby integrating the data between many Web Services easily. SOAP services do not use direct HTTP Web calls and therefore cannot be integrated as simplistically. The simplicity and ease of integration of RESTful Services enable agile data and front-end integration in the enterprise. Simple integration equals less time spent on mundane tasks and more time spent focusing on new development.

Service-driven design and development requires an inter-disciplinary approach that integrates the elements of CBA with SOA, REST, Business Process Management (BPM), and Event-driven architectures to enable building business services and coordinated processes that are flexible, agile, and facilitative of closer alignment with dynamic business models.

Service Characteristics

Services exhibit various characteristics that make them suitable for the architecture of Service-driven, distributed, and reusable software components and integration solutions. Let us examine the individual characteristics of services in more detail below.

Services are autonomous: Each service can be developed, deployed, maintained, and versioned independently. While Services are designed to be autonomous, the intent is not to isolate them. Individual services collaborate with other services through the mechanisms of orchestration and choreography to provide business solutions.

Services are loosely coupled: Each service is independent of the others and can be replaced or updated without breaking applications that use it, as long as the interface is compatible. Services should be designed in such a way that there is flexibility to evolve the interface without breaking the contracts with existing clients.

Services can be published, discovered, and invoked: Services can be addressed using an URL (an unique identifier of a Web resource). A service communicates with another service using interface driven messages and policies. Services can be published to a registry and discovered and invoked dynamically at runtime. The registry provides location transparency, thereby enabling the service location or deployment topology to change over time without affecting the way the service is invoked.

Services have the potential for reuse: Services have the potential to be reused across the enterprise. A Service can be designed in such a manner that the business logic that it encapsulates is independent of any particular business process or application, thus promoting its reuse.

Services exhibit statelessness: Services delegate state management to an external component to increase scalability. This delegation also reduces resource consumption by the service, enabling it to handle more requests.

Services share contract and schema: Contract defines the behavior of the service while Schema defines the structure and content of the messages. Services share contracts and schemas, not internal classes, when they communicate. This enables flexibility and interoperability of services.

Services abstract away the implementation: Services use standards-based interfaces to expose themselves and hide the implementation details. This enables services to be loosely coupled, leading to applications and integration solutions that are more easily maintainable.

Services are distributable: Services can be located anywhere on a network, locally or remotely, as long as the network supports the required communication protocols. Consumers address service providers through URL, enabling the locations and deployment topologies of service providers

to change or evolve over time with little impact upon the service consumer.

Services can be orchestrated and choreographed: Individual application services can be fine-grained or coarse-grained. Complex business services are composed of simpler services by combining individual application and business services in a process driven manner to service the consumer request. This mechanism is called *Orchestration.* Each invoked service may in-turn invoke other service providers, thereby leading to multiple layers of orchestrations, resulting in *Choreography.*

Services can be policy-driven: The contract and schema control the structural interface of a service. Policies can be used to control the semantic interface of services. Policies provide a set of configurable and interoperable semantics that govern the behavior of a service. This enables service level agreements and security requirements to be discovered and enforced at runtime.

Service Types

A service type is a broad classification used to indicate the type of service, based on the nature of the encapsulated logic, the reuse potential, and the relationship of the service to other services in the enterprise. Services can be classified as "task service," "entity service," and "utility service" (Erl, 2007).

- Task service is defined as a service that has a specific functional context and executes specific business process logic. A task service encapsulates the composition logic to orchestrate other services to complete its task.
- Entity service is associated with business entities such as purchase order, invoice, etc. and is generally implemented as a reusable service that is functional context agnostic.

- Utility service is also implemented as a reusable service that is functional context agnostic and encapsulates low level technology and platform specific functionality such as logging, notifications, and auditing, among others.

Service Portfolio

Service portfolio refers to the set of services created and maintained by an enterprise to solve specific business problems, and enhance the operational efficiency and flexibility of the business. Typically, a service portfolio is derived from a business service model that describes the business in terms of business services and business events. The service portfolio represents a categorized set of services from the business service model that is planned to be built or that has already been realized as service implementations. This is called the *top-down* approach to service identification. Service portfolio also includes those services that are identified by analyzing functionality within legacy systems that can be exposed as services. This is called the *bottom-up* approach to service identification.

Service-Driven Computing

Rapidly changing market conditions, competition, and regulatory compliance requirements faced by enterprises, demand an information technology infrastructure that is positioned to support constantly changing business models and requirements. Most enterprise applications were not designed to handle rapid adaptation to business changes, and this adds to another level of complexity in the IT landscape. Service-driven computing is based on the idea of composing new business services from existing application and business services through the mechanisms of Service Mediation and Service Composition. The Service-driven approach is programming language and operating system agnostic and uses standard architectural styles, languages, artifacts, and protocols.

SOA enables developers to quickly build complex applications and integration solutions by combining existing software assets with external components. Besides, legacy enterprise systems such as enterprise resource planning, customer information and relationship management systems, and supply chain management systems, can be enabled for service integration through adapters and exposed as services on the Enterprise Service Bus (ESB). This enables integration of previously isolated systems or "Silos" using a loosely coupled service mechanism instead of the traditional point-to-point integration methodology.

Traditional point-to-point integration requires the implementation of n times (n-1) (i.e. the product of n and n-1) integration points for bi-directional integration among "n" applications. Consider a large organization with 50 applications that need to be integrated with each other. This would require the development and implementation of 2450 custom point-to-point integrations – a large development and maintenance effort. On the contrary, by leveraging Service-driven architectural approaches to develop loosely coupled integration services that can mediate among consumers and providers, and by deploying them on an Enterprise Service Bus where the integration services can be shared among consumers and providers, one would need to develop and implement only "n" integration services, which are 50 implementations, versus 2450 for the point-to-point approach. A savings of 2400 implementations! It is easy to see the benefit of the Service-driven approach for enterprise integration.

Furthermore, the use of Web APIs in the enterprise to enable business efforts have provided mashups an incredible opportunity to impact the way software is developed in the enterprise. Enterprises have historically used proprietary APIs behind company firewalls. The private nature of what are considered Enterprise APIs stems from their purpose being different from consumer APIs, like Twitter API, Google Maps API, etc. Enterprise APIs traditionally handled mission critical data and services for the business that is a key to driving business value. What has changed in recent years is that enterprises are utilizing more Web-based public APIs (i.e. APIs that are made available to the general public for development of new applications) to enable functionality via the Internet. This is due to consumer demand; end users require that applications and data be available on multiple channels and devices, with near-continuous availability and speed.

RESTful Web APIs should not be thought of as simply service interfaces – these little pieces of code can carry dire business consequences and implications. Let us illustrate this with an example to show the dramatic role that RESTful APIs can play in the value of a business, namely, Mobile Banking (Vizard, 2012). Banking and payment services is a multi-billion dollar industry, with traditional financial institutions and non-traditional players (e.g. Google Wallet, Paypal, MineralTree, etc.) now competing fiercely for market share. These non-traditional players are able to compete because they offer financial services (in the form of API coding), which results in the creation of quick payment applications, and thereby payment services, at a fraction of the cost of traditional banking, resulting in thousands of dollars of savings for consumers and businesses.

APIs have made it possible for these non-traditional players to take the traditional functionality offered by banking institutions and combine that with their unique twist to offer payment services, such as Google and Paypal for consumer services and MineralTree for small and medium businesses. API-based services are generally more amenable to the Cloud, which makes them more easily accessible to consumers looking to use payment services without physical boundaries. The effect of these API services is a clear shift away from traditional banking services. This is more evident when one sees the trend of financial institutions also shifting to mobile services and Cloud Computing in an attempt to become relevant and regain market share. The use of APIs in mobile banking is just one example of how much business value APIs can bring to an enterprise.

Enterprises have seen increase in creativity and innovation by utilizing APIs in areas that they had prior to ignored, such as Social Media, Commerce, etc. Any enterprise can utilize APIs to create business opportunity. APIs can enable the enterprise to deliver more personalized services, drive customer growth, and through integration enable system flexibility. The Enterprise APIs of today are not proprietary, heavily-coded interfaces; instead, Enterprise APIs are typically RESTful Services and exhibit simplicity, standardization, Web exposure, multi-channel distribution capability, and reusability (Hinchcliffe, 2011). Enterprises can benefit by incorporating Enterprise APIs into the overall Service-driven strategy of the enterprise; and API-based Web Services, just like other Service-driven components, require an architectural approach and appropriate governance to ensure their quality.

Service-driven Computing uses services as building blocks to orchestrate and build complex applications from simpler ones, thus promoting the principle of reusable software components (Bell, 2008). It enables one to build complex business services from existing granular service components that can be managed together in a business process by the mechanisms of mediation, orchestration and choreography, without having to re-invent the wheel. After all, the goal of service-oriented architecture is to effectively align business with technology by empowering the Information Technology (IT) team to deliver applications that support and meet the dynamic needs of the business in an agile manner.

However, it is important to note that service invocations can be subject to network latency, network failure, and distributed system failures. Therefore, a significant amount of error detection, exception handling, and compensation logic must be associated with any service invocation. While services are built to last, service configurations are liable to change. Furthermore, security and trust models are likely to change with each system boundary crossing. Crossing system or enterprise boundaries is an expensive process, however, deployment of local objects designed to minimize such boundary crossings can make the system inflexible. A system that implements monolithic local objects may gain performance but duplicate a previously implemented functionality and create a system that is less agile and difficult to scale.

Service-driven computing will lead to increased intrinsic interoperability. Based on a vendor agnostic architecture model, Service-driven applications will enable an enterprise to evolve the infrastructure in alignment with business needs and provide the flexibility for vendor diversification in terms of platforms and products. Service-driven computing will help enterprises achieve increased ROI (return on investment) and lower TCO (total cost of ownership) due to increased agility and reusability inherent in the methodology. The following sections will delve into the SOA and RESTful architectural styles.

SOA SERVICE ARCHITECTURE

A SOA Service has two main components: the *Service Contract*, which is the interface that the service exposes to the outside world, and the *Service Implementation*, which is the program logic implemented in the service. A client (the Service Consumer) makes a request to a service (the Service Provider) in a manner that is consistent with the interface exposed by the service provider. The service implementation of the provider handles the execution of the program logic to service the consumer request and returns a service response to the consumer in accordance with the interface specified in the contract.

Figure 3 illustrates the components of a SOA Service, namely, the service contract, which represents the interface that the service exposes to the outside world, and the implementation, which is the program logic within the service. This is comparable to the front-office/back-office operations analogy in a business. While the front office works with the clients to facilitate their requirements, it is the back-office that actually implements and fulfills the needs of the clients.

Figure 3. Anatomy of a SOA service

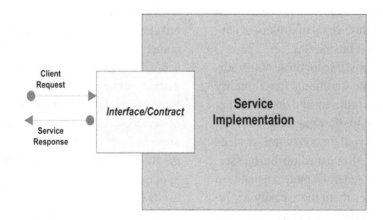

The Service Contract

SOA Services are defined by a standard interface which is in the form of a Web Service Description Language, a message structure which is in the form of an XML Schema Document (W3C, 2001b), and non-functional capabilities and requirements defined using WS-Policy (Web Service Policy) (W3C, 2007b). These XML standards are easily exchanged between systems and applications using standard protocols. The use of standardized interface and message structures enables systems to interoperate in a heterogeneous environment.

The WSDL (version 1.1) consists of a "port-Type" element that defines the operations supported by the service and the corresponding message structures for the input and output messages for each operation. The message types are defined by the "message" element in the WSDL. Figure 4 illustrates a WSDL 1.1 snippet that defines one operation named "list" that depends on input and output messages named "requestMessage" and "responseMessage" respectively. Note that the more recent WSDL 2.0 specification replaces the portType with an "interface" element and does not have separate message elements, messages are defined as part of the interface element.

The message structures are defined by the "message" elements that specify the parts of the

message. As shown in Figure 5, the input message, which is the input to the service provider, is of type "String" (inp1: String indicates that the XML namespace that the "String" type belongs to is "inp1"), and the output message, which is the output returned by the service provider, is of type "dirListMessage," which is detailed in the message structure in the message schema XSD file as shown in Figure 5. Each service can support multiple operations with each operation depending on different message structures.

A functional specification of a service contract consists of both the WSDL and the Message Schema. In addition to the functional items defined by these artifacts, the contract also includes non-functional items such as security requirements, transactional requirements, and Quality of Service (QoS) or Service Level Agreements (SLA), such as availability, scalability, reliability, and execution time, among others, as expected by the service consumers. These non-functional entities can be expressed in the form of policies. Any incompatible or non-backward compatible change in any of these policies can potentially affect the service contract and thereby affect the services that depend on the contract. These non-functional requirements are generally handled by attaching policies to services and service components or by configuration in the middleware (a platform that hosts

Figure 4. WSDL(1.1) snippet

```
<wsdl:message name="requestMessage">
    <wsdl:part name="request" element="inp1:String"/>
</wsdl:message>
<wsdl:message name="replyMessage">
    <wsdl:part name="reply" element="out1:dirListMessage"/>
</wsdl:message>
<wsdl:portType name="listfiles_ptt">
  <wsdl:operation name="list">
    <wsdl:input message="tns:requestMessage"/>
    <wsdl:output message="tns:replyMessage"/>
  </wsdl:operation>
</wsdl:portType>
```

Figure 5. XML message schema (XSD) snippet

```
<xsd:element name="dirListMessage">
    <xsd:complexType>
        <xsd:sequence>
            <xsd:element ref="hdr:Header" minOccurs="0"/>
            <xsd:element name="file" minOccurs="0" maxOccurs="unbounded">
                <xsd:complexType>
                    <xsd:sequence>
                        <xsd:element name="directory" type="xsd:string"/>
                        <xsd:element name="filename" type="xsd:string"/>
                        <xsd:element name="lastModifiedTime" type="xsd:string"/>
                        <xsd:element name="creationTimc" type="xsd:string"/>
                        <xsd:element name="size" type="xsd:string"/>
                    </xsd:sequence>
                </xsd:complexType>
            </xsd:element>
        </xsd:sequence>
    </xsd:complexType>
</xsd:element>
```

services and integration modules and serves to isolate the enterprise applications from the lower layers of the software infrastructure).

The WS-Policy is a specification published by W3C (World Wide Web Consortium) which provides a flexible and extensible grammar for expressing the capabilities and requirements of Web Services in the form of policies. A WS-Policy is a collection of policy assertions as shown in Figure 6. While a WSDL describes "how" and "where" a Web Service exchanges messages, the WS-Policy describes the capabilities and requirements of a Web Service, such as how a message

must be secured, whether and how a message must be delivered reliably, and whether a message must flow a transaction, etc.

Web Service Policy language is extensible, permitting child elements and attribute extensibility. WS-Policy also enables versioning by allowing service consumers to continue to use older policy alternatives in a backward compatible manner. This allows service providers to deploy new behaviors using additional policy assertions without breaking compatibility with consuming services that rely on older policy alternatives.

Figure 6. WS-policy snippet

```
<wsp:Policy>
    <sp:ProtectionToken>
    <wsp:Policy>
        <sp:KerberosV5APREQToken sp:IncludeToken=".../IncludeToken/Once" />
    </wsp:Policy>
    </sp:ProtectionToken>
    <sp:SignBeforeEncrypting />
    <sp:EncryptSignature />
</wsp:Policy>
```

Service Implementation

Service implementation concerns the actual business logic that is implemented in the service. This can be in the form of BPEL (Business Process Execution Language), Java, C++, C#, XSLT, etc. Implementation is also dependent on the technology used, such as, Java or.Net; what transport protocols are used to communicate, such as, HTTP (Hypertext Transport Protocol) or FTP (File Transport Protocol); what message protocols are used to package the message, such as, SOAP or JMS; what algorithms are used to compute the result; and what business processes are used in servicing the request. It is the goal of Service-driven methodologies to decouple the service interface from its implementation, such that changes in the implementation do not affect the interface. It is conceivable that the implementation of a service may evolve over time to provide for different levels of quality of service, different security implementations, etc., in addition to implementing more efficient algorithms and more elaborate business processes. From an architecture standpoint, it is significant to design service interfaces in such a way that the interface is able to provide a stable contract in the face of implementation dynamics.

Dependency on Implementation

It is generally believed that by leveraging the concept of "loose coupling" of services, Service-driven approaches enable one to insulate the service consumer from the implementation details of the provider. A common misconception is that, because services are defined through the interface and not by the implementation, changes in the service implementation will not affect service consumers. It is generally assumed that as long as the provider's service interface is unchanged, the provider implementation can change independently without affecting the consumer, thereby providing a high level of flexibility and extensibil-ity. This is true in some cases, depending on the type of implementation changes that are taking place in the service provider.

However, the above stated belief begins to blur when it is realized that service consumers actually depend on the service contract (and not just the interface), which consists of both functional and non-functional elements. It is the service contract that matters. As far as the functional aspect goes, that is controlled primarily by the interface. However, changes to non-functional elements such as QoS or security happen in the service implementation, and these can break a service contract that is relied upon by a consuming service. Let us take an example. Consider a service consumer "Consumer A" that has been using a secure service provider "Service A," that is access controlled through WS-Security (Web Service Security specification) (OASIS, 2004) username token. Let us say that at a later date, the implementers of "Service A" decide to enhance the security model of the service to provide for federated security through the use of SAML (Security Assertion Markup Language) (OASIS, 2005) tokens. In this case, there is no change to the service provider interface, just a change to the implementation of the service provider. After the new implementation of "Service A" is deployed, "Consumer A" will be unable to access "Service A" anymore.

This brings up a good point about the need for service versioning. Service versioning can prevent this classic problem of static interface with dynamic implementation changes affecting service consumers. Versioning is also very useful for dynamic interfaces with static or dynamic implementation changes.

Service Versioning

A major benefit of the Service-driven architectural style is its ability to efficiently deal with changes. Changes in business requirements can often be satisfied by either changing the existing business processes or by creating new business processes based on existing services. This approach enables the development of agile and maintainable systems through the process of assembly of service components using the concept of reusable services. Services can be shared by multiple business solutions, thus enabling parallel autonomous development of business services by disparate teams, each with its own delivery and maintenance schedules.

The concept of reusability enables any service to be used simultaneously in multiple enterprise solutions. Therefore, a change in one reusable service can produce a significant impact on several existing implementations and may require changes in all of them. This leads to high software maintenance costs, in addition to requiring a great deal of coordination between development teams. It also belies one of the key tenets of service-oriented architecture, which is that "services are autonomous." Autonomy is one of the main principles behind service orientation - services should be independently deployable and maintainable.

As seen in the previous section, adherence to the interface alone does not guarantee that the consuming service will be unaffected by certain types of implementation changes in the service provider. The service providers are not defined by the interface, but rather by the service contract, which depends not only on the functional aspects of the interface but also on the non-functional aspects such as pre- processing and post-processing conditions and SLA or QoS properties of the service on which the service consumer relies.

Consider a service that did not perform any validation of incoming parameters but was recently re-implemented to validate the input parameters. This is a pre-processing type situation that breaks the existing contract. Similarly, consider a provider service that was re-implemented to enhance the data analysis with more complex and accurate number crunching that caused its execution time to considerably increase from that of its former

implementation. An interactive consuming service that depended on this provider for a synchronous near real-time interaction in the past, would now find that the original contract has been broken. It is also important to note that different service consumers could be relying on different parts of the same service contract, and therefore service implementation changes should be validated against all existing service consumers to ensure that no contracts will be broken.

Service Versioning is the primary architectural approach that can be used to accommodate for changes in services during their life cycle. Versioning makes it possible for multiple implementations of the same service to coexist and allows for them to be individually addressable. There are options to consider when implementing versioning – should the entire service or just the individual operations that constitute the service be versioned? Versioning at the individual operation level enhances the flexibility for coarse-grained services.

When the change is limited to one or just a few operations in a service, the entire service does not have to be versioned off. This allows for specific operations of a service to be deprecated over time with newer implementations and minimizes the impact of the change to consumers. However, this approach of versioning individual operations of a service requires that each operation be deployed independently as a service. Versioning may also require the provision of a "façade" service (mediator) that implements a content based routing of the incoming messages to the appropriate version of the fine-grained or coarse-grained service that implements the correct version of the operation. The façade service will be the interface that is exposed to the service consumers.

As a general rule of thumb, any incompatible or non-backward compatible change in the service provider in terms of the interface or implementation will impact the service consumer and will therefore require the creation of a new version of the service provider. Irrespective of whether services are being versioned off at the "operation" level or at the "service" level, additional operations can be added to the façade service or the actual service without affecting existing consumers. However, removal or renaming of existing operations will cause the contract to break.

Similarly, backward-compatible changes in the message schema, such as adding optional elements to an existing data type in the schema or adding global elements or types, will not affect existing consumers. However, changing the attribute of an element from "optional" to "required," adding or removing an enumeration value, or deleting or renaming global data types will cause the message data structure to change in a non-backward compatible manner, and will cause the new service contract to be inconsistent with the existing contract. On the same lines, as discussed earlier, implementation changes that alter the QoS attributes and SLA requirements or introduce different pre- or post- processing conditions on the implementation will render the contract incompatible.

Scalable Service Versioning

In order to implement an easily scalable versioning mechanism for SOA service artifacts such as WSDL and Message Schema (XSD), it is recommended to use XML namespaces that contain the version number as part of the namespace for all non-backward compatible changes. These artifacts can then be organized into folders corresponding to the namespaces. A major and minor version numbering scheme can be adopted to facilitate maintenance of the files relating to the different versions. Minor version numbers (such as 1.1) can be used for backward compatible changes while major numbers (such as 2.0) can be used for non-backward compatible changes. An alternate way to make versioning scalable is by componentization of the artifact into logical partitions using multiple namespaces.

The SCA Model for Service Oriented Architecture

Service Component Architecture (SCA) is a set of specifications developed by the Technical Committee of OASIS (which is a non-profit, international consortium that creates interoperable industry specifications based on public standards such as XML), which specifies an extensible and portable model for architecture and assembly of SOA Service applications. The most recent update to the Service Component Architecture Assembly Model Specification version 1.1[1] was published on 31st May 2011. SCA extends and complements prior approaches for implementing services and builds on open standards such as Web services.

SCA is based on the idea that a business function is provided as a series of services, which are assembled to create solutions (Composites, as they are called) that serve a particular business need (OASIS, 2011). These Composites can contain both new services created as a result of a top-down design, as well as business functions from existing systems and applications, identified as part of a bottom-up design approach. SCA provides a flexible and extensible model for the creation and composition of services and service components and facilitates the building of reusable service components.

SCA defines an XML file format for its artifacts. These XML files define the portable representation of the SCA artifacts. SCA encompasses a wide range of technologies for service components and access methods which are used to connect the components. For components, there is support for different programming languages, frameworks, and environments commonly used with those languages. For example, SCA supports service implementations written using conventional object-oriented and procedural languages such as Java, PHP, C++, COBOL; XML-centric languages such as BPEL and XSLT; and also declarative languages such as SQL and XQuery. SCA supports a range of popular communication and service access mechanisms, such as Web services, Asynchronous and Synchronous Messaging, and Remote Procedure Call (RPC), among others.

The SCA Component

The basic building block in SCA is the Component, as illustrated in Figure 7. A component consists of a configured instance of an implementation. An implementation is the piece of program code providing business functions. Each business function is offered for use by other components as a Service. Implementations can depend on services provided by other components; these dependencies are called References. Implementations can have settable Properties, which are data values that influence the operation of the business function. The component configures the implementation by providing values for the properties and by wiring the references to Services provided by other components.

SCA Assembly Model

The SCA Assembly Model consists of a series of artifacts which define the configuration of Composites assembled from service components and the connections and the related artifacts which describe how they are linked together. The assembly model is independent of the implementation language.

SCA promotes the decoupling of service implementation and service assembly from the details of the infrastructure capabilities and access methods used to invoke services. SCA components operate at a business level and use a minimum of middleware APIs. Composites can contain components, services, references, property declarations, and the wiring that describes the connections between these elements. Composites can link components built from different implementation technologies, thus allowing appropriate technologies to be used for each business task.

The SCA Composite is illustrated in Figure 8. The components A and B implement the core logic, which can be implemented in any of the supported

Figure 7. SCA component (Adapted from OASIS Service Component Architecture Assembly Model Specification version 1.1, OASIS copyright 2011)

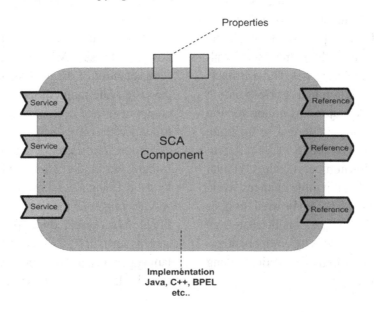

Figure 8. SCA composite (Adapted from OASIS Service Component Architecture Assembly Model Specification version 1.1, OASIS copyright 2011)

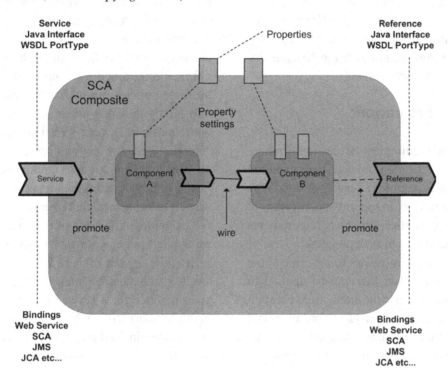

technologies, and are linked together through the wiring mechanism. Component A is exposed to the calling clients by promoting itself to a service with an appropriate access binding (Web Service, JMS, and JCA etc.). Similarly, component B links itself to an external service by promoting itself through the reference mechanism with a binding consistent with the external service.

Composites can be used as complete component implementations providing services, which in turn can be used as components within other composites, allowing for a hierarchical construction of business solutions, where high-level services are implemented internally by sets of lower-level services.

Composites are deployed within an SCA domain. An SCA domain typically represents a set of services, providing an area of business functionality that is controlled by a single organization. For example, for the accounts department in a business, the SCA Domain might cover all the financial functions, and it might include a set of composites dealing with specific areas of accounting, such as accounts receivable, accounts payable, general ledger etc.

Wires

The Wires provide more than a simple endpoint address; they provide a place to inject non-functional policy items into the system, such as security, auditing, and service-level agreements. These policy items are not part of the service providers or consumers, but properties of the wires that associate them in the model.

By decoupling the non-functional concerns from the core logic that provides or consumes services, it allows the developers to focus on the business logic without getting bogged down by security, auditing, and other concerns. Besides, policies dealing with security, auditing, or quality of service might concern other groups in the organization which might need to get involved in their specification and implementation. Furthermore, when policies change, the individual components that provide the core logic are not affected, thereby promoting reusability and increasing the maintainability of the software artifacts.

SCA Policy Framework

Non-functional requirements are an important aspect of service definition and need to be captured and expressed as part of the service design. SCA provides a framework to support specification of constraints, capabilities, and QoS requirements from component design to deployment.

SCA uses the term *policy* to describe some capability or constraint that can be applied to service components or to the interactions between services and references. Consider a non-functional requirement that mandates that all messages exchanged between a specific service consumer and a provider be encrypted to maintain message confidentiality. This requirement can be handled through the application of an encryption policy to this interaction.

In SCA, services and references can have *interaction policies* applied to them. These policies affect the runtime interaction between them. Service components can have *implementation policies* applied to them that affect how they behave within their runtime container. Provisioning of the policies depend on the runtime container for implementation policies and on the binding type for interaction policies. Some policies can be provided as inherent parts of the container or of the binding – for example, a binding using the "https" protocol will always provide encryption of the messages flowing between a reference and a service. A service that has interaction policies attached to it will require the references to honor them. In turn, each reference that has a set of policies attached to it defines how it will interact with any service to which it is wired.

SCA policies are held in policy sets that contain one or more policies expressed as WS-Policy assertions. Each policy set targets a specific binding type or a specific implementation type and is used to apply policies through configuration information attached to a component or composite. Multiple policies can be attached and organized into policy domains, where each domain deals with a particular aspect of the interaction, such as "message integrity" or "message confidentiality."

When multiple policies are applied to a particular policy domain, they represent alternative ways of meeting the requirements for that domain. For example, in the case of message integrity, if we applied policies for X509, SAML, and Kerberos, then any one of these tokens could be used to satisfy the message integrity requirement. It is good practice for a service provider to support multiple alternative policies within a particular policy domain so that it is accessible by a wide range of service consumers.

RESTFUL SERVICE ARCHITECTURE

A RESTful Service has two main components: the *Resource,* which is a conceptual mapping to a set of Web entities, and the *Service Implementation,* which is the program logic implemented in the service using a variety of technologies and programming languages. RESTful services do not need a service contract. However, WSDL 2.0 supports service contracts for RESTful services (Mandel, 2008).

Any information that can be named can be a resource such as a document, image, non-virtual objects (e.g. car), and collections of any of them. This abstract definition of a resource provides generality by encompassing many sources of information without artificially distinguishing them by type or implementation; and it also enables late binding of the reference to a representation (i.e. a sequence of bytes, plus metadata to describe those bytes; in other words the MIME type such as HTML, XML etc.), enabling content negotiation to take place based on characteristics of the request and removes the need to change existing links whenever the representation changes.

According to Fielding (2000), the REST architectural style is an abstraction of the architectural elements within a distributed hypermedia system (hypermedia is a logical extension of the term hypertext in which graphics, audio, video, plain text and hyperlinks intertwine to create a generally non-linear medium of information). REST ignores the details of component implementation and protocol syntax in order to focus on the roles of components, the constraints upon their interaction with other components, and their interpretation of significant data elements.

Unlike the traditional distributed object style (Chin & Chanson, 1991), where all data is encapsulated within and hidden by the processing components, the nature and state of the data elements is a key aspect of REST. The rationale for this design can be seen in the nature of distributed hypermedia. When a link is selected on a Web page, information needs to be moved from the location where it is stored to the location where it will be used, in most cases, by a human reader (Fielding, 2000). This is unlike many other distributed processing paradigms (Andrews, 1991; Fuggetta, Picco, & Vigna, 1998) where it is possible and usually more efficient, to move the "processing agent" (e.g., mobile code, stored procedure, search expression, etc.) to the data, rather than move the data to the processor; in other words, REST uses a pull based interaction style where consuming components pull representations of resources.

REST focuses on a shared understanding of data types with metadata, but limits the scope of what is revealed to a standardized interface. REST components communicate by transferring a *representation* of a resource in a format matching one of an evolving set of standard data types, selected dynamically based on the capabilities or desires of the recipient and the nature of the resource.

Whether the representation is in the same format as the raw source, or is derived from the source remains hidden behind the interface. The benefits of the mobile object style are approximated by sending a representation that consists of instructions in the standard data format of an encapsulated rendering engine. REST therefore gains the separation of concerns of the client-server style without the server scalability problem; and allows information hiding through a generic interface to enable encapsulation and evolution of services, and provides for a diverse set of functionality through downloadable feature-engines (Fielding, 2000).

REST components perform actions on a resource by using a representation to capture the state of that resource and then transferring that representation between components. All REST interactions are *stateless* where each request contains all of the necessary information, independent of any requests that may have preceded it. Every resource that is identifiable on the Web should have an identifier which is the URI. URIs form a global namespace that enables identifying the key resources by means of a global identifier. Service consumers typically send JSON or XML based service request calls to a resource (e.g. Web API exposed as a Web Service) and receives JSON or XML service responses back.

A RESTful Service URL has the following general form:

REST_METHOD http(or https)://www.website.com/resource/id

where

- REST_METHOD refers to the standard HTTP verbs described below.
- "http" or "https" refers to the transport protocol.
- "www.website.com" refers to the Internet address of the Web site.
- "resource" refers to the Web resource that is being addressed.

- "id" refers to the specific instance of the resource; this part could be several levels deep and refer to linked resources (e.g. cust_id/orders/order_id).

The following describes the standard interface utilized in REST, mirroring the HTTP verbs:

- **GET:** Retrieve the representation of a resource.
- **PUT:** Modify an existing resource or Create a new resource if it does not exist.
- **POST:** Create a new instance of a resource.
- **DELETE:** Delete the existing resource.
- **HEAD:** Obtain meta information about a resource.

An example Web API that provides services for managing "customers" and "orders" is described in the table below. Assume that "customers" and "orders" are provisioned as Web resources and "id" and "oid" indicated in the table refer to specific instances of the Web resources, respectively. In the RESTful methodology, only the methods supported by the generic HTTP interface operations are available to use unlike SOA Services where any number of operations can be constructed for a service. When exposing an application's func-

tionality in a RESTful way, one needs to adhere to the REST principles and restrictions. In order to argue that most of the typical business application logic can be exposed with a handful of RESTful operations, consider the example in Table 1 below which indicates the functionality that is exposed by an API and the corresponding RESTful service URI to invoke that API functionality.

RESTful URIs are logical entities that do not point to a corresponding unique physical resource. For example, */customers/id*, representing logical resources for different customers identified by the id, does not point to separate physical resources; instead, all of these logical resources point to only one physical resource which is the underlying "customers" resource that is exposed as a Web Service, which parses the logical resource URI and performs the requested operation to return the result to the consuming service in a negotiated or acceptable form.

On the one hand, there is significant business value to be gained from utilizing RESTful APIs in the enterprise; on the other hand, there are many technical considerations to incorporating APIs into an overall enterprise service architecture. While the biggest benefit to implementing APIs is simplicity, the biggest consideration is maintaining enterprise class security.

Table 1. Example of RESTful URI

API Functionality	RESTful URI
Get all customer details	GET /customers
Add a new customer	POST /customers
Get the details of a specific customer (referenced by id)	GET /customers/id
Update a specific customer	PUT /customers/id
Delete a specific customer	DELETE /customers/id
Get orders placed by a specific customer	GET /customers/id/orders
Get order details placed by a specific customer for a specific order (referenced by oid)	GET /customers/id/orders/oid
Update specific order for a customer	PUT /customers/id/orders/oid
Add a new order for a customer	POST /customers/id/orders
Remove specific order for a customer	DELETE /customers/id/orders/oid

Security

Security is a critical aspect for enterprises that should be built into the API architecture from the very beginning. Enterprise REST API endeavors should carefully evaluate whether the system meets the criteria for enterprise-class security measures (Woods et al., 2012); specifically authentication, data protection, and perimeter defense.

API Authentication allows one to validate whether the service request is from a legitimate source. The most dominant API authentication model is OAuth, and it is frequently used where large numbers of users are trying to access an API. OAuth works by creating a temporary token (i.e. valet key) utilized only during the period when the applications are communicating with each other. The primary lure of OAuth in the current API market is that it is simple to use, lightweight, and the current open standard.

Data protection is another important issue for Enterprise APIs, since these APIs may be transmitting enterprise data beyond the corporate firewall. Furthermore, in the case of Cloud storage, the enterprise cannot be certain where the data will be physically stored. SSL (secure sockets layer - https), which uses public key cryptography to encrypt/decrypt the request payload is the most common technology used for on-the-wire data encryption in RESTful Services; helping to ensure that data is protected after it leaves the enterprise boundary until it reaches any external service or storage.

Finally, perimeter defense is also an important component of enterprise-level security. Improper integration of various vendor APIs can cause gaps in the overall security of the enterprise, leading to a weakened perimeter every time data moves across the boundary of the enterprise firewall. Edge security (i.e. security of the connected systems) needs to become a part of the security policy to ensure that any such risks can be quickly detected and then resolved with appropriate measures.

The good part about API and security mechanisms is that it is an area that has lately received significant attention. The challenge lies in implementing and maintaining security protocols. API management tools can be used to create and manage security policies. Good API design patterns, such as API Gateway can provide better visibility and control over the API traffic, thereby enabling better enterprise security.

Service Granularity

Services can be defined from its coarsest-grain to its finest-grain, and broken out to their most discrete functions. There are several aspects to determining whether a service should be fine or coarse grained, such as, scalability, latency, persistence, dynamicity, etc. Typically, fine-grained services are easier to control; however they can cause performance and scalability problems that coarse-grained services are better equipped to handle.

This process of differentiating between fine- and coarse-grained services is extremely relevant in the context of Service-driven applications and creating appropriate APIs (Pautasso & Wilde, 2009). This correlates well with the notion of service composition in RESTful APIs in which the Web of resources is the most basic building block of data or functionality. RESTful Web Services should balance the tradeoff between being too fine-grained or too course-grained in terms of the resources that they target. The tradeoffs require careful understanding to determine how these services fit into the larger picture of the enterprise.

Service Versioning

In the realm of RESTful services, versioning is typically implemented by including the version number as part of the logical resource URI and by fronting the RESTful Web Service endpoint with a "façade" to redirect the requests to the appropriate version of the service.

LEVERAGING SOCIAL MEDIA AND CLOUD APIs IN THE ENTERPRISE

Social Media

Social networking has changed the way in which people are able to connect and interact with each other. RESTful APIs have played a large part in the area of social media applications. Some of the most notable social media APIs (Parr, 2009) include TweetDeck for Twitter and Facebook Connect.

Social Media APIs have the potential to draw out valuable end user information. Social media is important in enterprises today, to the extent that enterprises are often forced to incorporate social media applications into their business context. Those that fail to make good use of their internal and external social networks often end up holding the short end of the stick, in terms of valuable user insights that can be leveraged into business opportunities.

The reason social media APIs are effective is because of the social networking information that they are built on. While social networking information was a key to the creation of the initial social APIs, the introduction of the *Social Application Platform* (Reynaert et al., 2012) really served to take social APIs to the next level. Social application platforms, much like their name suggest, are the middleware platform tuned for running social applications on an Internet scale.

Social application platforms facilitate access to social networking information for application use. These platforms have drastically improved the usability of social media APIs by enabling to host developer applications directly within social networking websites, as opposed to supporting these applications on external websites that cannot fully utilize the functionality inherent in the social networking site. Therefore, applications can gain better insight into user bases, while still maintaining security and authentication policies to prevent information leak. Social application platforms have become increasingly popular

within the industry. Since then, the industry has made further progress with social media APIs in terms of more open APIs, better data portability, and more robust features to handle media content.

The key enabler to making use of social APIs in the enterprise is the enterprise view of their social networking information. Just as one may be able to map out their relationships through Facebook on a graph indicating strengths and types of relationships, the enterprise should also be able to create an Enterprise Social Graph (Woods, 2010) of their important business relationships. This enterprise social graph information combined with the power of social APIs can be leveraged to drive key business level insights about the customer base and drive creative growth opportunities. The social graph information can provide insight on organizational dynamics, data flow bottlenecks, market conditions, demand, operational gaps, etc. Combining this enterprise social graph information with APIs and applications that perform data analysis can provide a wealth of knowledge to the enterprise.

For example, Twitter has a REST based API[2] that is especially applicable to the idea of Social Media Analytics. This API enables access to the data and metrics offered by Twitter, which are mapped to resource endpoints. By accessing these endpoints, one can access specific data and metrics. For example, it is possible to collect information on the number of followers, number of tweets, number of favorites, etc., and then run analytics on this aggregated data. If one were collecting information on tweets and analyzing them to determine sentiment around a product, it would be possible to combine this sentiment data with social graph data that showed the network between users of the product, retailers, and product developers.

Using this information, one could analyze which user channels are most effective for selling the product, such as business partners, retailers, wholesalers, etc. Thereby, the analysis could lead to more targeted marketing and product sales efforts, and hopefully more revenue for various enterprises involved in the retailing chain. Combining these social media APIs and data sources into a Mashup application, can serve to aggregate both internal and external enterprise information and generate insights to leverage in the business.

Because of the importance of social graph, it is significant that the enterprise has access to the right social networking infrastructure and information. There are dozens of players in the market offering enterprise class capability in creating Social Infrastructure within the enterprise (e.g. Jive Engage Platform, IBM's Lotus Connections and Quickr, Cisco's Quad, Salesforce.com's Chatter). There are even more players offering enterprise class analytics tools to make sense of external social media talk.

To really round out the picture, companies are also starting to offer enterprise class social media APIs which tap into the social graph information and infrastructure of the enterprise; for example, TIBCO recently announced its Enterprise Social Graph API, which enables developers to tap into enterprise activity sources to build applications that leverage the social graph - enterprise interactions across colleagues, partners, files, processes, events, and activities. Considering all of these social tools together, the enterprise's effort to integrate with social media is becoming more actionable.

Cloud

Cloud Computing is a paradigm which "shifts the location of computing infrastructure to the network in order to reduce the costs associated with the management of hardware and software resources" (Vaquero et al., 2009). Cloud computing is perhaps the most well known area for using RESTful APIs within the enterprise. Cloud APIs (Linthicum, 2012) are interfaces that enable integration between the internal systems of the enterprise and the external Cloud Computing resources using RESTful Web Services enabling their consumption.

Within the relatively new field of Cloud API development, there is still debate over which technology to use. REST is popular among developers for Web APIs in general, and especially for Cloud, utilizing REST APIs has become a matter of simplicity and flexibility. However, some Cloud providers like Amazon have provided both RESTful Services and WSDL-based SOAP Services to avoid displeasing either camp.

Cloud APIs are divided by service area (Kleyman, 2012): Infrastructure, Platform, and Application. Infrastructure APIs provide Infrastructure as a Service (IaaS) through Web Services that provision and configure Cloud infrastructure resources, such as virtual machines, storage, network, etc. Platform Service APIs provide Platform as a Service (PaaS) that interfaces into specific development environments, to enable one to create, test, and deploy applications to that environment. Application APIs provide access to applications hosted on the Cloud in the form of Software as a Service (SaaS).

Cloud Provider APIs are generally unique to a specific provider of Cloud services. Utilizing the provider's API implementation is intended to increase service control. Provider APIs are usually RESTful, HTTP/HTTPS based, with built-in authentication keys to prevent unauthorized API calls. Cross-platform Cloud APIs can facilitate making a single, generic version of the multiple provider-specific API calls, thereby providing a higher level of abstraction; as well as benefit with respect to only having to utilize a single API call across heterogeneous Clouds, thus saving implementation time and reducing code complexity.

Consider a typical enterprise that interfaces with multiple Cloud providers. Each Cloud provider makes available a proprietary API interface to interact with their Cloud services. As a result, the mix of technologies creates an unorganized "Wild West" architecture approach (Woods et al.,

2012) within the enterprise. Appropriate security and transport is a key to ensuring that any Cloud endeavor is successful, without causing data leakage or harm to corporate information. Vendor specific Cloud APIs typically require different security and transport protocols to handle each of the Cloud domains of service, causing several different technologies and standards to be used in the enterprise to access similar services from multiple providers. As a result, efforts move away from building re-useable enterprise-wide solutions to one-offs. Maintaining individual Cloud solutions and API services can become a management nightmare.

One of the significant benefits of Cloud APIs is tackling the challenge of federation (Amrhein, 2011). Integrating Cloud services with the current enterprise environment can lead to the issue of coherency in management and operations. The typical approach is to implement service management systems for each service domain within the Cloud; in an enterprise view, this siloed management only adds complexity. Consider that any federation approach to services requires multiple sources of integration, such as service request integration (i.e. integration of internal system provisioning with IaaS resources), service management integration (i.e. integration of monitoring, authentication, authorization, etc) and service runtime integration (i.e. integration of data across internal and Cloud systems). Cloud providers can provision APIs that can perform all these required integration functions, such as, provisioning services, managing services, monitoring services, and securing services in a coherent manner across the different service domains.

However, as indicated earlier, Cloud APIs are not standardized yet, and therefore the problem of vendor competition reigns supreme with the Cloud. As the industry matures, it is quite likely that Cloud APIs will become more standard, and therefore easier to implement. Many in the industry are calling for a new open standard Cloud API, including Distributed Management Task Force

(DMTF), the Open Cloud Consortium (OCC) and the Cloud Security Alliance (CSA). Without standardization, it will increasingly become difficult to integrate various Cloud providers into the enterprise.

The justification for API usage in the enterprise is in considering the business value it offers, whether it is to use Social Media APIs to discover actionable insights or Cloud Computing APIs to reduce computing resource costs.

MEDIATION AND COMPOSITION OF SERVICES

Service Mediation

Service Mediation is an abstraction that decouples service consumers from service providers and provides protocol and message level mediations to enable connectivity between consumers and providers. This decoupling mechanism enables flexibility in terms of location transparency and dynamic selectability of service providers. Consumers can be unconcerned about where the provider is located and be unaffected by the change in provider URL. The mediation layer can also handle cross cutting concerns such as authentication, encryption, audit logging etc., across all service requests, thereby relieving individual service providers from having to deal with these common concerns. The service component that provides this mediation layer is commonly termed "Service Mediator."

Mediators can also provide transformation functionality, both in terms of transport protocol translation and data translation. Protocol translation is required when a service provider speaks a different transmission protocol from the service consumer. For instance, let us say that the consumer sends messages in the form of SOAP over HTTP protocol, but the provider only services SOAP over JMS transport protocol requests. The mediator would facilitate this connectivity between the consumer and provider through appropriate protocol translation.

Similarly, the mediator also facilitates data structure transformation from input structure to the data structure expected by the service provider. Consider an invoicing system where two or more service consumers invoke an "invoice" service provider by passing in invoices as input, each in a different format. The mediator can handle this variation in the input invoice data structure, by appropriately mapping or transforming them to the data structure expected by the provider service, thereby relieving the consumers from having to conform to the provider's data model.

Another significant capability of the mediator is message routing. Mediators can be used to route service messages to different providers (Pires et al., 2003) either through static definition of the routing scheme or through dynamic content or rules based routing schemes.

An ESB provides a Service-driven integration backbone with mediation capability. The Service Bus concept is analogous to a Computer Hardware Bus whose function is to allow components to be easily plugged in and out of the network without impacting other components that are on the bus. Service consumers and providers connected to an ESB do not communicate directly; instead, they interact via the ESB. This indirection allows the ESB to intervene in the message exchange and mediate the communication as well as monitor and log the transactions. At the heart of an ESB is a message oriented middleware that provides a reliable message transport mechanism. With the ability to offer protocol and data transformation, message routing, and message adaptations, an ESB enables location and transport protocol transparency; provides various message exchange patterns including synchronous and asynchronous exchanges, manages quality of service (such as security, transaction management, reliable delivery, etc) through policies and configuration, and implements content and business rules based routing of messages from consumers to providers.

Key benefits of the ESB are:

- Increased flexibility in terms of managing business requirement dynamics.
- Enterprise-wide deployment instead of point-to-point integrations.
- Management of cross-cutting concerns such as logging, auditing, security, and transaction management on a centralized basis; relieving individual consumers and providers from that responsibility.
- Configuration-driven interface.
- Ability to handle large volumes of messages that are expected in an enterprise.
- Providing a scalable and highly available messaging gateway.
- Incremental maintenance with near zero down-time (in a clustered mode).

Popular ESBs are IBM Websphere ESB, Oracle OSB, Mule ESB, JBoss ESB, Microsoft BizTalk ESB, etc.

Service Composition

Enterprise business solutions are created by combining individual fine-grained or coarse-grained services into business services. This act of combining simpler services to build more complex business services is termed Service Composition (Khalaf & Leymann, 2003). Service composition is a recursive mechanism where each service can combine several services and service components into a Composite or Mashup using orchestration and choreography techniques, and each service that makes up the composite can in turn be composed of multiple individual services.

There are two aspects to service composition – composition design and composite implementation.

Consider a service provider *orchestration* scenario where a service consumer is requesting a service provider to perform a specific service. Let us assume that the service provider cannot fulfill the service by itself and needs the output from other services to accomplish the consumer request. Therefore, the provider will call out to the other services, which provide granular functionality to the invoker, thus enabling the service provider to fulfill the consumer request. In other words, the service provider orchestrates the call-outs to other services in such a way that an end-to-end process flow is realized. Each of the granular called-out service is not tightly coupled with the service provider – they just expose an interface that the provider conforms to interact with them, thereby loosely coupling themselves to the provider.

Figure 9 illustrates the orchestration mechanism with a real world example. Consider attempting to make an airline reservation through an online system. The request details containing personal information, date of travel, itinerary etc., is delivered by the service consumer on behalf of the customer (customer fills out a Web form) to the service provider that provides this on-line reservation functionality. The service provider in-turn interacts with other services, such as, the availability service, the reservation service, and the billing service in a process-oriented manner to accomplish the different steps required to make the necessary reservation and deliver the confirmation details back to the customer.

Static and Dynamic Service Compositions

Static composition is a design-time activity at which time service components that are envisaged to be part of the composition are chosen and assembled together to create a service composition. This is a viable approach to composition as long as the service environment which includes the business partners, service components, and service providers do not change or change very infrequently.

However, consider the case where one or more entities of the environment changes. For example, there are newer service providers with better functionality, version changes have occurred in services, or old business partners have been replaced with new ones. In this case, it may be imperative to bind to the new services or providers and may also necessitate change to the business process. Under these circumstances, static compositions may be too restrictive. We need composition techniques that can transparently adapt to unforeseen changes in the business environment and requirements with minimal user intervention. This is called dynamic service composition.

Dynamic service composition will require tools for decomposing user and business requirements

Figure 9. Service orchestration

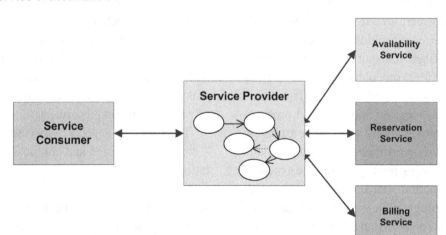

into abstract service descriptions, performing dynamic service discovery based on the requirements, and a business rules-driven composition engine that can assemble the composite at runtime by selecting the appropriate individual services that fit the needs of the business. Service providers can publish their services, along with their QoS attributes, in a Web Service Registry for discovery and assembly.

Composition Design

Two popular design approaches to composition are - hierarchical and conversational.

In the case of a hierarchical composition, the composite implementation is a black box to the service consumer and does not support any type of interaction with the consumer, except for its invocation. The consumer invokes the hierarchical composite and waits for results of the execution to be returned back to the consumer. This type of design is ideal for workflow type systems where each activity can be modeled as a composite, composed of hierarchical processes or tasks.

The other design pattern is the conversational composite pattern which permits the service consumer to control the execution of the service provider composite, based on the intermediate results of the execution. In both, the hierarchical and conversational composition patterns, the implementation of the composite service is opaque to the consumer. However, in the case of the conversational model, selected intermediate results are exposed to the consumer.

In the conversational pattern, the consumer and the provider maintain a peer to peer relationship by exchanging data and control messages. Figure 10 illustrates both patterns. Figure 10a indicates the hierarchical pattern where the service consumer interacts with a black box (service provider) by making a request and then receiving a response from the service provider at the end of processing. In contrast, Figure 10b indicates the conversational pattern where intermediate exchanges take place

Figure 10. a.) Hierarchical composition; b.) conversational composition

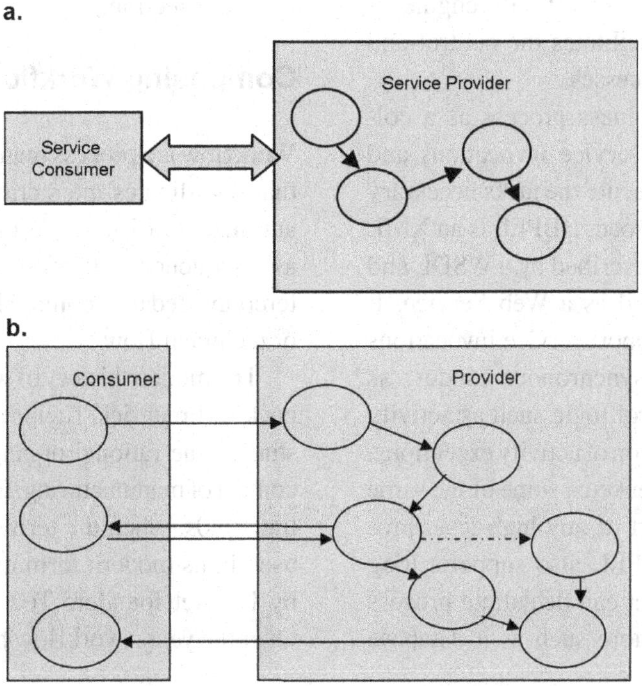

between the service consumer and the service provider. The conversational approach makes it possible to capture common business interactions such as negotiation, and result-driven actions between the consumer and the provider. Online booking of airline tickets is one such example where the route taken by the booking process is based on the conversation between the person initiating the booking and the booking service, which enables the customer to select the desired flight among provided options as part of the flight booking process.

Composite Implementation

Composites can be implemented primarily using orchestration and choreography mechanisms. Enterprises have to constantly modify and improve business processes to align with new business decisions, practices, and regulations, which make business processes highly dynamic in nature. BPEL (Business Process Execution Language) is one of the popular technologies that enable easy and flexible composition of SOA services into business processes. A BPEL Server provides the runtime environment and orchestration engine for BPEL processes and facilitates the control and monitoring of those processes.

BPEL models a business process as a collection of coordinated service invocations and related activities that execute the tasks necessary to realize the business process. BPEL is an XML based language and is described by a WSDL and therefore can be exposed as a Web Service. It has the capability to support service invocations in synchronous and asynchronous modes, as well as to provide control logic such as activity sequencing, parallelization of activity executions, while loop, case statement etc., some of the same capabilities that are part of any high level programming language. BPEL also supports long running transactions that can dehydrate process state in a persistence store such as a database

and facilitate fault management of long running business processes through compensating mechanisms (detailed discussion of the compensating mechanism is out of scope of this chapter, and is discussed in a following chapter).

The event-based approach is another interesting technique that can be used for orchestration of services. In this case, services publish events that are subscribed by other services. The events act as the dynamic and asynchronous enablers of service composition. The service consumer initiates the composition by publishing an event that is subscribed by a service provider. The service provider in-turn publishes another event that invokes other services, and this sequence of events dynamically assembles a composite service.

In the realm of Web APIs, Mediation and Composition mechanisms, such as, Piping and Wiring, are used to compose Mashup applications by coordinating and aggregating the various RESTful API and data sources. Lightweight resource composition (Hoyer et al., 2008) promotes the idea of reusing building blocks to address a variety of user needs and is very relevant to Enterprise Mashups which are discussed in detail in a later section.

Composing Workflow Services

Workflow is a process management methodology that coordinates interactions across manual and automated tasks. A Workflow depicts a process as a sequence of tasks or operations that are interconnected to accomplish the required business or technical flow.

The modern history of workflows can be traced back to Frederick Taylor and Henry Gantt, who studied the rational organization of work in the context of manufacturing. However, it was not until the 1980s, when the term "Workflow" was first used in its modern form in the software industry by FileNet founders Ted Smith and Ed Miller. Over the years, workflow has evolved from being a technology that was embedded within individual applications to being embedded in middleware, and shared across multiple applications.

BPM is a superset of workflow and deals with the definition, execution, and management of business processes and the coordination of activities across multiple applications with fine grained control. BPM takes a more structured approach and emphasizes a holistic methodology to coordinating work across all resources – people, information, machines, and systems.

As applications become increasingly distributed, there is a need for individual services to call other services to delegate work. Implementing these calls as asynchronous operations necessitates the support for handling call-backs and introduces complexity in these applications. Furthermore, some of these "called" services can be long running transactions. The incorporation of error handling and detailed end-to-end tracking in the applications to manage these asynchronous services can add additional complexity. These issues make asynchronous distributed applications complex to write and maintain. However, workflows are a natural way to express the coordination of asynchronous work, especially calls to external services. Workflows are also effective at representing long-running business processes. These properties of workflows (and BPM) make them ideally suited to building Service-driven process-centric applications in distributed environments.

Workflows (and BPM) enable a process-centric view of SOA Services, where business services are composed using business processes and application services. This synergy between them is referred to as Workflow Services and it facilitates the use of reusable services to build end-to-end business services in a process-oriented manner. Workflow Services also facilitate human interaction through asynchronous tasks that can be controlled by human actions such as completion of a document review, or assembly of a part in an assembly line. Workflow Services decouple business processes from the services that implement the tasks for these processes to provide a loosely coupled Service-driven environment.

Figure 11 illustrates a workflow service where a business process controls the workflow. Each of the workflow tasks invoke composite services that are deployed on the ESB. Specifically, the example relates to the online reservation system that first checks for the availability of seats before making the reservation and consequently generates the bill for the customer.

Figure 11. Workflow services

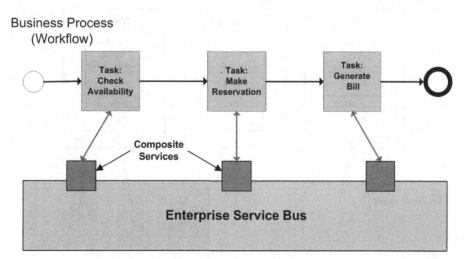

Composing Web APIs into Enterprise Mashups

Mashups are lightweight applications that use Web technologies, store no data or content themselves, source all data or functionality, and generate a result in which the sourced data and functionality retains the integrity of its intended purpose. This section focuses on Enterprise Mashups which are Mashup applications created for the enterprise to provide specific business value.

The business benefit of Enterprise Mashups is significant. For example, consider a business that receives customer service calls, including information about the caller, purchase history, etc. An Enterprise Mashup might take this information, along with the customer location information, and apply this to a Maps Web Service, and generate location-based, and therefore highly tailored, customer support responses. Being able to offer better customer support is just one business benefit that Enterprise Mashups can make possible.

Mediation and Composition mechanisms are used to compose Mashup applications by coordinating and aggregating the various Web services and data sources. Mashups can be composed by performing mediations at three levels (Lorenzo et al., 2009): data level, process level, and UI (User Interface) level. Enterprise Mashups typically use agile, low-cost, lightweight composition techniques. (Hoyer et al., 2008) describe the Enterprise Mashup Stack as illustrated in Figure 12. Enterprise Mashups are composed using both the Piping mechanism, where the mediation and composition takes place at the resource layer; and the Wiring mechanism, where the composition takes place at the Widget layer.

The Enterprise Mashup Stack consists of the following layers.

Figure 12. Enterprise mashup stack

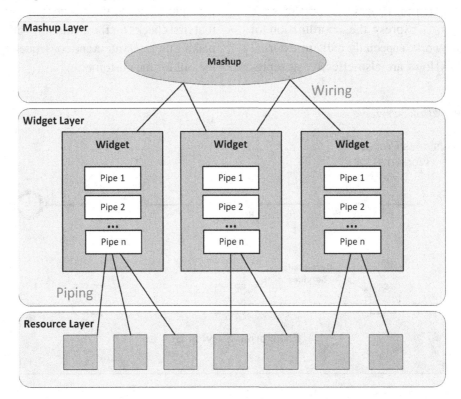

Resource Layer

This is the lowest level of the Mashup stack and contains the Web resources, such as content, data, or application functionality that are represented by resource URIs. These resources can be invoked using RESTful Web Service calls. Resources are typically created and exposed by using appropriate tools and technologies, such as, HTML, JavaScript, Servlet, Web Services etc.

Resources typically use the following data sources (Clarkin & Holmes, 2012):

- **Enterprise Data:** This represents the critical data that is a key to the business and is resident in databases and files in the enterprise.
- **External Data:** This represents data that is resident outside the enterprise, such as in business partner databases, Cloud Storage etc.
- **External Data Feeds:** RSS (Really Simple Syndication) and ATOM (Atom Syndication Format) data feeds, which are Web feed formats commonly used for distribution of Web content. These data feeds are in well-defined XML format, making for easy consumption of external Web data.

Widget Layer

This level of the Mashup stack represents Widgets (also called Gadgets) which encapsulate the functionality and data of the underlying resources. Mashup tools enable users to put a visual face in the form of a graphic on the Widget to enable users to easily identify the appropriate Widgets to use in their Mashups. Widgets are typically composed using the Piping mechanism. The Widget Pipes is similar to the UNIX Pipes concept that facilitates data processing by enabling the output of one command to be fed as the input to the next command in a processing chain of commands.

Pipes provide data mediations in a Widget. Data level mediation may involve converting data, filtering data, transforming data, merging data from different sources etc. The data may come from internal data sources as well as from external data sources and feeds (such as RSS). The data may be of different types, namely, structured (i.e. follows well formatted data model) or unstructured (i.e. natural text, no data model). The main goal of data mediation is to transform the input data into an useable structure or format for subsequent process level mediations. Unstructured data sources can be more difficult to mediate and may need pre-processing to decipher content and reformat into a structured data model. A Widget can implement multiple pipes to support variations to processing logic depending on the input parameters that is passed in during invocation of the Widget. For example, a weather Widget could have a pipe each to generate the temperature reading according to different temperature scales (Fahrenheit, Celsius, etc).

Piping is illustrated in Figure 13 as performing data integration by concatenating resources through data level operations (mediations) that filters, sorts, aggregates, transforms, creates feeds, calls services, etc, to generate data processing chains. Each pipe can interface with multiple resources, and can perform a variety of operations. For example, consider a Pipe that filters sports news feed resource for information such as soccer game results, game statistics etc, and then combines this data with another feed that provides soccer league player information, to generate a complete listing of soccer player information and related statistics.

Mashup Layer

A Mashup application performs Process level mediation by coordinating and integrating multiple Widgets (and therefore, the underlying resources) into a coherent process. This coordination in-

Figure 13. Piping

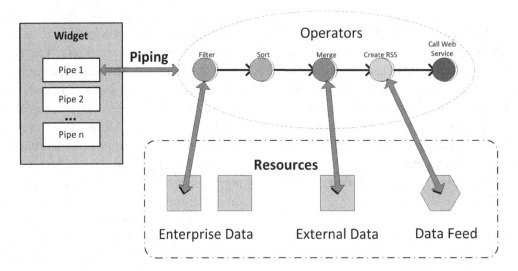

volves invoking individual services (exposed by Widgets) and aggregating their outputs to make an end-to-end process flow. In a typical enterprise setting, workflow languages like WS-BPEL (Web Service-Business Process Execution Language) are used to model the composition of the process flow. However, these languages are not very suitable in Mashup process integration for modeling the interactive and asynchronous process flows that are common in Mashup applications. Instead,

newly developed process composition modeling and programming languages such as MashMaker, Bite, and Swashup are used for process integration in the Mashup paradigm, that enable wiring the different Widgets together to create the required process flow.

Wiring at the Widget level as illustrated in Figure 14, enables users to develop a process flow by simply stringing the Widgets together to create an end-to-end process. This is accomplished by

Figure 14. Wiring

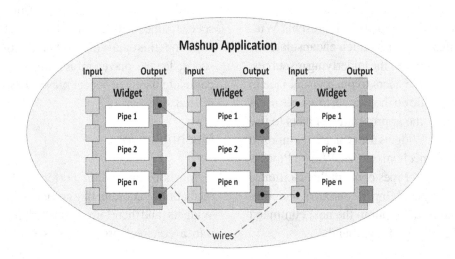

wiring the required Widgets together and performing "parameter mapping" by connecting the specific output parameter ports of one Widget to the appropriate input parameter ports of the next widget in the processing chain of Widgets. These input and output parameters are referenced by the pipes that constitute the Widget.

Once the desired functionality is achieved through wiring, the Mashup tooling can perform the required UI customization using technologies like AJAX (Asynchronous Javascript and XML), HTML, etc, for Web presentation. UI-level mediation is the customization of the user interface for end users. A user interface (UI) is needed to collect user information and display Mashup service result information in a user friendly manner. UI technologies used can be as simple as a HTML page or an interactive AJAX-based Web page. AJAX can enhance the Mashup consumer experience by enabling dynamic and interactive data display without requiring Web page refresh.

UI technologies are important for both server-side and client-side hosted Mashup applications.

Server-side Mashups integrate data and services on a remote server, and therefore only require the UI to display the final results in the client browser. However, client-side Mashups do the integration in the client browser (e.g. the AJAX-based Web page application does the process composition and displays the results in the Web browser), and therefore requires a more sophisticated UI.

Yahoo Pipes[3] is an example of a popular Mashup tool that is built with the concept of lightweight resource composition and mediation, and allows the Mashup developer to use simple programming commands and a drag-and-drop environment to compose Mashups.

SERVICE-DRIVEN DEVELOPMENT LIFE CYCLE

The typical life cycle of service-driven applications is comprised of six phases: Model, Realize, Assemble, Deploy, Monitor, and Govern. Figure 15 illustrates the service development lifecycle.

Figure 15. Phases of the service-driven development lifecycle

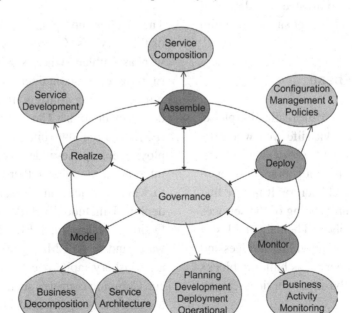

The Modeling Phase

The modeling phase in service-driven methodology is analogous to the traditional software development design phase. The primary activities performed in this phase are business process decomposition, service identification, and service architecture. Business process decomposition consists of breaking apart of the business process to identify new services that need to be developed or identify business functionality that can be mapped to existing reusable services - this is the top-down approach to service identification.

Additionally, service identification is also done in a bottom-up manner where business functionality encapsulated within legacy applications is identified as service candidates for exposing to business processes. Service identification typically happens in a hybrid manner involving both top-down and bottom-up analysis as described. The artifacts generated from service identification form the input to the next step in the modeling, which is the service architecture phase. Service architecture involves the design of service contracts and messages for SOA Services, and the identification of logical resources for RESTful Services. This phase also involves the design of service mediations and compositions to build business services.

The Realization Phase

The modeling phase leads to the realization phase. This is the phase in the service life cycle where the identified task services, entity services, utility services, Web resources, and Widgets are developed to realize the service architecture. It is here that the development and unit testing of the services and components take place. The deliverables of this realization phase are individual services and components that can be used as building blocks from which complex business services can be assembled.

The Assembly Phase

Service-driven approaches facilitate the building of complex business services from simpler services and components. The reusable building blocks comprising of services and components that were developed in the realization phase are assembled together to manufacture business services. The assembly happens by connecting the different components and services using smart wires that provide interface connectivity between services and components and also enable the injection of non-functional QoS requirements into the services.

In the case of Enterprise APIs, Mashups are assembled in this phase, and API brokering is performed to transform general purpose APIs from service providers into new APIs that is easier to consume for the enterprise by adding transformations that are specific to the business.

Service mediation and orchestration mechanisms enable composition of complex services in a process-oriented manner. Industry standard GUI tools are available to assist with the assembly process.

The Deployment Phase

The deployment phase involves the targeting of the Services, Composites, and Mashups that were assembled in the assembly phase to specific runtime service containers and middleware environments using configuration management and deployment tools. The Enterprise Service Bus (ESB) is a popular runtime environment for deploying enterprise-wide services and application integration modules. Other popular middleware to which services and integration solutions are deployed include IBM Process Server, Oracle Fusion Middleware, TIBCO Messaging Middleware; and to API Management Platforms, such as, Mashery, apiGrove (open source), Apigee, etc. Common concerns such as security and audit logging can be configured during the deployment phase, thus freeing up the Composite and Mashup developers from having to deal with those details in the development and assembly phases.

The Monitoring Phase

Monitoring of the Service-driven infrastructure helps to achieve high levels of operational integrity and enables the measurement and enforcement of service levels and policies. Runtime monitoring tools can help to perform Business Activity Monitoring (BAM) to measure key performance indicators (KPI), QoS parameters, service usage, and business data integrity. Faults and Alerts can be monitored to track runtime exceptions and warnings. Transaction monitoring helps to track service and data transactions end-to-end and Report generators and dashboards can generate and present user-friendly real time reports for executives and enterprise operation teams.

The Governance Phase

Governance specifies the rules and regulations for effective control of the service-driven environment. As services and Service Composites (and Mashups) proliferate in an enterprise, it increases the risk associated with the access and reuse of those service artifacts. As the service infrastructure evolves, there will be greater possibilities of policy violations and coding errors. It is not straightforward to govern these service assets, due to the responsibility and ownership requirements. Boundaries of applications and services fade, due to the fact that multiple service clients may use the same service provider to interact with different applications. This leads to management challenges when dealing with service maintenance.

When an application or service is retrofitted to tackle a new business requirement, the change can have a ripple effect on multiple services and applications, if the change is not governed effectively. Service governance is not specific to the operations phase; it must be applied at the planning, design, development, deployment, and operational stages of a project; in other words across the life cycle phases from modeling to monitoring, to be useful and cost-effective in the service-driven environment. Without doubt, service governance practices will introduce additional costs in the short term but lead to increased ROI in the long term, through reduction in the overall development and maintenance costs of the service environment.

DESIGN PATTERNS FOR SERVICE-DRIVEN METHODOLOGY

Standard design practices are traditionally documented as "design patterns" to provide software engineering design solutions to solve commonly encountered situations in the architecture and implementation of systems and applications. Service orientation has evolved from past design paradigms. New design considerations and techniques that are specific to the enterprise-centric approach of Service-driven computing have led to the formulation of service design and implementation patterns (Erl et al., 2008) that can help architect effective solutions for the service paradigm. The intent of this section is to provide a brief introduction to some of the useful design patterns that are applicable to the Service-driven environment, and not meant to provide a complete overview and detailed analysis of all applicable patterns.

The Service Façade pattern (Erl, 2008), which is inspired by the Façade pattern created by the Gang of Four (Gamma et al., 1994), is a key pattern that is frequently applied in service architecture. This pattern attempts to decouple the service contract from the service implementation by establishing an abstraction that can be exposed to the service consumers. The Service Decomposition pattern (Erl, 2008) is another popular pattern that enables a coarse-grained service to be split up into a number of fine-grained services and through the use of additional patterns such as Proxy

Capability (Erl, 2008) and Distributed Capability (Erl, 2008), ensures that this decomposition does not impact the interfaces of the original service and its consumers.

The Agnostic Service pattern (Erl, 2008) promotes the encapsulation of service logic as discrete reusable services which can be used to implement multiple business services. Encapsulating agnostic logic into discrete services facilitates service reuse and composability. Other patterns, such as Legacy Wrapper (Erl & Roy, 2008), and Service Data Replication (Erl, 2008), can be used to address integration and scalability related requirements. The Contract De-normalization pattern (Erl, 2008) enables one to increase the longevity of service contracts by helping to postpone service versioning requirements. It does this by allowing the interface to expose similar functionality at different levels of granularity, thus enabling the same contract to meet the needs of different service consumers. Alternatively, the Concurrent Contracts pattern (Erl, 2008) creates separate contracts for the same underlying service logic.

Services can be wrapped in atomic transactions with rollback features to provide transactional integrity using the Atomic Service Transaction pattern (Erl, 2008). Transaction management services can be implemented in the component layer and reused by multiple services. The Service Callback pattern (Karmakar, 2008) enables service providers to call back the consumer with its response, asynchronously. The asynchronous response approach enables the service consumers to continue processing without waiting for response from the provider and thereby increases efficiency and is especially useful with long running services.

Another significant pattern is the Enterprise Service Bus pattern (Erl, Little, Rischbeck, & Simon, 2008) that establishes a message broker between service consumers and providers and allows for a bus based integration methodology, versus the traditional point-to-point integration approach, leading to efficiency in the development and maintenance of integration solutions. The Enterprise Service Bus can perform protocol and data transformations and advanced message routing, including content and dynamic rule based routing of messages among the participant services.

To track and control the API services that are being used in the enterprise, the API Gateway pattern becomes relevant. Managing API user traffic into the enterprise requires the presence of a control point to funnel all information flow. The API Gateway design pattern (Woods et al., 2012) enables enterprise-class security, reliability and scalability of the enterprise API architecture.

The Asynchronous Queuing design pattern (Little, Rischbeck, & Simon, 2008) can be used to provide a highly available architecture by establishing a persistent central queue to store and retrieve messages to enable services to overcome the availability issues and provide robust asynchronous message communication. Event Driven Messaging pattern (Little, Rischbeck, & Simon, 2008) is another asynchronous mechanism that uses the publish-and-subscribe mechanism between services to generate and respond to events. The Service Agent pattern (Erl, 2008) delegates the cross-cutting concerns to agents that intercept and forward messages at runtime. Intermediate Routing pattern (Little, Rischbeck, & Simon, 2008) is an extension of the "Service Agent" pattern to help provide intelligent agent-based message routing and increase the scalability of services and compositions.

Examples of other types of patterns that have been documented include those that address grid computing, stateful service design, REST-based communication, security, versioning, dynamic messaging, runtime compensation, binary attachments, transformations, and many more.

EMERGING TRENDS

The main goal of service-driven approach is to enable the dynamic needs of the business in an agile manner. This requires techniques that will facilitate the dynamic configuration of services. Today, most service applications execute static business processes and Mashups that are pre-determined at design time. Furthermore, Service-driven applications experience dependability degradation throughout their lifetime and require continuous human intervention for remediation.

In the future, the expectation will be to architect services that can reconfigure themselves dynamically to satisfy changing business goals and requirements and to automatically compose optimized distributed business processes and Mashups. Services will also be expected to restructure themselves to account for changes in infrastructure topologies and capabilities and to perform accurate service discovery based on semantic requirements. They will be designed with the goal of providing adaptive processes and management services, as well as self-healing capabilities that will enable them to recover from unexpected exceptions and conditions. They will also be expected to dynamically provision security services that can detect and identify threats and protect against them; and facilitate automatic governance of complex environments.

Consider "dynamically configuring services" that can take into consideration changing user and business requirements, dynamic non-functional and semantic requirements, and infrastructure availability and capabilities, to automatically configure the composition to provide the required functionality with the best performance, security, and conformance to quality of service requirements. This is an area that current research is vigorously focused on.

A key challenge facing Service-driven architectural methodology is the absence of a standard federated service model that is robust and scalable enough to meet mission-critical needs of an organization and also provide data and service interoperability spanning multiple organizations of the enterprise. Service-driven implementations generally adhere to a complex centralized model that lacks the necessary flexibility, extensibility, and scalability for large enterprises.

The need for heterogeneous and dynamic context semantic description, on-the-fly service creation, efficient and semantically aware discovery of services, seamless and scalable deployment, on-demand services in the Cloud, dynamic migration, autonomous reconfiguration, provisioning to diverse user platforms ranging from hand-held mobile devices to supercomputers, and federated services across organizations of an enterprise or across enterprises will provide the momentum for research into new generation service technologies.

Data-centric APIs where data is brokered by the APIs rather than by custom data feeds will be a significant new business model for enterprises whose primary business is data. SIRI (Speech Interpretation and Recognition Interface) is one example of an application built on a data-centric API that uses a natural language user interface to answer questions. Provisioning access to data through APIs configured for various payment models will become more prevalent in the future.

Mobile applications are becoming the primary driver for API adoption due to the pervasiveness offered by the mobile technologies, and the need to access information from multiple devices and operating systems. There will be more research and focus on designing and implementing context-aware Mashups and autonomous composition. In the future, Mashups will possibly be the most common way to access back-end services in the enterprise. Effort will be expended to make services easily and smoothly mashed up to improve business agility and flexibility. Virtualization techniques to improve the synergy between Service-driven ecosystems and the Cloud are expected to be an area of significant research interest. In addition, new standards for Cloud APIs, security models, and RESTful Services should enable less vendor specific APIs and more focus on development of unique applications in an agile manner to meet the dynamic needs of businesses.

CONCLUSION

A service-driven architectural approach typically uses SOA to design and implement enterprise applications and integration solutions; though more recently, Web APIs are driving easy to use, agile, and low cost techniques for Service-driven development in the enterprise. Service-driven approaches enable the interaction and interoperability of services within and across enterprises and use services and service components as building blocks to orchestrate and build complex applications from simpler ones, thus promoting the principle of reusable software components.

This chapter set out to explore the characteristics of services and the principles and challenges of Service-driven approaches to software architecture and enterprise integration. It illustrated the structure and significance of SOA service contracts and emphasized the importance of service versioning to deal with changing needs of an enterprise. The concept of business services and reusable components was also presented. RESTful architecture for Web API was discussed, along with business value of REST Web APIs for Social Media and the Cloud. Mediation and Composition techniques were described for implementing SOA Composites, Workflow Services, and Enterprise Mashups.

In enterprises, software development for Web-based applications typically involves an assessment of user requirements, all of which cannot possibly be incorporated into the new software. Those requirements which are not included are still valuable for a specific group of enterprise users, and generally there are large numbers of unanswered requirements that cater to this smaller group of users, a phenomenon called the "Long Tail" of software requirements (Anderson, 2006). There exists motivation in many situations to enable Web-based software development that addresses these unmet requirements for specific business needs, and involves delivery of software that is low-cost and typically transient in nature, called Situated Software (Shirky, 2004).

As argued in (Schroth & Christ, 2007), SOA implementations cannot sufficiently cover the long tail of user needs because of the technical complexity of relevant standards, inflexibility to respond to dynamic business requirements within days, and importantly, limitations in integrating external end-user and partner software development efforts with enterprise development activities. Traditional SOA can add complexity to situations that can accept a simple and straightforward approach; complexity which typically leads to high costs for integration projects and inflexibility due to longer integration times. This is where APIs come into play.

In fact, API and SOA development can go hand-in-hand; for example, mashups are able to leverage the Web Services that SOA-centric organizations already have in place using transformational gateways (Ogrinz, 2009), and in turn produce new enterprise services with agility.

This chapter also discussed the typical phases involved in the service development life cycle and design patterns relevant to service design and implementation were explored. Standards and best practices were discussed appropriately.

Service-driven approaches to architecture have enabled the delivery of agile and easily maintainable applications and integration solutions. With the current research focused on the dynamic structuring and control aspects of the service architecture, Service-driven applications are expected to play a major role in the implementation of robust, adaptable, fault-tolerant, and dynamic enterprise applications that are closely aligned with the changing needs of the business.

REFERENCES

Alonso, G., Casati, F., Kuno, H., & Machiraju, V. (2004). *Web services: Concepts, architectures and applications*. Berlin, Heidelberg: Springer-Verlag.

Amrhein, D. (2011). *What's the big deal about cloud APIs*? Retrieved from http://cloudcomputing.sys-con.com/node/1842790

Anderson, C. (2006). *The long tail: Why the future of business is selling less of more*. Hyperion Books.

Andrews, G. (1991). Paradigms for process interaction in distributed programs. *ACM Computing Surveys*, *23*(1), 49–90. doi:10.1145/103162.103164.

Bell, M. (2008). *Introduction to service-oriented modeling*. Wiley & Sons.

Benslimane, D., Dustdar, S., & Sheth, A. (2008). Services mashups: The new generation of Web applications. *IEEE Internet Computing*, *12*(5), 13–15. doi:10.1109/MIC.2008.110.

Chin, R. S., & Chanson, S. T. (1991). Distributed object-based programming systems. *ACM Computing Surveys*, *23*(1), 91–124. doi:10.1145/103162.103165.

Clarkin, L., & Holmes, J. (2012). *Enterprise mashups*. Retrieved from http://msdn.microsoft.com/en-us/architecture/bb906060.aspx

Erl, T. (2007). *SOA principles of service design*. Prentice Hall.

Erl, T. (2008). *SOA design patterns*. Prentice Hall.

Erl, T., Karmakar, A., Roy, S., Little, M., Rischbeck, T., & Simon, A. (2008). *SOA patterns*. Retrieved from http://www.soapatterns.org

Erl, T., Little, M., Rischbeck, T., & Simon, A. (2008). *SOA patterns*. Retrieved from http://www.soapatterns.org

Erl, T., & Roy, S. (2008). *SOA patterns*. Retrieved from http://www.soapatterns.org

Fielding, R. T. (2000). *Architectural styles and the design of network-based software architectures*. (PhD Dissertation). Retrieved from http://www.ics.uci.edu/~fielding/pubs/dissertation/top.htm

Fuggetta, A., Picco, G. P., & Vigna, G. (1998). Understanding code mobility. *IEEE Transactions on Software Engineering*, *24*(5), 342–361. doi:10.1109/32.685258.

Gamma, E., Helm, R., Johnson, R., & Vlissides, J. (1994). *Design patterns: Elements of reusable object-oriented software*. Addison-Wesley Professional Computing Series.

Georgakopoulos, D., & Papazoglou, M. P. (2008). *Service-oriented computing*. The MIT Press.

Hinchcliffe, D. (2011). Enabling collaboration with open APIs. Retrieved from http://www.zdnet.com/blog/hinchcliffe/enabling-collaboration-with-open-apis/1594

Hoyer, V., Stanoesvka-Slabeva, K., Janner, T., & Schroth, C. (2008). Enterprise mashups: Design principles towards the long tail of user needs. Retrieved from www.alexandria.unisg.ch/export/DL/Volker_Hoyer/45602.pdf

Karmakar, A. (2008). *SOA patterns*. Retrieved from http://www.soapatterns.org

Khalaf, R., & Leymann, F. (2003). On web services aggregation. TES, LNCS 2819, 1-13. Berlin: Springer-Verlag.

Kleyman, B. (2012). Understanding cloud APIs and why they matter. Retrieved from http://www.datacenterknowledge.com/archives/2012/10/16/understanding-cloud-integration-a-look-at-apis/

Kunze, M. (2009). *Business process mashups: An analysis of mashups and their value proposition for business process management*. (Master's Thesis). Retrieved from http://bpt.hpi.uni-potsdam.de/pub/Public/MatthiasKunze/matthias_kunze.masters_thesis.pdf

Linthicum, D. (2010). Determining the business value of Web APIs. Retrieved from http://www.bickgroup.com/uploads/documents/determining_the_business_value_of_web_apis.pdf

Linthicum, D. (2012). Define and design cloud APIs, step by step. Retrieved from http://www.javaworld.com/javaworld/jw-06-2012/120612--how-to-define-a-cloud-api.html

Little, M., Rischbeck, T., & Simon, A. (2008). *SOA patterns*. Retrieved from http://www.soapatterns.org

Lorenzo, G. D., Hacid, H., Paik, H., & Benatallah, B. (2009). Data integration in mashups. *SIGMOD Record*, *38*(1), 59–66. Retrieved from http://www.sigmod.org/publications/sigmod-record/0903/p59.surveys.hacid.pdf doi:10.1145/1558334.1558343.

Mandel, L. (2008). *Describe REST web services with WSDL 2.0*. Retrieved from http://www.ibm.com/developerworks/webservices/library/ws-restwsdl/#describerestservice

OASIS. (2004). *Web services security v1.0*. Retrieved from https://www.oasis-open.org/standards#wssv1.0

OASIS. (2005). *SAML specification for SAML V2.0*. Retrieved from http://saml.xml.org/saml-specifications

OASIS. (2011). Service component architecture assembly model specification version 1.1. *OASIS Committee Specification Draft 08 / Public Review Draft 03.*

Oasis. (2013). *Website*. Retrieved from http://docs.oasis-open.org/opencsa/sca-assembly/sca-assembly-1.1-spec.pdf

Ogrinz, M. (2009). *Mashup patterns: Designs and examples for the modern enterprise*. Pearson Education.

Papazoglou, M. P., Traverso, P., Dustdar, S., & Leymann, F. (2008). Service-oriented computing: A research roadmap. *International Journal of Cooperative Information Systems*, *17*(2). doi:10.1142/S0218843008001816.

Parr, B. (2009). The evolution of the social media API. Retrieved from http://mashable.com/2009/05/21/social-media-api/

Pautasso, C., & Wilde, E. (2009). Why is the web loosely coupled? A multi-faceted metric for service design. In *Proceedings of the 18th International World Wide Web Conference*, Madrid, Spain.

Pires, P. F., Benevides, M. R. F., & Mattoso, M. (2003). Building reliable web services compositions. Web Databases and Web Services 2002, LNCS 2593, 59-72. Berlin: Springer-Verlag.

Reynaert, T., De Groefy, W., Devriesey, D., Desmety, L., & Piessensy, F. (2012). *PESAP: A privacy enhanced social application platform*. Retrieved from https://lirias.kuleuven.be/bitstream/123456789/356922/1/reynaert2012a.pdf

Schroth, C., & Christ, O. (2007). Brave new web: Emerging design principles and technologies as enablers of a global SOA. In *Proceedings of the IEEE International Conference on Service Computing*.

Shirky, C. (2010). *Situated software*. Retrieved from http://www.shirky.com/writings/situated_software.html

Twitter. (2013). *Website*. Retrieved from https://dev.twitter.com/docs/api

Vaquero, L., Rodero-Merino, L., Caceres, J., & Lindner, M. (2009). A break in the clouds: Towards a cloud definition. *SIGCOMM Computer Communications Review*, *39*, 50–55. doi:10.1145/1496091.1496100.

Vizard, M. (2012). *How APIs are fueling the mobile banking wars*. Retrieved from http://blog.programmableweb.com/2012/08/14/how-apis-are-fueling-the-mobile-banking-wars/

W3C. (2001a). *Web services description language (WSDL 1.1)*. Retrieved from http://www.w3.org/TR/wsdl

W3C. (2001b). *XML schema 1.1 recommendation*. Retrieved from http://www.w3.org/XML/Schema.html

W3C. (2007a). *Web services description language (WSDL) version 2.0*. Retrieved from http://www.w3.org/TR/wsdl20/

W3C. (2007b). *Web services policy 1.5 - Framework*. Retrieved from http://www.w3.org/TR/ws-policy/

Woods, D. (2010). *Building the enterprise social graph. Forbes*. Retrieved from http://www.forbes.com/2010/09/27/enterprise-social-media-technology-cio-network-woods_print.html

Woods, D., Thurai, A., Dournaee, B., & Musser, J. (2012). *Enterprise-class API patterns for cloud & mobile*. Retrieved from http://www.govhealthit.com/sites/govhealthit.com/files/resource-media/pdf/enterprise-api-patterns-1.pdf

Yahoo. (2013). *Website*. Retrieved from http://pipes.yahoo.com/pipes/

ADDITIONAL READING

Daigneau, R. (2011). *Service design patterns: Fundamental design solutions for SOAP/WSDL and RESTful web services*. Addison-Wesley.

Erl, T., Karmakar, A., Walmsley, P., & Haas, H. (2008). *Web service contract design and versioning for SOA*. Prentice Hall.

Linthicum, D. (2009). *Cloud computing and SOA convergence in your enterprise: A step-by-step guide*. Addison-Wesley.

Mulloy, B. (2012). *Web API design: Crafting interfaces that developers love*. E-book. Retrieved from http://offers.apigee.com/web-api-design-ebook/

Richardson, L., & Ruby, S. (2007). *RESTful web services: Web services for the real world*. O'Reilly Media.

Rosen, M., Lublinsky, B., Smith, K., & Balcer, M. (2008). *Applied SOA: Service oriented architecture and design strategies*. Wiley & Sons.

Schmutz, G., Liebhart, D., & Welkenbach, P. (2010). *Service oriented architecture: An integration blueprint*. Packt Publishing.

Yee, R. (2008). *Pro web 2.0 mashups*. New York, NY: Springer-Verlag.

KEY TERMS AND DEFINITIONS

Enterprise APIs: APIs used in the enterprise that make use of both internal and external data.

Enterprise Service Bus: An integration backbone abstraction for integrating applications using mediation, routing, and possibly business process management.

Mashup: Enables data aggregation and service integration and are created by combining existing API data and functionality in a coordinated fashion into a new application.

Mediation: A mechanism to resolve protocol and data inconsistency between services and enable connectivity between them.

Orchestration: A mechanism used to build a process flow by linking discrete services.

Service: A platform-independent computational entity that implements a specific business function.

Service Composite: A compound service entity that is composed of one or more services and service components.

Service Contract: An artifact used to publish the functional and non-functional behavior of a service.

Service-Driven: A design methodology that uses services as building blocks to build complex applications from simpler ones.

Service Governance: Set of procedures and processes used for effective administration of the Service-driven environment.

Service Policy: An artifact that defines the non-functional capabilities and constraints that can be applied to service components or to the interactions between services.

REST: An architectural style for creating Web Services that is the industry favorite for Web API development. The key abstraction of information in REST is a *resource*, which is a conceptual mapping to a set of entities.

Web APIs: Web-enabled APIs that perform inter-application communication over the network, using Web Service calls.

ENDNOTES

[1]   See Oasis (2013).
[2]   See Twitter (2013).
[3]   See Yahoo (2013).

Chapter 2
Enterprise Integration:
Challenges and Solution Architecture

Leo Shuster
Nationwide Insurance, USA

ABSTRACT

The purpose of this chapter is to discuss the current state and associated challenges of Enterprise Integration (EI). The chapter will explore EI's past, present and future, examine its path towards the current practices, and contemplate its future evolution. Synergies between Service-driven and other modern architectural approaches will be investigated. Major challenges associated with EI strategy and execution will be explored in depth. This will include organizational, technology, process, methodology, and governance challenges. In addition to the current state concerns, future trends and directions will be investigated and specific challenges outlined. A major part of this chapter will be devoted to defining and discussing modern solution architectures associated with EI. This will include current architectural best practices, technology constructs employed, design patterns, governance mechanisms, and implementation considerations.

INTRODUCTION

When Charles Darwin published his *Origin of Species* in 1859, he was not aware that his work would be applied to so many topics outside of biology. Yet, the evolutionary paradigm, survival of the fittest, and many other postulates from Darwin's work can be directly applied to a variety of other topics. Just like the Earth's species, Enterprise Integration has evolved over the years – from humble beginnings in data replication and messaging to ETL (Extract-Transform-Load) and

Service-driven mechanisms. The current integration approaches have evolved over the years and are all built on the deep foundation of integration knowledge and experience. Today, Service Oriented Architecture (SOA) plays a major part in Enterprise Integration.

SOA has significantly influenced the direction of Enterprise Integration. Many enterprise technologies such as BPEL, BPM, Business Rules, etc, enable Service-driven methodologies for enterprise integration. This chapter identifies SOA's influences and usage and primarily concentrates on the integration architectures.

DOI: 10.4018/978-1-4666-4193-8.ch002

What is Enterprise Integration?

Many definitions of Enterprise Integration exist. According to Gartner, it is the "unrestricted sharing of data and business processes among any connected applications or data sources in the enterprise." This is the simplest and the best definition of Enterprise Integration. It succinctly defines the core function of EI and draws connections between its past, present, and future.

The modern form of Enterprise Integration, Service-driven Application Integration is based on SOA. First described by Gartner (1996), Service Oriented Architecture (SOA) is a style of software architecture that is modular, distributed and loosely coupled. SOA-style applications use business components that are designed to be reusable across applications and enterprise boundaries. These components are invoked through *Services* that are based on well-defined interface definitions, and are independent of the underlying hardware and software platforms, as well as development language (Gartner, 1996). Service-driven Application

tion Integration uses SOA approaches to enable integration across the enterprise.

Considering the key differences between the Enterprise Integration and SOA definitions above, one can see the emphasis on integration with EI and reuse with SOA. Therein lays the core development in the maturation process of integration techniques – from basic application and data integration, to better componentized, reusable, and specialized code fragments.

Charles Darwin described human evolution from single cell organisms to the complex, intricate life forms we are today. Integration evolution can be described in similar terms. It started out as simple point-to-point communication and evolved into the complex Service-driven architecture style as shown in Figure 1.

Enterprise Application Integration (EAI), the first structured integration technique, became popular in the late 1980s, early 1990s. IT environments had matured to the point where multiple systems performed various critical functions and needed to be integrated with each other. The days

Figure 1. Evolution of enterprise integration

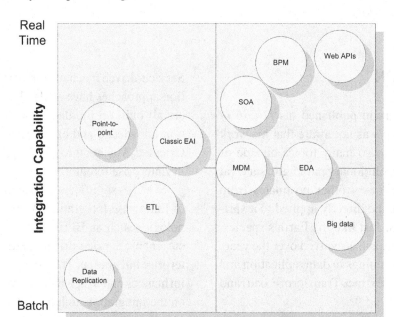

of monolithic mainframe applications were over. Shared responsibilities and the ever-maturing landscape of development tools, vendors, and technologies forced companies to think about integration.

Niels Bohr once said "All ingenious is simple." First integration techniques were simple but far from ingenious. They continue to be used today and still cause headaches for architects across the industry. These techniques were simple data replication approaches where data was copied from one system to another. While such approaches make sense in certain situations, they largely tend to cause problems, including duplication of data and related rules, increased storage costs, lack of real-time access, and higher support costs.

EAI products were designed to address these issues. They opted for a more real-time integration approach and quickly became popular. However, lack of standards and inability to easily switch between different EAI platforms became the downfall of classic EAI. Open standards transformed the integration world from EAI into Service-driven Application Integration.

Modern Enterprise Integration

Modern Enterprise Integration takes on a variety of different shapes. They include Web Services, Integration Adapters, Enterprise Service Bus (ESB), Business Process Management (BPM), Business Rules Management (BRM), Event Driven, Extract-Transform-Load (ETL), Master Data Management (MDM), and more. While attribution of these technologies and platforms to the integration space may not be completely obvious, it is necessary for a variety of reasons. They contain a number of important integration capabilities that are often facilitated through SOA-enabled interfaces. They represent the modern face of integration and provide next generation tools to simplify and streamline integration practices. Finally, many of these technologies are on the path

towards convergence and will form the foundation for the future Enterprise Integration platforms.

Web Service is the most popular integration technique that is used for enterprise integrations today. Web Services are software services that are exposed via standard Web protocols and enable clients (or consumers) to invoke the services over the network.

Integration Adapter is another popular integration technique. They are software entities that implement functionality to bridge the impedance mismatch between enterprise applications and technologies being integrated. These adapters are configurable and are generally JCA (Java Connector Architecture) standards compliant if Java technologies are utilized. They enable connectivity to enterprise applications and technologies such as SAP, PeopleSoft, Oracle, Siebel, FTP, MQ, etc.

Enterprise Service Bus (ESB) has become one of the most popular integration platforms used today. ESB is a specialized software component that can provide a central integration backbone for the enterprise with a variety of inbound and outbound adapters; the ability to route messages based on content, context, or specific rules; service orchestration and message transformation capabilities, among other features.

The popularity of Service-driven methodologies gave rise to BPM. Gartner defines Business Process Management (BPM) as "a management discipline that treats business processes as assets that directly improve enterprise performance by driving operational excellence and business agility." In simple terms, BPM is the discipline of identifying, modeling, automating, managing, and enhancing business processes. Because business processes are a key part of IT Systems operations and interactions, BPM plays a direct role in their integration. It is a higher-level integration activity, as systems are integrated across processes, not the other way around as in typical integration approaches.

Business Rules Management (BRM) has been around for a long time. It enables companies to externalize their rules and define them in a more readable and understandable format. Most powerful rules engines can present rules in an English-like language that requires virtually no programming experience to dynamically define data values and manage the rules. ESB and BPM use business rules to dynamically control message flow and process flow among the integrated applications as shown in Figure 2.

Event Driven Integration uses the Event Driven Architecture (EDA) style which is a step in the evolution of SOA. Sometimes referred to as "asynchronous SOA" or "publish-subscribe," EDA is the architectural style that relies on processing messages asynchronously rather than in real time. This is the most decoupled approach to integration, as neither the publisher nor the subscriber of the message has any knowledge of one another.

Extract-Transform-Load (ETL) tools and approaches enable large volume data manipulation and replication and are one of the oldest data integration mechanisms. Typical ETL tools come with capabilities to extract data from its source, transform it into the target format, and load it into the target data source. Modern ETL tools enable users to expose these operations in a batch as well as real-time mode. As a result, ETL platforms possess SOA and BRM capabilities.

All the techniques described above represent the modern Enterprise Integration landscape. It continues to evolve at a rapid pace. Current advances in mobile platforms, consumer devices, computing platforms, etc., force the integration approaches to move forward as well. Modern trends point to simplification and greater degree of business enablement. While the future is uncertain, it is clear that the Enterprise Integration landscape will continue to evolve rapidly and expand.

David Linthicum, a noted thought leader in the integration space envisions the next generation integration platform as having "the ability to connect to any number of source and target systems, on-premise or cloud-delivered, and to do so in a highly scalable and flexible way. There is also the ability to leverage core standards that lower risk and provide value, as well as the ability to provide pre-built integration solutions for vertical markets. Finally, and most important, there is the ability to quickly deploy and adapt to any changes in the business, which provides agility to accommodate any strategic changes in the business" (Linthicum, 2010). The modern Enterprise Integration landscape fully supports this vision. One can even go out on the limb and suggest that some of the modern integration platforms are already increasing business agility and providing significant value to the organizations.

Figure 2. SOA, BPM, and BRM synergy

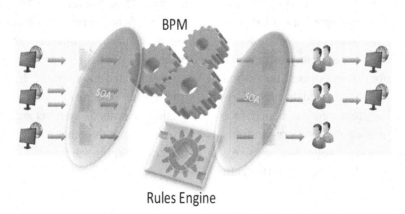

BACKGROUND

Integration represents the biggest IT problem enterprises typically face. Whether it is the integration between internal systems, across incompatible platforms, or with trading partners, the task is daunting, difficult, and never straightforward. Various architectural approaches and design patterns have been created to address the integration challenges. They have evolved from simple proprietary techniques to standards-based, ubiquitous mechanisms. Today, Service-driven architectural approaches are the predominant integration methodology. They are evolving and have incorporated additional methodologies such as BPM, ETL, EDA, etc.

Integration Challenges

Albert Einstein's famous saying "In the middle of difficulty lies opportunity" was not directed at integration. Yet, it fits perfectly. Integration challenges are vast and complex but when done right can be a significant asset to any organization. The difficulty is solving the integration challenges. The opportunity is making integration a strategic asset that renders the enterprise more mature and agile.

The Big Integration Problem

Why is integration so difficult? Many best IT shops struggle to adequately integrate their systems. Organizations that have been in business for a while have a gigantic web of integration mechanisms, tools, patterns, and approaches. They have data moving across their network in large quantities from one system to another. They have a slew of services that are exposed from a variety of applications. They have teams whose primary (and often only) job function is to maintain these integrations. Newer companies, not quite in the same league of integration nightmares, have similar challenges on a smaller scale.

Integrations are hard because they have to achieve a Sisyphean task of making systems, processes, and platforms understand each other. Just like King Sisyphus was punished by the Greek Gods to eternally roll the boulder to the hilltop just to have it roll down again, integration engineers have to continually adjust integration logic, models, and protocols to accommodate internal system changes that take place daily.

Tower of Babel presents another poignant analogy. Different systems, integration points, and trading partners are like the people building the Tower, who lost the ability to speak the same language. The function of the integration mechanisms is to ensure that everyone understands not only what the other integration partners are saying, but also what they mean. In short, the biggest challenge with integration is achieving syntactic and semantic clarity across all integration partners.

Douglas Adams in his novel *The Hitchhiker's Guide to the Galaxy* invented a universal translating device he called the Babel fish. With its help, anyone could understand anyone else regardless of what language they spoke or what planet they were from. Essentially, this was what integration solutions tried to create over the years – a universal translator capable of making every system understand all others. This is a virtually impossible task and as a result most who tried it failed.

Another big problem with integration is that IT systems constantly change. The translating mechanism that has been so painstakingly created eventually has to be modified to accommodate requirements changes, internal system updates, and a variety of other circumstances. This is tantamount to changing tires on a moving vehicle. While all systems need to continue to operate as expected in production, all internal changes as well as changes to the impacted integration mechanisms, need to be carefully choreographed to ensure they are done in complete unison.

As you can imagine, this leads to dramatic and frequent failures. Typical integration problems are directly related to the problems described above. Failure to accommodate internal system and data structure changes is the most typical integration issue. Lack of cooperation between integration teams leads to improper interpretation of new or updated data elements, or outright failures to translate the messages. Semantic changes in data being transmitted result in proper understanding, but improper interpretation and use of the data.

Spaghetti integration presents one of the most typical integration problems. The term relates to many point-to-point integrations as depicted in Figure 3 below. Many enterprises that do not have well defined integration architecture or an SOA program face this challenge. As integration needs are identified, they are addressed in vacuum without consideration of what exists and how these integrations are going to be managed in the long term. This organic integration proliferation leads to systems being dependent on each other and completely exposed to each other's internal changes. When one system changes, it may result in changes cascading through multiple integrations and related systems. In short – an integration nightmare!

All of these aspects represent the big integration problem: systems being dependent on each other, multiple point-to-point interactions, and the need to constantly keep up with changes being made to each system.

Types of Integration Challenges

Every enterprise faces a number of different integration challenges as shown in Figure 4. Regardless of the organization's level of maturity, types of technology and approaches it employs, political landscape, or culture, the types of challenges remain the same. In general, they can be classified as organizational, technological, process, governance, methodology, and shadow IT related.

Organizational Challenges

Organizational challenges stem from the company's structure and the specific way that integration services are provided. Ron Heifetz in his book *The Practice of Adaptive Leadership* said: "There is no such thing as a dysfunctional organization, because every organization is perfectly aligned to

Figure 3. Spaghetti integration

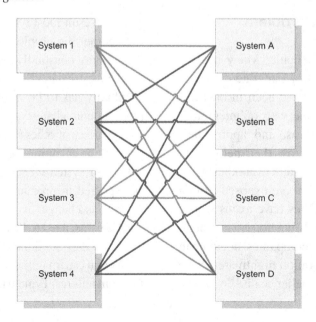

Figure 4. Types of integration challenges

achieve the results it gets" (Heifetz, 2009). This is especially true with integration and SOA program structure within the enterprise. A poorly conceived organizational structure tends to negatively impact even such great architectural paradigms as SOA. On the other hand, a well planned, constructed, and run organization will not only enhance the value provided by integration services but also create efficiencies and save money in the process.

A couple of examples will help visualize and contrast positive and negative examples of organizational structures. Many SOA thought leaders recognize that the most effective path to achieving maturity quickly is to establish a centralized SOA team. However, once the organization as a whole matures to the point that SOA is well understood across the enterprise - practices are accepted and widely followed, technology knowledge is widely spread, and many groups are trying to service-enable their own domains - transition from a centralized to a federated model should occur. Companies that start SOA initiatives but fail to establish a central SOA organization tend to achieve poor results and reach maturity a lot slower than their centralized counterparts.

Similarly, companies that federate too quickly before the right maturity level is achieved, find themselves in a SOA quagmire wherein different groups lacking proper guidance create something known as "Just a Bunch of Services," that deliver little value and complicate the integration space.

Another example of poor organizational structure is silos within individual departments or divisions that deliver similar integration services without any collaboration with, guidance from, or regard for the centralized team and processes. In this scenario, integrations and SOA can be accomplished in multiple ways resulting in increased costs, duplication of work, inconsistent practices, and poor overall results.

Technology Challenges

Technology challenges are a result of poorly selected integration technology platforms, improper architectural decisions, lack of skilled resources, and inappropriate use of technology. Some organizations spend a lot of time choosing the right integration platform only to use it in inappropriate ways. Others are easily swayed by the key vendors

– they buy the vendor's integration platform without much due diligence or understanding of what is being purchased. Sometimes, companies buy powerful integration platforms but outsource all operations, resulting in significant resource gaps when consultants leave. In other cases, companies throw ill-trained support resources at the newly selected technology.

Often enough, people developing integration solutions do not understand best practices or are not given proper guidance, which results in inappropriate, inefficient, and hard to maintain solutions. Alternatively, some companies and their technology leaders decide to utilize only a subset of the integration platform capabilities, which leads to subpar solutions, increased complexity, and inefficient use of powerful technology assets.

Upgrades tend to cause headaches as well. Once integrations or services are implemented on a specific version of a vendor platform, upgrades to this platform may have detrimental impacts on existing code. Unless an upgrade path is provided or the new version of vendor software is backwards compatible, companies will have to spend inordinate amounts of time migrating their implementations to the new version. Instead, organizations choose to remain on the old platform, which leads to lack of support and outdates technologies running in production.

Process Challenges

Process challenges deal with the lack of proper processes, governance mechanisms, and methodologies related to integration services. For any enterprise integration offering to be successful, processes must be well defined, communicated, and understood by everyone involved. If even a single element of the process landscape is not clear, inefficiencies, miscommunications, improper behavior, duplication of efforts, and other issues become the norm. Ensuring that all the processes are set up and executed correctly is probably the single most important task that

enterprises must complete to make the integration program a success.

Processes related to enterprise integration encompass such elements as engaging the integration team, reserving development environments, change management, release management, configuration management, etc. This includes all the steps involved in delivering everyday solutions and communicating across various teams.

Many organizations fail to properly define all the relevant processes. Imagine what havoc can result if even a single station is missing on an assembly line, not to mention two or three. This would be similar to failing to properly define processes guiding enterprise integration delivery. Many tasks would be skipped, end up incomplete, or not even considered. Alternatively, all the processes may be defined so rigorously and require so much time to execute that they impede progress and become bottlenecks themselves. Similarly, processes may be appropriately defined and well understood but ineffectively executed resulting in inefficient delivery, slowdowns, frustrations, and lack of good will towards the enterprise integration team.

Integration Governance Challenges

Establishing proper governance mechanisms is extremely important for successful implementation and maintenance of enterprise integration. These are the guardrails that keep the organization moving forward on the right path without ending up in the ditch. Governance mechanisms include such tasks as ensuring that the right architecture approaches, design patterns, technology platforms, and processes are utilized, validating results at each stage of the delivery lifecycle, defining decision routes, identifying governing bodies, guiding funding decisions, etc. Many books and articles have been written about IT and SOA Governance.

Potential for governance failures are too numerous to mention. Typical challenges come from: poorly defined or convoluted governance processes, improper process execution, lack of real enforcement authority by the governance bodies, ineffective or inappropriate decision making, lack of seamless integration with the rest of IT governance processes, and failure to catch problems. Many organizations struggle with governance. It is probably the most problematic area because it is so hard to get it right. Some companies put too much governance in place while others too little. Some make it too overreaching while others too lax. Even the most mature organizations struggle to execute governance in the most efficient way possible.

Methodology Challenges

Methodologies define how tasks are performed and what steps are taken in the delivery lifecycle. Most well known Software Development Methodologies define specific phases though which a development activity must pass, each of which outlines specific steps, roles, and deliverables. Enterprise Integration methodologies are very similar. They perform the same role, but are specific to integration tasks and activities. They too define steps, roles, and deliverables for each phase in the delivery lifecycle, but they also need to tightly integrate with the Software Development Methodologies being used across the enterprise.

It is easy to see where methodology related challenges lie. They stem from: methodologies being too rigid or too loosely defined, inappropriate role definitions, burdensome level of deliverables, too many steps, inability to scale, lack of understanding or appropriate training available, and improper execution. Methodologies are a typical strength for large enterprises, with the time and money to invest in defining and refining their methods. Smaller companies typically struggle with appropriately defining methodologies and executing them. Methodologies often take on lives of their own, becoming larger than the processes they intend to improve and support. People execute them without understanding, questioning or trying to improve them. Deliverables are often created just because the methodology calls for them, not because they are truly needed. In some instances, no descriptive documentation is produced.

Shadow IT Challenges

A specific type of integration problem deserves a separate mention. Since the integration landscape has expanded and now contains many complementary technologies, many of these can and often are owned by the business. Known as "Shadow IT," these groups operate their own integration practices and run their own integration platforms. IT governance and best practices do not extend into this area. This creates islands of disparate integration practices within the company.

While IT strives to balance delivery with long term thinking, business groups tend to only concentrate on delivering quickly and at the lowest cost. IT generally tries to identify and incorporate all of the Shadow IT groups, but this challenge is not quick or easy to solve. Often, IT is not even aware of the existence of these teams. Other times, business groups do not want to give up autonomy or do not trust IT to be as responsive to its needs as its own team can be.

Next Generation Trends

The technology landscape is always changing. The pace of innovation and introduction of new technologies, concepts, ideas, and approaches continues to accelerate. Disruptive technologies also emerge and tend to reshape not only the technology landscape but also how we approach integration as well. Commoditization of the Internet spurred the creation of *SOAP* (Simple Object Access Protocol), Web Services and ultimately SOA. The Web 2.0 revolution brought with it the emergence of *REST* (Representational State Transfer) and other lightweight communication methods. Many new disruptive technologies and patterns of behavior or usage of computing resources can be observed today.

Virtualization

According to Gartner, virtualization is the abstraction of IT resources that masks the physical nature and boundaries of those resources from resource users. Traditionally, virtualization was implemented within the enterprise boundaries. However, it is not limited to the enterprise anymore and has been extended as a fundamental aspect of the Cloud. Its biggest impact in the enterprise is in the deployment patterns for the integration platforms and their scalability aspects.

Cloud Computing

Cloud computing is probably the best example of a modern disruptor. It is causing a significant impact on how solutions are designed, deployed, and integrated. It is a double whammy – it does not only reshape technology approaches but also completely changes our way of thinking. It introduces a paradigm shift.

Gartner defines Cloud Computing as a style of computing in which massively scalable IT-enabled capabilities are delivered "as a service" to external customers using Internet technologies. Essentially, Cloud computing creates a way to abstract computing resources from their end users and enable the underlying platform to scale dynamically up and down based on demand. Cloud platforms are known as elastic compute nodes. Think of a rubber band – it can easily expand and contract based on whether it is being stretched or not. That is exactly how cloud computing is intended to behave.

Cloud computing has a significant impact on integration. Not only can data, services, and applications reside inside or outside the enterprise boundaries, they will need to be integrated together across these boundaries. Complexity increases drastically if you include Software-as-a-Service, BPM, orchestration, synchronous and asynchronous messaging, event handling, and security. Imagine services and systems that need to be seamlessly integrated across multiple hosting platforms, various security domains, and many physical locations.

David Linthicum stated the Cloud computing impact on integration quite well in his InfoWorld article. He observed that a core issue that arises as we toss our data out to the Clouds is the fact that at some point we need to sync that data with our existing "traditional" on-premises systems. This fact is often lost on those deploying to the Cloud until they attempt to drive business processes between the Cloud and on-premises resources. Linthicum suggested that there are a few ways to address this integration need, including software-based on-premises integration tools, on-premises appliance-based integration tools, and the cloud-delivered integration tools (Linthicum, 2009). Organizations need to understand which path is right for them.

Mobile Computing

Mobile computing is a major trend disrupting how systems are delivered and what integration patterns are used. With the introduction of smart phones, tablets, and other portable devices, more applications are being developed for these platforms. Since these devices have limited computing capacity and access the majority of its data via the network, communications to the server must be quick and lightweight.

As more enterprises make their data, applications, and platforms available through mobile devices, they have to change how data and services are exposed. Lightweight, simple communication mechanisms are preferred over the typical heavyweight, full-featured protocols like SOAP. Lightweight REST protocol becomes the norm. Other lightweight protocols are starting to emerge and will impact how mobile platforms integrate with each other and with the enterprise.

Social Computing

Social computing changes the way companies do business. While in the past, a company web site, toll free phone number, and a few affiliates were sufficient; today organizations must extend themselves beyond their boundaries into the social world. Those that are successful are seamlessly integrating their promotions, marketing, and product offerings across all the social computing platforms, establishing a consistent customer experience throughout all the communication channels, and mining the data acquired through these social interactions. In order to achieve this, enterprises must completely rethink their integration approaches, techniques, and tools.

Consumerization of IT

Consumerization of IT refers to the trend within the industry to enable a mobile workforce through the use of personal devices. In this environment, data, applications, and other essential tools must be made securely available on non-company owned equipment. While there are many potential solutions to solve this challenge, integration plays a key role because organizations should strive to make their employees equally productive regardless of the device or platform they use.

Big Data

Big Data emerged recently as one of the most important disruptive technologies. According to Gartner, Big Data is the term adopted by the market to describe extreme information management and processing issues that exceed the capability of traditional information technology along one or multiple dimensions, to support the use of the information assets.

Since big data deals with large, unstructured data, integration with the data stores becomes a challenge. This data cannot be easily interpreted or consumed. Specific knowledge of how to understand each data structure needs to exist.

Versioning and continuing changes to systems dealing with unstructured data become a part of life. The sheer volume of data requires radically new algorithms to be used to process and make sense of the hidden knowledge. Integration with external data sources introduces yet another challenge, as the amount of external data that needs to be processed can be significant. In short, big data is a big problem.

The Unknown

The disruptions do not end here. Many new technological innovations are just beyond the horizon. Even though we cannot see them today, this does not mean that we should not be prepared for their eventual rise. We should constantly be on the lookout for disruptive changes and put safeguards in place to minimize their impact.

INTEGRATION SOLUTION ARCHITECTURES

A famous American businessman Bernard Baruch once said, "If all you have is a hammer, everything looks like a nail." This is an especially powerful statement if related to software architecture. As technicians, we tend to fall in love with certain solutions and thus look at every problem through the lens of a predetermined approach. Yet, this is the worst thing an architect can do. We always need to consider every single tool on our tool belts, not just a favorite one.

Integration solution architectures cannot be looked at through the prism of a hammer. Every problem is different, and therefore every solution has to be different. We cannot fall into the trap of looking at every problem as a nail. We need to understand the situation and recognize the possible solution patterns that we can apply. A number of proven patterns, best practices, and technologies exist to make our choices well defined and easy. We just need to understand what they are and how to apply them.

Architecture Best Practices

There are many integration architecture best practices that have been developed throughout the years. Many wrong approaches have been tried and tossed to the side, while a number of proven techniques remain and are continually being improved. SOA brought a lot of new and interesting ideas to the integration world.

Hub-and-Spoke Architecture

Hub-and-spoke architecture was the first attempt to solve the big problem of point-to-point integrations. In this paradigm, a central hub would serve as a central integration mechanism for all the parties wishing to interact with each other. Integration mechanisms, protocols, transports, and contracts needed to be agreed to by all parties participating in the conversation. This approach is very similar to a hub model of major airlines, where flights come to a central hub and get distributed from to a large number of destinations as shown in Figure 5.

Even though hub-and-spoke architecture has many flaws, it continues to be used today in a

Figure 5. Hub-and-spoke architecture

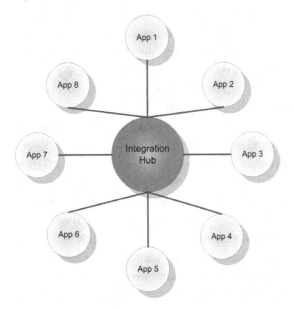

variety of scenarios. Its biggest problems of complexity in managing interactions between all the parties, scalability challenges, and lack of encapsulation have never truly disappeared but rather have been masked by applying this approach only to specific problems. As a general architecture approach, hub-and-spoke architecture still makes sense for data integrations, B2B communications, clearinghouse activities, and centralized processing. Consider this approach only in the scenarios when data or messages need to be processed in a central location or distributed from a central location to a variety of other systems.

Service Bus Architecture

The most prevalent integration architecture best practice today is the Service Bus as shown in Figure 6. This approach establishes a central integration mechanism known as a service bus that accepts, translates, and routes messages from consumers to providers. To best explain this concept, imagine a bus route where people are messages and stops act as consumers and providers. People (messages) get on the bus at one stop, ride on the bus until it is time to get off, and leave the bus at their desired stop. Service bus architectures behave in the same fashion. Consumers send their messages to the service bus, and it delivers the messages to the appropriate providers, which, in turn, respond to the consumers accordingly.

The key advantages of the service bus architecture lie in its ability to abstract consumers from providers, enable message routing, and establish a flexible integration mechanism. Consumers do not need to know who the provider of a specific capability is, as long as they receive the information they seek. Messages may be routed to different providers based on context, version number, or explicit rules. All of this is hidden from the consumer as well as the provider and is in the domain of the service bus itself. Typical service bus architectures provide contract verification, security and protocol reconciliation, message

Figure 6. Service bus architecture

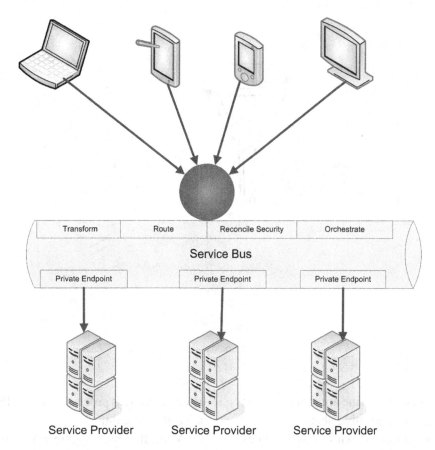

routing and transformation, orchestration, and monitoring capabilities.

The service bus architecture not only enables real time integrations, it also has the ability to facilitate asynchronous messaging. In this architecture approach, messages are sent to the service bus, but the consumers do not wait for a reply. There is also the "fire and forget" messaging pattern in which service consumers do not expect and will not get a response.

Event-Driven Architecture (EDA)

Event-Driven Architecture (EDA) as shown in Figure 7 is one of the latest developments in asynchronous event processing. According to Gartner, "Event-driven architecture (EDA) is an architectural style in which a component (or multiple components) in a software system executes in response to receiving one or more event notifications. An event is anything that happens, and an event object is a record of that event." EDA is also known as publish-subscribe, since it describes this approach very well.

EDA establishes a pattern of communication in which both consumers and providers are completely decoupled from each other. All they know about are the events they publish or consume. They do not know who published those events and who will consume them.

Sometimes referred to as asynchronous SOA, EDA represents the most decoupled way for two systems to interact with one another. This presents significant challenges, especially debugging problems that occur between events being published and consumed. Additionally, complex rules are

Figure 7. Event driven architecture

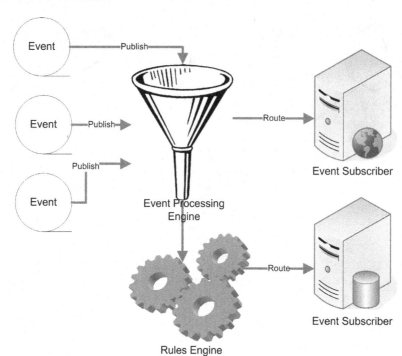

sometimes necessary to define appropriate event routing, aggregation, and subscribers.

A specific form of EDA known as Complex Event Processing (CEP) deserves a separate mention. This is the integration mechanism that correlates events to produce other events, make specific decisions, determine patterns, or process a group of related events. CEP is event processing that combines data from multiple sources to infer events or patterns that suggest complicated circumstances. CEP often relies on SOA platforms and Business Rules engines to enable complex processing and correlation of incoming events. Figure 8 shows how CEP operates.

Extract-Transform-Load (ETL) Architecture

Extract-Transform-Load is most widely used in data integrations. Its goal is to extract data from one source, transform it into the target format, and load it into the target data store, typically in a batch mode. This processing typically takes place at a central location.

While this architecture primarily applies to batch data replication, it is starting to gain traction in real time applications. Since ETL has a lot of similarities with service bus as well as hub-and-spoke functionality, it is not a far stretch to leverage existing transformations to return real time messages rather than loading data into a specific data store. The primary challenge here is to determine when to utilize ETL for real time interactions as opposed to its typical usage model of batch data movement.

Master Data Management (MDM)

Master Data Management (MDM) is a mix of data and real time integration mechanisms. Gartner defines MDM as "a technology-enabled discipline in which business and IT work together to ensure the uniformity, accuracy, stewardship, semantic consistency and accountability of the enterprise's

Figure 8. Complex event processing architecture

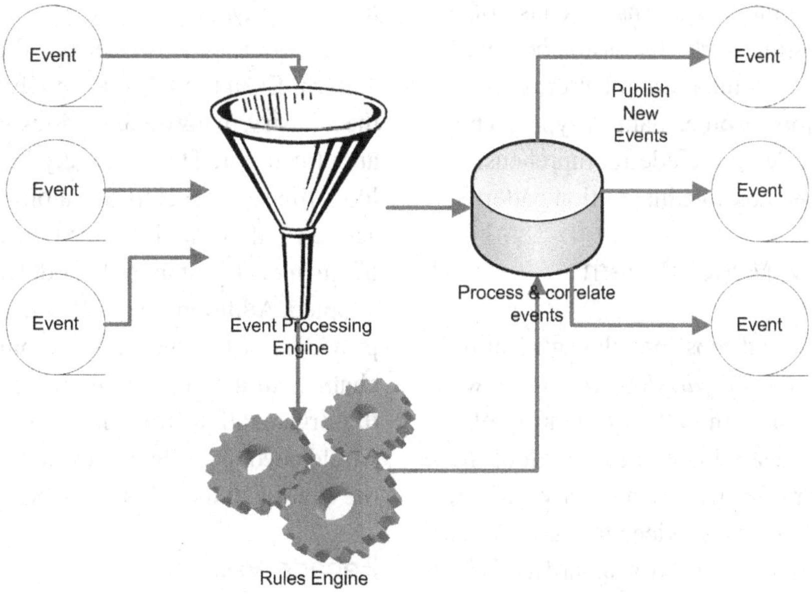

official, shared master data assets. Master data is the consistent and uniform set of identifiers and extended attributes that describes the core entities of the enterprise, such as customers, prospects, citizens, suppliers, sites, hierarchies, and chart of accounts." Essentially, MDM enables a centralized management of key enterprise entities. Access is often controlled through both ETL and Service-driven mechanisms. As a result, MDM can embody and incorporate both of these architectural styles.

Business Process Management (BPM)

Business Process Management is another powerful integration technique. Unlike all the previously discussed integration approaches, BPM can also involve system-to-human interactions. While the role of BPM is to automate business processes, BPM relies heavily on other integration techniques to access the data it needs for processing. Additionally, BPM can be viewed as a system integration mechanism that creates an automated way to perform work across a variety of systems and human tasks. WS-BPEL (Web Service-Business Process Execution Language) is a popular and standard executable language that is used for specifying actions within business processes and for controlling the interaction between business processes and Web services.

Integration Patterns

Integration architectures represent high-level building blocks of a comprehensive integration solution. Once you have selected a specific architectural approach, you need to decide how to design a solution that is going to run on top of it. This is where various integration patterns come in. They represent proven best practices of designing scalable, maintainable, and long lasting integration solutions.

Many of the integration patterns can be applied to multiple architectural approaches. In fact, these patterns are largely architecture and implementation agnostic. Therefore, they will not be discussed in the context of a specific architecture. Instead, each pattern will be described on its own with recommendations as to where it fits best.

A number of books and articles have been written about the integration patterns. (Hohpe

& Woolf, 2003) described a comprehensive set of enterprise integration patterns. Because of a large body of existing work, discussion here will be limited to specific integration patterns and a high-level mention of other pattern types. This section is not intended to include a comprehensive treatment of all the possible integration patterns.

Canonical Data Model Pattern

One of the oldest and most popular integration design pattern is *Canonical Modeling* as shown in Figure 9. This pattern calls for creation of a standard data or messaging model that all of the consumers either directly or indirectly utilize. The integration hub or a service bus can convert all incoming messages into a standard canonical format and perform operations against this format. This way, the central integration broker only needs to know and understand a single data model. This significantly reduces maintenance and support of all the central processing, orchestration, and routing logic. Resources working with the canonical model do not need to constantly learn

new data structures and can complete integration tasks quickly.

However, there are serious drawbacks to this pattern. Even though it is widely adopted across the industry, many organizations are apprehensive about using it. This is largely because it takes a long time to develop a canonical model from scratch or thoroughly understand all of the details of an industry standard model if one is being adopted. Additionally, if all of the consumers and providers utilize the same canonical model, any changes to it can have significant impact across the organization. Imagine how many interfaces would need to be changed when a new version of the canonical model is released.

Façade Pattern

A *façade pattern* (as shown in Figure 10) can prove very useful to minimize the impact of canonical model changes to the consumers. First defined by the Gang of Four (1994) in their book *Design Patterns,* the façade pattern represents a unified interface to the underlying functionality. In this

Figure 9. Canonical model design pattern

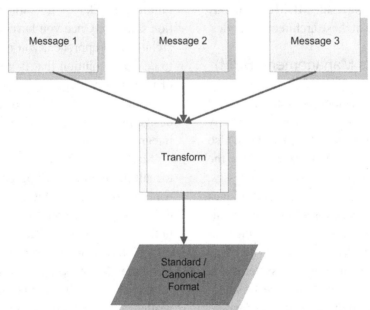

Figure 10. Façade design pattern

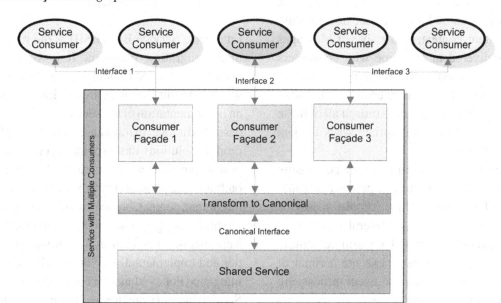

scenario, instead of exposing integration endpoints that expect canonical model based messages, simplified interfaces are defined that are not based on canonical model definitions. These messages are then translated into the canonical model under the covers, and all the processing is performed against canonical model based messages. Since consumers are not aware of the canonical model and do not use it directly, changes do not affect them.

Because integration interfaces are simplified and are no longer based on a standard data model, there may be a number of consumer specific interfaces defined in order to minimize the impact on the existing consumers. Transformations from a simple message model into the canonical format add processing overhead and lengthen the development lifecycle, since these transformations need to be developed, tested, and deployed. Overall, maintenance is increased since both the integration logic and transformations need to be managed.

Messaging, Routing, and Composition Patterns

All the other integration patterns can be broken up into three categories – messaging, routing, and composition. These patterns deal with how messages are delivered, routed, and composed. There are a lot of specific patterns related to these integration categories, but they will not be described here in detail. Instead, we will generalize each category and discuss what kinds of patterns fit into it.

Messaging patterns deal with how messages are constructed, delivered, and processed. This category of patterns deals with canonical modeling, facades, transformations, messaging protocols, delivery models, and processing logic. All of these design patterns strive to create a comprehensive solution space for dealing with different types of messages, delivery mechanisms and requirements, protocols, invocation types, and processing models. They cover the majority of situations we will encounter when integrating together various systems through a message-based interaction.

Routing patterns deal with how messages are routed by the central hub or service bus. Routing may be content, context, or rules-based. Messages may be delivered in real time with consumers waiting for a response from the providers. An asynchronous publish-subscribe mechanism may also be used. Routing patterns broach all of these scenarios and define appropriate ways to deal with all of them.

Composition patterns deal with composing messages together to create a new set of functionality. This may include simple scenarios of combining the output of several services, or complex processing based on simple atomic services composed so as to execute a chain of conditional logic. Complex event processing also falls into this category, as many messages need to be combined, broken up, aggregated, and conditionally processed based on system state or context. Compositions may encompass simple service orchestrations, complex choreographies, or possibly even automated business processes.

Overall, the universe of integration design patterns is very large. However, understating them and determining the right situations to apply the right design patterns is the key to successful integration implementations.

Types of Integration Technologies

Integration technologies are widely accepted as part of the IT landscape. They perform a variety of functions related to system, human, and data integrations. Many of these technologies implement the integration architecture best practices and patterns discussed above. While many of the platforms are designed to perform a specific task, a number of overlaps in functionality and capabilities exist. Some of the technologies have started to merge together to deliver a more seamless experience for end users.

Enterprise Service Bus (ESB)

Enterprise Service Bus (ESB) is the most common integration platform. It is very closely associated with SOA and has become popular when SOA hit the mainstream. ESBs represent an implementation of the service bus architecture described above. In most cases, these are software product solutions that provide a central integration mechanism with a variety of inbound and outbound adapters, ability to route messages based on content, context, or specific rules, orchestration facility, message transformation capabilities, and a number of other features depending on the vendor and implementation. Some ESBs come with integrated Policy Management, SOA Governance, Service Registry and Repository capabilities that reach into the SOA governance space. In some cases, ESBs are delivered as hardware appliances that are aimed at increasing throughput and efficiency of the platform.

ESBs derive their roots from several sources – EAI platforms, Message-Oriented Middleware (MOM) platforms, or modern modular platforms. Depending on how an ESB has matured and the roots from which it came, it may possess different features, characteristics, and strengths. In general, today's ESB implementations have more or less uniform characteristics and come with a relatively standard set of features.

According to David Chappell, a widely recognized pioneer in the ESB space, "the invention of the ESB was not an accident. The ESB is a result of vendors working with forward-thinking customers who were trying to build a standards-based integration network using a foundation of SOA, messaging, and XML" (Chappell, 2004).

Many ESBs incorporate a number of other integration technologies and capabilities that will be discussed below. This may include a BPM/BPEL engine to orchestrate or choreograph services, a rules engine to define business, transformation or transition rules, and possibly even an event-processing engine. Thus, ESBs are becoming a focal point for a number of integration technologies.

Business Process Management (BPM)

Business Process Management suites enable enterprises to automate business processes and integrate them with various systems and services. A typical BPM implementation provides the ability to design, test, simulate, deploy, and execute business processes. Most of them support BPMN 2.0 (Business Process Modeling Notation) that represents a standard convention for modeling processes. They may also include a BPEL engine to execute the business processes. Additionally, a Business Activity Monitoring (BAM) module that tracks and monitors the state of each process being executed is available in most BPM products.

If implemented as an enterprise asset, BPM heavily relies on SOA, WS-BPEL, and shared services to integrate with systems necessary to perform specific tasks within a process. Because these integrations reach across a number of processes, systems, and organizational boundaries, it is often necessary to treat the services consumed by BPM-enabled processes as enterprise assets. Thus, SOA and by extension the ESB, play a crucial role in the success of a BPM implementation.

Another platform that is typically closely associated with BPM is a Business Rules Engine. BPM products come with a rudimentary rules capability that is able to describe simple routing or logical decisions. For more complex decisions and processing, a robust and full-featured Business Rules Engine is necessary. Many BPM platforms come already bundled with a robust rules engine that seamlessly integrates with process design and execution. Many rules engines expose their executable rule sets as Web Services, which means that they may be consumed directly by the BPM/BPEL engine or via an ESB exposed endpoint.

Many BPM platforms rely heavily on an ESB to perform a variety of integration tasks. Thus, this represents another route for amalgamation of different integration capabilities and technologies.

Event Processing

While event processing by itself can be easily implemented on a MOM (Message Oriented Middleware) or ESB platform, a specific use case has spurred the creation of dedicated technology solutions. This use case is Complex Event Processing (CEP). As explained earlier, event processing is a method of tracking and analyzing (processing) streams of information (data) about things that happen (events), and deriving a conclusion from them. The goal of complex event processing is to identify meaningful events (such as opportunities or threats) and respond to them as quickly as possible.

Many vendors implement separate CEP solutions that help organizations filter, correlate, and process events. Events being processed by the CEP platform come from a variety of sources across the enterprise. To process them, CEP must rely on BPM, BRM, and ESB capabilities. BPM is needed to define and automate processes that each event needs to undergo to be properly processed. BRM is necessary to perform complex logic on incoming and outgoing events and ESB provides a common interaction and integration mechanism.

As a result, CEP solutions usually incorporate BPM, BRM, and ESB-like features or are tightly integrated with these offerings from the same or other partner vendors. As these platforms mature, they may become bundled with the rest of the supporting technologies.

Extract-Transform-Load (ETL)

Extract-Transform-Load architecture was discussed earlier. Most of the ETL tools implement this architecture in a very similar fashion. After all, a general ETL approach is quite simple and straightforward. Major differences lie in how each tool performs extract, transform, and load tasks, what underlying technologies are used, how each platform scales, and what additional features it offers.

Even though ETL is typically associated with batch data integrations, some of the ETL tools offer real time integration capabilities. This may serve as a poor man's ESB, if most of the services being consumed across the enterprise read data from enterprise repositories. Most likely, however, ETL generated services can be exposed through an ESB and consumed as enterprise services.

ETL tools contain a number of overlaps with other integration technologies. This includes message transformation, business logic, and event processing. Message transformation is at the core of each ETL platform. Business logic is needed to extract and transform complex data sets. Some ETL tools may act as event processors, in which case a specific ETL operation is performed in response to a predefined event.

Master Data Management (MDM)

Master Data Management, as discussed earlier, represents a central mechanism for managing key enterprise data entities. MDM vendors typically identify these master data entities and create an access layer for them through a well-defined set of APIs. Not surprisingly, these APIs are most often exposed as Web Services.

MDM products are based on a variety of integration mechanisms. They include ESB, ETL, and BRM. ESB-like capabilities are needed by the MDM API layer to expose a variety of interfaces to the consumers and manage access to the underlying data. Alternatively, MDM APIs may be defined uniformly as Web Services, in which case they need to be exposed through an ESB to achieve maximum effectiveness and efficiency. MDM relies heavily on ETL to move data to a central location or transform data into the standard format. BRM is needed to perform some of the more complex transformations or routing tasks.

Master Data Management is usually not successful without a strong SOA program. Quite often, MDM and SOA programs are executed in parallel and share many of the same technologies, approaches, and goals.

Implementation Considerations

Architecture is a logical representation of how the environment will look when the solution is actually implemented and running. The relationship between architecture and its implemented state is best described through a comparison of a class and an object. A class contains the code that describes how it will behave when it is instantiated and executed. An object is an actual instance of a class. A class should be aware of how it will be loaded into the memory, what resources it will consume, and how it will interact with the outside world. The compiler takes all this into account when it compiles the code and creates a class binary, and the class loader executes the binary code according to the instructions supplied by the compiled code. By the same token, when implementing specific architecture approaches, attention needs to be paid to how they will interact with the rest of the environment, what is the best way to deploy the solution, and what impact it will have.

Technology

Each architectural approach and best practice has some kind of associated technology parallel. For example, service bus architecture is typically implemented via an ESB, EDA is realized through a combination of ESB and a Business Rules Engine, ETL and MDM are supported by specific vendor tools, and so on. This is not accidental. Most of the architectural approaches discussed here were created before vendors started to manufacture product solutions for them. However, at this point of time, there are very few integration architectural approaches that do not have a technology implementation.

Many of the vendor products provide overlapping capabilities. The trick is to select the right product to solve the problem for the short and long term. While one product may offer most of the desired capabilities, some of the features may not satisfy current or future demands. For example, an ESB platform may offer rudimentary business process management capabilities that may be sufficient for near term requirements. However, in the long term, a more robust BPM solution will be necessary. Thus, we need to decide how to tackle the problem at hand and what solution should be selected for what use case.

It is often desirable to establish a common platform for some or most of the integration capabilities discussed in this chapter. A central ESB implementation is typical for most enterprises. Once this capability is established, a governance model should be put in place to identify the demand for and enable usage of this shared resource. This increases return on investment for the shared capability and decreases costs for everyone utilizing it.

Organization

Each integration capability brings a different organizational impact with it. Some are best suited to be owned and managed centrally, while others scale better in a federated mode. There may also be instances when a capability has to be created as a centrally managed asset, with the goal of federating it when a certain level of maturity is reached.

There are a couple of good examples for this. A BPM capability should characteristically be delivered in a federated mode. A central team would stand up, manage, and govern all the BPM run-time environments, while various teams perform the development of business process models across the enterprise. ESB typically falls into the "centralize then federate" scenario. The initial rollout of an ESB should be managed centrally, with a central team performing all the development on the platform. When the SOA program reaches a level of maturity in the enterprise, development on the shared ESB platform can start to be federated across the enterprise. This occurs when other teams

understand all the SOA concepts, are trained to develop their own services and integrations, have the need to service-enable their own areas, and when the central SOA team has strong governance mechanisms in place.

Other organizational realities need to be considered when rolling out integration capabilities. Politics and organizational structures play a huge role in the success or failure of enterprise-wide initiatives. If there is a strong business case and demand for these capabilities, as well as solid support from the organizational leadership, the initiative will succeed. If, however, support from the leadership is lacking and the enterprise is broken into strong silos, the centralized model will not work. Other factors might be the strength and influence of the architects across the organizations. With the lack of formal governance, architects can influence a number of areas or projects to adopt new technologies to solve their problems. This, in turn, may drive the demand for common solutions. It is important to ensure that all the organizational factors are considered when rolling out shared capabilities across the enterprise.

Funding

Funding is a crucial component in the success of integration initiatives. Since we are dealing with shared capabilities, it is always important to determine how they will be stood up and who will pay for them. These efforts are not cheap and are unlikely to be funded by individual business units. A central way to fund these initiatives must be determined.

Some organizations choose to pay for the shared capabilities through an overarching IT budget. Individual projects or business units would not be asked to share the costs. Once the capability is established, it continues to be managed and funded centrally. Other organizations, especially those that need to account for all the infrastructure usage at the activity or business unit level, establish a chargeback mechanism that estimates the portion of the funds that should come from each area using the shared asset.

There are many other funding mechanisms that companies use. The primary success factor is the ability for the enterprise to fund creation and management of the central capability. Individual business units should not be asked to fund the initial rollout or management of the shared asset, unless they intend to own it outright.

Culture

Organizational culture is one of those pesky little things that one forgets about when trying to push major initiatives through. Some organizations may be more susceptible to change than others because of their culture. Integration presents yet another dimension. Because it introduces shared capabilities that are offered primarily through vendor products, some organizational cultures may embrace this while others may reject it outright.

Consider those organizations that are used to implementing vendor products, dealing with third parties, and integrating applications together. Such enterprises will present fertile ground for shared integration assets. This would be a natural fit, because it would not be a far reach from the existing operating model. Shared integration capabilities may only improve the life of IT personnel and provide additional business enablement.

Alternatively, those organizations that are development shops and have very few third party applications will be overtly hostile to establishing shared integration capabilities. Most people that align with this culture would assume that they can just do this through code, and it would be better, cheaper, and easier to maintain. This kind of thinking is hard to change. Like the Titanic, this organization would be very slow to steer in any new direction, especially since the shift will be made away from custom development and towards configuring vendor provided platforms.

EMERGING TRENDS

François de la Rochefoucauld's famous quote "The only thing constant in life is change" can be easily applied to software. The pace of change and innovation is unprecedented. The adoption rate for new technology continues to accelerate. For example, iPad sold three million units in the first 80 days after its release, which is an enormous jump if compared to 350,000 DVD players sold in the first year.

The SOA and integration technology, architectures, and best practices will continue to change. Current trends point to consolidation in the business enablement and integration capabilities. As discussed earlier, more and more integration capabilities are being packaged into the BPM, BRM, ESB, and other products. At the same time, integration platforms are evolving beyond their typical technology roots and are striving to become business enablement tools.

Some more interesting trends are starting to emerge. Integration at the glass, or integration at the user interface level, is gaining momentum due to widespread adoption of various social media tools. Companies no longer have an option to align with one or two social media sites – they need to be active across all of them. They have to integrate their web sites and interaction channels with specific social media experiences, thereby posing an interesting integration problem.

Many web sites that allow other sites to be integrated with theirs, offer Web APIs to accomplish this. Integration platforms need to be able to incorporate adapters and connectors to enable easier integration with a variety of Web API interfaces and providers.

Proliferation of mobile devices are giving rise to the development toolkits aimed at keeping source code the same for a variety of mobile platforms. These toolkits enable developers to develop their applications once and specify the target deployment platform, which would trigger compilation into an appropriate executable module. While these approaches do not directly impact mobile integration practices, the mobile development toolkits are likely to start tackling integration problems once they gain momentum and are deployed at a number of large institutions. Close coupling with existing integration practices and platforms may move mobile development further into enterprise scale applications.

Yogi Berra provided by far the best perspective about the future when he said, "It's tough to make predictions, especially about the future." Many new trends in Service-driven architecture and integration are around the corner, but they are still invisible and unknown to us. Yet, as death and taxes, they are inevitable.

CONCLUSION

Integration is one of the most complex undertakings in software engineering. In its current form, it is infinitely more complex than ever. As the systems that need integration move farther apart, technologies become more disparate, and integration patterns become less uniform - the complexity of the integration problem increases exponentially. However, proven solution architectures, best practices, and design patterns provide a guiding light in the ever-changing landscape of software development and technology platforms. Using the techniques and approaches discussed in this chapter will ensure success of integration endeavors.

REFERENCES

Chappell, D. (2004). *Enterprise service bus: Theory in practice.* O'Reilly Media.

Gamma, E., Helm, R., Johnson, R., & Vlissides, J. (1994). *Design patterns: Elements of reusable object-oriented software.* Addison-Wesley Professional Computing Series.

Gartner, Inc. (n.d.). *IT glossary: Big data.* Retrieved from http://www.gartner.com/it-glossary/big-data/

Gartner, Inc. (n.d.). *IT glossary: Business process management (BPM).* Retrieved from http://www.gartner.com/it-glossary/business-process-management-bpm/

Gartner, Inc. (n.d.). *IT glossary: Cloud computing.* Retrieved from http://www.gartner.com/it-glossary/cloud-computing/

Gartner, Inc. (n.d.). *IT glossary: EDA (Event-Driven Architecture).* Retrieved from http://www.gartner.com/it-glossary/eda-event-driven-architecture/

Gartner, Inc. (n.d.). *IT glossary: Master data management (MDM).* Retrieved from http://www.gartner.com/it-glossary/master-data-management-mdm/

Gartner, Inc. (n.d.). *IT glossary: Service-oriented architecture (SOA).* Retrieved from http://www.gartner.com/it-glossary/service-oriented-architecture-soa/

Gartner, Inc. (n.d.). *IT glossary: Virtualization.* Retrieved from http://www.gartner.com/it-glossary/virtualization/

Heifetz, R. A. (2009). *The practice of adaptive leadership: Tools and tactics for changing your organization and the world.* Harvard Business Press.

Hohpe, G., & Woolf, B. (2003). *Enterprise integration patterns.* Addison-Wesley.

Linthicum, D. (2009). *The integration challenges of cloud computing.* Retrieved from http://www.infoworld.com/d/cloud-computing/integration-challenges-cloud-computing-157

Linthicum, D. (2010). *Moving to the next generation of data integration.* Retrieved from http://www.dataintegrationblog.com/data-integration-david-linthicum/moving-to-the-next-generation-of-data-integration/

KEY TERMS AND DEFINITIONS

Big Data: Ability to manage and process very large amounts of potentially unrelated and unstructured data.

Business Process Management (BPM): A practice of managing business processes as shared, enterprise assets.

Cloud Computing: Computing style that relies on elastic computing resources to provide all the necessary processing capacity or platform configurations to the interfacing systems.

Complex Event Processing (CEP): Event processing mechanism that correlates events to produce other events, make specific decisions based on event patterns, determine these patterns, or process a group of related events.

Enterprise Integration (EI): Sharing of data and business logic across systems in a single or extended enterprise.

Enterprise Service Bus (ESB): A platform that represents a central integration mechanism for exposing shared services, routing, transforming, and orchestrating messages, and defining and enforcing service policies.

Event Driven Architecture (EDA): Architectural style that relies on processing messages asynchronously rather than in real time.

Master Data Management (MDM): A practice of identifying and managing key enterprise data entities.

Service Oriented Architecture (SOA): Software architecture style that strives to establish a collection of business logic components that can be shared and reused across enterprise.

Chapter 3
Enterprise Integration:
Architectural Approaches

Venky Shankararaman
Singapore Management University, Singapore

Alan Megargel
Singapore Management University, Singapore

ABSTRACT

Enterprise Integration enables the sharing of information and business processes among the various applications and data sources within and beyond an organization. Over the years, due to changes in business requirements and availability of sophisticated technology, the architectures for integrating applications and data sources have evolved from simple point-to-point integration technique to more comprehensive architectures leveraging Service Oriented Architecture (SOA) and Event Driven Architecture (EDA). In this chapter, the authors trace this evolution, and examine the architectures in terms of complexity versus business benefit. The architectures are presented in a logical progression starting with the simplest form.

INTRODUCTION

Enterprise integration includes a broad set of activities that ensure both business processes and information technology applications are coordinated within and beyond the enterprise. It deals with solving a range of issues relating to business process definition, common data standards, architectural compatibility, technical interoperability, and organizational alignment (Lam et al., 2004; Lam et al., 2007).

First, let's examine why applications need to integrate. A stand-alone application that is purpose built and can fulfill all of its business functionality without sharing information with other applications would not need to be integrated. Any new functionality would be added incrementally, until the application becomes "monolithic." This style is reminiscent of the mainframe era, where one application and a set of terminals could operate an entire business.

We now know that monolithic applications are not flexible enough to adapt to today's ever changing business landscape. The speed of doing business is increasing. Customers are becoming more sophisticated and demanding better, faster,

DOI: 10.4018/978-1-4666-4193-8.ch003

and cheaper services, anytime and anywhere. In today's best practice architecture, business processes are decomposed into distinct components or applications integrated together to fulfill business functionality (Shankararaman et al., 2011). As a matter of necessity then, applications must integrate.

This chapter explores the various architectural styles for integrating applications, ranging from simple point-to-point messaging, to more comprehensive service-oriented and event-driven architecture styles. The integration patterns examined here vary in terms of complexity versus business benefit and will be presented in a logical progression starting with the simplest form.

BACKGROUND

A number of authors have attempted to classify enterprise integration based on integration approaches. One of the earliest classifications of enterprise integration is based on the point in the system where the integration occurs, namely, data, method, application or interface (Linthicum, 1999). For example, method integration focused on integrating one application with another by invocation of APIs in the second application; interface integration focused on screen scraping as a means for exchanging information; and data integration focused on the data where there is a direct exchange between the databases of the integrating applications.

More recently, Al Mosawi et al. (2006) proposed a more comprehensive classification for enterprise integration. The authors suggested two general categories, Category 1 and Category 2. Category 1 consisted of approaches that focused on data or process, which is similar to the classification proposed by Linthicum. Within this Category, they identified nine different approaches, namely, data integration, object integration, function or method integration, user interface integration, application interface integration, presentation integration, process integration, internal process integration, and cross-enterprise process integration. Category 2 consisted of approaches that focused on the architecture layers. Within this category they identified seven layers, namely, business architecture layer, business process layer, information architecture layer, inter-organizational layer, application layer, enterprise application layer, technology layer, and middleware integration layer.

Lam et al. (2007) take a very different approach by classifying integration approaches based on three categories namely enterprise application integration (EAI), B2B integration (B2Bi) and Web integration. Enterprise application integration dealt with integrating applications within the organization. The drivers included operational efficiency, customer relationship management, and business process automation. B2Bi dealt with integrating applications between two or more organizations. The drivers included supply chain management and B2B commerce. Web integration dealt with integrating an organization's existing application with new Web-based front-end applications. The drivers included E-Business and Web-channel services. In the same article, the authors suggested five categories of integration based on the level at which integration occurred, namely, presentation, data, application, service, and process integration. They then proposed four basic kinds of integration architectures, namely, batch integration, point-to-point integration, broker-based integration, and business process integration.

In this chapter, we build on the above approaches to classify enterprise integration but specifically focus on the architectural styles for integrating applications. We identify five different architecture styles:

- Point-to-point integration.
- Hub-and-spoke messaging.
- Service oriented architecture with enterprise service bus.

- Service oriented architecture with enterprise service bus and business process management.
- Event driven architecture.

Finally, we highlight some of the emerging trends in the area of enterprise integration. In the subsequent sections, for each style, using a diagram, we describe the architecture, discuss the business drivers, describe some use case scenarios and highlight the challenges. The architecture styles are organized according to their chronology, starting from point-to-point integration to event driven architecture.

ENTERPRISE INTEGRATION APPROACHES

Point-to-Point Integration

The simplest form of application integration is through direct Point-to-Point (P2P) connection between two applications using any number of different protocols and tools. Examples of P2P integration protocols, specifications, and tools include File Transfer Protocol (FTP), Java Remote Method Invocation (RMI), vendor independent peer-to-peer specifications like Common Object Request Broker Architecture (CORBA) (OMG, 2004; Maheswari et al., 2003), and vendor specific peer-to-peer messaging tools such as TIBCO Rendezvous (RV) (Maheswari et al., 2005). An example use case for a P2P integration using FTP is an auto insurance company receiving workshop reports from the garages sent as text file at the end of each day.

A P2P style of integration has its advantages. If the application developers on both ends of the integration agree on the protocol and data format to be used, then generally the integration can be developed quickly. The other advantage is low latency, since there is no intermediary between the applications. P2P integration is usually chosen by

design if it is the only way to achieve low latency requirements.

There are several disadvantages to a P2P style of integration. As the number of applications increases, the environment becomes more difficult to maintain as shown in Figure 1. Since the integration configuration details (e.g. documentation) are distributed among the end points, there is ever increasing chance that the documentation will become out of date, or even lost. Furthermore, with a P2P style of integration, applications are "tightly coupled" in a sense that any change in one application may impact many others, making the architecture "brittle" and inflexible to change.

Hub-and-Spoke Messaging

Once the number of applications in an enterprise reaches a certain threshold, the P2P style of integration becomes too complex to manage economically. "Middleware" is then introduced to implement a message-oriented *Hub-and-Spoke* style of integration, providing a central point of control sometimes referred to as a Message Broker. Message processing through the central

Figure 1. Point-to-point integration

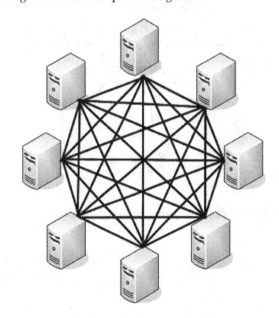

hub includes routing, splitting, and combining of messages. The hub decouples applications to some extent, in that changes on either side of the hub can be managed centrally as shown in Figure 2.

Message-Oriented Middleware (MOM) is an infrastructure that provides the means to transport messages between business applications, using a number of interaction patterns. Within a MOM, messages flow through a type of "Channel." The two basic types of channels are "Queue" and "Topic." Applications within an enterprise typically use common MOM vendor software to send and receive messages via queues and topics. Two of the most commonly used vendor software are TIBCO Enterprise Message Service and IBM Websphere MQ, both of which implement the Java Message Service (JMS) API standard (Yusuf, 2004).

Figure 2. Hub-and-spoke integration using a message-oriented middleware

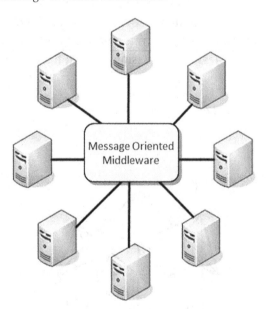

Figure 3. Point-to-point channel (queue)

The simplest implementation of a Queue is a point-to-point channel between a message sender and a message receiver as shown in Figure 3. A Queue, by definition, ensures that messages are received in First-In-First-Out (FIFO) order. Once a message is received by the Receiver, it is removed from the Queue. A persistent Queue can also guarantee message delivery such that if the Receiver becomes unavailable for any reason, the messages sent by the Sender will continue to accumulate (in the database or file system) within the Queue until the Receiver becomes available again. An example use case for a simple message queue is a piece of factory equipment that sends a continuous stream of measurement data to a factory information system (Hohpe et al., 2004).

One of the primary functions of a Message Broker is to route messages between queues as shown in Figure 4, using various types of routing logic. Content-based routing, for example, is typically performed based on information in the message header, or information at a fixed location (field name or offset) within the message body. Routing logic can be fixed at design-time, or can be made dynamic at runtime based on feedback from message senders or receivers. An example use case of a content-based message router is the dispatch of manufacturing work orders based on a factory code in the message header (Hohpe et al., 2004).

Besides a "Queue," the other basic type of messaging channel is a "Topic." A topic is the object of a *Publish-Subscribe* interaction pattern. Senders publish messages to a Topic, and receivers subscribe to the Topic as shown in Figure 5. All subscribers receive one and only one copy of a message sent by a publisher. A message in a

Figure 4. Message broker

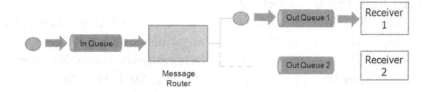

Figure 5. Publish-subscribe channel (topic)

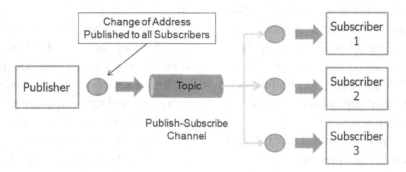

topic is configured with a Time to Live (TTL), such that the message will be removed from the Topic once its TTL has expired.

An example use case of the *publish-subscribe* pattern is in banking where multiple applications need to be updated, whenever a customer address changes. The publishing application need not know about the subscribing applications, as all it does is publish the message (customer address change) to the topic. Banking applications that have subscribed to the topic will receive the message (Hohpe et al., 2004).

In the three patterns mentioned above (point-to-point channel, message router, and publish-

subscribe), messages flow in one direction only, from sender to receiver. A natural extension of a simple queue then is to implement a pair of queues pointing in opposite directions, where one queue handles "Request" messages and the other queue handles "Reply" messages as shown in Figure 6.

In this context, a Request message is like an instruction, and a Reply message is like the result or status of the request. If the Requester needs to wait for the Reply before executing its next task, then this interaction is referred to as a Synchronous Request-Reply; otherwise, the interaction is referred to as an Asynchronous Request-Reply. Similar to a remote procedure call, a typical use

Figure 6. Request-reply

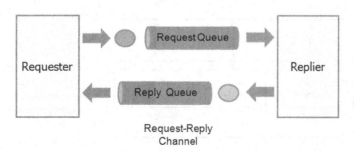

case for the Request-Reply pattern is to request for data to be Created, Read, Updated, or Deleted (CRUD) (Hohpe et al., 2004). In Asynchronous Request-Reply, the requester can send a number of requests and since the replies can arrive at any time in the future and in any order, a message correlation ID is used to match the reply message to the request message.

The main advantage of Hub-and-Spoke messaging over Point-to-Point integration is that changes are managed centrally at the hub rather than being distributing among all of the application end points. Message routing logic can be centralized. A MOM provides a set of interaction patterns, which can be implemented via an API (Hapner et al., 2002).

However, there are limitations. There is a tight coupling between the programming language and the message content, e.g., Java Messaging Service (JMS) requires specific fields in the message header. Data transformation still needs be performed by the sending or receiving applications where required. Each new integration must be explicitly developed, and as such, there is no opportunity for reuse. Reuse reduces development costs and enables business agility.

SOA with ESB

Service Oriented Architecture (SOA) has emerged as the dominant architectural style that enables business agility while reducing development costs (Woods, 2003). The primary integration design pattern that implements a SOA is the Enterprise Service Bus (ESB). In SOA, there is the concept of Service Consumers and Service Providers as shown in Figure 7.

Within an ESB, there are different layers of service components as shown in Figure 8. Consumer-facing Business Services (also referred to as Proxy Services) expose business functionality using standard data semantics and transport protocols; Atomic Services provide specific fine-grained application functionality, and Composite Services orchestrate multiple Atomic Services to provide end-to-end business services.

With an ESB, services are developed once and then used by multiple consumers. For example, a service called "GetOrderStatus" might be invoked by several service consumers using multiple channels, e.g., Internet Channel, Mobile Channel, B2B Gateway, and Order Entry. In pseudo code, each service consumer would invoke

Figure 7. SOA high level representation

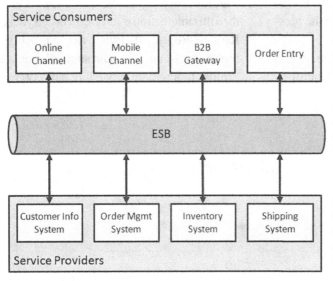

Service Consumers consume business services exposed via ESB using enterprise standard data semantics and standard transport protocols.

ESB exposes reusable business services using enterprise standard data semantics and standard transport protocols.

Service Providers expose business functionality and data using provider specific, native data semantics and native transport protocols.

Figure 8. ESB conceptual architecture

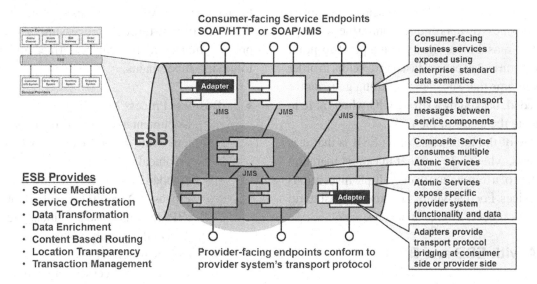

the service as follows: OrderStatus = GetOrder Status(OrderNumber).

The request and response parameters of services are typically published in a Service Catalog (also called a Service Registry) where application developers can conveniently find services to invoke. Many of the ESB tools leverage the Web Service technology, which is a standards based, vendor neutral XML based middleware framework. The key standards used include SOAP (Simple Object Access Protocol), WSDL (Web Services Description Language), and a host of additional standards, collectively called WS-*. These standards support SOA based enterprise solutions that ensure security, reliable messaging, transaction integrity, etc. (OASIS, 2012). Using these integration standards, the application generates a SOAP request based on the WSDL definition of the service interface (WSDL defines the Request, Response, and often Fault message formats in human and machine readable form).

The ROI (Return on Investment) on service development is quickly realized when two or more composite services reuse an existing service. SOA Governance can help track the overall development cost avoidance through service reuse. Cost avoidance through service reuse is one of the primary goals of a Service-driven methodology.

Besides cost avoidance, another primary goal of a SOA/ESB is flexibility such that changes and additions to the architecture can be made with little or no impact on service consumers. For example, if a company decides to replace its Order Management System, front-end applications (service consumers) would not need to make any software changes. This is made possible by the ESB which in effect decouples the front-end service consumers from the backend service providers through data abstraction. The service "GetOrderStatus" would still return "OrderStatus" using the same data structure and field names, regardless of the underlying Order Management System interface specifications.

A well implemented ESB reduces development costs through service reuse and enables business agility. However, there are organizational challenges to overcome. Typically, an ESB is centrally managed by a team of integration specialists who support company-wide integration requirements. Whenever a large enterprise is tasked to share a common enterprise platform, the gray areas of responsibility must be clarified. Questions arise such as – "Who owns what?" "Who pays?" and "Who decides what?" There is usually pushback from business owners by questioning the development of reusable services when a point-to-point integration is cheaper and faster to develop. In order to overcome these challenges, strong governance is needed, backed by a strong CIO who is able to mandate the usage of the ESB.

One of the limitations of an ESB is that it is stateless, which is to say that in cannot maintain the state of a transaction over multiple invocations of services. For that type of functionality, a stateful business process engine is needed.

SOA with ESB and BPM

Business processes are organizational assets that are central to creating value for customers. Customers, internal or external, perceive value from business processes rather than from standalone or individual functions. Since business processes are important assets of the enterprise, core processes that generate the most value to customers should be carefully managed (Shankararaman et al., 2007).

The singular objective of Business Process Management (BPM) is to achieve continuous process improvement. In order to improve a business process, or anything else for that matter, you have to be able to measure it. Business processes iterate continuously through a lifecycle consisting of four stages; modeling, simulation, execution, and analysis as shown in Figure 9.

Business process implementation is a large topic area covering process modeling and execu-tion across document centric workflow, and case management as well as process automation to achieve straight-through-processing. Business process implementation can be defined under the following subdomains:

- Business Process Modeling
  - ○ Documentation of a business system using a combination of text and graphical notation.
  - ○ Standard notations such as Business Process Modeling and Notation (BPMN) are used, which are understood by both business users and technical developers.
  - ○ Business processes are modeled, simulated and analyzed for optimum effectiveness and efficiency (Havey, 2005).
- Document-Centric Workflow
  - ○ Execution of document-centric and human-centric workflows.
  - ○ May consume business services via an ESB.
  - ○ Stateful long running processes.
- Business Process Orchestration
  - ○ Composition of complex business processes.
  - ○ System-centric, rather than human-centric.
  - ○ Business processes may consume services via an ESB.
  - ○ Stateful short or long running processes.

Figure 9. Business process lifecycle

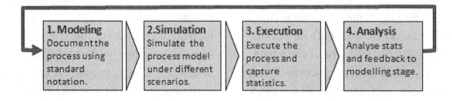

Business processes can be optimized for reuse across an enterprise much like business services exposed via an ESB can be optimized for reuse. The benefit of reusable assets is amplified when BPM and ESB patterns are used together. BPM and ESB patterns are expressed in the definitive "SOA Reference Architecture" as shown in Figure 10, published by The Open Group, a collaboration of industry partners and technology vendors.

A process-driven *Composite* application is comprised of a sequence of subprocesses or activities that invoke functionality in one or more distributed applications. An activity in the process can be human or automated. Human activities require a person to perform a task through an appropriate user interface, such as the task to approve a purchase request. Automated activities require the invocation of software functionality in an application through a service interface, such as a 'Create Purchase Order' service in an ERP application. The process-driven composite application requires BPM tools for modeling and configuring the process (e.g. through activities,

service interfaces, etc.), designing the user interfaces, and deploying and monitoring the execution of the process. It also requires SOA tools for exposing, discovering, and consuming application functionality as services.

Continuous process improvement through best practice BPM methodology is a journey. Improvements are realized incrementally through multiple iterations of the BPM life cycle. Many companies go through a process re-engineering phase, where effort is concentrated on the processes that are most critical to customer satisfaction. Typically, a process owner will implement manual and procedural improvements to human centric processes before introducing process automation. Increasingly more automation is introduced as the process moves through stages of maturity, until the process is completely automated. A process that is completely automated without any human steps is referred to as a "straight-through process." The business benefits of a process are proportional to its level of automation. Organizations may be at different stages of the BPM maturity shown in

Figure 10. SOA reference architecture (© Open Group 2009)

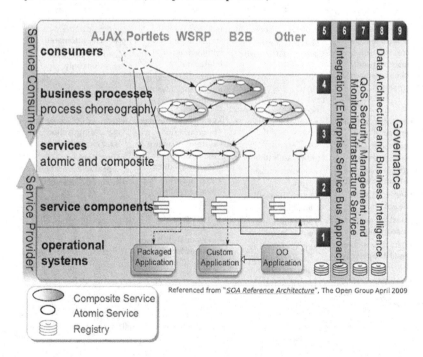

Figure 11. The integration architecture will vary according to the level of maturity. For example, an organization at Level 1 will most likely have hub-and-spoke architecture and organizations at Level 4 may be implementing SOA-ESB-BPM.

The business use cases for implementing the BPM and ESB patterns together span a multitude of different industries. Some examples are as follows:

- Banking
  - Loan Account Opening and Fulfillment
  - Collections and Handling of Non-Performing Loans
  - Customer Case Management
- Airlines
  - Flight Reservations
  - Ticketing
  - Loyalty Points Redemption

The above business processes may be highly automated, however, note that they are all initiated by a human. While BPM and ESB patterns are effective and efficient in executing business processes, there is some limitation in the way processes are started. With BPM, there is no capability to initiate a business process. Some external trigger in the form of human action, or scheduled or event based triggers are necessary to initiate a business process.

Event-Driven Architecture

Event-Driven Architecture or EDA is based on the concept that events drive business interactions. A business event is a noteworthy happening in the enterprise that introduces a change in its state, which in turn can trigger business processes. For example, a new sales order from a customer triggers the sales process, return of faulty goods

Figure 11. BPM maturity model

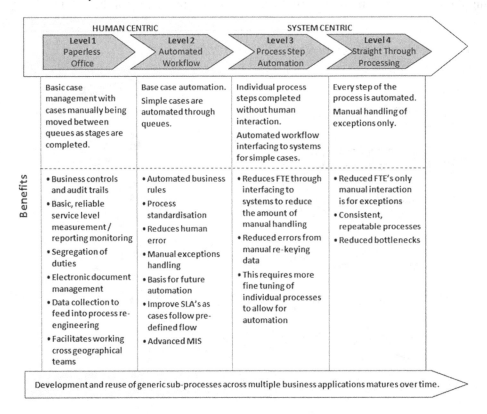

triggers the returns process, submission of the home loan application triggers the home loans process, and low inventory triggers the replenishment process (Luckham, 2002).

Event handling is nothing new to the integration community. However, in the past, these events have been mainly technical level events that triggered technical processes. For example, by monitoring low level events such as the "crash of a database application," the restart process that invokes a batch file to restart the database application can be triggered. Similarly, a message-driven application using the hub-and-spoke architecture, can monitor for certain "messages" and then invoke appropriate business function calls to handle the message.

Business Drivers

More recently, enterprises have become interested in proactively monitoring, analyzing, and acting upon higher level business events. For example, a large number of prepaid mobile phone subscribers withdrawing from a particular plan when the number of dropped calls exceeds two, or large number of retail bank customers changing their passwords at the same time. Monitoring, analyzing and acting upon such business events can add business value to the enterprise. In the mobile phone example, when the number of dropped calls reaches two, an action can be triggered to offer the customer additional discounts should they wish to recharge their account. In the banking example, monitoring and analyzing the password change event can lead to the deduction that customer accounts have been hijacked by an intruder and that the passwords are being changed by an automated program. Acting upon this intelligence can save the bank a substantial amount of money and enhance its reputation as a proactive customer oriented bank.

Furthermore, with ever increasing amounts of data, organizations have to find more efficient ways of analyzing data, and proactively acting upon this analysis in order to support decision making in real time. Having the right information at the right time with the right people and/or at the right place with the right context is essential in a data-driven enterprise. Ranadive and Maney argue that in addition, having the right information a little bit beforehand, is more valuable than having a lot of information six months later (Ranadive et al., 2011). This has led organizations to leverage EDA to drive their real time business intelligence strategy.

EDA Patterns

Using the concept of a business event, EDA helps to monitor, detect, report, and act in situations where a business opportunity, threat, or an exception occurs. In an EDA, the event source sends an event which is received by the event consumer. This interaction adheres to the following three principles (Schulte, 2008):

- The event consumer does not pull the event, rather the event is pushed to the consumer.
- On receiving the event, the consumer immediately acts on the event.
- The event does not explicitly contain the action that the consumer should perform on receiving the event.

Based on Schulte, EDA may be classified into the following patterns (Schulte, 2004), namely, Simple Event Processing, Complex Event Processing, and Event-driven Processes.

Simple Event Processing

Figure 12 shows the key components of Simple Event Processing (SEP). In this architecture pattern, the event source sends a business event such as the creation of a sales order or a purchase order, usually as an XML document. The event consumer is the receiving application that handles this business event and may trigger a business process such as the sales process or procurement process. The event is usually sent in real time

Figure 12. Simple event processing

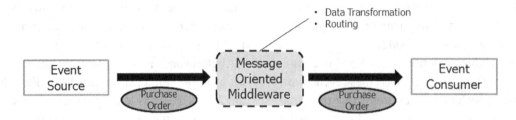

through publish-subscribe mechanism of a MOM infrastructure. The MOM can also add additional functionality such as data transformation and content based routing that was discussed under the hub-and-spoke messaging architecture.

A key limitation of SEP is the fact that only single events are processed at any one time. However, in an enterprise, a large number of business events can occur at the same time. A collective processing of these events can provide more valuable insight and help in decision making. Furthermore, all business events will not be significant and hence it is necessary to filter events that are critical to running the business.

Complex Event Processing

In Complex Event Processing (CEP) (see Figure 13), rather than pushing single events directly from source to consumer, they may be further processed by an event engine before being pushed to the consumer. This processing may involve

rules for filtering events, combining two or more simple events into a complex event, detecting event patterns, and detecting patterns that satisfy constraints. Once the simple events have been processed, the event engine can generate new derived events and send them to event consumers.

Following is an example scenario from the financial services domain (Adi et al., 2006). The event engine receives events from various sources such as ATM (Automated Teller Machine) applications, foreign exchange trading applications, core banking applications, and stock market applications. These events are filtered and aggregated, and additional new events are generated based on rules defined in the event engine.

Following are some example rules for this scenario as shown in Table 1.

When rules fire, the event engine will generate a new simple or complex event, which is received by the consumer application. In the above scenario, when Rule 1 fires, the fraud monitoring application receives the event with the account

Figure 13. Complex event processing

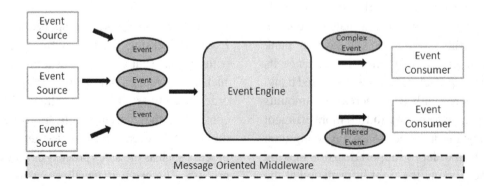

Table 1. Example rules in CEP

Rule No	Rule	Type of Rule	New Event Generated by Rule
1	If over $1500 are withdrawn within a 3 day period	Simple Filter Rule	Send a message to the fraud monitoring application informing the account details and total amount withdrawn
2	If SAP share price increases over 5% in a day trading	Simple Filter Rule	Send an alert to the trader application
3	If account balance exceeds $200K over a 3 month period and if $5000 are withdrawn every month	Complex Filter Rule (2 events are aggregated)	Send a message to the credit card marketing application giving details of the potential customer for the launch of a new credit card

number along with withdrawal details such as date, time, location, amount, etc.

Let us look at another use case from the financial fraud detection domain. A number of ATM withdrawal transaction events for the same customer within a short time frame are received by the event engine. The event engine then analyzes these events in real time using techniques such as discriminant analysis and neural networks (Widder et al., 2007). A suspicious event pattern is then detected, for example, the same card is being used in different geographic locations within a short time frame. This triggers another event to inform customer relationship manager of the probability of a fraud.

Event-Driven Processes

Event-Driven Processing (EDP) provides an enhanced form of EDA, where activities or entire processes are triggered by events. This is achieved through the use of a BPM layer. The BPM layer enables the control of process flows. When the process instance is executed, the BPM layer retains the state data of the running instances. The next step in the process is then triggered by the arrival of an appropriate simple or complex event, which

may cause the state data to change. Alternatively, a fresh instance of a process can be triggered by the arrival of an event. In either case, the BPM layer may then:

- Invoke the service application through a standard Web Service interface.
- Send a message event to a message-driven application.

Therefore, in an event driven process, both SOA and EDA are used. There are two possible patterns of EDP. In Figure 14, an event directly triggers a process instance. There is no event engine. This pattern is an extension of simple event processing with a BPM layer. The event source directly triggers the process instance. For example, the Web order management application, on receiving the customer request for a new order, triggers the sales order process in the BPM layer. Thus, a new instance of sale order process is executed. During this execution, the BPM layer invokes the Inventory application through a Web Service interface to check for available inventory, and sends a shipping order message event to the Shipping application. Additionally, the business process also sends a request for credit approval to the sales manager

Figure 14. Event driven processes

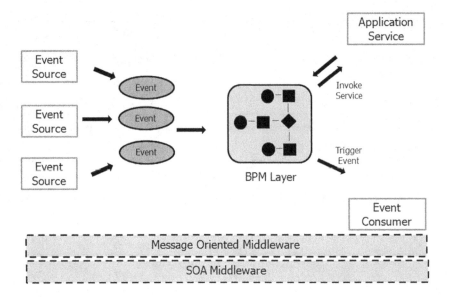

(by utilizing a mobile application running on a smart phone), and sends a billing order message event to the billing application.

Figure 15 illustrates the second EDP pattern. Once the events are filtered or combined into a complex event, the event engine passes them to the BPM layer. This pattern is an extension of the complex event processing with a BPM layer. The event engine filters or combines the events before passing them to the BPM layer. The BPM layer utilizes MOM or SOA middleware to invoke other application services or send another message to an event consumer. For example, consider the scenario from the financial fraud detection domain. A number of customers have changed their online banking passwords within a short time frame.

Figure 15. Event driven processes with BPM

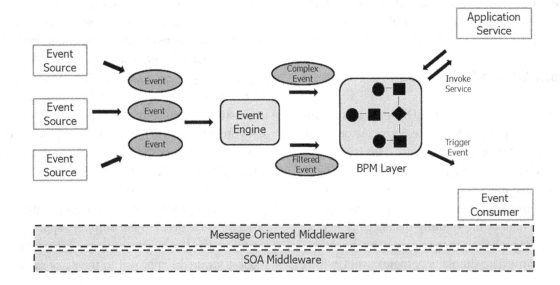

Each password change is received by the event engine. The event engine then analyzes these events in real time and a suspicious event pattern is then detected. This generates another event to trigger the IT fraud detection process in the BPM layer.

Though some organizations have implemented event driven solutions, this integration architecture is yet to mature. More importantly, organizations are exploring how to leverage current event streams in order to predict the future. For example, a shipping company receives event streams that indicate the possibility of labor strike at a key port. This information can be leveraged to plan the remediation in real time should this event actually occur. A major challenge is to improve the "analytical capability" so that incorrect predictions are not made. Organizations are yet to fully embrace Event-Driven Process Architecture.

Future integration architectures will have to support the emerging Cloud Computing paradigm. Cloud computing adoptions are on the rise due to possible reduction in datacenter resources and improved agility in meeting IT demands. However, many organizations will still have on-premises applications alongside those in the Cloud and will have to deal with the challenges that arise from integrating these applications.

EMERGING TRENDS

In this section, we identify two trends in relation to enterprise integration architectures, namely, Cloud Computing and RESTful services.

Cloud Computing

Cloud Computing provides a number of benefits that act as key drivers for its adoption. These drivers include: optimizing the use of hardware infrastructure, offloading the burden of managing various computing resources to the Cloud provider and thus minimizing IT management overhead, reducing capital and operating costs by obtaining resources on a need to basis and paying for what is used, and ensuring business agility by dynamically meeting the IT needs of the business by scaling up or down to suit rapidly changing market demands of the consumer (Amrhein & Quint, 2009; Plummer & Smith, 2009; Mell & Grance, 2009). The above drivers have encouraged a number of organizations to adopt Cloud Computing as a paradigm for offering enterprise solutions.

The movement of substantial number of enterprise applications to the Cloud infrastructure will lead to a number of integration challenges. For example, organizations will still have a lot of business applications that are not moved to the Cloud due to regulatory constraints such as HIPAA (Health Insurance Portability and Accountability Act), GLBA (Gramm–Leach–Bliley Act), and general security and NPPI (Non-Public Personal Information) issues. As a result, these on-premises applications have to be integrated with those in the Cloud. Additionally, organizations must also face the challenge of integrating Cloud-to-Cloud applications. An example would be integrating a best of breed SaaS (Software as a Service) application (e.g. CRM) in the Cloud with another best of breed SaaS application (e.g. ERP) in the Cloud.

These challenges can be addressed by leveraging the various integration architectures discussed earlier in this chapter. Following are three possible integration solution approaches, namely, Enterprise Application Integration tools, Web API Based Integration, and Integration-as-a-Service. Following is a brief discussion of these approaches, for more details and discussion on these one may refer to (Shankararaman et al., 2012).

Enterprise Application Integration Tools

Existing Enterprise Application Integration tools such as MOM, Message Brokers, BPM, and SOA platforms can be used for solving the Cloud integration challenges. There are two deployment options, namely, hosting the tools on-premises, and hosting the tools in the Cloud. Examples of these tools include TIBCO Business Works, SAP Netweaver Composition Environment, IBM Websphere Integration Server, Oracle Fusion Middleware, etc. They provide extensive functionality for data transformation, message routing, adapters for connecting to enterprise systems, graphical interface for modeling and orchestrating complex processes involving both human and automated activities. Additionally, they are proven technologies and have been widely used by many organizations. These tools can facilitate integration of on-premises applications with those hosted in the Cloud, as well as Cloud-to-Cloud applications.

Web API-Based Integration

Many vendors offer Web APIs to help integrate back end enterprise systems with their SaaS applications. For example, Salesforce.com provides APIs to integrate Saleforce.com CRM with the organization's ERP. The APIs offer opportunity for customized integration but at the cost of additional effort to code the APIs. APIs require custom coding to handle data translation, routing, and process automation. However, relying purely on APIs without using any integration middleware will lead to point-to-point solutions that can decrease the maintainability of the integrated applications.

Integration as a Service

The integration infrastructure and tools can be made available by the Cloud providers as services in the PaaS (Platform as a Service) layer of the Cloud. One may view this as a kind-of SaaS application that provides integration services rather than business application services. These tools are designed to deliver integration services securely over the Internet. Examples of vendor tools include Atomsphere from Dell Boomi, Informatica Cloud Platform from Informatica, Silver from TIBCO, and Cast Iron OmniConnect from IBM. These

tools are expected to exhibit all the characteristics of the Cloud such as self-service, elasticity, multi-tenancy and pay-as-you-use. They can facilitate integration of Cloud applications to on-premises applications, Cloud-to-Cloud applications, and also on-premises applications.

RESTful Services

REST (REpresentational State Transfer) is an architectural style that complements SOA. In contrast to Web Services technology framework that is based on SOAP and WSDL, REST architectural style is based on exchanging "plain XML" or any other valid Internet media type over the Internet. In REST, the services are exposed through an extensible set of resources identified by the Universal Resource Identifiers (URI). A standard set of methods are used to invoke these resources namely HTTP GET, PUT, POST and DELETE (Pautasso, 2008).

The key advantages of using REST include its simplicity, light-weight when compared to SOAP, and the use of Web-based standards. As a result, in recent years, REST has gained support and many REST based services are available on Google, Yahoo, Amazon, eBay, Facebook, etc. These services enable organizations to develop mash-up consumer applications that integrate enterprise systems with social media, mobile devices, location maps, etc.

CONCLUSION

In this chapter, we covered the various architectural patterns used in integrating enterprise applications and explored the evolution of the patterns over the years to meet the ever changing needs of the business. Event-driven businesses that predict and leverage customer behavior in real-time are becoming more common place. As the speed of doing business is increasing, there is increasing dependence on enterprise integration architecture that is massively scalable, that can execute at the speed of memory, is flexible to change, and is low cost to maintain. Application integration has become a key enabler to businesses of the 21st century and enterprises that practice modern integration architecture best practices will thrive.

REFERENCES

Adi, A., Botzer, D., Nechushtai, G., & Sharon, G. (2006). Complex event processing for financial services. In *Proceedings of the IEEE Services Computing Workshops*.

Al Mosawi, A., Zhao, L., & Macaulay, L. (2006). A model driven architecture for enterprise application. In *Proceedings of the 39th Hawaii International Conference on System Science*.

Amrhein, D., & Quint, S. (2009). *Cloud computing for the enterprise: Part 1: Capturing the cloud*. IBM Websphere Developer Technical Journal.

Brown, L. (2000). *Integration models: Templates for business transformation*. USA: SAMS Publishing.

Duke, S., Makey, P., & Kiras, N. (1999). *Application integration management guide: Strategies and technologies*. Hull, UK: Butler Group Limited.

Hapner, M., Burridge, R., Sharma, R., Fialli, J., & Haase, K. (2002). *Java messaging service API tutorial and reference*. Addison-Wesley.

Havey, M. (2005). *Essential business process modeling*. O'Reilly.

Hohpe, G., & Woolf, B. (2004). *Enterprise integration patterns: Designing, building, and deploying messaging solutions*. Addison-Wesley.

Lam, W., & Shankararaman, V. (2004). An enterprise integration methodology. *IT Professional,* Issue March/April Issue, 40-48.

Lam, W., & Shankararaman, V. (2007). *Enterprise architecture and integration: Methods, implementation and technologies*. USA: IGI Global. doi:10.4018/978-1-59140-887-1.

Linthicum, D. (1999). *Enterprise application integration*. Massachusetts, USA: Addison-Wesley.

Luckham, D. (2002). *The power of events*. Addison Wesley.

Maheshwari, P., & Pang, M. (2005). *Benchmarking message-oriented middleware: TIB/RV versus SonicMQ. In the Journal of Concurrency and Computation: Practice & Experience - Foundations of Middleware Technologies, 17(12), 1507-1526*. Chichester, UK: John Wiley and Sons Ltd..

Maheswari, P. (2003). Enterprise application integration using a component based architecture. In *Proceedings of the 27th Annual International Computer Software and Applications Conference* (pp. 557-562).

Mell, P., & Grance, T. (2009). The NIST definition of cloud computing. *NIST, Version 15*.

Object Management Group. (2004). *Common object request broker architecture (CORBA) Core Specification 3.0.3*. OMG Specification.

Pautasso, C., Zimmermann, O., & Leymann, F. (2008). Restful web services vs. "Big'" web services: Making the right architectural decision. In *Proceedings of the 17th international conference on World Wide Web* (pp. 805-814). ACM.

Plummer, C. D., & Smith, M. D. (2009). Three levels of elasticity for cloud computing expand provider options. *Gartner* ID Number G00167400.

Ranadive, V., & Maney, K. (2011). *The two-second advantage: How to succeed by anticipating the future just enough*. USA: Crown Business.

Schulte, R. (2004). Event-driven architecture: The next big thing. In *Application integration & web services summit*. Los Angeles, USA: Gartner.

Schulte, W. (2008). Tutorial for EDA and how it relates to SOA. *Gartner* ID Number G00155163.

Shankararaman, V., & Lum, K. E. (2011). Integrating a process-based composite application with ERP. *Annual international conference on enterprise resource planning and supply chain management,* Penang, Malaysia.

Shankararaman, V., & Lum, K. E. (2012). Integrating the cloud scenarios and solutions. In Aggarwal, A., & Bento, A. (Eds.), *Cloud computing service and deployment models: Layers and management.* IGI Global. doi:10.4018/978-1-4666-2187-9.ch009.

Shankararaman, V., Tan, W. K., Thonse, S., Gupta, M., & Deshmukh, N. (2007). *Aligning IT solutions with business processes: A methodological approach.* Pearson.

Themistocleous, M., & Irani, Z. (2001). Benchmarking the benefits and barriers of application integration. *Benchmarking: An International Journal, 8*(4), 317–331. doi:10.1108/14635770110403828.

Widder, A., Ammon, V. R., Schaeffer, P., & Wolff, C. (2007). Identification of suspicious, unknown event patterns in an event cloud. In *Proceedings of the 2007 inaugural international conference on Distributed event-based systems* (pp. 164-170). ACM Press.

Woods, D. (2003). *Enterprise services architecture.* O'Reilly.

Yusuf, K. (2004). *Enterprise messaging using JMS and IBM websphere.* Prentice Hall.

KEY TERMS AND DEFINITIONS

Architecture Style: An integration architectural style is a specific method of integrating applications, characterized by the features that make it notable. A style may include technology components, business drivers and standards. Integration architecture can be classified as a chronology of styles which changes over time.

Business Process Management (BPM): A discipline at the intersection between management and IT, encompassing methods, techniques and tools to represent, model, design, analyze, enact, and control business processes involving humans, organizations, applications, and documents.

Complex Event Processing (CEP): Advanced computations that can be performed on business events, for example calculating moving averages or totals, detecting instance of a pattern, finding trends in a set of events, etc.

Event Driven Architecture (EDA): An approach for designing and building applications in which events trigger messages to be sent between independent software components that are loosely coupled and unaware of each other.

Enterprise Integration: Deals with integrating applications residing within an enterprise, within two or more enterprises, between existing applications and the Web, and between applications in the Cloud and on-premises applications.

Enterprise Service Bus (ESB): An architecture pattern where reusable business services are exposed using enterprise standard semantics and standard transport protocols.

Message-Oriented Middleware (MOM): A software platform that provides the means to transport messages between business applications using a number of interaction patterns.

REpresentational State Transfer (REST): An architectural style, where a service exposes its capabilities through an extensible set of resources using Universal Resource Identifiers.

Service Oriented Architecture (SOA): An architectural approach for designing and building applications that tie services together and are defined by industry standard interfaces (e.g. Web Service Description Language).

Chapter 4
Mediating Message Heterogeneity in Service Compositions:
A Design Model

Prashant Doshi
University of Georgia, USA

Nithya Vembu[1]
University of Georgia, USA

ABSTRACT

Atomic Web Services (WS) may not always be sufficient for service requests. For such cases, several services may have to be assembled to create a new composite service of added functionality and value. Establishing message exchange between related but independently developed Web Services is a key challenge faced during WS composition which has hereto received inadequate attention. One of the challenges lies in resolving the differences in the schema of the messages that are input to and output from the Web Services involved. Data mediation is required to resolve these challenges. This chapter introduces a formal model for data mediation that considers the types and semantics of the message elements. Based on this model, it proposes methods for resolving different kinds of message-level heterogeneity. These methods are evaluated on synthetic and real-world pairs of Web Services, with the ultimate aim of integrating the data mediation techniques presented within WS composition tools.

INTRODUCTION

As reliance of the business and scientific community on services grows, service requests are becoming increasingly sophisticated. Atomic Web Services (WS), whose implementation does not involve other Web Services, are increasingly unlikely to be capable of satisfying such requests. Consequently, WS compositions in which multiple Web Services, both atomic and composite are assembled together to provide the required functionality, is becoming highly relevant.

DOI: 10.4018/978-1-4666-4193-8.ch004

Standardized interfaces, platform transparency, and the Web-based loosely-coupled nature of Web Services make their automated composition feasible. As a result, considerable attention has been directed to the problem of automatically determining the flow of control in a WS composition with the objective of satisfying the functional and non-functional objectives of the composition (Carman et al., 2003; Sirin et al., 2004; Pistore et al., 2005; Agarwal et al., 2005; Zhao & Doshi, 2009). While this is indeed a difficult task, the other key challenge in assembling Web Services to form executable compositions is in ensuring that the participating Web Services can "talk" with each other. In other words, the Web Services should be able to exchange messages and produce the output for the composition correctly.

However, given that Web Services are usually independently developed, their input and output message schemas (i.e., data models) are often heterogeneous. For example, similar data entities may have differing labels and types in the message schemas of different Web Services. A simple example of this may manifest in a StudentRecord WS that utilizes the attribute *grade* to represent a student's academic course performance while another student related WS uses the attribute *score* to represent the same. Nagarajan et al. (2007) list several message-level heterogeneities between Web Services, classified into attribute-level, entity-level and abstraction-level conflicts. Many of these heterogeneities are not new challenges; these have been highlighted previously in different contexts such as matching schemas of federated databases (Litwin & Abdellatif, 1986; Kim et al., 1993; Sheth, 1998; Rahm & Bernstein, 2001). Although by no means exhaustive, the classification does represent a variety of conflicts often found in practice. We use this set of potential heterogeneities between Web Services as our point of departure and mediate them. Specifically, the mediation involves identifying a nontrivial rule or mapping that transforms instances of a concept into instances of a related target concept. For example, grade may be used directly as score or it may need to be transformed into a numeric score.

We begin by noting that our focus is on *design-time mediation*, which precludes knowing the actual input and output parameters for the Web Services in the composition and thereby its use in the mediation. As a result, the mediation we perform is based on the schema only and represents a conservative approach to the extent of mediation that is possible. The diversity and complexity of potential resolutions make automatic elicitation of mediation rules difficult, and we do not pursue it here.

We take a formal approach toward data mediation between Web Services, and introduce a mathematical model of the message-level mediation problem. This concretely grounds the problem and promotes the development of general approaches toward message-level mediation between Web Services. Our model is sufficiently general in that it captures the different types of heterogeneity listed by Nagarajan et al. (2007) and the requirements for mediating them. The model includes a translator function that defines the set of syntactic and semantic rules that govern the transformation of message schemas. We implement the function in a *translator WS* whose interface is based on the model and its logic implements the rules. Because multiple types of conflicts may exist in a pair of Web Services participating in a composition, we prescribe a necessary ordering for identifying and resolving the different co-habiting conflicts.

This chapter represents a significant contribution toward addressing multiple types of data mediation between Web Services participating in a composition. We address several data conflicts – many of which are well known – adapted to the context of WS mediation. While the translator WS is well suited for inclusion between two Web Services that need mediation in an orchestration, it may be utilized in choreography as well. We discuss in detail how the translator WS resolves each type of conflict that we consider, and program these conflicts in synthetic Web Services for testing purposes. Furthermore, we also test it on some real-world Web Services involved in compositions.

BACKGROUND

Input and output messages of Web Services (or of the operations described using the Web Services Description Language, WSDL) must conform to message schemas (types in WSDL). In general, a message schema consists of the entity that describes the message and its typed attributes. Nagarajan et al. (2007) adapting previous discussions on schematic heterogeneities (Kim et al., 1993; Sheth, 1998) to the context of Web Services, comprehensively classify the syntactic and structural heterogeneity that could exist between similar WS message schemas into attribute-level, entity-level and abstraction-level conflicts. We briefly review each of these below and illustrate them using example Web Services (operations) from the academic domain.

Attribute-Level Conflicts: Occur between attributes of two message schemas that are semantically similar but differ in their naming labels and structure. These could be *naming conflicts* that arise when attributes that represent the same concept are named differently. For example, consider the output message of $\mathbf{WS_I}$ (retrieves student records) that must be mediated with the input message of $\mathbf{WS_J}$:

$\mathbf{WS_I}$: StudentRecord (*name*, *grade*) (string, float)

$\mathbf{WS_J}$: StudentRecord (*name*, *score*) (string, float)

Although the attribute names are different, *grade* and *score* are semantically similar and could be directly mapped. On the other hand, semantically dissimilar attributes may have identical names (homonyms). Note that we do not focus on attribute names that differ due to missing characters or misspellings as these could be trivially resolved.

Attribute conflicts may also manifest as *data representation conflicts* if similar attributes differ in their data types or representation formats. In the example above, this conflict would occur if *score* were of type integer instead of float. Furthermore, attributes may be identical in type as well, but differ in the measuring units. This type of *scaling conflict* could be mediated by employing scaling or shifting rules.

Entity-Level Conflicts: Analogous to attribute-level conflicts but apply to entities in the message schemas. For example, in the following operations of two Web Services:

$\mathbf{WS_I}$: Institution (*name*, *population*) (string, integer)

$\mathbf{WS_J}$: University (*name*, *population*) (string, integer)

A *naming conflict* exists between the entities although they refer to the same concept. However, entities with identical names could be semantically different.

A distinct conflict is the *schema isomorphism*, which occurs when the message schemas of two Web Services that need to be mediated have a differing number of attributes but refer to the same concept. For example, one of the message schemas may contain *address* as an attribute while the other may decompose address into its individual attributes such as *apt.no*, *street*, *city* and *zipcode*.

Abstraction-Level Conflicts: More difficult to resolve and include conflicts such as the *generalization* mismatch. For example, entities could be expressed at different levels of abstraction in the two message schemas.

$\mathbf{WS_I}$: PhDAlumnus (*name*, *department*, *email*) (string, string, string)

$\mathbf{WS_J}$: Alumnus (*name*, *department*, *email*, *type*) (string, string, string, string)

Entity PhDAlumnus is a specialization of Alumnus but the different names will prevent a straightforward mediation. This situation may analogously exist for attributes as well. Another conflict in this category is due to *aggregation* where an entity or attribute in a message schema could be an aggregate of the corresponding entity or attribute in the target schema.

A particularly complicated conflict occurs when an entity in a message schema appears as an attribute in the other schema. For example, consider,

WS$_I$: Course (*call no., name, semester*)

WS$_J$: Department (*course, semester,...*)

Here, Course entity in the schema of **WS$_I$** is modeled as an attribute, *course*, in the schema of the other WS.

Related Work

Mediating message-level heterogeneity is a key step toward successful execution of WS compositions. It has its roots in *schema mapping* techniques (Litwin & Abdellatif, 1986; Kim et al., 1993; Sheth, 1998; Rahm & Bernstein, 2001), but there has been a general scarcity in adapting those techniques to the relatively new problem of mediating between Web Services.

Web Services Modeling Ontology (WSMO) (Roman et al., 2005) is a conceptual framework for representing semantic Web Services. The main constituents of WSMO are ontologies, Web Services, goals and mediators. Mediators are used when heterogeneous situations arise, and they could be of different types such as O-O mediators, G-G mediators, W-G mediators and W-W mediators where O stands for ontology, G for goal and W for WS. The Web services modeling execution environment (WSMX) is an implementation for the WSMO framework, and currently the data

mediator component of WSMX implements only the O-O mediator from WSMO. Also in the context of WSMO, Cabral, and Domingue (2005) propose a broker-based mediation approach along the lines of the WSMX framework, in order to compose semantic Web Services. It focuses on specific conflicts and requires model references to ontologies.

Mrissa et al. (2007) present an approach based on their context model that extends WSDL specifications to allow inclusion of context information for resolving conflicts between semantic Web Services. Another context-based mediation approach (Li et al., 2009) for WS-BPEL processes uses the Context Interchange lightweight ontology that describes generic concepts. XPath functions are used to perform transformations based on the context differences between the service descriptions. The idea of using a common ontology to support mediation between Web Services is one of the ways we propose resolving conflicts, such as those involving data scaling.

The message-level conflicts addressed in this chapter were adapted from previous discussions on heterogeneities between database schemas (Kim et al., 1993; Sheth, 1998) by Nagarajan et al. (2007), which also proposed an approach for mediation utilizing the Semantic Annotations for WSDL (SAWSDL) schemaMapping (Farrel & Lauser, 2007) attributes. Using the mapping defined in the liftingSchemaMapping attribute, the output message of **WS$_I$** is mapped to an ontology instance which is then transformed to the input message of **WS$_J$** using the loweringSchemaMapping. As we mentioned previously, model references are only necessary for resolving some conflicts.

Pokraev et al. (2006) recognize semantic interoperability, which ensures that the messages exchanged between two systems have the same meaning to both, as key to systems integration, and requires the presence of a translation function, analogous to our translator WS, as a necessary condition to achieve it. BPEL for Semantic Web

Service (BPEL4SWS) (Nitzsche et al., 2007), an extension of BPEL 2.0, aims at message exchange independent of WSDL. Its mediate element is an extension of the BPEL Assign operator and may be used for ontology-based mediation (Nitszche & Norton, 2009). WSIRD (Spencer & Liu, 2004) is a rule-based engine that analyzes OWL-S descriptions to transform a message into the format of another.

Leitner et al. (2009) presents several mediation strategies that have been fused into their WS invocation framework, Daios (i.e. orchestrator), to resolve interface-level conflicts, although many types of conflicts remain unaddressed. The claim is that the approach is more flexible than middleware-based mediation approaches similar to ours because unlike those approaches, the communication between the client and the provider is not disconnected. Interestingly, Pokraev and Reichert (2006) observe that how the messages are exchanged between the client and provider Web Services may also need mediation. For example, the provider could be expecting two messages while the client provides just one. In this context, a mediator could be potentially helpful as well. In comparison, our focus in this chapter is to mediate the contents of the messages.

DESIGN MODEL FOR MESSAGE MEDIATION

The approach presented in this chapter is to interleave a translator WS before each WS invocation, except for the first, that is involved in the composition. The *orchestrator* will invoke the translator WS and provide it with the requisite input. We begin by introducing a formal mathematical model of the mediation problem, that also serves as the inspiration behind designing the interface of the translator WS.

Formal Model of the Mediation Problem

In order to mediate, we first formally model the mediation problem. A comprehensive model addressing the different message heterogeneities mentioned previously and enabling mediation is needed.

We define the data mediation problem as:

$$MD = \langle WS_I, WS_J, M_I, M_J, M_h, T \rangle$$

where:

- WS_I and WS_J are the Web Services involved in the mediation. Specifically, the message output by WS_I is considered to form the input message to WS_J.
- M_I is the set of messages output by WS_I. Usually, this set is a singleton.
- M_J is the set of messages input to WS_J. Usually, this set is a singleton.
- M_h is any message data available a priori and includes output from preceding WS invocations. This data may be combined with M_I for generating input M_J.
- $T: M_I \ \vec{\jmath} \ M_J \ \vec{\jmath} \ M_h \rightarrow \rho$, is the translator function, where ρ is the set of syntactic and semantic rules that govern the transformation of instances of schemas in messages M_I and M_h to the instance of schema in M_J. Note that the output of T may be null for some input indicating that mediation is unneeded or is not possible.

Furthermore, any message M is a tuple, $M = \langle MS, MR \rangle$, where $MS = \langle C, A, D \rangle$ is the *schema* of the message consisting of the ordered sets of entities, C, attribute(s), A, and corresponding data type(s), D. Typically, each attribute has a data type and the ordering of sets A and D establishes the correspondence between the attribute and its data type; *MR* is the representational format of the message (e.g., XML). An entity in **C**, $C=\langle N_c, MR_c \rangle$ identifies the particular data item in the message, where N_c is its label and MR_c is a reference to a knowledge model (e.g. ontology). An attribute in **A**, $A=\langle N_A, MR_A \rangle$ is defined analogously to an entity.

We will integrate message-level data mediation in compositions by utilizing a *translator WS* that implements the formal model. The translator WS (see Figure 1) implements the translator function *T*, taking messages M_I from WS_I, M_J from WS_J and M_h as input, and outputs appropriate rules. Based on the messages it sees, the translator may identify the conflict and select an appropriate transformation rule from its set of rules, *ρ*, to perform the mediation.

In general, we invoke the translator service before each invocation of a subsequent WS in the composition. This facilitates having the mediated messages for the subsequent WS. We consider four basic types of control flow constructs illustrated using two Web Services, w_1 and w_2, which are typically present in a composition; these could be linked with each other, and nested within

themselves and one another. As we show in Figure 2, we may interleave the *translator service*, *T*, between sequential service invocations, or prior to each concurrent service invocations in the control flow of the composition. We may similarly invoke the translator service prior to each service present in a conditional branch. If a single WS is invoked repeatedly in a loop and the output from its previous invocation is not utilized in the next invocation, we may invoke the translator service before entering the loop. On the other hand, if the output is utilized in the next invocation, it may need mediation and the translator is included within the loop. If more than one WS participates in a loop, the translator appears before each WS in the loop.

Figure 2 illustrates the translator WS, *T*, interleaved in four basic types of flow constructs that typically appears in a composition. These basic constructs may be linked and nested to form more complex compositions. The circles represent WS invocations and arrows represent the control flow in the composition.

Despite the different flow constructs, we utilize a general way of introducing the translator, and the mediation continues to require the output

Figure 1. (a) Translator WS interleaved between Web Services to be mediated as part of a larger composition (b) The translator WS returns the transformation rule

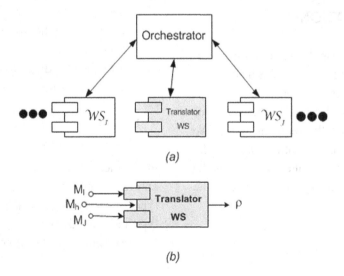

Figure 2. Translator service (T) interleaved in four basic types of flow constructs

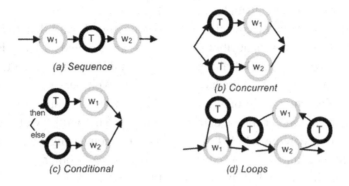

messages of the previous WS, the target input messages of the next WS and the messages on hand from prior WS invocations, as defined in our formal model. Therefore, each instance of the translator service in a composition represents an invocation of the same service but with different input messages. We observe that invocation of an additional WS adds overhead to the execution time of the composition, and therefore mediation calls should be used judiciously.

Resolution of the Conflicts

In this subsection, we describe how a translator may mediate the conflicts outlined previously thereby generating the transformation rules used by the function, *T*, in our model. In many cases, this requires the presence of auxiliary knowledge sources accompanying the schemas. The default language for specifying Web Services, WSDL, does not directly provide a way to specify such auxiliary information. However, World Wide Web Consortium recommendations such as the Semantic Annotations for WSDL (SAWSDL) (Farrel & Lauser, 2007) allow *model references*, which may be used to associate a WSDL component with a concept in some semantic model. We utilize these to add the knowledge sources.

Our focus in this subsection is on situations where the different conflicts exist in isolation. In the next subsection, we discuss transforming messages when multiple conflicts exist between two schemas.

Attribute-Level Conflicts: Attribute *naming conflicts* are identified by noting that the message schemas, M_I and M_J have identical entities (or entities that refer to the same concept) and a similar number of attributes, but the attributes' names are different. Consider the following example:

WS$_I$:M_I: StudentRecord (*name, grade*) (string, float)

WS$_J$:M_J: StudentRecord (*name, score*) (string, integer)

This conflict is resolvable if the translator decides that the attribute names, *grade* and *score*, in the two schemas are synonyms, otherwise it is not. An auxiliary knowledge source such as a lexicon or a thesaurus is sufficient for this purpose. Model references to ontologies, if present, could also be useful but are not needed. Therefore, we equip our translator WS with the ability to query WordNet (Miller, 1995) for finding synonyms and other related words in order to resolve naming conflicts. WordNet is a large lexical database for English in which words are grouped together into sets of synonyms, called "synsets." These are linked with each other using conceptual-semantic and lexical relationships.

In the previous example, a *data representation conflict* also exists because the attributes in M_I and M_J are deemed similar but differ in their data types. WSDL allows data types for attributes that are specified in the XML Schema Definition (XSD) (Biron & Malhotra, 2004), which is a language for describing XML schemas. In order to resolve this, we note that an XSD primitive data type could be numeric, string, date/time, URI, byte or object type. The conflict cannot be resolved if the two data types in question, D_I and D_J, belong to different categories (unless the actual instance is available, presenting a scenario that is outside the scope of this chapter). However, an exception is when the two types are string and URI. On the other hand, conflicts may not be resolved in a straightforward way even if the types are of the same category. This is because the different numeric types have varying allowed ranges and some types do not permit signed numbers. All of this complicates the mediation of this conflict; we comprehensively describe in the Appendix the different cases that are resolvable.

Another type of representation conflict that we consider occurs when matching attributes expect values along different scales. For example, the *length* and *width* attributes are expressed in different metric systems (another example is that the *cost* attributes differ in the currency). Consider the example:

WS$_I$:M_I: PaperSize ($\langle$*length*, http://sweet. jpl.nasa.gov/2.0/sciUnits.owl#centimeter$\rangle$, $\langle$*width*, http://sweet.jpl.nasa.gov/2.0/sciUnits. owl#centimeter$\rangle$) (float, float)

WS$_J$:M_J: PaperSize ($\langle$*length*, http://sweet.jpl. nasa.gov/2.0/sciUnits.owl#meter$\rangle$, $\langle$*width*, http://sweet.jpl.nasa.gov/2.0/sciUnits. owl#meter$\rangle$) (float, float)

The URIs in the message schemas above are model references to NASA's sciUnits ontology in its Semantic Web for Earth and Environmental Terminology 2.0 suite of ontologies (Raskin & Pan, 2003). These are associated with the attributes in M_I, and denoted as MR_a^I, and those in M_J are denoted as MR_a^J. References MR_a^I and MR_a^J indicate that the units of measurement in the two Web Services are different, resulting in the inability to assign the corresponding values directly. The ontology also provides the scaling rule for converting meters to centimeters, and between many other units, which is utilized by the translator WS.

Entity-Level Conflicts: Entity *naming conflicts* are identified by noting that the entity names in the two message schemas are synonyms possibly by finding the labels in a synset in WordNet. These conflicts are resolved analogously to attribute naming conflicts.

In order to identify and resolve *schema isomorphism conflicts*, consider the following example of such a conflict:

WS$_I$:M_I: Institution (*name, apt.no, street, city, zipcode*) (string, string, string, string, string)

WS$_J$:M_J: University (*name, address*) (string, string)

Having determined that the entities, Institution and University, can be mediated we seek to ascertain whether the attributes from *apt.no* onwards could be collectively mapped or an individual attribute be mapped to *address* in M_J. In the absence of accompanying model references, we are unable to determine that the concepts are semantically similar. Consequently, we may not resolve this conflict. However, consider the following model references to datatype properties in the *Address* ontology, which is a part of the ITTALKS project that developed multiple ontologies to enable a semantically rich interaction between intelligent agents (Cost et al., 2002):

$\langle$*apt.no*, http://daml.umbc.edu/ontologies/ittalks/address#aptnumber$\rangle$

⟨*street*, http://daml.umbc.edu/ontologies/ittalks/address#street⟩

⟨*city*, http://daml.umbc.edu/ontologies/ittalks/address#city⟩

⟨*zipcode*, http://daml.umbc.edu/ontologies/ittalks/address#zip⟩

and the model reference to a class for the *address* attribute in M_J:

⟨*address*, http://daml.umbc.edu/ontologies/ittalks/address#Address⟩

The presence of a relationship between the model references of the attributes in M_I and that in M_J – in the form of datatype properties of the referenced class – indicates an isomorphism conflict. Because the attributes in M_I are properties of the attribute in M_J, we may resolve this conflict by concatenating the values of the former attributes and provide them as input to the latter. SAWSDL's lifting and lowering schema mappings may also be used for resolving this conflict once it is identified (Nagarajan et al., 2007). For the case where the two Web Services are swapped, the isomorphism conflict continues to exist and may be resolved by decomposing the instance of *address* based on a delimiter such as a comma, and assigning the substrings to the individual attributes in M_J.

Another form of the schema isomorphism conflict exists in this example:

WS$_I$:M_I: Student (*name, id, phone, work_email, personal_email*) (string, string, string, string)

WS$_J$:M_J: University (*name, id, phone, email*) (string, string, long, string)

While attributes *name* and *id* are matched to their namesake attributes in M_J, we need to establish a relationship between the remaining attributes in the two schemas. Given model refer-

ences to the vCard ontology (Walsh, 2005) such as those below:

⟨*work_email*, http://nwalsh.com/rdf/vCard#workEmail⟩

⟨*personal_email*, http://nwalsh.com/rdf/vCard#personalEmail⟩

⟨*email*, http://nwalsh.com/rdf/vCard#email⟩,

We may reason from the vCard ontology that *work_email* and *personal_email* are subproperties of *email*, and thus identify the conflict, as we illustrate in Figure 3.

We may resolve it by assigning the value of either *work_email* or *personal_email* to the *email* attribute in **WS$_J$**. On the other hand, this conflict may not be resolved if the two Web Services are swapped. This is because instances of *email* in M_I cannot be unambiguously assigned either as an instance of *work_email* or *personal_email* in M_J.

Abstraction-Level Conflict: Consider the following example illustrating a *generalization conflict* between entities of schemas:

WS$_I$: M_I: PhDAlumnus (*name, department, email*) (string, string, string)

WS$_J$: M_J: Alumnus (*name, department, email, type*) (string, string, string, string)

While simple string similarity measures may reveal that PhDAlumnus is syntactically similar to Alumnus, we may not know the relationship between the two entities thereby precluding mediation. However, associated model references such as:

⟨PhDAlumnus, http://daml.umbc.edu/ontologies/person.owl#PhDAlumnus⟩

⟨Alumnus, http://daml.umbc.edu/ontologies/person.owl#Alumnus⟩

Figure 3. An illustration of the identification of the schema isomorphism conflict

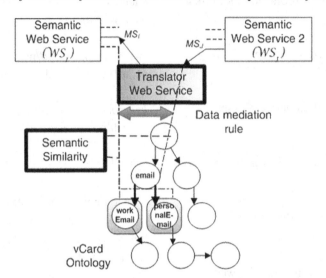

reveal that PhDAlumnus is a subclass of Alumnus in the person.owl ontology, and that this is a generalization conflict, as we illustrate in Figure 4.

Subsequently, we may resolve this conflict by assigning values of the attributes in M_I to the similarly-labeled attributes in M_J. However, the mediation is incomplete due to the presence of an additional *type* attribute in M_J. In general, we may resolve generalization conflicts by identifying a subclass relationship between the entities (or attributes). If an additional *type* attribute exists in the target schema, we may assign the label of the entity, N_c^I, to the attribute in M_J. The conflict could be mediated for the situation where the Web Services are swapped if the "type" attributes value in M_I matches syntactically to the label of the entity, N_c^J. In this case, the remaining attribute values in M_I may be simply assigned to those in

Figure 4. An illustration of identifying the generalization conflict between entity names

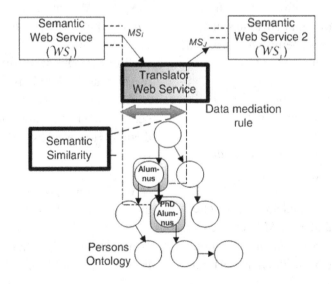

M_j. However, this requires knowing the value of an attribute, which is not possible in design-time mediation.

Another type of abstraction-level conflict is an *aggregation conflict* as illustrated in the following example:

WS$_I$: M_I: UndergradStudent (*name*, *id*, *department*, *email*) (string, string, string, string)

WS$_J$: M_J: StudentBody (*name*, *id*, *department*, *email*) (string, string, string, string)

Note that despite the reference to the entire student body, **WS$_J$** requests information about each individual student according to its attributes. Undergraduate students are part of the student body, which differs from being a specialization. WordNet includes holonym (and its inverse meronym) relationships between words, which our translator WS may exploit to identify and resolve this conflict. Additional support may come from associated model references, if any, which relate the two entities in a datatype or object property such as part-of. However, a resolution is not possible if the two Web Services are swapped.

The final conflict that we consider is the *attribute-entity conflict* for which the resolution is most challenging, but possible in some cases. Consider the example below:

WS$_I$: M_I: Resident (*name*, *address*, *phoneno*) (string, string, string)

WS$_J$: M_J: AreaInfo (*resident*, *address*, *phone*) (string, string, string)

First, we identify this conflict by observing that the entity label, N_c^I, appears in the attribute list of M_J, say as attribute A_j^I, or vice versa. We may resolve this conflict if attributes in M_J other than A_j^I are mapped with attributes in M_I or their values are available from the data in hand, M_h. Next, if a single attribute in M_I remains unmapped and if this

attribute is *name*, *id* or similar, we may assign its value to A_j^I. If multiple attributes remain as in the example in the Background section, the attribute whose label is syntactically closest to "name" or "id" is mapped. The conflict continues to exist if the two Web Services are swapped:

WS$_I$: M_I: AreaInfo (*resident*, *address*, *phone*) (string, string, string)

WS$_J$: M_J: Resident (*name*, *address*, *phoneno*) (string, string, string)

The conflict may be resolved if a single attribute in the new M_J remains unmapped and this attribute label is similar to "name" or "id." In the example above, we may assign the value of *resident* from M_I to attribute *name* in M_J. However, if multiple attributes remain unmapped in M_J then it is unclear which one should assume the value, and not all attributes in M_J may have values. Therefore, the conflict cannot be mediated in this case.

The approaches mentioned previously for resolving the conflicts are included in a rule set and utilized by the translator WS. In many of the above cases, model references are needed to enable mediation between Web Services. The presence of erroneous information such as an incorrect model reference further complicates the problem. Of course, we should check if the message data on hand (M_h) containing output messages from previous Web Services in the composition and from requestor is suitable for any entities or attributes in the target WS that remain unmapped.

Mediating Multiple Conflicts

In practice, Web Services that need mediation may exhibit multiple types of conflicts simultaneously. This motivates investigations into a particular order of checking for various conflicts with the objective of determining if the Web Services cannot be mediated, as quickly as possible. The ordering should also facilitate identifying the correct type of conflict. We present one such ordering in Algorithm 1, which also forms the algorithm of our translator WS. As we mentioned previously, Algorithm 1 may take recourse to the message data on hand, M_h, for resolving found conflicts.

Observe that the Algorithm shown above checks for any entity-level conflicts first and focuses on resolving those before proceeding to the attributes. This is because a failure in resolving these conflicts is indicative of the two message schemas referencing disparate concepts, which should not be mediated.

IMPLEMENTATION AND EVALUATION

As shown in Figure 1(b), the translator WS takes as input M_I from **WS$_I$**, M_J from **WS$_J$**, and M_h all of which are accessible to the orchestrator. While

Algorithm 1. Identify multiple conflicts between Web Services in order

```
1: Identify any entity naming conflict and attempt resolution
2: If entity naming conflict is identified but not resolved
3:      Return without mediation
4: Identify any generalization conflict at the entity level and attempt resolution
5: If generalization conflict is identified but not resolved
6:      Return without mediation
7: Identify any aggregation conflict at the entity level and attempt resolution
8: If aggregation conflict is identified but not resolved
9:      Return without mediation
10: Identify any attribute-entity conflict and attempt resolution (perform steps
2--10 if needed)
11: If attribute-entity conflict is identified but not resolved
12:      Return without mediation
13: If number of attributes in M_I and M_J are unequal
14:      Identify any schema isomorphism conflict and attempt resolution
15: If schema isomorphism conflict is identified but not resolved
16:      Return without mediation
17: If number of attributes in M_I and M_J are equal (after subtracting the number of
attributes that
        were collectively mapped in step 15) then
18:      Identify any attribute naming conflict(s) and attempt resolution
19:      If any attribute naming conflict is identified but not resolved
20:          Return without mediation
21:      Identify any data representation including scaling conflicts and attempt
resolution
22:      If data representation conflict is identified but not resolved
23:          Return without mediation
24:      Attempt to resolve unmapped attributes with M_h
25:      If conflict is not resolved
26:          Return without mediation
27: Return rules for successful mediation, ρ
```

the orchestrator could be a WS-BPEL (Web Service Business Process Execution Language) process, we utilized a Java client program for our evaluations.

Prior to invoking the translator WS, the orchestrator uses Apache AXIOM to parse the WSDL of the two Web Services that possibly need mediation resulting internally in a tree. Specifically, we use the pull parser to locate the ⟨wsdl: types⟩ elements in the WSDL definitions that enclose the message schemas. These are used to populate M_I and M_J (i.e., **C**, **A** and **D** in each).[2]

On invoking the translator WS, it uses Algorithm 1 to possibly resolve all considered conflicts that exist between the two message schemas while making use of the output messages from previous Web Services and the requestor as part of M_h if needed. If any of the conflicts remains unresolved, the translator WS signals a failure and the mediation is abandoned. Otherwise, for each conflict that is identified and resolved, a transformation rule is created. These rules constitute ρ and are built in XML using the Standard API for XML (StAX)

based builder that is available in AXIOM. They are returned by the translator WS as an extensible stylesheet language transformation (XSLT) file that will be applied on the output SOAP message data from WS_I in order to create a new XML file with added SOAP envelope for input to WS_J, when the composition is executed.

In Figure 5, we show an example XSLT file for resolving the data scaling conflict between schemas PaperSize in a preceding section.

We evaluate the implementation of our translator WS using pairs of Web Services from a repository of 9 synthetic WSDL/SOAP Web Services (each with a single operation) that sufficiently encompass the different conflicts, and 4 real-world Web Services obtained from the Web, all housed in an Axis2 Web server. We may choose among several pairs of these Web Services that require mediation, thereby permitting multiple test compositions. Each pair could be part of some type of flow in a composition. The Web Services and the mediating translator WS were invoked by a Java client program. While we comprehen-

Figure 5. Transformation rule in XSLT output from the translator WS

```
<xsl:stylesheet xmlns:xsl="http://www.w3.org/1999/XSL/Transform" version="1.0">
    <xsl:outputmethod="xml" indent="yes" omit-xml-declaration="yes"/>
    <xsl:template match="/">
        <xsl:element name="Parameters">
            <xsl:element name="Width_m">
                <xsl:apply-templates select="//Width_cm" />
            </xml:element>
            <xsl:element name="Height_m">
                <xsl:apply-templates select="//Height_cm" />
            </xml:element>
        </xml:element>
    </xsl:template>
    <xsl:template match="Width_cm">
        <xsl:value-of select="current()*0.01"/>
    </xsl:template>
    <xsl:template match="Height_cm">
        <xsl:value-of select="current()*0.01"/>
    </xsl:template>
</xsl:stylesheet>
```

sively evaluated with 13 test cases, we select 3 representative ones for illustration here. Additional test cases are available in (Vembu, 2011).

Test Case 1: We considered composing the following pair:

WS$_I$ getUnivInfo(): M_I: Institution(*name, people, ⟨address,* http://daml.umbc.edu/ontologies/ittalks/address#Address) (string, int, string)

WS$_J$ fileUnivAccreditationInfo(): M_J: University(*name, population,* ⟨*city,* http://daml.umbc.edu/ontologies/ittalks/address#City⟩, ⟨*state,* http://daml.umbc.edu/ontologies/ittalks/address#State⟩) (string, long, string, string)

Observe that several conflicts simultaneously exist such as entity naming, attribute naming, data representation and schema isomorphism. Beginning with the entity naming conflict, per Algorithm 1, the translator WS utilizes WordNet to realize that Institution and University belong to the same synset. Because the numbers of attributes in the two schemas are unequal, it checks for schema isomorphism. As concepts City and State are datatype properties for the class Address in the referenced ontology, it decomposes the *address* string using comma delimiters to obtain the *city* and *state* values. The attribute naming conflict is straightforwardly resolved by a call to WordNet, due to which the values of *people* may be directly assigned to *population*. Finally, a data representation conflict also exists between *people* with data type *int* and *population* with data type long, which is resolved by noting that the range of int falls within the range of long, and therefore the values may be directly assigned. Consequently, an XSLT file is generated with these rules.

Test Case 2: We consider composing a real-world WS for obtaining a stock quote (WebserviceX.net[3]) with an investment assistant WS (Nagarajan et al., 2007).

WS$_I$ getQuote(): M_I:
StockQuote(⟨*companyname,* ontologyURI#shareOf⟩, ⟨*stockticker,* ontologyURI#stockSymbol⟩, ⟨*stockquote,* ontologyURI#stockQuote⟩, ⟨*currentprice,* ontologyURI#price⟩, ⟨*change, ontologyURI#changeInValue⟩, ⟨open price,* ontologyURI#open⟩, ⟨*dayhighprice,* ontologyURI#high⟩, ⟨*daylowprice,* ontologyURI#low⟩, *volume, marketcap,* ⟨*yearrange,* ontologyURI#52WeekChange⟩) (string, string, string, double, double, double, double, int, string, double)

WS$_J$ investmentInfo(): M_J: Investment(⟨*name,* ontologyURI#shareOf⟩, ⟨*current_price,* ontologyURI#price⟩, ⟨*change,* ontologyURI#changeInValue⟩, ⟨*volume,* ontologyURI#Volume⟩, ⟨*bid_quantity,* ontologyURI#Quantity⟩, ⟨*investAmount,* ontologyURI#transactionAmount⟩) (string, double, int, double, double)

where ontology URI refers to http://lsdis.cs.uga.edu/projects/meteor-s/wsdl-s/ontologies/LSDIS_Finance.owl.

Notice that there are far less attributes in M_J and thus we focus on whether values are available for these. We find a link between "stock" in StockQuote entity and Investment in WordNet, which resolves the entity naming conflict. The translator WS did not identify any schema isomorphism conflict; although several attribute naming conflicts exist. One of these was resolved using simple syntactic string matching: *current_price* in M_J with *currentprice* in M_I, while, matching *name* with *companyname* was supported by the identical model reference as well. However, *bid_quantity* and *investAmount* in M_J remain expectedly unmapped with attributes in M_I. We expect to have this data on hand as part of M_h in order to make the investment.

Test Case 3: We compose another independently developed stock quote WS available on the

Web (Cdyne[4]) with the investment assistant WS. The stock quote WS is annotated using concepts from the ontologyURI as in test case 2.

WS$_I$ getQuoteDataSet(): M_I:
StockQuote($\langle$*stocksymbol*, ontologyURI#stockSymbol$\rangle$, $\langle$*currentprice*, ontologyURI#price$\rangle$, *lasttradedate*, $\langle$*stockchange*, ontologyURI#changeInValue$\rangle$, $\langle$*openamount*, ontologyURI#open$\rangle$, $\langle$*dayhigh*, ontologyURI#high$\rangle$, $\langle$*day low*, ontologyURI#low$\rangle$, *stockvolume*, *marketcap*, *prevCIs, changepercent*, $\langle$*fiftytwoweekrange*, ontologyURI#52WeekChange$\rangle$, *earnpershare*, *pe*, $\langle$*companyname*, ontologyURI#shareOf$\rangle$, *quoteerror*) (string, decimal, dateTime, decimal, decimal, decimal, decimal, int, string, int, string, string, string, int, string, boolean)

WS$_J$ investmentInfo(): M_J: Investment($\langle$*name*, ontologyURI#shareOf$\rangle$, $\langle$*current_price*, ontologyURI#price$\rangle$, $\langle$*change*, ontologyURI#changeInValue$\rangle$, $\langle$*volume*, ontologyURI#Volume$\rangle$, $\langle$*bid_quantity*, ontologyURI#Quantity$\rangle$, $\langle$*investAmount*, ontologyURI#transactionAmount$\rangle$) (string, double, double, int, double, double)

While this stock quote WS outputs a few more data items than the previous one, the mediation proceeds analogously to that of test case 2. A difference is that data representation conflicts also exist. Specifically, *currentprice* is a decimal in M_I but its corresponding attribute in M_J is of type double. The same is true for *stockchange* in M_I and *change* in M_J. Because the range of allowed values for decimal is within the range of double, the translator WS resolves this conflict by directly assigning the attributes' values.

CONCLUSION

Despite present capabilities and benefits of annotating WS interface descriptions with model references, the practice of including such annotations continues to be uncommon. Therefore, recognizing which types of conflicts may not need model references, such as entity and attribute naming differences, is important. We may further compensate for this by equipping the mediating Web Services with general-purpose lexicons such as WordNet and UMLS. While we focused on mediating the functional descriptions of Web Services involved in a composition, executing a composition may also require negotiating between the non-functional parameters of the Web Services. As part of our future work, we are looking into conflict types not covered in this chapter, and whether those could be mediated by the translator WS.

REFERENCES

Agarwal, V., Chafle, G., Dasgupta, K., Karnik, N., Kumar, A., Mittal, S., & Srivastava, B. (2005). Synthy: A system for end to end composition of web services. *Journal of Web Semantics*, *3*, 311–339. doi:10.1016/j.websem.2005.09.002.

Biron, P., & Malhotra, A. (2004). XML schema part 2: Datatypes second edition. *W3C recommendation*. Retrieved from http://www.w3.org/TR/xmlschema-2/

Cabral, L., & Domingue, J. (2005). Mediation of semantic web services in irs-iii. In *Workshop on Mediation in Semantic Web Services (MEDIATE)*, ICSOC (pp. 1–16).

Carman, M., Serafini, L., & Traverso, P. (2003). Web service composition as planning. In *Workshop on Planning for Web Services, ICAPS*, Trento, Italy.

Cost, R., Finin, T., Joshi, A., Yun, P., Nicholas, C., Soboroff, I., & Chen, H., · , Tolia, S. (2002). ITTalks: A case study in the semantic web and daml+oil. *IEEE Intelligent Systems*, *17*(1), 40–47. doi:10.1109/5254.988447.

Farrel, J., & Lauser, H. (2007). Semantic annotations for WSDL and XML schema. *W3C recommendation*. Retrieved from http://www.w3.org/TR/sawsdl/

Kim, W., Choi, I., Gala, S. K., & Scheevel, M. (1993). On resolving schematic heterogeneity in multidatabase systems. *Distributed and Parallel Databases*. doi:10.1007/BF01263333.

Leitner, P., Rosenberg, F., & Dustdar, S. (2009). Daios: Efficient dynamic web service invocation. *IEEE Internet Computing*, *13*, 72–80. doi:10.1109/MIC.2009.57.

Li, X., Madnick, S., Zhu, H., & Fan, Y. (2009). Reconciling semantic heterogeneity in web services composition. In *International Conference on Information Systems (ICIS)*.

Litwin, W., & Abdellatif, A. (1986). Multi-database interoperability. *IEEE Computer*, *19*(12), 10–18. doi:10.1109/MC.1986.1663123.

Miller, G. A. (1995). WordNet: A lexical database for English. *Communications of the ACM*, *38*(11), 39–41. doi:10.1145/219717.219748.

Mrissa, M., Ghedira, C., Benslimane, D., Maamar, Z., Rosenberg, F., & Dustdar, S. (2007). Context-based mediation approach to compose semantic web services. *ACM Transactions on Internet Technology*, 8.

Nagarajan, M., Verma, K., Sheth, A. P., & Miller, J. A. (2007). Ontology driven data mediation in web services. *International Journal of Web Services Research (JWSR)*, *4*(4), 104–126. doi:10.4018/jwsr.2007100105.

Nitzsche, J., Lessen, T. V., Karastoyanova, D., & Leymann, F. (2007). Bpel for semantic web services (bpel4sws). On the Move to Meaningful Internet Systems (OTM) - Volume Part I (pp. 179–188).

Nitzsche, J., & Norton, B. (2009). Ontology-based data mediation in BPEL (for semantic web services). Business Process Management Workshops, volume 17 of Lecture Notes in Business Information Processing (pp. 523–534). Springer.

Pistore, M., Marconi, A., Bertoli, P., & Traverso, P. (2005). Automated composition of web services by planning at the knowledge level. In *International Joint Conferences on Artificial Intelligence (IJCAI)* (pp. 1252–1259).

Pokraev, S., Quartel, D., Steen, M., & Reichert, M. (2006). Semantic service modeling - enabling system interoperability. In *International Conference on Interoperability for Enterprise Software and Applications (I-ESA)* (pp. 221-231).

Pokraev, S., & Reichert, M. (2006). Mediation patterns for message exchange protocols. In *Open INTEROP-Workshop on Enterprise Modeling and Ontologies for Interoperability* (EMOI), CAiSE (pp. 659-663).

Rahm, E., & Bernstein, P. (2001). A survey of approaches to automatic schema matching. *International Journal on Very Large Databases (VLDB)*, *10*(4), 334–350. doi:10.1007/s007780100057.

Raskin, R., & Pan, M. (2003). Semantic web for earth and environmental technology (SWEET). In *Workshop on Semantic Web Technologies for Searching and Retrieving Scientific Data*, ISWC.

Roman, D., Keller, U., Lausen, H., de Bruijn, J., Lara, R., Stollberg, M., & Polleres, A., · , Fensel, D. (2005). Web service modeling ontology. *Applied Ontology*, *1*(1), 77–106.

Sheth, A. (1998). Changing focus on interoperability in information systems: From system, syntax, structure to semantics. *Interoperating Geographic Information Systems,* 5-30.

Sirin, E., Parsia, B., Wu, D., Hendler, J. A., & Nau, D. S. (2004). HTN planning for web service composition using shop2. *Journal of Web Semantics, 1*(4), 377–396. doi:10.1016/j.websem.2004.06.005.

Spencer, B., & Liu, Y. (2004). Inferring data transformation rules to integrate semantic web services. In *International Semantic Web Conference (ISWC)* (pp. 456–470).

Vembu, N. (2011). *A translator web service for data mediation in web service compositions.* (Master's Thesis). Department of Computer Science, University of Georgia, Athens, USA.

Walsh, N. (2005). *Ontology on vCards.* Retrieved October 22, 2012, from http://nwalsh.com/rdf/vCard.ont

Zhao, H., & Doshi, P. (2009). A hierarchical framework for logical composition of web services. *Journal of Service Oriented Computing and Applications (SOCA), 3*(4), 285–306. doi:10.1007/s11761-009-0052-9.

ADDITIONAL READING

Blake, B. M. (2010). WSC-2010: Web services composition and evaluation. *IEEE Conference on Services Oriented Computing and Applications (SOCA)* (pp. 1-4).

Cardoso, J., Sheth, A., Miller, J., Arnold, J., & Kochut, K. (2004). Quality of service for workflows and web service processes. *Journal of Web Semantics, 1.* doi:10.1016/j.websem.2004.03.001.

Doshi, P., Goodwin, R., Akkiraju, R., & Verma, K. (2005). Dynamic workflow composition: Using markov decision processes. *Journal of Web Services Research (JWSR), 2*(1), 1–17. doi:10.4018/jwsr.2005010101.

Harney, J., & Doshi, P. (2008). Selective querying for adapting web service compositions using the value of changed information. *IEEE Transactions on Services Computing, 1*(3), 169–185. doi:10.1109/TSC.2008.11.

Medjahed, B., Bouguettaya, A., & Elmagarmid, A. K. (2003). Composing web services on the semantic web. *International Journal on Very Large Databases, 12*(4), 333–351. doi:10.1007/s00778-003-0101-5.

Milanovic, N. (2004). Current solutions for web service composition. *IEEE Internet Computing, 8*(6), 51–59. doi:10.1109/MIC.2004.58.

Rao, J., & Su, X. (2004). A survey of automated web service composition methods. In *Workshop on Semantic Web Services and Web Process Composition (SWSWPS)* (pp. 43-54).

Singh, M., & Huynhs, M. (2005). *Service-oriented computing: Semantics, processes and agents.* New York: Wiley.

Srivastava, B., & Koehler, J. (2003). Web service composition – current solutions and open problems. In *ICAPS Workshop on Planning for Web Services* (pp. 28-35).

KEY TERMS AND DEFINITIONS

Atomic Web Service: A Web service whose implementation does not invoke other Web services and is self contained.

Choreography: A type of WS composition in which the participating Web Services interact with one another according to their defined roles and without the presence of a central controller.

Data Mediation: A process of transforming data in order to facilitate interaction between entities.

Isomorphism: A mapping that preserves sets and the relationships between the elements of the sets.

Message Schema: An organization of the data that make up a message including the structure and syntax.

Message-Level Heterogeneity: The diversity in the messages exchanged by the Web Services participating in a composition.

Ontology: A rigorous formalization of the concepts and the relationships between the concepts that exist in a particular domain.

Orchestration: A type of WS composition in which a central controller interacts with the participating Web Services and guides the flow of control in the composition.

Web Service Composition: An assembly of Web services, which operates together as a single unit leading to new functionality.

ENDNOTES

[1] Nithya Vembu participated in this research while she was a graduate student in the Institute for Artificial Intelligence, University of Georgia, USA.

[2] XSD datatype restrictions become a part of D.

[3] http://www.webservicex.net/stockquote.asmx?WSDL.

[4] http://ws.cdyne.com/delayedstockquote/delayedstockquote.asmx.

APPENDIX

As mediation is performed at design time, following XSD data types are acceptable:

When category is numeric:

```
if D_J=decimal,double,float,integer, then accept values from D_I=any numeric type
if =int, then accept values from D_I=float, unsignedShort, byte, unsignedByte
if D_J=long, then accept values from D_I=decimal, float, int, short, unsignedInt,
unsignedShort,
byte, unsignedByte
if D_J=nonNegativeInteger, then accept values from D_I=positiveInteger
if D_J=nonPositiveInteger, then accept values from D_I=negativeInteger
if D_J=short, then accept values from D_I=byte, unsignedByte
if D_J=unsignedInt, then accept values from D_I=int, short, unsignedShort, byte,
unsignedByte
if D_J=unsignedShort, then accept values from D_I=byte, unsignedByte
```

When category is string:

```
if D_J=string or normalizedString, then accept values from D_I=any string type
```

When category is URI:

```
if D_J=anyURI, then accept values from D_I=string
```

When category is date/time:

```
if D_J=gDay, then accept values from D_I=date, dateTime by separating the 'Day'
part
if D_J=gMonth, then accept values from D_I=date, dateTime by separating the
'Month'
part
if D_J=gMonthDay, then accept values from D_I=date, dateTime by separating the
'Month-Day' part
if D_J=gYear, then accept values from D_I=date, dateTime by separating the 'Year'
part
if D_J=gYearMonth, then accept values from D_I=date, dateTime by separating the
'Year-Month' part
if D_J=date, then accept values from D_I=dateTime by separating the 'Date' part
if D_J=time, then accept values from D_I=dateTime by separating the 'Time' part
```

The second part of resolving data representation conflicts involves matching the XSD restrictions on the data types. Checking is done to ensure that they have the same kind of restrictions and that range/ Length-of-values $(D_J) \geq$ Range/Length-of-values (D_I).

Chapter 5

Improving the Quality and Cost–Effectiveness of Process–Oriented, Service–Driven Applications:
Techniques for Enriching Business Process Models

Thomas Bauer
Neu-Ulm University of Applied Sciences, Germany

Stephan Buchwald
T-Systems International GmbH, Germany

Manfred Reichert
University of Ulm, Germany

ABSTRACT

A key objective of any Service-driven architectural approach is to improve the alignment between business and information technology (IT). Business process management, service composition, and service orchestration, play major roles in achieving this goal. In particular, they allow for the process-aware integration of business actors, business data, and business services. To optimize business-IT alignment and to achieve high business value, the business processes implemented in process-aware information systems (PAISs) must be defined by domain experts, and not by members of the IT department. In current practice, however, the information relevant for process execution is usually not captured at the required level of detail in business process models. In turn, this requires costly interactions between IT departments and domain experts during process implementation. To improve this situation, required execution information should be captured at a sufficient level of detail during business process design (front-loading). As another drawback, existing methods and tools for business process design do not consider available Service-oriented Architecture (SOA) artifacts such as technical service descriptions

DOI: 10.4018/978-1-4666-4193-8.ch005

during process design (look-ahead). Both front-loading and look-ahead are not adequately supported by existing business process modeling tools. In particular, for many process aspects, appropriate techniques for specifying them at a sufficient level of detail during business process design are missing. This chapter presents techniques for enabling front-loading and look-ahead for selected process aspects and investigates how executable process models can be derived from business process models when enriched with additional information.

INTRODUCTION

Business process management (BPM) and process-aware information systems (PAISs) have become integral parts of enterprise computing and are used to support business processes at the operational level (Mutschler, Reichert, & Bumiller, 2008; Reichert & Weber, 2012; Weske, 2007). As opposed to function- and data-centric information systems, process logic is strictly separated from application code, relying on executable process models that provide the explicit schemes for process execution (Weber, Rinderle, & Reichert, 2007; Weber, Reichert, & Rinderle-Ma, 2008). This enables a *separation of concerns*, which is a well-established principle in computer science to increase maintainability and to reduce costs of change.

A particular challenge for process-aware information systems (PAIS) is *enterprise application integration*, i.e., to link the atomic activities of an executable process model with business functions implemented in heterogeneous, distributed application systems.

In this context, the emergence of Service-oriented architectures (SOA) and well-defined service principles (Erl, 2005) foster *process-centric* application integration in the large scale (Weber & Reichert, 2012). A Service-driven approach provides tools for encapsulating heterogeneous application functions as services with standardized interfaces. These services then can be composed and orchestrated in a process-aware manner based on a run-time component called *process engine*. Altogether, SOA enables enterprise application integration at a high level of abstraction, reducing the need for realizing application-to-application bridges prevalent in current practice (e.g. based on message exchange or remote procedure calls). In particular, any process activity may retrieve data from an application system (e.g. by invoking a corresponding service) and temporarily store it within the process engine. In turn, this data can be consumed, changed, or complemented when executing subsequent process activities (e.g. human tasks).

Another fundamental goal of a Service-driven approach is to improve *business-IT alignment* (Chen, 2008). In particular, a PAIS should meet the needs of the stakeholders involved in the business processes it implements and not reflect only the design decisions made by the IT department. A variety of issues related to business-IT alignment have been investigated in the ENPROSO (*Enhanced Process Management through Service Orientation*) project (Buchwald, Bauer, & Reichert, 2012; Buchwald, 2012). In particular, ENPROSO revealed that all aspects relevant for process automation should be defined at a sufficient level of detail during the design of business process models. Furthermore, existing artifacts should be reused in this context if available. With *front-loading* and *look-ahead*, this chapter presents two fundamental techniques for achieving these goals.

Front-loading enables the capturing of relevant aspects for process automation at a sufficient level of detail during business process modeling. For a *business process model*, it is not sufficient to only specify the activities, the rough control flow between these activities, and the abstract data objects or roles associated with them. Additionally, the designer of a business process model should capture information relevant for process execution, e.g., about actor assignments (Rinderle-Ma & Reichert, 2007; Rinderle-Ma & Reichert, 2009), user forms (Kolb, Hübner, & Reichert, 2012), and exception handling procedures (Reichert, Dadam, & Bauer, 2003). These and other aspects constitute relevant information for process implementers and therefore should be captured in business process models. They will be discussed in detail in this chapter. In particular, business process models shall be detailed enough to constitute a valuable artifact for process implementers. Note that the latter usually do not have detailed domain-specific knowledge.

Consequently, business process models must not leave room for misinterpretation, such that there is ambiguity in how a business process model is implemented. Only then, it can serve as an appropriate artifact for process implementation. In the current practice, however, many aspects required by process implementers are missing in business process models or only defined in an imprecise manner. This in turn results in significant delays during process implementation due to the need for additional interviews with process stakeholders at a late stage in the project, at which time the domain experts and project consultants involved in the design of the business process might no longer be available. As a direct consequence, in many cases, IT departments themselves decide on how to implement the imprecise or ambiguous specification of a business process model (Mutschler, Reichert, & Bumiller, 2008). This often results in faulty or incomplete process implementations.

Why are business process designers unable to create business process models with a sufficient level of detail fostering their automation in a PAIS? Firstly, domain experts and project consultants are neither aware of the particular aspects relevant for implementing a business process nor the level of detail required in this context, existing Service-driven methodologies do not emphasize this issue adequately. Secondly, business process designers

do not have the skill level for defining the IT aspects of a business process. Neither existing process meta-models like Event-driven Process Chains (EPCs) and Business Process Modeling and Notation (BPMN) nor contemporary business process modeling tools (e.g. ARIS Architect) provide appropriate techniques for defining IT aspects in a way comprehensible for business people and providing the required level of detail. For example, when using ARIS Architect and EPCs, it is not possible to express that a process activity Y must be performed by a person having role "hardware developer" and belonging to the same department as the user who performed the previous process activity X. Usually, business process modeling suites like ARIS only allow assigning a role to a process activity. However, this is not sufficient if more complex actor assignments (Rinderle & Reichert, 2005) need to be implemented.

In order to reduce implementation efforts, available SOA artifacts relevant for process implementation (e.g. technical service descriptions, service implementations, or entities of the organizational model) should be reused and referenced by business process models. We denote the inclusion of respective references in business process models as *look-ahead*. Existing Service-driven methodologies, however, do not provide techniques enabling such a look-ahead. Indeed, integrating SOA artifacts with business process models constitutes a non-trivial task. This is not surprising considering the fact that business process designers do not have the skills required to handle the technical specifications of IT artifacts. For example, a service implementing a particular activity of a business process model is usually described in a technical style. However, specification languages like WSDL are not comprehensible to business people having no or only little IT background. Also note that textual annotations of service descriptions, as provided by many IT departments, will be hardly comprehensible due to the large discrepancies existing between technical specifications and common business languages (e.g. technical artifacts like XSD data types are used to describe the input / output parameters of a service).

Front-loading and look-ahead can be applied to different process aspects (Reichert & Weber, 2012), including *control flow* (e.g. flexibility by design or inclusion of exception handlers), *data flow* (e.g. data types of process data elements), and *organizational entities* (e.g. actor assignments). However, techniques enabling business process designers to specify technical aspects or reference IT artifacts during business process modeling are still missing. This chapter analyzes the requirements for look-ahead and frontloading, and presents selected techniques in detail. In particular, the techniques suggested can be included in a corporate SOA methodology. For example, a governance committee responsible for the quality of business process models may only release models enabling front-loading and look-ahead. (Buchwald, 2012) presents a corporate SOA methodology for PAIS development, which covers front-loading and look-ahead as well. In early phases during business process design, modelers must capture front-loading data and refer to existing SOA artifacts to realize look-ahead. In a subsequent phase, respective information is then used for the technical specification and implementation of executable process models.

The remainder of this chapter is structured as follows: we first provide background information and introduce a scenario used throughout the chapter to illustrate basic issues and concepts. We then analyze for which process perspectives front-loading and look-ahead are useful. In this context, we elaborate general requirements and present front-loading and look-ahead techniques for selected process aspects. In particular, these techniques can be used by business process designers having only few IT skills. Front-loading will be illustrated for actor assignments, where we will present techniques for precisely specifying complex actor assignments during business process design. In turn, look-ahead techniques will

be illustrated along with the integration of service implementations in business process models. In this context, the challenge is to enable business process designers to find required services based on available documentation described at the business level. For both scenarios, we discuss how respective information can be utilized during process implementation. The chapter concludes with a summary and outlook.

BACKGROUND

The framework developed in the ENPROSO project comprises several methods that improve business-IT alignment when implementing business processes in a Service-driven environment. One of these methods bridges the gap between business process models on one hand and business process implementations (i.e. process orchestrations) as well as related technical specifications on the other (Buchwald, Bauer, & Reichert, 2012). For this purpose, different models are used.

One of these models – denoted Business-IT-Mapping Model (BIMM) – captures the dependencies between the steps of a business process model (e.g. specified in terms of an EPC) and the steps of the corresponding system process (i.e. technical implementation). As illustrated in Figure 1, a single step of a business process model may be realized in terms of multiple steps at the IT system level (i.e. mapping type "Split" is used). As example, consider an activity that allows a user to enter data via a form and then automatically store this data in an IT system. Such an activity will be implemented as a human task realizing the user interaction, followed by an automatically invoked service that writes the data into the respective IT system.

Note that a system process may contain additional steps not present in the corresponding business process model, such as using a mapping type "Insert," or performing a technical step such as writing data to a system log. In many cases,

Figure 1. Business-IT-Mapping Model capturing dependencies between process steps at different levels

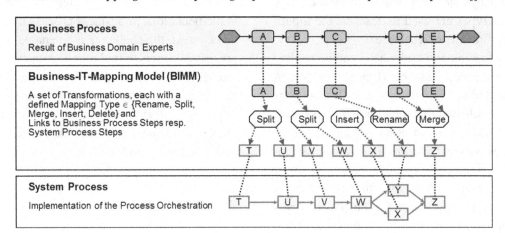

however, a business process step is just mapped to exactly one step of the system process. In this context, mapping type "Rename" must be applied if different labels shall be used for the respective step at the business and system process level. Mapping type "Merge" aggregates multiple steps of the business process to a single step of the system process. This mapping is useful in cases where the same person must perform a sequence of separate business activities to be realized by one and the same human task (in the implemented system process) to minimize required user interactions (Kolb, Hübner, & Reichert, 2012).

In general, a BIMM represents all dependencies between the steps of a business process model and that of the corresponding system process model (Figure 1). Based on respective mappings, for each business process step (e.g. A) the corresponding steps at the system level can be identified (e.g. T and U). Especially, when business requirements related to a business process step evolve, it will be easy to figure out which system level steps might have to be adapted. In summary, when using a BIMM, changes in business requirements may be quickly transferred to the operational level with reduced effort and cost compared to existing approaches.

Since a BIMM allows mapping the information defined at the business process level to elements of

the system process, it can be used as the basis for realizing *front-loading* and *look-ahead* as well. If business level information is changed after the first version of the business process model was released and process implementation has already started, the BIMM enables quick and easy identification of those steps of the system process affected by the change. For example, assume that the *actor assignment* of business process step A (Figure 1) is changed. Based on the given BIMM, it can be easily figured out that A is implemented by steps T and U in the system process. Assume further that only T represents a human task, whereas U corresponds to an automated service storing data. In this scenario, only the actor assignment of step T must be changed in the system process.

Related Work

Both front-loading and look-ahead are methods known in other domains as well. In the automotive industry, for example, *product engineering processes* apply *front-loading* to achieve a higher maturity level of the product in the early development phases. For this purpose, selected development activities are performed earlier than required. Based on existing, but still evolving CAD (Computer Aided Design) models of vehicle parts, it is checked whether the production of the vehicle might cause problems in future lifecycle phases (e.g. when producing the vehicles in the factory). *Look-ahead* is realized by investigating which vehicle parts (e.g. a specific electric motor) have been already used by other vehicle components or in other vehicle engineering projects and, therefore, might be reused in the current project.

With contemporary business process modeling tools, front-loading and look-ahead can be partially realized for selected process aspects (Enderle, 2009). For example, *flexibility flags* marking process regions with high flexibility demand can be realized by assigning *annotation objects* to the respective process steps. As will be shown, however, existing business process modeling tools do not provide an appropriate basis for business process implementation due to their restricted functionality as well as the incomplete and ambiguous specifications provided by them.

Generally, a Service-driven methodology should enforce both *front-loading* and *look-ahead*. In the following text, we will analyze Service-driven methodologies with respect to specific techniques.

SOMA (Service-Oriented Modeling and Architecture) enforces front-loading for some of the process aspects discussed in this chapter (Arsanjani et al., 2008). For example, flexibility flags can be realized during the identification phase. In turn, exception handlers and data objects may be defined during the specification phase. However, SOMA does not allow for querying existing service implementations to enable their reuse in business process models (look-ahead). Finally, front-loading in terms of early specifications of complex actor assignments or forms for human tasks is not supported.

Quasar Enterprise (Engels et al., 2008a; Engels et al., 2008b) allows adding flexibility flags to simple business process models as well. Like in SOMA, business rules can be used for this purpose. However, creating such rules requires special skills that business process designers usually do not have. Querying services based on

business criteria and hence reusing services based on look-ahead are not supported.

M3 for SOA (Deeg, 2007) constitutes a modeling method that uses different model types in the different phases of the process life cycle (Weber et al., 2009). However, it is not possible to define organizational aspects at a sufficient level of detail during business process design (initiation phase). Furthermore, data objects and business rules may be specified within a business process model although this is not directly supported in existing business process modeling tools. Look-ahead for existing data objects and services is not supported at all.

AVE (ARIS Value Engineering) (IDS Scheer, 2005) provides a methodology for BPM projects that is strongly connected with the ARIS toolset and EPC. Hence, for many process aspects, a sufficient (i.e. complete and unambiguous) support of front-loading or look-ahead is not possible. For example, complex actor assignments cannot be specified unambiguously when using AVE. Further, querying services in the service repository based on business criteria is only rudimentarily supported.

SOAM (SOA Method) allows for querying services and reusing them (Offermann, 2008; Offermann & Bub, 2009). However, other process aspects discussed in this chapter (e.g. front-loading through adding flexibility flags or precise actor assignment to business process models) is not supported. Other SOA approaches like OrVia (Stein et al., 2008), Project-Oriented SOA (Shuster, 2008), and SUPER (Weber et al., 2007) provide methodologies for developing process-oriented applications in a SOA (process applications for short). However, they only rudimentarily support the front-loading and look-ahead techniques presented in this chapter.

In summary, neither existing business process modeling tools nor SOA methods meet the requirements raised by front-loading and look-ahead in a sufficient manner. Some approaches enable front-loading of individual process aspects (e.g.

actor assignments or flexibility flags). During business process design, however, these aspects can only be defined at a rather abstract level, which hinders their direct realization during process implementation. Furthermore, SOA literature does not report on methods enabling front-loading or look-ahead. In particular, appropriate modeling techniques are still missing.

Application Scenario

Figure 2 depicts a business process dealing with product change management in the automotive domain. This simplified process will be used as an illustrating example throughout this chapter. Its purpose is to allow responsible users to request a change of a product (e.g. a vehicle) in its development or production phase. The requested change must be described and analyzed, its costs must be estimated, the request must be approved or rejected, and finally the change must be realized (in case of approval).

In Figure 2, the first process step (i.e. Step 1) deals with the creation of a new change request. This step may be performed by an actor who is allowed to start instances of the product change management process. Furthermore, the respective actor must provide information about the product change desired in Step 1. For this purpose, the actor edits a form and enters the required data, such as the reason for the change request, a technical description of the change, an estimation of

resulting costs and earnings, the deadline for realizing the change, and concerned objects (e.g. prototypes, production plants). Steps 2 and 3 are then performed to prevent unnecessary or costly change requests. More precisely, Step 2 constitutes an automated process step that classifies the change request according to the data provided by Step 1.

A change request will be considered as problematic, for example, if its estimated costs are too high, its deadline cannot be met, or it refers to a vehicle project that has already entered the production phase. For problematic requests, Step 3 is additionally performed, i.e., the manager (e.g. department head) of the change requestor then decides whether the processing of the change request shall be continued (e.g. for safety reasons). If a problematic change request is not considered as meaningful, it will be stopped in this early phase, otherwise it will be continued. Change requests classified as "non-problematic" in Step 2 will be continued anyway. Note that Step 2 reduces overall efforts for the department head, since he/she does not need to handle unproblematic requests.

The technical evaluation of the change request starts with Step 4. During this process step, a specialist identifies all product parts concerned by the requested change. This specialist must have the role of "hardware developer" and belong to the same department as the change requestor (i.e. the process starter). Step 5 is then executed multiple times in parallel according to the number of parts affected by the change. For each part identified

Figure 2. Product change management process

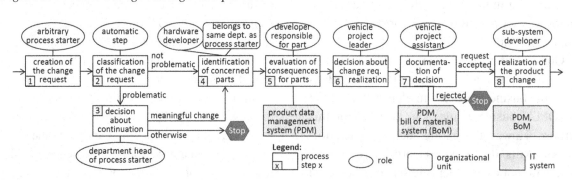

in Step 4, required technical changes, changes in product weight, estimated costs, etc. are evaluated. Thereby, each evaluation is performed by the developer responsible for the respective part.

As a prerequisite for Step 5, detailed information about product parts needs to be provided, e.g., by invoking a respective information service offered by the product data management system (PDM). After completing all part evaluations, in Step 6 the project leader decides whether or not the change shall be approved. In Step 7, a project assistant documents this decision, which is then automatically logged in several IT systems. To prevent undesired changes, change approval constitutes a prerequisite for changing part data (e.g. geometry data) in these systems. Following this, rejected change requests are stopped, whereas approved ones are realized by executing Step 8. The latter is performed multiple times by developers responsible for the concerned sub-system for which parts or entire components need to be changed. Finally, resulting data is stored in the PDM system and the BoM (Bill of Material) system.

REQUIREMENTS FOR FRONT-LOADING AND LOOK-AHEAD

This section analyzes the process aspects for which front-loading techniques are useful. In this context, we refer to the problems that will arise if respective aspects are not already specified during business process design. Furthermore, for each process aspect, we show an appropriate front-loading technique. Finally, general requirements for front-loading are summarized. Applying the same schema, issues related to look-ahead are presented. Selected approaches enabling front-loading and look-ahead are presented in the subsequent section.

Process Aspects for which Front-Loading is Useful

To better understand the benefits provided by front-loading, for the different aspects of a business process, we analyze the information that would typically be captured during business process design.

Organizational Aspect

In a business process model, an actor assignment defines the persons who may perform a particular process step (Rinderle & Reichert, 2005). In a later development phase, these actor assignments are then implemented at a technical level. During run-time, a process engine ensures that instances of this process step are only added to the work lists of authorized users. That means, only the persons that qualify for the process step (i.e. belonging to the actor set specified by the respective actor assignment) are allowed to perform this step. Therefore, the precise and complete specification of actor assignments at the business level is crucial for correctly and efficiently implementing them in a PAIS. However, the concrete implementation method depends on the process engine chosen. While certain process engines require program code in this context, others provide more sophisticated support for specifying actor assignments in terms of pre-defined templates whose parameters may be linked to entities (e.g. roles) of the organizational model of the company (e.g. the corporate directory) as well as the process instance data (e.g. to refer to the actual performer of a previous process step). At run-time, the process engine then uses the organizational model of the enterprise to determine the potential actors of a process step. An example of a process engine enabling this approach is AristaFlow BPM Suite (Dadam & Reichert, 2009; Reichert et al., 2009).

To better understand the challenge of defining actor assignments during the design of a business process model, we discuss how respective expressions may be specified when using a contemporary business process modeling tool. More precisely, for the business process model depicted in Figure 2, Figure 3 shows how the actor assignment of Step 4 can be expressed when using the ARIS modeling tool; remember that this step shall be performed by a person owning the role of "hardware developer" and belonging to the same department as the performer of the first process step (i.e. the change requestor).

Usually, a process step within an ARIS model only refers to the role an actor performing this step shall have. In some cases, in addition, "department objects" with unclear semantics are used (Figure 3a).

However, the information provided in this context is not sufficient to implement the process step in a way required to execute it by a process engine. As indicated by the dotted lines in Figure 3b, the exact department that the hardware developer belongs to is determined during run-time by taking the execution history of the process into account. With business process modeling tools like ARIS, however, it is not possible to express such inter-dependencies relevant for process execution. In fact, ARIS does not support any object type representing the actual performer of a particular process step. Furthermore, there is no relationship type allowing the process model designer to specify that the department assigned

to Step 4 shall be the one a particular actor (e.g. the performer of Step 1) belongs to.[1]

Note that there exist many similar scenarios not adequately covered by tools like ARIS due to the insufficient expressiveness of their business process modeling language. For example, in ARIS it cannot be expressed that a change request shall be approved by the head of that department to which the change requestor belongs, i.e., it is not sufficient to only assign a role "department head" to the respective process step (i.e. Step 3 in Figure 2), but to express this dependency as well. Similarly, a bank clerk applying for a credit must not approve this credit request or that a particular document must be checked by a person different from the one who created it (i.e. separation of concerns). In the latter example, again it might be necessary that the second specialist belongs to the same department as the first one (Figure 3b).

Regarding Step 4 in the model from Figure 3, an actor assignment like "role = 'hardware developer' AND department = department(performer(Step 1))" is required. In particular, incomplete information like "role = 'hardware developer'" (Figure 3a) prohibits the correct implementation of the desired behavior since the actor set corresponding to this expression would be too large (i.e. the set would include all hardware developers from arbitrary departments). In the subsequent section, several modeling techniques will be presented, which

Figure 3. An actor assignment defined (a) with ARIS and (b) including the additionally required dependencies

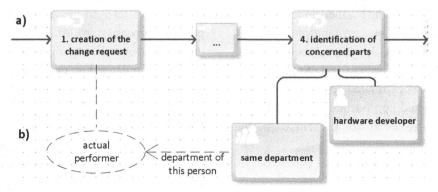

allow defining such complex actor assignments during business process design without requiring comprehensive IT skills.

Substitution rules constitute another element of the organizational perspective (Bauer, 2009). Basically, a substitution rule defines the actors who shall take over a particular process step in case its regular performers are absent (e.g. due to a business trip, sick leave, or holidays). Most process engines support substitution rules and hence prevent process steps from being solely assigned to the worklists of absent persons. Note that the latter might cause significant delays as well as high costs (e.g. due to deadlines missed) during business process execution. As a prerequisite for implementing substitution rules, however, for all processes and process steps, respectively[2], domain experts must specify which persons shall act as substitute. For example, consider Step 6 in Figure 2. From the information provided, it does not become clear for implementers who shall act as substitute of the vehicle project leader. Perhaps there exists a vice project leader or decisions are made by a project committee. Alternatively, the supervisor of the project leader might have this responsibility. The techniques we will present for defining actor assignments during business process design can also be used to realize front-loading of substitution rules.

An escalation rule defines notifications sent to specific actors or managers if a process step (representing a human task) is not started or completed within a pre-specified time period. In certain cases, it might be even required to automatically forward a delayed human task to another actor. For example, consider Step 5 (evaluation of consequences for parts) from Figure 2, for which multiple instances are concurrently processed by different developers. Manually monitoring these instances and their temporal constraints (Lanz, Weber, & Reichert, 2010; 2012) by a process administrator would require a huge effort due to the potentially large number of human tasks (even in the context of a single change request). Instead,

a process engine should allow for their automatic monitoring, and automatically trigger escalations in case of delays. Again, this necessitates the provision of respective information during business process design, i.e., domain experts should specify the escalations required in a specific context (e.g. violations of temporal constraints). Generally, it does not constitute a valid option to allow process implementers realizing escalation rules in an arbitrary way. This becomes obvious when considering the fact that in large companies, technical implementations are often outsourced to external contractors. However, the latter may have only low economic interest to invest any effort in clarifying ambiguities with domain experts. Altogether, front-loading is essential for all issues related to the organizational aspect.

Data Objects

The data objects of an executable process model have associated data types to precisely define the interface of the process model as well as its internal data flow (Reichert & Weber, 2012; Künzle, Weber, & Reichert, 2011). Usually, data is provided by the environment when starting a process instance. In turn, when completing a process instance, it may return output data back to its environment. Furthermore, when a process instance invokes a service during run-time (i.e. to execute a process step), input data required by this service are consumed from process data objects, whereas output data produced upon service completion are stored in corresponding data objects (Reichert & Dadam, 1998). For example, consider Step 5 of the process model from Figure 2, which invokes a service to read part data from a product data management (PDM) system. Thereby, the process provides the part number as input to enable the invoked service to identify the part concerned by the change and to return all part data required by the process.

A human task is often implemented as an electronic form (Kolb, Hübner, & Reichert, 2012;

Künzle & Reichert, 2011). Input data types then represent the information presented to the actor processing the form, whereas output data types correspond to the data that may have to be set for updatable form elements. Usually, data types are only roughly specified in process models at the business level, e.g., only the name and most relevant attributes may have been captured. This information, however, is not sufficient for implementing the interfaces of executable process models and callable services (including user forms) respectively.

Regarding data objects, front-loading may contribute to avoiding unnecessary analyses during process implementation. For this purpose, for each data object, all attributes (including their data types) relevant from a business perspective must be specified. Regarding our running example, for instance, this means that a domain expert must decide whether the part number assigned to Step 5 (and the service it invokes) shall have type integer or string, e.g., to store part numbers like "4711" or "C-284285-2012." Note that only domain experts will have the knowledge required in this context, for example, the first character of a part number encoding the vehicle project (e.g. C-Class) and the last 4 digits encoding the development year of the part. Hence, data type string (with a length of 13) must be assigned to the respective data object in the business process model. Finally, for each process step, data objects read or written must be described at a similar level of granularity to avoid further analyses or ambiguities in the process implementation phase.

Services

When a process step is executed, it invokes a service, hands over data objects to it, and receives service results that may change the existing process data. To enable front-loading, the services required for implementing the process must be described in detail within the business process model, i.e., it is not sufficient to only define service names as placeholders. For example, assume that Step 7 in Figure 2 requires a not yet implemented service documenting the decision about a change request in the BoM system. In this case, the service name itself (e.g. BoM_StoreChangeRequestDecision) will not be sufficient to implement the service. In addition, the functions to be provided by the service need to be specified, e.g., (1) storing the number of the change request in the BoM system, (2) assigning the parts affected by the change to this number, and (3) allowing for future modifications of this part if the correct change request number is referenced.

In general, for each service to be invoked by a process, its functionality, data types of its input and output parameters, and desired quality of service (QoS) properties like response time (Bodenstaff, Wombacher, & Reichert, 2008) need to be pre-specified. A process implementer may then use this information either to select an existing service or to develop a new one. In addition, the business process designer should specify which IT system shall offer this service. Regarding Step 5 from Figure 2, it makes a bit of a difference whether data is retrieved from the PDM or the BoM system.

Note that these two systems store different attributes for product parts. Furthermore, in a BoM system, new part versions only become available with delay (i.e. when reaching a higher release level). There exist process modeling tools that already allow defining services from a business perspective, to specify desired service functions and properties. To foster front-loading, respective tool support must be provided to domain experts during business process design. Finally, this must be ensured by an appropriate SOA methodology (including governance processes).

Flexibility

When implementing a business process, those points or regions need to be known for which a high degree of flexibility is required during process execution (Sadiq, Sadiq, & Orlowska,

2005; Weber, Sadiq, & Reichert, 2009; Reichert, Rinderle-Ma, & Dadam, 2009). Since these flexibility points differ from process to process, they need to be identified and specified by a domain expert together with the required kind of flexibility. For example, there might be process steps whose associated service implementation frequently needs to be exchanged due to evolving business requirements. Regarding Step 2 in Figure 2, for instance, there exist frequently changing criteria used for deciding on whether or not a change request is problematic. Since Step 2 constitutes an automated step, the decision algorithm is implemented by a corresponding service. In particular, this service implementation should be exchanged whenever requested by the business domain, if the decision algorithm or its underlying criteria change. Hence, a flexible implementation of the service call is required that allows exchanging the service implementation if required.

In practical settings, domain experts usually know the services whose implementation frequently changes. Hence, front-loading can be realized by flagging the process steps that use these services and annotating them with respective descriptions. Based on this information, it becomes clear that the service call needs to be implemented in a decoupled manner, such as, by using an enterprise service bus (ESB) or a message broker. Other process artifacts that may require a similar degree of flexibility (i.e. dynamic exchangeability) include branching conditions, business rules, actor assignments, and timeout limits. In particular, it must be possible to add flexibility flags and descriptions to these artifacts during the design of a business process model, if required.

As an example consider Figure 4, which shows a process step with an associated flexibility flag and description. More precisely, the latter indicates that the service implementation of this process step frequently changes. When using a contemporary process modeling tool like ARIS, respective flexibility flags and descriptions can be realized by creating a corresponding object type for them (or by deriving such an object type from an existing one if the tool does not allow creating new object types). A particular attribute of this object type should then encode the required kind of flexibility. Furthermore, it should be possible to describe the expected changes by using a documentation or comment attribute as usually offered by any process modeling tool for all object types. The flexibility requested in Figure 4, for example, can be implemented by specifying a corresponding business rule using a business rule engine and connecting it with the process implementation. Consequently, changes can be directly mapped to rule modifications without requiring any adaptation of the process implementation itself.

Figure 4. ARIS process step with a flexibility flag and description

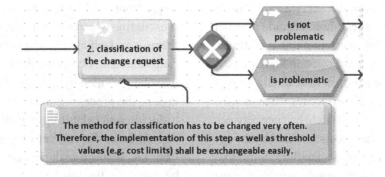

Exceptions

During the execution of a business process, it might become necessary to handle exceptional situations (Reichert & Weber, 2012). Examples of exceptions include failed service calls (e.g. the PDM system called by Step 5 might be not running), insufficient data quality (e.g. the data entered by a user in the context of a human task, e.g., Step1, might be incomplete or contradictory), and empty actor sets (e.g. no actor can be assigned to Step 4 after the only hardware developer of the respective department quit his job). Obviously, some of these exceptions can be anticipated and hence be automatically detected (e.g. failed service calls). Consequently, the IT department can detect them without need for domain-specific knowledge and no front-loading is required for exception detection. By contrast, insufficient data quality can be only detected if additional information is made available by a domain expert. For example, to detect that attribute values "vehicle project = Actros" and "part number = C-284285-2012" are contradictory, one must know that Actros is a commercial vehicle, while part numbers of kind "C-number-year" belong to the passenger car project C-Class.

While many exceptions can be detected without need for specific domain knowledge, exception handling itself usually requires domain knowledge and hence should be incorporated into business process models using front-loading. For example, a failed service call might be repeated infinitely in worst case. However, if a service call fails repeatedly, a domain expert should decide whether it should be repeated a certain number of times, an alternative service (e.g. causing higher costs) should be called, or a human task should be performed instead, to create service results manually. Thereby, the domain expert has to balance between the execution delays and costs incurred by the options available for exception handling. Similarly, if contradictory attribute values occur, it must be defined who shall correct the inconsistencies.

Finally, if the set of potential actors for a human task is empty, a process manager (i.e. a responsible actor) is required who manually re-assigns the task to an actor being able to perform it.

Forms

Usually, a user performing a human task fills in a respective form. As mentioned, the data fields displayed to the user or edited by the user are defined by the data types of the input and output data objects of the process step (Kolb, Hübner, & Reichert, 2012). For example, assume that the input data object of Step 3 (see the process model from Figure 2) corresponds to the change request produced in Step 1. Then the attributes of this data object will be displayed in respective form fields to the responsible department head and provide the basis for their decision.

Generally, a data object and data type respectively is used in the context of multiple process steps, i.e., its content is not optimized for a specific process step. Consequently, a data type often comprises more attributes than required or useful for performing a particular process step. In such a case, not all attributes shall be displayed to the performer of the process step (Künzle & Reichert, 2009; 2011). Regarding Step 3, for example, the department head shall only see selected attributes of the change request relevant for the decision, but not all technical details of the change as captured in the change request data object as well.

Regarding the user forms assigned to process steps, front-loading means that a domain expert must define which attributes shall be displayed to the user and which not. The same applies to form fields and data object attributes respectively that must be provided by the user. Generally, it is the task of the process designer and domain experts to decide which data object attributes shall be read or written in the context of a particular process step, i.e., respective design decisions should not be made by the implementer of the user form. As opposed to technical process specifications

(Reichert & Dadam, 1997; 1998), in most existing business process modeling tools, a data type does not contain information about mandatory and optional attributes. As a consequence, for an output data object of a process step, it is not always clear whether a particular attribute shall be realized as mandatory input field in the form.

For example, in Step 3 the department head may provide the decision as a Boolean value indicating whether to stop or continue the processing of the change request. Additionally, the department head may comment on the change request. Using front-loading, for instance, the domain expert may specify that the Boolean value representing the user decision is mandatory and hence shall be implemented as mandatory form field, whereas the comment shall be realized as optional field and certain attributes of the change request object shall be omitted. Regarding process steps, in general, for each attribute of its output data objects, a corresponding status ∈ {mandatory, optional, omit} shall be defined in the business process model. In turn, for each attribute of an input data object a status ∈ {show, omit} is required.

Besides the contents of a form, its design is crucial as well (Kolb, Hübner, & Reichert, 2012). Hence, front-loading should allow domain experts to provide information about the desired appearance of the form as well. Form implementers shall be supported by attaching drawings to process steps that define the positions of the data fields within the respective form as well as the labels to be displayed for the different form fields. Additionally, such a drawing might define the GUI control elements (e.g. text field, combo box, list, radio button, etc.) that shall be used for interacting with specific form fields and data objects respectively.

Other Process Aspects

Other process aspects for which front-loading is useful include transactional properties of a business process model and measurement points enabling process performance management. We

refer to (Enderle, 2009; Buchwald, 2012) for further details.

General Requirements for Front-Loading

Front-loading is a useful concept for a variety of process aspects and hence different techniques enabling it exist. Besides its particularities, which meet the requirements of a specific process aspect best, any front-loading technique should satisfy a number of general requirements:

- It must allow modeling the information required for implementing a specific process aspect from a business perspective; respective information shall be provided by a domain expert, to foster correct process executability, and increase process model quality.
- It must be comprehensible and easy to use for business process designers having no or only limited IT skills. In addition, the artifacts resulting from its use must be easy to read, i.e., they should be understandable to domain experts not having process management skills. Note that this is crucial for verifying the semantic correctness of the business process models.
- The specifications (i.e. artifacts) resulting from the application of any front-loading technique must be complete, i.e., their information content must be sufficient to implement the respective process aspect later on without need for costly interactions with domain experts.
- For each front-loading technique, a procedure shall be provided that allows transforming the respective business specification into a correct IT implementation. In principle, such a transformation shall be as efficient as possible. However, automatic, semi-automatic, and manual transformations have to be considered depending on the given application environment.

Process Aspects for which Look-Ahead is Useful

We describe the process aspects for which the existence of appropriate IT artifacts shall be checked during business process design in order to enable the reuse of these artifacts and hence to reduce process implementation efforts.

Organizational Aspect

As described in the context of front-loading, a business process model shall capture actor assignments, substitution rules, and escalations. Usually, respective information is defined in terms of expressions referring to organizational objects (OrgObjects for short). Examples of the latter include roles, departments, and competences. In a later development phase, i.e., during process implementation, these expressions must be transformed in a way that the resulting specifications are machine-readable, referring to real objects from the organizational model of the enterprise. During process execution, the organizational model is then used to determine potential actors of the respective process step. For this purpose, this model maintains all OrgObjects and their relations, as well as the assignment of concrete actors to them.

For example, to determine the potential actors of Step 4 in Figure 2, information about the employees, currently owning role "hardware developer" and belonging to the respective department, is utilized.

In general, the transformation of a business process model into an executable process implementation must not leave room for ambiguities. This necessitates that the OrgObjects referenced by a business process model are unambiguous, e.g., the label "hardware developer" used in the context of Step 4 should refer to a unique role. Ideally, a business process designer uses exactly the same names for OrgObjects as known in the organizational model of the enterprise. Concern-

ing the organizational aspect, this would ease the transformation from a business process model to an executable process implementation significantly. In turn, when using varying names for existing OrgObjects at the different levels, during process implementation, it might not be clear which OrgObject shall be actually referenced.

As a particular challenge, OrgObjects may correspond to IT artifacts not known and not self-explanatory to business process designers. Hence, additional information is required to enable these experts to refer to entities (i.e. OrgObjects) from the organizational model of the enterprise and hence to reuse them if favorable. For this purpose, the structure of the organizational model (e.g. object types like actor, role, department, and competence, as well as the relationship types between them) needs to be published in a way easily comprehensible to business process designers. Furthermore, the concrete instances of the different OrgObjects[3] must be published, e.g., the concrete roles or department names that may be used in a business process model (e.g. "hardware developer," "component architect"). Finally, appropriate support for querying OrgObject instances in the organizational model should be provided. Generally, such look-ahead increases the unambiguousness of a business process model. Further, it improves reusability of organizational objects, avoiding their redundant specification and hence reducing maintenance efforts.

When creating a business process model, even OrgObjects that do not exactly match the given requirements might be used. For example, consider Step 8 in Figure 2 and assume that OrgObject "sub-system developer" currently does not exist in the organizational model. A domain expert, however, might have the knowledge that all sub-system developers either possess role "component architect" or role "hardware developer." If both roles already exist in the organizational model, role = component architect OR role = hardware developer should be chosen as actor assignment to enable the reuse of existing IT artifacts.

Data Objects

When designing a business process model, data objects are used for specifying the data flow between process steps, e.g., the change request object produced by Step 1 (Figure 2) is consumed (i.e. read) by Step 2. Furthermore, data objects provide the basis for transmitting data between a process instance and invoked services (e.g. Step 5) or human tasks (e.g. Step 6). To enable look-ahead for the data perspective, existing data object types should be reused during the design of a business process model as well. Usually, for respective data object types, there already exist detailed specifications (e.g. UML class diagrams) or even implementations (e.g. Java class implementations). To enable the reuse of existing data object types through look-ahead, these should be easily accessible to business process designers and respective tools. As an advantage, efforts for designing, specifying, and implementing data objects are significantly reduced.

Even more important, business process models then refer to the same data types as existing services and human tasks. Due to this harmonization, the overall efforts for implementing the transformation of a data structure defined at the business level into another one used at the technical level can be avoided, such that, both the change management process and the service interfaces provided by the PDM system may refer to the same data type in the context of part data objects. Regarding our example from Figure 2, Step 5 calls a service of the PDM system to retrieve required part data. Due to the harmonization that can be achieved through look-ahead, there is no need for transforming the received part data, neither during the service call nor during business process execution.

Services

As discussed, a business process model may call a service to trigger an action (e.g. data delivery) in a foreign IT system. Basic to this are the ser-

vice interfaces that allow other applications to call specific service operations. Usually, service descriptions and service operations are published in a SOA repository. At process execution time, the SOA repository may then be used by an Enterprise Service Bus (ESB) to figure out the service endpoint before calling the service. Such a decoupling increases flexibility since it allows moving a service to another server without the necessity to modify all applications consuming this service. Furthermore, even changes of service signatures become possible, since an ESB may transform input or output data during the service call as well. All information required for endpoint lookup or transformation may be stored in a technical SOA repository like IBM WSRR (IBM, 2007). SOA repositories often manage large data volumes since they have to store information about service versions, business objects, usage contracts, and many other object types as well as their dependencies. A comprehensive meta-model of a SOA repository is presented in (Buchwald, 2012). Furthermore, SOA repositories are relevant in the context of semantic web services as well.

Regarding our running example, a SOA repository might be queried to search for already existing services that allow realizing Steps 5, 7 and 8. Unfortunately, services and their operations are often published only at a very technical level, e.g., using WSDL descriptions. However, such descriptions are not comprehensible to business process designers having no or only limited IT skills. Similar problems hold for textual service descriptions as offered by many IT departments as alternative to WSDL specifications. Usually, the language used in this context significantly differs from the one used by domain experts, especially when technical artifacts (e.g. XSD data type specifications for service parameters) are used.

To enable look-ahead, a service should be described in terms of a language (or graphical notation) easily understandable to business process designers. Furthermore, it must be easy to search for needed services and to access and understand related descriptions. Based on this, business process designers can find appropriate services and refer to them in corresponding process steps. Note that existing technical service specifications (e.g. service operations and the data types of their input/output parameters) then should be linked with these business level specifications to avoid unnecessary analysis and inquiries during process implementation.

For some process steps, no service might exist that precisely offers the required functionality. In such a situation, it might still be useful during business process modeling to refer to a service having similar functionality. For example, assume that for Step 5 in Figure 2, there exists no service delivering the part data based on the "part name" as input. Assume further that the PDM system already offers a service delivering respective data based on the "part number," which is not known within the change management process when executing Step 5. Before calling the respective service, therefore, the "part number" must be figured out based on the given "part name." This can be accomplished by introducing an automatically executed service or an interactive process step (human task) in the executable process model. Due to these changes in process behavior, this decision should be made by a domain expert during business process design.

To enable service look-ahead, existing services should be published and guidelines must be defined that enforce their reuse if favorable from an economic point of view. Usually, the reuse of existing services makes sense, and it does not only reduce efforts and costs for service implementation, but also eases service maintenance significantly. As a disadvantage, adjustments to the defined process logic might become necessary (see the example above). In certain cases, the costs resulting from such a restructuring are negligible, for e.g., if the sequence of already existing process steps is changed (e.g. determining the "part number" earlier as intended) or process steps (i.e. service calls) are added that can be completely automated (i.e. no additional human interactions become

necessary). Since domain experts are responsible for the design of business process models, they might also decide that an existing service shall not be re-used and a new one be requested instead, e.g., if costly human tasks become necessary or process quality suffers.

Business Rules

Business rules are used for implementing complex branching decisions within business processes. Step 2 from Figures 2 and 4, for example, automatically classifies a change request either as "problematic" or "not problematic." For problematic change requests, in addition, Step 3 must be executed in order to decide whether the processing of the change request shall be continued. Since the logic of the rule for deciding whether a change request is problematic might be rather complex and frequently change, it can be implemented using a business rule engine. The latter maintains business rules in a central repository and provides comprehensive support for rule execution. Even more important, by extracting complex rules from business process logic and implementing these rules separately in a business rule engine, rule changes can be accomplished without need for changing or re-deploying business processes and their implementation. Furthermore, sophisticated tools for defining or editing business rules are provided. Using these tools, domain experts without deep IT skills will be able to perform changes of a business rule (e.g. changes of the thresholds defined in the context of a business rule).

Look-ahead fosters the reuse of business rules. In particular, this helps avoiding unnecessary costs due to redundant implementation of already existing business rules. Note that such redundancies increase rule maintenance costs significantly and result in inconsistencies as well as unclear process behavior when business processes use different (and potentially degenerated) implementations of the same rule. For example, assume that there exists a business rule enabling customer classification (i.e. it characterizes a customer as standard, premium, or problem customer). There should be exactly one implementation of this classification rule that may then be reused in a variety of business processes. Only then, ambiguities can be avoided and it can be ensured that customers are classified and treated in the same manner for all business processes implemented. Altogether, look-ahead fosters such a reuse of business rules; as a prerequisite, business rules must be easy to find and be described in a way comprehensible to domain experts.

General Requirements for Look-Ahead

Generally, look-ahead presumes that existing technical specifications can be easily found by business process designers. For this purpose, a high-level description understandable for end-users of the respective business domain is required. How this description should look like depends on the respective process aspect. Besides these differences, look-ahead should meet a number of general requirements as well:

- For each process aspect requiring look-ahead during business process design, techniques for describing technical artifacts (e.g. service or business rule) at a certain level of abstraction are required. Appropriate descriptions are crucial when considering the fact that the selection of a particular artifact might influence the design of business process models (i.e. their structure). Furthermore, it must not be ambiguous for process implementers, which concrete technical artifact shall be (re-) used when implementing a specific step of the business process.

- The descriptions of the technical artifacts should be easy to understand for business process designers having only few IT skills. To enable them to find the required artifacts, advanced techniques for search-

ing in repositories and for browsing within descriptions are required.

- For any description of a technical artifact, its information content shall be complete, i.e., sufficient to enable decisions of business process designers on whether or not the artifact is appropriate for implementing a particular process step.

- A business process model may refer to the technical artifacts that shall be used during process implementation. For business process steps, therefore, it must be unambiguously specified which technical artifact shall be used for implementing them. Furthermore, corresponding references shall be stable, i.e., the identifier of the referenced artifact must not change. Then, a transformation into a process implementation becomes possible by using the implementation techniques offered by the process engine and substituting this identifier by the referenced implementation object (i.e. technical artifact).

FRONT-LOADING AND LOOK-AHEAD FOR SELECTED PROCESS ASPECTS

In the previous section, we introduced the basic principles of front-loading and look-ahead for different process aspects. This section provides more detailed insights into concrete techniques enabling front-loading for the organizational aspect or – to be more precise – for actor assignments. Furthermore, look-ahead is illustrated for the service perspective.

Front-Loading for Actor Assignments

As explained in the context of Step 4 from Figure 2 (and Figure 3 respectively), contemporary business process modeling tools allow defining actor assignments only at a rough and imprecise level of detail. However, this contradicts with the general requirements existing in the context of front-loading, e.g., ease of use for domain experts and availability of the information required by process implementers. In the following sections, we present selected techniques enabling front-loading for actor assignments. We further show how process implementers may transform the information generated by these techniques into a technical process implementation.

Approaches Enabling Business Process Designers to Define Actor Assignments

We present four modeling techniques for capturing actor assignments. According to the sequence in which they are presented, they offer increasing information content and functionality to users, while at the same time requiring extended support by business process modeling tools.

Approach 1: Free Textual Description of Actor Assignments

A simple modeling technique that can be realized in contemporary business process modeling tools is to describe the actor assignment of a process step in terms of free text. For capturing the respective text, annotation objects (Figure 4), process step attributes, or attached documents may be used depending on the given business process modeling tool. For example, in Figure 2, the following text might be assigned to Step 4: "The actor shall possess role 'developer' and belong to the same department as the change requestor." In principle, with this simple technique, a good information quality can be achieved. Furthermore, process designers do not need to have any specific competencies to apply this modeling technique.

As a drawback, however, the quality of the resulting actor assignment descriptions cannot be ensured, i.e., the textual descriptions might

be imprecise or ambiguous. In particular, process designers will be unable to guess and hence to use exactly the same names in their free text descriptions as the ones defined for OrgObjects (e.g. roles) in the organizational model of the enterprise. Regarding the above example (i.e. the actor assignment of Step 4), the provided free text refers to role developer instead of hardware developer. During process implementation, it has to be guessed (or inquired), which organizational object shall be used in fact. Furthermore, any combination of the different parts of an actor assignment (using AND / OR and respective priorities or brackets) might not be unambiguous. Finally, manual interpretations by the process implementer require mental effort.

Approach 2: Semantic Description of Actor Assignments

An extension of Approach 1 is to restrict the names of OrgObjects to a pre-defined vocabulary, i.e., to use an ontology. For example, when assigning a role name to a human task, the business process designer shall be forced to select this name from a pre-defined list. If the respective names of OrgObjects reference existing IT artifacts, this approach realizes look-ahead to a certain degree. A more advanced variant of this approach is to analyze the created descriptions automatically in order to detect references to OrgObjects. For this purpose, it must be checked whether the names used for OrgObjects are contained in the list of pre-defined names. In the example introduced in the context of Approach 1, for instance, such an analysis might reveal that the word "developer" shall correspond to a role name. Furthermore, a subsequent comparison with the pre-defined vocabulary might detect that this vocabulary does not contain role name "developer," but role names "software developer" and "hardware developer."

In such a scenario, the business process modeling tool shall ask the process designer to state the respective actor assignment more precisely.

Finally, the business process designer will then substitute role name "developer" with "hardware developer." Overall, Approach 2 results in more precise descriptions compared to Approach 1 since the names of OrgObjects become unambiguous. In turn, this reduces the effort for process implementers. As for Approach 1, however, costly analyses and interpretation of the arbitrarily structured parts of the textual actor descriptions are still necessary.

Approach 3: Template-Based Description of Actor Assignments

The drawbacks discussed in the context of Approaches 1 and 2 are resolved by Approach 3. Not only the names of OrgObjects, but also the other textual parts of an actor assignment are now based on pre-defined artifacts. To be more precise, a set of templates covering all relevant types of actor assignments is provided to business process designers. Figure 5 depicts examples of such templates.

To define an actor assignment of a process step, the business process designer selects a template and provides the names of the concrete OrgObjects that shall replace the template parameters (e.g. x or y in Figure 5). In order to avoid ambiguities, again, these names shall originate from a pre-defined vocabulary. Regarding Step 4 of our running example, for instance, template RoleAndDept(x, y) of Figure 5 will be selected. Furthermore, the following OrgObjects will be assigned to the parameters of this template: x = "hardware developer" and y = "department of actor working on process step 'creation of the

change request'." Overall, Approach 3 results in rather precise actor assignments. Only references to preceding process steps or process variables, as required in the context of dependent actor assignments, might be ambiguous. However, this can be improved with appropriate support of the business process modeling tool, e.g., only references to existing attributes (e.g. actor) of a process step shall be allowed.

In summary, process implementation efforts can be significantly reduced when using Approach 3. As a drawback, however, more complex actor assignments can only be expressed if a high number of specific templates considering all possible combinations of OrgObjects is provided (e.g. RoleAndDept, RoleAndCompetence, DeptAndGroup, and so forth).

Approach 4: Using Combinable Templates to Describe Actor Assignments

To cope with the combinatorial problem when pre-defining actor templates, Approach 4 only pre-defines elementary templates like Role(x) or Department(x). However, these may be combined by the business process designer to more complex actor assignments using Boolean operators (i.e. AND, OR, NOT). To which extent a business process designer will be able to define such combinations, however, depends on his mathematical skill level. Generally, one cannot expect that a domain expert will be able to correctly define Boolean expressions without any tool support. Therefore, any business process modeling tool

Figure 5. Examples of template-based descriptions of actor assignments

Template Name	Description
Role(x)	Potential actors must possess role x (e.g. x = 'hardware developer')
Department(x)	Potential actors must be members of department x
Competence (x)	Potential actors must have competence x (e.g. x = 'knowledge of German')
Group(x)	Potential actors must be a member of group x (e.g. x = 'Project Passenger Safety')
Supervisor(x)	Potential actors are supervisor of person x
RoleAndDept(x,y)	Potential actors have role x and are members of department y

should provide sophisticated support for defining actor assignments.

First, it must allow for the selection of elementary templates (Figure 6), the assignment of object names from a pre-defined vocabulary to template parameters, and the definition of references to process steps and process variables. Second, a business process modeling tool must allow combining the resulting actor assignments to more complex ones based on a collection of pre-defined and comprehensible combination types. The semantics of the latter must be appropriately explained to business process designers (see Figure 6b for an example), i.e., it will not be sufficient to present only a list of Boolean operators without further explanation.

Figure 6. Wizard for (a) selecting an elementary template and (b) combining templates

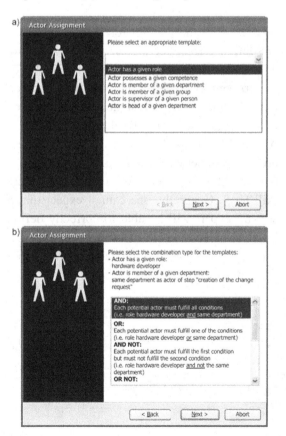

Transforming Actor Assignments of the Business Level to the Process Implementation

The actor assignments defined by domain experts for the different steps of a business process model (see upper part of Figure 1) must be transformed into technical actor assignments at the system process level (see lower part of Figure 1). We will shortly discuss how a process implementer may perform such a transformation as well as the method that may be used to identify the concerned step(s) of the system process.

Deriving Technical Actor Assignments

We have presented four approaches enabling front-loading of actor assignments. For all of them, technical actor assignments may be manually derived by the process implementer. In this context, the information made available through front-loading significantly reduces process implementation efforts. Furthermore, the efforts for analyzing this information (and perhaps for contacting domain experts for further clarification) decrease from Approach 1 to Approach 4. Furthermore, Approaches 3 and 4 allow for a semi-automatic generation of technical actor assignments. As described, Approach 3 suggests using exactly one template for describing the actor assignment of a particular process step in a business process model. When providing standard implementations for each of these business level templates, the process implementation tool will be able to automatically select the right implementation of an actor assignment for system process steps (see lower part of Figure 1).

Furthermore, if the names of OrgObjects are selected from a pre-defined vocabulary at the business process modeling level, the references to corresponding technical OrgObjects can be automatically generated as well. The only remaining ambiguous part concerns the handling of references to preceding steps within actor assignments (e.g. "actor of process step B shall belong to the same department as the actor of process step A"). Regarding such dependent actor assignments, the process implementer must transform the respective part of the information provided by the business process model manually.

In principle, the same procedure can be applied in the context of Approach 4, but with an important extension: the transformation tool generating the technical actor assignments for a system process step now has to consider that the respective business level specification may consist of several elementary templates (i.e. basic actor assignments) combined with Boolean operators. In particular, the transformation tool must check whether the used process engine actually supports the technical actor assignment derived from this.

Handling Mapping Types

When deriving technical actor assignments, another relevant issue concerns the relation between the steps of a business process model and the ones of its related system process model (Figure 1) – note that the latter provides the technical basis for any process implementation. While for certain process steps there exists a 1:1 mapping between these two levels, in other cases a process step from a business process model is split into several steps of the system process model or vice versa, i.e., several steps from the business process model are merged to one system process step (see Figure 1 for examples).

Figure 1 shows that the BIMM that we described in the background section is useful for deriving the system process step(s) corresponding to a particular step of the business process model. For example, regarding business process model step C in Figure 1, to which mapping type "Rename" is applied, it is obvious that the corresponding technical actor assignment must be defined for system process step Y. In particular, this step can be identified automatically when

implementing the process. In turn, mapping type "Split" is more difficult to handle for process implementers. Consider again Figure 1, where business process step A is realized by the two system process steps T and U. Regarding the actor assignment of step A, the process implementer then has to figure out which of the two system process steps shall be considered.

Basically, there exist several options for dealing with such splits:

1. The actor assignment of the business process model is used to generate the technical actor assignments for both system process steps independently, e.g., by assigning the same role to these two steps. However, then different actors (with same role) might perform the two steps.

2. The actor assignment of the business process model is used for generating the technical actor assignment of system process step T. For system process step U, the actor assignment 'Same performer as for step T' is chosen to ensure that both steps are performed by the same actor.

3. The actor assignment of the business process model shall be applied either to T or U if only one of these two steps constitutes a human task. Note that technical actor assignments are only required in the context of human tasks, but not for automatically performed system process steps (e.g. Web Service calls). When using mapping type "Split," in many cases, only one of the derived system process steps actually corresponds to a human task, while the other steps are automated ones.

Concerning mapping type "Merge," the corresponding system process step can be always identified unambiguously. However, since several steps of the business process model are merged to one system process step (e.g. in Figure 1, steps D and E are merged resulting in system process step Z), it should be checked whether there exist contradictory actor assignments of these different business process steps – this would be an error in the business process model. Regarding mapping type "Insert" (e.g. step X in Figure 1), usually, no technical actor assignment is required since this mapping type is solely used for technical activities executed without any user interaction. Finally, in the context of mapping type "Delete" (i.e. a process step of the business process model is not mapped to any step of the system process model), no transformation is required at all.

Note that the BIMM is not only useful when implementing a system process, but also in the context of later business process changes. For example, assume that a domain expert decides to change an actor assignment of a business process model during its implementation phase or even after deploying the IT artifacts of the implemented process. Based on the BIMM, it then will be easy to figure out, which system process steps are affected by this change. Furthermore, when taking the information provided by front-loading into account, changes of actor assignments at the business process level can be quickly and flexibly transformed into adaptations of the corresponding technical actor assignment. In turn, this increases both process flexibility and process quality in Service-driven environments.

LOOK-AHEAD FOR SERVICES

Taking the service aspect (i.e. calling a service to execute a process step), we exemplarily discuss how look-ahead can be realized. Firstly, we discuss selected approaches for publishing information about existing services in a manner comprehensible to business process designers. Secondly, we explain how service specifications, created by business process designers, can be used during process implementation.

Approaches for Publishing Services for Business Process Designers

We present three approaches for publishing information about existing services in a manner comprehensible to business process designers and enabling them to use this information in the context of look-ahead. The three approaches mainly differ in respect to the information source they use: a technical *SOA repository*, *business repository*, or business process modeling tool. Since each of the three approaches meets the requirements for service look-ahead, the approach best suited depends on the IT landscape and the business processes to be supported.

Approach 1: Extending the Technical SOA Repository

In many companies, for already implemented services, there exist technical descriptions (e.g. WSDL files) usually stored in a SOA repository. Obviously, such SOA repositories might serve as the basis for service look-ahead as well. However, the technical information provided by them is hardly comprehensible to business process designers. Therefore, additional information should be maintained to enable service look-ahead for business process designers as well. For this purpose, attributes capturing business information about implemented services should be added to the meta-model of the SOA repository. Examples of such attributes include textual service descriptions from a business perspective (i.e. the business function supported by the service), service category (e.g. category "data delivery" for the service used by Step 5), descriptions of the input / output data objects of the service (e.g. "part data that contains the attributes …"), the domain or IT system providing the service (e.g. "product data management in the context of vehicle development"), and contact person. Respective attributes can be used by business process designers in the context of service look-ahead, i.e., when searching for a service (e.g. based on category and domain) and deciding about whether a specific service matches the requirements of the given business process step.

Usually, it is possible to extend the meta-model of a (technical) SOA repository. Respective options are provided by SOA tools like WebSphere Service Registry and Repository (WSRR) (IBM, 2007) and CentraSite (Schneider & Vaughan-Brown, 2008). Extending a meta-model means that additionally required attributes may be created and added to the already existing SOA repository of an enterprise. However, note that the quality of Approach 1 does not only depend on the extension features of a SOA repository, but also on the definition and maintenance of complete and consistent service descriptions, i.e., information quality is crucial. The latter should be controlled by appropriate governance processes that ensure both completeness and comprehensibility of the service information provided. In particular, passing respective checks should be a prerequisite for releasing any technical service implementation.

Approach 2: Business Repository

As an alternative to Approach 1, the service descriptions comprehensible to business process designers can be stored in a separate business repository. In particular, a description of a business service may be also created if the specification of the respective technical (i.e. implemented) service is available, i.e., a corresponding entry in the SOA repository exists. Note that such a late business service specification enables domain experts to decide for any registered technical service whether it is meaningful from a business perspective, i.e., whether a corresponding entry shall be created for the business repository as well. The information to be maintained in a business repository is similar to the one covered by the additional attributes mentioned in Approach 1. Since a business repository focuses on the business aspect, however, it may comprise additional attributes and details.

In principle, a business repository does not contain any technical information about services (e.g. WSDL descriptions). However, service look-ahead must be able to determine the technical service (i.e. the implemented service) to be invoked when a particular step of the system process becomes enabled. For this purpose, each business service must be associated with a technical service, e.g., by adding references to technical services from the SOA repository to entries of the business repository. Alternatively, technical services from the SOA repository can be enriched with references to corresponding business services.

Offering a separate business repository relieves business process designers from browsing through technical SOA repositories when searching for a particular business service. Furthermore, the meta-model schema of a business repository meets the needs of business users, and does not have to take the requirements of IT departments, using the same repository (as in Approach 1), into account. Again, completeness and quality of the information captured in a business repository (e.g. service descriptions) must be ensured by establishing appropriate governance processes. Due to the co-existence of business repository and technical SOA repository, it must be ensured that the release of a technical service will be accompanied by the definition of a corresponding business service where appropriate.

Approach 3: Graphical Model in a Business Process Modeling Tool

Business process designers use high-level modeling tools for creating and changing business process models. Usually, a business process modeling tool represents its models in a graphical notation (e.g. EPC, BPMN). In particular, all models created with such a tool belong to the business level. Therefore, a business process modeling tool represents an appropriate source for business service descriptions as well. In particular, for business process designers, it will be most convenient if they are able to define or access business service specifications within the same tool.

To realize this approach, a business process modeling tool must allow creating and accessing descriptions of business services. As for other model components (e.g. process model, data model, and organizational model), a graphical notation should be provided for this, i.e., a special diagram type for modeling business services is required. As illustrated by Figure 7, the central element of such a diagram type is the business service itself. All relevant properties can then be described by objects connected to the respective business service. Taking the annotations provided in the context of Figure 7, one obtains a concrete example of the service required for realizing Step 5 in Figure 2.

More precisely, the business service has name "provide part data," its input (output) data object is "part number" ("part data"), it is provided by organizational unit "product data management," and so forth.[4] Each of these objects is at least described by its name. In addition, a textual description (i.e. a document) or another diagram may be assigned to the object. For example, a document attached to the organizational unit "product data management" may describe that this unit "belongs to the domain vehicle develop-

ment, centrally manages the PDM data for all business units, and realizes the operations of the PDM system." Furthermore, the output data object "part data" may be detailed through a business object diagram, which contains all attributes of data object "part data," e.g., name, weight, procurement costs, and responsible developer of the part.

As described in Stein (2009), ARIS supports *Service Allocation Diagrams*, which may be used to specify business services as well. Another object type that may be connected with business service objects to describe the corresponding business functions is "capability." Regarding the service example from Figure 7, related capabilities may describe that "part data is returned," "part is found by part number," "part data is delivered even for unreleased parts," and so forth. Finally, respective capabilities can be also used by business process designers to find an appropriate service in the context of service look-ahead.

Object type "software service type" (Figure 7) represents the technical service corresponding to business service "provide part data." For example, this object may contain the WSDL description of the technical service or refer to it, i.e., it is not intended for business process designers, but for process implementers.

Figure 7. The service allocation diagram of ARIS used for describing a (business) service type

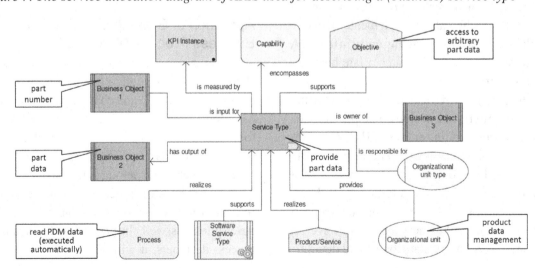

Comparing the Approaches

As major advantage of Approach 1, all relevant information is stored within one and the same SOA repository, i.e., both the technical and the business perspective are maintained in the same repository. Hence, the two perspectives can be easily kept consistent since no references have to be maintained across different tools. Furthermore, Approach 1 can be realized with moderate effort, especially if a technical SOA repository already exists. As a drawback, however, business process designers have to work with a repository that still is based on a rather technical structure.

Approach 2 avoids these disadvantages since business process designers do not work with a technical repository. In particular, the meta-model of the business repository may respect the specific requirements of business users without any restriction, e.g., it becomes possible to include additional business-related information, if required. As a drawback, Approach 2 requires additional realization efforts as well as efforts to keep technical and business information consistent across the two repository systems.

As major advantage of Approach 3, the graphical user interface of a modeling tool that the business process designer is familiar with is used. However, only object types offered by the respective modeling tool can be used (or the tool must be extended which might require high customization costs). Furthermore, respective information should be made accessible to all business process designers even if they are assigned to different development projects.

Realizing Service Calls in the Context of Process Implementation

When using Approach 1, the business process model directly refers to technical services. By contrast, when using Approaches 2 and 3, a business service is referenced instead. In turn, this business service refers to a unique technical service. By using the information provided by look-ahead, for process implementers, it becomes obvious which technical service shall be used for implementing a particular step in a business process model.

The presented BIMM (Figure 1) enables determining the system process step belonging to a given business process step. As discussed in the context of actor assignments, however, multiple steps of a system process may belong to the same business process step (i.e. mapping type "Split" is used). Even for this case, however, the respective step of the system process can be identified unambiguously if only one of these steps is realized through an automated service call and the other steps correspond to human tasks (e.g. consider business process step A and the two system process steps related to it, i.e., human task T and service call U). Only if several technical services and automated steps are assigned to the same business step, ambiguities might occur, requiring further analyses or inquiries.

Again, the BIMM is very useful when business requirements for already existing process implementations change. For example, the business division might decide that a different service shall be used for Step 5 in Figure 2 going forward, e.g., if a new BoM system is released offering more appropriate part data than the PDM system does. In such a situation, it is easy to adapt the process implementation. First, look-ahead allows deriving the required technical service unambiguously. Second, the existing BIMM allows deriving the system process steps affected by the change.

CONCLUSION AND OUTLOOK

In a Service-driven environment, business process design necessitates advanced techniques enabling front-loading and look-ahead. Both are crucial to realize process implementations that actually meet business requirements on one hand, but do not ignore the technical SOA environment existing in an enterprise on the other. The chapter analyzed the process aspects that benefit from front-loading and look-ahead and discussed general requirements for these two fundamental concepts. To provide detailed insights into how respective techniques can be transferred to practice, front-loading techniques were illustrated for the aspect of actor assignments. Thereby, focus was not on developing new modeling techniques, but to specify relevant information for implementing processes as early as possible during the process design phase. Furthermore, basic look-ahead concepts were illustrated for the aspect of services. A particular challenge in this context is to make existing technical services known to business process designers.

We explored different process aspects that may benefit from front-loading and look-ahead in general. However, business process designers must be also able to use the resulting methodology. In particular, they should not be burdened by the introduction of a large number of new techniques. Furthermore, front-loading and look-ahead should only be used for aspects not overextending the technical capabilities of business process designers (note that it depends on the skill level of a business process designer which aspects actually lead to an overextension). This means, in a PAIS development project, it has to be considered which process aspects are most relevant for front-loading and look-ahead and for which aspects it is realistic to use the techniques proposed. For the other aspects, the required information may be determined at later project phases or decisions can be made autonomously during the technical specification or implementation. Such a limited approach may be acceptable for certain process aspects or detail levels in order to keep business process design as easy as required.

The proposed approaches still have to be tested in real implementation projects in order to prove that they are applicable in the large scale and really result in significant benefits. The mentioned aspects and techniques may be used as a basis (similar to a checklist) for selecting the front-loading and/or look-ahead aspects that shall be included into the methodology of the given development project. It is reasonable to base this selection on experiences made during previous development projects. Using front-loading or look-ahead is recommended for process aspects whose clarification during process implementation resulted in considerable delays or whose transformation to the technical level caused erroneous process implementations due to missing details in business process models.

REFERENCES

Arsanjani, A., Ghosh, S., Allam, A., Abdollah, T., Ganapathy, S., & Holley, K. (2008). SOMA - A method for developing service-oriented solutions. *IBM Systems Journal*, *47*, 377–396. doi:10.1147/sj.473.0377.

Bauer, T. (2009). Substitution rules for task performers in process-oriented applications. [in German]. *Datenbank-Spektrum*, *9*(31), 40–51.

Bodenstaff, L., Wombacher, A., Reichert, M., & Jaeger, M. C. (2008). Monitoring dependencies for SLAs: The MoDe4SLA approach. In *Proceedings of the IEEE 5th International Conference on Services Computing (SCC 2008)*, Honolulu, Hawaii, USA (pp. 21-29). IEEE Computer Society Press.

Buchwald, S. (2012). *Increasing consistency and flexibility of process-oriented applications by service-orientation.* (PhD thesis). University of Ulm, Germany (in German).

Buchwald, S., Bauer, T., & Reichert, M. (2012). Bridging the gap between business process models and service composition specifications. In Lee, et al. (Eds.), *Service life cycle tools and technologies: Methods, trends, and advances* (pp. 124–153). IGI Global.

Chen, H. M. (2008). Towards service engineering: Service orientation and business-IT alignment. In *Proceedings of the 41st Hawaii International Conference on System Sciences*. IEEE Computer Society.

Dadam, P., & Reichert, M. (2009). The ADEPT project: A decade of research and development for robust and flexible process support - Challenges and achievements. *Computer Science - Research for Development, 23*(2), 81–97. Springer.

Deeg, M. (2007). SOA starts far beyond BPEL – Service-oriented business process modeling as basis for a SOA. *OBJEKTspektrum - Onlineausgabe* (in German).

Enderle, R. (2009). *Early modeling of process aspects relevant for process execution at a business level – Process modeling in a SOA.* (Master thesis). University of Ulm (in German).

Engels, G., Hess, A., Humm, B., Juwig, O., Lohmann, M., Richter, J. P., et al. (2008a). A method for engineering a true service-oriented architecture. In *Proceedings of the 10th International Conference on Enterprise Information Systems*, Barcelona (pp. 272-281).

Engels, G., Hess, A., Humm, B., Juwig, O., Lohmann, M., & Richter, J. P. et al. (2008b). *Quasar enterprise: Service-oriented design of applications landscapes.* Dpunkt-Verlag.

Erl, T. (2005). *Service-oriented architecture: Concepts, technology, and design.* Prentice Hall.

IBM. (2007). *WebSphere service registry and repository handbook.* IBM Redbook.

Kolb, J., Hübner, P., & Reichert, M. (2012). Automatically generating and updating user interface components in process-aware information systems. In *Proceedings of the 20th International Conference on Cooperative Information Systems (CoopIS'12)*, Rome, Italy, LNCS 7565. Springer.

Künzle, V., & Reichert, M. (2009). Integrating users in object-aware process management systems: Issues and challenges. In *Proceedings of the BPM'09 Workshops, 5th International Workshop on Business Process Design (BPD'09)*, LNBIP 43 (pp. 29-41). Springer.

Künzle, V., & Reichert, M. (2011). PHILharmonicFlows: Towards a framework for object-aware process management. *Journal of Software Maintenance and Evolution: Research and Practice, 23*(4), 205–244. Wiley. doi:10.1002/smr.524.

Künzle, V., Weber, B., & Reichert, M. (2011). Object-aware business processes: Fundamental requirements and their support in existing approaches. *International Journal of Information System Modeling and Design (IJISMD), 2*(2), 19–46. doi:10.4018/jismd.2011040102.

Lanz, A., Weber, B., & Reichert, M. (2010). Workflow time patterns for process-aware information systems. In *Proceedings of the Enterprise, Business-Process, and Information Systems Modelling: 11th International Workshop BPMDS and 15th International Conference EMMSAD at CAiSE'10*, Hammamet, Tunisia, LNBIP 50 (pp. 94-107). Springer.

Lanz, A., Weber, B., & Reichert, M. (2013). *Time patterns for process-aware information systems. Requirements Engineering Journal.* Springer.

Mutschler, B., Reichert, M., & Bumiller, J. (2008). Unleashing the effectiveness of process-oriented information systems: Problem analysis, critical success factors, and implications. *IEEE Transactions on Systems, Man, and Cybernetics, 38*(3), 280–291. doi:10.1109/TSMCC.2008.919197.

Offermann, P. (2008). SOAM – A method to concept enterprise software with a service-oriented architecture [in German]. *Wirtschaftsinformatik, 6*, 461–471. doi:10.1365/s11576-008-0094-1.

Offermann, P., & Bub, A. (2009). A method for information systems development according to SOA. In *Proceedings of the 15th Americas Conference on Information Systems*, San Francisco.

Reichert, M., et al. (2009). Enabling poka-yoke workflows with the AristaFlow BPM Suite. In *Proceedings of the BPM'09 Demonstration Track*, Ulm, Germany. CEUR Workshop Proceedings 489.

Reichert, M., & Dadam, P. (1997). A framework for dynamic changes in workflow management systems. In *Proceedings of the 8th International Workshop on Database and Expert Systems Applications*, Toulouse, France (pp. 42-48).

Reichert, M., & Dadam, P. (1998). ADEPT-flex - supporting dynamic changes of workflows without losing control. *Journal of Intelligent Information Systems*, *10*(2), 93–129. doi:10.1023/A:1008604709862.

Reichert, M., Dadam, P., & Bauer, T. (2003). Dealing with forward and backward jumps in workflow management systems. *Software & Systems Modeling*, *2*(1), 37–58. doi:10.1007/s10270-003-0018-x.

Reichert, M., Rinderle-Ma, S., & Dadam, P. (2009). Flexibility in process-aware information systems. *LNCS Transactions on Petri Nets and Other Models of Concurrency (ToPNoC)*, Special Issue on Concurrency in Process-aware Information Systems *LNCS*, *5460*(2), 115–135. Springer.

Reichert, M., & Weber, B. (2012). *Enabling flexibility in process-aware information systems: Challenges, methods, technologies*. Springer. doi:10.1007/978-3-642-30409-5.

Rinderle, S., & Reichert, M. (2005). On the controlled evolution of access rules in cooperative information systems. In *Proceedings of the 13th International Conference on Cooperative Information Systems (CoopIS'05)*, Agia Napa, Cyprus, LNCS 3760 (pp. 238-255). Springer.

Rinderle-Ma, S., & Reichert, M. (2007). A formal framework for adaptive access control models. *Journal on Data Semantics* IX Springer. *LNCS*, *4*, 82–112.

Rinderle-Ma, S., & Reichert, M. (2009). Comprehensive life cycle support for access rules in information systems: The CEOSIS project. *Enterprise Information Systems*, *3*(3), 219–251. doi:10.1080/17517570903045609.

Sadiq, S., Sadiq, W., & Orlowska, M. (2005). A framework for constraint specification and validation in flexible workflows. *Information Systems*, *30*(5), 349–378. doi:10.1016/j.is.2004.05.002.

Scheer, I. D. S. (2005). Business process management: ARIS value engineering – concept. *White Paper*.

Schneider, G., & Vaughan-Brown, J. (2008). The CentraSite community - Fast-tracking SOA governance using best-of-breed solutions. *White paper*. Software AG.

Shuster, L. (2008). *Project-oriented SOA. SOA Magazine*. XXI.

Stein, S. (2009). *Modelling method extension for service-oriented business process management*. (PhD thesis). University of Kiel, Germany.

Stein, S., Kühne, S., Drawehn, J., Feja, S., & Rotzoll, W. (2008). Evaluation of OrViA framework for model-driven SOA implementations: An industrial case study. In *Proceedings of the 6th International Conference on Business Process Management*, Milan (pp. 310-325).

Weber, B., Reichert, M., & Rinderle-Ma, S. (2008). Change patterns and change support features - enhancing flexibility in process-aware information systems. *Data & Knowledge Engineering*, *66*(3), 438–466. doi:10.1016/j.datak.2008.05.001.

Weber, B., Reichert, M., Wild, W., & Rinderle-Ma, S. (2009). Providing integrated life cycle support in process-aware information systems. *International Journal of Cooperative Information Systems, 18*(1), 115–165. doi:10.1142/S0218843009001999.

Weber, B., Rinderle, S., & Reichert, M. (2007). Change patterns and change support features in process-aware information systems. [Springer.]. *Proceedings of the CAiSE, 2007,* 574–588.

Weber, B., Sadiq, S., & Reichert, M. (2009). Beyond rigidity - dynamic process lifecycle support: A survey on dynamic changes in process-aware information systems. *Computer Science - Research & Development, 23*(2), 47-65. Springer.

Weber, I., Hoffmann, J., Mendling, J., & Nitzsche, J. (2007). Towards a methodology for semantic business process modeling and configuration. In *Proceedings of 2nd International Workshop on Business Oriented Aspects concerning Semantics and Methodologies in Service-oriented Computing* (pp. 176-187).

Weske, M. (2007). *Business process management - Concepts, languages, architectures*. Springer.

KEY TERMS AND DEFINITIONS

Business Domain: Part of the enterprise (e.g. department) owning and performing a business process.

Business Process Designer: A person who creates business process models by taking the perspective of the respective business domain, i.e. without respecting process implementation aspects in detail.

Business Process Modeling and Notation (BPMN): A standardized notation used to define business processes.

Domain Expert: An actor from a business domain usually not belonging to the IT department.

Enterprise Service Bus (ESB): A powerful communication infrastructure of a SOA.

Event Process Chain (EPC): A language for defining business process models.

OrgObject: An (organizational) object belonging to the organizational model of the enterprise.

Process Engine: A generic software product that is able to execute (specified) business processes.

ENDNOTES

[1] It is possible to add the name of the referenced process step 1 to the department object. In our example it may have name "same department as performer of step creation of the change request." Referencing the name as text (instead of an explicit edge), however, is not a proper modeling technique and may result in errors. In particular, such a text cannot be interpreted correctly if the name of the process step is changed in future. Additionally, this name is not unique if the same activity is added multiple times to the same business process model.

[2] In general, substitution rules should not be defined globally for a person or a business process. Instead, a substitution rule is necessary for each single process step (cf. Bauer 2009). For example, consider a team leader who is substituted by an experienced team member at a step in the change request process (e.g. step 5 in Figure 2: evaluation of consequences for parts). Regarding executive functions (e.g. approval to increase a budget), however, it is substituted by another team leader or even by his supervisor.

3   At business process design, normally, no concrete persons shall be referenced. Therefore, it is not necessary to publish information belonging to individual persons (e.g. their assignment to roles).

4   Respect that it is not necessary to use all (possible) object types depicted in Figure 7 for describing a specific business service. Only such objects shall be connected to a service type that really contributes to explain the purpose and function of this service.

Chapter 6

Maintaining Transactional Integrity in Long Running Workflow Services:
A Policy-Driven Framework

Stephan Reiff-Marganiec
University of Leicester, UK

Manar S. Ali
University of Leicester, UK

ABSTRACT

This chapter presents a framework to provide autonomous handling of long running transactions based on dependencies which are derived from the workflow. Business Processes naturally involve long running activities and require transactional behaviour across them. This framework presents a solution for forward recovery from errors by automatic application of compensation to executing instances of workflows. The mechanism is based on propagation of failures through a recursive hierarchical structure of transaction components (nodes and execution paths). The authors discuss a transaction management system that is implemented as a reactive system controller, where system components change their states based on rules in response to triggering of events, such as activation, failure, force-fail, completion, or compensation events. One notable feature of the model is the distinction of vital and non-vital components, allowing the process designer to express the cruciality of activities in the workflow with respect to the business logic. Another novel feature is that in addition to dependencies arising from the structure of the workflow, the approach also permits the workflow designer to specify additional dependencies which will also be enforced. Thus, the authors introduce new techniques and architectures supporting enterprise integration solutions that cater to the dynamics of business needs. The approach is implemented through workflow actions executed by services and allows management of faults through a policy-driven framework.

DOI: 10.4018/978-1-4666-4193-8.ch006

INTRODUCTION

Enterprise integration is significantly eased by the use of Service-driven architectural approaches as diverse systems can be encapsulated as Services which in turn can communicate readily through standard interfaces. This is further enhanced by the concept of executable (and possibly dynamic) Business Processes or Workflows which add a technical layer between the services and the business process as seen by a business analyst (Montangero, Reiff-Marganiec, & Semini, 2011; Gorton et al., 2009). However, enterprise integration is challenging and many of the challenges persist even in the Service-driven environment. One crucial aspect is that of ensuring correct transactional behaviour – both in the sense of not failing in states that are undesirable, and also in terms of attempting to complete the process (suitable concepts would be backward and forward recovery).

The database community has always strived to ensure consistency of data and allow for transactions to complete (possibly at a later stage or later attempt), or to be rolled back to a previous consistent state, and many solutions currently exist. It would seem straight forward to simply employ existing techniques; however, this is hampered by a number of new challenges arising in business processes. The two most crucial are the long running nature of business transactions and the delicate and complex nesting that naturally occurs. Database transactions usually complete within a matter of seconds and the most common solution for addressing the transactional integrity challenge involves some form of locking of resources. This is not applicable to business transactions, also often called *Long running transactions* (LRTs), these often span several days or even weeks (they typically involve humans making decisions such as approval of applications or time intensive operations such as shipping of physical goods) which clearly forbids any resource locking approach. Also, business processes often perform many actions in parallel or inside nested structures with complex control operators and this must be reflected in the transactions.

One of the important aspects in managing Long Running Transactions is in preserving consistency of the systems being involved in the LRT. This is done by guaranteeing that an LRT will always ensure that the data integrity is preserved and that systems are maintained consistently. This is made possible by ensuring that the execution of the LRT terminates in an accepted state from the business and the transaction modeling points of view. This will normally occur in the absence of a failure, but the same behaviour should manifest even if the LRT has not completed its normal path of execution due to a failure that causes termination of the LRT or diverts the execution to an abnormal path. This is usually achieved by adopting effective compensation and fault-handling techniques.

Workflows are usually composed out of workflow patterns (van der Aalst et al., 2000), and Bhiri, Perrin, and Godart (2006) have proposed transactional patterns to provide an understanding of the transactional consequences of workflow patterns. We have extended the concepts introduced in the transactional patterns to support multi-level nesting and we introduce the novel concept of *vitality* of actions, allowing the process designer to express the cruciality of activities in the workflow with respect to the business logic. We also present a framework based on propagation of failures through a recursive hierarchical structure of transaction components (nodes and execution paths). Our transaction management system COMPMOD is implemented as a reactive system controller, where system components change their states based on rules in response to triggering of events, such as activation, failure, force-fail, completion, or compensation events and policy rules enforce good transactional management at runtime.

We analysed a number of example business processes and derived the following list of aspects that we consider essential for a transaction management system to support. Aspects 1 to 3 are motivated by the structure of transactions and the fact that it is at the business level where a full understanding of the implications exists; aspect 4 facilitates to separate the actual process and any handling of exceptions in a clear and user-friendly way; and aspects 5 to 6 are requirements ensuring the practicality of the approach.

1. Multi-level nesting of transactions with reliable behavioral dependencies between transaction components and across hierarchy levels.
2. Definition of designer-order compensation patterns that reflect the business logic of the LRT.
3. Incorporating compensation logic into business logic of long running transactions through transactional dependencies.
4. Rule-based actions for managing execution and compensation control flow.
5. Automated method for propagating failure events through the hierarchical structure as a failure handling mechanism.
6. Automated method for performing compensation actions while the LRT execution is in progress, through backward and forward order compensations.

The work in this chapter focuses on handling failures that occur during the normal execution of the LRT (referred to as Failure Management) and the compensation handling mechanisms from a control flow perspective (referred to as Compensation Management). The failure-handling and compensation mechanism are incorporated into the business logic of the transaction through strict logical definitions of behavioral dependencies between transactional components. This chapter defines the structure of the workflow and the required dependencies, and explores the algorithms guiding the reactive controller. This will be presented in the context of the supporting architecture. The work will be placed in the context of the current state of the art in the domain.

The encoding of LRTs as workflows and hierarchical structures and the corresponding failure management has been presented before in Ali and Reiff-Marganiec (2012); however, the compensation mechanism presented in this chapter is novel.

This chapter is organized as follows. First, we describe the adopted transaction modeling paradigm, discussing workflow and transactional patterns. We then present the COMPMOD's LRT attributes, dependencies, and management rules; the recursive failure handling propagation mechanism, and the compensation mechanism with its rules and dependencies. Through examples and a case study we illustrate the mechanisms. We conclude by summarising and reflecting on future work.

BACKGROUND

Transactions

Database centric transactional models are well understood, supported in practice and provide a strong theoretical foundation for transactions. Transactions can be composed of sub-transactions where tasks and activities are transactions on their own. Failure atomicity and concurrency control are inherent within the models usually enacted through temporary resource locking. Recovery is mainly based on the notion of roll-back and compensation to restore the state of the system to the state before the failure had happened. Coordination support for multi-tasking and collaborative activities across organisations is limited and thus they are not applicable to heterogeneous and loosely coupled systems.

Conventional transactions are ACID transactions (Lewis, Bernstein, & Kiefer, 2001; Gray & Reuter 1993; Gray, 1981). ACID stands for Atomic, Consistent, Isolated and Durable – which represent four characteristics seen as desirable for transactions as they ensure stable results after a transaction completes (or fails). They have been developed in the context of tightly coupled systems, occur between trusted parties, and run over short periods of time (short-lived) – so they are generally the accepted model for databases. ACID transactions must either fully commit or fully roll back in case of failure.

In ACID transactions, any failure that occurs within the transaction will be rolled back and its effects are erased. In traditional database operations, a one-step operation is called an atomic operation where an operation does not conflict or interfere with other operations using the same database. More complex database operations are called transactions and involve multiple steps that must all be completed for the transaction to succeed. A traditional transaction is a single unit of work that is composed of two or more tasks. As databases are more distributed, some of the initial constraints have been loosened and protocols such as the two-phase commit (2PC) protocol (Mohan & Lindsay, 1985) have prolonged the lifespan and usefulness of ACID transactions allowing for transactions to span multiple local database systems.

However, these protocols and solutions do not address the needs encountered by long lived and complex transactions. For long-lived transactions, individual constituent sub-transactions maybe ACID, but the overall business transaction employs a compensatory approach to reverse or erase partial work. For this reason, a number of extended and relaxed transactional models have been proposed which relax some of the ACID requirements.

Nested Transactions (Moss, 1982) allow transactions to be nested within other transactions to form a tree structure, that is, a transaction is decomposed into a hierarchy of sub-transactions. A child can only start after its parent has started and a parent may terminate only after all its children have terminated. Each sub-transaction can either commit or roll-back. The 'commit' of a child will only take place if its parent commits. If a parent rolls back, all its children must roll back. This is applied in a recursive manner. This model has advantages: it provides full isolation, better failure handling, and allows concurrent execution of sub-transactions. The Open Nested Transactions Model (Weikum & Schek, 1992) is a generalization of nested transactions. It relaxes the isolation property by allowing the results of committed sub-transactions to be visible to all top level transactions. Sub-transactions can commit and release resources before their predecessor transaction successfully completes and commits. The abort of a top-level transaction requires roll-back for committed sub-transactions.

The Saga Transactional Model (Garcia-Molina & Salem, 1987) relaxes the full isolation requirement and provides an increased inter-transaction concurrency. A Saga divides a long running transaction into a sequence of ACID sub-transactions. Each sub-transaction has an associated compensating sub-transaction which can be executed in case the effects of its associate need to be undone. Saga describes a mechanism for handling LRT within relational databases. It supposes that a LRT is composed of a sequence of smaller inner transactions which could be interleaved with inner transactions from other Saga. Each inner transaction retains the ACID properties. The Saga itself is not ACID.

The most important feature of a Saga is its failure handling mechanism. There are two modes of recovery, backward recovery and forward recovery. Each inner transaction is provided by its own compensation handler which is responsible for cancelling or reversing the effects of its associated transaction. In backward recovery, if any of the inner transactions of a saga has failed, it is rolled back. The Saga then executes the compensation handler for all previously committed inner transactions, in reverse order; Forward recovery depends on the existence of save points. A save point is where the state of Saga is persistent. Hence, when a failure occurs, the Saga restarts execution from the save point. If one or more inner transactions have committed between the save point and the failure point, they first must do backward recovery by executing compensating transactions for these committed transactions and then restart from the save point.

Flexible transactions (Elmagarmid, 1992; Zhang et al., 1994; Mehrotra et al., 1992) propose approaches suitable for a multi database environment. Transactions are defined as global transactions and composed of sub transactions and a set of execution dependencies such as commit, alternative, and failure dependencies on sub-transactions. These models depend in their correctness on weak-atomicity of the global transaction by relaxing the 2-PC protocol. Failure recovery is handled by retriable and compensable transactions and hence flexible transactions provide better resilience to failures than traditional transaction models.

ACTA model (Chrysanthis & Ramamritham, 1990) presents a framework for specifying and reasoning about transaction structure, concurrency and recovery. The model formalizes the effects of transactions on other transactions and on objects through commit and abort dependencies, using predicate logic.

Business Processes and Workflows

Business Processes are usually defined by business analysts to capture the activities and their respective order and dependencies required to achieve some larger business goal. The result of such a process definition is a workflow. Modeling of such workflows is usually conducted in some graphical notation such as BPMN (White, 2004) or UML activity diagrams. However, there are other notations, such as YAWL (van der Aalst & ter Hofstede, 2005) which are graphical and textual and have formally defined semantics.

Workflow systems integrate, automate and manage business processes through flexible rep-

resentations of the control flow of their tasks. A Service-driven workflow process is composed of Web Services that relate to each other through workflow constructs such as sequence, split and join; to allow for sequencing, parallelism or choices in the control flow. A workflow management system is required to coordinate the sequence of service invocations within a process, to manage control flows and data flows between Web Services, and to ensure execution of the process as a reliable transaction unit (Yan et al., 2005).

(Kiepuszewski, ter Hofstede, & Bussler, 2000) provide formal definitions for arbitrarily structured and well behaved workflows. A structured work flow consists of symmetrical blocks of AND-split followed by AND-join or OR-split followed by an OR-join. A workflow is well behaved if "it can never lead to deadlock nor can it result in multiple active instances of the same activity." Their work shows that every structured workflow is well behaved and provides transformation techniques to transform non-structured workflows into structured ones.

(Reichert & Dadam, 1997; Reichert & Dadam, 1998), present a framework (ADEPT$_{flex}$) to support ad-hoc and dynamic deviations from premodeled Workflow (WF) activities. This framework is based on well-structured workflows and proposes a minimal and complete set of change operations to suport dynamic structure modification of a running workflow. Change operations are supported with correctness properties which ensures the correctness and consistency of the resulting WF graph by construction.

The workflow management system in (Müller, Greiner, & Rahm, 2004) is a step towards dynamic and automatic workflow adaptations in case of failure events. The management model is based on temporal rule-based approach to specify exceptions such as logical failures and perform necessary workflow adaptations as a failure recovery mechanism.

The work in (Casado et al., 2012) proposes an abstract model for dynamically modeling Web

Service transactions, based on BTP (Business Process Protocol) and WS-transaction standards. They apply a model-based testing tool to generate test scenarios, and evaluate the reliability of WS-standards in terms of failures.

The work in Qiu et al. (2005) presents a formal operational semantics BPEL (Business Process Execution Language) as a simplified version of BPEL4WS (omitting data handling semantics) to highlight its fault handling and compensation semantics. Activities are enclosed by scopes and each scope is associated with fault handler and compensation handler (default or programmed). An exception within a scope invokes its fault handler and if compensation is required, the fault handler invokes the compensation handler which associates compensation context with each activity. The compensation mechanism is based on accumulating compensation contexts of completed activities such that when a scope is compensated, compensation contexts are invoked in reverse order of their installation.

The work in (Butler, Hoare, & Ferreira, 2005; Butler & Ripon, 2005) proposes a compensating CSP (cCSP) modeling approach for LRTs based on Process Algebra (Hoare, 1978). Operational semantics of cCSP are modelled as follows: atomic actions are aggregated through sequencing, choice, and parallel operators to compose standard processes where processes can be aggregated as well to form a business process transaction. A compensable standard process is a process that is paired with compensating actions. The model provides execution and compensation primitives to control execution flow; SKIP for successful termination, THROW for throwing an interrupt, and YIELD to indicate that an interrupt is willing to yield between the execution of two processes. When an atomic transaction fails, sequential compositions of compensable processes are executed in reverse order while compensations of parallel compositions are accumulated in parallel.

Parallel Sagas are proposed in Bruni, Melgratti, and Montanari (2005) by adding increased expressiveness to LRT representations and the work is supported by a hierarchy of transaction calculi to model parallelism, nesting, and choices. The definition of compensation is part of the Saga (compensation pairs like cCSP) but provide a richer form of exception than cCSP. The model provides primitives to allow execution of alternatives to an aborted sub-transaction as well as discriminator choices.

In Kokash and Arbab (2011) REO (a channel-based exogenous coordination language) is used to model the behaviour of LRTs. The approach uses a set of basic REO channels to implement connectors such as sequence and parallel routing. Control flow is monitored through signalling and flow of message tokens through the circuits. Exception handling is implemented by coordinating sequential and parallel activities with compensation activities, where each activity is paired with a compensation activity. For example, an activity cancelled in a sequential flow leads to all previous activities being compensated by passing a cancel token.

Control Flow Intervention (CFI) (Moller & Shuldt, 2010) presents a flexible and automatic failure handling mechanism for Composite Web Services. If a failure of a service occurs at runtime, the failed service is dynamically replaced by a semantically equivalent service(s), thus achieving forward recovery. OWL-S profiles describing service semantics provide a formal framework to reason about semantically equivalent or similar services. The approach supports sequential executions only and parallelism is not addressed.

In our approach, a failure of a component service does not necessarily fail the LRT. By applying a combination of forward recovery (implemented by exclusive routing) and a failure propagation mechanism, it is possible to tolerate failures and prevent the LRT from early failure.

Workflow and Transactional Patterns

Bhiri, Godart and Perin (Bhiri, Godart, & Perrin, 2006; Bhiri, Perrin, & Godart, 2006; Bhiri, Perrin, & Godart, 2005) introduced transactional patterns. Control and transactional dependencies are defined for component Web Services and are mapped onto workflow patterns. Dependencies expressed in first order logic are employed to validate transactional behaviour of Web Service compositions. Galoul, Bhiri, and Rouached (2010) propose an event-driven approach where dependencies are defined in event calculus. These works discuss simple patterns such as AND-split or XOR-split, where a single service exists on each split branch. In addition, the way the dependencies are defined does not allow for nesting in the Composite Service. The failure handling and recovery mechanism is implemented through dependencies. We have drawn inspiration from that work, but provide solutions for multiple nested transactions.

Workflow patterns have been developed as part of an initiative commenced in 2000 by van der Aalst et al. (2000). They classify the core architectural constructs inherent in workflows in a language and technology independent way, thus allowing definition of fundamental requirements of business process modeling. Workflow patterns consider workflow specifications from a control-flow perspective and characterize a range of control flow patterns that might be encountered when modeling a business workflow. Following the initial work (van der Aalst et al. 2000), 43 control patterns were proposed in Russel, ter Hofstede, and Mulyar (2006). The patterns are classified as (a) basic control-flow patterns, (b) advanced branching and synchronization patterns, (c) structural patterns, (d) state-based patterns, and (e) cancellation patterns. Our approach, COMP-MOD, so far, implements the basic control-flow patterns: sequence, AND-split, AND-join, OR-split, OR-join, XOR-split, and XOR-join.

The concept of *transactional patterns* was introduced in Bhiri, Godart, and Perrin (2006). Transactional patterns are aimed at specifying flexible and reliable Composite Web Services. They are a convergence concept between workflow patterns and advanced transactional models (Elmagarid, 1992), and thus they combine the flexibility of work flow control patterns with the reliability of transactional models to ensure transactional consistency of service compositions. Transactional patterns define orchestrations between services in a composite web service by using dependencies to define how services are combined and how the behaviour of some given services influences the behaviour of some others. Dependencies are used to express the relationships that exist between services, such as sequence, alternative, compensation, activation, or cancellation. They also associate preconditions with service operations. Services can change their state based on internal behaviour or on external stimuli – both would be transitions, the latter being externally triggered and often referred to as external transitions.

The general definition of a dependency is:

Dependency: A dependency from service s1 to service s2 exists if a transition of s1 can fire an external transition of s2. (Bhiri, Godart, & Perrin, 2006).

It is assumed that a transition can be an internal or external transition, with internal transitions being fired by the service itself (e.g. *complete( ), fail( ),* or *retry( )*) and external transitions being fired by external entities (e.g., *abort( ), cancel( ),* or *compensate( )*).

Policies

Management rules (or policies) incorporate autonomy into systems by describing how a system is to adapt its behaviour under certain circumstances. The most common form in which the rules are described is that of an ECA (event condition action) rule, which presents an event-driven approach.

Policies have been used in many systems, with the most common occurrence being in access control (e.g., Siewe, Cau, & Zedan, 2003; Halpern & Weissman, 2003), in usage control (Zhang et al., 2005), in telecommunications (Turner et al.,

2006) and in service-oriented computing (Buscemi et al., 2007; Gorton & Reiff-Marganiec, 2006) are documented.

One of the first attempts in applying ECA rules approach in management of transactions in WF systems was in (Dayal et al., 1990) by using triggers for organizing long running activities. ECA rules have been used to adapt workflows and provide more fine-grained specification for service selection for tasks in (Müller, Greiner, & Rahm, 2004) and in database management systems (Paton, 1999; Widom & Ceri, 1996).

LRT's Transactional Attributes and Dependencies

An LRT is executed as a flat transaction, i.e. a sequence of nodes that are executed sequentially. A node can be an atomic node representing an atomic task (a single web service), or a scope node starting with a split pattern and ending with a join pattern of the same type. Each scope creates two or more execution paths that start from the split point and end at the join point (or synchronizer) of the scope. Each execution path is a sequence of one or more nodes executed in sequential order where nodes along the path again can be atomic or scopes. Through the rest of the discussion we will use the term component to refer to both nodes (atomic/scope) and execution paths.

Transactional Operators and Scopes

A scope starts with a split operator (OR, AND, or XOR) that is explicitly assigned while constructing the LRT. The model implicitly specifies a join operator of the same type to mark the end point of a scope. The join point is represented by a synchroniser in the WF schema. The type of operator used to define a scope influences the definition of transactional attributes and dependencies of its encapsulated components. Semantics of operators are adopted from the definitions of WF-patterns in Bhiri, Perrin, and Godart (2006). An AND opera-

tor creates a scope with parallel execution paths, and the scope is successfully completed if all its execution paths are successfully completed. An OR operator creates a scope with parallel paths where only a subset of these paths are executed during runtime, the executed paths are those whose enabling conditions are satisfied. An OR scope successfully completes if all its enabled activity paths are successfully completed. An XOR scope creates exclusive paths, the first path has the highest priority and therefore execution starts with the path with the highest priority.

If an exclusive path failed to complete, it is compensated in forward order until the split point of the scope is reached, and then next path (if one exists) is executed. Therefore, execution paths are assigned with the following transactional attributes: an execution path *hasAlternative*, if it was an exclusive path that has a path with lower priority in the same scope. In an OR scope, a path is *enabled* if and only if its branching condition is satisfied at runtime and hence, only enabled paths are activated. Each execution path has an ordered list of one or more nodes denoted by *nodeList*. Informally, a scope groups semantically related nodes together and we can formally define a scope node as follows:

Scope Node:

$$\forall_{i=1..m} p_i.nodeList$$
$$= splitNode_i \, and \forall_{i=1..m} nodeList_i.type$$
$$= \{ATOMIC, SCOPE\} : scope$$
$$= (operator, [splitNode_1 .. splitNode_m 1)$$
$$\rightarrow scope.pathList = [p_1 .. p_m]$$

where operator $\in$ {AND, OR, XOR}.

Consider some of the notations introduced here as they are used throughout this work. Components, i.e. scopes and paths, consist of ordered list of nodes. An object-oriented attribute dot-type notation is used to identify attributes of components. Nodes are either atomic or scope nodes, which is reflected in their type. p denotes a path (there might be indices to differentiate different paths).

When a scope is initially defined, a split operator and a list of split nodes are specified. The number of split nodes corresponds to the number of execution paths encapsulated within the scope. A split node can be an atomic node, or a scope node which facilitates the construction of nested scopes. When a node is appended to an existing execution path p_i, the node is appended to $p_i.nodeList$.

Vitality of Components

Each LRT component has a *vitality attribute*, allowing to specify whether a component is vital or non-vital. A vitality value {TRUE/FALSE} is assigned to each component either by *specification* or by *evaluation*. Vitality of atomic and scope nodes is assigned by specification, that is, according to the business logic of the LRT. Essentially, vitality allows the workflow designer to express whether a failure of the specific service can be tolerated and the workflow can proceed (an example of a non-vital task might be one sending a progress message to the invoking user – nothing in the process will be broken if the message is not sent). Vitality of execution paths is assigned by evaluation according to the following rules. A path is

- Vital if it encapsulates at least one vital node.
- Non-Vital if all the nodes it encapsulates are non-vital.

The transactional implication of the vitality measure of a component expresses the impact of unsuccessful completion of a component on its immediate superior[1]. For example, the failure of a vital node will fail its enclosing execution path. Vitality of components is utilised in the failure handling propagation mechanism proposed in this chapter.

Note that the decision of assigning the vitality value to nodes (atomic and scope) is based on the business logic of the LRT. It is important to note that our management/compensation model does not investigate or analyse the business logic of the LRT. It is always assumed by the model that the logic provided for the LRT at design time is what it is required from the transaction at the business level. Therefore, it is possible for a designer to define a scope node as a non-vital node, even when it encapsulates vital paths, without leading to an incorrect model.

Note that we make a fundamental assumption that workflows are structured in a well formed way where scopes are completely enclosed inside other scopes and do not overlap in random ways. This assumption makes the approach easier to explain and many of the practical workflows that we have encountered do fulfil this requirement, with the others that we came across allowing for easy syntactical rewrites bringing them into this structure.

However, the following logical restrictions are assumed by the approach with respect to design of scopes (and they are assumptions that could be considered for relaxation in the future):

Assumption 1: In an exclusive scope, all exclusive paths should have the same vitality measure, which is they must all be vital or non-vital.

Assumption 2: If all paths in a scope are non-vital, their encapsulating scope should be non-vital by specification.

Assumption 1 might be seen as quite restrictive, however, considering it at a more business-oriented level, it essentially says that if there is a choice, each of the alternatives that one could choose from are ultimately of equal vitality. Not having this assumption would allow for a kind of free choice between maybe doing something (or not) – the non-vital route – and a strong requirement of doing something and succeeding in it – the vital route. This seems simply wrong: consider a human decision in a notification task: you must send a letter (vital) or alternatively you could send an email (non-vital).

Execution States

During the execution life cycle of the transaction, the LRT and its components go through different execution states and they are marked with their current execution state. We list below the set of execution states for the LRT and each component. Figure 1 shows the state transition diagram of atomic nodes. State transitions are triggered by events. For example in Figure 1, when a completion of an atomic node is triggered, the execution state of the node changes from ACTIVATED to COMPLETED.

LRT.state = {*not-activated, activated, completed, failed, compensating, compensated, terminated*}

AtomicNode.state = {*not-activated, activated, completed, failed, compensating, compensated, skipped, aborted, terminated*}

ScopeNode.state = {*not-activated, activated, completed, failed, compensating, compensated*}

ExecutionPath.state = {*not-Activated, activated, completed, failed, compensating, compensated*}

Representations of Nested LRTs

We use two main representations of the workflows in our work: a workflow representation which allows to abstract away from sub workflows and a tree representation that is used by the propagation algorithm.

In our model we have two basic components: nodes and execution paths. A node can be an atomic node (a single web service) or a scope node – a set of semantically connected nodes (atomic and/ or scope). An execution path represents a trail of nodes that are executed in sequential order. An execution path reading of a scope node that it encapsulates is the same as an atomic node. In other words, scope nodes on an execution path are like black boxes that encapsulate execution paths and other nodes. Transactional dependencies are

Figure 1. State transition diagram for atomic node

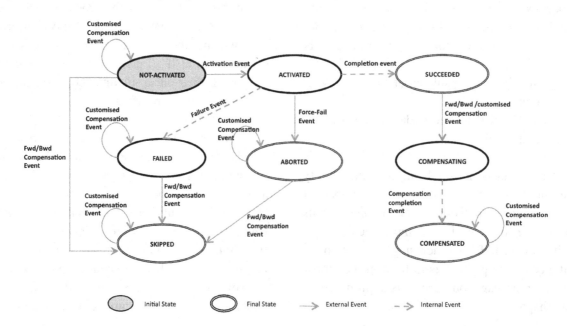

employed to model the transactional behaviour between transaction components. Transactional dependencies are defined between a component and its neighbours.

Workflow Model

The modeling method allows for multi-level nested transactions to address demands occurring in real cooperative business processes. In the representation model itself we see alternating levels of paths and nodes.

Figure 2 demonstrates a two level-nested LRT that consists of atomic nodes and nested scopes. Considering execution p_1 in $scope_2$, the path consists of an atomic node n_6 followed in sequence by a scope node $scope_{2.1}$ which in turn encapsulates three execution paths. As mentioned earlier, an execution path is a trail of nodes (atomic and/or

scope) that are executed in sequential order and we provide a nodeList attribute on path objects to express this: for example, $p_1.nodeList= [n_6, scope_{2.1}]$. Figure 2(a) shows the LRT with all nesting levels expanded and Figure 2(b) demonstrates the LRT with level 2 of the WF collapsed.

The main execution path of a transaction is regarded as level 0 in the workflow and denoted as p_0. If we collapse level 1 of the WF, the main execution path becomes a flat WF that executes the nodes in $p_0.nodeList= [n_1, n_2, scope_1, scope_2, scope_3]$ in sequential order (see Figure 3).

Hierarchical Structure Model

Transaction components –nodes and execution paths-- are linked together in a hierarchical structure (see Figure 4). Each component has a single superior and an ordered set of one or more inferiors.

Figure 2.

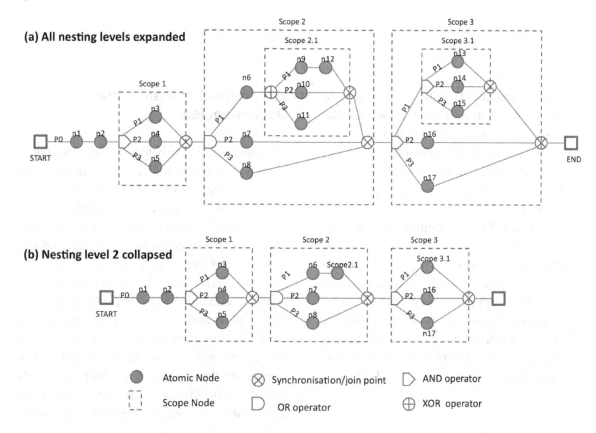

Figure 3. The main execution path

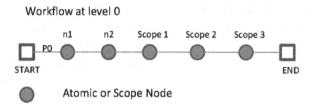

Figure 4. Hierarchical representation of LRT shown in Figure 1

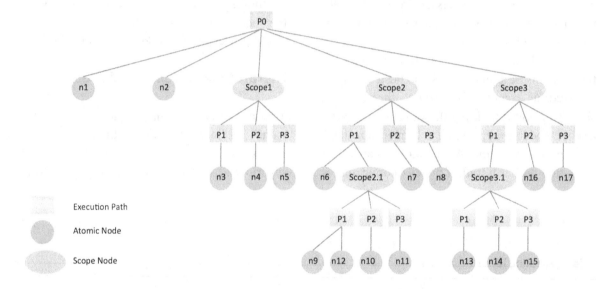

- **Node Component:** A superior of any node is the execution path that encapsulates the node. An atomic node is a leaf node that has no inferiors. A scope node has two or more inferiors which represents the number of split execution paths it encapsulates.
- **Execution Path Component:** The superior of any execution path is the scope node that encloses it. The main execution path of a LRT has a NULL superior. Each execution path has one or more inferiors. Inferiors of a path represent an ordered set of one or more nodes that the path encloses. The root of the recursive hierarchy is the main execution path of the LRT p_0.

Hierarchical Transactional Dependencies

As stated, transaction behaviour between components is expressed through dependencies. Transactional dependencies are defined: (a) between an execution path and its immediate outer scope, (b) between a node and its immediate outer execution path and, (c) between any two successive nodes on a sequence of the same execution path. This imposes the hierarchical relationship between components and facilitates hierarchical propagation of events. We expect dependencies to be defined in the WF representation and then mapped into the hierarchical structure to enforce the propagation mechanism through and across hierarchy levels. In terms of the hierarchy structure, transactional dependencies are defined between a component and its immediate superior and between a node and its immediate siblings (if any exist).

Dependencies such as activation, completion, failure, force-fail, compensation (forward/ backward/designer-tailored) and compensation-completion are defined in first order logic and in terms of sets of pre-conditions, that when satisfied at run time leads to an event being fired. In the scope of this chapter, we focus on failure and force-fail dependencies.

As we are using an event based mechanism to control state changes, it is meaningful to also express transactional behaviour in the same way. For that we allow components to raise events to notify other parts of the system of transactional requirements; such events are called transactional events in our approach.

The general definition for a behavioral dependency is:

Behavioral Dependency: A behavioral dependency exists from $component_j$ to $component_i$ if a state transition in $component_i$ can fire a transactional event for $component_j$:

$Dep(component_j): = preCond(component_i.state)$

As an example, for two successive nodes the activation dependency of the successor node stating that an activation event is fired for a successor node if its predecessor node has been completed or, if its predecessor node was not a vital node but failed to complete is defined as:

$ActDep(succNode). = (PredNode.State = COMPLETED) \lor (PredNode.Vital=FALSE \land PredNode.State=FAILED)$

Behavioral dependencies can also be defined between a set of sibling components and their immediate superior component, essentially extending Definition 3 to allow for any of a number of sibling nodes to fire a transactional event for the superior component:

$Dep(superior) =PreCond(Isibling_1.state..sibling_n.stateJ)$

Also note that the behavioral dependency defines a trivial compensation dependency, such that a state transition in $component_j$ can fire a compensation event for $component_i$.

Failure and Force-Fail Dependencies

Failure dependencies are defined for non-vital scope nodes and non-vital execution paths. Vital scopes and execution paths do not lead to events fired by dependencies; instead, such failure is assessed by the management rules discussed later. Table 1 shows a complete list of failure and force fail dependencies. Failure of all vital nodes in a path will fail the path (*path.nodeList $\leftarrow_{fail}$ path*; FD1); failure of paths in a scope will lead to failure of the scope (*scope.pathList $\leftarrow_{fail}$ scope*), dependent on the semantics of the scope operator. For example, FD3 states that an OR scope fails if all its enabled paths failed.

Force-fail is a counterpart for cancellation. When a vital concurrent path fails, its immediate outer scope fails. Force-fail dependencies force all active paths within a failed concurrent scope to cancel their executions, and subsequently all active nodes on paths are forced to fail. Force-fail dependencies are defined between components and their immediate superiors.

A force-fail dependency *component.superior $\leftarrow_{forcefail}$ component* means that failure of an activated component's superior will force the component to fail. For example FF1 states that an activated path will fail if its enclosing scope has failed. Consequently, all concurrently activated paths within a scope will force-fail if their immediate superior scope fails.

Table 1. Fail and force-fail dependencies

Dependency	Dependency Formula
Failure Dependencies	
FD1	$FailDep(pat\boldsymbol{h}) := \left(\bigwedge\limits_{1 \leq i \leq m} nodeList_i.State = FAILED \right)$ $where\, m = |pat\boldsymbol{h}.nodeList|$
FD2	$FailDep(ANDscope) := \bigwedge\limits_{\downarrow}(1 \leq i \leq m) \equiv [\![(path_{\downarrow}i.State = FAILED]\!]\,)$ $where\, m = |ANDscope.pat\boldsymbol{h}List|$
FD3	$FailDep(ORscope)_i := \bigwedge\limits_{1 \leq i \leq m} \begin{pmatrix} path_i.Enabled = TRUE \wedge \\ path_i.State = FAILED \end{pmatrix}$ $where\, m = |ORscope.pat\boldsymbol{h}List|$
FD4	$FailDep(XORscope) := \bigwedge\limits_{1 \leq i \leq m} [\![(path_i.State = FAILED]\!]$ $where\, m = |XORscope.pat\boldsymbol{h}list|$
Force-Fail Dependencies	
FF1	$ForceFailDep(pat\boldsymbol{h}) := immediateSuperior.State = FAILED$
FF2	$ForceFailDep(node) := immediateSuperior.State = FAILED$

FAILURE MANAGEMENT

Management Rules

Event Condition Action (ECA) rules in COMPMOD are used to model the expected execution behaviour of the LRT. When an event is fired, it triggers an ECA rule, and if the condition holds, an appropriate action takes place. ECA rules have the following pseudo generic form:

*ON event **IF** condition **DO** action*

The event part of the rule can be (a) an internal system generated event such as completion, failure, or cancellation of an atomic node or, (b) an external event fired as a result of a dependency condition satisfied for a component or, (c) a result of executing a transition event of a component. The condition part is one or more connected Boolean expressions that need to hold for the rule to be applied. The action is a sequence of one or more actions to be performed in case the rule is applied, and can in turn introduce new events needing to be handled.

COMPMOD Rules are classified into: activation, completion, compensation, failure, and propagation rules. As this chapter focuses on failure handling, we only list failure and failure propagation ECA rules in Table 2. Note that *fail* and *abort* are actions that lead to raising an event (fail or abort) but also have a side effect on the state of the respective component as follows:

if component.state=ACTIVATED

then component.state:=FAILED

ECA rules of COMPMOD reflect the following:

- The business logic of the LRT (e.g. FR4 states that if a node is vital and failed, its superior path fails).
- The semantics of a COMPMOD model (e.g. FFR2 states that if a force-fail event is fired for an activated atomic node, the node is aborted).

Table 2. Failure and propagation rules

Rule	Pseudo ECA-Rule statement
Failure Rules	
FR1	**ON** "internal failure/cancellation event fired for atomic node" **DO** fail(node)
FR2	**ON** FailDep(node)=TRUE **IF** node.type=SCOPE **DO** fail(node)
FR3	**ON** FailDep(path)=TRUE **DO** fail(path)
FR4	**ON** fail(node) **IF** node.vital= TRUE **DO** fail(node.superior)
FR5	**ON** fail(path) **IF** path.hasAlternative - FALSE and path.vital = TRUE **DO** fail(path.superior)
FR6	**ON** fail(p_0) **DO** fail(LRT)
Failure Propagation Rules	
FFR1	**ON** ForceFailDep(node) **IF** node.type=SCOPE and node.state=activated **DO** fail(node)
FFR2	**ON** ForceFailDep(node)=TRUE **IF** node.type=ATOMIC and node.state=activated **DO** abort(node)
FFR3	**ON** ForcefailDep(path)=TRUE **IF** path.state=activated **DO** fail(path)*

- The semantics of WF patterns (e.g. FR5 states that failure of a vital path that has no alternative, i.e. a concurrent or last exclusive path fails its enclosing scope).

Failure Propagation Mechanism

This work presents a recursive method for propagating vital failure events through the recursive hierarchical structure of LRT components. Propagation is in parallel with rule-based actions in order to reach a consensus about the execution state of LRT components and the LRT itself.

Within the context of the proposed hierarchical structure, the recursive failure propagation mechanism entails a combination of three types of propagation methods:

- **Bottom-Up Propagation:** Originates from failure of a vital atomic node and propagates up the hierarchy to its immediate superior path. If the failed atomic node exists on the main execution path p_0, the LRT fails.

- **Upwards Recursive Propagation:** Originates from failure of a scope node by repeating a bottom-up propagation to its immediate superior execution path in recursive fashion until a non-vital component is reached in the hierarchy or until the failure reaches the root of the hierarchy structure (p_0).

- **Downwards Recursive Propagation:** Originates from a failure of a scope node (vital or non-vital) by repeating a top-down propagation to its immediate activated paths until the propagation reaches all active atomic nodes within the failed scope's sub-hierarchy. This represents a means of forcing failure/cancellation of concurrently running nodes in a failed scope. Force fail only applies to concurrent scopes and in our model only applies to AND and OR scopes since a failed XOR is a result of a failure of all its exclusive paths.

- **Failure Propagation:** Always initiated by the failure of a vital atomic node and propagates recursively through vital component ancestors in the hierarchy structure to stop when a non-vital ancestor component is reached or when the root of the hierarchy is reached. As for Top-down propagation of failures, both vital and non-vital active components are force-failed.

If a vital failure propagates through the hierarchy structure of the LRT and reaches the root of the hierarchy p_0, the LRT fails. Figures 5 and 6 illustrate key parts of the failure propagation mechanism linked to dependencies and ECA rules (Tables 1 and 2). Figures 5 and 6 include compensation mechanisms that tie in with work presented in the next section.

The failure mechanism also handles failures of non-vital components. Failure of a non-vital atomic node could fail its enclosing path if the enclosing path was a non-vital path under the following two conditions (1) the enclosing path is an atomic path, i.e. encapsulates one node only, or (2) the node is the last node in the path and all other nodes in the path have failed. Failure of a non-vital path (Figure 6) will only fail its enclosing scope under two conditions: (1) it is an exclusive path (2) it has no alternative, i.e. it is the last exclusive path in the scope. From assumptions

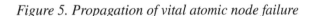

Figure 5. Propagation of vital atomic node failure

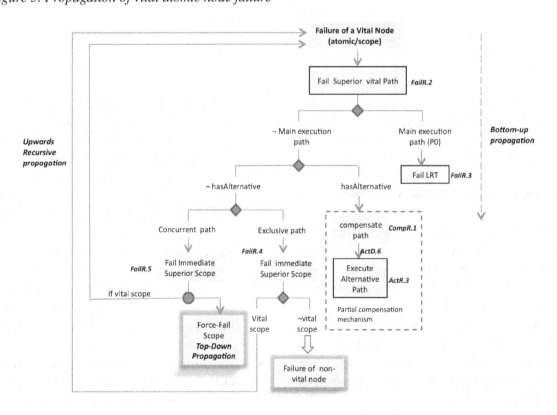

Figure 6. Failure handling mechanism for non vital nodes

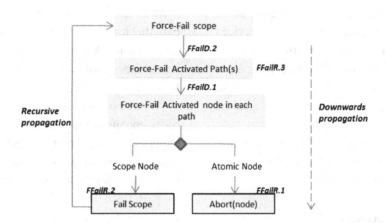

1 and 2 earlier, failure of a last non-vital exclusive path will fail a non-vital exclusive scope. Recursively, failure of a non-vital scope is treated as a failure of non-vital node.

To briefly illustrate the propagation mechanism, consider the LRT presented in Figure 4. Assume an execution instance with the following states of its components: n_1, n_2, $scope_1$ and $scope_2$ have completed, and $scope_a$ is activated. n_{17} is a vital node and has failed to complete. All other nodes and paths are vital apart from p_2 and n_{16}. All nodes and paths in the subtree are activated.

Following the propagation mechanism of Figure 4, failure of n_{17} will fail its superior path $scope_a.p_a$. This is not the main execution path and does not have an alternative but it is a concurrent path since its superior is an AND scope. $scope_a$. p_3 is vital by *evaluation* since it encapsulates vital node n_{17}. Therefore, the immediate scope of $scope_a.p_a$ which is $scope_a$ fails $scope_a$. is vital by *specification*, hence two actions take place: (a) the failure is propagated recursively one level up in the hierarchy to path p_0. (b) Force fail is recursively propagated in top-down order to cancel all activated components encapsulated by $scope_a$. Failure of p_0 will fail the LRT (FR6). Failure of $scope_a$ will force fail all its activated paths. At this point of execution, $scope_a.p_a$ has already failed while $scope_a.p_1$ and $scope_a.p_2$ are still activated

and therefore both are forced to fail. Force failing a path, fails the activated node in that path. Therefore, activated nodes n_{16} and $scope_{3.1}$ are forced to fail. $scope_{3.1}$ is a scope node and hence the force fail mechanism is recursively repeated one level down in the hierarchy to force fail $scope_{3.1}$'s activated components in same manner as scope3's activated components were forced to fail. In this example, failure of a vital node $scope_a$ on p_0 caused the LRT to fail. Our management/compensation model applies a reliable mechanism that controls failure of the LRT in designer-specific order that reflects the business logic of the transaction. In case of force failing a scope that has un-activated paths, these paths can never activate since their enclosing scope state is failed, ensuring correctness of the model and avoiding activation of paths in failed scopes.

COMPENSATION MANAGEMENT

While executing a long running transaction, faults might occur – often this is not a problem as alternatives can be probed and often the long running transaction can be successfully completed. Consider the scenario of booking a holiday; if one hotel is full one might find an alternative hotel and still get the desired rest. However, usually when faults occur, a path in the business process has been travelled along, possibly for quite some time, making commitments to specific services along the route. However, sometimes there is simply no alternative (or all alternatives have been explored – it is a small town on a remote island and all hotels are fully booked) and the long running transaction will fail.

In both cases we require compensation, and COMPMOD caters for this by supporting two types of compensation modes:

1. **Partial Compensation:** Occurs where some compensation actions take place while the LRT is executing in its normal mode (in the model the LRT state is *activated*). Partial compensation is applied to nodes, paths, and scopes in tolerance with failures and it primarily reflects WF semantics.

2. **Comprehensive Compensation:** Needed when an explicit consensus is reached about the failure of the LRT. The LRT starts its global compensation applying it to all successfully completed atomic nodes in a customised-order that is defined by the business process designer at design time. Comprehensive compensation mainly reflects the compensation logic of the business process.

We will now explore the two types of compensations in more detail. We will focus on Partial Compensation but also provide an overview of the Comprehensive Compensation and custom-order aspects.

Partial Compensation

Partial compensation is triggered by failure of an exclusive path that has an alternative. Exclusive scopes encapsulate paths that alternate each other in execution such that only one path is allowed to succeed. If an activated path has failed to successfully complete, which is mainly triggered by

a failure of a vital node on the path or by failure of all its encapsulated nodes, then all nodes on the path that have successfully completed (if any) are compensated. When the failed path has completed its compensation actions, an activation event is fired for its alternative path.

When compensating a path, the current state of its encapsulated nodes at the time the failure happened is important for deciding the compensating actions to be performed on these nodes, so we consider the following possible situations:

- The failed exclusive path might contain nodes that have succeeded, failed, or not been activated (i.e. the failure occurred before the node has been activated).
- Nodes might be scopes, and hence, if they were activated and some tasks had succeeded within the scope, then their work has to be compensated.
- The path is an atomic path that encapsulates a single node, and its failure has caused the failure of the path; the node could be either atomic or a scope.

We adopt two widely used terminologies in Transaction Processing: Forward Compensation and Backward Compensation and give them a precise definition in COMPMOD.

1. **Forward Compensation:** Used to refer to the compensation process of an exclusive path that has an alternative but failed to complete. Forward compensation starts by compensating the last node on the path and completes when the first node on that path has completed its compensating actions at which point the alternative path will be attempted.

2. **Backward Compensation:** Used to refer to the compensation process of a scope node that has previously succeeded or failed (i.e., some partial work could have succeeded within the scope). We define

backward compensation for scopes that are contained within potentially compensable paths. Backward compensation of a scope starts by compensating all its encapsulated paths concurrently in backward order. The backward compensation of each path is processed in the same manner as in forward order, that is, starting from last node and cascading compensation events along the nodes on the path until the first node on the path has completed its compensating actions.

A potentially compensable path is a path that can possibly, in case of tolerable failures and during the normal execution mode of the LRT, have some compensating actions applied to it. Hence, a forward compensable path and a backward compensable path (a path within a backward compensable scope) are both potentially compensable paths. Analogously, a node is potentially compensable if it is encapsulated with a potentially compensable path. In COMP-MOD, all potentially compensable components are defined with compensation dependencies. However, compensations of nodes on a compensating path are always performed in reverse order of their activations. Therefore, whether a path is in forward or backward compensation mode, the order by which nodes are compensated is always in reverse order of their activations.

We require some preliminary artifacts before we can consider compensation dependencies, one of these is concerned with formalizing the notion of being compensable, while the other looks at identifying nodes that must be compensated. For the former, we define an attribute for LRT components, *IsCompensable,* and its value is computed as follows:

1. The main execution path is not compensable since if it fails, the LRT has failed and we leave the normal execution mode of the LRT to start comprehensive compensation:

$$path = p_0 \rightarrow path.IsCompensable = FALSE$$

2. A path *IsCompensable* if the path has an alternative:

$$path.hasAlternative = TRUE \rightarrow$$
$$path.IsCompensable = TRUE$$

3. A scope node *IsCompensable* if its superior path *IsCompensable*:

$$scopeNode.\sup erior.IsCompensable =$$
$$TRUE \rightarrow scopeNode.IsCompensable$$

4. A path that has no alternative *IsCompensable* if it's superior scope *IsCompensable*. This applies to the case of concurrent paths (e.g. AND), and the last exclusive path in an exclusive scope (e.g. XOR).

$$scope.IsCompensable =$$
$$TRUE \land \neg scopeInferior.hasAlternative \rightarrow$$
$$scopeInferior.IsCompensable = TRUE$$

Items 3 and 4 do of course include the notion that compensation of some inner components depends on their enclosing environment, so if that environment can offer alternatives then they will be compensable; if the environment does not offer alternatives they will not be compensable.

It is intuitive that compensation is only required to undo actions of atomic nodes that succeeded (it is only those that might have an effect on the world), we need to be able to identify such nodes. Such atomic nodes can only exist on a successful path or failed path (there might be some nodes earlier on the path that succeeded) but never on not-activated paths or previously compensated paths. This can be further extended to enclosing scopes, where not-activated scopes will only contain not-activated paths.

So, we have two rules telling us which components can be skipped when considering compensations:

CR1: If the component was an atomic node that has not succeeded (i.e. it failed, was not-activated, or was aborted) or it was a scope node that was not activated, the node is skipped (i.e. its state is marked as SKIPPED).

CR2: If the component was a not-activated or previously compensated path, no action is taken for its compensation event; hence the state of the path does not change.

Compensation Dependencies

Considering compensations, we have two types of dependencies: those that we refer to as compensation dependencies and those that are called compensation completion dependencies. The former capture the targets for compensation events, while the latter are concerned with notifications of completed compensations. Compensation dependency exists

- Between a node and its successor (if any) if its superior path *IsCompensable,*
- Between a path and its superior scope if the superior scope *IsCompensable, and*
- Between the last node and its encapsulating path if the path *IsCompensable.*

Table 3 details the compensation dependencies. A compensation event is fired for the last node on a compensable path when the path has commenced its compensation (CompD.1) and is fired for a path when its superior scope has commenced its compensation (CompD.3). (CompD.2) enforces the reverse order of compensation activation such that a compensation event is fired for a node if its successor on the path has been compensated or skipped.

Compensation completion dependencies are defined for compensable paths and scopes to signal the end of their compensation process (Table 4) such that when fired, they are marked by a completion policy as COMPENSATED. Atomic nodes raise an event when compensation is completed (we assume that compensation completion is guaranteed to succeed) and the state of the node will be COMPENSATED. A path ends its compensation process when the first node in the path has either compensated or skipped (CpCompLD.1). To reach a consensus about compensation completion of a scope, we have to evaluate all possible states of its encapsulated paths at the time the scope has SUCCEEDED or FAILED.

Partial Compensation Mechanism

As with fault handling, partial compensation is automated through compensation policies (Table 5) and compensation completion policies (Table 6). All compensation policies contain a

Table 3. Compensation dependencies

Dep	Dependency Formula	Component
CompD.1	$CompDep(lastNode) = superiorPath.State = COMPENSATING$	Last node on a compensable path
CompD.2	$CompDep(node_1) =$ $superior.State = Compensating$ $\bigwedge \square (node_2 \ is \ COMPENSATED \ \lor \ node_2 is \ SKIPPED)$	A node that has a successor on a compensable path $node_2$=successor($node_1$)
CompD.3	$CompDep(path) = superiorScope.State = COMPENSATING$	Path within a compensable scope

Table 4. Compensation completion dependencies

Dep #	Dependency	Component
CpCompLD.1	$CpCompLDep(path) :=$ $(firstNode.State = COMPENSATED) \lor firstNode.State = SKIPPED)$	Compensable Path
CpCompLD.2	$CpCompLDep(scope) := scope.state = compensating \land$ $\left(\bigwedge_{i=1..m}(pathList_i.state = COMPENSATED \lor pathList_i.state = NOT-ACTIVATED\right.$	Compensable scope with m paths

Table 5. Compensation policies

Rule#	Compensation Policies	Component
CompR.1	**ON** *fail(path)* **IF** *path.hasAlternative and* *node.superior.state=ACTIVATED* **DO** *compensate(path)*	Exclusive path with alternative
CompR.2	**ON** *CompDep(path)* **IF** *LRT.State=ACTIVATED and (path.state=SUCCEEDED or path.state=FAILED)* **DO** *compensate(path)*	Compensable path previously succeeded or failed
CompR.3	**ON** *CompDep(node)* **IF** *LRT.State=ACTIVATED and node.Type=ATOMIC and node.State=SUCCEEDED* **DO** *compensate(node)*	succeeded Atomic node
CompR.4	**ON** *CompDep(node)* **IF** *LRT.State=ACTIVATED and node.Type=ATOMIC and (node.State=FAILED or node.state=NOT-ACTIVATED Or nodeState=ABORTED)* **DO** *skip(node)*	Non-succeeded atomic node
CompR.5	**ON** *CompDep(node)* **IF** *LRT.State=ACTIVATED and node.Type=SCOPE and (node.State=SUCCEEDED or node.state=FAILED)* **DO** *compensate(node)*	Succeeded or failed scope
CompR.6	**ON** *CompDep(node)* **IF** *LRT.State=ACTIVATED and node.Type=SCOPE and node.state=NOT-ACTIVATED* **DO** *skip(node)*	Not activated scope

Table 6. Compensation completion policies

Rule#	Compensation Policies	Component
CpCompLR.1	**ON** *"internal compensation completion event of atomic node"* **IF** *LRT.State=ACTIVATED* **DO** *compensated(node)*	Atomic node
CpCompLR.2	**ON** *CpCompLDep(path)* **DO** *compensated(path)*	Path
CpCompLR.3	**ON** *CpCompLDep(node)* **IF** *node.Type=SCOPE and node.state≠SKIPPED* **DO** *compensated(node)*	Concurrent Scope
CpCompLR.4	**ON** *compensated(path)* **IF** *path.IsExclusive and Path.superior.state=compensating* **DO** *compensated(path.superior)*	Exclusive path

consistency condition (*LRT.state=ACTIVATED*) to differentiate between the partial compensation mode and comprehensive compensation mode (*LRT.state=COMPENSATING*), such that compensation events are handled reliably in the correct mode of compensation.

The partial compensation mechanism operates as follows (Figure 7 and Figure 8 contain a graphical representation of some of the steps). Please note that the steps indicate which rules are applicable, however the reactive controller will be based on events available in the system and apply the correct rules automatically:

1. When a failure event is fired for an exclusive path with an alternative, the event is assessed by (CompR.1 - Table 5) and the path is marked COMPENSATING.

2. A compensation event fired for a compensable path is assessed by (CompR.2 - Table 5) and the path is marked COMPENSATING.

3. When a path commences its compensation, a compensation event is fired for the last node in the path (CompD.1 – Table 3).

4. When a compensation event is fired for an atomic node, if the node has succeeded, the event is assessed by (CompR.3 – Table 5) and the nodes start COMPENSATING.

5. When a compensation event is fired for an atomic node, if the node that has not been succeeded, the event is assessed by (CompR.4 – Table 5) and the node is SKIPPED.

6. When an internal compensation completion event is fired for an atomic node, the node is marked as COMPENSATED (CpCompLR.1 – Table 6).

7. A compensation event fired for a non-activated scope is assessed by (CompR.6 – Table 5) and the scope is SKIPPED.

8. A compensation event fired for a SUCCEEDED or FAILED scope is assessed by (CompR.5 – Table 5) and the scope starts compensating.

Figure 7. Compensation of path

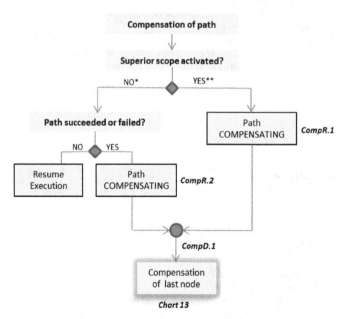

* A compensable path within a compensating concurrent scope
** An exclusive path within an activated exclusive scope

Figure 8. Compensation of node

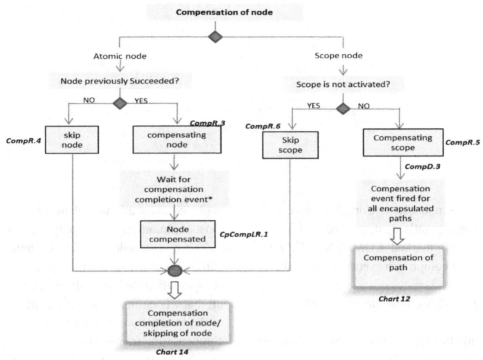

* It is assumed that the compensation of atomic node is guaranteed to succeed

9. When a scope commences its compensation, a compensation event is fired for all its encapsulated paths (CompD.3 – Table 3) and control goes to step 2.

10. When a node is COMPENSATED or SKIPPED, if the node was the first node in the path, a compensation completion event is fired for the path (CpCompLD.1 – Table 4) and the path is marked compensated by (CpCompLR.2).

11. If a COMPENSATED or SKIPPED node has a predecessor node, a compensation event is fired for the preceding node (CompD.2 – Table 3) and control goes to step 4 or 5.

12. When a compensation completion event is fired for an exclusive path within an activated exclusive scope, an activation event is fired for the next alternative path (ActD.6) and the node is activated by activation policy (ActR.3).

13. When a compensation completion event is fired for an exclusive path within a compensating exclusive scope, the scope is marked COMPENSATED by policy (CpCompLR.4 – Table 6).

14. When a compensation completion event is fired for a concurrent scope (CpCompLD.2 – Table 4), the scope is marked compensated by policy (cpCompLR.3 – Table 6).

For further illustration of the mechanism, let us consider the scope of a larger process depicted in Figure 9. Consider a scenario, where n_d, n_6 succeed, and non-vital n_7 fails which fails $scope_{2.1}$, p_2 by FailR.7, but $scope_{2.1}$ succeeds by CompLR.5. n_{11} is vital, but fails and thus p_1 fails by propagation.

In this scenario, $scope_{2.1}$ has succeeded and thus it is explored in the following manner: both paths p_1 and p_2 start compensating, n_6 and n_7 are explored because they are the last nodes on the

Figure 9. An example process to demonstrate partial compensation

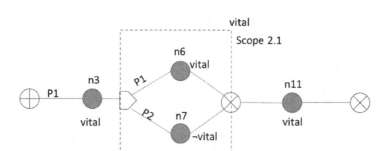

paths, n_6 is compensated (CompR.3) and n_7 is skipped. Subsequently p_1, p_2 and their enclosing $scope_{2.1}$ are all marked COMPENSATED by compensation completion events and policies.

Comprehensive Compensation

We will only briefly touch upon comprehensive compensation, highlighting the main ideas. The overall management in COMPMOD is similar to that presented for failure handling and partial compensation: that is a number of rules and dependencies are defined and enacted by the reactive controller.

Comprehensive compensation is engaged when a global failure of the long running transactions is recognized – that is there is no possibility to recover and complete the LRT in some alternative way. These failures are triggered by a failure of a vital node that is preceded by a hierarchy of vital ancestor components towards the top of the hierarchy (p_0), such that the failure propagates up the hierarchy structure and reaches the main execution path and consequently the transaction fails globally.

From the business point of view, a failed transaction means that it has failed to achieve its expected outcome. Both from a business perspective and also from a consistency of transaction's point of view, any task that has succeeded must be compensated. The question raised is how to apply compensations and in which order. The most common way is to apply compensations to tasks in reverse order of their completions which is commonly referred to as rolling back or backward compensation. In backward compensations, rolling back is enforced by the management model of the transactions and results in a long running compensating transaction.

With Web Services, tasks in a transaction can mean anything from a database update operation to sending email to a client. Thus, rolling back a transaction must depend on what the transaction was about. In real B2B applications, it is the case that business process logic requires that compensation logic diverges from the standard backward compensation order by freely incorporating compensation logic into business logic. The restricted backward recovery mechanism makes implementing an arbitrary order for compensations not a straight forward process and might force the business process designer to change the business logic of the transaction to comply with compensation logic requirements (or build very complicated compensation schemes into the original workflow making the workflow more complicated and distracting from the actual process).

COMPMOD model supports a customized compensation method that provides transaction designers with the flexibility of expressing their business process logic without putting compensation in mind. Compensation logic can then be mapped onto the business process in a very flexible way to meet business needs. The designer is allowed to specify compensation patterns on a subset or subsets of atomic nodes (component services) of an LRT. In Figure 10, such dependencies are indicated by dashed arrows. A compensation pattern decides the order by which the specified services are compensated, and will only be defined for parts of the LRT where the designer cares about the compensation order. Any other services that are not involved in any compensation pattern are compensated concurrently. This will increase the performance of the system in terms of time spent on the compensation process. Assignment of compensation patterns is restricted by *validity rules* to avoid deadlocks and violation of logic integrity. The general mechanism of comprehensive compensations guarantees the following:

- Each atomic node in the LRT is traversed.
- Each succeeding atomic node in the LRT is compensated.

- If there are customized compensation patterns, then the order of each pattern is enforced.
- Achieving (1-3) guarantees an explicit compensation completion state of the transaction.

We will not discuss the technical details of the implementation here, but mention that nodes are sorted into groups depending on whether:

- They can readily be compensated (i.e. they do not form part of a defined pattern or are the source node of a pattern (that is no user defined dependency points to it).
- They are a target node in a user defined dependency.

In the latter case, which includes nodes that might be both target and source, the node will have to wait until the nodes on the user defined path leading to them have been compensated and

Figure 10. A sample LRT with customized compensation dependencies

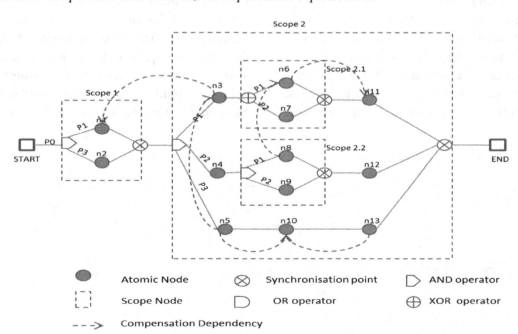

then they will move to the group of nodes that can readily be compensated. Once all the atomic nodes in the LRT are visited, a customized compensation completion event is fired for the LRT and it is marked as COMPENSATED.

e-Booking Example

We demonstrate our management and failure handling mechanism on an e-booking example depicted in Figure 11 to illustrate how an LRT can succeed in case of non-vital node failures. In this scenario, it is required to book a flight, a hotel room, and a car for a specific period as received by the *BookingOrder activity*. It is necessary to find a flight booking and a hotel room for requested dates and thus the nodes *Flight* and *Hotel* are assigned as vital nodes. It is desirable for *Make-Bookings* scope that a car rental is booked for the same dates, but this booking is not essential. In other words, if a car rental was not available, the *MakeBookings* is still successful from the business point of view – this is reflected in the non-vital nature of the node. All other nodes are vital. So, by evaluation p_1 and p_2 in *MakeBookings* scope are vital, while p_a is non-vital.

Activation of the LRT (ActR.1) triggers an activation event for p_0 (ActD.1). Activation of a path triggers the activation of the first node *BookingOrder* (ActD.2). The system waits for the *BookingOrder* to finish its execution. We assume

that a completion event has been fired for the node and the *BookingOrder is* marked SUCCEEDED (CompLR.1). Successful completion of *BookingOrder* activates *MakeBooking* scope (ActD.3) since *BookingOrder* is not the last node on p_0. Activation of *MakeBookings*, fires activation events (ActD.4) for p_1, p_2, and p_a encapsulated by *MakeBookings* and they are all activated by (ActR.3). Subsequently, and in the same manner as illustrated above, the first nodes on the concurrent paths are activated; *Flight*, *Hotel*, and *Car* and are executed concurrently. Assume that *Flight* succeeded and *Hotel* succeeded and the system is waiting for the *Car* node to finish its execution. Note p_1 and p_2 have succeeded by (CompLR.2).

To demonstrate how the completion and successful completion of concurrent scopes are dealt with in case of non-vital failures, we assume that the *Car* node fails to complete. Failure of the non-vital *Car* node fires a failure event for p_a (FailD.1) and thus p_a fails (FailR.7). Failure of p_a fires a completion event for *MakeBookings* since it is the last path to complete and hence *CompLDep(MakeBookings)=True*. *MakeBookings* has not failed since all its vital components succeeded and there is no failure event fired for the path since p_1 and p_2 have succeeded, hence *MakeBookings* succeeds by the completion policy (CompLR.5). Successful completion of *MakeBookings* activates *Payment*. If we assume

Figure 11. e-Booking example

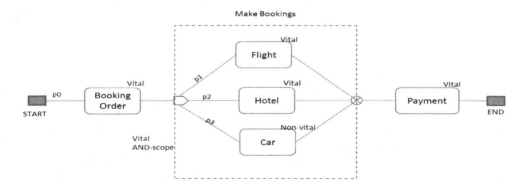

that *Payment* succeeds, then a completion event is fired for p_0 (CompLD.1) and policy (CompLR.2) succeeds p_0. The successful completion of the main execution path leads to the success of the LRT by (CompLR.3).

CONCLUSION AND FUTURE RESEARCH DIRECTIONS

We presented an approach for modeling and enacting failure recovery and compensation on nested long running transactions. The approach provides a novel model that makes explicit the propagation of failure events through the transactions. It also distinguishes two types of nodes - vital and non-vital - that allow a process designer to include activities in the design that are useful but where failure does not matter. We also introduced the idea of custom defined compensation dependencies in the context of final failure of an LRT. The designed propagation rules are enforced through a novel rule based management system, allowing for monitoring and controlling LRTs. Nested workflows are used as examples throughout.

One of the motivations for this work was the perceived lack of high level approaches to compensation handling: compensations are part of the business process and are best understood at the design level. Existing support in some BPM tools (e.g. TIBCO BW or IBM Process Server) and also existing work in exception handling for processes (Russell, van der Aalst, & ter Hofstede, 2006). Lerner, Christov, and Osterweil (2010) address the issue of "things going wrong" in a way that is akin to programming level solutions. They require detailed consideration of each individual case of possible failure and then a deliberate exploration of how to handle this. The presented work lays a foundation for abstracting away from specific errors and considering how failure and compensation should be handled in the situations that are

meaningful to address for the business analyst while dealing with all other cases automatically in standard ways defined through the framework and its policies. Programmatically this might mean that the tools implement the details of the framework through an exception handling mechanism, but this would be transparent to the user.

Direct future work includes implementation of an operational system reflecting this approach and its use in some larger case studies. There is also a growing interest in risk-aware business processes and our notion of vitality (combined with the proposed framework) could be one way of addressing this. However, this requires further study.

More generally, there are two areas of work that are required to better support transactions: workflow or business process design standards and workflow execution environments. For the former, much work has been done over the last few years with the introduction of BPEL (more as an implementation oriented mechanism) and BPMN (more targeted as a business requirements capture mechanism) in formulating and designing workflows. These efforts consider ideas of compensation and alternatives that can be engaged when repair is needed due to partial failure, but they are somewhat cumbersome to describe. In our work, we provide a good solution in terms of dependencies that automatically takes care of many of the issues that arise, letting the business analyst focus on the parts of the process where more customized dependencies are needed. Also, none of the mechanisms support the distinction of vital and non-vital parts of the process (with the only option being an alternative scope to capture non-vital aspects, making the flow less intuitive).

Regarding the execution environments, these are currently more of interpreters for workflows that largely leave transaction handling aside at the high level and assume that transactions are managed at lower levels in the execution environment, and possibly through the aforementioned repair routes. It would be desirable to include transaction management as a more native part of the workflow engines – and again as much of these work in an event based fashion, our approach should be able to provide a solution for ready implementation.

REFERENCES

Ali, M. S., & Reiff-Marganiec, S. (2012). Autonomous failure-handling mechanism for WF long running transactions. In *Proceedings of SCC 2012.*IEEE.

Bhiri, S., Godart, C., & Perrin, O. (2006). Transactional patterns for reliable web services compositions. *Proceedings of ACM, ICWE06*, 137–144.

Bhiri, S., Perrin, O., & Godart, C. (2005). Ensuring required failure atomicity of composite Web services. *Proceedings of ACM, WWW05*, 138–147.

Bhiri, S., Perrin, O., & Godart, C. (2006). Extending workflow patterns with transactional dependencies to define reliable composite Web services. In *Proceedings of AICT-ICIW '06* (pp. *145)*. IEEE.

Bruni, R., Melgratti, H., & Montanari, U. (2005). Theoretical foundations for compensations in flow composition languages. In POPL (pp. 209–220). ACM.

Buscemi, M. G., Ferrari, L., Moiso, C., & Montanari, U. (2007). Constraint-based policy negotiation and enforcement for telco services. In TASE 2007 (pp. 463-472).

Butler, M., Hoare, T., & Ferreira, C. (2005). A trace semantics for long-running transactions. *Communicating Sequential Processes, The First 25 Years*, 707-711.

Butler, M., & Ripon, S. (2005). Executable semantics for compensating CSP. *Formal Techniques for Computer Systems and Business Processes*, 243-256.

Casado, R., Tuya, J., & Younas, M. (2012). Testing the reliability of web services transactions in cooperative applications. *ACM,* 743-748.

Chrysanthis, P. K., & Ramamritham, K. (1990). ACTA: A framework for specifying and reasoning about transaction structure and behavior. *ACM,* 194-203.

Dayal, U., Hsu, M., & Ladin, R. (1990). Organizing long-running activities with triggers and transactions. *Proceedings of SIGMOD, 90,* 204–214. doi:10.1145/93605.98730.

Elmagarid, A. K. (1992). *Transaction models for advanced database applications*. Morgan Kaufmann.

Gaaloul, W., Bhiri, S., & Rouached, M. (2010). Event-based design and runtime verification of composite service transactional behavior. *Transactions on Services Computing (IEEE), 3*(1), 32–45. doi:10.1109/TSC.2010.1.

Garcia-Molina, H., & Salem, K. (1987). SAGAS. In *ACM International Conference on Management of Data (SIGMOD)* (pp. 249-259).

Gorton, S., Montangero, C., Reiff-Marganiec, S., & Semini, L. (2009). StPowla: SOA, policies and workflows. In ICSOC 2007 Workshops, LNCS 4907 (pp. 351-362). Springer.

Gorton, S., & Reiff-Marganiec, S. (2006). Towards a task-oriented, policy-driven business requirements specification for web services. Business Process Management, volume 4102 of LNCS, 465-470. Springer.

Gray, J. (1981). The transaction concept: Virtues and limitations. In *Proceedings of the 7th International Conference on Very Large Databases* (pp. 144–154). Tandem Computers.

Gray, J., & Reuter, A. (1993). *Distributed transaction processing: Concepts and techniques*. Morgan Kaufmann.

Halpern, J. Y., & Weissman, V. (2003). Using first-order logic to reason about policies. In *Proceedings of the Computer Security Foundations Workshop (CSFW'03)* (pp.187-201). IEEE.

Hoare, C. A. R. (1978). Communicating sequential processes. *Communications of the ACM, 21*(8), 666–677. doi:10.1145/359576.359585.

Kiepuszewski, B., ter Hofstede, A., & Bussler, C. (2000). On structured workflow modeling. In *Proceedings of the International Conference on Advanced Information Systems Eng. (CAiSE),* volume 1789 (pp. 431–445).

Kokash, N., & Arbab, F. (2011). Formal design and verification of long-running transactions with eclipse coordination tools. *Transactions on Services Computing, 2011*(99), 1–1.

Lerner, B. S., Christov, S., Osterweil, L. J., Bendraou, R., Kannengiesser, U., & Wise, A. (2010). Exception handling patterns for process modeling. *IEEE Transactions on Software Engineering, 183,* 162–183. doi:10.1109/TSE.2010.1.

Lewis, P. M., Bernstein, A., & Kifer, M. (2001). *Database and transaction processing.* Addison Wesley.

Mehrotra, S., Rastogi, R., Silberschatz, A., & Korth, H. F. (1992). A transaction model for multi-database systems. In *Proceedings of the 12th International Conference on Distributed Computing Systems (ICDCS)* (pp. 56–63). IEEE.

Mohan, C., & Lindsay, B. (1985). Efficient commit protocols for the tree of processes model of distributed transactions. *ACM SIGOPS Operating Systems Review, 19*(2), 40–52. doi:10.1145/850770.850772.

Moller, T., & Schuldt, H. (2010). OSIRIS next: Flexible semantic failure handling for composite web service execution. *Proceedings of IEEE, ICSC10,* 212–217.

Montangero, C., Reiff-Marganiec, S., & Semini, L. (2011). *Model-driven development of adaptable service-oriented business processes. Rigorous software engineering for service-oriented systems, LNCS (Vol. 6582).* Springer.

Moss, J. E. B. (1982). *Nested transactions and reliable distributed computing.* Cambridge, MA, USA: The MIT Press.

Müller, R., Greiner, U., & Rahm, E. (2004). Agentwork: A workflow system supporting rule-based workflow adaptation. *Data & Knowledge Engineering, 51,* 223–256. doi:10.1016/j.datak.2004.03.010.

Paton, N. W. (1999). *Active rules in database systems.* New York, NY: Springer Verlag. doi:10.1007/978-1-4419-8656-6.

Reichert, M., & Dadam, P. (1997). A framework for dynamic changes in workflow management systems. In *DEXA Workshop 1997* (pp. 42-48). IEEE.

Reichert, M., & Dadam, P. (1998). ADEPT flex - Supporting dynamic changes of workflows without losing control. *Journal of Intelligent Information Systems, 10,* 93–129. Springer. doi:10.1023/A:1008604709862.

Russell, N., ter Hofstede, A. H. M., & Mulyar, N. (2006). Workflow control flow patterns: A revised view. *Technical Report BPM-06-22.* BPM Centre.

Russell, N., van der Aalst, W. M. P., & ter Hofstede, A. H. M. (2006). Exception handling patterns in process-aware information systems. *Proceedings of the CAiSE, 06,* 288–302.

Siewe, F., Cau, A., & Zedan, H. (2003). A compositional framework for access control policies enforcement. In FMSE '03 (pp. 32-42). ACM.

Tan, C., & Goh, A. (1999). Implementing ECA rules in an active database. *Knowledge-Based Systems, 12*(4), 137–144. doi:10.1016/S0950-7051(99)00028-3.

Turner, K. J., Reiff-Marganiec, S., Blair, L., Pang, J., Gray, T., Perry, P., & Ireland, J. (2006). Policy support for call control. *Computer Standards & Interfaces*, *28*(6), 635–649. doi:10.1016/j.csi.2005.05.004.

Van der Aalst, W. M. P., & ter Hofstede, A. H. M. (2005). Yawl: Yet another workflow language. *Information Systems*, *30*(4), 245–275. doi:10.1016/j.is.2004.02.002.

Weikum, G., & Schek, H.-J. (1992). *Concepts and applications of multilevel transactions and open nested transactions* (pp. 515–553). Morgan Kaufmann Publishers.

White, S. A. (2004). Business process modeling notation. Object Management Group (OMG) and Business Process Management Initiative. Van der Aalst, W.M.P., Barros, A.P., ter Hofstede, A.H.M., & Kiepuszewski, B. (2000). Advanced workflow patterns. In Proceedings of Cooperative IS 2000 (pp. 18-29). Springer.

Widom, J., & Ceri, S. (1996). *Active database systems: Triggers and rules for advanced database processing*. Morgan Kaufmann.

Wieringa, R. (2003). *Design methods for reactive systems: Yourdon, statemate, and the UML*. Morgan Kaufmann.

Yan, S., Li, Y., Deng, S., & Wu, Z. (2005). A transaction management framework for service-based workflow. In *Proceedings of the International Conference on Next Generation Web Services Practices* (pp. 377-381).

Zhang, A., Nodine, M., Bhargava, B., & Bukhres, O. (1994). Ensuring relaxed atomicity for flexible transactions in multi-database systems. In *Proceedings of the ACM SIGMOD* (pp. 67–78).

Zhang, X., Parisi-Presicce, F., Sandhu, R., & Park, J. (2005). Formal model and policy specification of usage control. *ACM Transactions on Information and System Security*, *8*(4), 351–387. doi:10.1145/1108906.1108908.

KEY TERMS AND DEFINITIONS

Compensation: The undoing of the primary effects of having completed an activity.

Failure: The incapability of successfully completing an activity or workflow – failure can be partial with the possibility to recover or total with the outcome that the process overall fails.

Long Running Transaction: A transaction that spans a long period of time that can run into days, weeks, months, or years.

Management Rules: Rules describing the actions to be undertaken to manage failure and compensation under certain occurring events and conditions.

Task: An activity to be undertaken to achieve a business goal.

Vitality of Tasks: The contribution of the success of a task to the overall outcome of the business process.

Workflow: An artifact describing a process in terms of the activities to be undertaken and their relationships.

Workflow Pattern: A structure of activities and the flow between them that represents a specific business need.

ENDNOTES

[1] The immediate superior of node is its enclosing path and the immediate superior of a path is its enclosing scope (section 5).

Chapter 7
Access Control in Service Compositions:
Challenges and Solution Architecture

Aurélien Faravelon
Laboratoire d'Informatique de Grenoble, France

Stéphanie Chollet
Laboratoire de Conception et d'Intégration des Systèmes, France

ABSTRACT

Pervasive applications are entering the mainstream, but at the present time, exhibit significant security weaknesses. Service-driven architectural approaches facilitate the development of pervasive applications, however, security with respect to access control and data privacy of pervasive applications are currently not managed comprehensively from design time through run time. This chapter presents a use case emphasizing the security challenges for pervasive applications and proposes a novel, generative architectural approach, to include security in pervasive applications at design time. This is a model-driven approach based on models pertaining to access control management that respect the temporal constraints relating to pervasive applications. The approach is implemented with a design and runtime environment and the results of the validation applied to the pervasive use case are presented.

INTRODUCTION

Healthcare costs are skyrocketing as the world's population ages, due to these aging members requiring on average more frequent hospitalization. A solution to mitigate medical costs is to enable these senior citizens to receive medical care while remaining in their homes, by adapting houses to their needs. This includes regular monitoring and interaction with medical staff and family. *Pervasive computing*, which is integrating computational artifacts into the fabric of our daily lives, is a promising paradigm to enable a safe, and well-connected medical experience in homes. Technologies to perpetuate this kind of home environment already exist, including residential high-speed Internet connections and a wide range of home sensors for health monitoring. Coordinat-

DOI: 10.4018/978-1-4666-4193-8.ch007

ing communication between these various available computing units and technologies therefore becomes crucial. Furthermore, for privacy and security reasons, the access to these individual units must be controlled from the perspective of the entire system, to prevent situations in which a unit causes data leakage or other harm.

The software engineering community strives to produce new answers to these kinds of relevant challenges. Service Oriented Computing (SOC) (Papazoglou, 2003) is one of the answers. SOC relies on the notion of service that can manifest as anything from software to infrastructure. A service provides a set of well-defined characteristics and possesses a description that expresses both its functional and non-functional properties. Web Services are the best known services, but several other implementations exist, including UPnP, DPWS, and OSGi, all of which are especially interesting because they allow for exposing devices as services.

Services are assembled using Service-driven approaches based on Service Oriented Architecture (SOA). SOA provides mechanisms to specify, publish, discover and compose services. Service compositions are defined according to the control, which can be internal or external to the service. When the control is internal to the service, services interact directly. When the control is external, services are composed according to a directed graph that represents a process. Processes are traditionally specified through languages such as WS-BPEL (Web Service Business Process Execution Language) and then interpreted by an execution engine.

Two features of Service-driven architectural approaches are of particular interest. First, service consumers do not have to deal with the heterogeneity of services. Composition's elements are independent. Services can thus evolve independently. This is especially important when an application must rely on loosely coupled elements that were not meant to work together. Services may be substituted for one another as long as they implement the functional interface defined by the service provider. Next, since services are capable of late-binding, service-driven approaches address the dynamism of services.

However, Service-driven architectural approaches still suffer from some major hurdles. Dynamic service compositions are complex, especially when they have to enforce an access control policy defined at an application-wide level. Two main difficulties remain:

1. Services are highly heterogeneous as there are multiple technologies and varied implementations of them, as indicated earlier. As a consequence, developing dynamic service compositions require cross-technology skills that are rare.
2. Actual services are not necessarily known at design time of the application. Thus, the access control capabilities of the services cannot be trusted. Services may or may not offer access control capabilities and when they do so, they may not enforce the right access control features.

In this chapter, we will focus on the following pervasive application scenario:

- The house monitors the medical condition of its inhabitants.
- On a regular basis, the house generates reports:
  - Medical reports are available to physicians
  - Nurses can access reports necessary to perform their daily visits
  - Family members can read summarized reports to make sure that their relatives are OK.
- At any time, if the inhabitants are in danger, the house generates alerts and sends them to:
  - The physicians
  - The family members

- Physicians or family members can react to an alert by calling the house or remotely interacting with its parts, such as lights, in order to communicate with the occupants who are in danger.

Enabling pervasive communication can potentially jeopardize privacy since sensitive data is collected and transmitted outside the house. In the scope of this chapter, we assume that mechanisms exist to prevent messages from being intercepted by malevolent users. However, allowing remote interactions with devices in the house, such as windows, lights, sensors, or the heating system, may endanger the occupant's physical security. In the course of this chapter, we will configure the above scenario in order to safeguard the occupant's security and privacy.

Access control mechanisms can help protect both privacy and security, by restricting the access to actions and data. Sharing a coherent access control policy with the data owners (occupants of the house) may foster the acceptance and the reliability of the pervasive application. However, we identify challenges to access control design and enforcement in pervasive applications. Firstly, non-technical people (occupants of the house) may need to customize the access control policy. Thus, access control must be easy to understand and customize. Secondly, access control policies have to be fine-grained and contextual, such that the privileges and contextual information of users can be managed at runtime. Lastly, the pervasive application runs in a highly heterogeneous and dynamic environment which will require the adaptation of the access control policies to a wide range of platforms at runtime.

This chapter outlines the challenges in access control enforcement in service compositions, especially related to pervasive applications. As a possible answer to these challenges, a model-driven approach is presented for access control in service compositions. The chapter is organized as follows. First, some background information

on challenges in security and access control is presented. Then, a use case is introduced for application integration in the pervasive computing environment. From this use case, the current challenges pertaining to access control in service compositions are extracted. Then, the state of the works on this topic is presented. Finally, the architectural proposition is discussed. Eventually, future research directions are explored.

BACKGROUND

In this section, we establish the main challenges in access control enforcement. We emphasize the impact of the heterogeneity and the dynamism of services on the definition and enforcement of access control policies. We first provide a brief introduction to the notions of security and access control. We then define the notion of service and the security threats in service-driven computing. Finally, we emphasize the remaining challenges in the area of access control.

Security-Related Threats in a Service-Driven Environment

Services are computational elements that perform well-defined functions. They are self-describing because they possess a machine-readable description, which enables their consumption and composition. The notion of a service is platform-independent (Papazoglou, 2003; Sward et al., 2011). Services are the basic elements of a service-driven environment that aims to build applications by composing loosely coupled services. To do so, the service-driven architectural approach relies on three entities and the interactions among them:

- The *service provider* publishes its services in the *service registry*.
- The *service consumer* (client) discovers the services of interest by searching the service registry.

- The consumer invokes the services it has selected and binds itself to the service provider.

Figure 1 illustrates the service provider, the service registry, the client and their interactions.

Since the interaction among the three entities stated above is based on client-server principles, the service-driven methodology becomes exposed to security threats. We classify these threats into two sets. The first set encompasses the threats caused by a malevolent intruder. The intruder may spy into the network, leading to data leakage. The leakage may also derive from identity theft where the intruder may pretend to be an authorized user. The second set concerns domain-specific threats. For instance, when services are context-sensitive, i.e., when they need contextual information to perform their function or determine if a user can invoke them, contextual data may be inferred (Hengartner et al., 2006) from their use.

On the whole, all these threats endanger three properties (Jajodia et al., 2007):

- Data confidentiality, which guarantees that only authorized entities can access data.
- Data integrity, which ensures that only authorized software agents of users can modify data.

- Availability, which safeguards the access to a system and its resources.

Preserving these properties is necessary to build a reliable service composition. There is a wide range of security techniques that focus on one or more of these properties. Access control is one of them.

Notion of Access Control

Several security techniques focus on protecting one or more of the above stated properties. For instance, authentication, either with a login and a password or with a digital signature; and encryption, which forbids reading a set of data if an agent does not possess the right tools to decipher it; protect data confidentiality. Access control protects data confidentiality and data integrity by identifying forbidden data modifications. Access control also protects an application against denial of service by ensuring that only permissible actions are performed. This is accomplished by intercepting the access queries to an application to determine if they are permissible, *i.e.,* if they belong to an authorized agent (Samarati, 2000). Once the access control decision is made, it must be enforced.

Figure 1. Service-oriented computing

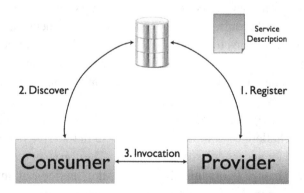

Access control definition and execution relies on three elements:

1. Access control models provide a vocabulary and a grammar to express access control policies. Most models allow formal verifications to prove that they respect access control properties.
2. Access control policies are composed of rules written according to a specific model. Policies are usually specific to an application.
3. Access control enforcement is performed by dedicated mechanisms.

Access control models are of great significance. Their expressiveness, *i.e.,* the concepts they rely on and their relations, constrains what access control designers can protect and how they can do so. Most models accommodate the same basic entities. Specifically, we identify four basic access control entities:

1. Objects are passive entities. They are the resources available in an application. Medical record, lights, or bells, for instance, are objects.
2. Subjects are active entities such as physicians or nurses. They request access to objects.
3. Actions are the access modes of the subjects to an application's objects. The primitives "write" and "read" are actions.
4. Constraints enable specification of the access criteria for an object.

Access control models differ by the range of constraints they accommodate and by the categorization of entities they offer. For instance, (Sandhu et al., 1996) proposes the Role-based Access Control Model (*RBAC*), in which the authors categorize users according to their roles, which are usually defined as organizational positions. Permissions are granted to these roles and not directly to users. As a result, the access control policy is expected to be more stable because or-ganizational roles are less likely to change than individual users. A wide range of purpose-specific access control models also exist (Barker, 2009). They largely serve to introduce new constraints, such as locational and temporal ones, as in Chae et al. (2006) and Damiani et al. (2007). They also provide specific ways to categorize users or objects as in Barker et al. (2008). However, the diversity of access control models leads to a wide range of access control mechanisms which does not work together.

The Attribute-based Access Control model (*ABAC*) is another interesting way to model access control. It provides a flexible framework that has proven to accommodate most specific access control models, like the RBAC model and Temporal Access Control model (Zhu et al., 2012). ABAC does not possess a contextual model, even though some authors have tried to formalize one (Yuan et al., 2005). The grammar of the eXtensible Access Control Markup Language (XACML) (OASIS, 2003), which is the implementation of ABAC by the Organization for the Advancement of Structured Information Standards (OASIS), is currently considered as the reference model for ABAC. Figure 2 summarizes the ABAC model entities.

As shown in Figure 2, an ABAC policy is composed of rules which constrain the values of a set of attributes. A rule is satisfied if and only if, all the constraints it is composed of are satisfied too. As such, ABAC's policies can be very fine-grained. Since anything can be an attribute, ABAC can be used to enforce RBAC access control, for instance. In this case, a subject's role is seen as an attribute. ABAC is also well-adapted to pervasive applications as it relies on three attribute sources, namely subjects, resources, and the application's environment.

When a subject tries to access a resource or, more generally, tries to perform an action, they trigger rules. The Policy Decision Point (PDP) evaluates these rules and transmits the decision to the Policy Enforcement Point (PEP) which applies the access control decisions. Figure 3 shows

Figure 2. The attribute-based access control model

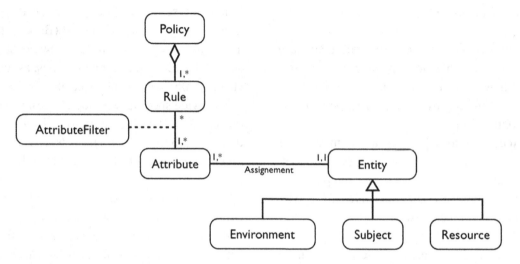

the PEP, the PDP, and the information sources necessary to enforce ABAC and their relations.

Access control is a well-mastered technique. Standards, such as XACML, offer flexible and efficient frameworks. The use of ABAC has been proposed in the framework of SOC (Yuan et al.,

2005) and there is a specific profile of XACML for Web Services (Abi Haidar et al., 2006). However, despite the apparent linkages between access control and SOC, access control is still not widespread in service compositions.

Figure 3. Architecture necessary to enforce attribute-based access control

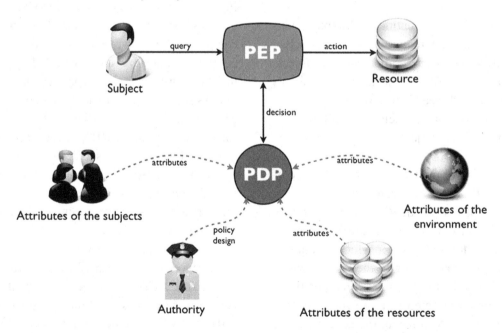

Challenges in Access Control for Service Compositions

There is a rich literature on access control in service compositions. However, most works focus on a specific service implementation, usually Web Services. Web Services are software pieces which realize a specific functionality (Srivatsa et al., 2007; Carminati et al., 2006). They are described with files written in the Web Service Description Language (WSDL) and communicate with the Simple Object Access Protocol (SOAP). Although Web Services do not natively accommodate security related features like access control, much work has been done to extend their descriptions to allow the specification of security properties.

The so called "WS-*" specifications[1] enable extending WSDL to improve its expressiveness. For instance, the WS-Policy[2] permits expressing a Web Service's restrictions in terms of security or quality of services. In terms of access control, WS-Policy is a subset of *XACML*, which enables expression of access control policies. WS-SecureConversation[3] allows the establishment of shared security contexts between participants. All of these specifications can be easily applied to devices exposed as services, according to the Device Profile for Web Services (DPWS)[4]. Indeed, DPWS respects the service-oriented architecture necessary to Web Services; however, DPWS is not used much in the pervasive computing domain.

Other service technologies such as the Universal Plug and Play (*UPnP*) are more widespread but rely on service concepts different from the ones that Web Services are based on. As a consequence, they necessitate technology-specific mechanisms to model and enforce access control. Furthermore, UPnP is a good example of a technology which cannot enforce security. UPnP does not provide authentication mechanisms and, as such, is mostly used in closed, limited environments, such as domestic networks. The heterogeneity of services and security capabilities make enforcement of access control very challenging in pervasive applications.

Access control is a well-mastered technique for specific technologies and domains (Hung et al., 2007), but access control models and enforcement mechanisms must be made technology-agnostic.

The second challenge is dynamism. Services are dynamic when they join and leave the network during runtime. Actual service compositions are usually ad hoc; developers cannot predict which services will be available at execution time, and moreover, the actual services must be chosen at runtime. Developers must therefore design a composition which is generic enough to be adapted at runtime with the available services. Service selection is often seen as a way to build an adaptive composition, thanks to late binding. The necessary services are only selected at runtime among actual services. Service selection is also seen as a way to enforce access control. For instance, Carminati et al. (2006), uses extended service descriptions to select services according to their access control capabilities. However, this method is vulnerable to the heterogeneity of services. The authors focus on Web services and extend WSDL with security properties. As a result, their work may not be applicable to other types of services.

Service selection only addresses part of access control enforcement. Indeed, some access control constraints, such as separation of duty, are not enforced at the level of a service. They are defined and must be enforced at the level of the entire composition. As a result, access control enforcement mechanisms must exist at the level of the composition, to manage the pieces of information necessary to process access control.

Consequently, the development of service compositions is of high technical complexity. Service compositions necessitate a strong expertise in several service technologies, interface description languages, and service communication protocols. Most of the time, services are not designed to work together. As a result, developers must write mediation code to allow the interaction between services with different data models. When access control is added to such service compositions, the developer must have a strong expertise in access control design and enforcement, since there are no established standards to express access control in service compositions, and therefore, implementations are technology-dependent. Identifying the links between access control and service composition is still a stringent process. Thus, access control enforcement is still often implemented as late code patches (Basin et al., 2006), which forbids having a comprehensive view of access control to ensure its efficiency.

Model-Driven Security

However separated they remain, access control and service compositions are gathered around the notion of the model. Indeed, access control policies rely on access control models and service compositions are often represented as models themselves. The Web Service Business Process Execution Language (WS-BPEL)[5], for instance, represents a service composition as a process, *i.e.,* a set of temporally ordered activities realized by services.

More generally, modeling is a common way to select a subset of an application's features and focus on them. It is also an efficient way to abstract away technical details and identify links between the different aspects of an application. Since models can be integrated into a generative approach, thanks to model-driven engineering, an application can be generated from its models. As models which present different views on an application can be related, an application can be generated from multiple related points of view.

In the field of service compositions, Orriëns et al. (2003) show that model-driven engineering is well-suited for service compositions. Compositions can be modeled without knowing which services will be actually available at runtime. Service selection allows choosing the suitable services at runtime.

In the field of security, *Model-driven Security* (MDS) is an implementation of model-driven engineering for secured applications (Basin et al., 2006). Specifically, the authors focus on relating RBAC access control policies to UML diagrams, such as class diagrams or sequence diagrams. The authors generate Enterprise Java Beans from these models. In Chollet et al. (2008), the authors prove that MDS is of interest in ensuring security of transfer in a service composition. In Wolter et al. (2007) and Rodríguez et al. (2007), the authors extend process models with authorization constraints and generate the related XACML code.

In brief, MDS is driven by two principles as shown in Figure 4.

1. **Abstraction:** Modeling is about selecting a specific view of an application. For instance, analysts do not need technical details as they mostly want to focus on what an application performs, not how it does so.
2. **Separation of Concerns:** Each point of view on an application is usually handled by a specific expert. For instance, the access control rules are relevant to a security expert. Separating concerns means providing tools to independently model an application from different points of view. Separation of concerns is often achieved by defining independent grammars and vocabularies for each viewpoint. These grammars and vocabularies are called "*metamodels*" (OMG, 2002).

Figure 4. Principles of model-driven security

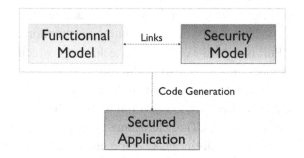

Metamodels are then related in order to enable relating a set of viewpoints. Eventually, model-to-code transformations can be used to generate an executable application.

Consequently, MDS is a promising solution to address the production of compositions of heterogeneous and dynamic services secured with access control. It gathers several experts around the application while providing them with the language they usually utilize. Furthermore, MDS shields the designers from technical complexity and builds generic specifications which can be easily reused and maintained.

However, MDS still needs to be adapted to the demands of access control in SOC.

This raises a couple of questions:

- Which metamodels are suitable for access control and service compositions and how do they relate to each other?
- Which transformations are required to conduct flow from the design to the execution level?

A MODEL-DRIVEN APPROACH TO ACCESS CONTROL IN HETEROGENEOUS SERVICE COMPOSITIONS

Use Case

As an illustrative example of application integration in the pervasive application domain, let us consider a smart home adapted to the needs of senior citizens or people requiring constant medical monitoring and attention. This home relies on a set of distributed computing services that belongs to several providers. As a result, these services must be integrated to provide an efficient pervasive environment.

The house relies on sensors, such as scales or cameras that record medical condition and move-

ments and analyze environmental parameters, such as temperature. All the devices are exposed as *UPnP* (UPnP Forum, 2008) or *DPWS* (Jammes et al., 2005; Zeeb et al., 2007) services. All the necessary software is exposed as Web Services. The application that runs the smart home consists of a composition of the available services, all of which are exposed on the Internet.

From the captured data, the application generates medical reports that contain detailed medical data and are transmitted to physicians. Nurses can access a subset of the information contained in medical records to provide daily care. The application also generates summarized reports that are available to family members. In case of danger, the application generates alerts that can be transmitted to physicians or family members.

As visible from the use case, access control is an organizational feature. The access rights of the physicians and the nurses derive from their position in the organization. They are also constrained by the home occupant's preferences. As a result, the consistency and the completeness of an access control policy is difficult to achieve. Such properties can only be guaranteed by capturing access control at the application level. In a service-driven methodology, applications are realized as service compositions. Access control must thus be captured at the level of a composition.

Architectural Approach

We propose a model-driven approach to the production of pervasive applications realized as service compositions secured by access control.

As shown in Figure 5, our approach is divided into two phases:

1. **At Design Time:** Designers capture the different aspects of the application through different views. To do so, we provide Domain Specific Modeling Languages (DSML) for two major views: service composition and pervasive access control. We also provide

Figure 5. Generative approach

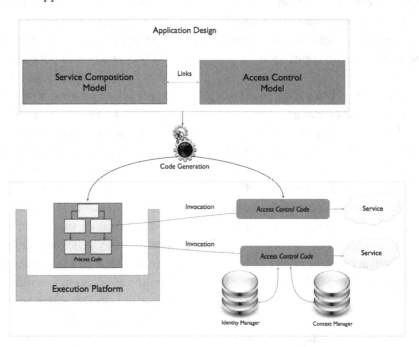

means to relate these views to foster communication between experts and stakeholders.

2. **At Runtime:** Automatic model-to-text transformations generate the appropriate code to secure services according to access control requirements and to the technology of the discovered services. We generate an executable service composition realized as a secured service orchestration. To do so, we add a dedicated repository to manage the pieces of information necessary to process and enforce access control.

In contrast with existing works on model-driven security, we take into account the specificities of service oriented architectures. In contrast with approaches which focus on generating access control of service composition code, we generate a complete composition from multiple points of view and provide a way to combine them. Against the wide-spread realization of access control as code patches, we take access control into account right

from design time. In contrast with technologies such as BPEL, we rely on abstract specifications which are made concrete at execution time only. As a result, we build reusable abstract compositions which are well adapted to a pervasive setting. Technology-dependent details are handled by proxies that are generated at runtime and that play the role of access control decision and enforcement points.

In contrast with approaches focused on domain-specific access control models, we rely on an access control model similar to the attribute-based access control model which is flexible enough to be adapted to a wide variety of scenarios. For instance, ABAC has applications in privacy management; the Enterprise Privacy Authorization Language (EPAL)[6] is a subset of XACML which can be used to model a company's privacy policy.

In contrast with works on pure ABAC, we provide primitives to guide access control. They are evaluated as attributes. This approach allows us to provide an intuitive language to model organizational access control.

Our solution to the orchestration of heterogeneous and dynamic services is implemented as a complete environment to model and execute such compositions and their access control policies. The execution environment provides a comprehensive way to execute the composition and enforce access control, *i.e.*, manage contextual information and notify users of what they have to do. In contrast with mainstream orchestrator, our tool allows security and business experts to work together. We now present our solution in detail by introducing our design and execution phases. We then delineate the implementation in our tool along with the validation of our work on the medical use case.

Design Phase

In the design phase, we extend the service composition with access control features. To do so, we compose a service composition metamodel and an access control metamodel.

Service Composition Metamodel

Our approach regarding service composition builds on the Abstract Process Engine Language (*APEL*) (Dami et al., 1998). As visible on the left-hand side of Figure 6, APEL is a high level process definition language. We chose APEL because it natively supports any type of service whereas other process languages, such as WS-BPEL, are dedicated to a specific technology. It contains the minimal set of concepts sufficient to specify a process:

- An Activity is a step in the process that results in the performance of a work, realized by a human or a computer. Activities can be made of sub-activities; they are then said to be composite. An activity has *Ports* representing communication interfaces. An Activity must be realized by a *User*.
- A Product is an abstract object that flows between activities, such as data. *Dataflows*

connect output ports to input ports, specifying which product variables are being transferred between activities.
- An Abstract Service can be attached to an activity. It represents a type of service to be called in order to achieve the activity.

Specifically, an Abstract Service is a service specification retaining high level information and ignoring as many implementation details as possible. Our model defines an abstract service in the following terms:

- A Signature defining the identifying name of the service, with its inputs and outputs in terms of products.
- Possibly, technology-specific information such as WSDL extracts for Web Services or SCPD (Service Control Protocol Description) extracts for UPnP services. Extracts only contain implementation independent information. For instance, no address is provided as is in a complete WSDL description.

Providing technology-specific information means that the service technology can be chosen beforehand by designers, which is frequently the case. This information enables generation of better, leaner code.

Access Control Metamodel

Most mainstream *access control metamodels* are built around the same core structure but their reuse is difficult because they are specific to an application domain. Most of them do not address access control for pervasive applications or processes. The ABAC model is a flexible metamodel, but it does not provide the primitives necessary to intuitively model access control policies. As visible on the right-hand side of Figure 6, we extend ABAC with concepts necessary to pervasive processes and provide mainstream primitives to

Figure 6. Service composition and access control metamodels

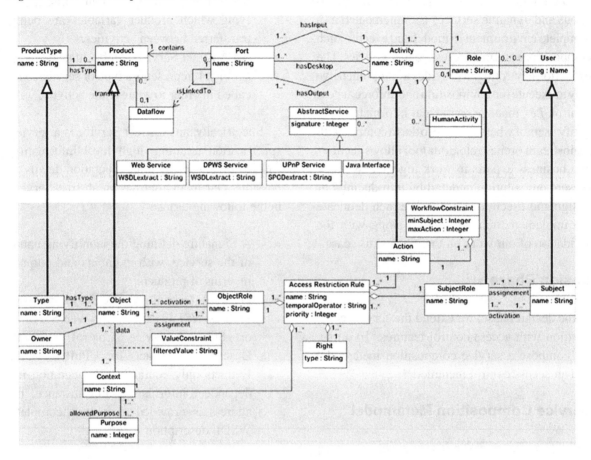

model access control. They are all evaluated as attributes. Specifically:

- A Subject is a user or a software agent that acts on the application. Subjects are categorized in *SubjectRoles* according to their position in an organization.
- An Object is any entity a Subject can affect. Objects can be categorized according to their functionalities such as *ObjectRoles*.
- An Action is an access mode of an Object.
- A Right is the modality of a Subject's relation to an Action. Rights are divided into permissions, obligations and prohibitions; they apply to SubjectRoles and ObjectRoles.

Several Access Control Rules may apply to the same set of Actions, ObjectRoles, and SubjectRoles. Access Control Rules are conditioned by:

- Context is a situation defined by a constraint over the values of a set of data. The Context entity captures the specificity of pervasive access control. An emergency situation – for instance, the home occupant falls – is a context.
- The satisfaction of workflow security patterns. We accommodate two of them, separation and binding of duties. Both of them restrict the number of *Subjects* that can intervene in a group of Actions, and the number of Actions each Subject can

perform. We gather these constraints under the name *Workflow Constraints*, which is the maximum number of Actions a set of Subjects can perform within a particular group of Actions.

When several Access Control Rules apply to the same set of Actions, ObjectRoles, and SubjectRoles, all of these rules cannot share the same conditions.

Linking Service Composition and Access Control Views

When designing an application from multiple points of view, two problems must be addressed (Vallecillo, 2010). First, the metamodels must be related in order to build complete specifications. Then, views must be synchronized *i.e.,* a mechanism must be provided to preserve coherency between views at execution. Figure 6 displays the relationships between the service composition and the access control metamodels.

Two points are of foremost interest: the classes from each metamodel to relate and the cardinalities of these relations. In the access control view, we define an Action as an access mode to an Object. In the process view, we define an Activity as an operation on a Product. In order to compose the two views, we express that an Action is a specific type of Activity constrained by access control rules. The Action class thus inherits from Activity. The same stands for Objects in the process views that are specific Products to which access is controlled.

Views are designed in conformity with their metamodel. Views are then composed according to the inheritance defined between the metamodels; each activity in the process specification is refined into several possible actions constrained with access control rules defined in the access control view.

Execution Phase

At runtime, available services cannot be trusted because they may not enforce access control. We secure a heterogeneous and dynamic composition in two steps:

- Before execution, orchestration and access control program code is generated from each view's specifications. To synchronize the view, insertion points of access control code in the orchestration are identified.
- At execution time, the access control code is inserted between the orchestrator and the available services.

Figure 7 displays the execution of a *pervasive orchestration* secured by access control. When a new service is discovered by the execution machine, a secured proxy is generated and registered in the registry. Thus, the registry only contains secured web services and the orchestrator cannot directly access non-secured services. Consequently, the composition cannot be executed without access control enforcement.

Access control enforcement relies on three components: the *Decision Point* evaluates the access control policy for a user in a given context; the *Context Manager* stores the path to contextual information sources such as users' smartphones or the composition's log file; and the *Identity Manager* stores the user roles and identities.

When a secured proxy is invoked, it calls the access control Decision Point. The proxy provides the Decision Point with the current user's name and the current Activity's name. The Decision Point retrieves the user's privileges from the Identity Manager and the necessary contextual information from the Context Manager. It then checks the access control policy according to the retrieved information and provides the secured proxy with a decision. If the user is allowed to access the current activity, the secured proxy invokes the

Figure 7. Execution architecture of a secured composition

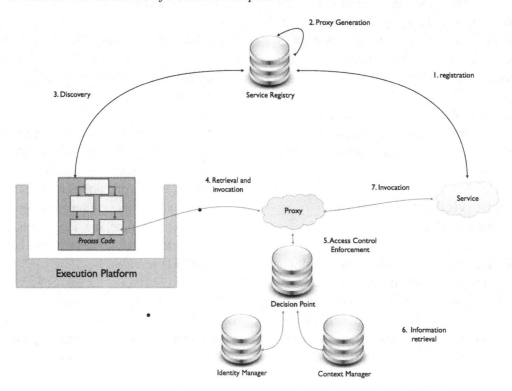

available service it protects. Otherwise, it rejects the invocation. Each communication between the proxy and the other components is secured with authentication.

Generating an Executable Access Control Policy

The Decision Point checks an executable access control policy derived from a process specification and its associated access control requirements. We generate the access control rules that apply to each Action and its temporal ordering from the designer's specifications. We gather all this information into an executable access control policy.

We see a composition secured by access control as temporally ordered flow of actions, i.e. of access rules. As we said earlier, we base our work on attribute-based access control. As such, we see a rule as a set of attributes with allowed values. As a result, we see an action as a set of

pairs of attributes and values. We allow the use of two connectors between constraints on attributes, namely "and" and "or." We forbid the use of negation in the head of the rules in order to make sure that our language is fully computable (Gottlob et al., 2000).

We model the temporal ordering of access control with Allen's algebra, which provides seven temporal operators to link events, as presented in Figure 8. Our events are the actions represented as a set of attributes. Actions can have duration which is represented as intervals.

We chose Allen's algebra against other formal temporal notations such as temporal logic, because it maps intuitively to the order and the temporal relations of a composition's activities. As a result, the grammar of our access control policies is given by the following regular expression:

$$((A,V)+ \; Oland|or \; (A,V)+)+$$

Figure 8. Allen's algebra

Operator	Symbol	Relations on Endpoints	Pictorial Meaning
x before y y after x	< >	(x+<y-)	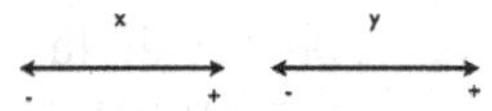
x equals y y equals x	= =	(x-=y-)^ (x+=y+)	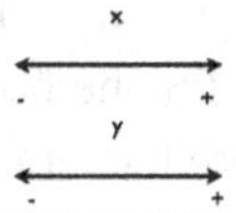
x meets y y meets x	m m	(x+=y-)	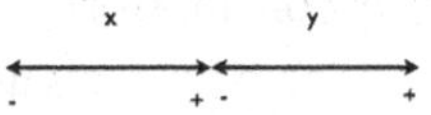
x overlaps y y overlaped by x	o oi	(x-<y-)^(y-<x+)^(x+<y+)	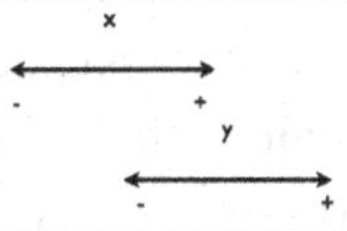
x during y y includes x	d di	(y-<x-)^(x+<y+)	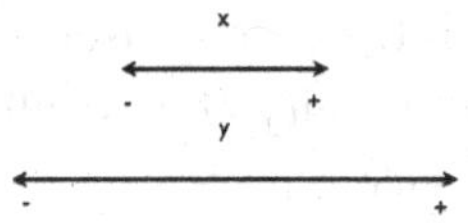
x starts y y started by x	s si	(y-=x-)^(x+<y+)	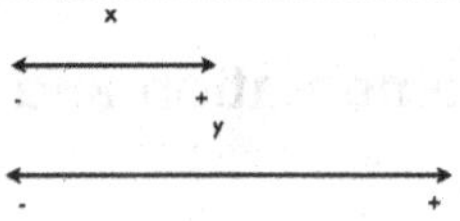
x finishes y y finished by x	f fi	(y-<x-)^(x+=y+)	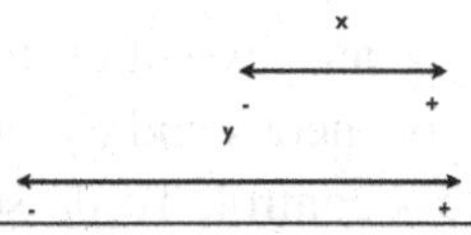

where A is an attribute and V the value it can take. O is a temporal operator.

One or several Workflow Constraints P, *i.e.,* Separation of Duties and Binding of Duties can be added to the composition. Such a constraint is represented by the following boolean constraint where MaxS is the maximum number of Subjects allowed to perform activities and MinA is the minimum number of Activities: P → MaxS and MinA.

Identifying Insertion Points and Enforcing Access Control at Execution

At execution, each Activity is realized by a service. Each available service is secured as it registers to the service registry by a proxy. The proxy is built at runtime according to the target service through code generation from a template. Each template is parameterized by a set of variables such as the endpoint to call or the service's implementation. Each variable is set with values from the actual service to protect. We rely on Java Emitter Templates (JET)[7] to perform code generation.

The proxy plays the role of a policy enforcement point. In order to generate it, for each method of the service to protect, we generate a secured method for the proxy. We insert a call to the policy decision point and the proxy then handles the obtained decision. If the call to the method is allowed, the proxy calls the raw service's method.

We generate a WSDL description for the proxy and expose it as a Web Service, thus rendering it transparent for the composition. As a result, we reduce the orchestration of heterogeneous services to the orchestration of a set of web services. Each proxy is responsible for dealing with the dynamism of the service it protects and for dealing with the technological details of its implementation. The proxy acts as an access control enforcement point. To do so, Figure 7 shows that the proxy intercepts the invocation and asks the Decision Point to check if the current user is allowed to access the current activity. If and only if, the proxy invokes the service it protects.

Implementation and Results

We have implemented our work as a complete modeling and execution tool for compositions of heterogeneous and dynamic services secured by access control. To do so, we have extended FOCAS, an orchestrator which executes APEL compositions. The resultant tool is composed of two parts:

- The Modeler permits composition and access control designers to specify the composition and its associated access control policy.
- The Composition Execution Engine is composed of the APEL orchestrator extended with an access control decision point and dedicated repositories to manage the pieces of information necessary to process access control.

We present in this section each part of our tool and its application to our use case.

A Medical Application Realized as a Secured Process

Figure 9 displays a subset of the activities necessary to realize the medical application as a use case. The figure also shows summarized access control rules associated with each activity. For instance, a medical alert may only be managed by a physician who is not opted out by the patient.

In the rest of this section, we will focus on this access control rule to which we add contextual constraints. For example, in order to manage a medical alert, a physician must be available, i.e., the physician must be on duty and not already managing an emergency or tied up in a meeting.

Modeling Environment

As shown in Figure 9, our modeling environment represents a composition as a temporally ordered flow of activities. We chose to provide a dedicated modeling environment to ease the specification process in two ways. First, we provide a user-friendly graphical tool. Also, since the modeling environment is based on our metamodels and links, all the obtained specifications are *de facto* in conforming to the metamodels and their links. Each activity possesses properties tab which can be edited. We have added a property tab dedicated to access control. In this tab, the access control designer can edit the access control rules applicable to each activity.

Access control is notoriously hard to express. To ease this difficulty, we provide the access control designer with a set of keywords, *i.e.,* the concepts from our access control metamodels. The translation from this high-level language to an executable policy is automatic in order to free the access control designer from technical complexities. The access control designer can access the attributes of these concepts using the name of the concept followed by a dot and the name of the attribute. We also allow access control designers to define their own primitives, such as the definitions of contexts, so that they can reuse them. In

Figure 9. Example scenario realized as a process and its access control

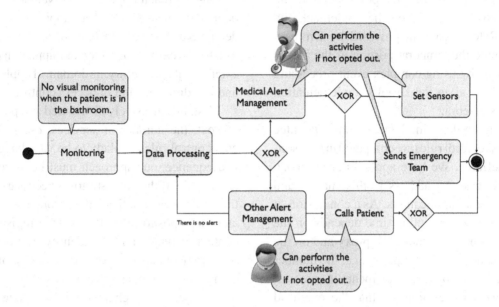

order to ease the access control designer's work, we also infer the temporal operators which control the flow of access control rules from the flow of activities in the service composition. All keywords of this high level language are used according to the grammar we have already described.

As a result, access control designers can specify complex policies while using an intuitive language.

For readability sake we authorize the following notations:

- Attributes can be prefixed with the name of their source with the words "actor," "resource," or "environment."
- The names of actions can be followed by the sign "=" in order to define the set of attributes which define them. The same stands for contexts.

For instance, the obtained policy for the three activities "Medical Care Management', "Other Alerts Managements" and "Calls the patients" reads:

Medical Care Management = (subject. role,Physician) and (subject.optedOut,false) and (subject.context,available) and (environment. context,emergency)

Other Alert Management = (subject.role,Family Member) and (subject.optedOut,false) and (subject.context,available) and (environment. context,emergency)

Calls Patient = (subject.role,Physician) or (subject.role,Family Member) and (subject. optedOut,false) and (subject.context,available) and (environment.context,emergency)

Medical Alert Management OR (Other Alert Management THEN Calls Patient)

Execution Environment

The execution environment is responsible for transforming the abstract specifications into concrete ones and running the modeled composition. We benefit from the APEL execution engine and run our process as an APEL composition. In terms of access control, computing temporal operators can be very costly. We rely on the implementation of the "Rete" algorithm provided by Drools[81]. We compute the temporal portion of the access control rule by using complex event processing methodology as in the Drool's implementation of Allen's algebra.

Relying on these implementations guarantee that access control rules are computed in a reasonable timeframe. We have applied our approach to the use case we address in this chapter and to several other applications. As a conclusion, it appears that the execution time depends on the time necessary to generate the proxy and on the size of the access control policy, *i.e.* the number of connectors and unitary elements it contains. So far, we have established that the overhead entailed by the use of our method is reasonable; it represents less than 10% of the execution time of the secured composition.

In summary:

- Design effort is focused on applications, not on implementation details. The abstraction level used to describe the secured application hides the complexity of the underlying technologies.
- Reuse of designs is enabled. The models can be independently reused. We have tested our approach with two service composition models (APEL and BPMN) and with many configurations of devices used in pervasive applications.

DISCUSSION AND FUTURE RESEARCH DIRECTIONS

We have proven the feasibility of our approach through its implementation. In this section, we discuss the extension points that we envision and future research directions in the field of service composition security.

Our approach appears to be valuable to reconcile technical views of an application, which demands a strong expertise in the area. We identified three reasons for which our approach can be extended: its scalability, its domain of application, and its administration of access control.

First, in a massively distributed and pervasive context, the number of services, users and access control rules is likely to be very large. As a consequence, our approach must be as scalable as possible. If the orchestrator is necessarily centralized, we can duplicate the enforcement points and the repositories – the service registry, the context manager, and the identity manager – in order to avoid a denial of service if one of these components happens to be overused.

Second, in this chapter, we have focused on extending APEL with access control features. However, in order to prove the independence of our approach from a specific process language or engine, we have also established links between access control and the Business Process Modeling Language (BPEL). We have successfully used our proxy generation scheme and repositories to build a composition of heterogeneous and dynamic services. We have based our testing on the Java Business Process Management engine, which runs processes expressed in BPMN. As a consequence, we believe our approach to be platform-independent.

Third, we have focused here on the specification of access control policy by an access control expert. In brief, we enforce the access control policy chosen by a company or a virtual organization. However, as we have mentioned, access control can also be used to protect privacy. As such, access control cannot be completely defined by a company. Indeed, privacy is a rather subjective notion. For example, data subjects, such as patients, may want to choose a specific medical practitioner. As a consequence, data subjects must be empowered with means to express their own access control rules.

Considering current legislation, such as the European Data Privacy Directive, it becomes clear that delegating part of the access control administration to data subjects ought to not only be available but also be legally obligated. Indeed, the directive states that personal data can only be processed when data subjects have consented or if the data provider is a public body. As a consequence, data subjects must be able to give such consent. In the case of pervasive applications, data subjects are both the owners and users of the data processed throughout the composition. As a result, users must be aware of and in control of data collection. Works such as Hengartner et al. (2006) investigate specific protection means for service users. We are currently investigating tools to allow users to specify their privacy preferences and weave them with a company's access control policy.

Apart from these immediate perspectives, our work on access control must be included in a broader reflection on security in service compositions. We envisage two long term perspectives in this field, namely extending model-driven security and inquiring into other security breaches, such as code hacking and statistical inference of protected pieces of data that can be used whenever non-functional properties are added to a service composition.

Model-driven Security has already been applied to several security aspects in several platforms. However, MDS has been applied only to one security feature of service compositions. This approach may not be enough. Indeed, authentication or other solutions aiming at ensuring security of transfer are necessary to ensure the efficiency of access control. As a result, security of transfer and access control should be designed at the same time. There is already work in progress which provides a metamodel for security of transfer and the relationship of this metamodel to a process metamodel; work is now needed at the modeling and the execution level to build a fully secured composition. At the modeling level, it is necessary to determine the relations between an access control and a security of transfer metamodel. Detecting potential conflicts is especially important. At the execution level, it is necessary to define how the two security views must be articulated to build a coherent security code.

We believe that two security threat types which could cause data leakage should receive careful attention. First, we have posited in this chapter that all the services are trustful and do not perform unlawful actions in order to gain access over sensitive data. This hypothesis may not always hold. As a result, trust should be part of the service selection criteria. There are a wide range of trust models, and investigating what trust must exist in a service remains an open question. Respecting the Service Level Agreement (SLA) may be a starting point. However, many approaches use logs as an evidence of a service or a software entity's behavior. Building models at runtime instead of relying on logs may be a fruitful way to extend Model-driven Security and as the basis of trust.

Secondly, even though access control prevents the disclosure of a specific piece of data during execution of a single query, it is well-known that the execution of seemingly unrelated queries may allow for obtaining unauthorized data. Against this threat, we think that our centralized approach is a good means to monitor the queries and the disclosed data. As a result, it is possible to define properties which are well-known to protect data against inference, such as k-anonimity (Sweeney, 2002) and to enforce them at execution time. So far, this approach has only been applied to location-based services (Gkoulalas-Divanis et al., 2010) and requires a deeper investigation, along with the enforcement of other privacy-preserving methods and properties.

CONCLUSION

In this chapter, we explored the challenges of securing pervasive applications, such as healthcare applications. Today, many pervasive applications are particularly useful in helping people with their everyday lives. However, many threats and attacks have not been sufficiently resolved, preventing the large scale utilization of these applications. The traditional approach to securing applications is by adding security patches to fill security flaws.

We have presented a promising model-based approach to take access control security into consideration at design time. The principle of our approach is to express a pervasive application as a service composition at a high level of abstraction, and, from that, generate the composition code with the security constraints.

This approach was divided into two parts:

1. First, the design step allowed us to express the pervasive application as a model with functional and security properties.
2. Second, the runtime step allowed us to generate the appropriate code to execute the application according to the available services.

REFERENCES

Abi Haidar, D., Cuppens-Boulahia, N., Cuppens, F., & Debar, H. (2006). An extended RBAC profile of XACML. In *Proceedings of the 3rd ACM workshop on Secure web services* (pp. 13-22). ACM.

Barker, S. (2009). The next 700 access control models or a unifying meta-model? In *Proceedings of the Symposium on Access control Models and Technologies* (pp. 187-196). ACM.

Barker, S., Sergot, M. J., & Wijesekera, D. (2008). Status-based access control. *ACM Transactions on Information and System Security, 12*(1). doi:10.1145/1410234.1410235.

Basin, D., Doser, J., & Lodderstedt, T. (2006). Model driven security: From UML models to access control infrastructures. *ACM Transactions on Software Engineering and Methodology, 15,* 39–91. doi:10.1145/1125808.1125810.

Carminati, B., Ferrari, E., & Hung, P. (2006). Security conscious web service composition. In *Proceedings of the International Conference on Web Services* (pp. 489-496). IEEE Computer Society.

Chae, H., Jung, J., Lee, J. H., & Lee, K. H. (2012). An efficient access control based on role attributes in service oriented environments. *In Proceedings of the 6th International Conference on Ubiquitous Information Management and Communication* (pp. 73-80). ACM.

Chollet, S., & Lalanda, P. (2008). Security specification at process level. *In Proceedings of the IEEE Service Computing Conference* (pp. 165-172). IEEE Computer Society.

Dami, S., Estublier, J., & Amiour, M. (1998). APEL: A graphical yet executable formalism for process modeling. *Automated Software Engineering, 5*(1), 61–96. doi:10.1023/A:1008658325298.

Damiani, M. L., Bertino, E., Catania, B., & Perlasca, P. (2007). GEO-RBAC: A spatially aware RBAC. *ACM Transactions on Information and System Security, 10*(1), 29–37. doi:10.1145/1210263.1210265.

Eclipse.org. (2013). *Website.* Retrieved from http://www.eclipse.org/modeling/m2t/?project=jet

Gkoulalas-Divanis, A., Kalnis, P., & Verykios, V. S. (2010). Providing K-Anonymity in location based services. *Science of Knowledge Discovery and Data Mining Exploration. Newsletter, 12*(1), 3–10.

Gottlob, G., Gradel, E., & Veith, H. (2000). Linear time datalog and branching time logic. In *Logic-Based Artificial Intelligence* (pp. 443–467). Kluwer Academic Publishers. doi:10.1007/978-1-4615-1567-8_19.

Hengartner, U., & Steenkiste, P. (2006). Avoiding privacy violations caused by context-sensitive services. In *Proceedings of 4th IEEE international conference on pervasive computing and communications* (pp. 222-231). IEEE Computer Society.

Hung, P. C. K., & Zheng, Y. (2007). Privacy access control model for aggregated e-health services. In *Proceedings of the IEEE Enterprise Distributed Object Computing Conference* (pp. 12-19). IEEE Computer Society.

Jajodia, S., & Yu, T. (2007). Basic security concepts. In *Secure data management in decentralized systems* (pp. 3–20). Springer-Verlag. doi:10.1007/978-0-387-27696-0_1.

Jammes, F., Mensch, A., & Smit, H. (2005). Service-oriented device communications using the devices profile for web services. In *MPAC'05 Proceedings of the 3rd international workshop on Middleware for pervasive and ad-hoc computing* (pp. 1-8). ACM.

Jboss.org. (2013). *Website*. Retrieved from http://www.jboss.org/drools/

OASIS. (2010). XACML v3.0 Core and Hierarchical Role Based Access Control (RBAC) profile version 1.0. Retrieved from http://docs.oasis-open.org/xacml/3.0/xacml-3.0-rbac-v1-spec-cs-01-en.pdf

OMG. (2004). Meta-Object Facility (MOF) specification, version 1.4, April 2002. Retrieved from http://www.omg.org/cgi-bin/doc?formal/2002-04-03

Orriëns, B., Yang, J., & Papazoglou, M. P. (2003). Model driven service composition. In *Proceedings in Service-Oriented Computing* (pp. 75–90). Springer-Verlag.

Papazoglou, M. P. (2003). Service-oriented computing: Concepts, characteristics and directions. In *Proceedings of the Fourth International Conference on Web Information Systems Engineering* (pp. 3-9). IEEE Computer Society.

Rodríguez, A., Fernández-Medina, E., & Piattini, M. (2007). A BPMN extension for the modeling of security requirements in business processes. *Transactions of the Institute of Electronics, Information and Communication Engineers. E (Norwalk, Conn.), 90-D*(4), 745–752.

Samarati, P., & di Vimercati, S. D. C. (2000). Access control: Policies, models, and mechanisms. In *Proceedings of Foundations of Security Analysis and Design* (pp. 137–196). Springer-Verlag.

Sandhu, R. S., Coyne, E. J., Feinstein, H. L., & Youman, C. E. (1996). Role-based access control models. *Computer, 29*(2), 38–47. doi:10.1109/2.485845.

Srivatsa, M., Iyengar, A., Mikalsen, T. A., Rouvellou, I., & Yin, J. (2007). An access control system for web service compositions. In *Proceedings of the IEEE Conference on Web Services* (pp. 1-8). IEEE.

Sward, R. E., & Boleng, J. (2011). Service-oriented architecture (SOA) concepts and implementations. In SIGAda (pp. 3-4).

Sweeney, L. (2002). k-Anonymity: A model for protecting privacy. *International Journal of Uncertainty. Fuzziness and Knowledge-Based Systems, 10*(5), 557–570. doi:10.1142/S0218488502001648.

UPnP Forum. (2008). UPnPTM Device Architecture 1.1. Retrieved from http://www.upnp.org/specs/arch/UPnP-arch-DeviceArchitecture-v1.1.pdf

Vallecillo, A. (2010). On the combination of domain specific modeling languages. In *Proceedings of The European Conference on Modeling and Applications* (pp. 305-320). Springer-Verlag.

W3.org. (2013). *Website*. Retrieved from http://www.w3.org/Submission/2003/SUBM-EPAL-20031110/

Wolter, C., Schaad, A., & Meinel, C. (2007). Deriving XACML policies from business process models. In *Proceedings of Web Information Systems Engineering* (pp. 142–153). Springer-Verlag. doi:10.1007/978-3-540-77010-7_15.

Yuan, E., & Tong, J. (2005). Attributed Based Access Control (ABAC) for web services. In *Proceedings of the IEEE International Conference on Web Services* (pp. 561-569). IEEE Computer Society.

Zeeb, E., Bobek, A., Bohn, H., & Golatowski, F. (2007). Service-oriented architectures for embedded systems using devices profile for web services. In *AINAW '07Proceedings of the 21st International Conference on Advanced Information Networking and Applications Workshops* (pp. 956-963). IEEE Computer Society.

Zhu, Y., Hu, H., Ahn, G.-J., Huang, D., & Wang, S.-B. (2012). Towards temporal access control in cloud computing. In *Proceedings of the IEEE INFOCOM* (pp. 2576-2580). IEEE Computer Society.

KEY TERMS AND DEFINITIONS

Business Process Execution Language (WS-BPEL): An XML-based language designed for specifying executable and abstract business processes via the orchestration of web services.

Devices Profile for Web Services (DPWS): A specification fully aligned with Web Services technology which enables discovery, description, messaging, and eventing on devices.

OSGi: OSGi is both a component-based platform and a service platform for the Java programming language. OSGi aims to facilitate the modularization of Java applications as well as the interoperability of such applications and services over various devices.

Pervasive Computing: Pervasive or ubiquitous computing corresponds to an information processing model where the user interacts naturally with their environment. The model proposed by pervasive computing consists of using the objects in the environment as a means of interaction between users and computer systems.

Service: Within SOA, a service is a unit of logic that enables a set of functionalities. Those functionalities are specified in a service description.

Service Oriented Architecture (SOA): An adjustable set of design principles which consists of well-defined composition units – services – to support the rapid development of applications. The central objective of this approach is to reduce dependencies among composition units, where a unit is typically some remote functionality accessed by clients.

Service Oriented Computing (SOC): Promotes the use of well-defined composition units – services – to support the rapid development of applications. The central objective of this approach is to reduce dependencies among composition units, where a unit is typically some remote functionality accessed by clients.

Universal Plug and Play (UPnP): A specification defined from an industrial initiative and is currently run by the UPnP Forum. The goal of this specification is to simplify connections between heterogeneous communicating devices and the construction of home networks.

Web Services: Web Services comply with the service-driven approach, meaning they can be described, published and discovered. A service provider can describe their service's functional and non-functional characteristics in a WSDL file and then register the service description in an

UDDI service registry. The main purpose of Web Services was to render applications available via the Internet or from within an Intranet.

WS-Security: An extension to SOAP to apply security to Web Services. Particularly, it defines three main mechanisms for integrating security properties in SOAP message: SOAP message signature to ensure integrity, SOAP message encryption to ensure confidentiality and the ability to attach security tokens for authentication.

ENDNOTES

[1]   The notation "WS-*" summarizes all the specifications about Web Services as their names usually start by the letters "WS."

[2]   See W3.org. (2013).

[3]   See OASIS. (2010).

[4]   See OASIS. (2010).

[5]   See OASIS. (2010).

[6]   See W3.org. (2013).

[7]   See eclipse.org. (2013).

[8]   See jboss.org. (2013).

Chapter 8
Architectural Practices for Improving Fault Tolerance in a Service–Driven Environment

Raja Ramanathan
Independent Researcher, USA

ABSTRACT

Enterprises that implement Service-driven applications face challenges relating to unprecedented scale, high availability, and fault-tolerance. There is exponential growth with respect to request volume in Service-driven systems, requiring the ability to provide multipoint access to shared services and data while preserving a single system image. Maintaining fault-tolerance in business services is a significant challenge due to their compositional nature, which instills dependencies among the services in the composition. This causes the dependability of the business services to be based on the reliability of the individual services in the composition. This chapter explores the architectural approaches such as service redundancy and design diversity, scaling, clustering, distributed data caching, in-memory data grid, and asynchronous messaging, for improving the dependability of services. It also explores the data scaling bottleneck in data centralization paradigms and illustrates how that presents significant scalability and fault-tolerance challenges in service-driven environments. Prevalent strategies to handle failure recovery such as backward and forward recovery mechanisms as well as the built-in mechanisms in WS-BPEL for exception handling and transactional compensation are discussed.

INTRODUCTION

Enterprise architects use service-driven architectural approaches to solve real-world computing and integration problems by leveraging Service Oriented Architecture (SOA) and REST (Representational State Transfer) Service architecture and their concepts of service abstraction to create services that are interoperable, autonomous, stateless, and language agnostic. To enable interoperability, services are designed to be loosely coupled, composable, and standards compliant. Service-driven approaches to architecture contrast with tightly coupled object-centric architectures where component interfaces are distributed to clients to enable them to talk to providers using a common protocol.

DOI: 10.4018/978-1-4666-4193-8.ch008

Enterprise systems built using service-driven approaches face a host of challenges relating to unprecedented scale. There is an exponential growth with respect to request volume in service-driven systems. Services are reusable entities that are shared among various applications in the enterprise, causing large volumes of service consumer requests and service provider responses to be generated. Furthermore, as business processes become increasingly automated, they contribute to enormous increase in processing and data load. The challenge for large-scale and data-intensive systems is to provide multipoint access to shared services and data while preserving a single system image. It is extremely important to architect for application scalability in order to handle the enormous load requirements of the service-driven environment. *Scalability* is the property of a system, application, or service that indicates how well it can handle increasing amounts of load in response to increasing processing demand. Enterprise architects are concerned with designing systems and applications that can scale dynamically to handle varying compute and data loads to satisfy the dynamic requirements of the business.

Service-driven architectural approaches introduce a set of new challenges to the continuous availability of services and systems. Service availability requires the elimination of all single points of failure within a given service and its dependents, while System (server/node) availability requires the elimination of the tight coupling between the System (server/node) and the Services that are hosted on it. *Fault-tolerance* is the indicator of how well a system or application can tolerate the failure of one or more hardware or software components and still continue to operate in an acceptable manner. Fault-tolerance ensures overall system or application availability, albeit at decreased throughput. Fault-tolerance is related to the *high availability* characteristics of the system. Highly available systems provide useful resources over a period of time and guarantee functional continuity within that time window. Enterprise architects place great emphasis on the operational reliability of systems and applications. In other words, they attempt to build highly available systems and applications that continue to operate in the event of hardware or software failures.

Service-driven approaches enable to distribute applications or services to multiple locations within an enterprise and off-premises. A Service-driven application is generally deployed in a server farm (group of servers) in a load-balanced manner. One of the goals of the Service-driven approach is to provision the application environment to handle large processing and data volumes by distributing the service entities for concurrent processing. By design, SOA and REST are intended to provide scalability; however, there are many challenges that need to be addressed before one can achieve true scalability. The challenges relate to the manner in which the application is coded and how the application performs data access and storage.

Service-driven architectural approaches decompose an application into coarse grained services and instances of each service are deployed on multiple servers. Each service is expected to be stateless, in other words, they do not retain any data with them across multiple calls. This data independence enables any instance of the service running on any server to service consumer requests, thus facilitating service scalability. However, the real world is far from the ideal situation, and services have to deal with data. Access and persistence of both session and application data causes the scalability bottleneck in service-driven environments. Service-driven applications compose complex business services by orchestration and choreography (which are service composition techniques) of finer grained application services. This causes data shuttling among services, which is affected by network latency. The latency effect is further exacerbated when the target services are distributed among servers that are spread out across the Wide Area Network (WAN), causing data to make long trips from one service to the next through the network. Effective scaling of such applications may not be easy.

Service-driven environments are different from traditional user-centric application environments in terms of the magnitude of the rate of consumption requests generated. In a typical service-driven environment, granular and reusable services are invoked by multiple applications at dramatically increased rates. Consequently, the technologies that were capable of handling traditional user loads are unable to keep up with the increased load requirements associated with a service-driven environment. It is critical to ensure the reliability and integrity of conversational state, such as the HTTP (Hypertext Transport Protocol) session state of Web Services, which are usually short-lived, but rapidly modified and accessed. The transient nature of the conversational state makes it particularly difficult to manage by traditional means.

Database persistence has been the traditional solution for saving conversational state, but this method does not meet the throughput and latency requirements of large-scale service-driven environments in a cost-effective manner. The alternative methodology has been to use in-memory solutions that utilize asynchronous updates, master/slave high-availability (HA) solutions, and static partitioning of data to address scalability issues. However, these solutions address the scalability problem at reduced reliability. Due to these scaling and dependability challenges, stateful applications are usually discouraged in service-driven environments.

This chapter explores the typical challenges faced by enterprises for implementing the scalability and fault tolerance in a service-driven environment and recommends architecture best practices to improve fault-tolerance for services. It provides guidelines for implementing scalability, reliability, and fault-tolerance for business services by presenting architectural approaches such as redundancy and design diversity, clustering, distributed data caching, in-memory data grid, and

asynchronous messaging. Typical fault recovery mechanisms used in enterprises implementing service-driven approaches are also covered.

BACKGROUND

Traditionally, enterprises that required high availability and fault-tolerance for applications satisfied that objective by building redundant datacenters; entire datacenters that duplicated the hardware, software, applications, and data of the original datacenter. The secondary datacenters were also used to offload traffic from the primary datacenter during times of peak usage and sometimes doubled up as a disaster recovery datacenter. However, during other times, the secondary datacenter sat idling, providing a low return on investment.

In service-driven environments, scalability, reliability and fault-tolerance are significant architectural considerations. Many enterprise applications depend on the Enterprise Service Bus (ESB) and other service components to continue application processing. Hence, services have to be seamlessly available to users and applications without interruption, even though there may be hardware failures, software faults, network congestion, database crash, or peak loads in the system. Services are expected to be highly available and fault-tolerant.

High availability is generally stated or measured in terms of the *"nines availability"* definition. The "nines" definition describes the number of minutes or seconds of estimated downtime with respect to the number of minutes in a full year (365 days or 525,600 minutes). Table 1 illustrates the "nines" terminology.

Table 2 shows a typical mapping of availability levels to the reliability classes.

Services may fail for many reasons including implementation errors, resource starvation, and network instability, among others. Service-driven applications have to employ fault handling techniques to cope with errors propagated by ser-

Table 1. "Nines" availability

Nines Terminology	% Availability	Downtime (minutes)	Downtime (per year)
1 Nine	90	52,560	36.5 days
2 Nines	99	5,256	4 days
3 Nines	99.9	525.6	8.8 hours
4 Nines	99.99	52.56	53 minutes
5 Nines	99.999	5.26	5.3 minutes
6 Nines	99.9999	0.53	32 seconds

Table 2. Reliability class

Reliability Class	Availability
Continuous	100%
Fault Tolerant	99.999%
Fault Resilient	99.99%
High Availability	99.9%
Normal Availability	99 - 99.5%

vices, and thereby ensure an end-to-end Quality of Service (QoS). WS-* Standards specifications, such as, WS-Reliability (OASIS, 2004) and WS-ReliableMessaging (OASIS, 2006) deal with faults at the transport level, however, there are no standards to deal with faults at the application level.

It is practically impossible to build a perfect system. As a rule of thumb, as the complexity of a system increases, its reliability deteriorates drastically, unless compensatory measures are taken. For illustration, consider a system comprising of 100 non-redundant components where each component is built at a reliability level of 99.99%. The reliability of the system is computed as a product of the individual component reliabilities which in this case approximates to 99%. However, by increasing the number of non-redundant components to 10,000, the reliability of the same system drops to an unacceptable reliability level of approximately 37%. In order to bump up the reliability of this system back to the 99% level will require that each component be built to a

reliability level of 99.999%, which could be cost prohibitive.

The principle of fault-tolerant computing is to accept that faults are inevitable and that they may lead to component failures (hardware, software, network, etc.). The ultimate goal of fault tolerance is the development of a dependable system. Fault-tolerant mechanisms have therefore focused on preventing system failures as a result of component failures. These fault tolerance mechanisms rely heavily upon the replication of components. Redundancy-based fault-tolerant strategies have long been used as a means to avoid disruptions in the service-driven environment despite the occurrence of failures in the underlying software or hardware components.

It is, however, estimated that the vast majority of faults originate from software (Gray & Siewiorek, 1991). In distributed service-driven applications, much of the complexity is located in the application layer, and the inherent design faults may elude detection despite rigorous and extensive testing. Therefore, traditional replication schemes, which can successfully handle hardware faults and transient faults caused by external disturbances, do not provide sufficient protection for tolerating software faults (Dubrova, 2002; Johnson, 1989).

The next section presents different architectural approaches that can improve the fault-tolerance of services and provides guidelines for enterprises to implement fault-tolerance in their service design.

ARCHITECTURAL APPROACHES FOR FAULT-TOLERANCE IN SERVICES

Service failures need to be detected and handled appropriately in order to provide fault-tolerance. Errors, faults, and failures, cause dependability issues. An error is a system state that may cause a subsequent failure; a failure occurs when an error reaches the service interface and alters the service behavior. A fault is the hypothesized cause of an error and is generally classified into design, physical, and interaction faults.

Faults happen due to incorrect specification, incorrect implementation, and external factors. They can also occur due to program faults, runtime errors, and network failures. Most of the errors and failures occur during service binding and invocation. Failures can be detected at both the individual service level and at the service composition level. Service faults can be classified into publishing fault, discovery fault, composition fault, binding fault, and execution fault as described below.

- **Publishing Fault:** The act of publishing a service involves deployment of the service code on the server(s) and the publication of the service description (service contract) for use by consuming services. It is possible for the service description to be faulty in terms of being incorrect or improperly formatted. Furthermore, service descriptions can also be incomplete such that the service provides more features than published, or refer to non-existent content or algorithms, or be incompatible with the deployed service in terms of communication protocol.
- **Discovery Fault:** Faults can happen during service discovery due to non-existent services or by finding the incorrect service during the service lookup.
- **Composition Fault:** Services compose new services from existing ones. There is a possibility of faults happening during service composition due to incompatibility in the services that are being linked together, in terms of incompatible service contracts and data, and unmet pre- and post-conditions such as validation, security, etc.
- **Binding Fault:** Service consumers and providers negotiate the conditions to execute the service during the binding phase. The binding may fault when access is de-

nied due to authentication, authorization, or due to protocol compatibility issues.
- **Runtime Fault:** Runtime faults occur when the service is executing. The service may fault due to faulty software or incorrect inputs.

As discussed earlier, failures are caused by errors and errors are caused by faults. Erradi et al. (2006) identified three types of failures in services, namely, Behavioral, Operational, and Quality of Service (QoS) failures. Behavioral failures refer to business logic related failures where the service fails to complete its task, or delivers incorrect results due to computational or logic errors. Operational failures relate to the underlying middleware and communication infrastructure. QoS failures concerns with service delivery failures in meeting the expected quality of service properties such as Service Level Agreement (SLA), security, response times, etc.

Service Redundancy and Design Diversity

Scalable environments promote fault-tolerance due to the fact that redundant copies of the services can be deployed on multiple servers, thereby providing backup instances of services which can continue to run even when the primary service fails.

Various approaches to achieving fault tolerance have been published by several authors (De Florio, 2009; Dubrova, 2002; Johnson, 1989; Diab & Zomaya, 2005). The common aspect of each of these methods is the use of a certain amount of redundancy to guarantee high availability and increased reliability of the system. Deployment of multiple instances of a particular software component in a distributed system has proven successful in improving the scalability, and the reliability of the system in the event of hardware and software failures.

The redundancy can be at the component level, process level, service level, or the system level. Usually, the components which have high probability of faults are chosen to be made redundant. The increase in complexity caused by the redundancy can be quite severe and may diminish the dependability improvement, unless redundant resources are allocated in a proper way.

Two kinds of redundancies are possible (Leu, Bastani, & Leiss, 1990; Salatge & Fabre, 2007):

- **Space-Redundancy:** Employs extra resources, such as hardware or software to mask faults. Space-redundancy can be further classified into hardware, software, and information redundancy, depending on the type of redundant resources added to the system. *Active-replication* and *passive-replication* are two types of space-redundancy. Active-replication is performed by invoking all service replicas at the same time to process the same request, and the first returned response or a voting outcome is considered as the final result. On the other hand, passive-replication first invokes a primary service candidate to process the request. Secondary replicas will be invoked only when the primary candidate fails. A scalable environment enables space-redundancy.
- **Time-Redundancy:** Uses extra computation or communication time to tolerate faults by repeating the computation or data transmission and comparing the repeated result with a previous copy of the result.

There are two different techniques that leverage the redundancy concept for implementing fault-tolerance in services and service components:

- **Single-Version:** Fault detection, containment, and recovery mechanisms are incorporated into the service software design; however, the same version of the service is redundantly deployed on multiple servers.
- **Multi-Version:** Each instance of the service is designed independently of one another; using different tools and techniques, and each of the different versions (that provide the same functionality) are deployed redundantly in multiple nodes.

The single-version scheme would obviously replicate the software fault in all instances of the deployed service. When two or more redundant components fault simultaneously, it is called a *common-mode fault*. Common-mode faults are caused due to dependencies between the redundant components that cause them to fail at the same time. Design faults can cause redundant copies of same service to fail under identical conditions.

An architectural approach that is generally used for overcoming the common-mode fault is the technique of *Design Diversity*. Diverse design methodology eliminates the dependencies by using different design rules, different software tools and techniques, and most often separate design teams to vary the design and implementation of the redundant copies of the same component or service. Multi-version techniques employ redundant service components, developed using the concept of design diversity, where redundant copies of the same component or service are designed and implemented differently from one another. The diversification scheme is based on the classic N-version programming (NVP) mechanism (Avizienis, 1985) for software fault tolerance that advocates the independent generation of "n" functionally-equivalent programs from the same functional specification. In the NVP model, all "n" programs execute simultaneously, and a decision algorithm determines a result from the individual outputs of the programs.

Therefore, instead of using identical replicas of the same software component, current software fault-tolerant techniques try to leverage the experience of hardware redundancy schemes, where the technique of design diversification of redundant components was implemented to withstand design faults. The rationale behind the diversification scheme is that by redundantly deploying multiple functionally-equivalent software components that are independently designed and implemented will reduce the likelihood of a software fault affecting multiple implementations simultaneously, thereby keeping the system operational despite software failures.

However, the multi-version schemes (such as NVP) do not take into account the changes in the operational status of any of the components contained within the redundancy scheme. Web services often suffer from temporary unavailability issues which may be the result of unavailability of dependent services, network connectivity failure, and network latency issues. The temporary unavailability of any specific Web service that is part of a service composition may cause the whole business service to fail. A redundancy based fault-tolerance scheme may not address such cases. The effectiveness of the redundancy based fault-tolerant scheme depends on the frequency with which the components become temporarily unavailable, and the effect of network latency on the business service.

The next section explores the typical approaches used in enterprises for scaling service-driven environments.

Scaling Approaches

The extent of the scalability of a business service is dependent on the scalability of individual services that make up the service composition. Therefore, it is important to understand the scalability hot spots of the service-driven environment before attempting to architect a suitable scaling solution.

There are three typical approaches to service distribution through Scaling – horizontal, vertical, and hybrid. Horizontal Scaling as shown in Figure 1, adds additional nodes with identical functionality to existing ones, and distributes the load among all the nodes using a load balancer to fan-out the incoming requests in an algorithmic manner. The most common algorithm for load balancing is round-robin that sequences the requests among the group of nodes that are being load-balanced.

Figure 1. Horizontal scaling

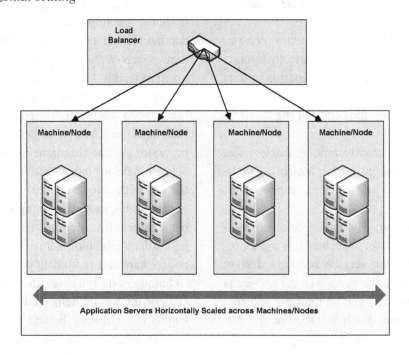

Vertical Scaling involves adding hardware, storage, or processing servers to a node to enable it to increase its processing capacity. As shown in Figure 2, multiple application servers are added to the same machine (node) to fully utilize the machine resources and increase the processing throughput.

One can also combine the schemes to create a hybrid model to maximize the benefit of both horizontal and vertical scaling as shown in Figure 3.

Figure 2. Vertical scaling

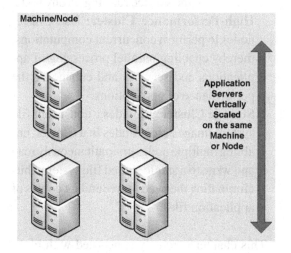

Scaling enables to distribute the work load among nodes/servers. This is especially useful in service-driven environments where individual services or composites (service composed of individual services) are distributed among multiple nodes/servers to enable load-sharing and fault-tolerance. As shown in Figure 1, the horizontally scaled servers are unaware of each other, however, share the work load due to the fact that client requests are distributed to them by means of a load balancer. On the other hand, if this group of nodes/servers communicated and worked together to present a single computing interface to the user, they would be referred to as a Cluster of nodes/servers (Baker, 2001). The next section explores Clustering as an architectural approach to facilitate not only load balancing, but also to provide higher reliability and a fail-over mechanism for services.

Clustering

The first inspiration for Cluster Computing was developed in the 1960s by IBM as an alternative to linking mainframes to provide a more cost effective form of parallelism. However, Cluster

Figure 3. Hybrid scaling

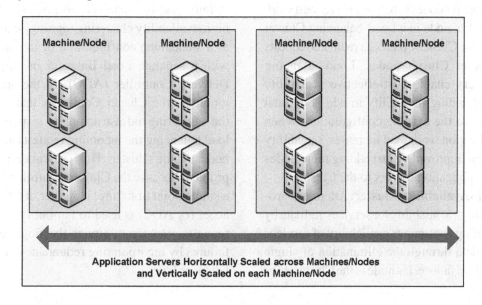

Computing did not gain momentum until the convergence of four important trends in the 1980s: high-performance microprocessors, high-speed networks, standard tools for high performance distributed computing, and the increasing need for large computing power for solving tough science problems and running commercial applications (Buyya, 1999).

Today, *Clustering* is one of the prevalent architectural techniques used for improving the scalability, high availability, and reliability of service-driven applications. A *Cluster* can be defined as a group of nodes/servers that communicate and work together to present a single computing interface to the user. Clustering facilitates load balancing and failover of applications and improves service availability by providing uninterrupted service through redundant nodes and servers that eliminate single points of failure (Buyya, 1999). When failure occurs in a Cluster, resources can be redirected and the workload can be redistributed.

Clusters are usually classified into four major types:

1. **Load-Balancing Cluster:** The Cluster Controller (software that controls and manages the Cluster) in a Load-balancing Cluster distributes the service requests among multiple Cluster nodes to balance the request work load. If a node in a Load-balancing Cluster fails, the Cluster Controller redirects requests to other Cluster nodes. Load-balancing Clusters enable cost-effective scalability by providing the ability to add additional nodes to the existing configuration. When application work load increases, scalability can be improved by just adding more nodes and application servers to the Cluster.

2. **High-Availability Cluster:** Attempt to provide high availability for services and data by enabling continuous availability of services and data through the elimination of single points of failure. If a node in the Cluster stops functioning, the Cluster failover mechanism kicks in to automatically shift the workload of the failed node to another node in the Cluster. This failover mechanism ensures continuous availability of critical applications and data. High-availability Clusters are designed to not only handle node or server failures, but also to provide for fault tolerance with regard to session data by persisting and distributing session state among the nodes in the Cluster. However, clustering works best with stateless services where the same consumer request can be processed by any instance of the service running on any node.

3. **High-Performance Cluster:** Use Cluster nodes to perform concurrent computations, thereby enabling parallel processing of applications and services and enhancing the performance of applications.

4. **Storage Cluster:** Provides a consistent file system image across nodes in a Cluster, enabling multiple nodes to simultaneously read and write to a single shared file system, thus eliminating the need for redundant copies of application files.

This chapter is mostly concerned with high-availability Clusters. In practice, most high-availability Cluster products also incorporate in-built load-balancing capability. Therefore, the high-availability clustering topology can be built as a standalone configuration or in conjunction with a separate Load Balancer or Application Delivery Controller (ADC). In the standalone topology, the Cluster Controller that is part of the clustering infrastructure is responsible for load balancing the incoming requests among the nodes of the Cluster. This presents a reliability problem because the Cluster Controller becomes a single point of failure. However, if a Load Balancer (or ADC) is used to fan-out the incoming requests, one can minimize the single points of failures by incorporating redundancy at the load balancer level.

Load balancing can be implemented independently of clustering as shown in Figure 1, when incoming requests need to be split out to multiple independent servers that have the same setup, but are unaware of each other. From a user's perspective, if services were operational on a node when the node went down, with just load balancing implemented without clustering, the session state of the service request that was being processed by the failed node would likely have been lost, resulting in the loss of the service request. However, with the implementation of the high-availability clustering for services and data, the failed service may fail-over to the other node and continue to process as if nothing had happened to the node. This is possible because of the persistence of the session state data in the high-availability Cluster.

Figure 4 illustrates an Application Server Cluster. A farm of Load Balancers feed incoming requests into a Web Server farm. The use of redundancy in the load balancing and web tiers enhance the high availability and failover capabilities of the system. It is important to avoid single points of failures and single points of bottlenecks in the system topology to enable high availability and reliability of the system as a whole. The Web Servers direct the requests to the individual nodes within the Cluster. The Cluster Controller handles failover of incoming requests when a node or application server fails. The backend database server should also be highly available (clustered) to prevent single points of failures and bottlenecks in data.

Cluster nodes can be configured to be either active or passive. When a node is active, it is actively handling incoming requests. When a node is passive, it is idle, and on standby waiting for a node to fail. In general, clusters can be configured

Figure 4. Cluster of application servers

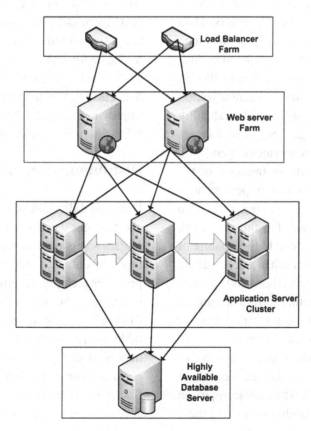

using different combinations of active and passive nodes. If a node fails or is shut down, the Cluster Controller can reallocate the server demand to the other nodes of the Cluster that have the resources available. This process is called *failover*. If an active node fails and there is a passive node available, the resources and services running on the failed node can be transferred over to the passive node. Since the passive node has no current workload, it will be able to assume the workload of the failed node. This mode of failover is sometimes called N+1 failover. However, if all nodes in a Cluster are active and a node fails, the resources and services running on the failed node can be migrated over (using the server/component migration mechanism supported by the Cluster) to another active node or can be split-up among several active nodes. In this case, the failed-over node(s) handle the additional processing load.

Services quite often have to deal with data stored and accessed in a distributed and parallel manner. Enterprise data services facilitate access to enterprise data for service consumers. Data services help to consolidate data operations such as store and query, enabling centralized control of data without the proliferation of data silos in the enterprise. However, this data centralization paradigm brings with it significant scalability and performance challenges. Scalability issues arise when many business services depend on a single data service, causing an overload of the back-end database and resulting in performance bottlenecks. The granularity of data services can also influence performance. On the one hand, fine-grained data services, due to their nature of returning too little data can result in increased data service invocations. On the other hand, coarse-gained data services can return too much data and unnecessarily bog down the network. In either case, application performance suffers.

Clustering can provide effective scaling of business services. However, data services don't scale in the same manner. The classic approach to implementing data scalability is by using static

data partitioning across database servers, each with its own dedicated backup database server to ensure availability. However, static data partitioning restricts dynamic increases to capacity, and requires massive over-provisioning to prevent peak loads from overwhelming the service; and leads to non-performing, difficult to scale, and expensive operations. In other words, data essentially becomes the scalability bottleneck. Furthermore, when a primary server fails, the backup server becomes a single point of failure in the system. A recommended solution is to use a transparent dynamic data partitioning mechanism such as an in-memory data grid (explained below) to achieve continuous availability and reliability for services.

Clustered databases are a commonly used solution for improving data availability. For example, Oracle Real Application Clusters (RAC) is a prevalent solution to enable an Oracle database to run across a Cluster of servers, thus providing increased availability and fault tolerance without the need for any application changes (Vallath, 2003). Similarly, IBM's pureScale DB2 Clustered Database provides high availability and fault-tolerance for DB2 databases.

The next section describes the distributed data caching mechanism (Paul & Fei, 2001) for improving the scalability, availability, and fault-tolerance of data services.

Distributed Data Caching

Data scalability can be improved at multiple levels. Services usually have to deal with two types of data – session data and application data. Both types of data can cause scalability issues. The prevalent technique to improving data scalability is by using the mechanism of *Distributed Data Caching*. Caches are implemented as an indexed table where a unique key is used for referencing data. Services satisfy data access requests by first checking the cache before hitting the database. Cache misses lead to the more expensive database accesses and cache updates. A distributed cache is used to cache only a subset of the data that is in the database, based on the needs of the applications at any point of time. The cache scales out across multiple nodes/servers, but presents a single logical view of the data to the applications and services. This can lead to drastic improvements in the performance and scalability of services.

Distributed Data Caching is illustrated in Figure 5 which shows a Distributed Cache Cluster that can scale horizontally across nodes, independent of the Application Server Cluster or the Database Cluster.

Various caching topologies can be used to perform Distributed Caching. The most prevalent techniques are Partitioned Caching, Partitioned-Replicated Caching, and Replicated Caching.

Figure 6 illustrates Partitioned Caching topology in which the cache is broken up into partitions, and each partition is stored in different cache servers in the Cluster. Each partition has different sets of data from the database.

Figure 7 illustrates the Partitioned-replicated Caching topology which is very similar to the Partitioned Cache topology in that the data is partitioned among several cache servers in the Cluster. However, there is an important difference. In this topology, a replica of each partitioned cache is maintained as a backup on secondary cache servers for failover. Should the primary cache server fail, the secondary cache will be activated to service consumer requests. Both of these caching methodologies enhance the scalability for

Figure 5. Distributed data caching

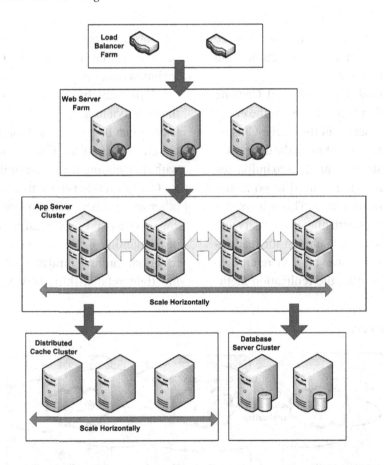

Figure 6. Partitioned cache

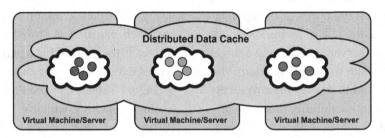

Figure 7. Partitioned-replicated cache

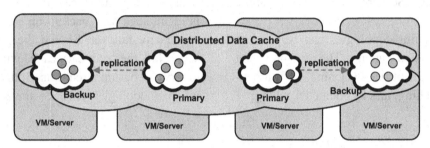

transactional data. As more cache servers are added to the system, increased transactional and storage capacities result.

On the other hand, the Replicated Caching topology illustrated in Figure 8, copies the entire cache to each cache server in the Cache Cluster. Thereby, every cache server has all the data available to service consumer requests, and unlike the other two topologies, do not need to go across servers in order to retrieve data. Therefore, replicated caching provides both high availability and performance and is a good solution for read-intensive environments. However, if there are frequent updates to the data, the replication meth-

odology does not perform well since every copy of the cache has to be synchronously updated to maintain data integrity.

High availability can be further enhanced through dynamic cache clustering, where cache servers can be provisioned for dynamic addition or removal from the Cache Cluster at run time without stopping the cache or the applications.

Composite Services that are composed of other services have a dependency on the constituent services and they must account for the lack of availability of those dependent services. The traditional architectural methodology for preventing tight relationships between components is

Figure 8. Replicated cache

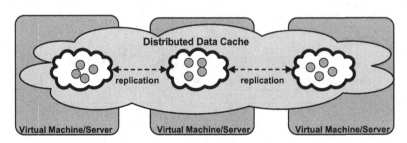

by either loosely-coupling or decoupling them from the dependent components. Consider business services that are dependent on data services for accessing and storing application data. If the underlying database or datastore that is used by these data services fail, the data services themselves will fail, leading to failure of the business services. In order to provide fault-tolerance under these conditions and improve the availability of the business services, data services should continue to operate for a period of time without hiccups for both data reads and data writes despite the failure of the database/datastore.

Figure 9 depicts the sequence of operations involved in cache requests. As discussed earlier, data values stored in the cache are indexed by a key. When a read request is made by a client (consumer) for a specific data item by specifying the corresponding key (e.g. read("A"), where "A" is the key of the data object stored in the cache); the cache is first checked to retrieve the data object that is indexed by that key. If the requested data is unavailable in the cache, which is termed a "cache miss," causes a read from the database to update the cache, and the cache then returns the result

to the requester. This is called the *read-through* mechanism.

Consider the case when data is requested to be written to the database (e.g. write("A," value), where "A" is the key of the data object and "value" is the data object that is to be stored). The write operation can happen in one of two modes – synchronous and asynchronous. In the synchronous mode, the write operation will first update the cache and synchronously update the backend database. This is the *write-through* mechanism. In the asynchronous mode, the cache will be updated, however, the backend database will not be updated immediately. The update of the database will happen asynchronously at a later time. This is called the *write-behind* mechanism. By incorporating a read-through/write-behind caching scheme, data inserts and updates are delayed being written to the database. As a consequence, data services can continue to operate even when the underlying datastore is unavailable, and synchronization with the database can take place later when the datastore becomes available. This will greatly improve the fault-tolerance and performance of business services.

Figure 9. Cache operation sequence diagram

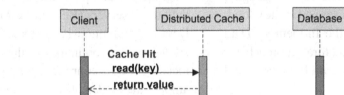

Most data in enterprise applications are relational in nature, which means that there are underlying relationships among the data entities that are captured in the database. That leads to an interesting point about managing these data relationships in the cache. For example, consider that "Customer" and "Order" data entities are stored in a database, and that they are related by a one-to-many relationship, i.e., for every customer there are one or more orders. When these entities are loaded into the cache, the cache will need to respect that relationship such that if a customer is removed from the cache, the corresponding order cache entries are also automatically removed from the cache. Object Relational Mapping (ORM) is generally used by data caching mechanisms to map relational data to objects in the memory and maintain the relationship among them. If the cache is unable to track and maintain data relationships among the entities, the data service will have to deal with it programmatically in order to maintain data integrity.

Enterprise applications need fast access to data for maximum performance. Distributed *In-Memory Data Grids* (IMDG) (Allcock, Chervenak, Foster, Kesselman, & Livny, 2005) combine distributed caching with powerful management tools to provide scalable solutions for managing dynamic data both on-premises and in the Cloud. The next section presents the In-memory Data Grid as an effective architectural approach for preventing single points of data bottleneck and single points of data failure.

In-Memory Data Grid

By providing speedy access to frequently used data, *In-Memory Data Grid* (IMDG) enables dynamic scaling of mission-critical applications by providing linear scalability to hundreds of servers. It improves resource utilization and enables significant increases in transaction rates while reducing data access response times. IMDG can protect the service-driven environment from the events of server failures and facilitate continuous data availability and transactional integrity.

In the IMDG, the data model is distributed across multiple virtual machines or nodes that may be either co-located or separated across multiple locations (Chervenak, Foster, Kesselman, Salisbury, & Tuecke, 2001). All data is stored in the RAM of the servers. Servers can be added or removed without disrupting the applications or services that run on the server. Custom APIs make it easy to query and store data in the data grid. The IMDG is resilient and is capable of automatic recovery from a single server or multiple server failure. Some examples of industrial strength IMGDs are IBM eXtremeScale, Oracle Coherence, Gigaspaces' XAP Elastic Caching, Hazelcast, VMware Gemfire, etc.

IMDGs are designed using a peer-to-peer architecture to prevent single points of bottleneck and single points of failure. Servers form a data mesh instead of a master-slave topology. IMDG stores the data in memory in order to achieve very high performance, and uses the concept of redundancy by replicating data objects and synchronizing them across multiple servers to provide for fault-tolerance. The data load is balanced across a Cluster of servers by using data partitioning, and providing a logical view of all data to all servers (Belalem & Meroufel, 2011). Data is synchronously replicated to at least one other server for continuous availability. Distributed locks are used to coordinate data synchronizations among the nodes. IMGD monitors the health of each node in the Cluster and if it detects an unhealthy or failed server, immediately activates healthy servers to assume the responsibility of the failed server to provide continuous operation without interruption of service or loss of data. IMDG maintains database integrity using the read-through, write-through, and write-behind caching strategies.

Figure 10 illustrates the IMDG mechanism. Consider that the data grid is clustered over three nodes/servers as shown in the figure. Clients

Figure 10. In-memory data grid data replication

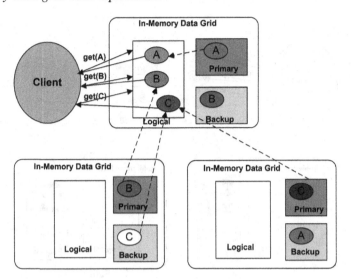

(consumer programs) make requests for data from service providers which in-turn interacts with the data grid to retrieve or store data in the underlying database. In the figure below, when client makes a read request, such as get(A), to obtain the value of the keyed data object "A," the data grid checks the local primary cache for a cache hit, and the data object "A" is returned. However, if the data object is not local, IMDG would have been able to retrieve it from another server's primary cache and return the data object to the requesting client. For example, consider the request for data object "C." This data object is not found in the local primary cache, so IMDG retrieves it from another server's data cache where it is stored in the primary cache. In other words, IMDG ensures a logical view of all data for applications, irrespective of the physical location of the data.

Enterprise data is typically stored in relational databases. However, the data grid caches only object data, not relational data. Therefore, object-relational mapping (ORM) is used to map relational data to data objects in the cache. Similarly, ORM is also used to decompose the object data back into the relational form by generating the SQL queries for inserts, updates, and deletes into the database. Since a single data object may

be composed of data from many database tables, the cost of retrieving objects from the database or storing decomposed objects in the database can be significant for applications in terms of the load on the database and the latency of data access. IMDG achieves low response times for data access by keeping the data in memory and in the object form, and by sharing that data across multiple servers. IMDG partitions the data across the grid, with each server being responsible for managing its own share of the total data set, thus avoiding single points of bottlenecks in the system. Applications may be able to access the required data without network communication and data transformation (such as ORM). In cases where network communication is required to access data, such as when the primary local cache is a miss, IMDG accesses data from the other nodes.

Figure 11 illustrates the mechanism used by IMDG to provide fault-tolerance. When one of the servers that hosts a part of the data grid fails, the IMDG retrieves the required data object from the backup copy on another working server. For example, consider the earlier use case of a client requesting for the data object "C" which is stored in the primary cache of another server in the Cluster. If that server hosting the data object

Figure 11. In-memory data grid operation with one failed virtual machine or node

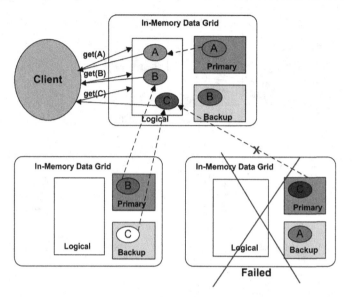

"C" fails as shown in the figure, the IMDG will retrieve that data object "C" from the backup cache of another active server. The IMDG ensures that replications of data objects are always available as a backup copy in one or more servers so that it can provide fault-tolerance against single and multiple server failures.

There are three typical architectural issues that need to be addressed in a distributed memory system. The first is data placement. This is related to partitioning the data among the servers such that the data is placed optimally for access. Next is data consistency. This is an issue because of the possibility of reading different values of the same data object from different servers due to data synchronization issues, and last but not the least is fault tolerance due to node or network failures. The CAP theorem (Brewer, 2004) states that you cannot simultaneously achieve all three goals of consistency, availability, and partitioning. IMDGs typically tradeoff with respect to these three concerns, to improve performance, provide ease of use, and support fault tolerant capabilities.

IMDGs use a distributed hash table (DHT) for partitioning data, where a hash value is computed based on the key that is used to access data, and that hash value is mapped to a node. Data items can be easily located by the hash value of the key. Therefore, a random read or a write operation would require only a single network hop at the worst case. However, it turns out that the single network hop, which is the worst-case scenario, also happens to be the common scenario when dealing with multiple data items, since chances are that they will reside on different nodes. Locality preserving hashes are sometimes used to ensure that specific types of data items are grouped together in particular nodes so that range queries could be carried out efficiently without hopping all over the Cluster to retrieve the data.

Services that implement the request/response messaging paradigm are called *Synchronous* services. In practice, not all services are synchronous; many of them work in an asynchronous manner where services continue to operate without waiting for the request to complete. For example, long-running business processes are good candidates for asynchronous messaging. The next section presents the asynchronous messaging paradigm for improving the flexibility in service distribution and fault-tolerance.

Asynchronous Messaging

Long-running business processes do not have the need to run synchronously. In other words, these types of processes send request messages to communicate with services and continue to operate without waiting for the request to complete, i.e., they initiate the request which returns immediately and the results are received asynchronously at a later time. This *Asynchronous Messaging* architecture (Hohpe & Woolf, 2003) decouples different processes and services within the system, allowing them to run at different speeds. The decoupled system allows for the most flexibility in service distribution and scaling. Some of the major benefits of asynchronous processing are: higher throughput, easier to load balance requests, fault tolerance, and support for intermittent system connections. The asynchronous model creates a perception of a faster system response time for users by allowing the different steps of the process to continue without having to wait for responses at each stage.

To support asynchronous messaging, the architecture must provide for some form of a queue to hold pending requests, and thereby enable each step of the process to send messages to these intermediate queues, instead of directly interfacing with the services. There is also the need for a correlation mechanism to facilitate the inter-linking of request and response messages.

In an asynchronous messaging system, the intermediate queues enable the request messages to be processed in an asynchronous manner. When a service is ready to process a request, it grabs one from the pending queue. Therefore, application scaling can be accomplished by simply increasing the number of services processing requests from the pending queue. The asynchronous architecture also improves fault-tolerance by insulating the business services from disruptions in dependent applications or services and intermittent network failures. If a hardware or software failure removes one of the processing steps, pending requests for that step will just be queued up until the service is restored. There will be no real impact on the previous steps in the process, although the overall processing time will likely be affected by the failure.

By combining the asynchronous messaging paradigm with *Distributed Queues* (queues that can be physically distributed across a Cluster and still provide a single logical view to the applications) and a clustered architecture that can migrate the queues from a failed server/node to the healthy server in the Cluster, it is possible to provide reliability and fault-tolerance for the messages that are being queued up. In the event the server that hosts a part of the distributed queue dies, the Cluster can migrate the queue subsystem from the failed server to a healthy server, and the redundant services running on the healthy server will be able to dequeue messages from the queue of the failed server and continue processing.

An asynchronous business process can work without having all parts of the workflow connected at all times. Consider a business process where one of the workflow steps is processed by a business partner. Assume that the connection between the systems (host and business partner) is only available on an intermittent basis or is established on demand. The business partner on their own schedule can connect to the host system and queue up one or more requests for the workflow process for asynchronous processing, or receive the results asynchronously from the workflow system for a previously executed step for further processing. The asynchronous processing architecture decouples the systems from one another and as a consequence prevents the failure of one system from affecting the other.

Enterprise messaging systems support reliable message delivery even in the presence of failures by ensuring that the message is delivered to the recipient or by communicating to the sender that the message failed to reach the recipient. However, the guaranteed delivery of a message from the service consumer does not guarantee that the message was successfully processed by the service provider. The service provider might have crashed while processing the message. Therefore, service level fault-tolerance will be required (as discussed in previous sections) to ensure that asynchronous messages are processed in the event of service failures.

Notifications are considered the most efficient way to track the status of an asynchronous message. In the *notification* methodology, the service consumer is notified only when the service provider registers a change in the message processing status. On the other hand, in the *polling* methodology, the service consumer may have to make multiple status requests to the provider in order to capture the change in status. In asynchronous processing, one is not waiting on each step to complete; however, it is significant to ensure the completion of the entire process without waiting indefinitely to receive the processing results. This is generally handled by implementing a time-out mechanism. Exceptions in the process are handled by the transactional compensation mechanism as described in the next section, which essentially involves rolling back the transaction in the database for actions that have already completed before the process as a whole failed.

Failure Recovery

The goal of fault-tolerance is to enable the system to continue to function despite faults being generated. Services do fault and there needs to be mechanisms in place to handle and recover from faults so as not to affect the integrity of data. Exception handling and transactional compensation are the two primary techniques used for fault recovery in service compositions (Tartanoglu, Issarny, Romanovsky, & Levy, 2003). Exception handling attempts to repair faults and allow the composite services to continue to run, while transactional compensation ensures that composite services terminate with data integrity when faults are un-repairable.

Two prevalent strategies to handle failure recovery are *backward recovery* and *forward recovery* mechanisms (Dobson, 2006; Liu, Li, & Xiao, 2007; Mikalsen, Tai, & Ravellou, 2002). Backward recovery is achieved by *rolling-back* all the actions that succeeded as part of a failed transaction so that the transactional state is restored back to the initial state that existed before the transaction executed. This is also called transactional compensation. Forward recovery is implemented by either ignoring the failed invocation (Ignore), or retrying the same invocation to the same service (Retry), or retrying the same invocation to a functionally-equivalent substituted service (Substitute). A hybrid approach of combining some of these strategies such as retrying for a specified number of times and then substituting the called service with a substitute service is also practiced.

Business Processes are widely used in a service-driven environment to implement Workflow Services. WS-BPEL (Web Service–Business Process Execution Language) is a prominent technology for controlling and managing business process execution. WS-BPEL has built-in mechanisms for exception handling and transactional compensation. BPEL provides scopes with fault handlers to handle faults in a similar manner to the try-catch mechanism in programming languages such as Java. BPEL scopes also provide for compensation handlers, which can facilitate to undo a failed transaction with a compensating transaction to bring the system back to its initial state.

When a fault occurs in BPEL, the execution flow moves from the activity that generates the fault to the fault handler that is in the scope that is immediately enclosing the faulting activity. If there is no immediately enclosing fault handler, then the execution moves to the process fault handler. On execution of a fault handler, all enclosed activities of the scope are forced to terminate. Once a scope catches a fault, it is considered to have not completed normally and is therefore not eligible for compensation. Only activities that have completed normally will be compensated by the compensation handler, which would include those activities in the enclosed scopes. Having terminated all enclosed active activities, all enclosed scopes are compensated. After that, the fault is thrown to the immediately enclosing scope to enable graceful termination of the business process.

CONCLUSION

This chapter explored the challenges faced by enterprises in terms of achieving high availability and fault-tolerance for business services. Several architectural approaches were discussed to provide guidelines for improving the fault-tolerance of service compositions. Concepts such as service redundancy and design diversity were presented to illustrate the fundamental methodologies for implementing fault-tolerant services. The chapter focused on architectural approaches such as scaling, clustering, distributed data caching, in-memory data grid, and asynchronous messaging as predominant methodologies that enterprises can use to achieve fault-tolerance with business services. The data scalability bottleneck was also examined and solutions were presented. Last but not the least, strategies to handle failure recovery as well as the built-in mechanisms in WS-BPEL for exception handling and transactional compensation were discussed.

The future of service fault-tolerance lays in context-aware adaptive solutions, where the fault-tolerant mechanism is aware of its operational environment and adjusts itself dynamically based on the current levels of redundancy employed, the operational status of the deployed resources, such as, dependability, load, execution time, and the evolution of voting outcomes, etc. These fault-tolerant systems will be self-tuning and self-healing by continuously monitoring the resources and their operational statuses. The Cloud ecosystem will also play a significant role in enhancing the scalability, high availability, and fault-tolerance of enterprise services due to its nature of elastic scalability and dynamic resource provisioning capabilities.

REFERENCES

Allcock, B., Chervenak, A., Foster, I., Kesselman, C., & Livny, M. (2005). Data grid tools: Enabling science on big distributed data. [Institute of Physics Publishing]. *Journal of Physics: Conference Series, 16*, 571–575. doi:10.1088/1742-6596/16/1/079.

Avizienis, A. (1985). The n-version approach to fault-tolerant software. *IEEE Transactions on Software Engineering SE, 11*(12), 1491–1501. doi:10.1109/TSE.1985.231893.

Baker, M. (Ed.). (2001). Cluster computing white paper. Retrieved from http://arxiv.org/ftp/cs/papers/0004/0004014.pdf

Belalem, G., & Meroufel, B. (2011). Management and placement of replicas in a hierarchical data grid. *International Journal of Distributed and Parallel Systems (IJDPS), 2*(6), 23–30. doi:10.5121/ijdps.2011.2603.

Brewer, E. (2004). Towards robust distributed systems. Retrieved from http://www.cs.berkeley.edu/~brewer/cs262b-2004/PODC-keynote.pdf

Buyya, R. (Ed.). (1999). *High performance cluster computing: Architectures and systems (Vol. 1)*. Prentice Hall.

Chervenak, A., Foster, I., Kesselman, C., Salisbury, C., & Tuecke, S. (2001). The data grid: Towards an architecture for the distributed management and analysis of large scientific datasets. *Journal of Network and Computer Applications, 23*, 187–200. doi:10.1006/jnca.2000.0110.

De Florio, V. (2009). *Application-layer fault-tolerance protocols*. IGI Global. doi:10.4018/978-1-60566-182-7.

Diab, H. B., & Zomaya, A. Y. (Eds.). (2005). *Dependable computing systems: Paradigms, performance issues, and applications. Wiley Series on Parallel and Distributed Computing*. Wiley-Interscience.

Dobson, G. (2006). Using WS-BPEL to implement software fault tolerance for web services. In *Proceedings of the 32nd EUROMICRO Conference on Software Engineering and Advanced Applications, IEEE Computer Society* (pp. 126-133).

Dubrova, E. (2002). *Fault tolerant design: An introduction*. Kluwer Academic Publishers.

Erradi, A., Maheshwari, P., & Tosic, V. (2006). Recovery policies for enhancing web services reliability. In *Proceedings of the IEEE international Conference on Web Services (ICWS'06), IEEE Computer Society* (pp. 189-196).

Hohpe, G., & Woolf, B. (2003). *Enterprise integration patterns: Designing, building, and deploying messaging solutions*. USA: Pearson Education.

Johnson, B. W. (1989). *Design and analysis of fault tolerant digital systems*. Boston, MA, USA: Addison-Wesley Series in Electrical and Computer Engineering.

Leu, D., Bastani, F., & Leiss, E. (1990). The effect of statically and dynamically replicated components on system reliability. *IEEE Transactions on Reliability, 39*(2), 209–216. doi:10.1109/24.55884.

Liu, A., Li, Q., & Xiao, M. (2007). A declarative approach to enhancing the reliability of BPEL processes. In *Proceedings of the IEEE international Conference on Web Services (ICWS'07), IEEE Computer Society* (pp. 272-279).

Mikalsen, T., Tai, S., & Ravellou, I. (2002). Transactional attitudes: Reliable composition of autonomous Web services. In *Workshop on Dependable Middleware Based Systems (WDMS)*, Washington, DC, USA.

OASIS. (2004). *Web services reliability*. Retrieved from http://docs.oasis-open.org/wsrm/ws-reliability/v1.1/wsrm-ws_reliability-1.1-spec-os.pdf

OASIS. (2006). *Web services reliable messaging*. Retrieved from http://docs.oasis-open.org/ws-rx/wsrm/200608/wsrm-1.1-spec-cd-04.html

Paul, S., & Fei, Z. (2001). Distributed caching with centralized control. *Computer Communications, 24*(2), 256–268. doi:10.1016/S0140-3664(00)00322-4.

Salatge, N., & Fabre, J. C. (2007). Fault tolerance connectors for unreliable web services. In DSN (pp. 51–60).

Tartanoglu, I. V., Romanovsky, A., & Levy, N. (2003). Coordinated forward error recovery for composite web services. In *Proceedings of International Symposium. Reliable Distributed Systems (SRDS '03)* (pp. 167-176).

Vallath, M. (2003). *Real application clusters*. Burlington, MA: Digital Press.

KEY TERMS AND DEFINITIONS

Cluster: A group of nodes or servers that work together to present a single system interface to the user. Clustering facilitates load balancing and failover of applications and improves service availability by providing uninterrupted service through redundant nodes and servers that eliminate single points of failure.

Distributed Data Caching: A data caching mechanism that scales out across multiple nodes or servers, but presents a single logical view of the data to the applications and services. A distributed data cache leads to drastic improvements in the performance and scalability of services.

Distributed Queue: A message queue that is clustered across servers such that each server has its own physical queue that is managed by a logical queue that is shared by all servers.

Fault-Tolerance: An indicator of how well a system or application can tolerate the failure of one or more hardware or software components and still continue to operate in an acceptable manner. Fault-tolerance ensures overall system or application availability, albeit at decreased throughput.

High Availability: Highly available systems provide useful resources over a period of time and guarantee functional continuity within that time window.

In-Memory Data Grid: An abstraction that combines distributed caching with replication techniques to provide a highly scalable, available, performant, and fault-tolerant data caching environment.

N-Version Programming: A technique that advocates the independent generation of "n" functionally-equivalent programs from the same functional specification and the simultaneous execution of all of them to obtain the result using a decision algorithm based on the individual outputs of the programs.

Object Relational Mapping: A mechanism used for mapping relational data to object data and vice-versa.

Scalability: A property of a system, application, or service that indicates how well it can handle increasing amounts of load in response to increasing processing demand. Service-driven applications require dynamic scalability to handle varying compute and data loads to satisfy the dynamics of the business.

Transactional Compensation: A technique for maintaining the data integrity in transactions when faults are un-repairable. The compensation is achieved by rolling back the transactions in the database for actions that have already completed before the process as a whole failed.

Write-Behind Caching: A caching mechanism which writes out the database in an asynchronous mode. The cache is updated synchronously but the update of the database is delayed and happens asynchronously at a later time.

Chapter 9
Governing the Service–Driven Environment:
Tools and Techniques

Leo Shuster
Nationwide Insurance, USA

ABSTRACT

The purpose of this chapter is to discuss tools, technologies, and practices employed to govern the service lifecycle in a Service-driven environment. Aside from defining the complete service lifecycle, the discussion will concentrate on specific approaches to governing each stage in the lifecycle and best practices associated with it. SOA governance methodology will be covered in great detail. The topics discussed will include SOA Governance program structure, methodology, processes, funding, value demonstration, and adoption levers. These governance mechanisms will be aligned with each stage in the service lifecycle, and appropriate applications will be identified accordingly. Current and future state of governance tools and technologies will be explored. Some examples of existing tools will be provided to highlight and support the assertions made throughout the chapter. Connection between stages in the service lifecycle and the governance tools and technologies will be identified and best practices explored.

INTRODUCTION

Imagine driving down an unpaved road at 60 miles per hour without road signs, traffic lights, markers, or guardrails to help you determine where you are going. How quickly would you end up in a ditch? That depends on many things – how good your driving skills are, how tough is the road, how well lit it is, etc. However, it is plainly evident that avoiding a ditch is virtually impossible in this situation.

The example highlights an important reality. No project or program that embarks on a journey through an unchartered territory can survive without a roadmap and a paved road with clearly marked signs, exits, and guardrails. This is especially significant for a program utilizing Service-driven architectural approaches. It can easily disintegrate without a well defined governance mechanism. SOA (Service Oriented Architecture) Governance is as necessary for the Service-driven approach to survive as the air is for people. Without it, any

DOI: 10.4018/978-1-4666-4193-8.ch009

Service-driven initiative will quickly become "Just a Bunch of Services," a collection of loosely organized, unmanaged, and unaccounted services, scattered throughout the enterprise.

SOA Governance

In simplest terms, *SOA Governance* is a mechanism for controlling and directing outcomes of a Service-driven program. It is the guardrails on the SOA highway, without which the SOA program would end up in a ditch. While SOA defines how services are built, SOA Governance specifies the rules by which it happens.

Brown et al. (2008) defined governance as "the need for a process or set of processes to ensure that where appropriate the laws, policies, standards, and procedures are being adhered to. It also should appropriately distribute the rights and responsibilities under which an organization makes decisions and operates." This definition can be applied to SOA Governance as well, considering that the target to which the rules are applied against is the SOA program.

The primary responsibility of SOA Governance is to ensure success of the SOA program. The goal of SOA is to increase business agility through loose coupling of applications and reuse of shared services. SOA Governance helps achieve these goals by enforcing standards, laying out guidelines, ensuring compliance, and driving correct behaviors. Most importantly, SOA Governance helps institutionalize SOA across the organization and creates a system of checks and balances to maximize the success of the SOA program.

The success of the SOA program is measured through a series of metrics defined to capture what is most important for the organization. One of the key outcomes of SOA Governance is the organization's ability to measure the value of the SOA program. With this comes the ability to improve those areas that are not performing well based on the collected metrics. Overall, SOA Governance

forces the organization to accelerate its maturity and effectiveness through a continuous cycle of evaluation and improvement.

SOA Governance cannot exist by itself. It is a part of a larger IT governance structure that controls every aspect of IT systems design, build, and implementation. SOA Governance covers the planning, design, development, and the operational aspects of Service-driven systems. It must rely on IT governance to provide guidance on tasks that fall outside its domain.

SOA is a subset of Enterprise Architecture. Enterprise Architecture is the overarching architecture strategy that the company employs to align business and IT strategies. It governs all of the aspects of business and IT architecture. Since SOA is one of the key business agility enablers, it falls in the Enterprise Architecture domain. By extension, SOA Governance falls under the purview of Enterprise Architecture precepts, rules, and guidelines. While SOA Governance defines rules that are more detailed and specific than those of Enterprise Architecture, they must still comply with the high level guidelines and the spirit of Enterprise Architecture principles.

SOA Governance can also intersect with business governance. Since SOA promises significant business agility, business is deeply involved in business process modeling, service identification, reuse opportunity identification, portfolio management, and funding decisions. Thus, SOA governance becomes a business imperative. Business stakeholders need to be involved in the SOA governance processes as much as IT and Enterprise Architecture.

An SOA Governance program is the formalized practice of executing SOA Governance activities. It typically consists of several key elements.

- **People:** Roles and responsibilities related to SOA Governance activities.
- **Processes:** SOA Governance processes that need to be executed.

- **Standards:** Set of policies, principles, and guidelines that the SOA Governance must enforce.

For any SOA Governance program to be successful, it must be well organized and formalized. Processes must be well defined and understood by everyone across the organization. The standards that the program enforces must be well documented, clear, and readily available. The people, roles, and responsibilities that participate in the SOA Governance activities must be clearly defined and accepted. Most importantly, there has to exist organizational and political support for the program from the very top of the organization. Without real teeth, the SOA Governance program will quickly become mired in political turf wars and irreconcilable differences.

Service Lifecycle

A Service-driven architectural approach manages the delivery and reuse of shared services. Since each service is managed independently, as a separate piece of software, its evolution can be described as a well defined lifecycle. It is similar to that of any software but has a number of unique characteristics due to a shared nature of each service, its shared deployment characteristics, and high degree of enterprise impact.

Typical stages in a *Service Lifecycle* are described in Table 1.

It is important to understand that a service can pass through each of its lifecycle stages multiple times until it reaches retirement as shown in Figure 1. The Service Versioning stage starts a new iteration of the entire lifecycle which results in a creation of a new service version. There may be multiple service versions running at the same

Table 1. Service lifecycle stages

Service Lifecycle Stage	Description	Details
Service identification	Identification of service candidates	This is typically the initial stage in the lifecycle, especially for new services.
Service analysis	Analysis of service requirements and existing service portfolio (inventory of services)	Many critical decisions related to current and future state of the service are made in this phase including fit into service portfolio, architectural direction, etc.
Service design	Detailed design of service interface, message model, and policies	Most of the low level decisions are made in this stage.
Service development	Development of all the service artifacts	This includes development of service interface, message model, policies, configuration, etc., as well as performing unit testing.
Service testing	Completion of various testing activities including integration, regression, performance, longevity, stress, etc.	Testing needs to take into account new and existing service requirements.
Service deployment	Deployment of service artifacts into the production environment	May need to include rudimentary smoke test.
Service run and management	Operational stage of the service that includes all of the run-time activities, metrics capture, and communications	This is where the actual service value is measured and ROI is tracked and communicated.
Service versioning	Creation of a new service version; starts a new cycle and kicks a new version to the service analysis stage	A new service version should be warranted and approved.
Service retirement	Retirement of one or several existing service versions	Service retirement criteria has to be met to be entered into this stage

Figure 1. Service lifecycle

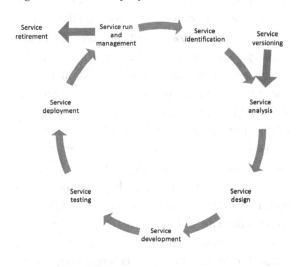

time. Each of them can reach retirement at different times depending on company's policies and its ability to migrate consumers to the new version of the service.

Different actors participate in different phases of the service lifecycle. These range from a service architect to a developer and support technician. While roles may be persistent across phases, their expected contributions and deliverables change from one phase to another. All of the roles and responsibilities will be defined in subsequent sections.

This chapter is organized as follows. SOA Governance program structure will be first introduced along with the methodology, processes, funding, value demonstration, and adoption levers. These governance mechanisms will be aligned with each stage in the service lifecycle, and appropriate applications will be identified accordingly. Next, current and future state of governance tools and technologies will be explored. Some examples of existing tools will be provided to highlight and support the assertions made throughout the chapter. Connection between stages in the service lifecycle and the governance tools and technologies will be identified and best practices explored.

BACKGROUND

SOA Governance is well covered in industry publications – from articles to white papers and books. Many leading minds in the SOA arena have voiced their opinions about how SOA Governance programs should be executed, what matters most, and how to make it successful. A number of standards bodies have defined their own SOA and SOA Governance frameworks. There is, however, no consensus on which frameworks and approaches work best. SOA Governance remains largely an art form rather than a scientific formula.

There are a number of common threads that can be seen across all the SOA Governance work produced to date. These include the need to establish the right organizational structures that fit specific corporate styles, creating a system of incentives to increase the adoption of SOA across the enterprise, seamlessly incorporating SOA Governance mechanisms into all the other IT and corporate governance structures, and, of course, closely managing every aspect of the service lifecycle.

The SOA platforms and subsequently SOA Governance tools have matured significantly since SOA first hit the mainstream. Today's technologies are much more seamlessly integrated with the entire SOA suite, development tools, and the rest of the enterprise than ever before. Nevertheless, many new and innovative SOA products continue to emerge. New frameworks, Cloud Computing offerings, infrastructure platforms, and many other solutions have been flooding the market. Organizations have many more choices today than they had even a few years ago.

Despite all the advancements in SOA technology and continued maturity of the SOA Governance frameworks, many organizations continue to struggle. Building a successful Service-driven approach is as elusive to many enterprises as when SOA was still in its infancy. While many proven techniques and approaches exist, companies are struggling to adopt them and make them work in their environment.

Service Categorization

Not all services are created equal. There are services that are used by a large number of applications and are deemed extremely valuable to the enterprise. There are those that are created as an abstraction layer on top of a third party vendor interface and are only relevant in a specific domain. Somewhere in between lay a number of other services. Their value can be monetary representing cost savings due to the scope of reuse or labor avoidance, related to opportunity cost of business being able to accelerate speed to market, or non-monetary representing reduced risk, better quality, and policy enforcement. An SOA Governance program must provide a clear guidance on how to categorize and value each of the services that fall under its guidance.

Before we define a comprehensive framework for assigning a value to each service, let's agree on the categories of services that can exist within an enterprise. Most services can fit into three distinct categories:

- Enterprise services
- Domain services
- Local services

Enterprise services are those services that are reused across organizational boundaries. This happens because the functionality they expose is needed by multiple organizations. Because different enterprises have different business unit and IT alignments, it is not always clear how to define an organizational boundary. A basic heuristic can be IT departments. Because services are typically consumed by IT assets, the IT organizational boundaries are most relevant for this categorization. It is important because different groups manage these assets and are impacted if

an enterprise service introduces a change. An enterprise service represents not only the biggest value to the organization but can potentially have the largest impact across the organization. Since many services are starting to be used directly by the business units, potentially even functional domain boundaries can be considered as possible delineation attributes for enterprise services.

Domain services are those services that are reused within a single organization, business unit, or functional domain. They may be reused by multiple applications or represent a high value for this domain. While the definition of a single domain is more straightforward than that of an organizational boundary, it is largely dependent on the corporate structure.

Local services are those services that are used by a single application. They are not reusable and are created specifically for this application. They are typically considered part of the calling application.

Erl (2007) categorizes services as entity, task, and utility. These are valid service characteristics, but they are related to the functional dimensions of the service rather than its organizational and governance aspects. Therefore, we will not use these categories in discussing SOA governance implications on different types of services.

As you can guess, enterprise services can have the most impact on the enterprise. As a consequence, enterprise services would typically garner more scrutiny, higher degree of urgency, more funding, and greater focus. Therefore, throughout this chapter, when discussing SOA Governance, we will only apply it to enterprise services unless other service categories are specifically called out.

GOVERNING THE SERVICE LIFECYCLE

Establishing a successful SOA Governance program is not an easy task. While it may seem simple on the surface, once you start looking deeper, you realize how many hidden currents and roadblocks there are. Service-driven architectural approach serves multiple masters. Even though it pursues an enterprise goal of creating shared services and increasing their reuse, these services are owned and consumed by various groups including a central SOA team, different business units, or even potentially external entities. This means that all the changes have to be carefully choreographed on the enterprise as well as the business unit level.

An SOA Governance program has to play a role of an orchestra conductor. It has to ensure that everything happens under its watchful eye, all the musicians (different departments) play from the same sheet of music, individual performers (specific asset owners) play the right notes, and the orchestra as a whole (enterprise) performs the musical piece as expected. In other words, SOA Governance has to ensure that everything that happens within the enterprise follows the rules, adheres to the established processes, and works together seamlessly.

We will discuss how to achieve this in the subsequent sections.

SOA Governance Program Structure

For any governance program to be successful, it must have the ability to do two things – incentivize the right behaviors and penalize the wrong behaviors. You cannot have one or the other – you must have both. In order to establish the right level of incentives and disincentives, enforce them effectively, and manage the exceptions, the appropriate structure must be put in place. This includes not only the organizational structures but also the processes that bind them together. Consequences of each decision and action must be clearly articulated and assigned to a specific governance body to enforce. The bottom line is that the entire structure of the SOA Governance program must be clearly laid out and aligned with the service lifecycle stages.

An SOA Governance program must have a clearly defined chain of authority. It must consist of the governance bodies that are empowered to make specific decisions. These bodies include:

- **SOA Governance Board:** Oversees all aspects of the Service-driven approaches.
- **Architecture Review Board:** Oversees all architectural decisions across the enterprise.
- **Executive Review Board:** Establishes and aligns business and IT strategies.

According to Biske (2008), "The most important thing is to have your governance efforts match the culture of the organization, presuming that your organization is already effective in its decision making and policy setting processes." Organizing the SOA governance program structure that closely aligns with the company's culture, decision making processes, and authority distribution, would remove a lot of barriers and improve its adoption.

As mentioned before, SOA Governance has to seamlessly integrate with the rest of the IT Governance mechanisms. However, the specific IT Governance bodies are not discussed or described here. We will focus principally on the SOA Governance structures and processes.

The general relationships between the governance bodies specified above are depicted in Figure 2.

Each of the specific processes that connect SOA governance bodies together will be discussed in subsequent sections. However, it is important to outline what they are.

- **Service Identification Process:** Identifies reusable service opportunities, classifies services, and serves as an entry point for service delivery lifecycle.
- **Service Delivery Process:** Defines governance processes and mechanisms related to service delivery.

Figure 2. SOA Governance bodies and their relationships

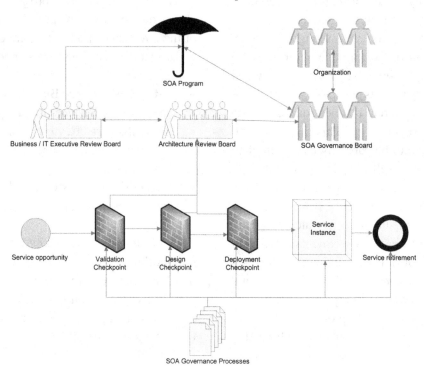

- **SOA Vitality Process:** Maintains the applicability and currency of SOA technology and reference architecture.
- **SOA Exception and Appeals Process:** Allows projects to appeal the noncompliance of a solution design decision or an investment.
- **SOA Communications Process:** Aims to educate about and communicate the SOA architecture across the organization.
- **Business/IT Executive Review Board Process:** Helps provide guidance for the Service-driven initiatives.

The structure of each of the governance bodies discussed above can differ from company to company. However, their basic charter and organization should remain consistent. Table 2 defines what each body strives to achieve and what roles need to participate in it.

Each SOA governance body has a specific role related to the service lifecycle. Since specific governance tasks and activities need to be performed in each phase, one or several governance bodies should be responsible for them. See Figure 3.

Even though different organizations may have different ways of dealing with governance activities and assigning responsibility for them, general tasks in a mature SOA program should all be consistent. It goes without saying that every enterprise that embarked on a SOA journey should travel towards maximum maturity level. Tasks and practices outlined in Table 3 are the mark of a mature organization.

All the details behind processes, standards, and individual roles and responsibilities related to governing the entire service lifecycle are discussed in subsequent sections. The information here provides a roadmap for all these discussions.

Table 2. SOA governance bodies

Governance Body	Objectives	People/Roles
SOA Governance Board	• Oversees all aspects of the SOA program • Approves and manages SOA Governance standards and processes	• Enterprise/Chief Architect • SOA lead architect • SOA development team lead • Architecture and development representative from each IT department • Infrastructure architect • Security architect • Data architect • Business service owners
Architecture Review Board	• Oversees all architectural decisions across the enterprise • Approves and manages architecture standards and processes	• Enterprise / Chief Architect • Architecture representative from each IT department • SOA architect • Infrastructure architect • Security architect • Data architect
Executive Review Board	• Establishes and aligns business and IT strategies • Provides guidance on business and IT investment priorities	• CIO • CFO • COO • Business executives from each business unit

Figure 3. SOA governance bodies and service lifecycle

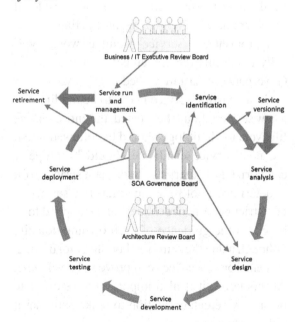

SOA Governance Methodology

Like any other extensive enterprise program, SOA Governance needs to follow a prescriptive approach. Everyone involved should know when specific processes need to be executed, what control gates exist, what deliverables are expected, and who is supposed to be involved. In order to achieve this, a comprehensive methodology must be established.

There are several critical processes for which a methodology needs to be established. They include:

- Service delivery methodology
- Project management methodology
- Service hosting methodology

Each of these cover an important portion of the SOA Governance program and provide prescriptive guidance on how these processes should be handled.

Service Delivery Methodology

Service delivery methodology deals with identifying what should be expected during a service delivery lifecycle. This methodology will not cover all the phases in the service lifecycle, just the ones dealing with delivering a new service or modify-

Table 3. SOA governance bodies' responsibilities in the service lifecycle

Service Lifecycle Phase	Governance Body	Roles and Responsibilities
Service identification	SOA Governance Board	• Validate service opportunities • Categorize services
Service analysis	None	
Service design	SOA Governance Board	• Align service design with enterprise inventory
	Architecture Review Board (or its subcommittee)	• Ensure design follows SOA standards • Accept/reject service design
Service development	None	
Service testing	None	
Service deployment	SOA Governance Board	• Accept/reject service deployment into production
Service run and management	SOA Governance Board	• Metrics collection and communication
	Executive Review Board	• Review metrics • Recommend strategic changes • Provide service adoption targets
Service versioning	SOA Governance Board	• Ensure new service version is warranted
Service retirement	SOA Governance Board	• Accept/reject service retirement proposal • Communicate decision to all impacted parties

ing an existing one. Figure 4 contains a high level depiction of the service delivery methodology, its specific gates and deliverables.

The methodology defines what is expected during each phase of service delivery. It is important to recognize that there are some references to the Service Registry, which will be discussed later in this chapter. For the sake of this discussion, only interactions with this tool will be addressed, not the mechanics of actually performing the expected tasks.

A service delivery kicks off with identification of a service candidate. Once this happens in the Analysis phase and some details of the service demand are understood, the decision needs to be made if an existing service meets the requirements. If there is a service with a close match, a determination whether it can be reused as-is should be made. If, in fact, the service matches the requirements perfectly, no additional steps are necessary aside from requesting for the new consumer to be on-boarded, which includes allowing access to the service, updating service policies, and ensuring adequate performance and scalability of the service given the additional volume.

The reuse decision may not be very straightforward. There may be a number of factors considered to determine whether reusing an existing service is appropriate. A Service Architect would typically make this recommendation, and the SOA Governance Board may need to approve it.

If an existing service needs to be modified or a new service should be created, the entire service lifecycle methodology should be followed. First, the new service candidate should be properly categorized as enterprise or domain service. If it is determined not to be an enterprise service, a less strict governance model can be applied to it, based on the guidance of each owning domain, although using the same methodology for domain and enterprise services can prove to be valuable. At this point, it is also important to re-evaluate prior service categorization to make sure that it did not change.

Once a service has been validated and categorized, it should be registered as a new delivery candidate in the Service Registry. If we are updating an existing service, a new service version needs to be registered. Situations may arise when a new service candidate is later rolled into an existing

Figure 4. (Top) Service delivery methodology: analysis, design, build; (bottom) service delivery methodology: test, production, run

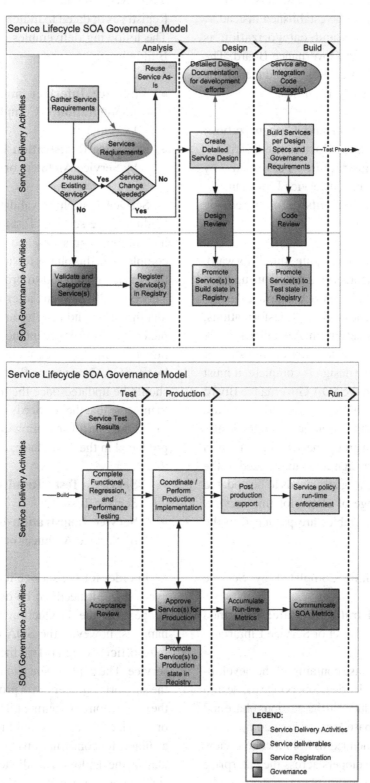

service. In this case, service candidate registration should be removed and a new version of an existing service should be established instead.

Service validation and categorization is performed by the SOA Governance Board. The following deliverables are being produced in the Identification and Analysis phases:

- **Service Validation and Categorization:** Performed by SOA Governance Board.
- **Service Registration:** Performed by Service Architect or Service Librarian.
- **Service Requirements:** Completed by Service Analyst.

Service Design phase is quite straightforward. In this phase, technical service details are updated or created. This includes service interface design, message model, orchestrations, transformations, and run-time policy definition. A detailed service design document is created that contains all of these items. Once the design is complete, it must be reviewed by both the SOA Governance Board and the Architecture Review Board to ensure that it complies with the standards and no design concerns exist. Both groups need to formally sign off on the service design for it to proceed to the next phase. Service Registry needs to be updated to reflect the change of status for this service. The following deliverables are produced in the Design phase:

- **Service Design:** Completed by Service Architect.
- **Service Registration Update:** Performed by Service Architect or Service Librarian.

Service Build phase contains all the development activities. Service developers take the design documentation produced in the previous phase and build the services based on it. Upon completion, it is highly recommended to hold a code review with other SOA developers across the enterprise to ensure maximum quality of the produced code.

Once the code has been completed and certified, it is moved into the test environment and Service Registry is updated to indicate the correct status. The following deliverables are produced in the Build phase:

- **Service Interface and Underlying Implementation:** Completed by Service Developers.
- **Service Registration Update:** Performed by Service Architect or Service Librarian.

Service Test phase validates quality and feasibility of the service. Tests such as functional, integration, regression, and performance are all completed in this phase. Results are reviewed, and the service is allowed to proceed to production. This typically happens after a number of defect identification and resolution iterations are completed. Test results acceptance is signed off by the project team. Any exceptions should be resolved by the SOA Governance Board. Service Registry should be updated once the testing is completed to indicate that the service is ready to be deployed to production. The following deliverables are produced in the Test phase:

- **Service Test Results:** Performed by Service Testers.
- **Service Registration Update:** Performed by Service Architect or Service Librarian.

In order for the service to enter the Run lifecycle stage, it needs to be deployed first which happens in the Production phase. Before this happens, however, the SOA Governance Board must officially sign off on the deployment of the service. The deployment should be performed by the support engineers with proper access rights to the production environment. The Service Architect or Service Librarian should mark the service as available for consumption in the Service Registry. During the deployment, all the appropriate access rights should be granted to the new consumers of the service, run-time policies applied, and infra-structure refreshed if necessary. Some organizations require a formal acceptance of the service by key stakeholders including business service owners and business / IT users.

The Run phase consists of monitoring the service in the production environment, providing necessary support, fixing production defects, and collecting usage metrics. Monitoring and metrics collection can be performed by automated tools. Operational and usage reports should be easily accessible for the SOA Governance Board to be able to provide all the relevant statistics to the IT and business executives.

Even though many companies will not have a Service Registry platform, this methodology uses it as a general concept that can be implemented by any tool, even as simple as an Excel spreadsheet. It is not the Service Registry platform that is important but rather the actions performed against it.

While this methodology appears sequential, it can be utilized in conjunction with any type of software delivery approach – *agile, iterative, waterfall*, etc. Rather than thinking of each phase as a pre-requisite to the next, think about the expected deliverables, processes, and governance mechanisms that are defined. Even agile software development methodologies can incorporate them into their structure and ensure that all the steps are followed throughout the service delivery lifecycle.

SOA Project Delivery Methodology

Projects are the primary means for an IT organization to deliver its work. Almost everything IT does is structured as a project. However, due to its enterprise nature and the goal of creating shared services, SOA is incompatible with the project-based software delivery lifecycle. Project and SOA program goals are often in conflict. A project's primary objective is to deliver the functionality requested by the business on time and on budget.

The Service-driven initiative strives to maximize service reuse, drive efficiencies, and increase agility across the enterprise. Even though most SOA efforts start small and expand over time from one project to the next, it is typically hard to reconcile these goals. Without a clear vision, roadmap, and guiding principles established upfront, project-based SOA activities will lead to failure of the Service-driven initiative as a whole.

Brown (2007) noted an important problem with a project-driven approach. He posed a number of very important questions related to it. "Who, in silo-oriented projects, has the responsibility for revising the total architecture— both business processes and systems? Who defines the needed services?" Not surprisingly, the answers are not promising. "In most enterprises, the silo-based development processes do not contain explicit tasks for determining who should be doing what – either during development or in the revised business process. You either give the requirements to the silo's development team or tell the team to go determine what the requirements are" (Brown, 2007). Brown's conclusion is that this kind of process doesn't scale.

Projects are delivered using specific software development methodologies (SDM). Each company may have their own SDMs defined. They, however, can be split into two general categories – waterfall and agile. A Waterfall SDM is a sequential software development process, in which progress is seen as flowing steadily (like a waterfall) through several phases. An Agile SDM promotes creation of working software through short iterative cycles. Regardless of the SDM used, SOA governance activities and mechanisms should be aligned with it to ensure best results.

In a W*aterfall methodology*, one phase of software development is followed by another, everything happens sequentially as shown in Figure 5. Waterfall methodologies align well with the service lifecycle. Each specific deliverable

Figure 5. Typical interaction between waterfall and SOA methodologies

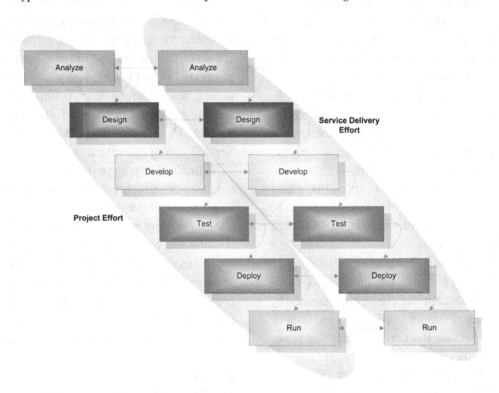

mandated by the SOA program and specific SOA governance methodology employed becomes a part of the deliverables for each SDM phase.

To most effectively align service-oriented efforts with *Agile Methodologies,* an overarching governance mechanism needs to be established. It will guide the delivery of all the shared services through a series of iterations. While each of the iterations continues to deliver working code, the team delivering shared services accumulates the related requirements and adjusts the service design and implementation accordingly as shown in Figure 6.

Projects are the primary driving forces behind service identification and implementation. While there may be some top-down approaches where services are built in anticipation of the demand, projects produce by far the largest chunk of service candidates than any of these anticipatory efforts. When a service is designed and developed to ad-

dress specific project needs, it is almost never fully reusable. New consumers invariably need changes introduced to the service to comply with their requirements. This typically involves field changes or additions, new operations, addition or removal of major entities, and even potentially business logic changes. The biggest SOA secret is that services are almost never reused as-is – changes and integration costs are practically unavoidable.

In order to make services truly reusable and ensure maximum leverage, service lifecycle should be centrally managed. Regardless of who is actually delivering shared services in your IT organization, a single view should be created to understand all the service identification, lifecycle management, and pipelining activities. The service portfolio modeling and service build out plan will also become inputs to this process. All of the disparate service requirements supplied by different

Figure 6. Typical interaction between agile and SOA methodologies

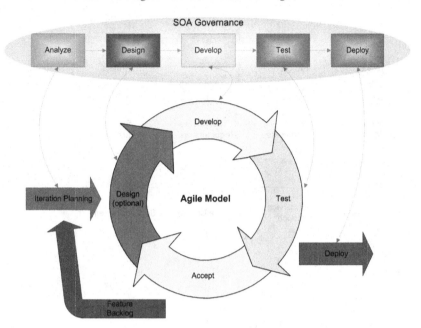

projects should be accumulated together to create a comprehensive view of each service's pipeline and roadmap as shown in Figure 7.

Project design and underlying architecture should also recognize the profound impact of service orientation on project's final deliverable. Application design should recognize services and related technologies that are included as part of the solution. All of this should be included as part of the overall design and managed accordingly. While service design can be completed separately from the application design, the final results should be integrated together to form a comprehensive view of the delivered solution.

The keys to successfully aligning project and service architectures are in achieving the following success factors:

- Early identification of service reuse or creation opportunities.
- Alignment of application and service designs.
- Comprehensive end-to-end application architecture.
- Service architecture flexibility.

Once these factors can be consistently realized from one project to another, project and SOA efforts will become more streamlined and efficient.

It is important to understand the complete project demand across the enterprise to establish a comprehensive *Service Pipeline* and release picture. Each project would supply its requirements and constraints to the service release mechanism, which would provide the completed services. Integration between these two efforts should be virtually seamless to ensure consistent delivery supporting both project needs and SOA goals.

Governance mechanisms should be put in place to recognize and ensure proper alignment between the project and service delivery efforts. Governance processes should be tightly coupled with the specific software development methodologies used by the enterprise as shown in Figure 8.

Service delivery efforts, just like projects, must comply with all the IT governance policies. It becomes even more important because changes to a single service can have significant impact on a large number of systems.

Without an effective funding model in place, it will be nearly impossible to reach both project

Figure 7. Service pipeline management

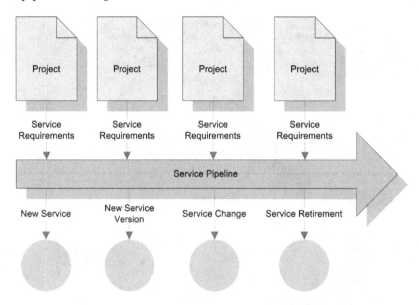

Figure 8. Integration between SDM and SOA governance

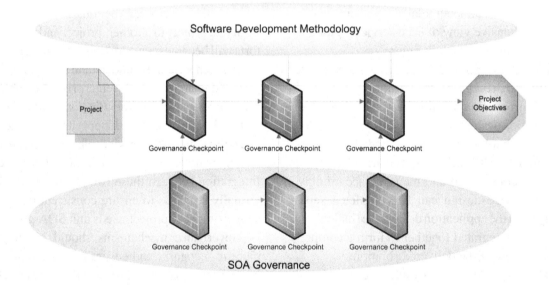

and SOA goals at the same time. IT organizations need to determine the most appropriate funding model for them and follow it. From the project perspective, the following considerations need to apply.

- Projects should not be unduly burdened to deliver enterprise functionality.

- Funding approach should entice projects to meet SOA goals as well as their own objectives.
- SOA funding processes should fit seamlessly into the existing project funding mechanisms.
- Project estimating, forecasting, and budgeting approaches should be in line with

the same activities related to the service delivery efforts. Both processes should be integrated to ensure smooth delivery.

For an SOA project delivery methodology to be successful, it must incorporate all the elements described here – SDM alignment, project pipelining, governance alignment, and funding.

SOA Hosting Methodology

SOA hosting methodology deals with hosting of the services and their endpoints. It is important to consider where each service instance resides based on what function it performs in the enterprise. Because different services have different value to the enterprise, distinct scalability characteristics, and different management needs, they may need to be hosted in different locations.

Service category plays a very important role in the hosting decision. Hosting decision largely depends on the service category, as shown in Table 4. The reason that service endpoints and implementation hosting decisions are separated is because ESBs (Enterprise Service Bus) can act as mediators as well as actual hosts for services. Enterprises may choose to create "virtual" services – services that have no physical implementation. As a result, both the endpoint and service implementation will reside on the ESB.

The most important factors in the hosting decision are how many consumers the service has, what its availability characteristics should be, and

Table 4. Service hosting decision direction

Service Category	Endpoint Hosting Decision	Service Hosting Decision
Enterprise	ESB or another central enterprise SOA platform	ESB or another enterprise scale platform
Domain	Domain ESB or another domain SOA platform	Domain ESB or another domain scale platform
Local	Application platform	Application platform

its overall value to the enterprise. As a general rule, all of the enterprise service endpoints should be hosted on the central ESB or an equivalent platform. It should be engineered for maximum scalability, performance, and uptime. Even though domain services may have similar requirements as those of enterprise services, it is often not warranted to host them on the enterprise platform because their value does not merit enterprise treatment and an enterprise team is often not the right entity to manage domain services. Domain services, by definition, only serve a single domain, which does not justify spending more money and effort to host them on an enterprise platform. If a domain ESB exists or a domain SOA environment has been established, this presents the most optimal platform to host domain services and their endpoints. Some companies, however, have chosen to only have a single central ESB that host both enterprise and domain services.

SOA Governance Processes

An SOA Governance program usually encompasses a number of processes. These cover all aspects of governing the service lifecycle and are aimed at managing such aspects as the SOA Maturity, SOA program execution, design-time governance, development-time governance, implementation-time governance, run-time governance, and change-time governance. We will discuss them in detail below.

SOA Maturity Model

SOA Maturity model defines different levels of an SOA program, from the lowest to the highest. It creates a roadmap for moving from one level to the next by defining specific characteristics and goals that should be reached at each level. There are a number of maturity frameworks that can be employed here. You can pick one that suits your organization best. One framework that can be served as a measuring stick for all others is

Table 5. COBIT governance maturity levels

COBIT Governance Maturity Level	Description
0 - Non-existent	Complete lack of any processes. The enterprise has not recognized that this is an area to be addressed.
1 - Initial/Ad-hoc	There is evidence that the enterprise has recognized that this is an area to be addressed. There are, however, no standardized processes; instead, there are ad-hoc approaches that tend to be applied on an individual or case-by-case basis.
2 - Repeatable but intuitive	Governance processes have developed to the stage at which similar procedures are followed by different people undertaking the same task. There is no formal training or communication of standard procedures, and responsibility is left to the individual. There is a high degree of reliance on the knowledge of individuals and, therefore, errors are likely.
3 - Defined Process	Governance procedures have been standardized, documented, and communicated. It is mandated that these processes should be followed; however, it is unlikely that deviations will be detected and corrected.
4 - Managed and Measurable	Governance authorities monitor and measure compliance with governance procedures and take action where processes appear not to be working effectively. Processes are under constant improvement and provide good practice. Automation and tools are used in a limited or fragmented way.
5 – Optimized	Governance processes have been refined to a level of good practice, based on the results of continuous improvement. Governance is used in an integrated way across the enterprise to improve quality and effectiveness, making the enterprise quick to adapt.

COBIT (Control Objectives for Information and related Technology) that provides an IT Maturity Model derived from the Software Engineering Institute's Capability Maturity Model (CMM) as shown in Table 5.

There are typically a number of dimensions across which the maturity level of the SOA program is measured. Different organizations can define the dimensions and criteria that are important to them. In general, these dimensions include:

- **Business:** Measures business attitude towards SOA.
- **Organization:** Determines the level of organizational readiness related to SOA.
- **Program Management:** Assesses maturity of Service-driven initiatives and project management practices.
- **Governance:** Evaluates maturity of SOA governance practices, processes, and supporting technology.
- **Architecture:** Gauges the level of SOA architecture definition, clarity, and adoption.

- **Technology:** Measures the maturity, type, and capability of the SOA related technology deployed in the enterprise.
- **Operations and Management:** Evaluates maturity of the service and SOA technology run-time management, monitoring, and scalability practices.

To correctly measure where you are in each dimension across the SOA maturity continuum, you need to define what it means to reach each maturity level. Once the matrix of dimension/maturity level definitions has been filled out, you can clearly see where you are and what you need to do to proceed to the next maturity level.

Program Level Governance

SOA program encompasses all the SOA efforts across the enterprise. This includes all of the projects with SOA or related deliverables, SOA technology implementations or changes, and service portfolio management. All of these efforts need to have visibility at the top level to ensure correlation of risk and impact. Any duplicate efforts need to be caught early and merged into a single work stream. The same should occur with the efforts that may have potential synergies.

These activities are best performed by the SOA Governance Board. It needs to have clear visibility into all of the SOA program activities across the enterprise and manage them accordingly. This work should be split into two distinct streams – service portfolio management and service technology management.

To properly manage the complete portfolio of services, the SOA Governance Board needs to clearly define what it represents and identify all potential and actual impacts to it. Service portfolio should be modeled as early in the life of the SOA program as possible. It will define a blueprint for what services should be created and where they would fit. Depending on the industry or an organization, these models may already exist. For example, the insurance industry has a variety of capability and entity models including ACORD, IAA, and others. A service portfolio model defines a complete list of business capabilities and associated services. In many instances, services may not be fully defined and will be flushed out as part of ongoing project work.

It is the responsibility of the SOA Governance Board to establish and manage the service portfolio. Recall that it has to review and validate all the service candidates in the Analyze phase of the service lifecycle. This is where the impact to the service portfolio should be identified. The SOA Governance Board should determine where in the portfolio the new service fits, or, in case of a change, who is impacted by it. Service portfolio should be updated to indicate services in production when new services are deployed or existing ones updated. This would occur in the Deploy service lifecycle phase.

If an impact to existing service consumers is identified, the SOA Governance Board should notify them and ensure that the impact is properly mitigated. The effort causing the impact may need

to be postponed, slowed down, or redirected to allow the impacted consumers to appropriately plan to accommodate the change. The SOA Governance Board may determine that the change is too impactful and guide the specific effort to create a new version of the service instead.

Managing SOA technology changes requires similar, if not greater, rigor. Depending on how these technologies are deployed, the impact to making any upgrades, infrastructure changes, or anything that would disrupt operations of services running on these platforms may be significant. If enterprise services are deployed on a central platform, making changes to it has to take into account disruptions in its operation and impact on many areas within the enterprise. Despite a lesser scope of impact for domain services regardless of whether they are deployed on an enterprise or domain platform, the same level of rigor and care should be applied.

The SOA Governance Board should manage any changes to the SOA infrastructure through a separate process. All requests for infrastructure changes, SOA platform upgrades, or new technology introductions must be approved or sponsored by the SOA Governance Board as shown in Figure 9. Without the official sanction, no changes should be allowed to occur.

The service portfolio management and service technology management processes need to be executed in conjunction with one another. They should not be managed in isolation. The SOA Governance Board needs to create a program level plan for managing all of the service and technology requests. This should be paired with a forward looking roadmap indicating planned changes that will eventually result in real efforts.

Design-Time Governance

The service delivery methodology calls for a number of things to occur that culminate in completion and approval of the service design. This includes service categorization and registration

Figure 9. SOA governance technology change management process

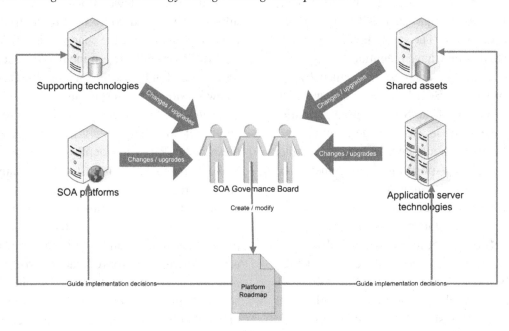

in the Identification phase, service requirements definition in the Analysis phase, and creation of service design and updating service registration in the Design phase. It also defines two governance processes that take place in these phases – service validation and categorization in the Identification phase and Service Design Review in the Design phase. The role of SOA Governance is to ensure that all the deliverables are properly furnished and all the processes are followed.

The service delivery methodology defines who is responsible for the specific deliverables and executing governance processes. Table 6 below details these responsibilities.

There are three key governance processes in the service design phases – service validation, categorization, and design review. Service validation is triggered by service candidate identification. This process, performed by the SOA Governance Board, takes service candidate information as the input and validates that it is, in fact, a candidate for a shared service and it fits into the service portfolio. Successful service validation triggers the service categorization

process. It is also performed by the SOA Governance Board. The expected outcome from this process is to determine service category – domain or enterprise – and ensure that the appropriate path is followed through the remaining service lifecycle phases based on the service category.

Table 6. Service design roles and responsibilities

Service Lifecycle Phase	Deliverable/ Process	Performed By
Service identification	Service validation	SOA Governance Board
	Service categorization	SOA Governance Board
	Service registration	Service Architect/ Service Librarian
Service analysis	Service requirements	Service Analyst
Service design	Service design	Service Architect
	Service registration update	Service Architect/ Service Librarian
	Service design review	Architecture Review Board (or its subcommittee)

Service design review process is initiated once the service design is completed. The Service Architect working on the service design should contact the Architecture Review Board to schedule the review. A predefined format for the review deliverables and proceedings should exist. Successful review will result in the service delivery efforts proceeding to the next phase, while a rejection will need to be considered by the project team and trigger appropriate changes to the service design. If the team feels that the rejection was improper or other overriding factors exist, it can appeal the decision to the Executive Review Board. This governance body can choose to override the Architecture Review Board's decision, which will allow the service to proceed into development.

Development-Time Governance

Service development results in executable service code to be produced and unit tested. Service design and requirements should be taken into account when developing the service. Non-functional requirements for all the service consumers should be addressed. Additionally, service implementation should follow all the SOA standards, best practices, and guidelines.

According to the service delivery methodology, a variety of roles (Table 7) participate in the service development efforts, a number of deliverables are expected, and one governance process should be executed.

Table 7. Service development roles and responsibilities

Deliverable/Process	Performed By
Service interface	SOA Developers
Service implementation	SOA or Domain Developers
Service registration update	Service Architect / Service Librarian
Service code review	Peer Review Committee

In the majority of organizations, service consumer endpoint for enterprise services will reside on the ESB. It is, therefore, the job of the central SOA team (if one exists) to create the endpoint, expose it to the consumers, and wire it with the underlying service implementation. If the underlying service provider resides in a domain system, it is the job of the domain team that owns it to create or modify it. There may also be situations when both the endpoint and service implementation are owned by the central SOA team, in which case both deliverables will be its responsibility.

Upon completion of the development work, both the interface and service implementations should be reviewed by a Peer Review Committee. Each organization will choose to implement this process differently. However, to ensure maximum quality of the service, a group of peers should review the work of the project team and provide formal feedback as well as approval to proceed.

The Service Architect or Service Librarian assigned to the service or the project should update Service Registry information to indicate that the development is complete.

Once service development has been completed, the service needs to be tested. A variety of tests need to be performed, which include:

- Functional testing
- Regression testing
- Performance testing
  - Against specific consumer's non-functional requirements.
  - Against cumulative non-functional requirements for all the service consumers.
- Stress testing
- Longevity testing

In the Service Testing phase of the service lifecycle, the service delivery methodology calls for two deliverables and execution of one governance process as shown in Table 8.

Table 8. Service testing roles and responsibilities

Deliverable/Process	Performed By
Service testing	Service Testers
Service registration update	Service Architect/Service Librarian
Service acceptance review	Service Consumer(s) SOA Support Team

There may be several different testing groups that perform a variety of tests described above. For the simplicity of the discussion, we will refer to all them as Service Testers. The results of the service testing along with all the supporting documentation produced to date should be reviewed by the teams or groups that will be consuming the service as well as the SOA support team that will be responsible for supporting it. It may be possible that one of these groups requires additional information or is not ready to accept the delivered service. In this case, the acceptance review should be considered incomplete and the process should be repeated again when all the concerns have been addressed.

Implementation-Time Governance

Upon successful completion of the service testing cycles, the service can be scheduled to be deployed into production. This is one of the most important steps in the service lifecycle and therefore should be performed with utmost care. The following deliverables and processes (Table 9) are mandated by the service delivery methodology.

Table 9. Service implementation roles and responsibilities

Deliverable/Process	Performed By
Service deployment	SOA Support Team
Service registration update	Service Architect / Service Librarian
Service deployment approval	SOA Governance Board

Before the service can proceed to production, the SOA Governance Board must approve its deployment. This has to be done in a formal way. No production release can be scheduled unless the approval is granted. If the service fails to garner the approval, any and all concerns should be addressed and another deployment request review should be scheduled. If the team feels that the request was improperly rejected or the timeline to address all the concerns is too onerous and creates too much risk, the decision can be appealed to the Executive Review Board.

When the deployment is scheduled, only those members of the SOA Support Team with access to the production environment should perform it. The service deployment process should follow all the IT Governance processes employed at the enterprise level including release and configuration management practices. As part of the deployment process, the service should be marked available for consumption in the Service Registry.

Run-Time Governance

Once the service is deployed to production, it needs to be managed with the same rigor as any other enterprise asset. Monitoring and alerting should be setup to ensure that any problems that occur with the service are immediately reported and handled. A dedicated support team should be handling all of these incidents as well as fixing production defects.

As part of the service deliverables, specific service policy definition should be created or updated. A service policy defines all of the non-functional requirements including Service Level Agreements (SLA), security information, performance characteristics, etc. Each service consumer may call for a different policy to be defined. Regardless of how the organization chooses to handle this, service policies should be enforced as strictly as possible.

Technologies to define and enforce service policies at run time have been in existence for a while. Mature SOA enterprises will benefit from deploying these technologies and automating service policy enforcement. These tools will not only help formalize how service policies are defined and supported but also help determine how to handle specific policy violations. For example, you can decide to dynamically provision another server if a service's SLA is breached.

It is important for the SOA Governance program to understand all the service metrics including consumption, incident, outage, and reuse metrics. These can be collected manually, but if a run-time SOA governance platform is deployed, it can collect all this data automatically. The SOA Governance Board should accumulate this data and communicate it to the Executive Review Board and other SOA stakeholders at least monthly.

Change-Time Governance

Service changes can be identified at any phase in the service lifecycle. Ideally, a change should be handled as any other request and be taken through all the service lifecycle phases. If a change is caused by a production defect, it needs to be made immediately but later taken through the normal service lifecycle process to ensure that the same defect is not reintroduced in the next service iteration.

Service versioning strategy should be created and employed to guide the decision making process when a service change is requested. In general, a non-breaking change to the service, or a change that will not impact its consumers, will result in an update to the service without the need to create a separate version. Any breaking change should trigger a creation of a new service version. Each organization should define how many concurrent versions of the same service can exist at the same time, the timeframe for retiring a service version, and all the communication processes that are initiated when a new service version is created or an old one is being retired.

When a service has reached its retirement age, the service retirement process should be triggered.

Service retirement may be prompted by a variety of factors including reaching the maximum number of supported versions, need for service deprecation, switch to a new implementation, etc. These criteria are set up-front and are monitored by the SOA Governance Board and service architects. The service retirement process starts when a need to retire a service has been identified. The SOA Governance Board then approves it and informs all the service consumers of the decision. The SOA team should subsequently establish specific service retirement plans. Service retirement should have well defined timeline with clearly communicated end of life date. If consumers are not able to migrate to one of the other service versions prior to the retirement date, they need to petition the SOA Governance Board to extend the timeline. In some instances, it may be prudent to retire the service from the enterprise environment and allow the teams still needing it to deploy it in their own environments.

Funding

Funding for an SOA program is like air for people. Without the proper levels of funding, the Service-driven initiative cannot survive. Just like any enterprise asset, if it is not properly fed and cared for, the Service-driven initiative can disintegrate very quickly. Think about the plants you have around the house. If you don't water them frequently enough, you will one day find them wilted.

SOA requires constant attention. It is an enterprise asset, and, as such, demands utmost attention and care. Many systems across the organization heavily depend on it. Any problems, failures, or downtime can have significant negative repercussions throughout the enterprise. Therefore, SOA, as a program, set of enterprise assets, and governance practices, needs to be constantly maintained and funded.

Funding should be of paramount importance to the SOA program. Without it, no new services can be delivered, SOA platforms cannot be adequately maintained, the program cannot be matured, and value cannot be delivered to the organization. All aspects of the SOA program require funding. This includes the program itself, SOA infrastructure, and service delivery function. Funding approaches for each one of these will be discussed in this section.

SOA Governance Program Funding

SOA Governance program consists of a set of processes, practices, and standards. They need to be constantly maintained, managed, and improved. Someone needs to be in charge of executing the processes, ensuring that all the standards and followed, and no governance mechanisms are breached. To achieve these goals, a dedicated team of people needs to be put in place. It doesn't matter where this team is located and what specific roles exist on it, but it is important to ensure that this team has enough funding to achieve its goals.

Funding required for these activities is needed to support the team working on the SOA Governance program. It makes little sense to do anything other than determine the appropriate team size and fund it from the department budget that owns the SOA Governance program. The budget has to be attached to the team size, which should be calculated based on the workload of its individuals. The budget should be reset every year to validate that the team size is optimal and no changes are needed.

SOA Platform Funding

SOA platform is an amorphous term. It may mean different things to different people and organizations. Most typical SOA programs introduce some infrastructure and software components that are shared across the enterprise. This may include ESBs, service management technology, a Registry/ Repository, etc. Thus, when referring to an SOA platform, we denote the totality of shared infra-

structure and enterprise software as prescribed by the overarching SOA program.

There are three possible ways to establish and maintain the SOA platform:

1. Identify appropriate projects to acquire/ extend new/existing SOA platform
2. Fund the SOA platform centrally
3. Fund the SOA platform through a hybrid approach whereas the funds are provided through both central and projects sources

Regardless of how the SOA platform is funded, it has to be managed centrally by the SOA team. All the support, management, and continued evolution of the SOA platform should be the responsibility of the central SOA team. Federation of the SOA assets can only be considered when the Service-driven initiative reaches a significant level of maturity and strong SOA Governance practices exist.

Under the project funding model, projects would fund a build out or extension of specific SOA capabilities. This rarely happens, as these platforms and infrastructure needed for them are costly and cannot fit into the project budget. In those rare circumstances when a project can afford these big ticket items, it only creates more problems than it solves. Unless an agreement is reached upfront with the SOA team to transition the ownership of the asset once the project is delivered or actually have the SOA team work on building out or upgrading the specific SOA capability, the project will almost never deliver anything aimed at enterprise consumption. This is because projects do not have the charter to do this. Rather, they are intended to deliver specific capabilities to the business. Thus, the project funding model rarely works unless the SOA team is the one doing the work.

The best and most widely utilized approach is central funding for the SOA platform. In this model, funds to establish and maintain the SOA platform are procured centrally and no projects or departmental budgets are impacted. This is by far the best approach, as it mitigates all the initial and ongoing funding issues as well as owner-ship concerns. Convincing the IT leadership to allocate funds for these activities is not always easy, however.

Some organizations that require activity based costing to be applied to all the assets establish chargeback mechanisms for using the SOA platforms. In this situation, the SOA platform build-out and expansion is funded centrally but business units using the platform are charged a fee designed to recoup the ongoing investment. The fees can be calculated based on the degree of usage, flat allocation, or some other formula agreed upon by IT finance.

The hybrid approach to funding SOA platforms is often applied when projects, business units, the SOA team, or all of the above are looking to build out a new capability or expand an existing one but do not have enough funds to do it. In this scenario, one or multiple projects or business units pool their funds with the SOA team in order to achieve a specific goal. The SOA team manages the effort and delivers the capability, but the work is accountable to the projects that help fund it. The most significant issue that can arise in this situation is the dependency on the new capability from one or more projects. If the SOA team is unsuccessful in delivering the results then projects will have to look for alternatives, which would most often mean withdrawing the originally promised funds.

SOA Delivery Funding

Shared services can be delivered through a variety of efforts – projects, SaaS (Software as a Service) utilization, third party vendor purchases, central service portfolio planning, etc. Funding plays an important role in whether these efforts deliver truly shared services or point integrations. For the purposes of this discussion, we will outline funding implications related only to enterprise services.

The structure of the Service-driven initiative may impact where funding is most relevant and impactful. Funding decisions can be broken into the following categories:

- How is public endpoint creation and support funded?
- How is private endpoint creation and support funded?

Most mature organizations deploy an ESB to expose public enterprise service endpoints. These are the endpoints that are being consumed as shared services and are registered in the Service Registry. The public endpoints connect to private service endpoints that may be hosted elsewhere and expose capabilities from other systems. If these systems are not owned by the SOA team, it is the responsibility of their asset owners to establish and maintain the private endpoints. In a situation when a public endpoint represents a virtual service with no private endpoint or the private endpoint is owned by the SOA team, this is who is considered the owner and makes all the relevant decisions. Thus, funding decisions need to apply to the public endpoints, ESB integration flows, and private endpoints.

For those services whose private endpoints reside on platforms not owned by the SOA team, funding situation is quite straightforward. It is the responsibility of the system owner to maintain the private endpoint. Thus, any changes to this endpoint are managed and funded by its owner.

It is a relatively standard practice in the in-dustry to establish a central SOA team to own all the public enterprise service endpoints and ESB integration flows. In this case, the creation and support of these assets becomes the responsibility of the SOA team. While support budgets are usu-ally aligned with the owner of the asset, funding approaches for building new services or modifying existing ones can vary. There are several different funding mechanisms that can be utilized to fund the creation of public interfaces and ESB flows. The most widely used approach to funding all SOA work is to rely on individual projects. If a project has a need to create or extend an enterprise service, it is expected to provide 100% of funding for it. This doesn't always work well, as some of the costs are not directly attributable to the project requirements, project and SOA team timelines and priorities do not match, or projects cannot afford to pay full price for all the SOA activities.

Another path that some organizations take is to fund all the SOA work centrally. This way, projects do not have to pay anything for the work but do have to help the SOA team prioritize and schedule this work. This is by far the simplest approach but is not always practical, as it would require a high degree of ongoing investment in the SOA area.

Sometimes, a hybrid approach is used. Here, some portion of funding is provided by the project, while the rest is supplied by the SOA team. This approach is needed when neither team has enough funds to complete the work. It works well if both the project and SOA teams agree on the funding amount upfront and both are accountable for delivering the work.

Demonstrating Value

To be successful, the Service-driven initiative has to demonstrate value. Since it represents a significant enterprise investment, the investors, namely IT and business executives have to be reassured that their money were used wisely and are generating positive returns. Just like any business seeking investment dollars, SOA program has to prove that it can generate value to its investors. If it does not, it will not be able to secure any additional funding. Since the SOA program needs to request funding in every budget cycle, the pressure to show consistent returns is constant.

There are three components to demonstrating value – defining metrics that need to be collected, collecting them, and communicating results. Spe-

cific steps and success factors for each of these activities are described below.

Defining Metrics

Metrics are the core measurements that we take to determine how well or poorly we are doing at a particular task. Peter F. Drucker, the famous influential thinker on management theory and practice, who coined the term "knowledge worker" (Drucker, 1957) once said, "What's measured improves." To understand something, we must measure it. To improve its performance, we must understand what the measurements tell us. SOA is no different.

In order to understand how the Service-driven initiative performs, a set of key SOA metrics must be defined. They should be geared towards measuring critical components of SOA. Typically, three areas of the SOA program are targeted – SOA platform, services, and ROI.

The SOA platform is a combination of infrastructure and software used to support the SOA program. There are several key metrics that are important in measuring performance of the SOA platform. We will omit the typical operational metrics and will concentrate only on those that are specific to SOA and related platforms.

The primary benefits reached through utilization of a variety of SOA platforms can be categorized and monetized in several ways.

- **Productivity Efficiency:** Productivity gains experienced as a result of utilizing the SOA platform.
- **Testing Efficiency:** Testing improvements realized through the use of the SOA platform.
- **Runtime Efficiency:** Operational savings related to the SOA platform.
- **Platform Consolidation:** Savings associated with elimination of redundant platforms and increased residency of shared platforms.

On top of efficiency metrics, other operational metrics should be captured. They include but are not limited to the following metrics.

- Operational
  - Number of services per server (residency rate)
  - Number of service calls (per time period)
  - Number of service consumers
  - Number of service calls per consumer
  - Most/least consumed services
  - Average response rate per service
  - Effective service support rate = # of services supported/total $ expense
  - Cost of platform support (per platform) = total support expenditures
  - Cost of platform maintenance (per platform) = total software expenses + total additional hardware expenses
  - Server CPU and memory utilization
- Quality
  - Number of failures
  - Number of bugs reported per service
  - Number of tickets logged
  - Average time required to resolve a bug (per service)
- Governance
  - Number of policies implemented
  - Number of policies enforced
  - Number of policy infringements
  - Number of SLAs enforced
  - Number of SLA infringements
  - Number of automated governance processes

There are typically three types of SOA metrics related to service delivery – IT, business, and financial. Each represents a view relevant to a specific group participating in the service lifecycle and is focused on maximizing their understanding of how SOA impacts them. They are detailed in Table 10.

The ROI calculations can be made based on the types of savings and efficiencies achieved through the SOA platform and service delivery activities. The actual ROI calculations and results may differ from one organization to the next.

Collecting Metrics

Once metrics are defined, they can start being collected. Organizations can choose approaches they feel best for doing this. Some may opt to do this through automation and integration, while others will federate the responsibilities across various teams that are involved in the process. Regardless of how it is accomplished, all the measurements should end up in a single database to ensure complete and timely reporting.

Collecting measurement data should be performed as efficiently as possible. Automated data feeds into a central repository should be setup if at all possible. There may be a variety of systems that contain pertinent information. Creating a standard representation of each metric and transforming data into this format as it arrives should make the collection and reporting process more efficient.

Table 10. Typical service delivery metrics

IT Metrics	Business Metrics	Financial Metrics
• Number of services created • Number of services reused • Service reuse ratio • Projects/applications utilizing shared services • Service performance	• Efficiencies associated with service reuse • Integration time savings • Opportunity cost related to faster product delivery	• Cost savings/avoidance • Service delivery ROI • Reduction in project and maintenance costs

Communicating Results

The SOA Governance Board should create a set of standard reports that it will communicate to all the SOA program stakeholders on a regular basis. These may include but are not limited to:

- Financial reports
- Service build reports
- Service usage reports
- Cost savings and ROI reports
- Operational reports

Ideally, these reports should be available through a dashboard that is supported by the central metrics repository. Different views may be setup to address specific stakeholder needs. For example, C-level executives will see macro level information, while operations managers may only see performance and uptime data.

Increasing Adoption

Metrics can be used not only to report the status of the SOA program but also to incentivize its adoption across the enterprise. The Executive Review Board may setup specific adoption targets for the SOA program, which, in turn, will generate specific objectives for each business unit. When metrics are collected, results are compared against the targets. Each business unit performance can then be evaluated.

To increase SOA adoption, this is exactly what should happen. Specific SOA adoption targets should be set and continually evaluated. The key to success is to attach specific incentives or punitive measures to each adoption target. Institutionalizing SOA adoption and formalizing how it is measured will lead to unequivocal success of the penetration and maturity of Service-driven initiatives.

SOA GOVERNANCE TOOLS AND TECHNOLOGIES

The journey from the beginning of the Service-driven initiative to its eventual maturity is an arduous one. It is full of boulders, crossroads, dead ends, giant chasms, and many other barriers that prevent travel in a straightforward fashion. To help clean out the path, automated machinery is often necessary. This machinery takes the form of SOA governance tools that help define, automate, and execute SOA governance processes.

There are a number of different SOA governance platform types. They can be described as Registry and Repository, Service Run-time Management, and Integrated Suites. Each of these tools has a different set of capabilities that it offers. Integrated suites combine all of the capabilities together to create a comprehensive set of functionality. In the subsequent sections, we will examine each of these SOA governance platforms, identify the capabilities they offer, and provide recommendation on their usage.

Registry and Repository

Service Registry became popular early in the SOA maturation process. It provided a way to register services and make them discoverable through a common protocol. These products quickly evolved beyond their traditional roots to start hosting metadata about the services. This gave rise to the *Service Repository* part of the platform. Today, we hardly ever see a standalone service registry. It is inevitably paired with a repository that enables storage of all kinds of metadata related to service artifacts and lifecycle.

A typical Registry and Repository platform offers the following capabilities:

- Service catalog
- Service metadata repository
- Service versioning
- Service discovery
- Service policy authoring

There are a number of commercial as well as open source vendors that provide Registry and Repository platforms. Besides these basic capabilities, these products also include SOA governance automation and enforcement mechanisms including:

- Ability to track service consumers
- Service lifecycle management
- Relationship tracking
- Integration with one or several ESB products
- Design-time governance

These SOA governance automation features make Registry and Repository platforms more valuable. They provide capabilities that SOA programs need to reach the next level of maturity. In fact, the service delivery methodology described earlier in this chapter can significantly benefit from these features. All of the governance tasks prescribed by it can be automated, which can streamline all of the processes and increase the overall productivity of the SOA organization.

Design-time governance can be very important to ensure that the service delivery follows the correct path and complies with all the governance mechanisms. They can be explicitly defined and enforced throughout the design and development portions of the service lifecycle. Additionally, automatic enforcement of SOA standards can be performed as part of this process.

Integration with an ESB can be valuable, as it enables services to be deployed directly onto the target ESB platform. This can simplify release and configuration management activities, as all of the metadata is managed and executed from a single environment.

Registry and Repository products can also offer integration with run-time management platforms. These capabilities include:

- Deployment of service policies to the target enforcement platform.
- Collection of run-time metrics.
- Proactive capacity management.

These capabilities transform Registry and Repository platforms into complete integrated suites. They would now contain a comprehensive set of functionality that covers the entire service lifecycle, from inception to run-time.

Deployment of service policies to the Service Run-time Management platform is an important capability for a number of reasons. It enables service policies to be managed centrally and deployed from a single location. They can be versioned and associated with specific service versions. Finally, run-time behavior of services can be fully designed and tested together with the service, not separately. This closes the final step in the service delivery lifecycle that is often omitted or ignored.

Collection of service run-time metrics can prove beneficial to the reporting of SOA performance and cost impacts. As discussed above, increased level of automation in metrics collection leads to better quality and accuracy of the reports.

Proactive capacity management can be achieved through consuming and interpreting notifications received from the run-time platforms. If a spike in consumption is observed, a ticket can be issued to the infrastructure team to provision additional capacity. Alternatively, in a virtualized or cloud enabled environment, that provisioning can happen automatically without any human involvement.

Some Registry and Repository platforms offer run-time management capabilities on top of everything else. This represents by far the most comprehensive set of features and may prove most valuable, although it may come with a prohibitive price tag.

Service Run-Time Management

The primary goal of the service *run-time management* platforms is to enforce run-time policies that are created at the design time. Service policies may consist of the following elements:

- Security
- Service Level Agreements
- Reliability
- Atomicity
- Transactionality

These are just the primary, most frequently used policy types. There may be a number of others that are described in the policy definition and enforced at runtime.

The main capabilities supplied by the service run-time management platforms include the following:

- Run-time policy enforcement
- Standards enforcement
- SLA violation visibility
- SOA activity monitoring
- Alerting
- Collection of run-time metrics
- Proactive capacity management

Run-time policy enforcement is the key capability of the platform. It reads the policy definition and monitors it for every consumer. If a violation is detected, an alert could be sent out or, if more proactive options are available, additional instances of the service could be spun up or non-performing instances isolated or killed. As discussed above, proactive capacity management can also be employed to address SLA failures.

The main benefits of using service run-time management platforms lie in not only automating service policy enforcement, monitoring, and alerting, but also in establishing a bullet proof SOA runtime environment. Run-time management closes the gap in the SOA governance automation

efforts. Combined together with a Registry and Repository, run-time management platform provides end-to-end visibility of the service lifecycle and associated SOA governance processes, enables complete SOA governance automation, and can facilitate metrics collection and dissemination.

EMERGING TRENDS

SOA governance has had time to mature. Its practices and methodologies are well known and widely used across the industry. However, the industry itself doesn't stand still. It continues to move forward, innovate, develop new models, and evolve in unpredictable ways. SOA practices have to keep up and change with it.

A number of interesting technology trends is forcing a transformation of the SOA program and the corresponding governance practices. They include:

- Cloud Computing
- Social Computing
- Web API Management
- Consumerization of IT

While there are a few other important trends that impact the technology industry as a whole, they have little to no effect on the SOA practices.

Impacts of the Cloud Computing on SOA are probably the easiest to understand. With Cloud, compute nodes becoming a part of the service deployment targets. SOA governance mechanisms need to be able to govern them in the same fashion as all the internal deployment targets. Therefore, service delivery methodology needs to take Cloud Computing into account ensuring that all the appropriate design and run-time choices are made throughout the service delivery lifecycle. Policies would need to change to ensure that they incorporate Cloud platform SLAs and authentication modes.

Run-time service management platforms need to be made aware of the Cloud run-time environment to ensure that they can adequately manage it. Finally, Cloud Computing, as discussed earlier, can significantly simplify proactive capacity management and spikes in service utilization. Run-time service management tools need to be modified to seamlessly integrate with Cloud Computing platforms to take advantage of its dynamic provisioning capabilities.

Social Computing approaches are widely used in consumer facing applications. Many websites enable their users to like pages or content elements, post their opinions, and share specific pages with their network of friends. Some of the business applications are starting to employ the same types of features, allowing users to interact with the applications and other users in a more social way. SOA governance may also be susceptible to this direction. A number of SOA governance mechanisms can benefit from these social interactions including service identification and categorization, design reviews, etc. Some of the SOA vendors are starting to offer Social Computing features in their packages.

Consumerization of IT adds another wrinkle to the SOA governance program. With consumers using their own devices to do the work, access to services can come from anywhere and in a variety of formats. An increased usage of AJAX, JSON, and REST, puts a larger burden on the SOA governance mechanisms to appropriately govern these types of services.

SOA Governance lacks standardization of practices. A number of standards bodies have attempted to bridge this gap by creating their own standards proposals for SOA and SOA governance practices, service delivery methodologies, and a number of other aspects of the SOA program. Even though there is little agreement across the industry on a single set of standards, the convergence is taking place and will eventually yield a semblance of industry accepted practices.

As the SOA practices continue to evolve, they become more closely intertwined with other technology practices such as BPM, Business Rules, Event Processing, and others. As this occurs, SOA governance practice needs to be expanded to incorporate these new aspects of the SOA program. Additionally, governance realms across all these programs need to be aligned to ensure seamless integration and management. At some point in the future, many of these technologies and practices will completely merge with SOA and become an indiscernible part of it. This will lead to expansion of SOA governance mechanisms and practices, along with an impact on the existing standards.

CONCLUSION

SOA governance is critical to the success of the SOA program. Without its guidance, all of the best efforts will quickly disintegrate in the face of political resistance, lack of cooperation, and unsustainable funding. If the enterprise is serious about establishing a successful Service-driven initiative and sustaining it over the long term, it must be willing to invest into creating and maturing the SOA governance program.

There is no single SOA governance practice or mechanism that is more important than the other. They are all equally valuable. However, the order in which they are implemented matters. You cannot start with automation before designing and bullet proofing your processes first. Or you cannot invest into organizational constructs and mechanisms before securing a stable source of funding. You need to decide what matters most to you in the SOA governance program and start from there. Some organizations choose to start from the conceptual program layout and establish a maturity roadmap that continually adds more and more capabilities and processes to the program. Some start by implementing a run-time governance tool and identifying all the rogue services in their portfolio. There is no right or wrong place to start. The enterprise needs to determine what makes most sense for the organization, in terms of the goals to achieve and the level of maturity to attain over time. Once those elements are in place, the enterprise is well on its way towards success with its SOA program.

REFERENCES

Biske, T. (2008). *SOA governance*. Packt Publishing.

Brown, P. C. (2007). *Succeeding with SOA: Realizing business value through total architecture*. Addison-Wesley Professional.

Brown, W. A., Laird, R. G., Gee, C., & Mitra, T. (2008). *SOA governance: Achieving and sustaining business and IT agility*. IBM Press.

Drucker, P. (1957). *Landmarks of tomorrow*. New York: Harper & Row.

Erl, T. (2007). *SOA principles of service design*. Prentice Hall.

KEY TERMS AND DEFINITIONS

Domain Services: Those services that are reused within a single organization, business unit, or functional domain.

Enterprise Services: Those services that are reused across organizational boundaries.

Enterprise Service Bus (ESB): A middleware solution that enables interoperability among heterogeneous environments using a service-oriented model.

Local Services: Those services that are used by a single application.

Representational State Transfer: (REST): A distributed system framework that uses Web protocols and technologies.

Service Lifecycle: All of the stages of a service evolution, from inception to retirement.

Service Registry and Repository: A tool that contains all the service metadata and allows services to be discovered.

SOA Governance: Mechanism for controlling and directing outcomes of a Service-driven initiative.

SOA Governance Board: A governance body that oversees all aspects of the SOA Program.

Virtual Services: Services that have an end point exposed through an ESB but have no physical implementation outside of ESB.

Chapter 10
Coordinating Enterprise Services and Data:
A Framework and Maturity Model

Keith R. Worfolk
AvantLogix, USA

ABSTRACT

The critical inter-dependencies between Enterprise Services and Enterprise Data are often not given due consideration. With the advent of Cloud Computing, it is becoming increasingly important for organizations to understand the relationships between them, in order to formulate strategies to jointly manage and coordinate enterprise services and data to improve business value and reduce risk to the enterprise. Enterprise Services encompass Service-driven applications deployed on-premises in the enterprise data centers as well as in the Cloud for the "extended enterprise." Enterprise Data Management encompasses the cross-application enterprise-level perspective of data in an information-sharing enterprise, and the critical business data that is created, maintained, enriched, and shared outside the traditional enterprise firewall. This chapter discusses and proposes best practice strategies for coordinating the enterprise SOA & EDM approaches for mutual success. Primary coordination aspects discussed include: Service & Data Governance, Master Data Management, Service-driven & EDM Architecture Roadmaps, Service Portfolio Management, Enterprise Information Architecture, and the Enterprise Data Model. It recommends a facilitative Service-driven Data Architecture Framework & Capability Maturity Model to help enterprises evaluate and optimize overall effectiveness of their coordinated Service-driven & EDM strategies.

INTRODUCTION

Strategies for Service-driven & Enterprise Data Management (EDM) architectural approaches have traditionally been treated as separate, disparate programs and initiatives in organizations, from a business requirements perspective as well as from an information technology (IT) implementation perspective. Yet there are critical overlapping and interdependent components, processes, and quality checkpoints of each strategy for which coordination becomes necessary to ensure mutual success.

DOI: 10.4018/978-1-4666-4193-8.ch010

Pursuing these strategies as unrelated approaches with disconnected objectives and measures of success may risk failure of both strategies and cause an organization's Service-driven & EDM initiatives to execute poorly and fall short of delivering the expected business results. However, the tendency for organizations to address their Service & Data strategies in isolation is evolving to a more enlightened perspective.

A study by the Data Warehousing Institute (CIO CSG, 2008) found that poor data quality costs U.S. businesses hundreds of billions of dollars annually. If data trapped in silo applications is "bad data," then imagine the issues when, via enterprise services, bad data from many applications is commingled. Bottom line, applications connected via a Service-driven integration strategy are not worth much if data in them is flawed. Data integration projects account for a growing percentage of the overall integration market, especially as enterprise services projects take hold; but such projects may fail if they don't incorporate an EDM strategy to address complex and expensive data problems in the enterprise (CIO CSG, 2008). With the advent of Cloud Computing, it is increasingly important for organizations to understand the relationships and interdependencies between Enterprise Service & Data so that strategies for leveraging and growing these assets are jointly managed and coordinated for mutual success.

With Cloud Computing, Enterprise Services comprise an organization's Service Oriented Architecture (SOA) as well as its evolving Cloud Services Architecture to make up the organization's "extended enterprise." Similarly, EDM encompasses the cross-application enterprise perspective for data management needed in any large information-sharing enterprise, but gains additional significance and business impact when its critical data is created, enriched, maintained, and shared outside its enterprise firewall, the case when Cloud Services are part of the organization's extended enterprise.

A positive trend in recent years has been for rational organizations and consultancies to in-creasingly realize the need to better coordinate their Service-driven & EDM strategies. The more progressive organizations readily understand such strategy coordination as a necessary foundation from which to improve its overall organizational effectiveness. Even risk averse and slow-to-change organizations know their existing SOA & Master Data Management (MDM) strategies and initiatives need coordination if either is to be successful (Dreibelbis et al., 2008). MDM addresses designated Master Data (MD) of the organization, and thus the most highly governed subset of its enterprise data (i.e. business-critical data in the enterprise warranting highest levels of enforced quality). Thus, reach of EDM, and MDM, is evolving necessarily as organizational strategies include Cloud Services, and they must appropriately manage critical data assets across the extended enterprise (Thoo, 2009).

While SOA & MDM strategy coordination is an important step for most organizations, it is only a starting point towards more comprehensive strategy coordination necessary to successfully support robust Service-driven & EDM approaches (Chandras, 2011). But this can be a reasonable and meaningful early step in the necessary evolution of strategic planning and execution that this chapter represents and hopes to accelerate within IT industry thought leadership, and in particular, among organizations pursuing Service-driven strategies. Organizations that coordinate their Service-driven & EDM strategies can go beyond mitigating their risks of bad data propagation via enterprise services to realize opportunities for optimizing their:

- Business value of both Enterprise Services and Enterprise Data, leading to:
  - Decreased business services development and maintenance costs.
  - Increased utilization of business services and data services (i.e., process efficiencies).
  - Increased information asset quality and reuse.

- Economies of scale and scope by capitalizing on synergies of key Service-driven & EDM processes, infrastructure, tools, and roles and responsibilities, leading to:
  - Increased organizational effectiveness.
  - Increased process efficiencies, and automation opportunities and utilization.
  - Decreased infrastructure costs.

If key components of its Service-driven and EDM strategies are taken into account in a coordinated fashion, an organization can realize the opportunities to optimize the benefits of these strategies by harnessing the power of synergistic enterprise services and data, including assets residing and processing in the Cloud. Conversely, organizations that don't coordinate these strategies can limit their value and effectiveness, and cause them to fall short of expectations, from the perspective of the IT implementation team as well as the executive team. We will define coordination points for Service-driven & EDM strategies, and analyze their synergies, dependencies, and interrelated components and processes in the context of internally focused IT organizations as well as those that extend an organization's Enterprise Services & Data beyond the firewall by employing Cloud Services.

This chapter prescribes a facilitative Service-driven Data Architecture (SD/DA) Framework & Capability Maturity Model (CMM) to help organizations evaluate and optimize benefits of their coordinated Service-driven & EDM strategies, while taking into account Cloud Services of the extended enterprise. The SD/DA Toolkit (Framework & CMM) provides an approach and guidelines for evaluation, refinement, and maturity towards improving overall effectiveness of an organization's proactively coordinated Service-driven & EDM strategies. The SD/DA Toolkit is an evolving body of work for over 25 years, having been applied and refined in 40 large strategic programs/projects across multiple industries, to manage and architect large Services & Data development initiatives. Some began as focused SOA, EDM, MDM, Data Warehouse, or Business Intelligence projects, but quickly revealed the need to include coordinated Services & Data strategies.

This chapter also illustrates how to apply and adapt the SD/DA Framework & CMM for a specific organization's needs, demonstrating how this can be utilized in an evaluative assessment (i.e. to establish a baseline or perform periodic assessment), as well as in the development of a strategic roadmap of coordinated Service-driven & EDM initiatives for organizational effectiveness and maturity.

BACKGROUND

SOA strategies and initiatives have been a driving force in the creation of business services for a long time, and SOA success has always been underpinned by the value of the data it serviced. Quality of an organization's data, within service transactions as well as in metadata for describing, configuring, and efficiently executing services, is understood to be crucial for a successful SOA and made possible through Data Governance (Inbar, 2008). As maturing service-focused organizations grow towards more progressive Service-driven strategies, and incorporate Cloud Services in an extended enterprise, it is increasingly clear across the IT industry that an organization's business services (i.e., its business processes automated by services) are only as effective as its data. Measures of data effectiveness (quality) include accuracy, consistency, completeness, and timeliness across all services and systems that address related sets of data. Data Governance needs to support success of services, preferably under a broader, coordinated EDM strategy designed to accommodate an organization's Service-driven strategy.

Figure 1 expresses a simple yet powerful truth that SOA often guides an organization's progress

Figure 1. Smooth sailing, powered by SOA and underpinned by EDM, with clouds on the horizon

via its business services and automated processes (the "wind in its sails"), hence its organizational efficiencies. Key to effectiveness of such services and automation is the organization's underpinning of data quality, which can promote (via EDM/MDM) or demote service stability, reliability, and integrity. Also shown in Figure 1, Cloud Services are arriving (or already here) for most organizations, extending the reach of Services & Data in the extended enterprise. The advent of Cloud Services provides third-party options and opportunities to organizations, while increasing the need to actively coordinate and mature now extended Service-driven & EDM strategies. Cloud Computing does little to solve the new, expanded Enterprise Services & Data integration problems it creates. It will not stop silo computing from being too prevalent in the industry; as more abundant commodity computing power is made available, Cloud Services could yield a bigger mess – only faster.

What has been missing so far in the IT industry has been a consistent approach to effectively coordinate an organization's Service-driven & EDM strategies, and a way to accomplish this across the extended enterprise. Vendors will gladly sell public or private Cloud solutions, but the organization needs to have an overarching strategy to effectively integrate service logic and extended enterprise data (across a broad environ-

ment). This is where SOA value lives on, in modern Service-driven architectures and approaches that include coordination with EDM strategies; this is becoming increasingly more important, now that the IT industry is cloud-enabling all products and services (Oliver, 2012).

Master Data

Master Data (MD) is the consistent and uniform set of identifiers that describe core entities of the enterprise that can be used across multiple business processes. Example entities are:

- **Parties:** Customers, prospects, people, employees, vendors, suppliers, or trading partners.
- **Places:** Locations, offices, regional alignments, or geographies.
- **Things:** Accounts, products, services, events, assets, contracts, or policies.

MD is not all enterprise data, but the subset required for sharing and standardization; its definitions change rarely and it is often referenced by business processes, transactions, and reusable services. Using an organization's Enterprise Data Model, Master Data scope includes the sets of subject area elements maintained in a Metadata repository. Master Data Services for manipulating and reusing the MD objects is utilized for sharing data across IT systems, applications, services, and users.

Master Data Management

While a Service-driven approach enables integration and data exchange through services, such integration is marginally useful without a common vocabulary of data content and structure. Master Data Management (MDM) defines how an organization's enterprise establishes and maintains such vocabularies. To fully implement a Service-driven program, organizations must first address MDM. Without focus on MDM in the broader context of EDM, it becomes inefficient to communicate information about transactions, since there is no common understanding of business objects to which services and events can refer to.

MDM encompasses such areas as Customer Data Integration and Product Information Management. MDM supports conformance, auditing, reporting, and a single view of data. MDM includes areas of Identity Management and Business Intelligence systems, and data quality and data integration activities. When organizations use enterprise-level MD, needs for separate departmental versions of truth are alleviated. In regards to MDM and *Metadata* (data that describes data entities) Management:

- Although users often say they want a single view of data, what they really want are multiple views for stakeholder types; where Metadata directly relates to MDM, and the reference of one interpretation or view of the Master Data to the source of truth data can be managed via Metadata.
- There are real-time impacts between data stores and data usage, requiring metadata-driven transformations of in-flight data. Such progressive Service-driven capabilities raise new data issues beyond those

normally addressed by EDM, MDM, and Data Governance for static data.

MDM deals with Service & Data Governance, Stewardship processes, data quality, and Metadata Management. Packaged solutions generally tout domain MDM remedies, but lack subject area integration or Metadata Management; thus, MDM is crucial for an organization's drive towards EDM.

MDM and Service-Driven Approaches

MDM and Service-driven architectural approaches have typically evolved separately but share many similar design principles. For example:

- **Contract:** Interfaces in MDM, and service definitions i.e. WSDL (Web Service Description Language) in Service-driven approaches.
- **Reusability:** Data conformance in MDM, and atomic and composite service designs in Service-driven approaches.
- **Discoverability:** Data through the MD repository in MDM and services through the Services Registry in Service-driven approaches.
- **Abstraction:** Source data system complexity with MDM, and underlying service complexity with Service-driven approaches.

Additional Service-driven paradigms also contribute to the maturity of MDM. For example, MDM does not typically embrace the Service-driven principle of loose coupling. But extending MDM with loose coupling (i.e. a federated MD Service approach) allows support for service semantic conformance. Loose coupling should be applied internally to create an agile MDM system. Such a service-enabled MDM system provides data quality, conformance, and other MDM functionality as enterprise business or data services, and can be enabled for human, application, business service, or external party consumption. MDM systems can further be configured to handle extensible data types (i.e., XML, HTML, PDF, etc.) to expose the MD model of the Enterprise Data Model for service consumption. Information Architects can then develop unifying schemas to merge content types. With XML being increasingly adopted as the standard for information exchange, barriers to content convergence via business or presentation services become mitigated.

The Case for Coordinated Service-Driven and EDM Strategies

Coordinated Services and Data is now a focus area (as shown in Figure 2) for most Chief Information Officers (CIOs). Organizational enterprise data initiatives (e.g. Customer/Product Data Integration, MDM) are realized as key drivers for SOA programs/projects (CIO CSG, 2008). An organization's data management house must be in order (via EDM/MDM) before its Service-driven strategy can succeed (Griffen, 2005). Without an EDM strategy to address a high-quality and consistent data foundation for an organization, its services can propagate bad data to more applications and more users, faster than ever; this dependency is only exasperated by an expanding Cloud footprint for an organization's Enterprise Services.

The survey findings in Figure 2 are not unusual; other surveys and case studies show the need for organizations to implement a robust and coordinated EDM strategy to support their Service-driven strategy. A recent study found that although there is an increasing comfort level for CIOs to adopt Cloud Services, the most pressing concern is around data integration issues between internal applications and Cloud Services. No surprise then, that the next greatest concerns of Cloud adoption in the study is in knowing where their data resides (i.e. which data in what applications and where hosted), followed by developing workflows across internal/external domains (i.e. integration of the extended enterprise's data,

Figure 2. The CIO perspective (© 2008, IDG research services. used with permission)

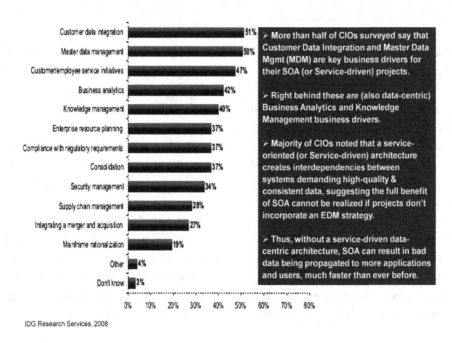

IDG Research Services, 2008

services, and workflows). Thus, leading barriers to Cloud adoption according to CIOs are related to issues which can be resolved by effectively coordinating Service-driven and EDM strategies (Kass, 2012).

Starting Small and Focused: SOA and MDM Coordination

As organizations embrace the need to coordinate their Service-driven & EDM strategies, different organizations are adopting coordination approaches in varying capacities and at different starting points. There has generally been a lack of consistency and established best practices for how organizations should coordinate their Services & Data. A recent trend emerging in the IT industry is pointing to a reasonable starting place for organizations to initiate coordination of their Service-driven & EDM strategies, albeit initially in a more focused way, involving their SOA and MDM strategies.

MDM is now understood to be foundational for SOA success, which in turn extends the reach of MDM and its high-quality Master Data via enterprise services (Dreibelbis et al., 2008). It's an organization's business information that makes SOA valuable; and Data Services are needed to add value to the information of various data sources by making information more available to users, processes, and applications, and improving its relevance and cost-effectiveness. MDM is a key enabler for such architecture to promote and facilitate Data Services foundation and SOA in general, a single location from which to manage the organization's Master Data (i.e., customers, accounts, products, etc.) that underpins key business processes across the enterprise. Thus, an effective SOA infrastructure needs good data, and effective Master Data can be created within and shared by a good SOA (McKendrick, 2010).

While SOA facilitates business functionality and automation as services, it doesn't guarantee the quality of data on which it operates; this serious gap is filled by including MDM within a Service-driven architecture. MDM provides consistent understanding and reliability of MD and standard mechanisms for its usage. MDM also plays a key role in evolving an organization's MD by centralizing its maintenance and governance (Dreibelbis et al., 2008). Starting with a coordinated SOA and MDM program is a reasonable first step for some organizations, but is limited to only address Master Data and internal enterprise services.

Other areas of data should be coordinated as well with a Service-driven approach; key metadata associated with services, but not considered Master Data, may be critical to defining, configuring, and executing the services. It's reasonable to expect such metadata should be managed for quality (e.g. via EDM, and Data Governance, beyond traditional MDM) and coordinated with associated services (e.g. within a Service-driven strategy and an extended enterprise). Also, since organizations categorize data differently, with only a subset of common industry standard Master Data defined, there is usually other critical data supporting or transacted by an organization's services, warranting high quality, yet is not traditional MD. Therefore, coordinating an organization's SOA and MDM strategies falls short in scope when considering the Data & Services needing management and coordination in enterprises.

The "Perfect Storm" for Service-Driven and EDM Strategies that Extend to the Cloud

Many interrelated factors across industries are recently and simultaneously creating an environment ripe for organizations to develop their Service-driven and EDM strategies and programs in parallel, leading to necessary collaboration and coordination. These conditions are further being shaped by the growth of Cloud Services as an industry force upon both these strategies and in how they should be coordinated. Figure 3 lists several key contributing industry events that together have

Figure 3. The "perfect storm" for coordinated service-driven and EDM strategies and cloud services

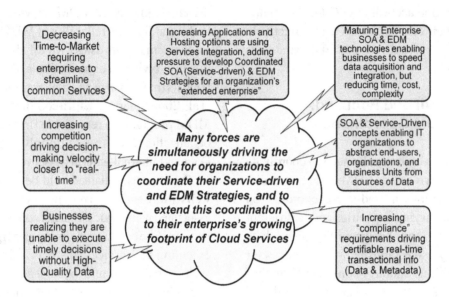

resulted in the "Perfect Storm" driving strategic corporate requirements and initiatives for these strategies and their coordination. Recent major catalyst events across industries that created this "Perfect Storm" include:

- High quality data is increasingly required to enable timely corporate (and enterprise) level decision-making.
- Real-time (or near) decisions are regularly required as competition increases and market cycle times accelerate across industries, providing impetus for real-time services and data accessibility.
- Common services are now expected, and should be optimized, in order to accommodate decreasing time-to-market pressures in many industries.
- With increasing frequency and maturity, packaged applications and hosting options are delivering "out of the box" standardized Web services and/or Software as a Service (SaaS) capability, raising requirements for coordinated Service-driven, EDM, and Cloud Integration strategies.

- Maturing Enterprise Services (via Service-driven approaches) & EDM technologies are enabling businesses to meet requirements for faster data acquisition and workflow integration, while reducing time, cost, and solution complexity.
- Organizations require their applications and end users to utilize an abstraction layer rather than sources of data directly, enabled by a Service-driven approach and integrated Data Services layer.
- Certifiable transactional information in (at least near) real-time, for both data and metadata, is increasingly part of compliance requirements.

Each factor individually could spur companies to coordinate and optimize their Service-driven & EDM strategies; but several occurring at once make a compelling argument for organizations to pursue strategic coordination in order to stay competitive. Beyond the private sector, U.S. Government IT officials have reported simultaneous contributing factors, such as a budget crisis, available Cloud solutions, and a new generation of federal IT leaders open to such options, providing impetus for a program to develop the uniform framework FedRAMP (Federal Risk & Authorized Management Program) for Cloud solutions (Corbin, 2012). It promotes a "do it once, use many times" philosophy, as an extension of SOA towards a mature Service-driven enterprise and pragmatic utilization of Cloud Services. The program, a response to the Government's "perfect storm," exposes needs for Service-driven & EDM strategy coordination.

This chapter introduces the SD/DA Framework as an effective and flexible tool to assess and drive necessary coordination between Service-driven & EDM strategies and initiatives. The SD/DA Toolkit includes a CMM and reference-able guidelines for how an organization should apply the Framework & CMM to establish an initial baseline of Service-driven & EDM capabilities; then to progressively improve on the baseline to gain benefits from resulting Service-driven & EDM strategy coordination. The Framework & CMM was originally designed for SOA and EDM strategy coordination, but, presented here, has evolved for Service-driven & Cloud Services environments. While the SD/DA Toolkit doesn't preclude the need for more comprehensive and detailed Service-driven & EDM focused programs, it:

- Identifies key dependencies and synergies between an organization's Service-driven and EDM strategies, while emphasizing related components of these strategies to be coordinated.
- Promotes a more comprehensive enterprise vision of Service-driven & EDM initiatives, emphasizing interdependencies and coordination points for organizations pursuing either strategy.
- Facilitates coordination of strategic IT initiatives for systems and infrastructure to support priorities, dependencies, and synergies of highly effective Service-driven & EDM approaches.

- Provides guidance for organizations seeking to improve their supporting Service-driven and EDM processes (e.g. project/program management, governance, and stewardship).
- Demonstrates capability maturity levels for organizations to progress towards evolving their Service-driven and EDM capabilities and synergies in a coordinated fashion.

A FRAMEWORK FOR COORDINATED SERVICE-DRIVEN AND EDM STRATEGIES

Having established reasoning and needs for an organization to coordinate its Service-driven and EDM strategies in order to optimize these interdependent strategies for mutual success, we lay out an effective approach with supporting best practices to accomplish this strategy optimization.

Guiding Principles

In this chapter, Guiding Principles (GPs) are identified for organizations to apply as part of an effective approach to coordinate Services and EDM strategies; GPs are recommendations and insights in planning and executing the strategies in a Service-driven environment. Based on this, we present the SD/DA Framework & CMM designed to help organizations improve their effectiveness by coordinating strategies.

Service-Driven and EDM Strategy Coordination: Guiding Principle #1

Organizations pursuing Service-driven & EDM strategies should consider overlaps and interdependencies of both strategies early in planning, and make appropriate accommodations and adjustments in execution:

- When pursuing a Service-driven strategy – Consider which transactional or service-related data and metadata should be governed within a broader EDM strategy, and perhaps as Master Data.
- When pursuing an EDM (or MDM) strategy – Consider if a Service-driven strategy is underway or anticipated. If so, consider transactional or service-related data / metadata that should be governed by the EDM or MDM strategy.

Whether starting with a Service-driven strategy perspective, or a data-centric EDM/MDM perspective, coordination with the other strategy is needed to ensure mutual success. For example, Data Governance should be applied to all Master Data and Metadata supporting or transacted by the organization's Service-driven strategy (Loshin, 2010).

Service-Driven and EDM Strategy Coordination: Guiding Principle #2

An organization's Service and *Data Governance* approaches are explicitly and undeniably intertwined:

- Information Quality Management (via EDM or MDM) is a necessary foundation for a Service-driven strategy and the success of Enterprise Services.
- Services that create or manipulate data (especially MD) should be governed for EDM success.
- Cloud Computing does not materially change, only extends, the needs described in 1 and 2, leading to coordinated Service & Data Governance across the extended enterprise.

At an enterprise level, key coordination points for an organization's Service-driven & EDM strategies are:

- Service Governance and Data Governance.
- Strategic Initiatives for Services, MDM and related Metadata.
- Service-Driven Architecture Roadmaps and EDM Architecture Roadmaps.
- Service Portfolio Management, Enterprise Information Architecture, and the Enterprise Data Model.

These high-level coordination points, each representing strategic organizational levels, roles, and initiatives, and IT components, to be coordinated, should be incorporated into an organization's overall IT Strategy. This enables coordination to be facilitated as part of its overarching Strategic Initiatives Portfolio and Enterprise Architecture Roadmap management (i.e. under guidance of an overall Program Management Office). Within the context of planning and implementing these coordination points, services include both Web Services that reside and are processed in an organization's fire-walled enterprise as well as those that are hosted, maintained, and executed outside the organization's immediate control as part of its extended enterprise. Similarly, the organization's critical data is now also hosted and utilized both within and outside its firewall, to be processed, enhanced, modified, and maintained internally or in the Cloud. Thus, the organization is actively employing third-party applications and services running in the Cloud, and these services may be further integrated with internal services as part of comprehensive workflows, generally reusing enterprise data (including MD).

EDM Framework and Component Considerations

We'll first consider strategic coordination needs and opportunities of an organization's Service-driven and EDM strategies from the data perspective, specifically by considering the industry established EDM framework and best practices (i.e. since data is an underpinning enabler for strategic initiatives of enterprise services). While there are variations on EDM frameworks, the one presented in Figure 4 is typical and applies to many organizations. After analyzing this from the data side, we'll consider the services perspective for strategy and component relationships and coordination points of an organization's Service-driven and EDM approaches.

Regardless of which side we look at, results are consistent and reinforcing. In reviewing known Service– Data relationships and potential coordination points, we see that applying such an EDM framework allows us to inventory strategic data components for an organization that has significant overlaps, dependencies, and synergies (i.e. strategic interdependencies) with Service-driven components. This helps an organization identify where it should focus its efforts (initiatives) to coordinate and mature its Service-driven and EDM strategies for optimal effectiveness.

The general EDM Framework in Figure 4 shows major components to consider in how they impact (or are impacted by) Service-driven approaches: Data Governance, MDM, Metadata Management, Enterprise Information Architecture, Data Security & Privacy, Data & Process Monitoring and Controls, and Data Quality, Profiling and Metrics. Typical strategic EDM initiatives for organizations consist of activities addressing one or (likely) more components simultaneously. For example, to address Data Governance or MDM, an organization usually must consider other related components such as Data Quality, Profiling & Metrics, or Data Security & Privacy (to name a few).

Practically, most strategic EDM initiatives address several components in coordination simultaneously, and set strategic priorities and objectives up front to emphasize goals for designated primary components, other inter-related components are selectively applied in support of

Figure 4. A typical EDM framework

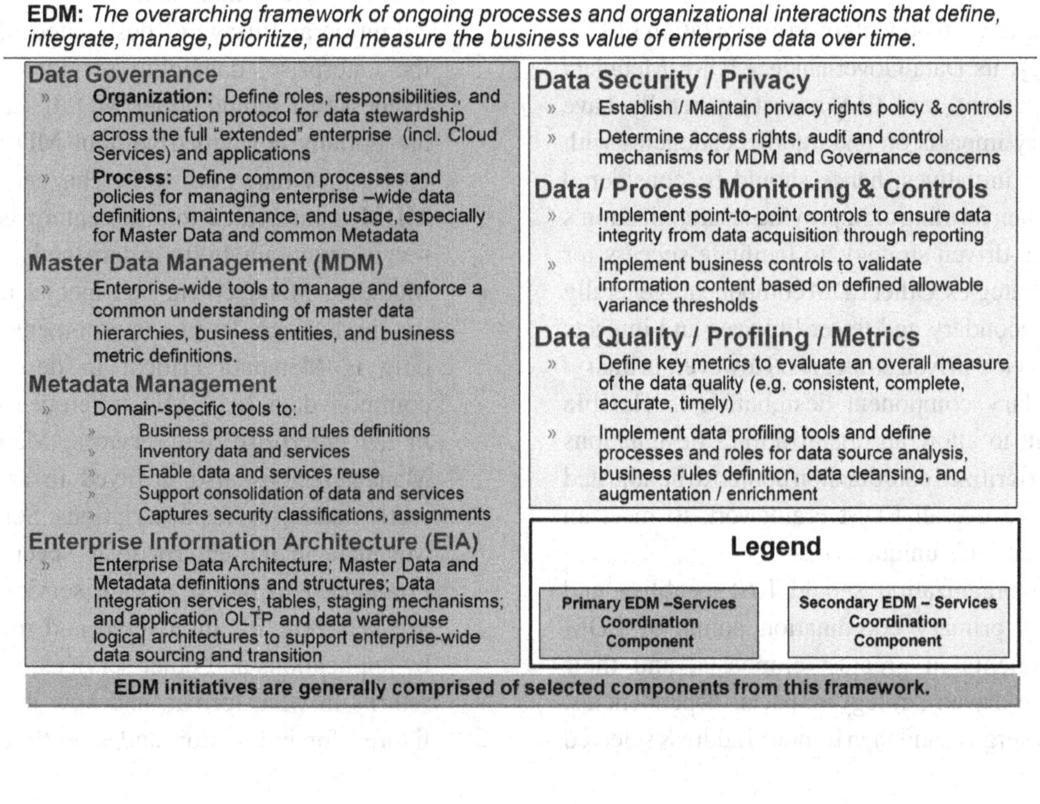

EDM: *The overarching framework of ongoing processes and organizational interactions that define, integrate, manage, prioritize, and measure the business value of enterprise data over time.*

Data Governance
- **Organization:** Define roles, responsibilities, and communication protocol for data stewardship across the full "extended" enterprise (incl. Cloud Services) and applications
- **Process:** Define common processes and policies for managing enterprise –wide data definitions, maintenance, and usage, especially for Master Data and common Metadata

Master Data Management (MDM)
- Enterprise-wide tools to manage and enforce a common understanding of master data hierarchies, business entities, and business metric definitions.

Metadata Management
- Domain-specific tools to:
  - Business process and rules definitions
  - Inventory data and services
  - Enable data and services reuse
  - Support consolidation of data and services
  - Captures security classifications, assignments

Enterprise Information Architecture (EIA)
- Enterprise Data Architecture; Master Data and Metadata definitions and structures; Data Integration services, tables, staging mechanisms; and application OLTP and data warehouse logical architectures to support enterprise-wide data sourcing and transition

Data Security / Privacy
- Establish / Maintain privacy rights policy & controls
- Determine access rights, audit and control mechanisms for MDM and Governance concerns

Data / Process Monitoring & Controls
- Implement point-to-point controls to ensure data integrity from data acquisition through reporting
- Implement business controls to validate information content based on defined allowable variance thresholds

Data Quality / Profiling / Metrics
- Define key metrics to evaluate an overall measure of the data quality (e.g. consistent, complete, accurate, timely)
- Implement data profiling tools and define processes and roles for data source analysis, business rules definition, data cleansing, and augmentation / enrichment

Legend

Primary EDM –Services Coordination Component	Secondary EDM – Services Coordination Component

EDM initiatives are generally comprised of selected components from this framework.

the primary components and their established goals. This way, the organization ensures its EDM initiative has priorities and component emphases (i.e. isn't "boiling the ocean," addressing too many EDM components at once).

While identifying EDM components that have highly significant, primary impacts on a Service-driven strategy, and conversely those that are highly impacted by Service-driven approaches/ initiatives, we see that those having direct major impacts (in either direction) are primary EDM coordination points with respect to Service-driven strategies. Other EDM components have secondary impacts and are emphasized less, in support of specific strategic initiatives. Secondary components have fewer linkages and cross-dependencies with Service-driven strategies and components, so don't warrant as much focus for an organization when coordinating and optimizing its Service-driven and EDM strategies.

Service-Driven and EDM Strategy Coordination: Guiding Principle #3

Among the components of an organization's EDM strategy, its Data Governance, MDM, Metadata Management, and EIA aspects generally have primary impacts on and interdependencies with service initiatives, hence should be considered first when forming or improving an organization's Service-driven strategy, to facilitate success for both strategies. Other EDM components generally have secondary and fewer linkages and impacts for Service-driven strategies. However, primary/ secondary component designation is flexible enough to allow an organization's designations (and prioritized coordination points) to be adjusted from the overall EDM Framework to meet an organization's unique needs.

An organization should first establish and address primary coordination points of EDM components in greatest emphasis, and their Service-driven strategy impacts, dependencies, and synergies, and then it should address selected secondary components that may be pertinent for coordination within its environment and strategic initiatives. By analyzing major components of the EDM Framework, we see these key interdependencies with a Service-driven strategy and initiatives:

- Data Governance is clearly needed to ensure that only well-managed and consistent data is utilized within and transacted by services. Without this, inconsistent and silo data will run rampant in an organization's services and applications, including those that reside in the Cloud.

- Expecting services to primarily utilize MD, then MDM is necessarily a primary component in support of an organization's services initiatives, including access to well-defined MD by Enterprise Services as well as proven MD Services (i.e. to read/ update MD, link Metadata to MD elements, and establish relationships between MD elements). MD Services can be orchestrated within complex service workflows. Without MDM, there is a lack of common definition and usage of designated MD in the enterprise, damaging services effectiveness that should utilize MD. If services are initially developed without MD references, they may need to be changed once MDM is integrated into the enterprise, so service maintainability is damaged.

- Metadata Management has special meaning in Service-driven environments; not only is Metadata critical in describing common data (e.g. MD, reference data) in the enterprise and services, Metadata Management is also involved in and directly tied to service descriptions. Selected Metadata in the enterprise is specifically established to describe each service (i.e. WSDL), how it's discovered and invoked by applications and other services, what it returns in what format, and how it's configured for integration and workflow, etc.

Similar to MDM, this component is critical to service functionality and transacted information (i.e. content payload) between applications, services, and data stores, including those in the Cloud.

- Enterprise Information Architecture (EIA) is the conceptual architecture and infrastructure that supports the organization's Data Architecture, including its Master Data and Metadata definitions and structures. It includes supporting data integration services, tables, staging, and on-line transaction processing (OLTP) mechanisms, as well as data warehouse logical architectures that facilitate enterprise-wide data sourcing and transitions associated with MD, Metadata, and all governed data. The EIA and its infrastructure is intended to enable and facilitate efficiencies for the information (i.e. all managed data) and related services for the organization's MD, Metadata, and data warehouse needs. It's the data architecture that underpins the organization's enterprise architecture, creating efficiencies for most Service-driven and EDM strategy interdependencies.

From a high-level perspective, organizations that fail to sufficiently coordinate their Service-driven & EDM strategies will inherently cause their Enterprise Services & Data to evolve disparately, rather than synergistically in support of each other and a well-managed Enterprise Architecture (EA). In short, without necessary coordination, organizations have to find other ways to answer the following:

- How will MD/Metadata utilized by services and shared in transactions be managed effectively?
- How will services be launched and maintained to only utilize standardized MD, Metadata, and other data under EDM juris-diction (rather than services using inconsistent, unmanaged silo data)?
- How will an organization ensure that its integration of processes, services, and data, and the overlapping roles, responsibilities, and stewardship for all data utilized within or made available by services are collaboratively managed by parallel Service & Data Governance programs?

Service-Driven and EDM Strategy Coordination: Guiding Principle #4

Services and applications in a Service-driven environment need consistent and reliable data. If there is insufficient data quality or integrity, and for example, if duplicate records or inconsistent data definitions are the norm, then applications and Enterprise Services (including Cloud Services) which cut across many transactions (i.e. the heart of any Service-driven strategy) cannot function well or be reused confidently.

In regards to Service-driven and EDM strategy coordination; EIA is a relatively new, refined primary component of EDM that:

- Is made up of both Business Process Architecture and complementary Information Architecture sub-components and supporting resources.
- Creates policies and standards for the use of enterprise data.
- Includes domain lead resources with responsibility to determine the information type, content, and quality delivered by services (working with Service & Data Governance staff, processes).
- Consists of "bridge" staff resources, those who understand the business but can also communicate with the technical staff (e.g. the enterprise information knowledge workers of the organization).

Figure 5 shows how EDM Framework components generally fit with major Service-driven components. It also conceptually demonstrates how the EIA works with organizational business processes and Service-driven components, and is guided by Service & Data Governance within coordinated Service-driven and EDM strategies. This illustrates how the EIA is leveraged by a Service-driven strategy; it includes the enterprise data model that services will utilize in designs. Hence, the EIA organization and roles work closely with MDM and Metadata Management components; it also coordinates pertinent data integration and quality issues, best practices, and tools between Service-driven and EDM strategy execution efforts.

Service-Driven Framework and Component Considerations

As we reviewed the EDM perspective of service and data component inter-dependencies, we now take a look at a typical Service-driven Framework and its components (see Figure 6).

- **Service Governance and IT Services Management:** Includes organizational

process governance and stewardship of services throughout their lifecycle, and also regular and, in many cases, automated IT monitoring and performance management of the services and related data flows, which feeds metrics back into the fine-tuning of governance and system policies.

- **Workflow Management Services and Business Rules:** Includes definition/configuration tools, and related business rules management, to ensure service and data accuracy and performance in automated workflows. Definition/configuration attributes are maintained in key business process management & workflow management systems/tools in the service environment, incorporating a business rules engine to guide service orchestration and data relationship integrity in and between services (e.g. under guidance of Service & Data Governance).

- **Access and Security Services:** They facilitate functional integration by providing the necessary supporting security capabilities (i.e. authentication, authorization, encryption, and virtual private network) for integration. They enable Presentation

Figure 5. EDM framework components with service-driven intersections and coordination points

Figure 6. A typical service-driven framework

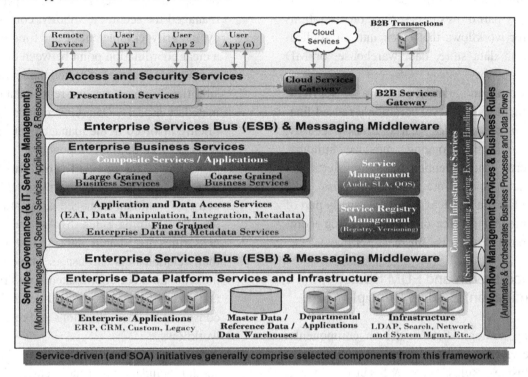

Services that provide user interface wrappers to internal services, workflows, and data, to create a consistent user experience of internal applications and portals, and provide extensions of internal services and data for external B2B & Cloud Services workflow integration.

- **Enterprise Business Services:** Includes composite business-level services and applications built from service orchestration. Composite Services/Applications are abstracted to represent complex business processes, and considered coarse- or large-grained as they are built on fine-grained data elements and Application Access & Data Access Services for Enterprise Application Integration. Its Service Management provides Service Auditing capabilities to manage Service Level Agreements and Quality of Service attributes, and its Service Registry Management provides a central

repository for business services with capabilities for discovery and service versioning of individual/groups of services.

- **Enterprise Service Bus (ESB) and Messaging Middleware:** The common messaging bus that facilitates communications and transactions between applications and services for invocation and workflow orchestration (i.e. backbone of Service-driven environments and information flow).

- **Enterprise Data Platform Services and Infrastructure:** Includes finest-grained services which facilitate access to and distribution of discrete data elements for service processing, and integration of the Data layer of the enterprise architecture (including application data stores, data warehouses, MDM repositories, tools) with all services and applications relying on its data. These services are not generally invoked by themselves, but are generally part of business service orchestrations for workflows that reach into an application data store, data warehouse, or MD repository.

- **Common Infrastructure Services:** Includes low-level commonly reused fine-grained services such as access, security, monitoring, logging, message building, error and exception handling, alerts and notifications, etc. Like Enterprise Data Platform Services, these are usually part of broader service orchestrations (e.g. composite Enterprise Business Services).

Service-Driven and EDM Strategy Coordination: Guiding Principle #5

Among strategic Service-driven components, the Service Governance, Workflow Management and Business Rules, Access & Security Services, Enterprise Business Services, Enterprise Service Bus, and Enterprise Data Platform Services have primary impacts on and dependencies with an organization's EDM strategy; the impacts and interdependencies with these needs to be considered first and foremost when forming or improving an organization's EDM strategy.

Typical Service-driven initiatives for an organization comprise activities to address several components simultaneously, in coordination. When considering how EDM components are impacted by such a service environment, most Service-driven components play a key role in an organization's coordinated Service-driven & EDM strategies and initiatives. In particular, these strategic Service-driven components have primary impacts on an organization's EDM strategy and components:

- **Service Governance:** Data Governance processes and quality checkpoints should ensure all services are using the right data and metadata, and that any proliferation

of data for or by services is appropriately managed for accuracy, validity, consistency, integrity, completeness, and timeliness; a clear coordination point between the two governance organizations and their responsibilities. For most service-related data and metadata aspects, Data Governance is explicitly involved in the management of the other Service-driven components.

- **Workflow Management and Business Rules:** Metadata Management should encompass common managed automation & workflow routing rules, SLAs, and business rules for shared data and services, their relationships and usage. These components should be coordinated across EDM and service strategies for well-defined and consistent business decisions and resulting workflows.

- **Access & Security Services:** MDM should include appropriate security classifications for all MD and user (role) categories, as well as security-controlled services (perhaps by their data). Also, Metadata Management should maintain the descriptions and rules that guide the handling and interactions of each classification for accessing and updating common data and service attributes.

- **Enterprise Business Services:** MDM should ensure availability and managed releases of MD to support all Enterprise Business Services (EBSs), whether fine-grained data access or composite business services. Metadata Management should ensure all EBSs utilize appropriate Metadata (for workflow management or business rules, or SLAs). EIA, as facilitator of MDM and Metadata architecture and infrastructure, should be referenced and influenced by planned releases of EBSs.

- **Enterprise Data Platform Services:** MDM and EIA should have similar impacts on Data Platform Services as for Enterprise

Business Services, though at this more fine-grained level of data store services, they provide mostly a reference for services and their data store relationships.

- **Enterprise Service Bus (ESB):** Metadata Management should provide the configuration rules for the ESB to support all enterprise service transactions and message processing between services and applications, as well as between different layers or domains of the enterprise architecture.

Service-Driven and EDM Strategy Coordination: Guiding Principle #6

An important foundation of service normalization is a service's relationship with its specific underlying data, and hence these aspects need to be highly coordinated:

- The objective of *service normalization* is to eliminate redundancy and missed functionality, and to deliver a meaningful partitioning of functionality for users of related applications and services.
- Systematic normalization of Service-Data relationships enable normalization of service designs with the underlying (enterprise) data model. Such approaches establish linkages and ownership/stewardship relationships between services and data elements upon which they rely.

Without coordinated services and data, service developers may be tempted to create data stores or data marts that support their unique domain of services/data, which further causes unnecessary propagation of un-governed data and non-enterprise databases. This can damage both an organization's Service-driven and EDM strategies.

As shown in Figure 7, there are four degrees of Service–Data normalization in designs, from immature to very mature processes and organizations:

- **"Wild West":** Virtually non-existent, only ad-hoc (pockets of) Service–Data design coordination, no method to the madness; minimal coordination via enlightened projects, designers.
- **Ownership/Stewardship:** Service designs build on (and influence) data designs for all elements utilized by or shared between services of an initiative. Identified data designs are precursors, inputs to separate service designs, which influence data design evolution (reactive coordination).
- **Encapsulation:** Service and Data designs are jointly created/updated; they co-exist

Figure 7. Degrees of progressively mature service data design coordination

Four degrees of progressively mature Service – Data Design Coordination:

1. "Wild West"	2. Ownership / Stewardship	3. Encapsulation	4. Object
➤ Non-existent or Ad Hoc (pockets of) Coordination	➤ Service Design builds upon (and influences) Data Design for all Data utilized by or shared via Services	➤ Service and Data Designs are Jointly Coordinated (co-created and maintained) with traceability	➤ Service and Data Designs are One & the Same ➤ Service implementation takes Data Ownership to a higher level where Master Data value is known only within the Services

Service–Data Design Coordination levels are part of an overall maturity model for Service-driven organizations and programs.

with robust traceability and are jointly managed and applied in development and Service & Data maintenance activities. Service or Data designs may drive the other so long as they are jointly updated and coordinated in initiatives and release management (proactive coordination).

- **Object:** Service and Data designs are one and the same (object designs); comprehensive designs are part of strategic EIA designs, and Service implementation takes Data ownership to a level where MD value is known inside the Service and interface designs for applications and end-users.

- **Service:** Data Design normalization maturity levels are part of an overall CMM for coordinated Service-driven and EDM strategies and programs. Most organizations attempting to coordinate/normalize their Service & Data Designs have made it to an Ownership/Stewardship level. But organizations should reach the Encapsulation level of design coordination before seeing major benefits in design and development efficiencies, maintenance costs, and (Service and Data) asset value. Moving from a lack of normalization to mature coordinated Service–Data designs (Encapsulation, Object) is achieved within an overall process to increase maturity of Service-driven & EDM strategies, processes, and tools. But Object level of Service – Data design coordination may not make sense for an organization, especially if its MD isn't stable yet, for example. Organizations should plan to attain an Encapsulation level of Service–Data design coordination, and then see if cost-benefit analysis justifies further efforts to reach an Object level.

This normalization process should be well managed by Service & Data Governance leadership and processes to ensure appropriate reuse

of services and data. Such reuse is prudent most of the time, unless service or data requirements are new or existing designs or implementations require updates. It's up to the Service and Data Governance bodies to evolve, manage, and communicate roadmaps of reusable services and data for development, maintenance, and coordinated release management activities. Service Governance can selectively advocate development of new/improved services if it makes business sense. And Data Governance would usually promote reuse of existing Master Data or managed Metadata, but decreasing over time as managed data stabilizes, there can be business reasons to extend or change standard data.

Service-Driven and EDM Strategy Coordination: Guiding Principle #7

For highly effective Service or Data Governance, an organization should consider instituting a Hybrid governance approach that includes key aspects of both Federated and Centralized approaches:

- A Federated approach should be used for domain-specific assets to allow domain implementation flexibility and efficiency.
- A strong centralized approach should be used for shared enterprise-wide assets, standardized processes, tools, and best practices.

Figure 8 shows major Governance approaches for Services & Data that exists within organizations, sometimes differing between approaches in parts of the organization. These range from mostly non-existent or "Ad Hoc," through a collaborative distributed Federated approach, and some organizations settle on a highly centralized Dictatorship. Another option is for a Hybrid approach (to consolidate the best of Federated and Dictatorship approaches) that can work most effectively for Service & Data Governance, especially in a mature, coordinated Service-driven and EDM strategy.

Figure 8. Continuum of service and data governance approaches

Governance approaches from Ad Hoc to Highly Centralized organizations, and taken further to a desired Hybrid approach:

Ad Hoc	Federated	Dictatorship	Hybrid
⌐ Non-existent or Ad Hoc (pockets of) Governance ⌐ Lack of Enterprise Coordination, but may have minimal Governance processes and roles developed out of necessity within some Domains	⌐ Coordinated independent efforts between various Domains, but lack of overarching cohesive approach. ⌐ Standards, Best Practices, & Tools are inconsistent by Domain. ⌐ Inconsistent Coordination Points with Business for Requirements, Testing, Release Management, etc.	⌐ Totally Centralized Control of all "governed" assets ⌐ Everything is coordinated, but only at a centralized management level ⌐ High Centralization comes at a cost of local (Domain) efficiency and flexibility (e.g. edicts emanate from "The Tower")	⌐ Coordinated independent efforts between various Domains that share common assets ⌐ Standards, Best Practices, Tools are coordinated to be consistent as practical between Domains ⌐ Coordination Points with the Business are consistent for Requirements, Testing, joint Release Management, etc. ⌐ Hence, a Federated approach to facilitate Domain implementation flexibility, but with ⌐ Centralized Governance of shared and standardized Enterprise-wide processes, tools, and assets

Thus, the Governance approaches we consider in fulfilling this Service-driven strategy are:

- **"Wild West":** Virtually non-existent or simply ad-hoc and uncoordinated pockets of governance. There is a lack of overall enterprise coordination, but there may be minimal governance processes and roles developed out of specific project necessity and only within a few enterprise domains.

- **Federated:** Coordinated independent efforts between various Enterprise Services or Data domains; selected enterprise coordination, but inconsistent standards, best practices, and tools as they are within control of each business or technical domain. Lack of overarching cohesive approach and coordinated management, and may include inconsistent coordination points with the business for requirements, testing, release management, etc., due to varying domain controls.

- **Dictatorship:** Centralized control of all governed service or data assets. Hence, all assets under Governance are considered from an enterprise perspective and coordinated as such, rather than to meet domain-specific needs. However, assets coordinated at this high-level of management can come at a cost to domain efficiency and flexibility for assets that are primarily domain-specific.

- **Hybrid:** Selected benefits from Federated and Dictatorship approaches; coordinated independent efforts between domains that share common Services or Data. Standards, best practices, and tools are consistent between domains, and business coordination points for each asset's lifecycle (e.g. requirements, development, release management, etc.) are consistent between domains. A Federated approach is implemented within domains for selected flexibility, balancing this with centralized management of standardized Enterprise Services or Data assets, processes, and tools.

Transitioning through these approaches can be seen as a maturity model for Governance. While "Wild West" is a problem in lack of control and coordination, Dictatorship swings too far to overly centralize all decisions regarding enterprise, as well as domain-specific assets. Sufficient maturity may be achieved as a Hybrid approach, whether referring to Service or Data Governance, and especially when coordinated.

Service-Driven and EDM Strategy Coordination: Guiding Principle #8

If an organization does not have a Center of Excellence (COE) to support either its Service-driven or EDM strategies and missions, then it should define and establish one in order to support both strategies in a coordinated fashion. However, if an organization already has a COE, consider expanding its mission to include both Service & Data development and integration considerations, including best practices and tools within a single, comprehensive COE.

There are advantages and economies gained by not letting domains pursue and maintain their own version of enterprise assets; there are also advantages and efficiencies for local control of domain-specific assets.

Hence, a mature Service-driven or EDM strategy includes the development and management of such a supporting Center of Excellence (COE). Furthermore, in the case of an organization's well-coordinated Service-driven and EDM strategies, a singular comprehensive Service – Data COE can meet the objectives for both strategies more effectively than separate COEs. However, despite overlapping roles, responsibilities, dependencies, and potential synergies, there is the undesired

tendency for an organization to develop disparate and mostly uncoordinated Service-driven and EDM COEs while pursuing both strategies; this should be avoided.

As shown in Figure 9, an organization should consider establishing such a comprehensive COE. This consists of more than a traditional SOA or EDM COE, and provides a design, development, prototyping, and testing sandbox for the development and integration of both services and data. Such a COE should provide all the processes, best practices, and tools of both the Service-driven and EDM environments, and it should facilitate all strategic service and data architecture, design, development, and testing coordination to achieve mutual maturity. Figure 9 also demonstrates that such a COE will closely coordinate with Service Governance and Data Governance, as well as the EIA, and all of these will be coordinated for overall enterprise architecture and IT Governance concerns. Furthermore, some of the key components managed within each of the Governance programs will also have instances of these components residing within the COE.

A Service-driven strategy leads an organization to implement an EIA and infrastructure in support of its Services & Data, including a common Data Services layer to support producers and consumers with consistent information. Service categories within the Data Services layer are:

- **Enterprise Data Services:** Encompass all services directly around the data (create, retrieve, update, etc.). Also, service enablement of traditional MDM functionality such as data quality and data harmonization across participant systems is exposed as Enterprise Data Services.
- **Enterprise Metadata Services:** Encompass services around metadata (e.g. retrieve MD schema of customer, etc.). Service designers and developers creating

Figure 9. Framework for mature services data center of excellence

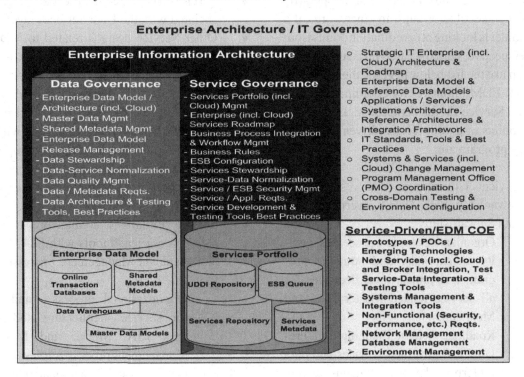

business services, and consumers, must reference the organization's MD schemas, exposed as Enterprise Metadata Services.

- **Enterprise Data Platform Services:** Support all services around the service and data platforms, including management, monitoring, and reporting.

Within all services, and across all Data Service categories, common infrastructure service methods for search, access, creation, update, deletion, management, monitoring, and reporting functionality should be made available. An organization can evaluate or plan for maturity of its Enterprise Data Services layer by systematically designing and releasing core Data Services and answering such questions as:

1. Are business services able to avoid impacts of changes in repositories/databases being accessed?

2. Do services typically only have to access one repository to read or update information?

3. Are the repositories being accessed designed to avoid overlapping/redundant information?

4. Can the Data Service layer provide a single version of truth for MD?

5. Are Data Services semantically integrated with data providers to define/maintain the MD?

6. Is the Enterprise MD model exposed for consumption by the Data Services?

Key Service-Driven and EDM Strategy Coordination Points

Summarizing from and building upon main findings of the Service-driven & EDM framework considerations discussed, we elaborate on key coordination areas that are recommended for these strategies. The coordination points are organized by the Service-driven and then EDM perspectives in order to facilitate understanding and adoption by different stakeholder groups. In other words, if a stakeholder is looking at coordination points from one perspective, perhaps based on a current role, they can use the list below to guide their Service-driven & EDM initiatives for coordination.

For a Service-driven perspective, key coordination points of a joint service-driven and EDM strategy program are:

- Service Governance and its Service Stewardship with Data Governance and Data Stewardship.
  - Organizational roles, processes, quality checkpoints, and strategic program and project-level decisions for all service related Master Data and Metadata.
  - Roadmap Release Planning for all related and governed services and data (enterprise-level, domain-specific, and extended enterprise).
  - Strategic decisions related to MD transacted by services or sent over the ESB.
- Services and Cloud Portfolio and Management with the EIA and its Enterprise Data Model.
  - Roadmap Release Management for all related services and data of the Services & Cloud Portfolio Management and the EIA.
  - Service-Driven Release Management with EIA Release Management for services utilizing EIA data.
- Service architecture and design with MD defined for, and MDM associated with, these services (i.e. strategic and tactical decisions related to the service designs and related data designs and implementation, and the ESB that utilizes or distributes MD on behalf of these services).
- Service initiatives architecture and designs with MDM and Metadata Management.

- Service-driven architecture and designs associated with the Data Services layer.
- Other Service designs related to MD and Metadata for Enterprise Infrastructure, Data or Business Services.
- Service designs with related Metadata for or used by these services, and hence, Metadata Management associated with the services (i.e. Service-driven component associated Metadata, including service WSDL and/or ESB configuration or security settings).
- Service initiatives architecture and design processes and tools with EIA, MDM, and Metadata Management processes and tools.
  - Organizational processes and roles for service architecture and roles with EIA, MDM, and Metadata Management processes/roles.
  - EA Release Management, including technical architecture supporting the ESB and integration points to managed data stores and consumers, and EIA and database references.
  - Service architecture tools and artifacts with those for EIA, MDM, Metadata Management.
- Service-driven initiatives enterprise service architecture and development teams with EIA, MDM, and Metadata Management staff/roles (i.e. initiative-level service architectural processes/roles with those for EIA, MDM, Metadata Management).
- Enterprise-level service-driven assets (i.e. Enterprise Architecture, Services Model, and Services and Cloud Portfolio Management) with EDM assets (EIA, MDM, Metadata Management).
  - EA and the Service Model with the EIA.
  - Service Model with MDM.
  - Service and Cloud Portfolio Management and its Release

Management with MDM Release Management.

○ Service Model and service-driven component-specific Metadata (e.g., WSDL and ESB configuration) with Metadata Management.

Similarly, from an EDM perspective, coordination points for joint service-driven and EDM strategies are:

- Data Governance and Data Stewardship with Service Governance and Service Stewardship.
    ○ Organizational roles, processes, quality checkpoints, and strategic program and initiative-level decisions for all service-related MD and Metadata.
    ○ Roadmap Release Planning for related and governed services and data.
    ○ Strategic decisions related to MD transacted by services and/or sent over the ESB.
- EIA and its Enterprise Data Model with Services and Cloud Portfolio Management and its Release Management.
    ○ Roadmap Release Management for related and governed services and data.
    ○ EIA Release Management and Service-driven architectural Release Management for the services utilizing data in the EIA.
- MD defined for and MDM associated with services (i.e. strategic and tactical decisions related to MD transacted by services and/or sent over the ESB).
- MDM and Metadata Management with Service-driven initiatives for architecture and design, including:
    ○ Data Services layer architecture and designs.

○ Other related MD and Metadata for (Infrastructure, Data, or Business) service designs.
- Designs for Metadata defined for, or used by, services, and hence, the Metadata Management.
- Processes associated with these services (i.e. Metadata directly associated with Service-driven components, such as WSDL or ESB configuration or security settings).
- EIA, MDM, and Metadata Management processes/tools with Service-driven initiatives for architecture and design processes/ tools.
    ○ Organizational processes/roles for EIA, MDM, and Metadata Management with service architecture processes/roles.
    ○ EA Release Management, including technical architecture supporting the EIA and its databases, and the ESB and integration points to the databases and data consumers.
    ○ Tools/artifacts for EIA, MDM, and Metadata Management with Service-driven architecture tools/artifacts.
- EIA, MDM, and Metadata Management staff and roles with Service-driven initiatives for enterprise service architecture and development teams (i.e. initiative-level processes / roles for EIA, MDM, and Metadata Management with Service-driven initiatives for architectural processes and roles).
- Enterprise-level EDM assets (EIA, MDM, and Metadata Management) with enterprise-level Service-driven assets (e.g., EA, Service Model, and Services & Cloud Portfolio Management).
    ○ EIA with EA and the Service Model.
    ○ MDM with the Service Model.
    ○ MD Release Management with Services and Cloud Portfolio

Management, and Release Management.

○ Metadata Management with the Service Model and Service-driven component-specific Metadata (e.g. WSDL and ESB configuration).

In a mature Service-driven and EDM environment that is further establishing or maintaining coordinated COE capabilities, here are other key coordination points for a joint Service-driven & EDM strategy:

- Service-Driven and EDM COE(s) with Service – Data Governance, EIA, and its Enterprise Data Model.
  ○ COE organization processes/roles with Service & Data Governance processes/roles.
  ○ COE roadmap development and releases with EIA releases and its accompanying Enterprise Data Model.
- Service-driven and EDM COE with Services & Cloud Portfolio Management, and Release Management.
- COE Roadmap development, releases with Services & Cloud Portfolio Management and Release Management.
- Program Management Office (PMO) initiatives for prioritization, decision criteria, and status reporting for Service-driven and EDM initiatives, including COE-related activities and releases.

SD/DA Framework

Both the framework and CMM introduced here are for a coordinated Service-driven Data Architecture (SD/DA), which is built on the data architecture that supports a Service-driven environment. Such a Framework and CMM is an important evaluative and planning tool to support coordinated Service-driven and EDM strategies and initiatives. The

SD/DA Framework (Figure 10) is not intended to supplant full-fledged (Service-driven or EDM) frameworks, but complements these to specifically identify synergies and dependencies, as well as evaluation criteria and maturity phases of the strategies for effective coordination. With some adjustments, the SD/DA Framework and CMM can be used as a comprehensive Service-driven or EDM strategy tool, but it is intended primarily to gauge and drive an organization's strategic capabilities for coordination and joint maturity of service-driven and EDM strategies.

Service-Driven and EDM Strategy Coordination: Guiding Principle #9

A service-driven approach (including its underlying SOA) and EDM are integral parts of the same Enterprise Architecture puzzle, and neither can mature successfully without the other. As with the many dependencies and synergies for the simultaneous implementation of both these strategies, an appropriately defined common framework and capability maturity model can be leveraged to evaluate organizational readiness as well as to plan roadmap initiatives for these strategies in a coordinated fashion.

This framework offers a consolidated perspective from which coordinated Service-driven and EDM strategies can be evaluated, and for which roadmaps of initiatives can be created to improve an organization's capabilities and maturity. The determination of an organization's strategic readiness for its combined Service-driven and EDM capabilities throughout these domains will help gauge overall maturity in this regard. This necessarily includes some stand-alone Service-driven and EDM capabilities, but emphasizes the synergistic nature of these strategies and their dependencies and coordination points. When considering how to apply the SD/DA Framework to an organization's combined Service-driven and EDM strategies, the following guidelines apply:

Figure 10. Service-driven data architecture (SD/DA) framework overview

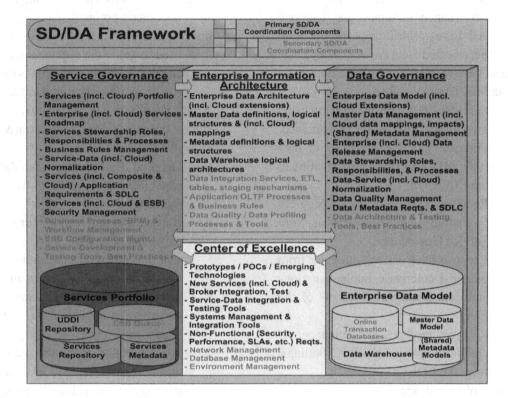

- Not all components of each domain carry the same weighted priority for achieving well-coordinated and mature Service-driven and EDM strategies.
- Primary components are those that directly impact the decisions and approaches for the maturity and coordination of these strategies, while Secondary components are utilized for context and in support of approaches to coordinate the Primary components.
- Primary components are usually addressed in greater detail and emphasis than Secondary components when evaluating an organization's maturity and/or formulating a roadmap of initiatives to achieve greater coordination and maturity.
- Primary/Secondary designation of components can be adjusted for a specific organization's needs.

The SD/DA Framework consists of 4 domains of capabilities that are highly interrelated as follows:

- Service Governance (including Services Portfolio components)
  - Provides input, guidance, service prioritization to EIA, Data Governance, and the COE.
  - Receives EDM strategy coordination input and prioritization from Data Governance.
  - Receives feedback and guidance, including prototype and POC (Proof of Concept) findings from the COE.
- Enterprise Information Architecture
  - Provides feedback and guidance from practical enterprise-level implementations and data quality assessments to Data Governance.

○ Receives Service and Data Governance guidance and (Service and Data) prioritization inputs from Service and Data Governance.

- Data Governance (including Enterprise Data Model components)
  ○ Provides EDM coordination input and prioritization to Service Governance.
  ○ Provides input, guidance, and data (incl. MD, Metadata) prioritization to the EIA, COE.
  ○ Receives Service-driven strategy co-ordination input/prioritization from Service Governance.
  ○ Receives feedback and guidance from practical enterprise implementations and data quality assessments of the EIA.
  ○ Receives feedback and guidance, including prototype and POC findings, from the COE.
- Center of Excellence
  ○ Provides feedback and guidance, including prototype and POC findings, to Service and Data Governance.
  ○ Receives input, guidance, (service and data) prioritization from Service and Data Governance.

Fine-Tuning the SD/DA Framework in the Enterprise

Evolving the SD/DA Framework for an organization's specific needs, initially and as Service-driven and EDM strategies mature, involves the following steps:

1. Determine/Confirm Primary and Secondary components (see Figure 10) for the organization's strategic needs as well as its most urgent strategic initiatives.
   a. Include the organization's full set of assets (e.g. external services and data

in the Cloud) when defining Primary/Secondary components.
   b. Resulting (adjusted) framework will be used to guide the organization's strategy development as well as supporting roadmap, programs, and initiatives.
2. Apply the framework to evaluate current state of coordinated Service-driven & EDM strategies.
   a. Detailed as needed for granularity of capabilities and initiatives to improve maturity.
   b. Rate each component for current state capabilities relative to desired (current or future) state; readout of how well current Service-driven and EDM processes, architecture, services, and data meet strategic (current or future) needs.
   c. A color-coded or number rating system may be utilized to evaluate each component's capabilities relative to desired capabilities; use the organization's methods for evaluation.
3. After evaluating an organization's current state using the framework, next inventory all initiatives underway (or will be starting soon) that will impact the rating of each component's current state.
4. Determine the desired future vision of the enterprise based on the same SD/DA Framework utilized to evaluate current state.
   a. Done for, or organized by, short- (e.g. next business quarter), intermediate- (e.g. 1 year), or long-term (e.g. 2+ year) goals as needed for a specific program's effectiveness.
   b. If long-term focus is desired, it's useful to organize this further into intermediate accomplishment checkpoints.
5. Determine the most urgent gaps to be filled between current state (plus known initiatives) for the timeframe involved and the desired

future state of SD/DA capabilities. Identified gaps may be detailed into intermediate steps (e.g. prerequisite projects) as needed, with goals and milestones.

6. Upon evaluating gaps in SD/DA capabilities, identify/define initiatives to achieve the future state.

7. Prioritize/schedule strategic, gap-filling initiatives to achieve desired SD/DA capabilities, part of a coordinated Service-driven & EDM Roadmap (i.e. key subset of overall EA Roadmap).

Several SD/DA Framework domains have both business- and IT-related components. There are potential business and IT initiatives to be planned and executed in a coordinated fashion, necessary to drive improved capabilities within domains. When developing or refining a specific SD/DA Framework for an organization, some components or their defined interrelationships may be adjusted if it makes sense for the way the business or initiatives are organized. The Framework can be applied in a flexible and agile way, as long as it doesn't compromise ability to progress Service-driven & EDM strategies, and their coordination, to greater maturity. Organizations may selectively emphasize key business or IT components as needed for their situation, but the level of overall and domain-specific maturity should be consistently defined and reported, according to the established SD/DA Framework for that organization.

The SD/DA Capability Maturity Model

Complementary to the SD/DA Framework for evaluating and maturing organizational capabilities, is its CMM for planning and executing appropriate Service-driven & EDM initiatives. This section describes a typical SD/DA, since increasing organizational maturity and Service-driven & EDM strategy coordination will increase the capabilities of the SD/DA. Figure 11 is a conceptual view of a typical SD/DA, with an

EIA / Data Integration Layer at its heart. Shared data and Data Platform Services are reused in all Service layers. There are generally several layers and domains of services in a robust SD/DA, shown in the diagram as two (but may be more) SOA / ESB domains of shared services (and buses) to address levels of services abstraction for different functional domains of the enterprise.

The SOA / ESB layers abstract "gold standard" (source of truth) data sources from Service consumers such as end-users in the User Experience & Presentation Layer and Operational/3rd Party Systems/Cloud Services. This abstraction facilitates workflow management, service orchestration and composite business services, and service automation. Workflow management, using business rules (and metadata), facilitates decisions for service discovery/invocation, notifies consumers of workflow progress, routes messaging, and manages process SLAs to provide a powerful architecture for optimizing Enterprise Services & Data assets. Figure 12 shows SD/DA strategy building blocks along a maturity path that leads to managed Services & Data as complementary corporate assets.

Each CMM phase and its building block have implications for EDM & Service-driven capabilities. It's intended that all building blocks of a strategy level be fulfilled before that level is reached by an organization, though it's not unusual for an organization to attain building blocks at different levels, allowing some interpretation in setting the SD/DA maturity level of the organization. However, lower phase level building blocks can be prerequisites to higher level ones, so lower building blocks should generally be fulfilled before declaring higher maturity levels during assessment. Some Data Governance components are prerequisites to MDM, which is a prerequisite to EDM; aspects of these are prerequisites for Enterprise Business Services, which is a prerequisite to maturing the SD/DA enterprise. In building a roadmap of initiatives to achieve organizational maturity under guidance of a SD/

Figure 11. Conceptual service-driven data architecture (SD/DA)

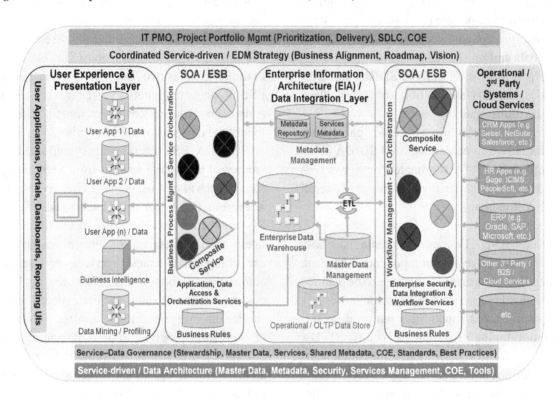

Figure 12. SD/DA CMM levels and progressive building blocks

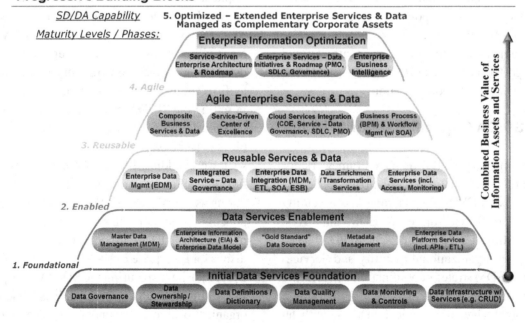

DA CMM, pay attention to foundational building blocks (i.e. candidates for high priority initiatives).

Color-coding guidelines suggested for SD/DA Framework domains/components (in Figure 10) can be utilized when analyzing maturity levels of each CMM building block, for consistency in rating and reporting, or can be tailored to an evaluation scheme that works in the organization. A more detailed SD/DA CMM table is shown in Figures 13 and 14, addressing both Service-driven & EDM

perspectives, and can be an essential cheat sheet for focus in the organization or a program/project.

Figures 13 and 14 show additional detail for developing the organization according to progressive SD/DA maturity levels, and further ties these to implementation steps along identified Dimensions of the Enterprise (i.e. Strategy, Process/Management, Metrics/Reporting, People/Roles, Services/Applications, Data, and Architecture) for SD/DA programs/initiatives. Figure 13 fo-

Figure 13. Service-driven data architecture (SD/DA) CMM and business dimensions

SD/DA CMM	Initiation Turn The Lights On		Deployment Evolve Capabilities		Agility Optimize Results	
Maturity Level / Dimension	**0. Ad Hoc**	**1. Foundational**	**2. Enabled**	**3. Reusable**	**4. Agile**	**5. Optimized**
Strategy	Uncoordinated, Line Of Business driven	>Business Process Integration >Separate visions for each of Services, Data, & Enterprise Architecture	>Common IT Strategy >Initial but separate for Services & Data >Master Data >Cloud Services awareness, analysis	>Services Portfolio >Enterprise Data (Information as Service) >Selected Cloud (3rd Party) Services >BPM & Workflow Automation	>Enterprise (incl. Cloud) Services Roadmap >Enterprise Data (incl. Cloud extensions) >Processes through Services composition	>Service-driven Enterprise Architecture & Roadmap >Enterprise Business Intelligence guidance >Mix & match Business and context-aware capabilities for independent svc centers
Process / Management	Ad hoc, LOB-centered "Governance" Manual data reconciliation Firefighting Ad-hoc workflow	>Data Governance >Data Ownership / Stewardship >Repeatable Data reconciliations >Data discovery techniques >Master Data analysis	>Separate SDLCs for Services & Data >Master Data Mgmt >Metadata Mgmt >Mature Data Governance (incl. MD & selected Metadata) >"Gold Standard" Data sources & definitions >Service Governance & Stewardship >Separate Services and Data Development & Test processes, tools >Single version of key Business Rules >Reactive, disconnected SDLC processes >Tactical Cloud Services analysis	>Coordinated Services–Data SDLC >Enterprise Data Mgmt >Services Portfolio Mgmt >Integrated Service–Data Governance, and part of IT Governance >Focused initiatives to improve information quality and delivery >Selected Cloud Service implementation >BPM & Workflow Orchestration >Standardized Business Rules Mgmt >Mature Services and Data Development & Testing processes, tools	>Service-driven Center of Excellence >Cloud Services SDLC Integration (incl. COE, Governance, PMO) >Mature Service–Data Governance >Mature BPM & Workflow Orchestration via Business Rules >Proactive Data & Services analysis, alerts >Quality measurable, linked to strategy >Integrated Service–Data Development & Testing processes, tools	>Enterprise Services– Data Initiatives & Roadmap (PMO, SDLC, Governance) >Enterprise-wide BI processes >Integrated Service-Data Governance matures >Evolving Service-Data & IT Governance via Policy, Corp. Performance Mgmt >Corporate Performance Mgmt >Closed-loop data / services integrity (e.g. Total Quality Management)
Metrics / Reporting	Ad hoc, LOB-specific, tactical	>Cross-domain, but ad hoc and tactical	>Common cross-LOB for short-term planning >Selected Service & Data Governance supporting	>Strategic cross-LOB >Service–Data Governance >PMO (incl. Service–Data initiatives tracking) >Selected SLA tracking	>Strategic Enterprise-wide metrics, reporting >Enterprise (incl. Cloud) SLA supporting	>Enterprise BI >Performance Mgmt >Enterprise-wide, Automated & Configurable w/ Governance >Advanced analytics
People / Roles	LOB-Specific Functional Skills & Organization No Enterprise Roles for Services, Data	>Shared LOB / cross-domain Skills & Organization >Data Architecture, Modeling, ETL, etc. >Database Mgmt >Environment Mgmt	>Strategic cross-LOB & IT Enterprise Mgmt >Enterprise Architecture >Service Governance & Stewardship >MDM >Services & Data Development & Testing >Services & Data Security >Network Mgmt	>Emerging Enterprise Asset Portfolio Mgmt & Organization >Evolving roles to support Services Portfolio Mgmt >BPM planning & definition >New Cloud Services architecture & integration roles	>Strategic Enterprise Asset Portfolio and Skills Mgmt >Integrated Services– Data Development & Testing	>Dynamically aligned Skills & Asset Portfolio Mgmt via Strategic Governance

Figure 14. Service-driven data architecture (SD/DA) CMM and technology dimensions

SD/DA CMM		Initiation Turn The Lights On		Deployment Evolve Capabilities		Agility Optimize Results
Maturity Level / Dimension	**0. Ad Hoc**	**1. Foundational**	**2. Enabled**	**3. Reusable**	**4. Agile**	**5. Optimized**
Services / Applications	Opportunistic, un-reusable Applications, Services & Data	>Data Infrastructure Services >Some reusable, but unplanned services >No coordination b/t Services and Data >Basic Data Access Security Services	>MDM appl., tools >Composite Services >Enterprise Infrastructure Services >Data Platform Services (incl. ETL, Data Integration) >Transactional Data Security Services >Basic Enterprise Services Bus, config.	>Data Transformation Services >Enterprise Data Platform Services (incl. Access, Integration, Security, Monitoring) >Service-Data Normalization >Orchestrate-able Security Services >Mature ESB config.	>Services–Data Roadmap >Process Integration via BPM & Composite Business Services >Cloud Services Integration >Integrated Service–Data Business Rules >Optimized ESB configuration	>Dynamic Assembly & Process Integration of Composite Applications via Context-Aware Invocation >Mature Service–Data (incl. Cloud) Normalization >Adaptive ESB configuration
Data	Application-specific silos of data Limited data integration Inconsistent Data definitions, usage Reconciliation sheets No centralized Governance, nor prescribed tools, best practices	>Data Definitions / Dictionary >Data Quality Mgmt >Data Profiling >Data Monitoring & Controls >Only some reusable and verifiable Data >Master Data and Metadata definitions & logical structures >Domain or LOB islands of data	>Master Data Mgmt >Metadata Mgmt >Mature Metadata to support Data Access & Security Services >Enterprise Data Model >"Gold Standard" Data Sources >Common Data tools >Canonical Enterprise Models >Data Warehouse >Data Mining & Proactive Profiling	>Enterprise Data Mgt >Integrated Data–Service Governance >Services Portfolio driven Data priorities >Enterprise-wide Data Services >Enterprise MD mappings >Data–Service Normalization >Standardized Data Transformations >Enterprise Data tools (Modeling, Architect)	>Data–Services Roadmap >Enterprise Data Model (w/ Cloud extensions) >Data–Service (incl. Cloud) Normalization >Enterprise Data Release Mgmt >Cloud Services Integration >Master Data / Cloud extensions mappings >Enterprise Business Data Dictionary	>Virtualized Data Services and Semantic Data Vocabularies >Mature EDM >Process and tools are integrated >Domain-specific Master Data Model (incl. Cloud) extensions
Architecture	Monolithic multiple Architectures, LOB-Specific Partial architectures inconsistently applied Few services, little reusability Limited, disconnected domain architectures Disparate platforms, technologies, toolsets	>Layered Architecture w/ Enterprise Standards >Data Services layer >Data Infrastructure >Shared Domain Integration points >Long-term Enterprise Architecture vision >Technologies & Tools shared b/t Domains >Data Warehouse logical architectures >Databases w/ On-Line Transaction Processing, Business Rules	>Common EA view >EIA, incl. Enterprise Data Architecture >MDM Integration >Metadata Mgmt integration >Security Services layer >Services Infrastructure (incl. ESB & UDDI Repository) >Services-supporting Network Mgmt >Data Warehouse Integration >Workflow Integration >Common technologies, tools, and best practices	>EA centrally managed by Architecture & Governance >Enterprise Data Integration >Data Transformation Services Integration >Integrated Workflow & Business Rules engine >Standardized technologies, tools, best practices >Workflow Integration & Orchestration tools, best practices >ESB Configuration tools, best practices	>Enterprise Architecture Roadmap >Service-driven COE >EA version-controlled & evolved via Roadmap >Cloud Services Integration >Enterprise Business Services >Workflow Mgmt Services >Business Rules Engine >Domain Reference Architectures >Mature standardized technologies, tools, and best practices	>Service-driven EA >Dynamically Re-Configurable Services Environment w/ Virtualization >Enterprise Business Rules Engine >EA-Integrated Workflow Mgmt & supporting Business Rules in planned releases >Architectural tools, processes are performance- and metrics-driven

cuses more on the business strategy and organizational aspects (Business Dimensions), while Figure 14 concentrates more on the technological aspects (Technology Dimensions); taken together, these give a comprehensive view for an organization's SD/DA maturity.

Each strategic CMM Dimension can progress (left to right in the table) through increasing SD/DA maturity levels. Roadmaps of progressive capabilities for each Dimension can be combined with other dimensions' progressive maturity plans, when defining and executing the organization's vision and Enterprise Architecture Roadmap (comprehensively, and for each SD/DA program/initiative).

Most organizations have achieved a degree of centralized data sources, but have inconsistent management of Services and Data, thus, they are partially Enabled and possibly Reusable in maturity, but have a ways to go to be Optimized.

Another observation is that organizations generally fall within the Deployment major phase in maturity, but far from achieving Agility. In fact, some capabilities of very mature organizations were not achievable until recently due to modern Service-driven & EDM (and Cloud) management tools.

To optimize such strategies in coordination, organizations must progress in maturity along multiple dimensions, as we develop a coordinated service-driven and EDM strategy program. The CMM table (Figures 13 and 14), and building blocks diagram (Figure 12), can be a reference for stakeholders and implementers in planning and executing their Service-driven & EDM initiatives.

FUTURE INDUSTRY RESEARCH DIRECTIONS

Research will continue to converge the concepts of Service-driven, EDM, and Cloud Services strategies and architectures. It will divest from on-premises systems to large-scale systems distributed across the enterprise and the Cloud. A significant impetus for this evolution in industry research will be the increasing Cloud solution options for most common business applications, which will subsequently spur new Cloud application management solutions, brokers, and infrastructure. Cloud integration, Cloud systems management, including flexible/agile virtualization and configuration options, with extended enterprise workflow management will become industry norms. Also, Cloud Computing will continue to strain existing service and data management concerns.

Companies that adopt Cloud solutions will accept that their critical will be managed both internally/externally; they will deem an internal repository as the "gold master," which may periodically and selectively synchronize with external sources, but it will remain more comfortable as internal. This can't always be the case; however,

as more applications move to hosted solutions for organizations, an external master will become accepted for key Master Data, etc. Another trend this will spur is the need for data management (and MDM) that is also external to the organization. Once data is generally accepted to be master outside the firewall, organizations must then govern this data with appropriate diligence at the (external) source. This puts additional pressure on Cloud Service providers / brokers for data quality SLAs, and customer access to their data, including from outside hosted application interfaces. Such dynamics will evolve, which will change the ways in which services and data are coordinated, but not diminish the need to do this.

CONCLUSION

The future is bright for Service-driven approaches, especially those that extend to Cloud Services, and the advent of Cloud Computing has driven the need and urgency for Service-driven & EDM strategy coordination. Even with SOA, there was a need to coordinate services and data, but now in maturing Service-driven enterprises, and with the incorporation of Cloud Services, such coordination is critical and should be raised to a higher priority so it can yield greater benefits. To not coordinate and mature Service-driven & EDM approaches now puts more distributed assets at risk than ever. This chapter demonstrated the strong case for coordinated Service-driven & EDM strategies and capabilities in organizations. It identified strategic Service-driven & EDM components that require attention to facilitate appropriate levels of coordination and strategy maturity. Best practices were presented in the form of guiding principles to assist enterprises in the definition and transition to an appropriate governance model for an organization. The SD/DA Toolkit was introduced to assist in the evaluation of organizational maturity as well as in developing prioritized, sequenced roadmaps of initiatives to achieve a future state vision of an organization's desired SD/DA strategic level of capabilities.

Organizations should develop an appropriate Service – Data Governance program and a SD/DA CMM for their organization. This needs to be initially coordinated at the highest level of leadership to enable potential to achieve optimal business value for the organization and its services and data. This is job one, and perhaps the highest priority building block towards coordinated Service-driven & EDM capability maturity.

Furthermore, as an organization's Service or Data Governance model is being developed and adopted, it should be closely coordinated for processes, quality checkpoints, and ownership with the other (Data/Service) evolving Governance model. Organizations have not usually developed these strategies and governance models to be coordinated at the start; instead, these are usually found already underway as independent efforts. It is important to adopt and adapt appropriate processes and quality checkpoints between these initially separate governance structures, and to redefine roles and responsibilities to support a more enlightened and coordinated Service – Data Governance. Also, if the organization has an overarching program or project management organization (PMO) that plans and funds initiatives, especially for Enterprise Architecture that span services and data, this coordination should be taken into account in the form of prioritized initiatives to lay progressive building blocks for achieving advanced SD/DA maturity levels.

Moreover, as Governance models and processes are expanded and stabilized for additional enterprise data scope and functional service areas of the organization, related processes and checkpoints (e.g. MDM, Metadata Management, and Service–Data Stewardship) should also expand to encompass this scope with increasing maturity as expressed via the SD/DA CMM. Thus, the organization should develop and scale a specific and progressive CMM with selected joint initiatives, and shared Service and Data Governance responsibilities with coordinated processes and communications. This should be complemented with internal education to inform Service development and EDM staff resources and stakeholders of how to effectively leverage each other during joint service and data development.

Keep in mind that many business processes and transactions use and reuse services and data, and may demand security, accountability, integrity, and performance across heterogeneous (and often multi-enterprise) transactions (including B2B, Cloud Service scenarios). Both service and data reuse increases interdependence of applications and services, further complicating management efforts, which is another reason to evolve towards greater levels of Service-driven and EDM maturity, in a progressive and coordinated fashion. Further, make sure that both business- and data-modeling analysts are involved in service design, in addition to service analysts. This ensures that services reflect business functionality rather than technical partitioning of software or data stores. A well chartered COE can help facilitate the bringing together of diverse stakeholders early and often to establish and drive necessary coordination during software development lifecycle (SDLC) stages of requirements, design, development, and testing of coordinated Service-driven and EDM initiatives.

Lastly, promote a culture of information-sharing and collaboration in the organization. This is the underpinning of successful Service-driven, EDM, and more progressive Service-driven Data Architecture (SD/DA) programs. The organization should make this part of its culture (for many reasons) to especially be a catalyst for the skills, communications, and cross-organizational collaboration that enable coordinated Service-driven and EDM optimization.

REFERENCES

Chandras, R. (2011). 10 tenets of enterprise data management. *InformationWeek Software.* Retrieved from www.informationweek.com/software/information-management/10-tenets-of-enterprise-data-management/229203011

CIO CSG. (2008). How to avoid the hidden pitfalls on the road to SOA: The case for a comprehensive data services framework. *CIO 2 CIO Perspectives.* Retrieved from www.ncr-bdpa.org/whitepapers/SOA_InformaticaWP.pdf

Corbin, K. (2012). Government moves toward cloud computing 'Perfect Storm'. *CIO.* Retrieved from www.cio.com/article/700337/Government_Moves_Toward_Cloud_Computing_Perfect_Storm

Dreibelbis, A., Hechler, E., Milman, I., Oberhofer, M., Run, P., & Wolfson, D. (2008). *Enterprise data management: An SOA approach to managing core information.* IBM Press.

Griffen, J. (2005). Get your data management house to enable service-oriented architecture. *Information Management.* Retrieved from www.information-management.com/issues/20050901/1035565-1.html

Inbar, D. (2008). Data governance for SOA success. *ebizQ: The insider's guide to BPM.* Retrieved from http://www.ebizq.net/topics/soa_security/features/10560.html

Kass, D. H. (2012). CIOs warming (and moving) to cloud technology. *CIO.* Retrieved from www.cio.com/article/710090/CIOs_Warming_and_Moving_to_Cloud_Technology

Loshin, D. (2010). *Data governance, data architecture, and metadata essentials.* Retrieved from http://www.sybase.com/files/White_Papers/Sybase_Data_architecture_and_data_governance_WP.pdf

McKendrick, J. (2010). *SOA strengthens master data management, which returns the favor.* Retrieved from www.zdnet.com/blog/service-oriented/soa-strengthens-master-data-management-which-returns-the-favor/4443

Oliver, A. (2012). Long live SOA in the cloud era. *InfoWorld.* Retrieved from www.infoworld.com/d/application-development/long-live-soa-in-the-cloud-era-205107

Thoo, E. (2009). Data in the cloud: The changing nature of managing data accessibility. *Gartner RAS Core Research.* Retrieved from www.gartner.com/id=902416

ADDITIONAL READING

Erl, T. (2010). *SOA design patterns.* Prentice Hall.

Hohpe, G., & Woolf, B. (2005). *Enterprise integration patterns.* Addison Wesley.

KEY TERMS AND DEFINITIONS

Enterprise Architecture: The IT architecture overview from the enterprise perspective, including all broadly used IT assets of systems, applications, services, data, databases, networking components, and their integration; the strategic IT assets of the organization, and how they fit together.

Enterprise Business Services: Composite Services that provide business functionality for the enterprise.

Enterprise Data Management: Encompasses the cross-application enterprise-level perspective of data in an information-sharing enterprise, and the critical business data that is created, maintained, enriched, and shared outside the traditional enterprise firewall.

Enterprise Information Architecture: A conceptual architecture and infrastructure that supports the organization's Data Architecture, including its Master Data and Metadata definitions and structures.

Enterprise Service Bus (ESB): The technical messaging bus that facilitates integration among services in a Service-driven environment.

Master Data: A single source of business data used across multiple systems, applications, and/or processes.

SD/DA: A framework to provide guidance to evaluate and optimize benefits of the coordinated service-driven and EDM strategies of an enterprise.

Service Oriented Architecture (SOA): Complete Web service platform for the EA, including the inventory of services maintained in a WSDL repository, the ESB, a rules engine, and the standards and protocols that are configured to enable the discovery and invocation of the services by systems, applications and humans as appropriate.

Web Services Description Language (WSDL): The XML description for defining web service discovery, invocation, and behavior within a SOA or Service-driven environment.

Chapter 11
Enabling Vendor Diversifiable Enterprise Integration:
A Reference Architecture

Lloyd Rebello
Independent Researcher, Canada

ABSTRACT

Without effective architectural oversight, enterprises risk stifling their ability to innovate, because vendor products are too tightly woven into their key business processes, which impedes the evolution of their technology environment in support of business needs. Vendors gain negotiation leverage due to monopoly on the technology that supports key enterprise processes and capabilities. The goal of this chapter is to provide practical guidance on business flexibility advantages through carefully managed vendor diversification options for enterprises that are implementing Service-driven applications and integration solutions. The approach presented in this chapter recommends adherence to four basic principles, namely, owning the ability to control delivery channels and integration, compartmentalizing concepts into fulfillment roles in the Service-driven enterprise, using a vendor agnostic enterprise service interface, and owning the key data. The dual reinforcing concepts of ownership and control underpin the vendor diversification opportunities. A reference architecture is presented that distills these principles into a conceptual model that can be applied to any enterprise. A real world transportation and logistics business enterprise integration project is used as an example to illustrate the advantages of using vendor agnostic principles in a Service-driven environment.

INTRODUCTION

Vendor dependencies that are not carefully managed can limit an organization's vendor diversification options which inhibit its business flexibility, putting the organization at a negotiation disadvantage for contracts and system enhancements. As described by Vivek Kundra, former US Federal CIO, "vendor lock-in include reduced negotiation power in reaction to price increases and service discontinuation because the provider goes out of business" (Kundra, 2011).

Organizations that have undergone large integrated package migrations or that have attempted

DOI: 10.4018/978-1-4666-4193-8.ch011

to modernize legacy systems to be repurposed for Web or mobile environments, will have at least in part experienced the challenge that this chapter aims to address. Vendor negotiations start from a position of disadvantage when vendor's products and solutions are so tightly woven into the key business processes of the enterprise that the organization no longer has any leverage to negotiate with.

These organizational technology challenges are captured in software architecture anti-patterns (Koenig, 1995), which result from the mismanagement of vendor dependencies within the architecture. The *Vendor Lock-in* anti-pattern occurs when the organization becomes completely dependent on the vendor's implementation. When upgrades are done, software changes and interoperability problems occur, and continuous maintenance is required to keep the system running...In addition, expected product features are often delayed, causing schedule slips and inability to complete desired application software features" (Vlissides, Brown, & Meszaros, 2012). The authors cite an increase in risk and cost and potential inability to deliver on necessary business outcomes. The solution they offer is to introduce an isolation layer between the applications and the vendor software, which in modern computing is consistent with service-oriented architecture infrastructure (backplane) acting as a mediation and isolation layer.

The Stovepipe Enterprise anti-pattern results from "Multiple systems within an enterprise are designed independently at every level. Lack of commonality inhibits interoperability between systems, prevents reuse, and drives up cost; in addition, reinvented system architecture and services lack quality structure supporting adaptability" (Vlissides, Brown, & Meszaros, 2012). The authors cite brittle, monolithic system architectures that cannot be extended to business needs and cannot be reused or interoperate with the rest of the enterprise driving up costs and reducing the value of technology investments. The authors

suggest that a combination of strategic planning (enterprise architecture) and open standards adoption to effectively manage this problem which is consistent with the approach expressed in this chapter.

The combination of an isolation layer, open standards, and enterprise architecture practices, will put the organization in a better position to manage the aforementioned challenges; however, it will not provide the assurance that they will have the necessary business agility required to succeed in their respective markets. In the modern multi-vendor scenario with architectures developed over decades, there are so many different options (with varying levels of effectiveness) for both the isolation layer and the practices of the enterprise architecture. The isolation layer and enterprise architecture approaches can in general be complimented by considering the technology architectures from a few key perspectives to ensure the desired architectural quality is achieved. This chapter aims to provide one such perspective, the perspective of vendor management in the architecture through service driven approaches, which results in higher levels of vendor diversification options, and can be considered a measure of architectural quality.

The proposed solution starts with service orientation, and the application of a few key principles to maintain vendor boundaries in the enterprise systems, to build a highly flexible business solution platform with *Service Oriented Architecture* (SOA). These principles include owning the ability to control delivery channels and integration, compartmentalizing concepts into fulfillment roles in the Service-driven environment, using a vendor agnostic enterprise service interface, and owning the key data.

This chapter presents a way to consider a key value perspective (vendor diversification) so as to ensure flexibility by managing vendor dependencies effectively. This will also translate directly into more general purpose architectural and business flexibility for Service-driven solutions. The result of such analysis will be a more effective architecture in the long term and a more capable business enablement platform.

BACKGROUND

The industry has general agreement on the core value proposition of service orientation and associated primary benefits. Essentially, SOA increases the flexibility both at the architecture and the organization levels. Architecturally, it improves the efficiency, reuse, integration, and evolution of solutions. From the organization's perspective, it promises business solutions that are more aligned to the business and its processes, at less total cost of ownership, increased business agility, increased flexibility, and shorter times to market (Rosen, Lublinsky, Smith, & Balcer, 2008; Newcomer & Lomow, 2004; McGovern, Ambler, Stevens, Linn, Sharan, & Jo, 2003).

The Open Group cites the benefits of SOA as "...A major benefit of SOA is that it delivers enterprise agility, by enabling rapid development and modification of the software that supports the business processes" (The Open Group, 2012).

Erl (2005) lists the primary SOA advantages as increased intrinsic interoperability, increased federation, increased vendor diversification options, increased business and technology alignment, increased ROI, increased organizational agility, and reduced IT burden.

Erl (2012) explains *vendor diversification options* and the value to the organization as, "this represents an important state for an enterprise in that it provides the constant freedom for an organization to change, extend, and even replace solution implementations and technology resources without disrupting the overall, federated service architecture. This measure of governance autonomy is attractive because it prolongs the lifespan and increases the financial return of automation solutions."

From an organizational outsourcing viewpoint, the point is not to actually avoid outsourcing in the case of key capabilities, but rather to control and maximize the organization's ability to leverage those capabilities. It can be advantageous for an enterprise to engage with vendors to enhance the organization's capabilities, and in such scenarios, some vendors move from being just suppliers to becoming strategic partners, but generally the organization might want to preserve the option to move to another vendor should it become necessary in the future.

Gottfredson, Puryear, and Phillips (2005) present the case for capability control and leverage focus. Now, globalization, aided by rapid technology innovation, is changing the basis of competition. It's no longer a company's ownership of capabilities that matters, but rather its ability to control and make the most of critical capabilities, whether or not they reside on the company's balance sheet. Outsourcing is becoming so sophisticated that even core functions like Engineering, R&D, Manufacturing, and Marketing can and often be moved outside.

Erl (2008) clarifies the goal, not to increase the number of vendors, but to be able to replace vendors when necessary. It is not a goal of service-orientation to increase the vendor diversity within enterprises, instead, the objective is to provide a constant option for diversification so that when existing products and technologies are no longer adequate, they can be extended or even replaced with whatever else the marketplace has to offer without disrupting the established, federated service layer.

A key stated advantage of SOA is that a service orientation promotes flexibility at the architecture level which translates directly into business flexibility in terms of being able to develop new solutions, support new channels (e.g. mobile devices) and enable the enhancement of the existing functionality. However, the management of the vendors within the architecture presents a direct impact on the ability of the organization to realize the promise of SOA.

The two concepts – ownership and control – provide a basis of the approach presented in this chapter. SOA enables an architectural model that provides an organization with the ability to ensure that it has the necessary options to support its business execution with technology.

Firstly, if vendors are allowed to control key, core, or critical processes, then those vendors have leverage over the enterprise because there is a dependency on those vendors for a mission critical aspect of the business. Secondly, in the cases where it is not possible to change the processes, services, or data that vendors manage, then there is obvious dependence on those vendors to make changes, fixes or enhancements. This is not necessarily always bad, except the fact that there is very little leverage to negotiate with those vendors for services when the enterprise has become too tied to those vendors to implement services. If that vendor is the only party that can augment a service, then the organization is at their mercy for time to deliver and the cost to do so. While this situation may never manifest in the environment, it still is in the organization's best interest to protect the ability to run the business on its own terms.

Another challenge is the fact that vendor products normally come equipped with an architecture, which may not be designed for the level of flexibility that the future business requires (even when using open standards). It can be challenging to understand where vendor products fit into the architecture, especially without a reference model to map their product architectures onto. Also, while reviewing their product, it is easy to get oriented toward their way of doing things (existing product models, architectures, and APIs). The risk here is that one can easily lose sight of where the vendor product should fit in, versus where that particular vendor believes they should plug-in to the architecture.

These challenges can be made manageable by carefully considering the vendor diversifiable perspective when integrating new systems or services onto the platform. There are a number of ways that an organization may get locked into a vendor, thus, limiting vendor diversification options. Technically these ways include tight coupling (e.g. direct API access); point-to-point integration (i.e. two systems talking directly to each other, without a mediating layer); not owning the key data (e.g. key data is in a vendor package proprietary database, not ever being sourced out into an enterprise data layer), and contractual in terms of not building in the correct clauses (such as exits) and vendor performance agreements (i.e. SLAs).

Following along the lines of the Architecture Tradeoff Analysis Method (ATAM), which formalizes the analysis of quality attributes and architectural approaches that support business drivers in light of the risk themes (Bass, Clements, & Kazman, 2001); the enterprise architecture can be seen as informing the selection between a series of competing decisions and associated tradeoffs. This chapter presents one dimension, the vendor management dimension (to enable vendor diversification options), and a way to consider and effectively manage that dimension through a series of principles to improve architectural quality and business flexibility.

Governance of Vendor Diversification

In order to enable flexible, vendor diversifiable enterprise integration, the organization should plan and govern the technology architecture and integration of vendor products in a thoughtful and deliberate manner. The Service-driven approaches for the organization should be considered from the vendor diversification perspective, which provides business flexibility by ensuring that efforts to innovate are not hand-cuffed by mistakes in the management of the technology architecture. As stated previously and presented below, four basic principles should be employed by the architecture team in order to ensure that the organization maintains maximum technical flexibility in relation to enterprise integration:

Principle 1: Own the ability to control delivery of channels and integration.

Principle 2: Compartmentalize concepts into fulfillment roles in the service-driven environment.

Principle 3: Implement vendor agnostic enterprise service interface.

Principle 4: Own the key data.

Owning the Ability to Control Delivery of Channels and Integration

A fundamental concept to ensure retaining control over the technology architecture and maximizing the business agility and ability to innovate is to maintain control over the channels and integration. Figure 1 illustrates an enterprise view of channels and integration. *Channels* refer to the

paths (e.g. browser) that users of services take to interact with them, which generally would include internet browser, mobile phones, tablets, telephones (IVR – interactive voice response), kiosks, and in person. Integration refers to the set of systems, both inside and outside the enterprise that communicates and exchanges information in order to cooperatively fulfill and deliver a service (or set of services). Why is it so important to own the channels and integration? The short answer is that this is as close as an enterprise can come to being able to guarantee the quality of service that the organization delivers to its customers, and being in control to be able to evolve the current service offering.

For channels, the rule of thumb to use is to determine whether a new channel can be added or whether the system that manages the interaction with that channel seamlessly can be replaced (without service disruption to existing channels). For integration, the rule of thumb is similar – can a new system be added or is it possible to replace

Figure 1. Generic multi-channel, multi-vendor, enterprise view of channels and integration

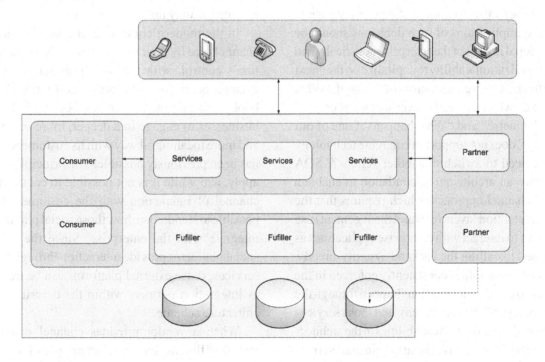

any system in the integration "chain" without disrupting any of the other systems? If the answer is no, then a vendor has leaked too far beyond what should be the compartmentalized boundary. Putting a service (or system) into a *compartmentalized role* aims to have that service (or system) do a single discrete job so it can most easily be replaced if the need arises.

Probably the biggest challenge to this concept is the fact that the architecture, because of the business drivers, is constantly being pushed to evolve rapidly and deliver new business value. As new ways to engage the customers emerge, and in order to capitalize on new market opportunities, the organization strives to get new products to market quickly. In such scenarios, the architecture quality may not always come first, unless architecture is seen as an enabler. The reality is in some cases, it just may not always be faster than "just dropping something in" in an ad hoc way. However, a platform based approach offers a series of advantages over the ad hoc option. A mature platform may not add much time to the schedule while reducing risk and offering a series of technical advantages such as security, availability, and a standardized technology infrastructure that can be leveraged.

The implications of such decisions should be considered in light of the enterprise holistically and the organization's ability to capitalize on the "next big thing." The organization must ask itself, "What do we do when we need to overhaul some or all of our channels?" and "What happens if one of our vendors' does not support an emerging technology or we need to switch to another vendor?" SOA provides an architectural foundation to enable a multi-channel approach, which requires that the user interaction layers (channel management) use services to interact with enterprise applications as opposed to calling the backend systems directly.

If the principle is consistently enforced in the enterprise that all interactions happen through the service layer (Service-driven), and those services manage the application capabilities in the architecture, then the enterprise is largely insulated from

major vendor management challenges that result from vendor (architecture) mis-management. For example, by being too far removed from a process that the vendor controls, causes the organization to lose the ability to change the flow of it. The implications can be serious when that process is mission critical or related to a core business capability. If vendors touch customers (interacting through channels such as the browser or mobile devices) then the quality of service delivered by the vendor (which may be poor) is a direct representation of the organization.

A similar concept holds for system to system integration, and if the organization allows vendors to manage integrations with other vendors, without the service layer acting as a "hub" in the process, then the enterprise runs the risk of being too far removed from the integration chain, and thus less able to understand it, manage it, or change it. Unless a vendor provides a specialized service for a channel (e.g. mass email, reporting) or foundational service (e.g. enterprise service bus, monitoring), then generally it is ideal that the enterprise retains control over the management and delivery of those services. In the case of key services, it may turn out to be vital.

In the modern computing era, key customer channels are by their nature, out of the organization's control, with the most prevalent current example being Social technologies. Twitter, Facebook, LinkedIn, and others are key channels for businesses to engage in a deeper, more intimate and more meaningful way with its customers than has been previously possible. The principles still apply, and while it is not possible to control the channel of interaction with the customer, it is possible to standardize how those social platforms integrate with the enterprise. Since the major social platforms provide interaction through Web services, those external platforms can be treated as integration partners within the described architecture scheme.

When a vendor provides channel delivery and fulfillment services, when possible, the organization should not allow that vendor to control the process end to end. In other words, vendors should not be delivering the content and user interaction flow to the channel and directly calling their backend without going through the enterprise SOA layer. Ideally, the vendor would deploy or integrate into the portal or multi-channel technology and their services would become part of the fulfillment architecture of the enterprise SOA. This is not always practical, but in the cases of key or mission critical capabilities, it may be worth the investment.

Compartmentalizing Concepts into Fulfillment Roles

Compartmentalizing the SOA and the fulfillment of services into a set of roles allows for easier management of vendors and their solutions in relation to where they should fit in to the enterprise (not where they desire to). Part of the challenge is that when a vendor brings an offering to the

enterprise, often times it is a finished product with a set of solution decisions already made. The problem lies in the fact that these product solution decisions may not align with the best interests of the enterprise. The organization's best interest may not always align with what is most beneficial to a vendor.

A straightforward way to manage this is to develop *fulfillment roles* for the Service-driven environment (a functional view of the architecture), and segment vendors both by technology tiers and business functional aspects. Figure 2 shows an example view of tiers and fulfillment roles.

This principle is highly related to the first principle to control the channels and integration, and can be tested by questioning whether any fulfillment role in the enterprise could be fulfilled by a different service or vendor. The two principles together are mutually reinforcing and in combination provide a strong basis for vendor (architecture) management. The rule of thumb here is that the enterprise should have the option to replace the

Figure 2. Example view of tiers and functional fulfillment roles

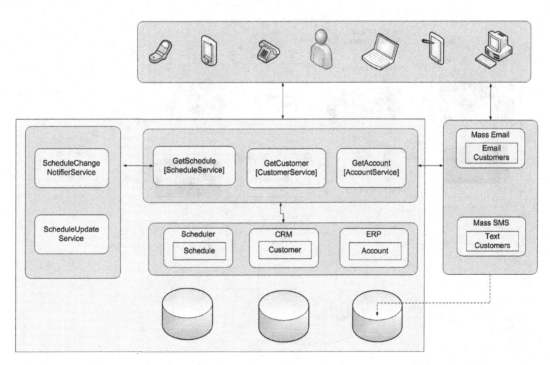

vendor that implements any service or replace the technical capability wholesale. The same vendor may assume many roles in the architecture; however, each role they fulfill should be sufficiently compartmentalized to provide the option to vary the service provider. Essentially, the enterprise strives to create a set of "boxes" for services and fulfillment and then ideally fit the technology capabilities neatly in to those "boxes." Even if a vendor offers end to end services (which is normal), the organization may still want to force them into the architecture roles.

It may not be always practical to pursue this principle. A key question to ask in order to decide whether it is worth pursuing the principle for a particular solution is whether it is a critical aspect to the evolution of the business (and architecture). In those cases where it is not critical, consider relaxing the rules if necessary.

Implementing Vendor Agnostic Enterprise Service Interfaces

The enterprise service interface(s) and the enterprise schema(s) constitute the integration contract across the enterprise. As much as it is realistic, the goal is for this enterprise service interface to be vendor agnostic. The challenge lies in the fact that the vendor schemas/APIs/interfaces are specialized to their products and dictate how the vendors view the enterprise integration (see Figure 3). Unfortunately, the current vendor approaches may not necessarily align with the long term multi-vendor compatible interface for the enterprise.

While challenging, it is important to start from the position of attempting to structure the services with the organization in mind first and the vendor's architecture second. In two previous large scale Service-driven industrial implementations,

Figure 3. Enterprise interfaces and vendor specific fulfillments

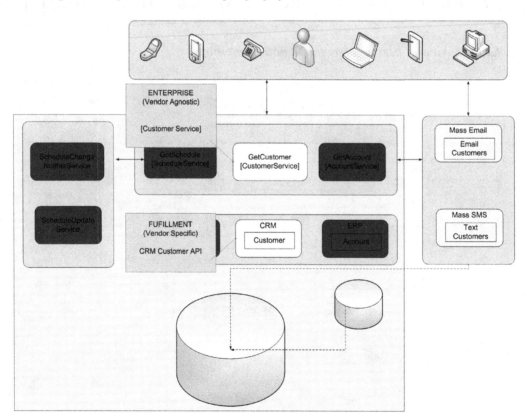

a pattern of intelligent routing was implemented after the fact, and in both cases this was made possible by having a service orientation and a vendor agnostic enterprise service interface.

Enterprise service interfaces need to be designed to route the invocations transparently to the most appropriate fulfillment service. For example, consider a scenario where there are a set of optimizer services that optimize an itinerary for a customer. The actual optimizer that is called at runtime may be dependent on a complex set of criteria, so the calling client system should not decide which one to invoke. The routing intelligence factors in the criteria to decide on the right service to fulfill the request. The client system can invoke the same interface, but the intelligent routing module introspects the message to determine the appropriate destination.

Similarly, when looking to vary or replace a key capability in the architecture without major disruption to the dependant systems, it is necessary to be as loosely coupled to the current vendor implementation as possible. This allows replacement vendor implementations to be integrated with the least amount of disruption. If the enterprise service represents services as modeled in the enterprise and not the vendor's services, then this loose coupling can be achieved through a public interface (enterprise services) in tandem with a private interface (fulfillment services), see Figure 4.

By implementing best practice concepts such as loosely coupled standards based integration, the enterprise can have a long lived, robust service interface model. This also sets up for services to be used in ways that may not have been initially planned, which can be extremely valuable. The earlier example of introducing an intelligent routing capability behind the service interface was applied onto an existing solution (after the fact) and was made possible by loosely coupled, standards based integration. Another common high value scenario is with development teams building value add services on top of the standard enterprise services and enhancing them in ways not originally planned.

An example might be that there is a generic customer service that provides a calling system with all the customers in a data set and allows for making standard searches. Now consider that one of the enterprise development teams is doing advanced customer segment targeting, and they develop a specialized aggregation service that allows systems to find all customers in a demographic segment that have a certain purchasing trend (e.g. affluent and bought a product in the last month) built on top of the existing basic service that other teams can now utilize. The original team may not even be aware of this new service, and they did not have to plan for it, but it has been made possible through the use of standards and loosely coupled integration. This layering of services through enhancement, aggregation, and composition is an illustration of the long term SOA value proposition.

Owning the Key Data

With the above stated principles, at times it may make sense to bend and flex, consistent with the goals of the enterprise. In stark contrast, there should never be any bend on the principle of "Owning the Key Data," primarily for two reasons. The first, data is a *core enterprise asset*, valuable over a very long period of time and it should be leveraged from many different utilization perspectives. Secondly, if the enterprise does not own the data in an outsourced situation, the vendor in possession of the data also possesses an undue amount of negotiation leverage. There is an interesting, but often less explored angle with vendors, the fact that vendors who manage data in the applications within the enterprise may also pose a risk to the enterprise. Whenever vendors manage key processes and data even within the enterprise data center with proprietary databases

Figure 4. Variability built on standardized enterprise interfaces and schemas

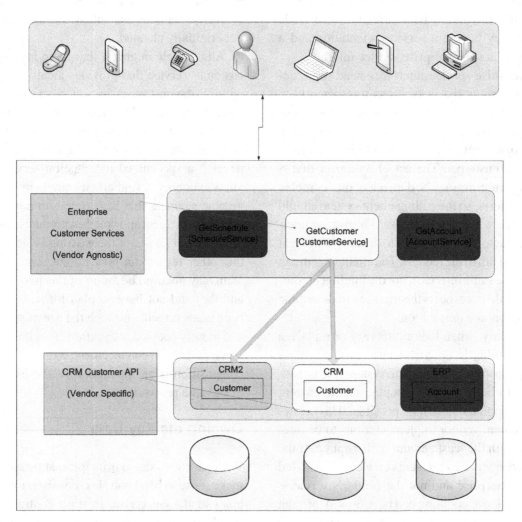

or schemas, then the enterprise is in a position of disadvantage with regard to the stability and continuity of the business.

External channels such as social platforms (e.g. Twitter, Facebook, LinkedIn, etc.) hold key information outside of the enterprise about the organization, products and customers. At a minimum, that data should be brought back to the enterprise in order to link it to the related enterprise data and metrics. There are tools and techniques to continuously monitor those social platforms (e.g. watching twitter #hash tags and occurrences of key phrase related to the organi-

zation and products) to leverage that data in the organization's data driven decisions.

The bottom line is that the enterprise should always strive to own its key data.

Techniques for Enabling Vendor Diversification

- **Decoupling Endpoint Awareness from Services:** If a service specifically references an end point other than through a symbolic reference (e.g. "AccountService" or "AddAccount"), the flexibility to change the underlying service provider is unnecessarily complicated through coupling. Strive to make services flexible by insulating the actual end-points from them.

- **Service Mediation:** Use of a mediation infrastructure in terms of a commercial ESB (Enterprise Service Bus) or an alternative to facilitate the separation of callable interface from the underlying service fulfiller will enable intelligent routing, service evolution, and the opportunity to change the underlying service fulfillers. This can be achieved with common industry practices and technologies.

- **Integration Standards and Protocols:** Use of technology standards such as Web Services and JCA (Java Connector Architecture) Integration Adapters is the recommended industry defacto standard way to achieve enterprise integration. Open standards and protocols enable vendor diversification since most major vendors have been supporting these standards for many years.

- **Being Business-Driven:** An often cited requirement for SOA success is that service drivers be business driven, not technology driven. This is logical when one considers that it is a stronger business case to better engage customers and drive innovation versus reducing technology costs and producing more elegant architectures. The technology governance team benefits from the business leadership understanding the Service-driven advantages and the value proposition to them (in business terms). If this understanding is achieved, then when the organization is under time pressure to deliver to the market, there will be leadership support to keep solutions on the Service-driven platform.

- **Effective Governance:** Implementation of the aforementioned principles requires strong governance in place in order to cor-

rectly manage the architecture evolution. Governance team must examine solutions and align them with the long term business objectives of the enterprise, while ensuring the technical health and quality of the solution. Assessment of technical quality should factor in the principles presented in this chapter to avoid incurring long term disadvantages.

Reference Architecture

The Vendor Diversifiable Enterprise Integration reference architecture presents a model based on the principles presented in this chapter, which an organization can apply to their enterprise. The positive side effect of the principle based approach is that while the focus is on effectively maintaining the control of the architecture by keeping vendor dependencies at bay, it generally will also produce more technically sound architectures.

The major layers in the reference architecture, as shown in Figure 5, provide guidance for effective application of the presented principles. The layers follow.

Multi-Channel Service Delivery Layer

While managing all channels in a consolidated and centralized manner is not absolutely necessary, it will provide advantages such as layering common look and feel, security, and the ability to leverage common architectural framework and functional components across the customer's client devices. There are several approaches to achieving *multi-channel service delivery*, including "rolling your own," using portal products and multi-channel products. According to the "Owning the ability to control delivery channels & integration" principle, this layer promotes the adherence to this principle by being a single, central, consolidated layer, and enables control over the service delivery to different channels of communication.

Figure 5. Vendor diversifiable service oriented reference architecture

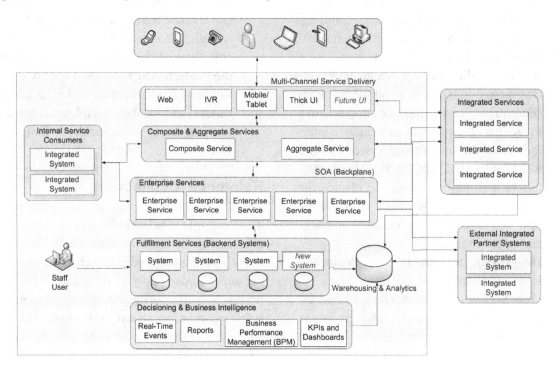

Composite and Aggregate Services Layer

The composite and aggregate services layers, referred to as Basic Services (Krafzig, Banke, & Slama, 2004), utilizes the more fundamental services and business processes, commonly referred to as *Process-centric Services* (Krafzig, Banke, & Slama, 2004). The services in this layer enhance the basic and generic services through composition and orchestration to provide more specialized and sophisticated functionality.

Enterprise and Fulfillment Services Layer

The enterprise services layer consists of key services that provide generic utility and data entity type services and acts as an intermediary between the Process-centric services and the specialized fulfillment services. According to the "Owning the key data" principle, the enterprise must always

strive to own the key data. This means that when working with vendors, a plan should be made for all key data to flow out of systems both in and outsourced into the enterprise data framework (whether it is data warehouses, federated data, master data, virtualized data, big data or equivalent). This increases the value of that data and protects the organization from being overly dependent on a vendor for their key data.

Service Consumers

The enterprise and fulfillment services provide value to the systems within and external to the enterprise. It is good practice to consider the clients of the services when developing them, to make the interaction with the service layer as usable and functional as possible. Many service layers suffer from unnecessary complexity that could be hidden from the client systems. A couple of ways to hide complexity in an interface are by using default settings and introducing the concept of advanced options. As a cautionary note, as the service infrastructure scales, data load may increase (after broad SOA adoption). As message volumes increase in the enterprise, there may be a need to implement SLAs for the service consumers in order to control their call volumes over an interval of time.

Integrated Services and Integrated Service Partners

Over the past several years, with the emergence of on-demand externally sourced services and Cloud Computing, it has become necessary for Service-driven enterprises to plan their architecture and infrastructure to accommodate the integration of both external services and external partners. Google, Amazon, and several other major online providers offer customers a rich set of services (integrated services) through their Web APIs to build their own business specific value upon. One example is Google Maps, where enterprise customers can use their internal enterprise services to integrate with and enhance the base Google maps to solve their specific business problems, such as, enhancing the map to display hospitals and clinics that provide a certain medical treatment. This can then evolve and expand to more specialized map services.

Enhanced Vendor Diversification Options

With ownership of delivery across the service channels managed consistently in one layer, the vendor diversification options are increased through centralized control and interface standardization. Contrast this approach with the one where several vendors deliver parts of the solution in a proprietary manner and some vendors own processes end to end. The reference architecture provides the guidance to structure the application layers in a loosely coupled manner to enable flexibility with vendors, technologies, and implemen-

tations. This facilitates enhancements to vendor delivered services and makes it easier to replace vendor provided services, if necessary. Invariably, at some point in the future, the enterprise may have a need to replace a major vendor either due to lack of performance or intolerable vendor risk levels. As described in "Why New Systems Fail" (Simon, 2010), vendor divorce may be necessary from a consistent pattern of mutual antagonism, unmet expectations, or poor customer service.

The service layers (composite & aggregate, enterprise services and fulfillment services) create the *isolation layer* solution described in the vendor lock-in antipattern (Vlissides, Brown, & Meszaros, 2012). This builds business flexibility by maintaining separation from the channels, integrated partners, integrated consumers and back-end systems. The combination of a loosely coupled interface from the implementation (enterprise service layer and fulfillment services), along with the use of open standards and best practices, maximizes the variability of any part of the solution. This is well demonstrated by the fact that composite and aggregate services can be built on top of existing services without changing the underlying enterprise services themselves. This separation also provides the highly advantageous option of replacing a back-end fulfilling service implementation.

Beyond the vendor diversification advantage, this approach leads to a structurally sound architectural model, and while the increase in layers and interchange in some cases may present performance challenges to overcome, practical massive scale solutions have proven the approach in the real world. Organizations such as Amazon employ leading edge solutions such as caching, delayed consistency and data synchronization, while calling hundreds of services at a time (Vogels, 2007) to gain the business advantages from the architectural structure, while still meeting the challenging everyday operational performance and availability demands of extremely large scale systems. The dual reinforcing concepts of ownership and control, the ownership of channels, the core services, the key data and control over their evolution, underpin the vendor diversification opportunities.

In order to effectively manage such broad reaching concepts, it is necessary to organize around them. The management goal is to develop organizational structures or competency centers that can advance the architectural agenda while not inhibiting the overarching business agenda, which is to deliver value to customers. Sample practice areas might include business transformation, business process re-engineering, business architecture, enterprise architecture, service-oriented architecture, enterprise data, IT strategy and the multi-channel management.

Reference Architecture: Case Scenario

To illustrate the reference architecture and it's principles in practice, the following section presents a real-world example with a scenario exploration for the future state architecture.

The organization considered is a large transportation provider with major systems including scheduling, optimization, customer service, and vehicle logistics. The problem space for this architecture is essentially a fleet of a few hundred vehicles, with a variable route per vehicle (dynamically changing during the day), which presents complex schedule, vehicle logistics and service delivery challenges.

Historically, at this organization, with most of the existing systems using point to point integration, existing vendors would have been the only vendors that could be considered for enhancements and evolution of the existing products (locked-in), because the architecture would not have made it cost-effective to introduce new vendor's products. However, by evolving to a Service-driven architecture and incorporating the outlined principles, the organization was able to leverage the flexibility and extensibility of the vendor diversifiable architecture.

Figure 6 illustrates an example logistics and scheduling system architecture diagram derived from the reference architecture. Several scenarios

Figure 6. The example logistics and scheduling system architecture

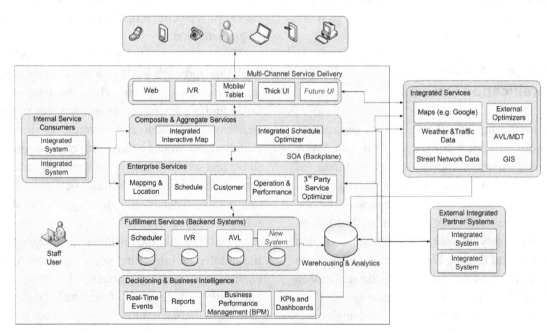

that illustrate the vendor diversifiable principles were considered. In the first scenario, there is a need to replace the existing Interactive Voice Response (IVR) system in the enterprise. Figure 7 illustrates a point-to-point integration approach on the left and a Service-driven design on the right that is neatly structured in comparison to the point-to-point 'spaghetti' architecture.

The point-to-point approach has systems directly integrating with each other, leading to strong coupling and conceptually a leakage of systems beyond a healthy boundary. On the other hand, when the integration is managed through the SOA layer and messaging is developed based on an enterprise schema (as opposed to being coupled to a vendor schema, in accordance with principle #3), it allows the replacement of a particular vendor's product with minimal disruption to the other vendor's systems and services. SOA enables the potential for flexibility, and applying the presented principles helps to ensure meet that promise for flexibility.

The above Service-driven approach creates loose coupling through a mediator layer and by using an enterprise schema which separates request messages from their transactional fulfillment. This has several advantages, and in this example most notably is that it increases the vendor diversification option to a level where the IVR vendor from an integration perspective is interchangeable (obviously the specifics of the phone system and staff interface still require

migration). In this scenario, since the integration channel was controlled (principle #1) via the SOA backplane and the IVR fulfillment role was effectively compartmentalized in the architecture (principle #2); and there was a vendor agnostic IVR service interface (principle #3); collectively the application of these principles made possible the near seamless (integration) replacement of the existing IVR system. The fact that the data was under the organization's ownership and control (principle #4), meant that when the new product was implemented, the existing data just needed to be migrated to the new product's repository.

Consider a second scenario dealing with the introduction of a second Automatic Vehicle Location (AVL) system into the architecture (see Figure 8). The AVL works with the onboard vehicle device that transmits GPS locations to notify systems of the current location of the vehicle, and inform the scheduler of the vehicle proximity to target locations. Part of the service delivery fleet was to be outsourced to contract providers and those vehicles used a different set of onboard devices and a different AVL system than was currently in production (both run simultaneously under the same scheduler and optimizers).

Lock in was avoided in this case through architectural flexibility via compartmentalization (principle #2) and the enterprise service (principle #3), which allowed the best solution (another vendor) to be integrated into the enterprise service interface and also allowed the two differ-

Figure 7. Replace IVR – point-to-point approach vs. service-driven integration

Figure 8. Additional AVL system integration

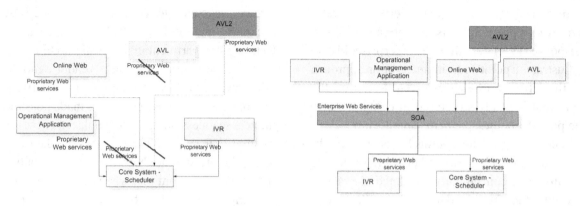

ent AVL systems to look generally uniform so they could co-exist harmoniously.

Simulating system behavior and AB Testing (testing two system behavior variants on two different user population samples) is a powerful concept in complex systems. Enterprises may do this to present marketing offers or to better engage customers. If there is an optimization hypothesis that needs to be tested before rolling out that functionality to the entire user base, AB testing is a commonly employed approach. The scenario under consideration here is a set of schedule optimizations in the scheduler that could be tested on a segment of the fleet as shown in Figure 9.

This simulation would use an optimizer, factoring in new or different optimization parameters

(e.g. historical performance averages, performance in weather conditions, performance with street construction, historical impact of special events, traffic trends day of month and time of day, etc.). Once the hypothesis is proven, the "test segment" behavior can then be scaled out to the entire production fleet. The ability that makes this possible "after the fact" to introduce A/B Testing into the solution is the control over channels (principle #1), because channel control enables the segment to be recognized (and behavior altered), and the enterprise services (principle #3) allow routing to the compartmentalized (principle #2) fulfilling backend system.

One of the strengths of standards based, open integration service models is that services can-

Figure 9. AB testing and field simulation

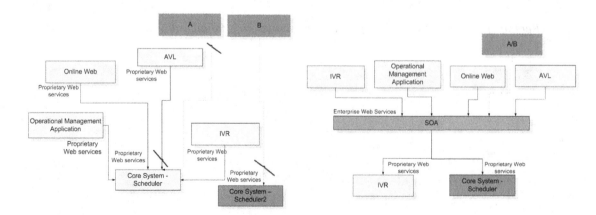

not only be consumed by planned consumers, but also be consumed by consumers that were not anticipated. It is not just that one may have unexpected service consumers, these consumers may use the services in unexpected ways and they may also enhance, aggregate, expand and compose those services in ways not anticipated. It is often cited that some of the most valuable uses of products and services are the unintended applications (Tuomi, 2002). Figure 10 illustrates some example service enhancements, where several services are enhanced.

Of particular note from the vendor diversification perspective is that this can be a major difference in the enterprise integration between integrating two disparate systems using vendor specific and customized point-to-point integration solutions versus laying the foundation for enterprise flexibility and extensibility (i.e. SOA). In other words, it is the difference between "just getting it to work" and building a platform for the future. In the vendor specific point-to-point model, as services grow, the problem of evolving the solution is amplified since there may not be a straightforward way to layer new functionality and integrate new services into the existing proprietary and customized architecture.

Service-driven best practices set the stage for diverse service consumption and enhancement through the practice of layered services, where one layer of services, the basic or general purpose services, is then enhanced by the composite/aggregating services or process services. Since a layer in the service architecture (process services) is actually enhancing another layer (basic services), the service enhancement model is established and can be utilized in practice. The use of enterprise services (principle #3) based on broadly adopted Web Service standards enables the creation of layers upon layers of services.

The service driven approach, when utilizing open standards with SOA, creates the opportunity to operate services with location transparency, since theoretically, endpoint location is not important (however having services distributed in practice may have performance and other implications). In an architecture where service request and fulfillment are separated (a mediator such as an ESB, provides routing), it is possible to implement a hybrid model of services located in many data centers and utilizing external service providers. de Vadoss et al. (2013) explains the SOA Cloud Computing opportunity – "From the perspective of SOA, Cloud Computing, especially with public Clouds, brings options to extend one's own architecture and processes beyond an organization's existing boundaries; and enable more meaningful, more collaborative, and potentially more agile interactions with partners and customers."

Figure 10. Building on top of services

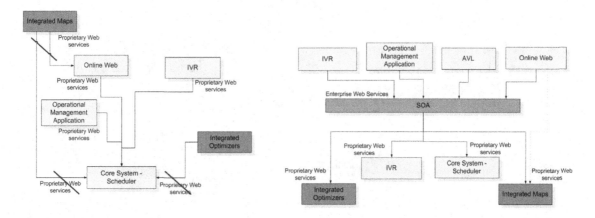

A combination of the current major industry trends in outsourced services including Software as a Service (SaaS), Platform as a Service (PaaS), and Infrastructure as a Service (IaaS), all have the potential to be made valuable and to offer the organization real advantages. Figure 11 illustrates an example of how the solution under review could distribute services to Cloud based offerings. It is worth noting that in this particular example, that all communications occurred asynchronously and there were delays of a few seconds built into the model. In this scenario, the control over channels and integration (principle #1) enabled the organization to move them off-premises, the enterprise services (principle #3) and related routing infrastructure allowed the routing of service fulfillment to the correct service in the correct data centre, the compartmentalization (principle #2) allowed for services like maps and optimizers to be integrated into the architecture, and data ownership (principle #4) gave the organization confidence to move services outside of its walls knowing that the key data assets are eventually brought back to the enterprise.

CONCLUSION

Organizations looking to maximize their SOA capability to enable a competitive pace of innovation and increase their business agility are recommended to consider managing their Service-driven approaches according to the principles outlined in this chapter. Enterprises should (along with other key factors) consider their architecture from the perspective of how well it allows them to diversify their vendors.

Vendors that are not managed correctly for key capabilities, present the organization a real risk in terms of lack of vendor diversification options, which can stifle innovation. Vendors that are not managed effectively within the architecture and that control key processes and data, present an operational risk to the technology environment and may have too much leverage in contract negotiations. The principles presented in this chapter can enable the organization to own its channels, have properly compartmentalized vendor roles, have vendor agnostic enterprise service interfaces, and own the key data, which will not only facilitate managing the vendors' more effectively in the architecture, but also result in the positive side effect of technically sound architectures.

As Service-oriented architecture and Service-driven approaches continue to evolve, so too should

Figure 11. Moving services to the cloud – service-driven integration

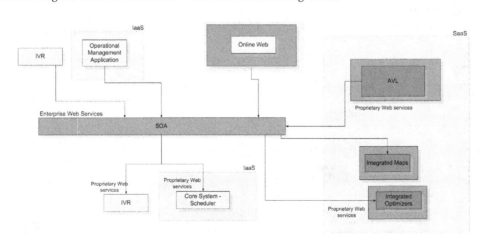

the maturity of organizations in considering the different organizational perspectives in the architectures. There could be further formalization in the application of principles like the ones presented in this chapter and the other core organizational concern perspectives such as Security, Availability, Performance, etc.

If some aspects of SOA can be formalized based on best practices becoming standard practices, it is possible then to measure architectural quality against that standardized model. In this chapter, the vendor management architecture perspective was explored and these concepts could be further formalized to quality metrics that could measure how well (or not) an architecture promotes vendor diversification options. An example could be to measure the level of compartmentalization of a vendor within the architecture, based on how coupled the rest of the architecture is to this part of the solution. This would answer the question whether the vendor fulfilling the role in the architecture could be replaced with measures such as how much additional effort it would be to replace the fulfillment aspect of those services or how many upstream systems would be directly impacted. Metrics could be derived that collectively result in a score rating of how diversifiable that aspect of the architecture is. Similarly, other perspectives could be explored, that formalize the assessment of Service-driven approaches from other more mature and formalized perspectives such as Risk, Value, etc.

The vendor diversifiable perspective of the architecture, which is one key dimension of architectural consideration, can be effectively managed through the principles presented in this chapter. In most solutions, this should not be the only dimension considered (and may not be the highest priority dimension). There may be potential tradeoffs to increase vendor diversification options, and other dimensions may be weighed more heavily in the prioritization scheme such as Risk, Performance, and Time to Market. The principles presented in this chapter, while only one dimension

of architecture concern in enterprise integration, will still provide organizations a real opportunity to enhance their technical platform for innovation and ensure vendors are managed correctly within their Service-driven environments.

REFERENCES

Bass, L., Clements, P., & Kazman, R. (2001). *Evaluating software architecture: Methods and case studies*. Upper Saddle River, NJ: Addison-Wesley Professional.

de Vadoss, J., Lascelles, F., Rischbeck, T., Wilhelmsen, H., Plunkett, T., & Little, M. et al. (2013). *Service-oriented infrastructure: On-premise and in the cloud*. Upper Saddle River, NJ: Prentice Hall.

Erl, T. (2008). *SOA design patterns*. Upper Saddle River, NJ: Prentice Hall.

Erl, T. (2012). *Increased vendor diversification options*. Retrieved July 1, 2012, from http://www.whatissoa.com/increased_vendor_diversification_options.php

Gottfredson, M., Puryear, R., & Phillips, S. (2005). Strategic sourcing: From periphery to core. *Harvard Business Review*, R0502J. PMID:15724581.

Koenig, A. (2005). Patterns and anti-patterns. *Journal of Object-Oriented Programming*, Vol. 8.

Krafzig, D., Banke, K., & Slama, D. (2004). *Enterprise SOA: Service-oriented architecture best practices*. Upper Saddle River, NJ: Prentice Hall.

Kundra, V. (2011). *Federal cloud computing strategy*. Retrieved July 1, 2012, from http://www.cio.gov/documents/federal-cloud-computing-strategy.pdf

McGovern, J., Ambler, S., Stevens, M., Linn, J., Sharan, V., & Jo, E. (2003). *A practical guide to enterprise architecture*. Upper Saddle River, NJ: Prentice Hall.

Newcomer, E., & Lomow, G. (2004). *Understanding SOA with web services*. Addison-Wesley Professional.

Rosen, M., Lublinsky, B., Smith, K., & Balcer, M. (2008). *Applied SOA: Service-oriented architecture and design strategies*. Indianapolis, IN: John Wiley & Sons.

Simon, P. (2010). Why new systems fail: Revised edition: An insider's guide to successful IT projects. Boston, MA: Course Technology PTR.

The Open Group. (2012). *SOA and enterprise architecture*. Retrieved July 1, 2012, from http://www.opengroup.org/soa/source-book/soa/soa_ea.htm

Vlissides, J., Brown, K., & Meszaros, G. (2012). *Stove pipe enteprise*. Retrieved July 1, 2012, from http://sourcemaking.com/antipatterns/stovepipe-enterprise

Vlissides, J., Brown, K., & Meszaros, G. (2012). *Vendor lock-in*. Retrieved July 1, 2012, from http://sourcemaking.com/antipatterns/vendor-lock-in

Vogels, W. (2007). *Availability & consistency or how the CAP theorem ruins it all*. Retrieved July 1, 2012, from http://www.infoq.com/presentations/availability-consistency

ADDITIONAL READING SECTION

Chappel, D. (2004). *Enterprise service bus*. Sebastopol, CA: O'Reilly Media.

Erl, T. (2005). *Service-oriented architecture: Concepts, technology, and design*. Upper.

Erl, T. (2007). *SOA principles of service design*. Upper Saddle River, NJ: Prentice Hall.

Hohpe, G., & Woolf, B. (2004). *Enterprise integration patterns*. Boston, MA.

Newcomer, E., & Lomow, G. (2005). *Understanding SOA with web services*. Boston, MA.

Saddle River, NJ: Prentice Hall.

Software Engineering Institute of the Carnegie Mellon University. (2013). *The capability maturity model integration web site*. Retrieved from http://www.cmmiinstitute.com

The Oasis Reference Model for SOA. (2012). *Website*. Retrieved from https://www.oasis-open.org/committees/tc_home.php?wg_abbrev=soa-rm

Web Services Standards Overview. (2012). *Website*. Retrieved from http://www.innoq.com/soa/ws-standards/

KEY TERMS AND DEFINITIONS

Consumer: A system that will invoke or call services that are part of the SOA.

Enterprise: The entire organization including all aspects and interests of the business.

Interface: A system that provides a mechanism for other systems to integrate (or interface) with it, primarily with messaging in this context.

Schema: Refers to XML Schema definitions.

Service: A callable interface exposing business functionality that has a downstream effect on underlying systems or data and normally will provide data in response.

Service Oriented Architecture (SOA): An architectural pattern of designing services to achieve enterprise advantages.

Chapter 12
Enterprise Mobile Service Architecture:
Challenges and Approaches

Longji Tang
FedEx, USA

Wei-Tek Tsai
Arizona State University, USA & Tsinghua University, China

Jing Dong
Hewlett-Packard, USA

ABSTRACT

Today, enterprise systems are integrated across wired and wireless networks. Enterprise Mobile Service Computing (EMSC) is a recent development style in distributed computing, and Enterprise Mobile Service Architecture (EMSA) is a new enterprise architectural style for mobile system integration. This chapter introduces the concepts of EMSC, discusses the opportunities, and addresses mobile constraints and challenges in EMSC. The mobile constraints include aspects relating to mobile hardware, software, networking, and mobility. Many issues such as availability, performance, and security are encountered due to these constraints. To address these challenges in EMSC, the chapter proposes seven architectural views: Enterprise Mobile Service, Enterprise Mobile Service Consumer, Enterprise Mobile Service Data, Enterprise Mobile Service Process, Enterprise Mobile Service Infrastructure, Enterprise Mobile Service Management, and Enterprise Mobile Service Quality. Each is described with principles, design constraints, and emerging technologies. In order to illustrate a practical implementation of EMSA, the chapter presents a major shipping and delivery services enterprise as a case study to describe the integration of Service-driven mobile systems in the enterprise.

DOI: 10.4018/978-1-4666-4193-8.ch012

INTRODUCTION

In a service-oriented enterprise architecture (Tang, 2011; Tang, Bastani, Tsai, Dong, & Zhang, 2011), there are two major components – services and service consumers. Traditionally, end service consumers access the system mainly through personal computers (PCs), such as desktops and laptops (notebooks) in an end-to-end system. With development of wireless communication and technologies, such as 3G and 4G (Amjad, 2004; Choi, Dawson, & La Porta, 2010), mobile and non-PC devices (tablets and others), such as iPhone, iPad, iPod, and Android-based mobile devices are overtaking PCs as the most widely used communication and Internet access devices. Canalys reported that 488 million smart phones were shipped in 2011, compared to 415 million client PCs that were shipped by vendors in its report "Smart phones overtake client PCs in 2011" (Canalys, 2012). Moreover a recent IDC report revealed that PCs will slip in market share from 35.9% in 2011 to 25.1% in 2016, as Android-based devices will grow from 29.4% share in 2011 to become a market leader in 2016 with 31.1% share. Devices running iOS will grow from 14.6% to 17.3% market share by 2016 (IDC, 2012).

Mobile devices are becoming the major interface for consuming services that are not limited to general phone services, but also include email, internet, entertainment, and social media services. Recently, use of enterprise services, such as mobile search, mobile ecommerce (M-commerce) (Amjad, 2004) - shopping and shipping, and mobile payment, from mobile devices are growing rapidly.

Enterprise mobile computing began from first-generation smart phones such as IBM Simon Personal Communicator, the first smartphone released in 1993 (Esposito, 2012). The IBM Simon had a simple operating system called DatalightROM-DOS, 16 MHz CPU, 1 MB RAM and 1 MB storage. Its features included sending and receiving facsimiles, e-mails and cellular pages.

It also included many applications including an address book, calendar, appointment scheduler, calculator, world time clock, electronic note pad, handwritten annotations and standard and predictive touchscreen keyboards. Around the same time, there were significant developments in Europe and Asia too. For example, Nokia N9000 Communicator came to the market in 1996 and offered pretty much the features that IBM Simon offered but had a mechanical keyboard instead of the touchscreen keyboard. Many generations of communicators followed. The first "Symbian" smart phone was Nokia N9210 in 2001. These devices were based on the Symbian OS that was a multitasking OS, supported video capturing and viewing, had browsers, navigation software, email clients, etc. Several handsets from Korea and Japan also came to the market that used Symbian OS since 2001. The first generation mobile devices also included Palm Treo 600, and first generation Blackberry, etc.

The modern era of Enterprise mobile service computing started with the release of the Apple iPhone in the summer of 2007 (Esposito, 2012). The iPhone defined a new generation of smart phones. Smart mobile devices, such as Apple iPhone, Google Android devices, Microsoft Windows 7 and Windows 8 smart phones, have a multitasking operating system (Firtman, 2010), a full desktop browser, Wireless LAN (WLAN, also known as Wi-Fi) and 3G/4G connections, a music player, and supported several of the following features (Firtman, 2010): Mobile Web, GPS (Global Positioning System) or A-GPS (Assisted GPS), Digital compass, Video-capable camera, Bluetooth (Firtman, 2010), Touch and gesture support (Firtman, 2010) that allowed an user to touch a screen or make a movement to issue commands, 3D video acceleration, and Accelerometer.

The features and capabilities of modern smart phones and smart mobile devices (including tablets, iPad, and iPod) provide a portable channel to connect to enterprise services through mobile applications and web interfaces. The mobile channel is regarded as an extension of the Internet and the enterprise network.

Mobile computing has been growing at a staggering rate across the developed nations. The following Table 1 shows the mobile subscription trend. Although not all mobile subscribers perform mobile computing, specifically in developing countries, the dramatic growth of mobile data plan and internet plan subscriptions in developed countries shows that demand of mobile computing is greatly increasing.

Mobile computing is expected to continue its spectacular growth rate over the next five years. Portio Research predicts that mobile subscribers worldwide will reach 6.5 billion by the end of 2012, 6.9 billion by the end of 2013, and 8 billion by the end of 2016 (Portio Research, 2012).

Erickson forecasts that mobile subscriptions will reach 9 billion in 2017, of which 5 billion will be mobile broadband connections (Portio Research, 2012). The trend of continuous mobile growth is changing the enterprise business customer space as shown in Figure 1.

At the same time, this trend is greatly increasing the demands of mobile applications and mobile services. Each time a mobile ad is displayed it creates what is termed an "impression." Compared to 2010, total impressions per user on mobile apps in November of 2011 grew 122%, in which shopping and services increased 105% (Taptu Report, 2010). The widespread mobile consumer adoption creates a new communication and commerce channel for enterprises, such as mobile sales and services (e.g. shopping and shipping), mobile payments and account access, customer self-services, customer incident report-

Table 1. Global mobile subscriptions in 2011 (data from Portio Research, 2012)

	Global	Developed Nations	Developing Nations	The Americas
Mobile cellular subscriptions (millions)	5981	1461	4520	969
Per 100 people	86.7%	117.8%	78.8%	103.3%
Fixed telephone lines (millions)	1159	494	665	268
Per 100 people	16.6%	39.8%	11.6	28.5%
Active mobile broadband subscriptions (millions)	1186	701	484	286
Per 100 people	17.0%	56.5%	8.5%	30.5%
Fixed mobile broadband subscriptions (millions)	591	319	272	145
Per 100 people	8.5%	25.7%	4.8%	15.5%

Figure 1. Extending enterprise customer space to mobile user space

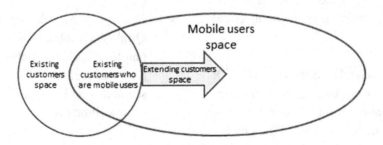

ing, notification and recalls, customer relationship management (CRM), and remote asset monitoring and control including real-time security alerts.

To meet this increasing demand for mobile commerce and services, service providers and enterprises are building and improving their mobile infrastructure, applications, and services constantly. The developing trends are not only impacting the business models of the enterprise, but also its Service-driven enterprise architecture. Specifically, these are some questions to ponder:

- Can service-oriented enterprise architecture meet the challenges from both mobile service demand and mobile device constraints?
- Can enterprises integrate their existing services and create new mobile services for the mobile world?

New architectural approaches are emerging, such as the *Enterprise Mobile Service Computing* (*EMSC*) and *Enterprise Mobile Service Architecture* (*EMSA*) to provide solutions to the challenges in the mobile realm.

This chapter starts out by discussing the issues of enterprise mobile computing. It then explores general concepts of EMSC, their standards, such as wireless network standards as well as mobile web standards; protocols, such as HTTP/HTTPS and languages such as HTML5; and architectural styles, such as SOAP-based Web Services and RESTful Web Services. The core of the chapter delineates EMSA as a Service-driven architectural approach to building and integrating mobile systems. EMSA includes several architectural views as follows:

- **Enterprise Mobile Services (EMS):** EMSs encompass existing enterprise services, Web applications, Cloud services, and specific mobile services. The charac-

teristics of mobile services and their design principles are discussed.

- **Enterprise Mobile Service Consumers (MSC):** The enterprise mobile service consumers include different mobile devices, such as iPhone, iPad and Android-based devices. The interaction patterns between enterprise mobile service consumers and *EMS* are presented. Mobile client computing (how to consume *EMS*) is also discussed.
- **Enterprise Mobile Service Process (EMSP):** The EMSP is a set of composed and managed services executed in mobile platforms and environments, and consumed by mobile devices for completing a complex business process.
- **Enterprise Mobile Service Data (EMSD):** The mobile context is a set of dynamic data that is applied for enabling context-awareness in EMSA.
- **Enterprise Mobile SOA Infrastructure (EMSI):** The EMSI is part of Enterprise SOA (Service Oriented Architecture) Infrastructure, which is a glue to connect wireless network to enterprise services and services in the Cloud.
- **Enterprise Mobile SOA Management (EMSM):** Due to the multitude of mobile devices and mobile platforms, it is critical to have appropriate management practices in place for managing the enterprise mobile service architecture. In this chapter, The *EMSM* principles are described and discussed.
- **Enterprise Mobile Service Architecture Quality Ontology (EMSQ):** The quality ontology includes mobile security, mobile performance, mobile availability, mobile scalability and mobile reliability. These aspects will be discussed.

Finally, the chapter presents a case study and discusses the challenges of *EMSC* and *EMSA* in both research and practice. The challenges include mobile enterprise integration and real-time service computing.

BACKGROUND

Mobile computing is a distributed computing model that allows mobile devices and their applications to connect/interact with other mobile devices, mobile applications, and servers or services in a wireless communication environment. It is designed for people who travel or work outside the boundaries of their organizations or homes and enables them to communicate, play, and work, by using mobile devices anywhere and anytime. The mobile computing model extends the traditional computing model which requires one to use stationary computing devices that are connected to the internet or the enterprise network through wire. Mobile computing has two major characteristics that differentiate it from other forms of computing (Turban, McLean, & Wetherbe, 2006):

- **Mobility:** Implies both physical and logical computing entities that can move, in which the physical computing entities include mobile users and mobile devices that change their locations. The logical entities are instances of running mobile applications, sensors, and mobile agents with wireless connection. The user carrying a mobile device can initiate a real-time connection with other mobile devices and systems if they can connect to a wireless network.

- **Broad Reach:** Mobile users can theoretically be reached at any time. As long as users carry an open device with power, they can be reached instantly, provided they don't block messages or not accept calls for some duration of time.

The above stated characteristics generate five value-added attributes of mobile computing as shown in Table 2.

Enterprise mobile computing is a new kind of mobile computing model which is designed for enterprises extending their business, infrastructure, and services to the mobile space – mobile users and wireless network. The characteristics of mobile computing and their value-added attributes in Table 2 make enterprise mobile computing an important business and IT strategy.

Specifically, enterprise mobile computing is listed as number one and number two in 2012 top strategy technologies by Gartner's report (Gartner, 2012) in which the "Media Tablets and Beyond"

Table 2. Value-added attributes of mobile computing

Value-Added Attributes	Description
Ubiquity	Ubiquity refers to the state and capacity of being available at any location and at any given time. A mobile device such as a smartphone or PDA offers ubiquity.
Instant connectivity	Mobile devices enable users to connect easily and quickly to the intranet, Internet, other mobile devices, services, and database anywhere and anytime.
Convenience	It is convenient for users to operate in the mobile environment. All they need is an Internet enabled mobile device such as a smartphone.
Personalization	Mobile device is owned by individual person with his/her personal choice and usage plan. Mobile devices can be customized for individual consumers.
Localization of products and services	Knowing the user's physical location at any moment is the key to offering relevant products and services. Users can easily search and find the products and services nearby (within the realm of security constraints).

is listed as number one and the "Mobile-Centric Applications and Interfaces" is listed as number two. The fast expanding technology of cellular communications, wireless LAN, and satellite services has been making it possible for mobile users to access enterprise information anywhere and anytime. Figure 2 illustrates the evolution of mobile computing (Reed, 2010; Esposito, 2012).

General Constraints of Mobile Computing

Mobile computing has its constraints and concerns for enterprises. This section describes general constraints of modern mobile computing. Deepak et al., described several mobility constraints and is-

sues of first generation mobile computing (Deepak & Pradeep, 2012). A. K. Gupta characterized the constraints of modern mobile computing as three aspects based on performance impact (Gupta, 2008). The three aspects are:

- Mobile device constraints
- Network constraints
- Mobility constraints

Despite mobile devices getting more powerful since iPhone released in 2007, and modern mobile connection speeds becoming comparable to fixed-line broadband, there are still constraints to be dealt with in the mobile space.

Figure 2. Evolution of enterprise mobile computing

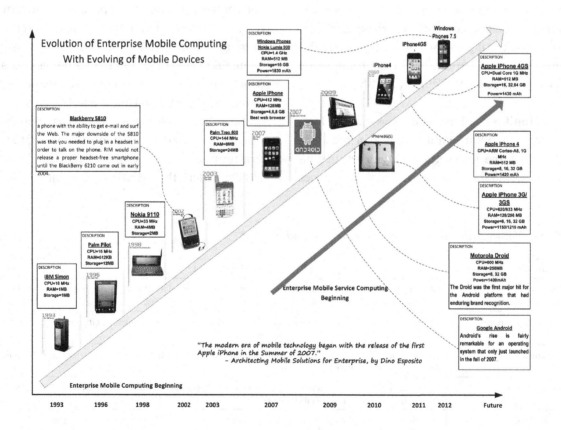

Mobile Device Constraints

The constraints mainly include hardware constraints, software constraints, and communications constraints:

- **Hardware Constraints:** The characteristics of mobile computing hardware are defined by the size and form factor, weight, microprocessors, primary storage, secondary storage, screen size and type, means of input, means of output, battery life, communications capabilities, expandability and durability of the device. Table 3 lists hardware data of today's typical smartphones - both iPhone 4GS and Android smartphone.

From Table 3, one can see that the limited size and means of input/output are big constraints for designing mobile application interfaces and browsers. Mobile device's limited capacity also impacts running large applications and storing large amounts of data. Moreover their short battery life impacts system stability, service availability and performance. Compared with PCs, camera and sensors are advantages in most mobile devices. They enable enterprises to create new applications and services using mobile camera and sensor technology.

- **Software Constraints:** Mobile devices utilize a broad variety of system and application software. The primary system software is mobile operating system (MOS). The MOS constraints greatly impact mobile application software design and capacity for consuming enterprise mobile services. Popular MOS examples are iOS 5.x, Android OS 4.x, Windows 7.x, Palm OS 1.x. MOS impacts application design through application programming interface (API) for applications and services. MOS also impacts architecture and deployment of mobile applications and services.

- **Communication Constraints:** Mobile device can communicate with other mobile devices through wireless networking and send short messages by SMS service. The ability of a mobile device to communicate with wired information systems and services, such as enterprise applications and services, and Cloud-based services is significant for mobile computing. The communication capabilities of mobile devices directly impact mobile application design.

Table 3. Hardware of iPhone 4GS and Android smartphone

Device name	Size (in) Weight	Display	Input	CPU	GPU	Capacity	Camera	Battery
iPhone 4GS	4.54x2.31x0.37 (in) 140 g	3.5 inches (89 mm) diagonal 1.5:1 aspect ratio widescreen LED backlit IPS TFT LCD 640×960 resolution at 326 ppi	4 buttons switch microphones, touch-screen, acceleration, orientation	800 MHz dual-core ARM Cortex-A9	PowerVR SGX543MP2	Memory 512 MB Storage 16/32/64GB	8 MP back-side illuminated sensor HD video (1080p) at 24/30 frame/s IR filter	3.7 V, 5.3 Wh (1,430 mAh)
Nexus one	4.7x2.35x0.45 (in) 130 g	3.7 in (94 mm) AMOLED with resolution of WVGA (480x800 pixels)	touch-screen, Micro-USB; 3.5 mm	1 GHz, Qualcomm QSD8250 Snapdragon	chipset, Adreno 200 GPU	512 MB RAM, microSD slot (supported up to 32 GB)	Rear: 5 Mpx, autofocus, LED flash, Geo-tagging, video recording Front: NO	1400 mAh Internal Rechargeable Li-ion User replaceable

From Table 4, one can see that iPhone 4GS and Nexus One can communicate using several different wireless communication standards, unlike older smartphones such as Nokia 1100.

Mobile Network Constraints

Mobile network constraints are focused on the connection behavior between mobile devices and mobile network providers in a wireless environment. The type and availability of the communication medium significantly impacts the type of mobile computing application that can be created. Although wireless networking has greatly improved, such as from 2G to 3G (Amjad, 2004), 4G (Choi, 2010) and Wi-Fi (WLAN IEEE 802.11) (Amjad, 2004), the wireless networks (Cellular networks) have some limitations (Deepak, 2012), such as packet loss, high latency due to power restriction and available spectrum, and mobility constraints, specifically in boundary of different networks, weak signal coverage area or strong signal interference area. Advanced mobile broadband (high speed cellular networks),

such as 3G and 4G, have different Max Downlink (*MDL*) for stationary clients and moving clients, for instance 4G $MDL_{stationary\ client}=1\,\mathrm{Gbps}$, but $MDL_{moving\ client}=100\mathrm{Mbps}$.

Mobility Constraints

In general, mobility is a characteristic of mobile objects. In mobile computing, the mobility is a quality attribute of the mobile computing system that includes mobile computation and communication. Figure 3 shows the relationship between mobility and mobile computing. The mobile objects typically move in three spaces – physical, network, and information spaces. The mobility in different spaces has different impacts to mobile computing. The mobility constraints can be defined as adaptability and fault-tolerance of mobile computing systems.

- **Mobility Constraints in Physical Space (MCPS):** Mobile computing systems should adapt to the mobile behaviors of network disconnection and reconnection,

Table 4. Network and connectivity of mobile devices

Mobile Device	Network	Connectivity
iPhone 4GS (2011)	2G - GSM 850 / 900 / 1800 / 1900 and CDMA 800 / 1900 3G - HSDPA 850 / 900 / 1900 / 2100 and CDMA2000 1xEV-DO	Wi-Fi (802.11) (2.4 GHz only) Bluetooth 4.0 **Combined GSM/CDMA antenna:** quad-band GSM/GPRS/EDGE (800 850 900 1,800 1,900 MHz) Quad-band UMTS/HSDPA/HSUPA (800 850 900 1,900 2,100 MHz) Dual-band CDMA/EV-DO Rev. A (800 1,900 MHz) GLONASS, GPS
Nexus One (2010)	GSM 850 / 900 / 1800 / 1900, 3G HSDPA 900 / 1700 / 2100	Wi-Fi 802.11 a/b/g, Bluetooth v2.1 with A2DP, A-GPS
Nokia 1100 (2003)	GSM (2G)	

Figure 3. Relationship of mobility and mobile computing

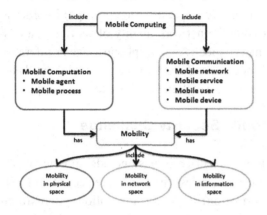

and poor connection as mobile users and devices move in their physical locations (space).

- **Mobility Constraints in Network Space (MCNS):** Mobile computing systems should adapt to the mobile behaviors of possible poor performance in a complex network topology space with multiple links and routers when mobile application and service connections are moving in the network space.

- **Mobility Constraints in Information Space (MCIS):** Information space consists of the large amounts of data scattered in the information superhighway – the Internet (and Cloud). Mobility in information space means mobile users and applications access the information space when moving in their physical space.

Mobility of mobile software components will negatively impact a mobile service system's quality of service (QoS) (Taylor, 2010), in which QoS mainly includes availability, performance and scalability. The possible temporary disconnection during application code migration process when moving in the physical space can cause certain components to be unavailable for a short time. The high volume mobile access in peak time, with

poor wireless connection, can cause poor system performance. Mobile computing systems should adapt to the mobile behaviors of possible poor performance and scalability when high volume mobile users and mobile applications access the information superhighway – the Internet (Cloud) or access enterprise mobile services in private data centers.

CHALLENGES OF ENTERPRISE MOBILE COMPUTING

The mobile computing constraints described in the last section are also the constraints of enterprise mobile computing. Additionally, there are also other challenges that are significant to the architecture of enterprise mobile systems as listed below.

Mobile Connection Challenge

Modern enterprise applications and services are built to communicate with networks and the Internet. Users access enterprise applications and services through an enterprise network infrastructure. The network connection is the bridge to enterprise applications and services. The mobile connection between mobile devices and enterprise applications and services often disconnect or are of poor connection quality due to mobility and device portability. The mobile connect behavior causes poor availability and performance of enterprise mobile systems. Therefore one can map the connection issues to reliability, availability, performance, and fault-tolerance challenges for designing enterprise mobile systems.

Mobile Heterogeneous Network Challenge

Unlike most of the stationary computers that stay connected to a single network, mobile devices run into more heterogeneous network connections.

While they leave the range of one wireless network transceiver and are routed to another, they may need to change transmission speeds and protocols as well. In some other situations, for instance, where a mobile device in adjacent cells overlap or where it can be plugged in for concurrent wired access, it may have to access several networks simultaneously. Moreover, mobile devices may need to switch interfaces, for example, when switching from cellular coverage to Wi-Fi. The heterogeneous network connectivity makes mobile networking much more complex than traditional networking (Amjad, 2004).

Mobile Performance and Scalability Challenge

Because of limited bandwidth, high latency, and mobility of mobile computing, mobile performance and scalability is an important issue. Mobile Internet access is generally slower than direct cable connections, using technologies such as GPRS and EDGE, and more recently 3G as well as 4G networks. These networks are usually available within range of commercial cell phone towers. Higher speed wireless LANs are inexpensive but have limited range (see Table 5).The speed of mobile computing depends on wireless network speed. Table 6 shows max speeds of different wireless networks. The slower networks cause higher latency. A research of mobile Web performance showed that "60% of all mobile users expect websites to load as fast as in a regular browser. But, 75% of all users experience slow load times as their #1 issue" (Tjepkema, 2011).

The above Tables 5 and 6 show maximum or average transfer capacities of single link between an access point and a terminal. However, they do not cover the overall performance of wireless access networks, which is out of scope of this chapter. The mobile network performance is no longer about ensuring that the network is up, it isn't even about ensuring that capacity is available

and coverage is provided as expected. It has become a combination of all three of these elements (availability, capacity, and coverage) in order to provide the network quality of service that customers expect. As smartphone usage proliferates, the devices and applications themselves will also become part of the network performance equation.

Mobile Security Challenge

Mobile security issues include mobile device security, wireless infrastructure security, mobile information (data), and information systems (apps and services) security. Forman and Zahorjan (1994) addressed mobile security risk since 1994. Amjad (2004) discussed mobile and wireless communication security. Dwivedi et al. (2010) described information security issues in mobile computing. Furthermore, the stealing and destruction of mobile devices are raising a big mobile security, trust, and privacy issue; since personal identity, email and sensitive data, such as bank account details can be stolen.

Some enterprises are adopting BYOD (Bring Your Own Devices) strategy (Borg, 2011) to improve employee productivity and flexibility. If employee's devices (iPhone, iPad, etc) with business data and sensitive corporate information are stolen or destroyed, then enterprises will be at risk. To preserve mobile device's integrity (different devices connect to different service providers) and prevent the cellular network from malicious attacks, the manufacturers of mobile devices and mobile network operators control access to critical mobile components, such as the file system, Internet services, multimedia features, Bluetooth, GPS, and communications, through a rights management system, such as signed keys from a Certificate Authority. However, this is not enough to protect enterprise mobile service systems from malicious attacks through mobile channels, because mobile networks are more broad, more dynamic and easier to access than

Table 5. Wireless network speed comparison (Fling, 2009; IEEE 802.16; LTE Forum, 2011

Wireless Network	Standard Description	Theoretical Max Data Speed
2G	Second Generation wireless network standard	
GSM	Global System for Mobile communication	12.2 KB/sec
GPRS	Global Packet Radio Service	60 KB/sec
EDGE	Enhanced Date rate for GSM Evolution	59.2 KB/sec
HSCSD	High-Speed Circuit-Switch Data	57.6 KB/sec
3G	Third Generation wireless network standard	
W-CDMA	Wideband Code Division Multiple Access	14.4 MB/sec
UMTS	Universal Mobile Telecommunication System	3.6 MB/sec
UMTS-TDD	UMTS + Time Division Duplexing	16 MB/sec
TD-CDMA	Time Divide Code Division Multiple Access	16 MB/sec
HSPA	High-Speed Packet Access	14.4 MB/sec
HSDPA	High-Speed Downlink Packet Access	14.4 MB/sec
HSUPA	High-Speed Downlink Packet Access	5.76 MB/sec
4G	Third Generation wireless network standard	
LTE	Long Term Evolution	100 MB/sec
LTE Advanced	Long Term Evolution Advanced	1 GB/sec
WiMax	IEEE 802.16e	128 MB/sec

their fixed network counterparts. Making enterprise mobile service systems secure is a definite challenge.

Enterprise Mobile Service Architecture

This section presents a new architectural style – Enterprise Mobile Service Architecture (EMSA) as a solution to addressing the challenges of enterprise mobile computing by presenting principles, design guidelines and best practice recommendations. The EMSA is a hybrid architectural style composed of enterprise mobile computing (EMC), enterprise SOA (ESOA), as well as enterprise Cloud service architecture (ECSA) as defined and specified in Tang (2011), Tang, Bastani, Tsai, Dong, and Zhang (2011), and Tang, Dong, Peng, and Tsai (2010). Figure 4 shows the relationship of EMSA and other enterprise architectural styles.

The EMSA consists of several architectural views as indicated below:

- Enterprise Mobile Service (EMS)
- Enterprise Mobile Service Consumer (MSC)

Table 6. Comparison of data rate and access range (Amjad, 2004; IEEE 802.11)

Wireless Technology	Data Rate	Access Range
Bluetooth	1 Mbps	10 meters
UWB	50 Mbps	<10 meters
IEEE 802.11a	Up to 54 Mbps	<50 meters
IEEE 802.11b	11 Mbps	100 meters
IEEE 802.11g	Up to 54 Mbps	100 meters
IEEE 802.11n	Up to 600 Mbps	
IEEE 802.11ac	Up to 1300 Mbps	
HiperLAN/2	Up to 54 Mbps	30 meters
GSM (2G)	9.6 Mbps	Cell sizes 10 to 20 KM KM
3G Cellular	Up to 2 Mbps	Cell sizes 5 to 10 KM
WLL (LMDS)	Up to 37 Mbps	2 to 4 KM
FSO	100 Mbps to 2.5 Gbps	1 to 2 KM
Satellites	64 Kbps	thousands of miles

Figure 4. Relationship between EMSA and other architectural styles

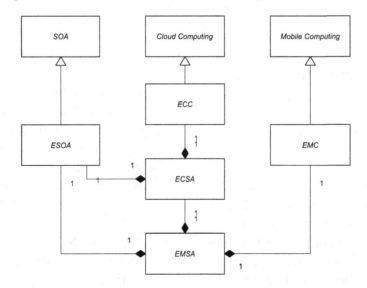

- Enterprise Mobile Service Data (EMSD)
- Enterprise Mobile Service Infrastructure (EMSI)
- Enterprise Mobile Service Process (EMSP)
- Enterprise Mobile Service Management (EMSM)
- Enterprise Mobile Service Quality Attributes (EMSQ)

The relationship among the architectural views of EMSA is shown in Figure 5.

Figure 5 is based on the framework proposed in Tang's PhD Thesis "Modeling and Analyzing Service-Oriented Enterprise Architectural Styles" (Tang, 2011). The EMSA architectural views

describe the hybrid enterprise architectural style which includes components and connectors that form an enterprise mobile service system. The figure also depicts the design constraints in terms of the mobile quality attributes and their relationship with the other architectural views.

The EMSA style is an abstraction of a family of concrete enterprise architectures that can provide design principles and guidelines for designing concrete enterprise mobile service architecture. By Taylor's definition of architectural style, "An architectural style is a named collection of architectural design decisions that are applicable in a given development context, constrain architectural design decisions that are specific to a particular

Figure 5. Relationships among architectural views of EMSA

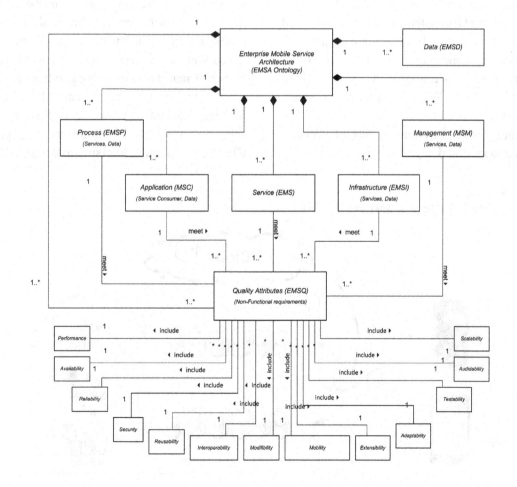

system within that context, and elicit beneficial qualities in each resulting system" (Taylor, 2010). The EMSA style defined in this chapter can be applied to any enterprise mobile service development context as a high level architectural pattern. The EMSA style will be used for evaluating FedEx enterprise mobile service architecture in the case study section. The rest of this section describes all the architectural views of *EMSA* and provides guidelines and best practices.

Enterprise Mobile Service (EMS)

The manufacturers of mobile devices often provide built-in services, such as native SMS service, Email service, mobile Web Services, and Cloud services. For example, iPhone 4S provides online services App Stores, such as, iTunes store, iBook store and iCloud. EMS is defined as the service in Enterprise SOA Systems that can be accessed from mobile devices for enabling enterprise *m-Businesses* (mobile businesses) (Amjad, 2004), such as m-Commerce (m-B2C and m-B2B), m-CRM, m-ERP, Wireless Advertising (Gao, 2010), etc.

Figure 6 indicates three kinds of services exposed to mobile devices:

- Existing enterprise services
- Mobile specific services
- Cloud services

These services can be categorized based on different architectural styles as shown in Table 7.

Hirsch et al. described the standards, design principles and applications of SOAP-based Web services in (Hirsch, Kemp, & Llkka, 2006). It is found that *RESTful Web Services* are more suitable in many areas of enterprise mobile service computing.

Table 8 maps constraints in mobile computing to a solution with RESTful Web Services. It illustrates that RESTful Web service is a better alternative for architecture choice for many mobile computing systems. However, it does not mean that SOAP-based Web service will go away. Because of its message-level security feature and well-defined message contract, it will still be suitable for many mobile enterprise applications. However, SOAP-based Web service needs to continue improving its performance and reducing bandwidth.

A solution architecture with RESTful Web Service and mobile Cloud service is shown in Figure 7, in which the Cloud can be a private Cloud or any public Cloud such as Amazon Cloud,

Figure 6. Enterprise mobile services

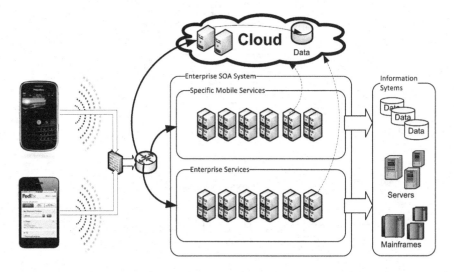

Table 7. Mobile services with different architectural styles

Mobile services	Description
Component-based services (Tang, 2011)	The service is built based on component architectural style such as J2EE, .NET, etc. Communication is based on RPC (such as RMI) and XML over HTTP.
SOAP-based Web services (Tang, 2011)	The service is built based on WS-* architectural style (EWS-*) and uses SOAP as its communication protocol and conforms to Web Service standards.
RESTful Web Services (Tang, 2011)	The service is built on REST-based Web-oriented architectural style REST (Alshahwan, Moessner, & Carrez, 2010), and *EWOA (Enterprise Web Oriented Architecture)*. HTTP/HTTPS are its communication protocols.
Cloud Services (Tang, 2011)	Infrastructure as a Service (IaaS), Platform as a Service (PaaS), Software as a Service (SaaS)

Table 8. RESTful services as a solution to challenges of mobile computing

Constraints of Mobile Computing	Advantage of RESTful Web services
Limited device capacity of hardware and software.	Architecture simplicity: Client-server model with unified service interfaces.
Limited bandwidth and battery power.	SOAP-based Web services use XML-based messages that need higher bandwidth and consume more power. RESTful JSON-based messages needs less bandwidth and consumes less power for processing.
Multitude of devices and Rich content in small mobile devices.	SOAP-based Web services support XML data format only, RESTful Web services support multiple media types: HTML, plain text, XML, JSON, PDF, Atom and more.
Performance and scalability issues.	Cacheable – boots performance. Stateless – increases scalability.

Figure 7. Solution architecture with RESTful mobile service or mobile cloud service

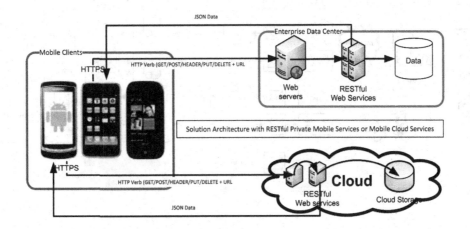

Google Cloud or Microsoft Cloud (Dinh, Lee, Niyato, & Wand, 2011; Sahu, Sharma, Dubey, & Tripathi, 2012; Tang, 2011; Tang, Bastani, Tsai, Dong, & Zhang, 2011).

Adopting Cloud services for enterprise mobile service computing is a new trend which is called Mobile Cloud Computing (Hong, 2011; Dinh, 2011). The Cloud can help enterprises to meet some of the challenges of mobile service computing. The IaaS can help enterprises to build highly dynamic, scalable, and highly available mobile infrastructure services. The PaaS can help enterprises to develop, deploy, and run mobile applications and services quickly and in a cost-effective manner. The SaaS can provide additional mobile service capacities.

Enterprise Mobile Service Consumer (MSC)

Mobile devices are provisioned with applications that can access and consume services locally or remotely. Enterprise mobile service consumer can be defined as any mobile application or user interface that is provisioned in the mobile devices,

and that can access and consume enterprise mobile services for enabling enterprise m-Business. This chapter emphasizes on mobile Web applications (Esposito, 2012; Firtman, 2010), and interfacing of mobile devices to enterprise SOA systems with Web technology, such as Web Services, Ajax, Javascript (JQuery mobile), and HTML5 (Esposito, 2012).

When stationary devices, such as a PC or wireless laptop accesses enterprise web services (SOAP-based or REST-based) through wired connection or WEB access point network, the request is directly routed to the Internet. However, with mobile devices, such as iPhone or Blackberry, when accessing enterprise web services through the Internet, the request/response has to be routed through the wireless operator's cellular network and wireless operator's proxy servers. Therefore mobile devices exhibit greater latency when compared to stationary devices for sending message requests to or getting responses from the enterprises services.

Figures 8 and 9 illustrate the typical Web service styles used for mobile computing. SOAP uses the same URL for all interactions. The SOAP

Figure 8. Interaction pattern of mobile service consumers and SOAP-based mobile web services

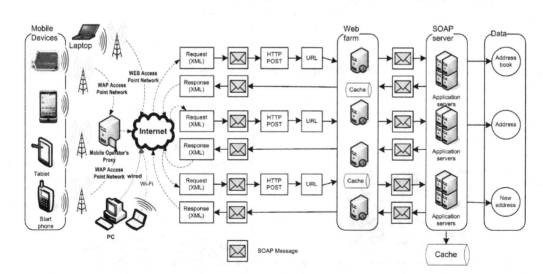

Figure 9. Interaction patterns of mobile service consumers and RESTful mobile web services

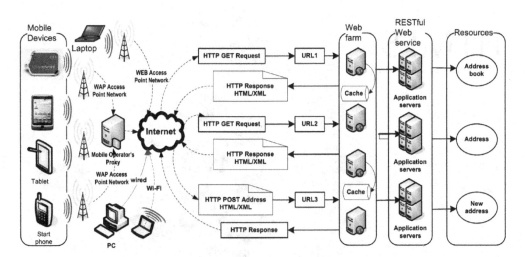

server parses the SOAP message to determine which method to invoke. All SOAP messages are sent with HTTP POST requests. However, REST uses different URLs to address resources. The Web server dispatches a request to a handler (URL addresses a handler) and REST maps the request to standard HTTP methods.

RESTful mobile service interaction is simpler than SOAP-based Web services. Therefore mobile services lean towards using RESTful Web Services. Mobile applications are becoming an important consumer for enterprise services; however, they face many challenges with respect to device variations and constraints.

HTML5 is the next generation hypertext language that brings new solutions to some of these issues. HTML5 enables mobile users to experience richer Web applications and improved usability. HTML5 compliant Mobile browsers reclaim the rendering of rich Web content from third-party plug-ins.

HTML5, shown in Figure 10, provides advanced features to build sophisticated mobile Web sites, and helps resolve challenging issues of *EMSA* as shown in Table 9.

Enterprise Mobile Service Data (EMSD) and Mobile Context

Tang described general SOA data entity (Tang, 2011; Tang, Dong, Peng, & Tsai, 2010), that includes various service descriptions, and infrastructure configuration data. SOA Data Entity is also applicable to the Data part of EMSD. However, mobile computing is different from traditional distributed computing. In desktop computing, most parameters in the environment are relatively stable, and has constant context. Likewise, notebook/laptop computers are designed for stationary use so there is usually little variation in the situation surrounding their usage. In contrast, the environment of ultra-mobile computing is characterized by change. The mobile context is a dynamic data set.

In IoT systems (Internet of Things) (Logica, 2012; Hwang, Fox, & Dongarra, 2012), mobile users will be able to dynamically discover and interact in an impromptu manner with heterogeneous computing environments and physical resources encountered during their roam (Kunze, Zaplata, Turjalei, & Lamersdorf, 2008). Mobile context can be used for enabling this kind of context-aware mobile service systems. Several authors (Kaltz, Ziegler, Lohmann, 2005; Kunze, Zaplata, Turja-

Figure 10. HTML5 new technology and API

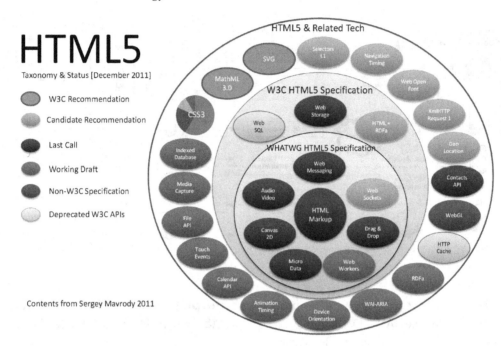

Table 9. HTML5 features for mobile computing

Constraints & Issues of Mobile Computing	HTML5 features
Limited capacity of hardware and software.	Rich features for supporting modern mobile Web applications.
Limited bandwidth and battery power. Issues on mobility, such as lost connection, out of coverage areas.	HTML5 documents use a manifest to list all dependent external resources (i.e. CSS files, JavaScript libraries, etc.). Mobile browsers can use the manifest to cache an entire Web application for offline use, allowing mobile users to interact with a Web app while roaming in and out of coverage areas.
Issues with variable devices and rich content in small mobile devices.	The Web Storage API allows documents to persistently store data in a mobile browser. Mobile browsers can write data in one browsing session and read it in the next session.
Issues in performance and scalability.	HTML5 processing speeds are improving, with the notable exception of CSS 3D transforms. Has AJAX support – asynchronous communication. Has Websocket support – this reduces HTML message overhead and provides duplex communication and lower latency. Supports real-time Web applications.

lei, & Lamersdorf, 2008) define mobile context concept and discuss its application.

The mobile context can be defined as a set of dynamic data that is applied for enabling context-awareness in EMSA style systems. The context-awareness is defined as a service capacity with full awareness of current service execution environment that includes location, time, and

Table 10. Mobile context and context awareness

Mobile Context	Description	Examples
Physical context	Real physical environment which is accessible by using sensors and other resources deployed in the environment.	User Location Traffic condition
Time context	Real time of any activity executing in the mobile system.	Time: minutes, seconds Day, week, month and year
Computing context	Capacity and resources of mobile computing that can be detected by the mobile system.	Device capacity Wireless type
User context	User information which the mobile system can be aware of.	User profile People nearby Current social situation

user information. Table 10 describes four types of mobile context (Bellavista, Corradi, Fanelli, & Foschini, 2012) in EMSA. The mobile context can be applied in mobile systems to provide context awareness for applications. Enterprise mobile service providers, such as Google and Facebook, make their services dynamically adaptable to the environment of mobile devices and mobile Web clients by using mobile context-awareness.

Physical context and time context are applied for monitoring mobile service systems, such as detecting error, traffic jam monitoring for providing vehicle routing information, etc. User context awareness provides automatic recommendation and situation-based adaptation of services and products.

Enterprise Mobile Service Process *(EMSP)*

Tang et al. specified and discussed the general enterprise service process (ESP) in ESOA style (Tang, 2011; Tang, Bastani, Tsai, Dong, & Zhang, 2011). The ESP is a set of composed and managed services for completing a complex business process, such as online shopping or shipping workflow, or any business transaction process. The EMSP is an extension of ESP in enterprise mobile

integration. The EMSP can be defined as a set of composed and managed services executed in mobile platforms and environments, and consumed by mobile devices for completing a complex business process. Traditionally, humans participate in an ESP, by logging in and providing information so that workflow execution can proceed, such as in insurance policy claim or inventory control. In the mobile realm, user interaction screen is delivered directly to the mobile user's device. Mobile service process can enable real-time, contact-aware and adaptive workflow. In this chapter, the design principles, architecture, and application of the following three types of enterprise mobile service processes are discussed:

- Mobilizing existing ESP consumed by stationary computers, such as PCs and workstations. This type of EMSP includes m-B2C, m-B2B, m-B2G (mobile business to government), m-G2B (Amjad, 2004), which are extensions of B2C, B2B, B2G, and G2B. Figure 11 is a high level view of mobilized ESP. The basic steps for mobile-enabling existing ESP are:
  - Adding mobile devices as consumers of existing ESP.

Figure 11. High-level view of mobilizing enterprise business processes

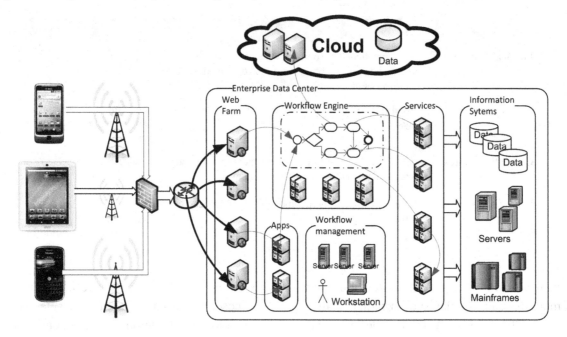

- ◦ Adding mobile access point in enterprise service infrastructure.
- ◦ Building mobile apps in devices for enabling to run end user work processes, such as JQuery mobile or HTML5-based mobile Web apps.
- ◦ Exposing existing enterprise service processes to mobile user's App space through a mobile-enabled interface gateway or broker, such as WSI which is based on SOAP Web service. Recently, RESTful Web services are being adopted for improving performance. Enterprise Web Oriented Architecture style process is extended to EMSP.
- ◦ Enabling an existing workflow engine in application servers of enterprise data centers to execute workflow within a mobile communication environment.
- ◦ Providing EMSM for monitoring and managing life cycle of mobile workflow.

- ◦ Addressing performance, availability, and security.
- • Provisioning mobile-based *EMSP* processes for completing a business task in mobile computing environment, such as in mobile Web Mashups, mobile social service processes, and context-based and context aware workflow (Hackmann, Haitjema, Gill, & Roman, 2006). The basic steps for implementing mobile-based *EMSP* are:
- ◦ Providing a light workflow engine in the mobile device, such as "Sliver" (Hackmann, Haitjema, Gill, & Roman, 2006) which is a BPEL workflow process execution engine for mobile devices that can execute business processes.
- ◦ Using visual representations of workflow.
- ◦ Integrating activity execution with mobile core platform features, such as iOS and objective-C or Android OS and java mobile platform.

○ Standardizing mobile interfaces and definitions to existing activities.

○ Enabling service discovery mechanism and service connection for each activity.

○ Addressing issues relating to mobility, adaptability, performance, availability, and security.

There are two types of mobile specific service processes that take advantage of mobility – mobile context, adaptability, real-time and sensor capacity. They are:

- Context-aware mobile service workflow.
- Agent-based mobile service workflow.

One of benefits of context-awareness for mobile workflow is to increase the adaptability of mobile workflow, so that mobile workflow can be successfully and more effectively executed in a dynamic and mobile environment. The mobile service composition for context-aware cooperation (Kunze, Zaplata, Turjalei, & Lamersdorf, 2008) is a good example. Figure 12 shows an initiator who is not capable of executing an ad-hoc process requiring several mobile and stationary services. The context-awareness helps the process to find other devices or services in its vicinity for remote access if local application is not available. The Cisco and GE location-aware mobile healthcare workflow solution is another good industry example (Horwitz, 2011). The solution is already benefiting from real-time data on the location and movement of mobile equipment and patients through the GE AgileTrac RFID network to make smart decisions to improve care delivery and hospital operations.

- Using mobile Cloud service processes consisting of a set of Web services in the public Cloud and a set of Web services in the private Cloud.

Majority of services in the process and workflow engine are located in the enterprise data centers. However, for mobile Cloud service processes, the service process as well as the majority of services and service process engines as well as management systems is located in the Cloud data centers. The architecture principles used in this case are a combination of the principles used in both mobile and Cloud computing paradigms.

Figure 12. Context-aware cooperation for mobile process composition

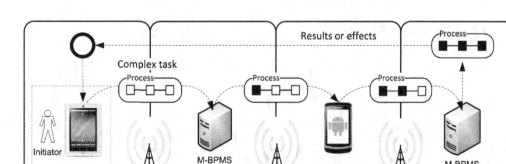

Enterprise Mobile Service Infrastructure (EMSI)

The SOA infrastructure is the heart of *ESOA* (Tang, Dong, Peng, & Tsai, 2010), and it supports the transformation of business in an enterprise or between enterprises into a set of managed services or repeatable business tasks, that can be accessed over a network when needed. The network can be a local network, the Internet, or a wireless network. The *EMSI* is an extension of SOA infrastructure defined in *ESOA* style. One of the challenges of enterprise mobile computing is that the *EMSI* depends on one or more wireless networks operated by mobile network providers, such as AT&T, Verizon, etc. Any of the requests from any mobile service consumer to an enterprise mobile service (*EMS*) must go through the operator's backbone. Therefore the backbone impacts reliability, performance, security, and availability of enterprise mobile services. Choosing the right backbone with solid service level agreements is a very important consideration for enterprise mobile service infrastructure. Figure 13 shows a typical enterprise mobile service infrastructure with two parts:

- Wired SOA infrastructure that is in the enterprise data center.

- Wireless infrastructure that is outside of the enterprise.

There are three major types of wireless networks in *EMSI* including:

- Cellular wireless networks.
- Wireless LAN network (Wi-Fi).
- Satellite networks.

The core of EMSI includes the following components:

- Existing wired infrastructure.
- Mobile applications and services.
- Mobile operating systems.
- Mobile devices.
- Mobile endpoint security agents.
- Mobile network which includes WLAN (Wi-Fi), 2G/3G/4G wireless networks, and/or satellite network.
- Enterprise network security perimeter, such as firewall (Mobile security is discussed in a later section).
- Tunnel gateway such as MEAP services.
- Authentication service and user directory such as SSO and LDAP service.
- Application servers.
- Data storage.
- Content repository.

Figure 13. Enterprise mobile service infrastructure

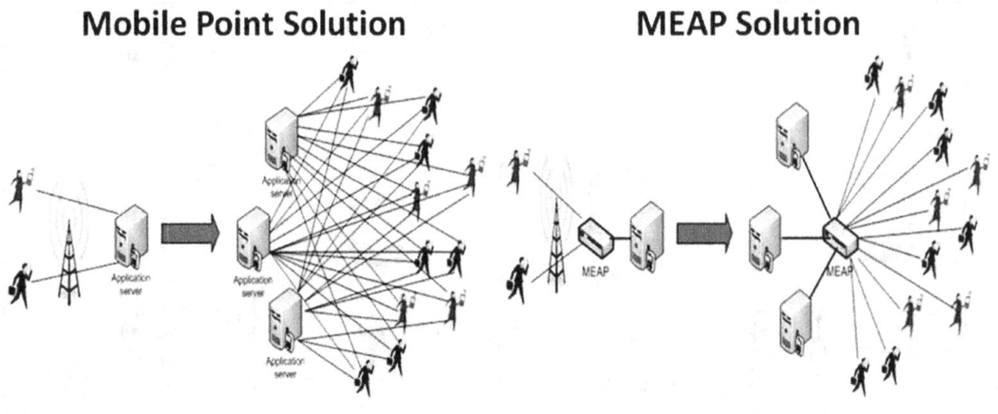

As the EMSI is an extension of the SOA infrastructure, the infrastructure ontology defined in (Tang, 2011) shows that EMSI is a connector for all of the components that include the components in EMS, Enterprise Mobile Service Consumer, and EMSP. The architectural constraints of EMSI are parts of EMSQ.

Mobile service management and mobile service quality are important aspects that impact the delivery of enterprise mobile services. The next two sections deal with these aspects.

Enterprise Mobile Service Management (EMSM)

The EMSM is an extension of the SOA Management of ESOA style. As discussed earlier, mobile service computing is different from traditional service computing. Except for following general SOA management principles, the EMSM has its specific aspects and principles based on mobile constraints, specifically on mobility, real-time, and highly dynamic behaviors. For instance, mobile web content is different in many ways from Web-to-desktop content. The mobile world is fragmented; there are hundreds of mobile device models, with different form factors, operating systems, and browsers. On the PC-Web world this is not an issue since both user interfaces and delivery mechanisms has been standardized for years. However, in the mobile world, web content must be routed to the user through an operator network, and additional operator specific content may be added during the download. Also, different devices render content differently, so when the Web server detects a specific device type it may choose to send a variant of the generic content to the requesting device. Finally, different devices are capable of handling the various components of a download differently (for example, images, text, and third-party content), which can dramatically vary download time.

The comparisons of Web content on a mobile device and on a desktop are shown in Table 11.

Table 11 shows challenges in EMSM, specifically the following issues:

- Mobile Device Management (including BYOD management) (Borg, 2011; 2012)
- Mobile Network Management
- Mobile Data and Context Management
- Mobile Service and Apps Management
- Mobile Performance and Security Management
- Mobility Management

Mobile Enterprise Applications Platform (MEAP) is a multi-channel gateway for enterprise

Table 11. Difference between mobile web content and PC web content

Web Content on a Mobile Device	Web Content on a PC
The mobile device connects to the mobile operator network.	PC connects to the ISP (Internet Service Provider)
Every mobile request goes through the operator's backbone. The wireless networks can be dynamically changed by mobility. Finally, the request is routed to the Internet for downloading content from web servers.	ISP routes through the Internet to download content from web servers.
Content server may send different content depending on device capability.	Content server sends same content for every request.

Figure 14. Comparison of mobile point solution and MEAP solution

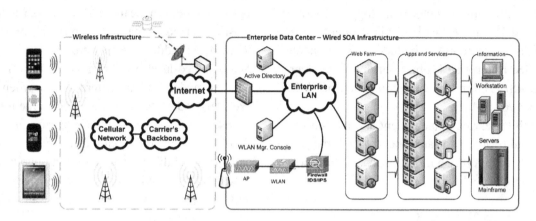

mobile application management. A comparison of Mobile Point Solution and MEAP Solution is shown in Figure 14. Obviously, MEAP solution facilitates higher manageability that can provide more operational flexibility and cost control for enterprises (Sybase, 2011). MEAP addresses the difficulties of developing mobile software by managing the diversity of devices, networks, and user groups at the time of deployment and throughout the mobile solution's lifecycle.

Mobile application and service monitoring is one of the most important components of *EMSM*. Without a monitor in the *EMSM*, performance and security management is not possible. MEAP is a middleware that manages connectivity and security, and can integrate with mobile monitors. For small and middle size enterprises, Cloud-based mobile service and application management is one of solutions. The Compuware Gomez provides a SaaS Cloud mobile monitoring service that can monitor both mobile websites and native mobile application experiences across platforms such as iOS and Android (Compuware, 2012).

Enterprise Mobile Service Quality Attributes (EMSQ)

Tang et al. proposed a SOA quality tradeoff ontology that has a set of architectural constraints for designing general enterprise SOA style systems. An *ESOA* system should meet certain SOA quality attributes to achieve required Service Level Agreement (SLA) and Quality-of-Service (QoS). Gafni (2008), Garofalakis, Stefani, Stefanis, and Xenos (2007), Tang (2011), and Tang, Dong, and Zhao (2011) list the following major SOA quality attributes for general enterprise SOA information systems:

- Performance
- Reliability
- Scalability
- Reusability
- Maintainability
- Security
- Cost
- Interoperability
- Availability
- Flexibility
- Manageability
- Agility
- Simplicity
- Consciousness
- Accountability

Tang (2011) shows that all quality attributes are not equal and there are constraints when trying to meet different attributes, such as the flexibility which may impact performance. The tradeoff of SOA quality attributes is one of the key design principles for designing enterprise SOA systems. The *EMSQ* is an extension of SOA quality attributes in *EMSA*. Gafni (2008), and Garofalakis, Stefani, Stefanis, and Xenos (2007) describe major quality attributes specifically for mobile service computing and includes adding the following quality attributes to the above list:

- Adaptability
- Mobility

Mobile Performance: An enterprise mobile service system may consist of different components (web services, web farm, application servers, data storage, and mobile devices) and connectors (wired network, wireless network, Cloud, and sensor network, even satellite network). The Figure 15 shows a simple end-to-end mobile service system. In the sample case, the elapsed time for a mobile device to get data from the enterprise web service is about $T_{mobile} = t1+t2+t3+t4+t5+t6$ (seconds). On the other hand, for a stationary device PC, the elapse time will be $T_{PC}=t0+t4+t5+t6$ (seconds). Since $t3 \approx t0$, the performance of the end-to-end mobile service system greatly depends on the performance of the networks in *EMSI*, specifically on its wireless network performance. Tables 5 and 6 show that different mobile communication standards have different wireless network performance. For instance, 4G is not only faster than 3G, but also provides more QoS for mobile systems

(Choi, Dawson, & La Porta, 2010). Moreover, Wi-Fi standard IEEE 802.11ac is much better than IEEE 802.11a, since the data rate (up to 1300 Mbps) of IEEE 802.11ac is much faster than that (54Mbps) of IEEE 802.11a.

Different wireless service providers support different standards with different cost, therefore properly choosing mobile standards and their operators is the first consideration. From Tables 3 and 4, it can be seen that different mobile devices have different performance. Choosing wireless carrier and selecting supported mobile devices are tied to the cost attributes. Form architecture design point of view, mobile service system design with different approaches also greatly impacts application level mobile performance. For example, adopting RESTful Web service may have better performance than using SOAP-based Web service in mobile SOA system. However, its security issues needs to be addressed in RESTful mobile Web service system design. We have also shown that mobility has negative impact on mobile performance in the section on Mobility Constraints.

Mobile Security: The mobile application and communication security has been addressed in the book "Engineering Wireless-Based Software Systems" (Gao, 2006). The InformationWeek reports on the State of mobile security (InformationWeek, 2012) shows that mobile security is a concern for enterprise mobile users. The mobile device is more vulnerable than a wired computer. Therefore, building end-to-end mobile security

Figure 15. End-to-end performance of mobile service system

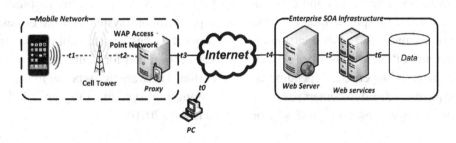

into a mobile service system is an important consideration in *EMSA*. Both wired as well as the wireless infrastructure of the enterprise needs to be secured. One should not only consider the traditional security mechanisms, such as authentication and authorization of users, multi-level security check point and access control, but also consider mobile device security, wireless network security, mobile application security, and mobile data as well as content security (Díaz & Ekman, 2011; Dwivedi, Clark, & Thiel, 2010). In general, *Enterprise mobile security* includes the following core functions:

- User authentication (including PIV card).
- Device, mobile app and enterprise services access control.
- Stored data encryption and end-to-end encryption for sensitive data, such as credit card.
- Application whitelist/blacklist.
- Content filtering and malware protection.
- Security event monitoring, logging, and response.
- Data leak protection and removable storage control.

Enterprise mobile users include employees, registered customers, and other users. Enterprise mobile service system should consider defining different policies for access control to enterprise resources based on the different security levels required for each resource. Evidently, employees can be allowed to access more resources with higher security level than registered customers and other users. The registered customers can be allowed to access more resources and app features than other users. For public mobile Cloud services, the registered or subscribed customers can be divided into different subscriber classes, such as Gold, Silver, Copper, etc. depending on their SLA and payment. Gold customers pay more than Silver and Copper customers, and will be

allowed to access more resources and features. Other mobile users may only be allowed to access limited resources and features.

Mobile Adaptability: Mobile adaptability can be defined as the ability that a mobile service system or mobile application can adapt to the mobile environment where mobile devices are in different mobility spaces such as physical space, network space, and information data space. The mobile adaptive behavior discussed earlier arises due to a certain mismatch between mobile service or supply, and service consumer demand for resources. The mismatch often happens in low-level system resources, such as bandwidth, memory, CPU or battery power (Othman, 2008). There are many different approaches for achieving adaptability in different circumstances and scenario. Kakousisa et al., investigates software adaptation of mobile and ubiquitous computing in Kakousisa, Paspallisa, and Angelos (2010). The general mobile software system adaptation loop is shown in Figure 16.

The Table 12 shows different types of mobile adaptability and corresponding strategies, framework, and architecture.

Mobility: This section describes the impacts to other system quality attributes by mobility as well as its impacts to system design. Enterprise architecture for Mobility extends enterprise service and application computing capacity and communication channels from non-mobile paradigm to mobile paradigm, however, the mobility of software components may negatively impact the QoS of mobile service system (Taylor, Medvidovic, & Dashofy, 2010), such as availability and performance due to the fact that system may be unavailable or may be slow during the migration process. To overcome mobility's negative aspects, mobile systems should be designed with support for certain adaptability as detailed in the last section and for fault-tolerance as described earlier. There are two types of mobility in mobile computing systems (Taylor, Medvidovic, & Dashofy, 2010):

Figure 16. System adaptation loop in mobile and ubiquitous computing

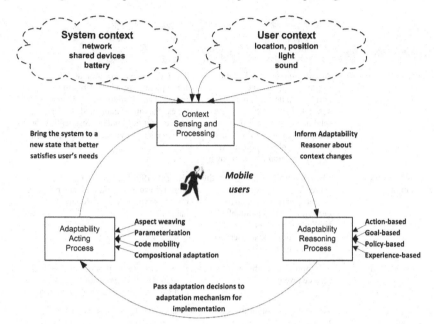

- **Physical Mobility:** The ability that mobile users with their devices can access information systems unimpeded while they are moving across different physical locations.
- **Logical/Code Mobility:** The capacity that the modules or components in the mobile system can dynamically move across servers during system execution.

There are two kinds of logical mobility (LM) (Fuggetta, Picco, & Vigna, 1998; Taylor, Medvidovic, & Dashofy, 2010).

- **Stateful Mobility, or Strong Mobility (SM):** This is the ability of a system to allow migration of both code and the execution state of an executing unit to a different computing environment.
- **Stateless Mobility, or Weak Mobility (WM):** This is the capacity of a system to allow just code movement across different computing environments.

Table 13 shows a classification of logical mobility mechanism.

Compared with non-mobile client-server style system in which the server has know-how logic and resources needed for providing a given service, the distribution of such know-how logic (code) and resources varies across the components in mobile systems. There are three types of mobile code systems for supporting *Logical Mobility* (Fuggetta, Picco, & Vigna, 1998; Taylor, Medvidovic, & Dashofy, 2010; Reed, 2010): remote evaluation (see Figure 17), code-on-demand (see Figure 18), and mobile agent (see Figure 19) as shown in Table 14.

Adopting proper architectural style is important when designing mobile service systems. The design guideline for selecting appropriate style is shown in Table 15. Fuggetta, et al., evaluated several code mobility technologies and discussed applications as well as issues of code mobility in Fuggetta, Picco, and Vigna (1998). The technology of Logic/Code mobility is a promising solution for the design and implementation of large-scale distributed mobile systems because it

Table 12. Types of mobile adaptability

Adaptability	Description	Strategies, Frameworks, Solution Architecture
Client and server adaptability	Application-aware adaptation is to use a collaborative partnership between mobile systems (OS) which provides total transparency: apps are completely aware of mobility and each mobile application copes with mobility on its own.	The Odyssey is a solution architecture for application-aware adaptation by multiple applications using diverse data types (Satyanaryanan et. al, 1995). However it does not address replication of objects and dynamic reconfiguration.
Server/Network adaptability	The mobile adaptability is in the server /network level for handling network adaptive behavior, such as available bandwidth changes, disconnection due to user move, or bad battery.	(Baggio, 1998) proposed a mechanism to store information, and replicate or cache objects when network disconnection happens.
Proxy adaptability	The mobile adaptability is in the service proxy.	(Fox, et. al., 1996) proposed a TranSend system which is application-transparent and supports dynamic reconfiguration.
Proxy and client adaptability	The mobile adaptability is in both the proxy and client.	MobiGATE (Zheng, et. al, 2010) is application-transparent and supports dynamic reconfiguration. It applies coordination theory for mobile service composition and configuration.
Middleware adaptability	The mobile adaptability is handled by mobile middleware that supports QoS-aware or policy-based adaptability.	(Keeney, et al, 2007) discussed several mobile middleware for mobile adaptability, such as reflective middleware, and policy-based middleware. (Bellavista, et. al, 2001) proposed agent-based middleware. (Nahrstedt, et. al, 2001) proposed a QoS-Aware mobile middleware.
Client adaptability	The mobile adaptability is handled by dynamic user interfaces and on-demand-code.	Using on-demand-code, such as Javascript and other technologies, like HTML5, CSS3 (Esposito, 2012) to create dynamic user interface for adapting to different types of mobile devices.

overcomes drawbacks of traditional client-server computing. As the execution units belong to different users, and computation environments are managed by different organizations; and communication may take place through an insecure infrastructure (Internet), the security is a concern to use logical/code mobility technology. Dwivedi, Clark, and Thiel (2010), Fuggetta, Picco, and Vigna (1998), and Ramdous and Kannan (2002) provide security solutions to code mobility.

We covered the major quality attributes in enterprise mobile service architecture. Gafni (2008) proposes a framework for quality metrics in mobile-wireless information systems. The author builds quality metrics and maps each metric to issues of mobile-wireless computing, such as "Narrow band," "Connection stability," and "Security and privacy." Moreover, the author also builds a mapping from mobile quality metrics to standard quality characteristics.

Table 13. Classification of logic mobility mechanism

Mobility Mechanism / Logic Mobility	Code and Execution State Management	Data Space Management
Stateful/Strong Mobility	Migration |-Proactive |-Reactive Remote cloning |-Proactive |-Reactive	Binding removal Network reference Re-binding By copy By move

Stateless/Weak Mobility	Code shipping
	|-Standalone code
	    |-Synchronous
	    |-Asynchronous
	       |-Immediate
	       |-Deferred
	|-Code fragment
	    |-Synchronous
	    |-Asynchronous
	       |-Immediate
	       |-Deferred
	Code fetching
	|-Standalone code
	    |-Synchronous
	    |-Asynchronous
	       |-Immediate
	       |-Deferred
	|-Code fragment
	    |-Synchronous
	    |-Asynchronous
	       |-Immediate
	       |-Deferred	

Figure 17. Remote evaluation

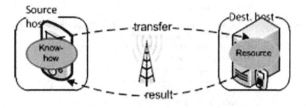

Figure 18. Code-on-demand

Figure 19. Mobile agent

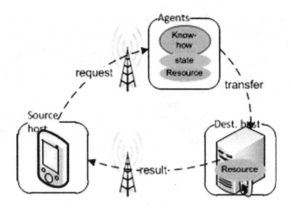

Table 14. Architecture of Mobile Systems with Logic Mobility Mechanism

Type of System	Architecture Description	High-Level Diagram
Remote Evaluation (REV)	There are source hosts and destination hosts. A component in source host has know-how logic but not the resources needed for performing the service. The component is transferred from source host to destination host where it is executed using the available resources. The result of the execution is returned to the source host.	*Figure 17.*
Code-on-Demand (COD)	The needed resources are available in a host A which does not have know-how logic. The subsystem in host A requests the component (s) providing the know-how logic from remote host(s), such as host B. The logic will be executed in host A.	*Figure 18.*
Mobile Agent (MA)	A software component (MA) located on a given host A, which has know-how logic, some of execution state and has access to some of the resources needed to provide a service. The MA with its state and local resources may migrate to destination host that may have remaining resources needed for providing the service.	*Figure 19.*

Case Study: Enterprise Mobile Solution

FedEx is a successful transportation/shipping company in the world. Its mobile solution (Fe-dex Mobile) is a noteworthy implementation in enterprise mobile service computing. FedEx mobile solution includes mobile web solution and mobile sensor–based real-time services. The FedEx mobile web solution consists of:

Table 15. Appropriate architectural styles for different systems

System Design Style	Client-Server	Remote Evaluation	Mobile Agent
Non Mobile	Appropriate	Code represented as data. Code receipt and execution must be programmed explicitly.	Code and state represented as data. Execution and state restore must be programmed explicitly.
Mobile with Weak Mobility	Degenerated code Unnecessary execution units are created	Appropriate	State represented as data. State restoring must be programmed explicitly.
Mobile with Strong Mobility	Degenerated code. Unnecessary execution units are created. Unnecessary state migration.	Unnecessary overhead for migration. Unnecessary state migration.	Appropriate

- Mobile App Store which carry mobile applications for different mobile devices with different OS such as iPhone/iPad, Android and Blackberry.
- Core services, such as shipping, tracking, rating, scheduling, pickup, and find location.
- A solid SOA infrastructure (Data Center Knowledge, Feb 2011) as a foundation of its enterprise mobile service architecture.
- Secure communication and data access with its user management and remote control to protect its business and enterprise services.

FedEx CIO Rob Carter in his "Dominant Design" presentation (InformationWeek, 2011) in InformationWeek provides an in depth look at how FedEx is building its data centers which are based on SOA and private/hybrid Cloud enterprise infrastructure architecture. Its core components include virtualized servers, modern network, intelligent storage, and SOA software architecture. The enterprise infrastructure architecture is the foundation of FedEx mobile solution.

Another FedEx mobile solution is to provide sensor-based real-time mobile services. The new product SenseAwareSM powered by FedEx (ZD-Net, 2011) shows that sensors and the Internet of things (IoT) will dominate its mobility strategy in the future. This device is dropped into a package and can relay back location, temperature, data and even radioactivity levels if needed. Internet of Things (IoT) is one of the emerging technologies (Logica, 2012; Hwang, Fox, & Dongarra, 2012). Enterprise mobility as well as mobile service computing is basic technology for IoT realization. The sensors connect many different disciplines, including customer service, data management, analytics, and business intelligence.

Unlike traditional mobile devices, wireless sensors are standard measurement tools which can be part of a mobile device or a wireless sensor device, equipped with transmitters to convert signals from process control instruments into a radio transmission. The radio signal is interpreted by a receiver which then converts the wireless signal to a specific desired output, such as an analog current or data analysis via computer software. Wireless sensors are very useful in infrastructure-free environments, such as sensor networks, ad-hoc networks for monitoring physical or environmental conditions such as temperature, sound, pressure, etc., and to cooperatively pass their data through the network to a main location. FedEx SenseAware can be used for customers monitoring shipment in-transit condition in near real-time. If an enterprise has infrastructure-free environments or ad-hoc networks like FedEx, then enterprise wireless sensor service architecture is an important part of the enterprise mobile solution architecture.

As we briefly described, FedEx enterprise mobile solution is built on its solid enterprise SOA mobile architecture which is an instance of *EMSA* architectural style described in this chapter. As we defined in *EMSA*, the architectural style consists of seven architectural views. Let us examine the FedEx mobile architecture and see how it maps to a concrete *EMSA* style architecture.

- FedEx mobile architecture consists of a set of mobile Web services (*EMS*) – such as FedEx mobile ship, mobile tracking, mobile locator, etc., which support its core business and provide online and offline services to its employees, customers and public users. More information is available from the FedEx mobile portal[1].
- FedEx mobile architecture provides its mobile applications in Apple store (iOS), Google store (Android OS), and BlackBerry world, for mobile service consumers (*MSC*).
- FedEx mobile architecture is built on its hybrid private enterprise SOA infrastructure and integrates its existing infrastructure to the enterprise wireless sensor network (*EMSI)* through its SenseAware mobile innovation product and Rackspace Cloud.
- FedEx mobile architecture supports mobile workflow (*EMSP*) and allows mobile users to complete shipping process by using mobile devices.

- FedEx mobile architecture is designed with its mobile enhanced SOA management system (*EMSM*) for managing and securing its data center infrastructure and providing quality of service (QoS) for its mobile users (*EMQS*).
- FedEx mobile architecture is designed and implemented for meeting quality requirements, such as security, performance, scalability, and availability (Babcock, 2011). FedEx mobile architecture improves its QoS by adopting new technologies and standards, such as x86 virtualized Linux platform, high-speed WLAN, and 3G above Cellular network. Recently, FedEx adopted Bluetooth wireless technology for its data collection device, the FedEx PowerPad, which gives FedEx couriers wireless access to the FedEx network, thereby enhancing and accelerating the package information available to its customers[2].

Figure 20 describes a high-level view of FedEx mobile service architecture based on public information (Carter, 2012; InformationWeek, 2011; Data Center Knowledge, 2011; ZDNet, 2011; Babcock, 2011).

FUTURE RESEARCH DIRECTIONS

EMSC is a rapidly developing trend in enterprise IT. *EMSA* is still in its infancy and is expected to grow substantially through future research work and practices. However, some of the open issues and challenges, such as dynamic resource provisioning, higher availability, performance, and scalability, need further research and development.

Future research trends in mobile computing are pointing in the following directions:

- Extending enterprise mobile service computing to enterprise mobile Cloud service computing (*EMCSC*) (Dinh, Lee, Niyato,

Figure 20. FedEx enterprise mobile service architecture (used with permission)

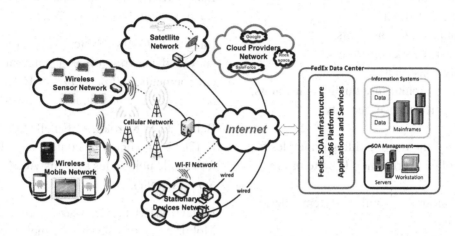

& Wand, 2011; Hong, Chonho, Dusit, & Ping, 2011).

- Extending *EMSA* style to enterprise mobile Cloud service architecture (*EMCSA*) which is a hybrid style of *ECSA* style (Tang, 2011) and *EMSA* style.
- Enhancing *EMSI* capacity and scalability by using Cloud IaaS (Dinh, Lee, Niyato, & Wand, 2011).
- Utilizing Cloud computing principles, such as dynamic resource provisioning, to enterprise mobile service computing design (Hong, Chonho, Dusit, & Ping, 2011).
- Extending mobile service to SaaS for mobile users.
- Utilizing Storage as a service for improving mobile storage challenge.
- Developing real-time mobile web applications for supporting IoT (Hwang, Fox, & Dongarra, 2012).
- Developing mechanism for mobile QoS-awareness and SLA-awareness (Tang, Dong, & Zhao, 2012).

CONCLUSION

This chapter presented the opportunities, challenges, issues, and solutions of enterprise mobile service computing. A case on FedEx mobile solution illustrates practical enterprise mobile service architecture. The *EMSC* as a new paradigm of distributed computing and a new architectural style brings great opportunity to enterprise businesses. Mobile applications and services build a new channel between enterprise business and its customers. However, *EMSC* faces many challenges and issues as discussed earlier. The main challenges include:

- Mobile device hardware and software challenge.
- Mobile connection challenge.
- Mobile heterogeneous network challenge.
- Mobile performance and scalability challenge.
- Mobile security challenge.

To solve those challenging issues, the chapter proposes an architectural style – *EMSA* as an architectural solution which provides design guidelines for enterprise mobile application and service system. The *EMSA* includes a set of design constraints, principles and high-level common structure – components, connectors and infrastructure. The mobile system design constraints include:

- Hardware constraints.
- Software constraints.
- Communication constraints.
- Wireless network constraints.
- Mobility constraints.
- Enterprise architecture quality constraints, such as performance, security.

In summary, the major guiding principles for architecture of enterprise mobile systems are:

- Work around mobile system design constraints.
- Meet enterprise software architecture quality and system non-functional requirements.
- Tradeoff quality attributes and achieve a balanced whole quality (*EMSQ*).
- Utilize mobile context in system design, such as designing for context-aware and location-aware.
- Apply Logic/Code mobility appropriately.
- Choose the right style of mobile services for maximum performance.
- Integrate mobile applications with enterprise core services.
- Build mobile App stores for supporting multiple mobile devices.
- Build enterprise mobile service infrastructure (*EMSI*) as a foundation.
- Build enterprise mobile service management (*EMSM*) to guarantee end-to-end QoS and SLA.

REFERENCES

Alshahwan, F., Moessner, K., & Carrez, F. (2010). Evaluation of distributed SOAP and REST mobile web services. *International Journal on Advances in Networks and Services, 3*(3&4), 447–461.

Amjad, U. (2004). *Mobile computing and wireless communications*. NGE Solutions, Inc..

Babcock, C. (2011). *6 lessons learned from FedEx private cloud*. InformationWeek.

Baggio, A. (1998). System support for transparency and network-aware adaptation in mobile environments. In *Proceedings of ACM Symposium on Applied Computing*, Feb. 27th – March 1.

Bellavista, P., Corradi, A., Fanelli, M., & Foschini, L. (2012). A survey of context data distribution for mobile ubiquitous systems. *ACM Computing Surveys, 45*(1).

Bellavista, P., Corradi, A., & Stefanelli, C. (2001). Mobile agent middleware for mobile computing. *IEEE Computer,* March Issue, 73-81.

Borg, A. (2011). *Mobility becomes core IT*. Retrieved from http://event.on24.com/ event/29/75/81/rt/1/documents/slidepdf/mobile_latest_march_28.pdf

Canalys. (2012). *Smart phones overtake client PCs in 2011*. Retrieved from http://www.canalys. com/newsroom/smart-phones-overtake-client-pcs-2011

Carter, R. (2012). *Enterprise mobility management 2012. The SoMoClo™ Edge*. Aberdeen Group.

Choi, H., Dawson, T., & La Porta, T. (2010). Network integration in 3G and 4G wireless networks. In *Proceedings of 19th International Conference on Computer Communications and Networks (ICCCN)* (pp. 1-8).

Compuware. (2012). *Mobile monitoring webpage*. Retrieved from http://www.compuware.com/application-performance-management/mobile.html

Data Center Knowledge. (2011). *Fedex opens Colorado Springs data center*. Retrieved from http://www.datacenterknowledge.com/ archives/2011/02/17/fedex-opens-colorado-springs-data-center/

Deepak, G., & Pradeep, B. S. (2012). Challenging issues and limitation of mobile computing. *International Journal of Computer Technology & Applications*, *3*(1), 177–181.

Díaz, L., & Ekman, U. (2011). Introduction to mobile ubiquity in public and private spaces. *Digital Creativity*, *22*(3), 127–133. doi:10.1080/14626268.2011.606819.

Dinh, H. T., Lee, C., Niyato, D., & Wand, P. (2011). *A survey of mobile cloud computing: Architecture, applications, and approaches. Wireless Communications and Mobile Computing*. Wiley.

Dwivedi, H., Clark, C., & Thiel, D. (2010). *Mobile application security*. McGraw-Hill.

Esposito, D. (2012). *Architecting mobile solutions for the enterprise*. Microsoft Press.

FedEx Mobile. (2011). *Website*. Retrieved from http://www.fedex.com/us/mobile/index.html?location=desktop

Firtman, M. (2010). *Programming the mobile web*. O'Reilly.

Flinn, J., & Satyanarayanan, M. (1999). Energy-aware adaptation for mobile applications. In SOSP-17 Kiawah Island, SC, December.

Forman, G.H., & Zahorjan, J. (1994). The challenges of mobile computing. *IEEE Computer*, April Issue, 38-47.

Forum, L. T. E. (2011). *Website*. Retrieved from http://lteworld.org/blog/lte-advanced-evolution-lte

Fox, A., et al. (1996). Adapting to network and client variability via on-demand dynamic distillation. In *Proceedings of 7th Internet Conference on Architectural Support for Programming Languages and Operating Systems (ASPLOSVII)* (pp. 160–170).

Fuggetta, A., Picco, G. P., & Vigna, G. (1998). Understanding code mobility. *IEEE Transactions on Software Engineering*, *24*(5). doi:10.1109/32.685258.

Gafni, R. (2008). Framework for quality metrics in mobile-wireless information systems. *Interdisciplinary Journal of Information, Knowledge, and Management*, *3*, 23–38.

Gao, J., & Ji, A. (2010). *Building an intelligent mobile advertising system. The International Journal of Mobile Computing and Multimedia Communications (IJMCMC)*. January Issue.

Gao, J., Shim, S., Mei, H., & Su, X. (2006). *Engineering wireless-based software systems*. Artech House Publisher.

Garofalakis, J., Stefani, A., Stefanis, V., & Xenos, M. (2007). Quality attributes of consumer-based m-commerce systems. In *Proceedings of the 2007 ICETE-B Conference,* Barcelona, Spain, 28–31 July (pp. 130–136)

Gartner. (2012). Gartner identifies the top 10 strategic technologies for 2012. *Gartner Report*. Retrieved from http://www.gartner.com/it/page.jsp?id=1826214

Gupta, A. K. (2008). Challenges of mobile computing. In *Proceedings of 2nd National Conference on Challenges & Opportunities in Information Technology, March 29* (pp. 86-90).

Hackmann, G., Haitjema, M., Gill, C., & Roman, G. C. (2006). Sliver: A BPEL workflow process execution engine for mobile devices. In *Proceedings of 4th International Conference on Service Oriented Computing (ICSOC)*.

Hirsch, F., Kemp, J., & Llkka, J. (2006). *Mobile web services architecture and implementation*. Wiley. doi:10.1002/9780470017982.

Hong, T. D., Chonho, L., Dusit, N., & Ping, W. (2011). *A survey of mobile cloud computing: Architecture, applications, and approaches. Wireless Communications and Mobile Computing.* Wiley.

Horwitz, B. (2011). Cisco, GE combine location-aware technology to track patients, equipment. *eWeek.* Retrieved from http://www.eweek.com/c/a/Health-Care-IT/Cisco-GE-Combine-LocationAware-Technology-to-Track-Patients-Equipment-569466/

Hwang, K., Fox, G. C., & Dongarra, J. J. (2012). *Distributed and cloud computing: From parallel processing to the internet of things.* Elsevier.

IDC. (2012). *Nearly 1 billion smart connected devices shipped in 2011 with shipments expected to double by 2016.* Retrieved from http://www.idc.com/getdoc.jsp?containerId=prUS23398412

IEEE. (n.d.). *IEEE 802.11. IEEE 802.11 Standards.* Retrieved from http://www.ieee802.org/11/

IEEE. (n.d.). *IEEE 802.16.* Retrieved from http://standards.ieee.org/findstds/standard/802.16e-2005.html

Information Week. (2011). *FedEx CIO Rob Carter: Dominant design.* Retrieved from http://www.informationweek.com/video/1178266432001

Information Week. (2012). *Report 2012 on state of mobile security.* Retrieved from http://reports.informationweek.com/abstract/21/8792/security/research-2012-state-of-mobile-security.html

Kakousisa, K., Paspallisa, N., & Angelos, G. (2010). A survey of software adaptation in mobile and ubiquitous computing. *Enterprise Information Systems, 4*(4).

Kaltz, J. W., Ziegler, J., & Lohmann, S. (2005). Context-aware web engineering: Modeling and applications. *Revue d'Intelligence Artificielle, 19*(3), 439–458. doi:10.3166/ria.19.439-458.

Keeney, J., Cahill, V., & Haahr, M. (2007). *Techniques for dynamic adaptation of mobile services, handbook of mobile middleware* (Bellavista, P., Ed.).

Kunze, C. P., Zaplata, S., Turjalei, M., & Lamersdorf, W. (2008). Enabling context-based cooperation: A generic context model and management system. In *11th International Conference on Business Information Systems (BIS 2008)* (pp. 459–470). Springer.

Logica. (2012). *The Internet of things.* Retrieved from http://www.logica.com/we-do/internet-of-things/related-media/brochures/2012/the-internet-of-things/

Nahrstedt, K., Xu, D., Wichadakul, D., & Li, B. (2001). QoS-aware middleware for ubiquitous and heterogeneous environments. *IEEE Communications Magazine,* (November Issue), 2–10.

Othman, M. (2009). *Principles of mobile computing and communications.* Auerbach Publication.

Portio Research. (2012). *Latest mobile state.* Retrieved from http://mobilethinking.com/mobile-marketing-tools/latest-mobile-state

Ramdous, S., & Kannan, G. (2002). Security of mobile code. *Journal of Cryptology, 2*(1), 1–12.

Reed, B. (2010). A brief history of smartphones. *Network World.* Retrieved from http://www.networkworld.com/slideshows/2010/061510-smartphone-history.html

Sahu, D., Sharma, S., Dubey, V., & Tripathi, A. (2012). Cloud computing in mobile computing. *International Journal of Scientific and Research Publications, 2*(8).

Satyanaryanan, M., Noble, B., Kumar, P., & Price, M. (1995). Application-aware adaptation for mobile computing. *ACM SIGOPS Operating Systems Review, 29*(1), 52–55. doi:10.1145/202453.202464.

Sharma, D., & Singh, R. K. (2011). QoS and QoE management in wireless communication system. *International Journal of Engineering Science and Technology (IJEST)*, *3*(3), 2385–2391.

Sybase. (2011). *Mobility advantage*. Retrieved from http://www.sybase.com/files/White_Papers/Sybase_SUP_MobilityAdvantagePlatform_wp.pdf

Tang, L. (2011). *Modeling and analyzing enterprise service-oriented architectural styles*. (PhD Thesis). CS of University of Texas Dallas.

Tang, L., Bastani, F. B., Tsai, W. T., Dong, J., & Zhang, L. J. (2011). Modeling and analyzing enterprise cloud service architecture. *Technical Report UTDCS-26-11*. Dept. of Computer Science, Univ. of Texas at Dallas.

Tang, L., Dong, J., Peng, T., & Tsai, W. T. (2010). Modeling enterprise service-oriented architectural styles. *Service Oriented Computing and Applications (SOCA)*, *4*, 81–107. doi:10.1007/s11761-010-0059-2.

Tang, L., Dong, J., & Zhao, Y. (2011). SLA-aware enterprise service computing. In Cardellini, V., Casalicchio, E., Branco, K. C., Estrella, J., & Monaco, F. J. (Eds.), *Performance and dependability in service computing: Concepts, techniques and research direction*. IGI Global Publishing. doi:10.4018/978-1-60960-794-4.ch002.

Tang, L., Zhao, Y., & Dong, J. (2009). *Specifying enterprise web-oriented architecture. High Assurance Services Computing* (pp. 241–260). Springer. doi:10.1007/978-0-387-87658-0_12.

Taptu. (2010). The state of the mobile touch web. *Taptu Report, January*. Retrieved from http://robertoigarza.files.wordpress.com/2009/07/rep-the-state-of-the-mobile-touch-web-taptu-2010.pdf

Taylor, R. N., Medvidovic, N., & Dashofy, E. M. (2010). *Software architecture: Foundations, theory, and practices*. Wiley.

Tjepkema, J. (2011). Guidelines for a successful mobile customer experience. *Mobile Convention Amsterdam*, 19 April.

Turban, E., McLean, E., & Wetherbe, J. (2006). *Information technology for management* (5th ed.). Wiley & Sons, Inc..

W3C. (2012). *HTML5 Editor's Draft 7*. Retrieved from http://dev.w3.org/html5/spec/

ZDNet. (2011). *Fedex CIO carter: Next era of internet is sensor based computing*. Retrieved from http://www.zdnet.com/blog/btl/fedex-cio-carter-next-era-of-internet-is-sensor-based-computing/61315

Zheng, Y., Chan, A., & Ngai, G. (2010). Applying coordination for service adaptation in mobile computing. *IEEE Internet Computing*, 61–67.

ADDITIONAL READING

B'Far. R. (2005). Mobile computing principles. Cambridge Press.

Bruneo, D., Puliafito, A., & Scarpa, M. (2007). *Mobile middleware: Definition and motivations, handbook of mobile middleware* (Bellavista, P., Ed.).

Chihani, B., Bertin, E., & Crespi, N. (2011). A comprehensive framework for context-aware communication systems. In *15th International Conference on Intelligence in Next Generation Networks (ICIN'11)*, Berlin, Germany.

Laukkanen, M., & Helin, H. (2003). Web services in wireless networks: What happened to the performance. In *International Conference on Web Services ICWS 03* (pp. 278–284). CSREA Press.

Malek, S. et al. (2009). An architecture-driven software mobility framework. *The Journal of Systems and Software*. Elsevier.

McKinley, P. K. et al. (2003). Composable proxy services to support collaboration on the mobile internet. *IEEE Transactions on Computers*, *52*(6), 713–726. doi:10.1109/TC.2003.1204828.

Nexus Telecom. (2007). Whitepaper on MMS service monitoring. Retrieved from http://www.nexustelecom.com/documents/whitepapers/whitepaper_mms_service_monitoring.pdf

Noble, B., et al. (1997). Agile application-aware adaptation for mobility. In *Proceedings of the 16th ACM Symposium on Operating System Principles* (pp. 276–287). ACM Press.

Spaceport. (2012). *Spaceport perfmarks report*. Retrieved from http://spaceport.io/spaceport_perfmarks_report_2012_3.pdf, 2012

Yoder, J. W., Balaguer, F., & Johnson, R. (2001). Architecture and design of adaptive object models. [ACM Press.]. *SIGPLAN Not.*, *36*(12), 50–60. doi:10.1145/583960.583966.

KEY TERMS AND DEFINITIONS

Architectural Style: A set of principles that provides an abstract framework for a family of systems. An architectural style improves partitioning and promotes design reuse by providing solutions to frequently recurring problems.

Enterprise Mobile Cloud Service Computing (EMCSC): Mobile Cloud Computing (MCC) is a mobile computing technology that leverages unified elastic resources of varied Clouds and network technologies toward unrestricted functionality, storage, and mobility. The EMCSC is a kind of MCC in which its systems are built on service-oriented enterprise architectural styles. EMCSC is an amalgam of four foundations, namely enterprise service computing, Cloud computing, mobile computing, and networking.

Enterprise Mobile Service Architecture: An architectural style for enterprise mobile service computing. It is an extension of enterprise service-oriented architecture (ESOA) style for enterprise mobile computing.

Enterprise Mobile Service Computing: A kind of Mobile Computing in which the mobile computing system is built on service-oriented enterprise architectural styles.

HTML5: Markup language for structuring and presenting content for the World Wide Web. It is the fifth revision of the HTML standard (created in 1990 and standardized as HTML4 as of 1997) and as of September 2012, is still under development.

Mobile Adaptability: The ability of a mobile service system or mobile application to adapt to the mobile environment where mobile devices are in different mobility spaces such as physical space, network space, and information data space.

Mobile Application: A computing program running in mobile device.

Mobile Application Server: Any application server which supports mobile applications and services.

Mobile Computing: Human–computer interaction where a computer is expected to be transported during normal usage. Mobile computing involves mobile communication, mobile hardware, and mobile software.

Mobile Content Repository: Any content repository which stores content for mobile applications and services.

Mobile Data Storage: Any storage or database which stores data for mobile applications and services.

Mobile Device: A small, hand-held computing device (including notebooks, tablets and smartphones).

Mobile Endpoint Security Agent: A mobile agent for managing mobile endpoint security, in which the mobile endpoint security means that the security of access point from any mobile device to enterprise network.

Mobile Network: A wireless network which includes WLAN, WWAN, 2G/3G/4G wireless networks, ad-hoc networks, satellite networks.

Mobile Service: A software service running either in mobile device or remote servers, such as web service, for providing any service for mobile users and mobile applications.

Mobility: Mobility includes physical mobility and logic or software mobility. The physical mobility refers to ability of movement of the components (mobile users and mobile system hosts) across different physical locations, while still being able to access an information system unimpeded. The logic mobility refers to the ability that a piece of software can move cross hardware hosts during the mobile computing system's execution.

RESTful Web Service: A kind of web service which is built based on the REST architectural style which uses the HTTP protocol.

Web Services: A method of communication between two electronic devices over the Web (Internet) using SOAP protocol or RESTful style.

ENDNOTES

[1]   See FedEx Mobile. (2011).
[2]   See FedEx Mobile. (2011).

Chapter 13
Extending
Service–Driven Architectural
Approaches to the Cloud

Raja Ramanathan
Independent Researcher, USA

ABSTRACT

Today, most enterprises own their IT infrastructures. In the future, it may well be more cost effective to use infrastructure and software provided by entities that are specialized in provisioning infrastructure and services on a need and usage basis. This is the Cloud Computing model. The Cloud enables ubiquitous, elastic, and on-demand network access, which can be rapidly self-provisioned. Information Technology is beginning to migrate to the Cloud, where dynamically scalable, virtualized resources, are provided as a service over the network. Currently, IT leaders focus on managing on-premises, centralized, and service-driven methodology, to deliver services and integration solutions for their businesses. In the future, they will be expected to deliver and manage a network of flexible services that are federated across on-premises and outsourced infrastructures. This chapter explores the capabilities and service models offered by the Cloud and the challenges of extending the Service-driven architectural approaches to that paradigm. It presents design principles and implementation guidelines to architect application services in the Cloud ecosystem. Finally, the chapter takes a look ahead at the future of Cloud Computing.

INTRODUCTION

Enterprises are constantly interested in improving business agility, growth, and profitability, while at the same time, reducing expenses, and implementing better management of risk and compliance. By adopting a service-driven approach to architecture, IT leaders are positioning their enterprise information technology to closely align with the dynamic needs of their businesses, thereby serving their business in an efficient and cost effective manner. Currently, those IT leaders focus on managing on-premises, centralized, and service-driven methodology, to deliver services and integration solutions. In the future, they will be expected to deliver and manage a network of

DOI: 10.4018/978-1-4666-4193-8.ch013

flexible services that are federated across on-premises and outsourced infrastructures.

Today, most enterprises own their IT infrastructures. But in the future, that certainly does not have to be the case. It may well be more cost effective to use infrastructure and software provided by entities that are specialized in provisioning infrastructure and services on a need and usage basis. By leveraging economies of scale, such providers will be able to supply the required processing power, software applications, and platforms at a lower cost, than could be achieved by enterprises internally. This is especially the case when business needs change constantly, resulting in drastic fluctuations in the required processing power, storage, and complexity of software to address the changing needs of the business. This model of renting and paying for computing power and software on an as-needed basis from a third party is called *Utility Computing*.

The idea of Cloud Computing is not new; it dates back to the 1950's in the form of Utility Computing. The concept of Utility Computing was pioneered by Professor John McCarthy, a well-known computer scientist who initiated time-sharing in late 1957 on modified IBM 704 and IBM 7090 computers (McCarthy, 1983). McCarthy expected that corporations would be able to sell computing resources through the Utility Computing model. As expected, different organizations paid service bureaus such as IBM and other mainframe providers who offered computing power and database storage to large organizations from their world wide data centers. To facilitate this business model, mainframe operating systems evolved to include process control facilities, security, and user metering.

Since then, several other implementations have tried to leverage that Utility model including:

- **Desktop Hosting Services:** InsynQ launched on-demand desktop hosting services in 1997 using HP equipment.

- **Utility Data Center:** HP introduced the Utility Data Center in 2001 by incorporating multiple software utilities to form a software stack. Services such as "IP billing-on-tap" were marketed.

- **Grid Computing:** The Grid concept involved combining computers from multiple administrative domains to form a distributed computing environment (Foster & Kesselman, 1998). This environment was composed of many networked and loosely coupled computers acting together to perform very large tasks. The Grid technology has been applied to solve computationally intensive scientific, mathematical, and academic problems based on a pay-per-use model.

- **Volunteer Computing:** Many research experiments that depend on compute intensive tasks, met their needs by exploiting idle computing resources available through volunteers (Sarmenta, 2001). This model provided researchers with access to supercomputer-like performance in a cost-effective manner. This is based on the grid computing model.

- **Web Hosting:** This service allows individuals and organizations to host their websites on Web servers provisioned by datacenters of other companies for a fee.

- **Application Service Provider (ASP):** A model where software companies offer applications for remote access by clients through networks for monthly fees (Smith & Kumar, 2004). The ASP model exempts clients from the capital and operational expenditure of procuring, installing, and maintaining commercial off-the-shelf (COTS) software and the underlying hardware infrastructures.

- **Online File Sharing:** A model where websites enable Internet users to share their files online. For example, Flickr users can share their photos over the Internet. In this model, shared artifacts are hosted on public spaces that can be accessed by clients over the Internet from anywhere and at anytime.

- **Social Networks:** A variety of websites connect users interested in specific subjects. Examples are YouTube, Wikipedia, Facebook, etc. All these networks allow their users to share their ideas and resources, such as, presentations, videos, pictures, etc., in an easy and efficient manner.

Cloud computing has evolved from this Utility Computing model. Various technologies converged together to enable the emergence of Cloud Computing, such as broadband high speed internet access that enabled access to large data files from far away distances; Grid Computing, which provided a distributed computing model that facilitated the use of underutilized computing resources in the enterprise to process compute-intensive tasks faster, and Service Oriented Architecture (SOA), which enabled software vendors to offer their products as services and facilitated the orchestration of reusable components to create business services in an agile manner.

The National Institute of Standards and Technology (NIST), defines Cloud computing as follows:

Cloud Computing is a model for enabling ubiquitous, convenient, on-demand network access to a shared pool of configurable computing resources (e.g. networks, servers, storage, applications, and services) that can be rapidly provisioned and released with minimal management effort or service provider interaction (NIST, 2011a).

Information Technology is beginning to migrate to the Cloud, where dynamically scalable, virtualized resources are provided as a service over the Internet. Cloud computing is making it possible for enterprises to access and create applications on virtual servers that scale dynamically to meet demand. While Service-driven architectural approaches are traditionally applied to on-premises infrastructure and applications, the Cloud enables enterprises to create applications and infrastructures that are completely remote and accessible through the network. Examples for Enterprise Cloud Systems include Amazon's EC2, Amazon's S3, IBM's SmartCloud, VMWare's vCloud, and Google's App Engine. To appreciate the scale at which these Clouds operate, consider Amazon's EC2 Cloud that is made up of almost half-a-million servers (Liu, 2012).

There are potentially significant financial benefits to building applications in the Cloud. There is no investment in capital equipment or data centers. You can ramp up use of an application without large investments in physical infrastructure. With computing available on a "Utility" basis (i.e. as a pay-per-use service) from Cloud Service Providers, and with the ability to provision resources as needed in a dynamic manner through self-service, makes a strong case for moving to the Cloud.

Consider the case of The New York Times publication that needed to convert 11 million articles and images in its archive to PDF format. By using the open-source implementation of the *MapReduce* framework (Dean & Ghemawat, 2004), "Hadoop," on Amazon EC2 Cloud with 100 simple Web Service instances running in parallel, the task was completed in just 24 hours for less than $300, which would otherwise have taken an estimated seven weeks to complete, if processed sequentially in the traditional manner (Phipps, 2009).

However, there are several challenges with Cloud Computing in terms of API (Application Programming Interfaces) Standardization, Security, and Governance, etc., which need to be tackled to make Cloud a serious enterprise initiative. Currently, each Cloud provider has its own specific APIs for managing its services. The Cloud industry is still in its infancy, where each vendor has its own proprietary technology that tends to lock in customers to their services. Lack of standards can cause enterprises to fear of vendor lock-ins which presents a barrier to Cloud adoption. Grossman points out that the current state of standards and interoperability in Cloud Computing is similar to the early Internet era where each organization had its own network and data transfer was difficult. This changed with the introduction of TCP and other Internet standards. However, these standards were initially resisted by vendors just as standardization attempts in Cloud Computing are being resisted by some vendors (Grossman, 2009).

SOA and Cloud Computing are closely related. SOA is an architecture methodology for implementing loosely coupled and reusable services, while Cloud is a delivery mechanism where infrastructure, platforms, and/or software are provided as services. While SOA is concerned with mechanisms for creating tighter business-IT alignment, Cloud Computing is about providing ease of access to and usage of hardware, software, and networking resources as services in a cost-effective and dynamic manner and uses a repeatable methodology to enable elastic scalability of resources. While SOA applies the service principle to application software within the enterprise, Cloud Computing applies the same principle at the application, infrastructure, and platform levels, and with respect to inter- and intra- enterprises.

From an architectural standpoint, Cloud Computing can be considered as the next logical step beyond SOA. SOA provides a foundation for moving to the Cloud. The architectural aspects of a Service-driven environment can be extended to the Cloud. In addition, Cloud Computing can strengthen existing service-driven initiatives and contribute directly to current SOA activities. There is strong agreement among technology leaders and analysts that for enterprises to extend successfully to the Cloud will require having a well designed service-oriented architecture to provide the foundation needed for Cloud Computing. To-

gether, SOA and Cloud technologies will provide a collaborative services-based solution.

RESTful (Representational State Transfer) Web API Services are being utilized in Cloud environments (Linthicum, 2012) to enable integration of the Cloud Services with the enterprise and provide benefits in terms of simplicity, agility, and low cost for managing and controlling Cloud resources. One of the significant benefits of Cloud APIs is tackling the challenge of federation (Amrhein, 2011).

This chapter is focused on exploring the capabilities of the Cloud and the challenges of Cloud Computing. It presents Service-driven architectural approaches as an essential foundation for enterprises looking to extend to the Cloud. The chapter describes the Cloud ecosystem in terms of the business benefits, service model offerings, standards, deployment models, and challenges; and provides guidelines and best practices for architecting application services for the Cloud.

BACKGROUND

SOA and Cloud architecture share several features. Both use the service principle and the delegation principle to delegate work to one or more services that perform the actual work. They also optimize resource utilization by enabling sharing of services by multiple applications or users. Both SOA and Cloud architecture promote loose coupling thus reducing dependencies with the other parts of the system. As a consequence, changes in a specific part of the system have limited impact on the overall system, leading to a quality system with lower maintenance costs. SOA can provide the backbone to enable enterprises to easily access Cloud services. With SOA already in place in the enterprise, it may be faster and more secure to take advantage of Cloud Computing.

SOA and Cloud architecture are also different in many ways. On the one hand, SOA focuses on the business. Services in SOA solve business problems. In other words, services in SOA are horizontal. On the other hand, services in the Cloud are vertically layered according to typical software stacks. The lower tiered services support the upper tiered services to deliver applications. SOA deals with application and integration solution architecture where you solve a business problem by abstracting out the services, whereas, Cloud architecture deals with IT delivery of infrastructure, platforms, and applications as services, and therefore does not deal directly with solution to a specific business problem.

Specific types of applications are natural candidates for the Cloud. Applications that perform computation on a massive scale or use storage on a massive scale, applications that require high availability and reliability, applications that expect large processing load variances over a specific duration, and applications that need to collaborate across enterprise boundaries, are good candidate applications for the Cloud. For example, data mining, batch processing, financial back-office, large nightly builds, image processing and document processing applications are excellent candidates for the Cloud. These applications reap significant benefits in terms of dynamic resource availability, reduced infrastructure administration, and lower costs, by processing in the Cloud.

There are typically three different ways in which an enterprise can accommodate growth in processing demand. The first approach is called the "Scale-up," where the enterprise is required to invest in larger and more powerful computers to accommodate the increase in processing requests due to the monolithic nature of its application software. This approach requires huge investments in hardware, software, and infrastructure and does not lend itself well to an agile business model.

The second approach is the "Scale-out," where the enterprise is able to scale its infrastructure horizontally and incrementally by adding only the necessary number of extra servers and other infrastructure as required to meet the increased demand.

Such enterprises typically use SOA to develop applications and deploy them using a clustered topology enabling them to take advantage of the loose coupling and scalability of services. Here, additional resources are added incrementally, thus insulating the enterprise from large IT expenses.

The third approach is the "Cloud," where resources are dynamically elastic and can be easily self-provisioned as needed. This is the most cost-effective model for scaling up or down and also protects against idling resources by enabling enterprises to scale down when processing demand falls.

To manage Cloud resources of various types, a provider-consumer resource model must exist that describes the mechanism by which that offering is presented and consumed. The service offering model defines entities for the service consumer and the service provider. The consumer can then request an instance of a service offering.

There are three standard Cloud Computing offering models, as defined by NIST, and all of them are based on the service concept: Infrastructure as a Service (IaaS), Platform as a Service (PaaS), and Software as a Service (SaaS). In addition, IBM defines a fourth model called Business Process as a Service (BPaaS)

IaaS

The capability provided to the consumer is to rent processing, storage, networks, and other fundamental computing resources where the consumer is able to deploy and run arbitrary software, which can include operating systems and applications. The consumer does not manage or control the underlying Cloud infrastructure but has control over operating systems, storage, deployed applications, and possibly select networking components (e.g. firewalls, load balancers) (NIST, 2011a).

In the IaaS service model, consumers have access to virtual computers, network-accessible storage, network infrastructure components, and other fundamental computing resources on which they can install, create, deploy, manage, and monitor arbitrary software. IaaS consumers have the capability to access these computing resources over the network and are billed according to the amount or duration of the resources consumed, such as CPU hours used, or the volume of data stored/retrieved and the duration for which the data is stored. Examples of IaaS consumers are: enterprise datacenters and small businesses.

PaaS

The capability provided to the consumer is to deploy onto the Cloud infrastructure consumer-created applications using programming languages and tools supported by the provider (e.g. Java, Python,.Net). The consumer does not manage or control the underlying Cloud infrastructure, network, servers, operating systems, or storage, but the consumer has control over the deployed applications and possibly configuration settings for the application hosting environment (NIST, 2011a).

In the PaaS flavor, the provider supplies the infrastructure and also the middleware and programming tools. In other words, the PaaS provider supplies the entire development platform. Consumers of PaaS are application developers', testers', deployers' and administrators, who configure, publish, manage, and monitor applications in the Cloud. PaaS consumers are billed based on the number of login accounts as well as the processing workload, database storage, network resources consumed by the applications, and the duration over which the PaaS platform is used.

SaaS

The capability provided to the consumer is to use the provider's applications running on a Cloud infrastructure and accessible from various client devices through a thin client interface such as a

Web browser. The consumer does not manage or control the underlying Cloud infrastructure, network, servers, operating systems, storage, or even individual application capabilities, with the possible exception of limited user-specific application configuration settings (NIST, 2011a).

In the SaaS service model, applications in the Cloud are accessible to the SaaS consumers through the internet or private networks. SaaS consumers are generally end users who directly use software applications, or administrators who configure applications for end users. For example, rather than buying a CRM (Customer Relationship Management) package to run the customer application in the enterprise, the end users in the enterprise that rely on a CRM package to perform their job are provided access to the software on the internet that is provisioned as a CRM service in the Cloud. SaaS consumers are billed based on the number of end users, the time of use, the network bandwidth consumed, and the amount of data stored or the duration of stored data.

BPaaS

Business process services are any business process (horizontal or vertical) delivered through the Cloud service model (multi-tenant, self-service provisioning, elastic scaling, and usage metering or pricing) via the Internet with access via Web-centric interfaces and exploiting Web-oriented Cloud architecture. The BPaaS provider is responsible for the related business function(s) (IBM, 2010).

Figure 1 illustrates the aspects of a Cloud.

A traditional on-premises SOA system includes business services, middleware platforms (both hardware and software) and tools, and supporting infrastructure in terms of CPU, storage, networks, etc. These elements of an on-premises system can be mapped to the different types of Cloud services. The business services relate to SaaS in the

Figure 1. Aspects of the cloud

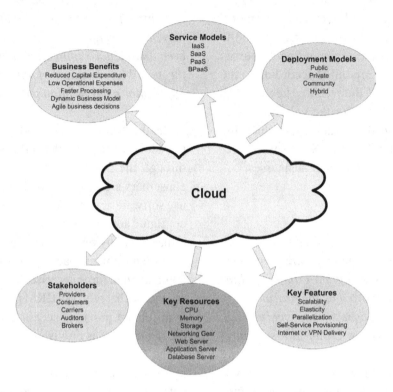

Cloud, the hardware and networking infrastructure relate to IaaS in the Cloud, and the middleware platform and tools relate to PaaS in the Cloud. In other words, the fundamental elements are similar; however, the delivery and usage models are different. The value proposition of the Cloud is a natural extension of the model provided by the on-premises system.

The cross cutting concerns in SOA such as integration, quality of service, and governance are significant concerns for both SOA and Cloud architectures and solutions. Each of the functional layers in both SOA and Cloud architectures may have interactions with capabilities in the cross cutting layers.

THE CLOUD ECOSYSTEM

Cloud providers are in the business of transforming various aspects of the IT computing stack into commodities that can be rented for use by consumers for a specific duration of time. For example, online storage can be procured from a Cloud provider in terabytes for the next six months. Along the same lines, hardware infrastructure or technology platforms to operate Web-based, middleware, and other applications can be rented from the Cloud, based on usage requirements.

Large-scale data processing brings many challenges with it. It is often difficult to obtain as many machines with specific CPU processing capabilities as needed by an application at a moment's notice. Even if one could obtain all the CPU power needed, it is challenging to distribute and coordinate a large-scale data processing job on a network of machines. Moreover, there will be a need to provide for fault tolerance and application fail-over. Also, when the load varies dynamically, one might have to scale the infrastructure up or down relatively quickly. Finally, when the large job is complete, one is stuck with all the additional resources that were provisioned to handle the job. Cloud architectures are designed to address these issues very well by encapsulating complex reliability and scalability logic in the underlying services of the Cloud.

Business Benefits of Cloud Computing

Cloud can provide significant business benefits to enterprises. In order to meet dynamic business challenges, traditional IT organizations constantly upgrade computing hardware and system software, configure and deploy new applications, and monitor and administer systems and applications. This is a time consuming and cost-intensive activity that can sometimes take too long to accomplish, leading to reduced business value for the enterprise. With Cloud Computing, businesses can reap the benefit of agility and cost-effectiveness of technology and enable IT to enhance alignment with the business. Significant benefits are listed below:

- **Cost Effective Business Model:** A large-scale data center will cost an enterprise a fortune in terms of investments in real estate, hardware, and operations. The big upfront costs can drastically slow down or completely halt a project due to the extent of approvals that may be required to materialize the project. With Cloud Computing, the enterprise is not bogged down by high upfront infrastructure costs, and has great flexibility and opportunities to implement new projects to serve the business.
- **Low Operational Costs:** Cloud Computing pricing model is "Utility" style. In other words, the consumer is billed only for the infrastructure and software that is used and the duration for which it is used, which translates into low operational costs.
- **Agile Business Model:** Enterprises can leverage the elasticity and scalability inherent in the Cloud to speed up business processing. For example, consider a compute- or data- intensive activity (that is conducive

to parallelization) that consumes 100 hours to process a job when running on a single server. In the Cloud environment, the same job can spawn hundred individual application instances running in parallel on 100 virtual servers and have the results aggregated in about an hour. The elasticity of the Cloud enables an enterprise to exploit the parallelization capability of applications and gain faster results in a shorter time frame leading to an agile and cost-effective business model (Armbrust, 2009). On the flip side, when the business volume decreases during some periods of the year, the enterprise can easily scale-down the infrastructure and avoid the wasteful expenditure of idling resources.

Based on these business benefits, it is not hard to envisage that enterprises will embrace the Cloud Computing model inevitably. Cloud Computing provides the enterprise with a massive pool of diverse computing resources such as powerful servers, networking gear, data storage, middleware, and varied applications and services, without capital expenditure. Enterprises that want to exploit the Cloud advantage should appropriately prepare themselves by embracing Service-driven architectural approaches in their organizations. The Cloud is primarily accessed through a service interface. Service protocols and standards are ingrained in the Cloud architecture. Potentially, the Cloud service catalog will grow rapidly with time, enabling enterprises to find services that they need from the readily available portfolio. There is also the option for enterprises to orchestrate new services from existing services available in the Cloud.

The Cloud can change the way enterprises think about data, collect data, and manage data. Cloud services are pervasive, thereby lending themselves to connecting across businesses, people, experiences, and time. This encourages enterprises to combine data with context information and increase relevancy of the data. The Cloud also shifts the burden of application integration from users to the providers, thus enabling consumers to interact with one composite application rather than having to interact with each of the individual applications or services in the workflow. For example, let's say a car manufacturer needs to trace parts and material flowing through an extended supply chain. If the enterprises in the supply chain can share information by publishing to the Cloud storage, and provision a Cloud application service (composite application) that can access this shared data to perform the required analytics and then supply results to the manufacturer, it will reduce the integration burden on individual organizations, and enable overall cost reduction for the solution.

While the Cloud will transform business capabilities and deliver a great deal of benefit to the businesses, moving from a centralized on-premises IT architecture to a public infrastructure can present new risks to the business. With the use of appropriate security standards and governance practices, it is possible to reduce the risk to the enterprise. Furthermore, since the infrastructure in the Cloud may not be owned by the enterprise, it is imperative to have detailed SLA (Service Level Agreements) in place before committing the business to the Cloud. The proliferation of Cloud Computing promises business agility and cost savings in technology infrastructure. However, mass adoption of Cloud Computing may depend greatly on the ability of the Cloud providers to address concerns such as Portability, Interoperability, and Security.

Cloud Deployment Models

NIST defines four deployment models for operating a Cloud infrastructure: public, private, community, and hybrid (NIST, 2011a).

- **Public Cloud:** A Public Cloud is owned by an organization that is in the business of selling Cloud Computing services, and serves a multitude of clients. The Cloud infrastructure and services are provided to the general public over a public network.
- **Private Cloud:** A Private Cloud is owned and managed by the consuming enterprise or by a third party, and is hosted on-premises in the enterprise. Access to the private Cloud is restricted from the general public.
- **Community Cloud:** Consumers that share concerns such as mission objectives, security, privacy and compliance policy, collaborate together to create a Community Cloud. It is very similar to Private Clouds, and is owned and managed by the group of participating enterprises or by a third party, and may be hosted on-premises in an enterprise, or outsourced to a hosting company. Community cloud consumers can access their local cloud resources as well as the resources of other participating enterprises.
- **Hybrid Cloud:** A Hybrid Cloud is composed of two or more clouds (on-premises private, on-premises community, off-premises private, off-premises community or public) that remain as distinct entities but are bound together by standardized or proprietary technology that enables data and application portability.

NIST also specifies a Cloud Computing Reference Architecture that defines five major actors as shown below. Each actor is an entity that participates in a transaction or process and/or performs tasks in Cloud Computing (NIST, 2011b).

- **Cloud Provider:** A person, organization, or entity responsible for making a service available to interested parties.
- **Cloud Consumer:** A person or organization that maintains a business relationship with, and uses services from a Cloud provider.

- **Cloud Carrier:** An intermediary that provides connectivity and transport of Cloud services from Cloud Providers to Cloud Consumers.
- **Cloud Auditor:** A party that can conduct independent assessment of Cloud services, information system operations, performance, and security of the Cloud implementation.
- **Cloud Broker:** An entity that manages the use, performance, and delivery of Cloud services, and negotiates relationships between Cloud Providers and Cloud Consumers.

A Cloud consumer may request Cloud services directly from a Cloud provider or via a Cloud broker. A Cloud auditor conducts independent audits and may contact the others to collect necessary information.

Technical Aspects of Cloud Computing

The Cloud Computing model exhibits significant characteristics. Enterprises that are considering moving to the Cloud should carefully examine the following technical aspects of Cloud Computing.

Virtual Machine as a Unit of Deployment

Virtualization creates a layer of abstraction between a virtual machine (VM) and the physical hardware such that software stacks can be deployed and redeployed on the VM without being tied to a specific physical server. This enables multiple VMs to run on the same physical machine. Virtual machines enable a dynamic datacenter where servers provide a pool of resources that can be harnessed as needed. By decoupling application deployment from server deployment, VMs facilitate rapid deployment and scaling of applications.

Virtual machine that is pre-configured to perform a specific task such as a Web server or a Database server is called a Virtual Appliance (VA). VA enhances the ability to create and deploy applications rapidly. VMs and VAs are the units of deployment in the Cloud. VMs are controlled by a *Hypervisor*, which is a specialized operating system that creates and manages the VMs. The hypervisor runs on a host machine and controls all the virtual machines (also called guest machines) that run on that host machine. The hypervisor presents a virtual operating platform to the guest machines and manages their execution.

The Cloud implements virtualization on a massive scale. The goal of virtualization is to potentially centralize administrative tasks while improving scalability and hardware-resource utilization.

Virtualization can facilitate migration (or transition) of virtual machines from one physical machine to another. SOA and Virtualization are a natural fit. The goal of SOA is to design services with increased flexibility and agility. Due to its very nature, SOA is capable of offering even greater flexibility by leveraging virtualization, whereby, each service can now be hosted individually in its own virtual server with one physical server supporting multiple services running in its own optimized virtual environment. Furthermore, virtualization provides the ability to transition services seamlessly from one physical server to another, allowing for fault-tolerance and failover in a controlled manner.

Service Delivery Over the Network

Cloud computing extends the existing Service-driven trend of making services available over the network. By using a well architected Internet-based service delivery model, applications in the Cloud can be made available anywhere and at any time.

Self-Service Provisioning and Pay-Per-Use Model

Cloud provides a *Self-service provisioning* infrastructure model where anyone with a credit card can purchase computing infrastructure and software for use, and a Web interface or API can be used to create VMs on demand and deploy applications on them as needed, without service provider intervention. Cloud providers don't require a long-term contract for services; they provide services on the basis of a pay-per-use model with minimal or no upfront costs and usage-based pricing that is dependent on the actual usage of resources. This model is similar to those used by utility and phone companies. Cloud providers typically use one of the following billing methods: fixed pricing (e.g. VM offered at a fixed monthly cost), and variable pricing by resource consumption or actual duration of use.

In the Cloud, the resources assigned to a certain virtual machine can be re-allocated by the VM hypervisor to allow other virtual machines to utilize the same resources based on the combined workload and configuration policies. This makes billing models based solely on allocation inadequate in the Cloud ecosystem. As a result, Cloud providers typically identify the smallest unit (atomic unit) of the billable items that will be available as a service to customers and use this atomic billable unit to drive data collection, billing, and reporting.

Multi-Tenancy

The ability for multiple customers (tenants) to share the same applications and/or computing resources without infringing upon each other is termed Multi-tenancy. It is through multi-tenant architectures that Cloud services achieve high cost efficiencies, economies of scale, and improved processing speeds. These cost benefits must be balanced with the need for individual tenants to secure their data and applications. In other words, a balance must be struck between sharing and security in multi-tenant architectures. In IaaS, tenants share infrastructure resources such as hardware and data storage. SaaS tenants share the same application (e.g. Salesforce.com), and hence the same database and tables.

The majority of security concerns in the virtualized infrastructure relate to the co-residency of virtual machines operated by different customers. Cloud providers try to alleviate this concern through VM segmentation and isolation using techniques such as VM introspection that inspects VMs to provide details about the resident applications and their configuration and facilitates the application of security policies dynamically based on this introspection. The extent of multi-tenancy is based on how much of the core application can be shared across tenants. The highest degree of multi-tenancy permits the database schema to be shared. On the other hand, in the lowest degree of multi-tenancy, only the IaaS and PaaS layers are shared, with dedicated SaaS layers for each tenant.

Elastic Scalability

While Scalability denotes the capacity to increase the nodes in a cluster of servers, elasticity represents the ability to dynamically increase or decrease the number of nodes in the cluster. The size of the data set, the level of parallelization, and the number of requests processed are all increased in the same proportion as the increase in the number of nodes in the cluster. In a perfectly scalable system, the average time needed to execute a request remains constant when all the parameters of the cluster grow linearly. *Elastic scalability* in the Cloud enables a cluster to dynamically expand or contract in size depending on the load in the system. The goal is to transparently scale out network or application services without the operational disruption that often occurs when scaling services up or down.

Service virtualization enables a service to be transparently scaled up or down with no negative impact to that service and to the dependent applications and services relied upon by that service. Service virtualization presents multiple instances of the service to appear as one resource and is necessary to achieve the desired level of transparency in dynamically scalable environments. Client services need to know only about the virtual service, which shields them from the volatility that may be occurring behind the scenes to ensure that demand is met with appropriate capacity.

High Availability

Availability of a system is generally measured as a ratio of the mean time between failure (MTBF) and the sum of mean time to repair (MTTR) and MTBF. Stated as an equation:

Availability A = MTBF/(MTBF+MTTR)

Therefore, system availability can be increased by either increasing the MTBF or reducing the MTTR.

Redundancy is often used as a general approach to increasing the availability of a system. The redundancy approach works well at all levels of a system, including redundancy in hardware, software, services, storage, and network. Redundant servers facilitate migration of resources and services from a failed server to a backup server by a process called *failover*. Stateless failover is the simplest approach where no application state is maintained between the failed server and the backup server. The alternative is stateful failover where the existing state of the service or application in the failed server is also transferred to the backup server. Stateful VM migration is implemented by most hypervisors to transparently migrate VMs in a continuous manner from the failed to the backup server to improve system availability in the Cloud.

Programmable Infrastructure

Traditionally, in an on-premises enterprise computing paradigm, architects design the server topology and application deployment model for deploying applications in a static infrastructure environment. In the Cloud, the enterprise IT can use the Cloud provider's Web API to map the application to a fleet of virtual machines, and rapidly scale the infrastructure as the application evolves to accommodate workload increases to the point where it might engage thousands of virtual machines to cater to a spike in demand. The ability to program infrastructure dynamically puts enormous power in the hands of the IT organization.

Service Composition

In the SOA paradigm, applications are composed by assembling and configuring different service components to realize a business process. The same concept applies to the Cloud where virtual appliances, hardware components, and software components are assembled and configured to compose infrastructure, platform, and software services that can be easily consumed.

Security

Cloud Computing environment requires new ways of thinking about security. Cloud services are consumed in a rather different manner than on-premises applications and infrastructure. Due to their platform specific nature, Cloud service providers typically do not distribute SDKs (Software Development Kits), instead they publish APIs that developers can leverage to access and control Cloud services, such as, IaaS, PaaS, SaaS, and BPaaS. Furthermore, Cloud service providers sell subscriptions and not licenses as is typically done in the on-premises environment. This leads to issues of data ownership and recovery that are unique to the Cloud service model.

In the public Cloud, the service provider is largely responsible for security of the service stack. For enterprises adopting Cloud services, this leads to limited visibility into the provider's security controls and also decreases the opportunity to deploy enterprise specific additional security mechanisms in the Cloud. Traditional enterprise security is based on single tenancy requirements and is characterized by control of devices, infrastructure, data, and processes within the enterprise firewalls. With Cloud, information and infrastructure resides outside the perimeter of the enterprise and is constantly evolving. Security controls must therefore be available on demand and requires a security policy framework that can be consistently applied to achieve isolations and trust zones in the presence of dynamic workloads.

Virtualization alters the relationship between the Operating System (OS) and the hardware. This challenges traditional security perspectives. A potential risk is the compromise of the VM hypervisor. At the scale of the Cloud, such a risk would have a drastic impact on the tenants. Another security concern with virtualization relates to allocating and de-allocating resources in the VM such as local storage. During the deployment and operation of a VM, data is written to the physical memory. If the data is not cleared before reallocating the memory resource to the next VM, there is a potential for data exposure.

In the spring of 2009, leading technology companies such as IBM, Cisco, SAP, and EMC, among others, announced the creation of an "Open Cloud Manifesto"[1] calling for more consistent security and monitoring of Cloud services. However, Amazon, Google, Salesforce.com, and Microsoft did not participate in the effort suggesting that broad industry consensus may not be imminent in the near future.

Lack of standards in Cloud security has led each Cloud service provider to furnish proprietary security methods. Meanwhile, industry groups such as Distributed Management Task Force (DMTF), the Open Cloud Consortium (OCC) and the Cloud Security Alliance (CSA) are working towards the standardization goal. The CSA has released a set of security standards specific to the Cloud referred to as the Cloud Controls Matrix (CCM), which is organized in thirteen domains and consists of about 100 controls and assessment guidelines that span a diverse range of best practices, for ensuring security in the Cloud. The CCM also includes several regulatory and compliance mandates, including PCI, HIPAA, ISO/IEC, NIST and COBIT. The CSA has also created the Security Trust and Assurance Registry (STAR) to enable customers to get insight on the security measures implemented by the various Cloud providers. Then there is the Storage Networking Industry Association working on security standardization related to Cloud storage. The CIO Council of the US federal government has also laid out guidance on Cloud security controls.

Emerging security patterns and practices such as information classification models, federated identities, and context–based authorization are attempting to address these security challenges. In the Cloud, security controls must be applied across the virtual infrastructure so that workloads are consistently protected as they are migrating over VMs. It is imperative to have security mechanisms to support dynamically constructed relationships between virtual resources such as virtual networks, virtual storage, and virtual machines.

Portability and Interoperability

Cloud consumers should have the flexibility to move their data and applications across multiple Cloud environments at low cost and with minimal disruption to their businesses. Furthermore, it should be possible to communicate between and among multiple Clouds with little effort and be able to use the same data and services across multiple Cloud providers with a unified management interface. Portability and Interoperability in the Cloud will enable users to take advantage of multiple providers without having to lock-in to a single vendor, thus facilitating effective risk and cost management.

Each Cloud service model may have different requirements for portability and interoperability. IaaS requires the ability to migrate and run applications on a new Cloud. This necessitates capturing virtual machine images (VMs) from the existing Cloud and migrating them to the other Cloud, which may be using different virtualization technologies. For SaaS, the focus is on data portability, and requires the ability to extract data and perform backups in a standard format.

Keahey et al. (2009) investigated the issues with developing interoperability standards and summarized the main goals of achieving interoperability between different IaaS providers as being machine-image compatibility, contextualization compatibility, and API-level compatibility. Image compatibility is an issue as there are multiple incompatible virtualization implementations such as the Xen, KVM, and VMWare hypervisors. When users want to move entire VMs between different IaaS providers, from a technical standpoint this can only work when both providers use the same form of virtualization. Contextualization compatibility problems exist because different IaaS providers use different methods of customizing the context of VMs, for example, setting the operating system's username and password for access after deployment is done in different ways. Finally, there are no widely agreed APIs between different IaaS providers that can be used to manage virtual infrastructures and access VMs.

For machine image or VM compatibility there is an ongoing attempt to create an open standard called the *Open Virtual Machine* Format (OVF). At the API-level for PaaS, "*AppScale13*," an open source effort to re-implement the interfaces of Google App Engine, is aiming to become a standard. For IaaS management, Amazon EC2's APIs are quickly becoming a de-facto standard, popularized through their open source re-implementation "*Eucalyptus.*"

Cloud Computing can benefit from standardized API interfaces as generic tools that manage Cloud infrastructures can be developed for all offerings. However, standardized interfaces alone do not prevent vendor lock-in. For an interoperable Cloud, there is a need for standardization in protocols and software artifacts to unlock more of the potential benefits from Cloud computing.

Governance

Guo et al. (2010) define governance in the Cloud as "the processes used to oversee and control the adoption and implementation of Cloud-based services in accordance with recognized policies, audit procedures and management policies." While Cloud Computing alleviates some IT responsibilities of the enterprise, governance isn't one of them. The highly abstracted, on-demand, and dynamic nature of Cloud-based services pose technical challenges in executing information governance. In the on-premises model, lax governance did not pose a significant risk to the enterprise since infrastructural and service components were still within the perimeters of the enterprise firewall.

However, Cloud Computing adds layers of abstraction and makes it tedious to track the dependencies across the distributed infrastructure. Understanding these dependencies is critical to ensuring the adherence to a broad range of business, regulatory, security, legal, and operational requirements. The goal of Cloud governance is to ensure that information is securely shared among authorized users and partners of the enterprise, that retention policy is adhered to, and that proper logs are maintained for auditing purposes.

Lack of a proper governance strategy when adopting the Cloud can leave enterprises with SaaS silos and Cloud islands, leading to poor data consistency and security. Due to the dynamic nature of the Cloud, traditional governance processes that require human intervention may not be work well in this agile environment. Effective governance in the Cloud may require automation to ensure that the right security levels and access policies are applied in a dynamic manner; that workloads are dispatched to the proper environments, and that data is protected and maintained in the correct jurisdiction, among others.

Cloud governance is more than policy and process definition and enforcement. It involves supporting business strategy and ensuring service value, service quality, and security. A comprehensive Cloud governance model should define processes and policies for service development, secure use of infrastructure, secure and effective consumption of services, and operational aspects; adjust existing organizational structure by way of refactoring roles and responsibilities to better support Cloud Computing; and introduce new tools and techniques to automate and implement successful governance of the Cloud ecosystem.

SOA Standards and the Cloud

In January of 2012, The Open Group, which is a global consortium of more than 400 member organizations with a mission to enable the achievement of business objectives through IT industry standards, announced the availability of two new industry standards that enable enterprises to effectively integrate fundamental elements of SOA and Cloud Computing into a solution or Enterprise Architecture, namely, SOA Reference Architecture (SOA RA), and the Service-Oriented Cloud Computing Infrastructure Framework (SOCCI) (The Open Group, 2012).

The Open Group SOA standards that are applicable to the Cloud include:

- The SOA Ontology which defines service and SOA concepts that can be used as a basis for describing Cloud Services, and extended using specific extension ontologies for the Cloud.
- The SOA Reference Architecture, a vendor neutral blueprint for creating and evaluat-

ing SOA Solutions which defines the functional and cross cutting concerns for SOA and the Cloud.
- The SOA Governance Framework that defines a governance reference model that can also be applied to the design, development, and operation of Cloud Services. The SOA governance best practices can be extended to the Cloud ecosystem.
- The Service Integration Maturity Model that determines the level of service use in an organization. The "virtualized and dynamically reconfigurable" maturity level applies to Cloud services.
- Security for Cloud and SOA, a joint workgroup between SOA and Cloud Workgroups in "The Open Group," defines security considerations for both Cloud and SOA.
- Service-Oriented Cloud Computing Infrastructure Framework describes the concepts and architectural building blocks necessary for infrastructures to support SOA and Cloud initiatives.

Cloud Reference Architecture

NIST published a Cloud Reference Architecture in September 2011. As shown in the reference architecture in Figure 2, a Cloud provider uses a layered approach to provide services. The upper most layer is the *Service* layer. The Service layer defines the interfaces that consumers can use to access Cloud services. Three service models are provided in this layer – the IaaS, the PaaS, and the SaaS. SaaS applications can be built on top of PaaS components and PaaS components can be built on top of IaaS components. This stacking dependency is not necessary, and each of the service components can stand by itself. For example, a SaaS application can be implemented and hosted on virtual machines from an IaaS Cloud or it can be implemented directly on top of Cloud resources without using IaaS virtual machines.

Figure 2. Cloud reference architecture (referenced from NIST Cloud Computing Reference Architecture, Special Publication 500-292, Sept. 2011)

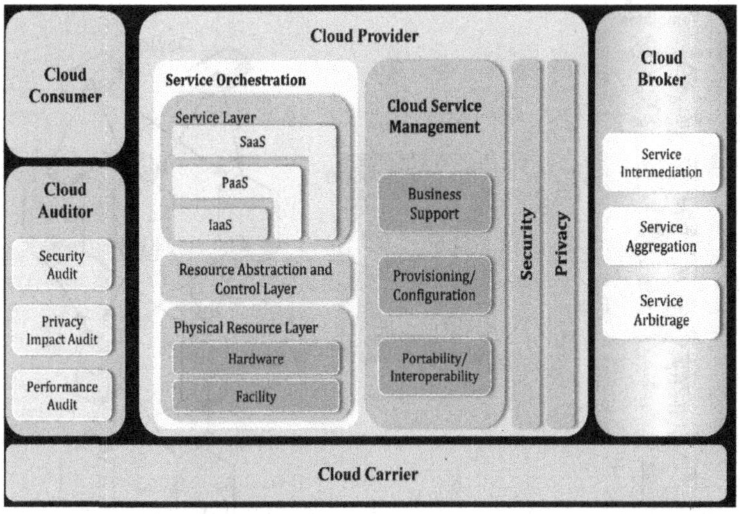

The middle layer in the reference model is the *Resource Abstraction and Control* layer. This layer contains the system components that Cloud Providers use to provide and manage access to the physical computing resources through software abstraction. Examples of resource abstraction components include software elements such as hypervisors, virtual machines, virtual data storage, and other computing resource abstractions. The resource abstraction ensures efficient, secure, and reliable usage of the underlying physical resources. The control aspect of this layer refers to the software components that are responsible for resource allocation, access control, and usage monitoring. This is the software fabric that ties together the numerous underlying physical resources and their software abstractions to enable resource pooling, dynamic allocation, and measured service.

The lowest layer in the stack is the *Physical Resource* layer, which includes all the physical computing resources. This layer includes hardware resources, such as computers (CPU and memory), networks (routers, firewalls, switches, network links and interfaces), storage components (hard disks) and other physical computing infrastructure

elements. It also includes facility resources, such as heating, ventilation and air conditioning (HVAC), power, communications, and other aspects of the physical plant.

The Cloud Service Provider (CSP) interface provides access to the logical endpoints of the service catalog, service manager, and the security manager. These endpoints provide the means to interact with service entities (such as VMs, networks, storage, and applications).

Consider an example for how a deployer in a Cloud consuming enterprise would provision and deploy a simple three-tier Web application into the Cloud as shown in Figure 3. The following steps are involved:

1. From a library of pre-configured virtual machine images, the deployer selects one or more Load Balancers, Web Servers, Application Servers, and Database Server appliances taking into account the redundancy requirements.

2. Next, the deployer configures each appliance to make a custom VM image. The Load Balancer is configured to serve the Web servers in a round-robin manner. The

Figure 3. Example cloud deployment process

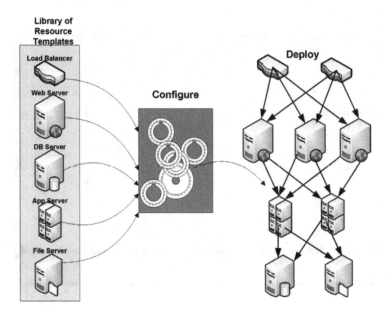

Web Server is populated with static content by uploading content to the storage Cloud. The Application Server appliance is configured for the required resources such as data sources, message queues, etc., and the Database Server appliances are populated with data required by the application. All of these operations are managed through the Cloud provider APIs.

3. Then, the deployer layers custom application code into the new virtual infrastructure using the Cloud APIs to access and deploy to the virtual machines.

4. Finally, the deployer chooses a deployment template to specify the deployment topology. Based on the template selected, the Cloud deployment manager service grabs the configured VM images for each layer and performs the necessary plumbing to tie them together in the Cloud by automatically handling networking, security, and scalability requirements.

ARCHITECTING APPLICATION SERVICES FOR THE CLOUD

The Cloud is designed to provide conceptually infinite scalability and on-demand elasticity. To leverage the capabilities of the Cloud, it is imperative to architect application services that can take advantage of the dynamic nature of the Cloud.

As part of developing architecture for the Cloud applications, the first step for the enterprise is to define a Cloud architecture strategy that details the business goals and expectations from the Cloud and scopes out the service and deployment models for migrating applications to the Cloud. Once a strategy is concretized, the next step is to start planning for the Cloud migration initiative. This is followed by application architecture, business process architecture, data architecture, integration architecture, and security architecture that leverages the virtualization, scalability, and elasticity of the Cloud. Finally, the enterprise Cloud Governance policies and mechanisms have to be defined and implemented.

Best practices and guidelines for architecting application services for the Cloud are presented below.

Leverage Scalability and Elasticity

Enterprises are challenged to meet stringent SLA requirements for their users even under peak load conditions by providing high assurance in terms of Quality of Service (QoS) metrics such as response times, high throughput, and service availability. Resource allocation that is planned on the basis of the average load can lead to cost-effectiveness when the load is at expected levels, however, with peak load, performance issues occur. Not meeting the SLA can discourage customers and impact revenue for the enterprise. On the other hand, if resource allocation is planned based on the peak workload, resources may remain idle most of the time and not be cost-effective. The on-demand and elastic nature of the Cloud enables the infrastructure to be closely aligned with the actual demand, thereby increasing overall utilization and leading to reduced cost. Elasticity is the ability to scale computing resources up or down with minimal effort. Cloud application services have to be architected to internalize the concept of elasticity so as to leverage the scalability of the Cloud and gain maximum benefit.

A scalable application service exhibits several characteristics:

- Provides a proportionally better performance by increasing the computing resources that are available to it.
- Are resilient, i.e. they can handle variability in allocated resources.
- Can run in a heterogeneous environment.

Traditionally, applications and services were built for fixed and pre-provisioned infrastructure. Enterprises have never had the need to provision servers on a regular basis. As a result, most software architectures do not address the dynamic infrastructure model of rapid deployment or reduction of hardware. There needs to be a change in the mindset when dealing with the Cloud, where application architects can take advantage of the vast scale and rapid resource provisioning capabilities, both in terms of scaling up when more resources are required and scaling down when the load on the application has reduced.

By leveraging elasticity in the application architecture, one can take advantage of the dynamic scaling capability of the Cloud. For example, consider an energy utility company that processes millions of transactions during the daytime but only a few hundred thousand during the night from 11 pm till 4 am the next morning. Infrastructure that was used to run the daytime volume will be idling during most of the night. With an application that leverages the elasticity in the Cloud, the enterprise can reduce the cost of operating resources by dynamically scaling up the computing power and storage allocated during the daytime, and scaling down the resources during the night; and thereby expect the application to perform optimally during both peak and off-peak situations.

When migrating application services to the Cloud, it is important to realize that there may be a mismatch in resources between the on-premises environment and the Cloud, and it may be necessary to map the current on-premises system specifications to those available in the Cloud. It is certainly possible that the virtual machine (VM) in the Cloud may not match the exact specification of the resources that one needs to operate the application. For example, consider that the Cloud VM has only 4GB of RAM allocated to it while the on-premises application server provisioned 8GB of RAM for the application. Similarly, let's say that the virtual database instance in the Cloud is specified to handle a smaller number of insertions per second compared to the on-premises database.

As we know, the Cloud provides abstract resources that can be dynamically provisioned to accommodate application demand. Therefore, even though the individual server VM or the database instance VM may not provide the required resources or performance specification, one can request for and provision additional VMs as needed to satisfy the requirement. For example, consider that the Cloud VM did not provide the required amount of RAM as stated earlier, and that the enterprise needed to provision additional VMs – 2 VMs with 4GB of memory in each, to match the on-premises configuration of 8GB.

The Cloud is architected to facilitate this scenario through the use of distributed data cache/data grid across multiple servers to maintain the integrity and availability of data for the resident applications running across multiple servers. Therefore, by ensuring that the application is scalable, it can be distributed across multiple servers, thereby, mitigating the issue of resource availability on individual VMs.

Similarly, if the application is database insert intensive and needs better performance with data insertions into the database, it can benefit from *Sharding*, a distributed data partitioning mechanism that involves horizontal partitioning of the database across multiple database instances. With a partitioned database topology in the Cloud, data insert-intensive application instances can be appropriately provisioned to take advantage of the data partitions for a given processing range of data. Thus, applications can be appropriately designed and provisioned to accommodate for virtual resource and performance limitations in the Cloud.

There are several use cases for leveraging elasticity in applications. If scaling requirement is pre-determined to be periodic and happens at fixed intervals such as daily, weekly, or monthly, then *proactive cyclic scaling* is the appropriate elastic strategy. The other use case is based on scheduled events where scaling needs to take place when there is a surge in transactions due to scheduled business events. This is the *proactive events-based elastic strategy*. The third strategy is *auto-scaling* that is purely based on workload demand and is implemented by monitoring the workload and generating triggers to automatically scale the infrastructure up or down based on demand.

Auto-scaling enables dynamic allocation and de-allocation of hardware resources in the Cloud. Auto-scaling mechanisms can also detect VM instance failures and launch replacement instances. VM images of application software can be kept preloaded in additional VMs (i.e. as a virtual appliance) so that these appliances can be provisioned very quickly through auto-scaling, when required. A typical issue with this automatic allocation scheme is the possibility of *thrashing* that can be caused by frequent variation of workload, leading to VMs being added and released on every sample, causing significant overhead. A desirable solution would require the ability to accurately predict the future workload on the system and allocate or deallocate resources a priori, so that the application can be ready to handle the load increase or decrease when it actually occurs.

Leverage Fault Tolerance

The Cloud is architected for reliability and fault-tolerance. The dynamic and elastic scalability of the Cloud enables replication of VMs, automatic detection of VM failures and launch of replacement instances in the case of failure. The VM hypervisor enables VM failover through stateful and continuous migration of VMs (live-migration). VM check-pointing establishes periodic recovery points to enable restarting/resuming a VM from the last checkpoint, and distributed messaging queues enable guaranteed delivery of messages among applications. The in-memory distributed data cache/grid that facilitates redundant storage of data objects across the cluster, handles data integrity during VM or server failures. The use of clustered databases enables data integrity, scalability, and reliability of data. Enterprises can leverage the inherent fault-tolerance capabilities in the Cloud without having to handle the complexities of fault-tolerance in their applications.

Leverage Loose Coupling

Another SOA design principle that is very much applicable to the Cloud is the principle of "Loose Coupling." Components and services in SOA are designed to be loosely coupled through the interface (service contract) to minimize the side-effects caused by modifications and implementation changes to related components/services, and thereby consequently improving the maintainability of software. The same principle is applicable to the Cloud where virtualization is the norm. Virtualized IaaS, PaaS, SaaS, and BPaaS services enable loose coupling by presenting a generic interface for interaction. The actual implementation of that interface happens and evolves at runtime without affecting the participants. Loose coupling among components and services enables to isolate the various layers of the application such that the changes in one layer do not cause side-effects on other layers.

Leverage Parallelization

Traditionally, writing parallel application code required highly trained developers with the ability to program complex job coordination and concurrency. Parallel systems were developed as unique solutions to solve specific problems. The complexity involved in developing parallel code inhibited the broad adoption of massively parallel processing. MapReduce (Dean & Ghemawat, 2004), a framework pioneered by Google, overcome many of these issues by abstracting the details and giving developers control over parallelism without having to deal with the underlying execution semantics of the code.

MapReduce provides a programming model and an associated implementation for processing and generating large data sets. It involves specification of a "mapping" function that maps a key/value pair to a set of intermediate key/value pairs, and a "reduce" function that merges all intermediate values associated with the same intermediate key. Many real world tasks are expressible in this model. Programs written in this functional style are automatically parallelized and executed on a large cluster of commodity machines. The run-time system handles the partitioning of the input data, scheduling the program's execution across a set of machines, handling machine failures, and managing the required inter-machine communication.

Cloud application architects should internalize the concept of parallelization when designing application services for the Cloud. The Cloud makes parallelization effortless due to its ability to replicate resources through dynamic scaling. Application services can be designed to leverage parallelism for all data processing activities such as when requesting or persisting data, processing data, and executing applications in the Cloud. The Cloud is designed to handle massively parallel operations. Applications can perform parallel processing by spawning up slave worker nodes to process tasks in parallel. This is easily done in the Cloud by provisioning the slave nodes through a few API calls.

Leverage Cloud API for Coherency in Service Management

Integrating Cloud services with the current enterprise environment can lead to the issue of coherency in management and operations. The typical approach is to implement service management systems for each service domain within the Cloud; in an enterprise view, this "silo-ed" management only adds complexity. Consider that Cloud federation approach to services requires multiple sources of integration, such as service request integration (i.e. integration of internal system provisioning with IaaS resources), service management integration (i.e. integration of monitoring, authentication, authorization, etc) and service runtime integration (i.e. integration of data across internal and Cloud systems). Cloud providers can provision APIs that can perform all these required integration functions, such as, provisioning services, managing services, monitoring services, and securing services in a coherent manner across the different service domains.

Reduce Data Latency

It is imperative to plan data residency when dealing with the Cloud in terms of whether to keep the data on-site or in the Cloud. It is generally a good practice to store data in close proximity to the computing resources from the point of view of data latency. However, this may not always be possible or practical. Distributed data caches and In-memory data grids such as IBM eXtremeScale, Oracle Coherence, Gigaspaces' XAP elastic cache, Hazelcast, VMware Gemfire, etc., can alleviate the data residency issue by distributing data across the cluster of servers and making it available closer to where it is needed for processing.

Data residency is important in the Cloud environment due to the internet latencies involved when shuffling data back and forth between the Cloud and the enterprise data center. Furthermore, Cloud charges are generally based on bandwidth in and out of the Cloud, making it cheaper to house data in the Cloud. If processing happens in the Cloud, and a large quantity of data resides outside the Cloud, it makes economic sense to house that data in the Cloud and perform parallel queries against that dataset to improve query response times, rather than store that data on-site. Similarly, if data is generated in the Cloud, then it makes sense to deploy the applications that consume that data in the Cloud to take advantage of the in-cloud free data transfer and lower latencies. Conversely, if the data is static, such as, images, video, audio, etc., then it might be better to cache that static data closer to the end user thereby lowering the transfer bandwidth.

Establish Access Security

Security is a shared responsibility in the Cloud. In traditional IT, one organization has control over the entire stack of computing resources and the entire life-cycle of the systems. The Cloud paradigm shifts the "control" aspect to a collaborative model. Cloud providers and consumers have differing degrees of control over the computing resources in a Cloud system. They design, build, deploy, and operate Cloud-based systems in a collaborative manner. Security is now a shared responsibility. Appropriate security controls have to be put in place for the supported service models by the concerned parties. Security should be implemented in every layer of the Cloud application architecture. Physical security is typically handled by the Cloud provider. However, network and application-level security is generally the responsibility of the enterprise. For example, deploying and maintaining the Security Account Management System is typically the responsibility of the Cloud provider, whereas, setting up the authentication and authorization credentials for the applications deployed in the Cloud environment is generally the responsibility of the consuming enterprise.

One of the issues hampering the broad adoption of Cloud Computing in the enterprise is identity management. Most IT organizations rely on *Microsoft Active Directory* for managing identities in their enterprise. In the Cloud, identity management typically requires a federated approach for exchanging identity information securely between partners and providing access control and authorization seamlessly across applications and services that may be using different identity management frameworks. There are challenges that must be solved by enterprises in any federated application environment. Organizations have to provide single sign-on (SSO) to applications and services across disparate security domains without having to manage partner users in terms of provisioning and un-provisioning their identities in the enterprise directory over time. A trust mechanism must exist in order to allow users authenticated in one domain to be trusted in a second domain.

The Cloud consumers' establish their identity to the Cloud and receive appropriate credentials, such as a session identity token. An identity token may also be obtained through an external identity provider that has a trust relationship with the Cloud service provider. Authenticated users are allowed to access the Cloud infrastructure and applications and partner applications through the federation of security credentials. It is the Cloud provider's responsibility to ensure that all security credentials, personal information, and personally identifiable information are properly protected in the Cloud.

Popular identity federation products are Microsoft's Active Directory Federation Services (ADFS) 2.0, IBM's Tivoli Federated Identity Manager (TIM), Oracle's Identity Federation, RSA Adaptive Federation, etc. Many Cloud vendors support federation standards such as Security Assertion Markup Language (SAML). Federation enables interoperability through well-established standards and facilitates enterprise partners to share less information about the user and still achieve authentication and authorization of the user on the other domain.

Security Policies and constraints (as in SOA) can play a major role in the management of security in the Cloud. A number of different security policies relating to access control, authorization control, encryption, traffic filtering to detect and prevent intrusions, etc., can be applied to offerings in the service catalog to control and manage the security in the Cloud realm.

Protect Data in Transit

Data needs to move from the Cloud to the enterprise and vice versa. If exchange of sensitive and confidential information takes place between the browser in the enterprise and the server in the Cloud, it would be prudent to configure SSL on the server instance using certificates. The public key included in the certificate authenticates the server to the browser and serves as the basis for creating the shared session key used to encrypt the data in both directions. SOA typically uses WS-Security standards for authentication, encryption, and data integrity to maintain end-to-end security

of data in web services, which can be applied to secure SaaS services in the Cloud. There is also the possibility of provisioning a Virtual Private Cloud which will provide logically isolated resources within the Cloud, and connect those resources directly to the enterprise datacenter using industry standard encrypted IPSec VPN connections, thus protecting data in transit.

Protect Data at Rest

Data at rest is as equally important to protect, if not more, as the data in transit. It is a good practice to encrypt sensitive and confidential data that is stored in the Cloud using either the built-in encryption facilities or by using standard encryption tools such as PGP. In this case, the application service needs to be designed to decrypt data before processing the retrieved encrypted data. However, it is a challenge to manage the keys used for encrypting the data at rest. On the one hand, if the encryption keys are lost, one may lose the ability to access that data. On the other hand, if the keys are compromised, the data may be at risk. It is necessary to have a sound tooling strategy for key management.

Plan for Disaster Proofing

Besides securing the integrity and privacy of data, a Cloud application architect will also have to consider the means to protect the data from disasters by backing up periodic snapshots of data in the Cloud storage. Furthermore, it is necessary to have a plan to update VM patches regularly and develop automated security check scripts that can be run periodically.

Establish New Tasks for Administrators

In the Cloud ecosystem, the tasks of the system administrators shift from the routine installation and configuration of hardware and software systems in the enterprise data center to managing resources in the Cloud through scripting and Web interfaces. Administrators can use the Cloud Service API to implement automated and repeatable deployment processes for launching and bootstrapping VMs. VM bootstraps are generally parameterized by server role (i.e. app server, db server, slave server, etc.) enabling the VM to allocate appropriate resources and configure itself based on its role during launch.

The database administrator would also experience a shift in the tasks from routine database instance administration to implementing horizontal partitioning (Sharding), query parallelization, asynchronous replication etc., using a combination of Web API and scripts.

Prepare for a Hybrid Model

Enterprises may consider *Hybrid Cloud* models wherein some applications or services run on-premises while others use the Cloud for additional computing power and storage. This enables the enterprise to use the current infrastructure (on-premises traditional datacenter or private cloud) for normal load and overflow excess workload to the Cloud with minimal effort and cost, dynamically, as and when needed. This model may provide the best of both worlds.

EMERGING TRENDS

Today, Cloud providers offer their infrastructure as isolated platforms, which make it difficult for consumers to switch between providers without significant additional costs. In order to reach a large customer base, providers must host environments that are highly adaptable and offer interoperability and portability. Clouds need to be open on as many levels as possible to achieve economies of scale in terms of users, devices, and applications, without being commoditized. Cloud Providers generally try to address as many use cases as possible in a generic solution without offering the performance

and capabilities needed for specific consumers. Moreover, for business processes and services spanning multiple providers, a simple Cloud provisioning model is insufficient. It is expected that in the future, the Cloud paradigm will extend substantially to hybrid and cross-provider models spanning federated Clouds. These are mostly academic and research topics at this time but are moving towards commercialization.

Currently, it is neither easy for an existing application to make use of the Cloud capabilities, nor is it straightforward to develop new applications that fully exploit the Cloud features. The reason being that the current programming languages do not natively support the scalability, elasticity, and parallelization features of the Cloud. This necessitates the use of specialized frameworks such as MapReduce to take advantage of the replication and parallelization features of the Cloud. Extensions to existing programming languages have to be developed to natively address the aspects of distribution, parallelization, and replication that cater to horizontal and vertical scaling of applications.

Security in the Cloud is typically achieved through access control and encryption of data and exchanges. However, data is decrypted before being processed by the Cloud applications, and therefore data will be always accessible to the Cloud provider, irrespective of the encryption. Distrust of data security in the Cloud is one of the most important reasons that enterprises are hesitant to dive into the Cloud. In the future, data encryption modes that support remote computing without decryption, using complex techniques such as homomorphic encryption, will be used to provide for high levels of data security. This should encourage enterprises to take a serious look at the Cloud for even their most sensitive applications.

New applications must be enabled to manage and adapt themselves autonomically on a large scale. Mobile devices and "Internet of Things" (IOT) are invading the planet at a fast pace. Providing availability of Cloud solutions on mobile systems will lead to increased communication and data traffic that can exceed the current physical connection and processing limitations, and make the current network management methodologies inadequate. In order to support future usage scenarios, the autonomic management systems of these mobile devices and IOT need to evolve from using a static dedicated resource management model to a dynamic resource management model, where heterogeneous resources will be discovered, and dynamically attached to and detached from. One approach being considered is to extend the Cloud service offering model to provide network connectivity as a service, i.e., Network as a Service (NaaS). In that case, the network must become as elastic as the Cloud, and provide for the requested quality of service in terms of bandwidth and latency, as required by the application or the consumer. Software-defined Networks (SDN) may prove to be a valuable concept in this context as it will enable developers and architects to define the data flow across the routed network.

The day when applications will cease to be aware of physical hardware is not too far off. Applications will continue to function even if the underlying physical hardware fails or is removed or replaced. Applications will adapt themselves to fluctuating demand patterns by deploying resources instantaneously and automatically, thereby achieving highest utilization levels at all times. In the future, scalability, security, high availability, bandwidth, latency, fault-tolerance, and elasticity will be configurable properties of the application architecture and will be an automated and intrinsic part of the platform on which they are built.

Today, you can build applications in the Cloud with some of these qualities by following the guidelines highlighted in this chapter. Best practices in Cloud Computing architectures will continue to evolve as researchers focus on enhancing the Cloud and building tools, technologies, and processes that make it easier for developers and architects to develop and deploy applications to the Cloud that leverages the full capability of the Cloud.

CONCLUSION

The Cloud is the future in IT Computing. It not only provides almost infinite elasticity, flexibility, and scalability to application services, but also offers significant cost benefits to the business from an IT infrastructure perspective and the ability to connect with customers, partners, and suppliers, like never before. However, without a well designed Service Oriented Architecture in place, enterprises will find it difficult to reach the Cloud.

Service-driven approaches are an essential foundation for emerging technologies like the Cloud.

The Cloud will enable real-time delivery of products, services, and solutions over the Internet. It will become essential to businesses because of its capability to deal with rapid change in external markets. Therefore, it is vital that business and technology leaders begin considering how they will operate in a Cloud environment. To meet this challenge, IT leaders must take a fresh approach to their IT architecture, moving away from static, internal, monolithic, and centralized architecture. Adopting a service-driven architectural approach will enable IT leaders to address today's critical challenges, while at the same time, provide for a solid foundation for the enterprise to adopt Cloud for tomorrow.

REFERENCES

Amrhein, D. (2011). *What's the big deal about cloud APIs?* Retrieved from http://cloudcomputing.sys-con.com/node/1842790

Armbrust, M., Fox, A., Griffith, R., Joseph, A. D., Katz, R., Konwinski, A., et al. (2009). *Above the clouds: A Berkeley view of cloud computing.* Retrieved from http://www.eecs.berkeley.edu/Pubs/TechRpts/2009/EECS-2009-28.pdf

Dean, J., & Ghemawat, S. (2004). MapReduce: Simplified data processing on large clusters. Paper presented at *OSDI'04: Sixth Symposium on Operating System Design and Implementation,* San Francisco, CA.

Foster, I., & Kesselman, C. (1998). *The grid: Blueprint for a new computing infrastructure.* Morgan Kaufmann.

Grossman, R. L. (2009). The case for cloud computing. *IT Professional, 11*(2), 23–27. doi:10.1109/MITP.2009.40.

Guo, Z., Song, M., & Song, J. (2010). *A governance model for cloud computing.* Paper presented at the Management and Service Science (MASS).

IBM. (2010). *IBM MI and IPR definition bridge between Gartner and IDC, August 19.*

Keahey, K., Tsugawa, M., Matsunaga, A., & Fortes, J. (2009). Sky computing. *Internet Computing, IEEE, 13*(5), 43–51. doi:10.1109/MIC.2009.94.

Linthicum, D. (2012). *Define and design cloud APIs, step by step.* Retrieved from http://www.javaworld.com/javaworld/jw-06-2012/120612--how-to-define-a-cloud-api.html

Liu, H. (2012). *Cloud computing, distributed system, research results.* Retrieved from http://huanliu.wordpress.com/2012/03/13/amazon-data-center-size/

McCarthy, J. (1983). *Reminiscences on the history of time sharing.* Retrieved from http://www-formal.stanford.edu/jmc/history/timesharing/timesharing.html

NIST. (2011a). The NIST definition of cloud computing. *NIST Special Publication 800-145.*

NIST. (2011b). The NIST cloud computing reference architecture. *NIST Special Publication 500-292.*

Opencloudmanifesto.org. (2013). *Website.* Retrieved from www.opencloudmanifesto.org

Phipps, S. (2009). What's the *New York Times* doing with Hadoop? *InfoWorld.* Retrieved from http://www.infoworld.com/d/open-source/whats-the-new-york-times-doing-hadoop-392

Sarmenta, L. F. G. (2001). *Volunteer computing.* (Ph.D. thesis). MIT. Retrieved from http://www.cag.lcs.mit.edu/bayanihan/

Smith, M. A., & Kumar, R. L. (2004). A theory of application service provider use from a client perspective. *Journal of Information and Management.*

KEY TERMS AND DEFINITIONS

Auto-Scaling: The act of scaling computing resources up or down automatically depending on the computing workload through monitoring and triggering mechanisms.

Cloud Computing: A computing model where dynamically scalable, virtualized resources, are provided as a service over the Internet. Cloud computing makes it possible for enterprises to access and create applications on virtual servers that scale dynamically to meet demand.

Elasticity: The power to scale computing resources up or down with minimal effort.

Loose Coupling: The mechanism of building components and services without requiring tight dependencies on each other is termed Loose Coupling. Loose coupling among components and services will facilitate to isolate the various layers of the application such that the changes in one layer does not cause side-effects on other layers.

Multi-Tenancy: A sharing model that enables multiple customers to share many of the same resources without infringing upon each other. Multi-tenancy in the Cloud distributes the cost and enables economies of scale.

Scalability: The ability to adjust computing resources dynamically based on demand is called Scalability. Scalability can be implemented horizontally across servers or vertically on each server.

Self-Service Provisioning: The act of being able to dynamically provision computing resources through an user interface without having to request the provider directly to provision the required resources.

Utility Computing: A computing model where computing power and software is used and paid for by renting from a third party on an as needed basis, just like one would pay to the utility provider for consuming electrical power based on usage. This model is also known as a pay-per-use model.

Virtualization: An abstraction that enables software stacks to be deployed and redeployed without being tied to a specific physical server. Virtualization enables a dynamic datacenter where servers provide a pool of resources that can be harnessed as needed.

ENDNOTES

[1]   See opencloudmanifesto.org. (2013).

Compilation of References

Abi Haidar, D., Cuppens-Boulahia, N., Cuppens, F., & Debar, H. (2006). An extended RBAC profile of XACML. In *Proceedings of the 3rd ACM workshop on Secure web services* (pp. 13-22). ACM.

Adi, A., Botzer, D., Nechushtai, G., & Sharon, G. (2006). Complex event processing for financial services. In *Proceedings of the IEEE Services Computing Workshops*.

Agarwal, V., Chafle, G., Dasgupta, K., Karnik, N., Kumar, A., Mittal, S., & Srivastava, B. (2005). Synthy: A system for end to end composition of web services. *Journal of Web Semantics*, *3*, 311–339. doi:10.1016/j.websem.2005.09.002.

Al Mosawi, A., Zhao, L., & Macaulay, L. (2006). A model driven architecture for enterprise application. In *Proceedings of the 39th Hawaii International Conference on System Science.*

Ali, M. S., & Reiff-Marganiec, S. (2012). Autonomous failure-handling mechanism for WF long running transactions. In *Proceedings of SCC 2012.*IEEE.

Allcock, B., Chervenak, A., Foster, I., Kesselman, C., & Livny, M. (2005). Data grid tools: Enabling science on big distributed data.[Institute of Physics Publishing]. *Journal of Physics: Conference Series*, *16*, 571–575. doi:10.1088/1742-6596/16/1/079.

Alonso, G., Casati, F., Kuno, H., & Machiraju, V. (2004). *Web services: Concepts, architectures and applications.* Berlin, Heidelberg: Springer-Verlag.

Alshahwan, F., Moessner, K., & Carrez, F. (2010). Evaluation of distributed SOAP and REST mobile web services. *International Journal on Advances in Networks and Services*, *3*(3&4), 447–461.

Amjad, U. (2004). *Mobile computing and wireless communications.* NGE Solutions, Inc..

Amrhein, D. (2011). *What's the big deal about cloud APIs?* Retrieved from http://cloudcomputing.sys-con.com/node/1842790

Amrhein, D., & Quint, S. (2009). *Cloud computing for the enterprise: Part 1: Capturing the cloud.* IBM Websphere Developer Technical Journal.

Anderson, C. (2006). *The long tail: Why the future of business is selling less of more.* Hyperion Books.

Andrews, G. (1991). Paradigms for process interaction in distributed programs. *ACM Computing Surveys*, *23*(1), 49–90. doi:10.1145/103162.103164.

Armbrust, M., Fox, A., Griffith, R., Joseph, A. D., Katz, R., Konwinski, A., et al. (2009). *Above the clouds: A Berkeley view of cloud computing.* Retrieved from http://www.eecs.berkeley.edu/Pubs/TechRpts/2009/EECS-2009-28.pdf

Arsanjani, A., Ghosh, S., Allam, A., Abdollah, T., Ganapathy, S., & Holley, K. (2008). SOMA - A method for developing service-oriented solutions. *IBM Systems Journal*, *47*, 377–396. doi:10.1147/sj.473.0377.

Avizienis, A. (1985). The n-version approach to fault-tolerant software. *IEEE Transactions on Software Engineering SE*, *11*(12), 1491–1501. doi:10.1109/TSE.1985.231893.

Babcock, C. (2011). *6 lessons learned from FedEx private cloud.* InformationWeek.

Baggio, A. (1998). System support for transparency and network-aware adaptation in mobile environments. In *Proceedings of ACM Symposium on Applied Computing,* Feb. 27th – March 1.

Baker, M. (Ed.). (2001). Cluster computing white paper. Retrieved from http://arxiv.org/ftp/cs/papers/0004/0004014.pdf

Barker, S. (2009). The next 700 access control models or a unifying meta-model? In *Proceedings of the Symposium on Access control Models and Technologies* (pp. 187-196). ACM.

Barker, S., Sergot, M. J., & Wijesekera, D. (2008). Status-based access control. *ACM Transactions on Information and System Security*, *12*(1). doi:10.1145/1410234.1410235.

Basin, D., Doser, J., & Lodderstedt, T. (2006). Model driven security: From UML models to access control infrastructures. *ACM Transactions on Software Engineering and Methodology*, *15*, 39–91. doi:10.1145/1125808.1125810.

Bass, L., Clements, P., & Kazman, R. (2001). *Evaluating software architecture: Methods and case studies*. Upper Saddle River, NJ: Addison-Wesley Professional.

Bauer, T. (2009). Substitution rules for task performers in process-oriented applications.[in German]. *Datenbank-Spektrum*, *9*(31), 40–51.

Belalem, G., & Meroufel, B. (2011). Management and placement of replicas in a hierarchical data grid. *International Journal of Distributed and Parallel Systems (IJDPS)*, *2*(6), 23–30. doi:10.5121/ijdps.2011.2603.

Bellavista, P., Corradi, A., & Stefanelli, C. (2001). Mobile agent middleware for mobile computing. *IEEE Computer*, March Issue, 73-81.

Bellavista, P., Corradi, A., Fanelli, M., & Foschini, L. (2012). A survey of context data distribution for mobile ubiquitous systems. *ACM Computing Surveys*, *45*(1).

Bell, M. (2008). *Introduction to service-oriented modeling*. Wiley & Sons.

Benslimane, D., Dustdar, S., & Sheth, A. (2008). Services mashups: The new generation of Web applications. *IEEE Internet Computing*, *12*(5), 13–15. doi:10.1109/MIC.2008.110.

Bhiri, S., Perrin, O., & Godart, C. (2006). Extending workflow patterns with transactional dependencies to define reliable composite Web services. In *Proceedings of AICT-ICIW '06* (pp. *145*). IEEE.

Bhiri, S., Godart, C., & Perrin, O. (2006). Transactional patterns for reliable web services compositions. *Proceedings of ACM, ICWE06*, 137–144.

Bhiri, S., Perrin, O., & Godart, C. (2005). Ensuring required failure atomicity of composite Web services. *Proceedings of ACM, WWW05*, 138–147.

Biron, P., & Malhotra, A. (2004). XML schema part 2: Datatypes second edition. *W3C recommendation*. Retrieved from http://www.w3.org/TR/xmlschema-2/

Biske, T. (2008). *SOA governance*. Packt Publishing.

Bodenstaff, L., Wombacher, A., Reichert, M., & Jaeger, M. C. (2008). Monitoring dependencies for SLAs: The MoDe4SLA approach. In *Proceedings of the IEEE 5th International Conference on Services Computing (SCC 2008)*, Honolulu, Hawaii, USA (pp. 21-29). IEEE Computer Society Press.

Borg, A. (2011). *Mobility becomes core IT*. Retrieved from http://event.on24.com/event/29/75/81/rt/1/documents/slidepdf/mobile_latest_march_28.pdf

Brewer, E. (2004). Towards robust distributed systems. Retrieved from http://www.cs.berkeley.edu/~brewer/cs262b-2004/PODC-keynote.pdf

Brown, L. (2000). *Integration models: Templates for business transformation*. USA: SAMS Publishing.

Brown, P. C. (2007). *Succeeding with SOA: Realizing business value through total architecture*. Addison-Wesley Professional.

Brown, W. A., Laird, R. G., Gee, C., & Mitra, T. (2008). *SOA governance: Achieving and sustaining business and IT agility*. IBM Press.

Bruni, R., Melgratti, H., & Montanari, U. (2005). Theoretical foundations for compensations in flow composition languages. In POPL (pp. 209–220). ACM.

Buchwald, S. (2012). *Increasing consistency and flexibility of process-oriented applications by service-orientation*. (PhD thesis). University of Ulm, Germany (in German).

Buchwald, S., Bauer, T., & Reichert, M. (2012). Bridging the gap between business process models and service composition specifications. In Lee, et al. (Eds.), *Service life cycle tools and technologies: Methods, trends, and advances* (pp. 124–153). IGI Global.

Buscemi, M. G., Ferrari, L., Moiso, C., & Montanari, U. (2007). Constraint-based policy negotiation and enforcement for telco services. In TASE 2007 (pp. 463-472).

Butler, M., & Ripon, S. (2005). Executable semantics for compensating CSP. *Formal Techniques for Computer Systems and Business Processes*, 243-256.

Butler, M., Hoare, T., & Ferreira, C. (2005). A trace semantics for long-running transactions. *Communicating Sequential Processes, The First 25 Years*, 707-711.

Buyya, R. (Ed.). (1999). *High performance cluster computing: Architectures and systems (Vol. 1)*. Prentice Hall.

Cabral, L., & Domingue, J. (2005). Mediation of semantic web services in irs-iii. In *Workshop on Mediation in Semantic Web Services (MEDIATE)*, ICSOC (pp. 1–16).

Canalys. (2012). *Smart phones overtake client PCs in 2011*. Retrieved from http://www.canalys.com/newsroom/smart-phones-overtake-client-pcs-2011

Carman, M., Serafini, L., & Traverso, P. (2003). Web service composition as planning. In *Workshop on Planning for Web Services, ICAPS,* Trento, Italy.

Carminati, B., Ferrari, E., & Hung, P. (2006). Security conscious web service composition. In *Proceedings of the International Conference on Web Services* (pp. 489-496). IEEE Computer Society.

Carter, R. (2012). *Enterprise mobility management 2012. The SoMoCloTM Edge*. Aberdeen Group.

Casado, R., Tuya, J., & Younas, M. (2012). Testing the reliability of web services transactions in cooperative applications. *ACM,* 743-748.

Chae, H., Jung, J., Lee, J. H., & Lee, K. H. (2012). An efficient access control based on role attributes in service oriented environments. *In Proceedings of the 6th International Conference on Ubiquitous Information Management and Communication* (pp. 73-80). ACM.

Chandras, R. (2011). 10 tenets of enterprise data management. *InformationWeek Software*. Retrieved from www.informationweek.com/software/information-management/10-tenets-of-enterprise-data-management/229203011

Chappell, D. (2004). *Enterprise service bus: Theory in practice*. O'Reilly Media.

Chen, H. M. (2008). Towards service engineering: Service orientation and business-IT alignment. In *Proceedings of the 41st Hawaii International Conference on System Sciences*. IEEE Computer Society.

Chervenak, A., Foster, I., Kesselman, C., Salisbury, C., & Tuecke, S. (2001). The data grid: Towards an architecture for the distributed management and analysis of large scientific datasets. *Journal of Network and Computer Applications, 23*, 187–200. doi:10.1006/jnca.2000.0110.

Chin, R. S., & Chanson, S. T. (1991). Distributed object-based programming systems. *ACM Computing Surveys, 23*(1), 91–124. doi:10.1145/103162.103165.

Choi, H., Dawson, T., & La Porta, T. (2010). Network integration in 3G and 4G wireless networks. In *Proceedings of 19th International Conference on Computer Communications and Networks (ICCCN)* (pp. 1-8).

Chollet, S., & Lalanda, P. (2008). Security specification at process level. *In Proceedings of the IEEE Service Computing Conference* (pp. 165-172). IEEE Computer Society.

Chrysanthis, P. K., & Ramamritham, K. (1990). ACTA: A framework for specifying and reasoning about transaction structure and behavior. *ACM,* 194-203.

CIO CSG. (2008). How to avoid the hidden pitfalls on the road to SOA: The case for a comprehensive data services framework. *CIO 2 CIO Perspectives*. Retrieved from www.ncr-bdpa.org/whitepapers/SOA_InformaticaWP.pdf

Clarkin, L., & Holmes, J. (2012). *Enterprise mashups*. Retrieved from http://msdn.microsoft.com/en-us/architecture/bb906060.aspx

Compuware. (2012). *Mobile monitoring webpage*. Retrieved from http://www.compuware.com/application-performance-management/mobile.html

Corbin, K. (2012). Government moves toward cloud computing 'Perfect Storm'. *CIO*. Retrieved from www.cio.com/article/700337/Government_Moves_Toward_Cloud_Computing_Perfect_Storm

Cost, R., Finin, T., Joshi, A., Yun, P., Nicholas, C., Soboroff, I., & Chen, H., · , Tolia, S. (2002). ITTalks: A case study in the semantic web and daml+oil. *IEEE Intelligent Systems, 17*(1), 40–47. doi:10.1109/5254.988447.

Dadam, P., & Reichert, M. (2009). The ADEPT project: A decade of research and development for robust and flexible process support - Challenges and achievements. *Computer Science - Research for Development, 23*(2), 81–97. Springer.

Damiani, M. L., Bertino, E., Catania, B., & Perlasca, P. (2007). GEO-RBAC: A spatially aware RBAC. *ACM Transactions on Information and System Security, 10*(1), 29–37. doi:10.1145/1210263.1210265.

Dami, S., Estublier, J., & Amiour, M. (1998). APEL: A graphical yet executable formalism for process modeling. *Automated Software Engineering, 5*(1), 61–96. doi:10.1023/A:1008658325298.

Data Center Knowledge. (2011). *Fedex opens Colorado Springs data center.* Retrieved from http://www.datacenterknowledge.com/archives/2011/02/17/fedex-opens-colorado-springs-data-center/

Dayal, U., Hsu, M., & Ladin, R. (1990). Organizing long-running activities with triggers and transactions. *Proceedings of SIGMOD, 90*, 204–214. doi:10.1145/93605.98730.

De Florio, V. (2009). *Application-layer fault-tolerance protocols.* IGI Global. doi:10.4018/978-1-60566-182-7.

de Vadoss, J., Lascelles, F., Rischbeck, T., Wilhelmsen, H., Plunkett, T., & Little, M. et al. (2013). *Service-oriented infrastructure: On-premise and in the cloud.* Upper Saddle River, NJ: Prentice Hall.

Dean, J., & Ghemawat, S. (2004). MapReduce: Simplified data processing on large clusters. Paper presented at *OSDI'04: Sixth Symposium on Operating System Design and Implementation,* San Francisco, CA.

Deeg, M. (2007). SOA starts far beyond BPEL – Service-oriented business process modeling as basis for a SOA. *OBJEKTspektrum - Onlineausgabe* (in German).

Deepak, G., & Pradeep, B. S. (2012). Challenging issues and limitation of mobile computing. *International Journal of Computer Technology & Applications, 3*(1), 177–181.

Diab, H. B., & Zomaya, A. Y. (Eds.). (2005). *Dependable computing systems: Paradigms, performance issues, and applications. Wiley Series on Parallel and Distributed Computing.* Wiley-Interscience.

Díaz, L., & Ekman, U. (2011). Introduction to mobile ubiquity in public and private spaces. *Digital Creativity, 22*(3), 127–133. doi:10.1080/14626268.2011.606819.

Dinh, H. T., Lee, C., Niyato, D., & Wand, P. (2011). *A survey of mobile cloud computing: Architecture, applications, and approaches. Wireless Communications and Mobile Computing.* Wiley.

Dobson, G. (2006). Using WS-BPEL to implement software fault tolerance for web services. In *Proceedings of the 32nd EUROMICRO Conference on Software Engineering and Advanced Applications, IEEE Computer Society* (pp. 126-133).

Dreibelbis, A., Hechler, E., Milman, I., Oberhofer, M., Run, P., & Wolfson, D. (2008). *Enterprise data management: An SOA approach to managing core information.* IBM Press.

Drucker, P. (1957). *Landmarks of tomorrow.* New York: Harper & Row.

Dubrova, E. (2002). *Fault tolerant design: An introduction.* Kluwer Academic Publishers.

Duke, S., Makey, P., & Kiras, N. (1999). *Application integration management guide: Strategies and technologies.* Hull, UK: Butler Group Limited.

Dwivedi, H., Clark, C., & Thiel, D. (2010). *Mobile application security.* McGraw-Hill.

Eclipse.org. (2013). *Website.* Retrieved from http://www.eclipse.org/modeling/m2t/?project=jet

Elmagarid, A. K. (1992). *Transaction models for advanced database applications.* Morgan Kaufmann.

Enderle, R. (2009). *Early modeling of process aspects relevant for process execution at a business level – Process modeling in a SOA.* (Master thesis). University of Ulm (in German).

Engels, G., Hess, A., Humm, B., Juwig, O., Lohmann, M., Richter, J. P., et al. (2008). A method for engineering a true service-oriented architecture. In *Proceedings of the 10th International Conference on Enterprise Information Systems,* Barcelona (pp. 272-281).

Engels, G., Hess, A., Humm, B., Juwig, O., Lohmann, M., & Richter, J. P. et al. (2008). *Quasar enterprise: Service-oriented design of applications landscapes.* Dpunkt-Verlag.

Erl, T. (2012). *Increased vendor diversification options.* Retrieved July 1, 2012, from http://www.whatissoa.com/increased_vendor_diversification_options.php

Erl, T., & Roy, S. (2008). *SOA patterns.* Retrieved from http://www.soapatterns.org

Erl, T., Karmakar, A., Roy, S., Little, M., Rischbeck, T., & Simon, A. (2008). *SOA patterns.* Retrieved from http://www.soapatterns.org

Erl, T., Little, M., Rischbeck, T., & Simon, A. (2008). *SOA patterns.* Retrieved from http://www.soapatterns.org

Erl, T. (2005). *Service-oriented architecture: Concepts, technology, and design.* Prentice Hall.

Erl, T. (2007). *SOA principles of service design.* Prentice Hall.

Erl, T. (2008). *SOA design patterns.* Upper Saddle River, NJ: Prentice Hall.

Erradi, A., Maheshwari, P., & Tosic, V. (2006). Recovery policies for enhancing web services reliability. In *Proceedings of the IEEE international Conference on Web Services (ICWS'06), IEEE Computer Society* (pp. 189-196).

Esposito, D. (2012). *Architecting mobile solutions for the enterprise.* Microsoft Press.

Farrel, J., & Lauser, H. (2007). Semantic annotations for WSDL and XML schema. *W3C recommendation.* Retrieved from http://www.w3.org/TR/sawsdl/

FedEx Mobile. (2011). *Website.* Retrieved from http://www.fedex.com/us/mobile/index.html?location=desktop

Fielding, R. T. (2000). *Architectural styles and the design of network-based software architectures.* (PhD Dissertation). Retrieved from http://www.ics.uci.edu/~fielding/pubs/dissertation/top.htm

Firtman, M. (2010). *Programming the mobile web.* O'Reilly.

Flinn, J., & Satyanarayanan, M. (1999). Energy-aware adaptation for mobile applications. In SOSP-17 Kiawah Island, SC, December.

Forman, G.H., & Zahorjan, J. (1994). The challenges of mobile computing. *IEEE Computer*, April Issue, 38-47.

Forum, L. T. E. (2011). *Website.* Retrieved from http://lteworld.org/blog/lte-advanced-evolution-lte

Foster, I., & Kesselman, C. (1998). *The grid: Blueprint for a new computing infrastructure.* Morgan Kaufmann.

Fox, A., et al. (1996). Adapting to network and client variability via on-demand dynamic distillation. In *Proceedings of 7th Internet Conference on Architectural Support for Programming Languages and Operating Systems (ASPLOSVII)* (pp. 160–170).

Fuggetta, A., Picco, G. P., & Vigna, G. (1998). Understanding code mobility. *IEEE Transactions on Software Engineering*, 24(5), 342–361. doi:10.1109/32.685258.

Gaaloul, W., Bhiri, S., & Rouached, M. (2010). Event-based design and runtime verification of composite service transactional behavior. *Transactions on Services Computing (IEEE)*, 3(1), 32–45. doi:10.1109/TSC.2010.1.

Gafni, R. (2008). Framework for quality metrics in mobile-wireless information systems. *Interdisciplinary Journal of Information, Knowledge, and Management*, 3, 23–38.

Gamma, E., Helm, R., Johnson, R., & Vlissides, J. (1994). *Design patterns: Elements of reusable object-oriented software.* Addison-Wesley Professional Computing Series.

Gao, J., & Ji, A. (2010). *Building an intelligent mobile advertising system. The International Journal of Mobile Computing and Multimedia Communications (IJMCMC).* January Issue.

Gao, J., Shim, S., Mei, H., & Su, X. (2006). *Engineering wireless-based software systems.* Artech House Publisher.

Garcia-Molina, H., & Salem, K. (1987). SAGAS. In *ACM International Conference on Management of Data (SIGMOD)* (pp. 249-259).

Garofalakis, J., Stefani, A., Stefanis, V., & Xenos, M. (2007). Quality attributes of consumer-based m-commerce systems. In *Proceedings of the 2007 ICETE-B Conference,* Barcelona, Spain, 28–31 July (pp. 130–136)

Gartner, Inc. (n.d.). *IT glossary: Big data.* Retrieved from http://www.gartner.com/it-glossary/big-data/

Gartner, Inc. (n.d.). *IT glossary: Business process management (BPM)*. Retrieved from http://www.gartner.com/it-glossary/business-process-management-bpm/

Gartner, Inc. (n.d.). *IT glossary: Cloud computing*. Retrieved from http://www.gartner.com/it-glossary/cloud-computing/

Gartner, Inc. (n.d.). *IT glossary: EDA (Event-Driven Architecture)*. Retrieved from http://www.gartner.com/it-glossary/eda-event-driven-architecture/

Gartner, Inc. (n.d.). *IT glossary: Master data management (MDM)*. Retrieved from http://www.gartner.com/it-glossary/master-data-management-mdm/

Gartner, Inc. (n.d.). *IT glossary: Service-oriented architecture (SOA)*. Retrieved from http://www.gartner.com/it-glossary/service-oriented-architecture-soa/

Gartner, Inc. (n.d.). *IT glossary: Virtualization*. Retrieved from http://www.gartner.com/it-glossary/virtualization/

Gartner. (2012). Gartner identifies the top 10 strategic technologies for 2012. *Gartner Report*. Retrieved from http://www.gartner.com/it/page.jsp?id=1826214

Georgakopoulos, D., & Papazoglou, M. P. (2008). *Service-oriented computing*. The MIT Press.

Gkoulalas-Divanis, A., Kalnis, P., & Verykios, V. S. (2010). Providing K-Anonymity in location based services. *Science of Knowledge Discovery and Data Mining Exploration. Newsletter, 12*(1), 3–10.

Gorton, S., & Reiff-Marganiec, S. (2006). Towards a task-oriented, policy-driven business requirements specification for web services. Business Process Management, volume 4102 of LNCS, 465-470. Springer.

Gorton, S., Montangero, C., Reiff-Marganiec, S., & Semini, L. (2009). StPowla: SOA, policies and workflows. In ICSOC 2007 Workshops, LNCS 4907 (pp. 351-362). Springer.

Gottfredson, M., Puryear, R., & Phillips, S. (2005). Strategic sourcing: From periphery to core. *Harvard Business Review*, R0502J. PMID:15724581.

Gottlob, G., Gradel, E., & Veith, H. (2000). Linear time datalog and branching time logic. In *Logic-Based Artificial Intelligence* (pp. 443–467). Kluwer Academic Publishers. doi:10.1007/978-1-4615-1567-8_19.

Gray, J. (1981). The transaction concept: Virtues and limitations. In *Proceedings of the 7th International Conference on Very Large Databases* (pp. 144–154). Tandem Computers.

Gray, J., & Reuter, A. (1993). *Distributed transaction processing: Concepts and techniques*. Morgan Kaufmann.

Griffen, J. (2005). Get your data management house to enable service-oriented architecture. *Information Management*. Retrieved from www.information-management.com/issues/20050901/1035565-1.html

Grossman, R. L. (2009). The case for cloud computing. *IT Professional, 11*(2), 23–27. doi:10.1109/MITP.2009.40.

Guo, Z., Song, M., & Song, J. (2010). *A governance model for cloud computing*. Paper presented at the Management and Service Science (MASS).

Gupta, A. K. (2008). Challenges of mobile computing. In *Proceedings of 2nd National Conference on Challenges & Opportunities in Information Technology, March 29* (pp. 86-90).

Hackmann, G., Haitjema, M., Gill, C., & Roman, G. C. (2006). Sliver: A BPEL workflow process execution engine for mobile devices. In *Proceedings of 4th International Conference on Service Oriented Computing (ICSOC)*.

Halpern, J. Y., & Weissman, V. (2003). Using first-order logic to reason about policies. In *Proceedings of the Computer Security Foundations Workshop (CSFW'03)* (pp. 187-201). IEEE.

Hapner, M., Burridge, R., Sharma, R., Fialli, J., & Haase, K. (2002). *Java messaging service API tutorial and reference*. Addison-Wesley.

Havey, M. (2005). *Essential business process modeling*. O'Reilly.

Heifetz, R. A. (2009). *The practice of adaptive leadership: Tools and tactics for changing your organization and the world*. Harvard Business Press.

Hengartner, U., & Steenkiste, P. (2006). Avoiding privacy violations caused by context-sensitive services. In *Proceedings of 4th IEEE international conference on pervasive computing and communications* (pp. 222-231). IEEE Computer Society.

Hinchcliffe, D. (2011). Enabling collaboration with open APIs. Retrieved from http://www.zdnet.com/blog/hinchcliffe/enabling-collaboration-with-open-apis/1594

Hirsch, F., Kemp, J., & Llkka, J. (2006). *Mobile web services architecture and implementation*. Wiley. doi:10.1002/9780470017982.

Hoare, C. A. R. (1978). Communicating sequential processes. *Communications of the ACM, 21*(8), 666–677. doi:10.1145/359576.359585.

Hohpe, G., & Woolf, B. (2004). *Enterprise integration patterns: Designing, building, and deploying messaging solutions*. Addison-Wesley.

Hong, T. D., Chonho, L., Dusit, N., & Ping, W. (2011). *A survey of mobile cloud computing: Architecture, applications, and approaches. Wireless Communications and Mobile Computing*. Wiley.

Horwitz, B. (2011). Cisco, GE combine location-aware technology to track patients, equipment. *eWeek*. Retrieved from http://www.eweek.com/c/a/Health-Care-IT/Cisco-GE-Combine-LocationAware-Technology-to-Track-Patients-Equipment-569466/

Hoyer, V., Stanoesvka-Slabeva, K., Janner, T., & Schroth, C. (2008). Enterprise mashups: Design principles towards the long tail of user needs. Retrieved from www.alexandria.unisg.ch/export/DL/Volker_Hoyer/45602.pdf

Hung, P. C. K., & Zheng, Y. (2007). Privacy access control model for aggregated e-health services. In *Proceedings of the IEEE Enterprise Distributed Object Computing Conference* (pp. 12-19). IEEE Computer Society.

Hwang, K., Fox, G. C., & Dongarra, J. J. (2012). *Distributed and cloud computing: From parallel processing to the internet of things*. Elsevier.

IBM. (2007). *WebSphere service registry and repository handbook*. IBM Redbook.

IBM. (2010). *IBM MI and IPR definition bridge between Gartner and IDC, August 19*.

IDC. (2012). *Nearly 1 billion smart connected devices shipped in 2011 with shipments expected to double by 2016*. Retrieved from http://www.idc.com/getdoc.jsp?containerId=prUS23398412

IEEE. (n.d.). *IEEE 802.11. IEEE 802.11 Standards*. Retrieved from http://www.ieee802.org/11/

IEEE. (n.d.). *IEEE 802.16*. Retrieved from http://standards.ieee.org/findstds/standard/802.16e-2005.html

Inbar, D. (2008). Data governance for SOA success. *ebizQ: The insider's guide to BPM*. Retrieved from http://www.ebizq.net/topics/soa_security/features/10560.html

Information Week. (2011). *FedEx CIO Rob Carter: Dominant design*. Retrieved from http://www.informationweek.com/video/1178266432001

Information Week. (2012). *Report 2012 on state of mobile security*. Retrieved from http://reports.informationweek.com/abstract/21/8792/security/research-2012-state-of-mobile-security.html

Jajodia, S., & Yu, T. (2007). Basic security concepts. In *Secure data management in decentralized systems* (pp. 3–20). Springer-Verlag. doi:10.1007/978-0-387-27696-0_1.

Jammes, F., Mensch, A., & Smit, H. (2005). Service-oriented device communications using the devices profile for web services. In *MPAC'05 Proceedings of the 3rd international workshop on Middleware for pervasive and ad-hoc computing* (pp. 1-8). ACM.

Jboss.org. (2013). *Website*. Retrieved from http://www.jboss.org/drools/

Johnson, B. W. (1989). *Design and analysis of fault tolerant digital systems*. Boston, MA, USA: Addison-Wesley Series in Electrical and Computer Engineering.

Kakousisa, K., Paspallisa, N., & Angelos, G. (2010). A survey of software adaptation in mobile and ubiquitous computing. *Enterprise Information Systems, 4*(4).

Kaltz, J. W., Ziegler, J., & Lohmann, S. (2005). Context-aware web engineering: Modeling and applications. *Revue d'Intelligence Artificielle, 19*(3), 439–458. doi:10.3166/ria.19.439-458.

Karmakar, A. (2008). *SOA patterns*. Retrieved from http://www.soapatterns.org

Kass, D. H. (2012). CIOs warming (and moving) to cloud technology. *CIO*. Retrieved from www.cio.com/article/710090/CIOs_Warming_and_Moving_to_Cloud_Technology

Keahey, K., Tsugawa, M., Matsunaga, A., & Fortes, J. (2009). Sky computing. *Internet Computing, IEEE, 13*(5), 43–51. doi:10.1109/MIC.2009.94.

Keeney, J., Cahill, V., & Haahr, M. (2007). *Techniques for dynamic adaptation of mobile services, handbook of mobile middleware* (Bellavista, P., Ed.).

Khalaf, R., & Leymann, F. (2003). On web services aggregation. TES, LNCS 2819, 1-13. Berlin: Springer-Verlag.

Kiepuszewski, B., ter Hofstede, A., & Bussler, C. (2000). On structured workflow modeling. In *Proceedings of the International Conference on Advanced Information Systems Eng. (CAiSE),* volume 1789 (pp. 431–445).

Kim, W., Choi, I., Gala, S. K., & Scheevel, M. (1993). On resolving schematic heterogeneity in multidatabase systems. *Distributed and Parallel Databases.* doi:10.1007/BF01263333.

Kleyman, B. (2012). Understanding cloud APIs and why they matter. Retrieved from http://www.datacenterknowledge.com/archives/2012/10/16/understanding-cloud-integration-a-look-at-apis/

Koenig, A. (2005). Patterns and anti-patterns. *Journal of Object-Oriented Programming,* Vol. 8.

Kokash, N., & Arbab, F. (2011). Formal design and verification of long-running transactions with eclipse coordination tools. *Transactions on Services Computing, 2011*(99), 1–1.

Kolb, J., Hübner, P., & Reichert, M. (2012). Automatically generating and updating user interface components in process-aware information systems. In *Proceedings of the 20th International Conference on Cooperative Information Systems (CoopIS'12)*, Rome, Italy, LNCS 7565. Springer.

Krafzig, D., Banke, K., & Slama, D. (2004). *Enterprise SOA: Service-oriented architecture best practices.* Upper Saddle River, NJ: Prentice Hall.

Kundra, V. (2011). *Federal cloud computing strategy.* Retrieved July 1, 2012, from http://www.cio.gov/documents/federal-cloud-computing-strategy.pdf

Kunze, C. P., Zaplata, S., Turjalei, M., & Lamersdorf, W. (2008). Enabling context-based cooperation: A generic context model and management system. In *11th International Conference on Business Information Systems (BIS 2008)* (pp. 459–470). Springer.

Kunze, M. (2009). *Business process mashups: An analysis of mashups and their value proposition for business process management.* (Master's Thesis). Retrieved from http://bpt.hpi.uni-potsdam.de/pub/Public/MatthiasKunze/matthias_kunze.masters_thesis.pdf

Künzle, V., & Reichert, M. (2009). Integrating users in object-aware process management systems: Issues and challenges. In *Proceedings of the BPM'09 Workshops, 5th International Workshop on Business Process Design (BPD'09)*, LNBIP 43 (pp. 29-41). Springer.

Künzle, V., & Reichert, M. (2011). PHILharmonicFlows: Towards a framework for object-aware process management. *Journal of Software Maintenance and Evolution: Research and Practice, 23*(4), 205–244. Wiley. doi:10.1002/smr.524.

Künzle, V., Weber, B., & Reichert, M. (2011). Object-aware business processes: Fundamental requirements and their support in existing approaches. *International Journal of Information System Modeling and Design (IJISMD), 2*(2), 19–46. doi:10.4018/jismd.2011040102.

Lam, W., & Shankararaman, V. (2004). An enterprise integration methodology. *IT Professional,* Issue March/April Issue, 40-48.

Lam, W., & Shankararaman, V. (2007). *Enterprise architecture and integration: Methods, implementation and technologies.* USA: IGI Global. doi:10.4018/978-1-59140-887-1.

Lanz, A., Weber, B., & Reichert, M. (2010). Workflow time patterns for process-aware information systems. In *Proceedings of the Enterprise, Business-Process, and Information Systems Modelling: 11th International Workshop BPMDS and 15th International Conference EMMSAD at CAiSE'10*, Hammamet, Tunisia, LNBIP 50 (pp. 94-107). Springer.

Lanz, A., Weber, B., & Reichert, M. (2013). *Time patterns for process-aware information systems. Requirements Engineering Journal.* Springer.

Leitner, P., Rosenberg, F., & Dustdar, S. (2009). Daios: Efficient dynamic web service invocation. *IEEE Internet Computing*, *13*, 72–80. doi:10.1109/MIC.2009.57.

Lerner, B. S., Christov, S., Osterweil, L. J., Bendraou, R., Kannengiesser, U., & Wise, A. (2010). Exception handling patterns for process modeling. *IEEE Transactions on Software Engineering*, *183*, 162–183. doi:10.1109/TSE.2010.1.

Leu, D., Bastani, F., & Leiss, E. (1990). The effect of statically and dynamically replicated components on system reliability. *IEEE Transactions on Reliability*, *39*(2), 209–216. doi:10.1109/24.55884.

Lewis, P. M., Bernstein, A., & Kifer, M. (2001). *Database and transaction processing*. Addison Wesley.

Li, X., Madnick, S., Zhu, H., & Fan, Y. (2009). Reconciling semantic heterogeneity in web services composition. In *International Conference on Information Systems (ICIS)*.

Linthicum, D. (2009). *The integration challenges of cloud computing*. Retrieved from http://www.infoworld.com/d/cloud-computing/integration-challenges-cloud-computing-157

Linthicum, D. (2010). Determining the business value of Web APIs. Retrieved from http://www.bickgroup.com/uploads/documents/determining_the_business_value_of_web_apis.pdf

Linthicum, D. (2010). *Moving to the next generation of data integration*. Retrieved from http://www.dataintegrationblog.com/data-integration-david-linthicum/moving-to-the-next-generation-of-data-integration/

Linthicum, D. (2012). Define and design cloud APIs, step by step. Retrieved from http://www.javaworld.com/javaworld/jw-06-2012/120612--how-to-define-a-cloud-api.html

Linthicum, D. (1999). *Enterprise application integration*. Massachusetts, USA: Addison-Wesley.

Little, M., Rischbeck, T., & Simon, A. (2008). *SOA patterns*. Retrieved from http://www.soapatterns.org

Litwin, W., & Abdellatif, A. (1986). Multi-database interoperability. *IEEE Computer*, *19*(12), 10–18. doi:10.1109/MC.1986.1663123.

Liu, A., Li, Q., & Xiao, M. (2007). A declarative approach to enhancing the reliability of BPEL processes. In *Proceedings of the IEEE international Conference on Web Services (ICWS'07), IEEE Computer Society* (pp. 272-279).

Liu, H. (2012). *Cloud computing, distributed system, research results*. Retrieved from http://huanliu.wordpress.com/2012/03/13/amazon-data-center-size/

Logica. (2012). *The Internet of things*. Retrieved from http://www.logica.com/we-do/internet-of-things/related-media/brochures/2012/the-internet-of-things/

Lorenzo, G. D., Hacid, H., Paik, H., & Benatallah, B. (2009). Data integration in mashups. *SIGMOD Record*, *38*(1), 59–66. Retrieved from http://www.sigmod.org/publications/sigmod-record/0903/p59.surveys.hacid.pdf doi:10.1145/1558334.1558343.

Loshin, D. (2010). *Data governance, data architecture, and metadata essentials*. Retrieved from http://www.sybase.com/files/White_Papers/Sybase_Data_architecture_and_data_governance_WP.pdf

Luckham, D. (2002). *The power of events*. Addison Wesley.

Maheshwari, P., & Pang, M. (2005). *Benchmarking message-oriented middleware: TIB/RV versus SonicMQ. In the Journal of Concurrency and Computation: Practice & Experience - Foundations of Middleware Technologies, 17(12), 1507-1526*. Chichester, UK: John Wiley and Sons Ltd..

Maheswari, P. (2003). Enterprise application integration using a component based architecture. In *Proceedings of the 27th Annual International Computer Software and Applications Conference* (pp. 557-562).

Mandel, L. (2008). *Describe REST web services with WSDL 2.0*. Retrieved from http://www.ibm.com/developerworks/webservices/library/ws-restwsdl/#describerestservice

McCarthy, J. (1983). *Reminiscences on the history of time sharing*. Retrieved from http://www-formal.stanford.edu/jmc/history/timesharing/timesharing.html

McGovern, J., Ambler, S., Stevens, M., Linn, J., Sharan, V., & Jo, E. (2003). *A practical guide to enterprise architecture*. Upper Saddle River, NJ: Prentice Hall.

McKendrick, J. (2010). *SOA strengthens master data management, which returns the favor.* Retrieved from www.zdnet.com/blog/service-oriented/soa-strengthens-master-data-management-which-returns-the-favor/4443

Mehrotra, S., Rastogi, R., Silberschatz, A., & Korth, H. F. (1992). A transaction model for multi-database systems. In *Proceedings of the 12th International Conference on Distributed Computing Systems (ICDCS)* (pp. 56–63). IEEE.

Mell, P., & Grance, T. (2009). The NIST definition of cloud computing. *NIST, Version 15.*

Mikalsen, T., Tai, S., & Ravellou, I. (2002). Transactional attitudes: Reliable composition of autonomous Web services. In *Workshop on Dependable Middleware Based Systems (WDMS),* Washington, DC, USA.

Miller, G. A. (1995). WordNet: A lexical database for English. *Communications of the ACM, 38*(11), 39–41. doi:10.1145/219717.219748.

Mohan, C., & Lindsay, B. (1985). Efficient commit protocols for the tree of processes model of distributed transactions. *ACM SIGOPS Operating Systems Review, 19*(2), 40–52. doi:10.1145/850770.850772.

Moller, T., & Schuldt, H. (2010). OSIRIS next: Flexible semantic failure handling for composite web service execution. *Proceedings of IEEE, ICSC10,* 212–217.

Montangero, C., Reiff-Marganiec, S., & Semini, L. (2011). *Model-driven development of adaptable service-oriented business processes. Rigorous software engineering for service-oriented systems, LNCS (Vol. 6582).* Springer.

Moss, J. E. B. (1982). *Nested transactions and reliable distributed computing.* Cambridge, MA, USA: The MIT Press.

Mrissa, M., Ghedira, C., Benslimane, D., Maamar, Z., Rosenberg, F., & Dustdar, S. (2007). Context-based mediation approach to compose semantic web services. *ACM Transactions on Internet Technology, 8.*

Müller, R., Greiner, U., & Rahm, E. (2004). Agentwork: A workflow system supporting rule-based workflow adaptation. *Data & Knowledge Engineering, 51,* 223–256. doi:10.1016/j.datak.2004.03.010.

Mutschler, B., Reichert, M., & Bumiller, J. (2008). Unleashing the effectiveness of process-oriented information systems: Problem analysis, critical success factors, and implications. *IEEE Transactions on Systems, Man, and Cybernetics, 38*(3), 280–291. doi:10.1109/TSMCC.2008.919197.

Nagarajan, M., Verma, K., Sheth, A. P., & Miller, J. A. (2007). Ontology driven data mediation in web services. *International Journal of Web Services Research (JWSR), 4*(4), 104–126. doi:10.4018/jwsr.2007100105.

Nahrstedt, K., Xu, D., Wichadakul, D., & Li, B. (2001). QoS-aware middleware for ubiquitous and heterogeneous environments. *IEEE Communications Magazine,* (November Issue), 2–10.

Newcomer, E., & Lomow, G. (2004). *Understanding SOA with web services.* Addison-Wesley Professional.

NIST. (2011). The NIST definition of cloud computing. *NIST Special Publication 800-145.*

NIST. (2011). The NIST cloud computing reference architecture. *NIST Special Publication 500-292.*

Nitzsche, J., & Norton, B. (2009). Ontology-based data mediation in BPEL (for semantic web services). Business Process Management Workshops, volume 17 of Lecture Notes in Business Information Processing (pp. 523–534). Springer.

Nitzsche, J., Lessen, T. V., Karastoyanova, D., & Leymann, F. (2007). Bpel for semantic web services (bpel4sws). On the Move to Meaningful Internet Systems (OTM) - Volume Part I (pp. 179–188).

OASIS. (2004). *Web services reliability.* Retrieved from http://docs.oasis-open.org/wsrm/ws-reliability/v1.1/wsrm-ws_reliability-1.1-spec-os.pdf

OASIS. (2004). *Web services security v1.0.* Retrieved from https://www.oasis-open.org/standards#wssv1.0

OASIS. (2005). *SAML specification for SAML V2.0.* Retrieved from http://saml.xml.org/saml-specifications

OASIS. (2006). *Web services reliable messaging.* Retrieved from http://docs.oasis-open.org/ws-rx/wsrm/200608/wsrm-1.1-spec-cd-04.html

OASIS. (2010). XACML v3.0 Core and Hierarchical Role Based Access Control (RBAC) profile version 1.0. Retrieved from http://docs.oasis-open.org/xacml/3.0/xacml-3.0-rbac-v1-spec-cs-01-en.pdf

OASIS. (2011). Service component architecture assembly model specification version 1.1. *OASIS Committee Specification Draft 08 / Public Review Draft 03.*

Oasis. (2013). *Website.* Retrieved from http://docs.oasis-open.org/opencsa/sca-assembly/sca-assembly-1.1-spec.pdf

Object Management Group. (2004). *Common object request broker architecture (CORBA) Core Specification 3.0.3.* OMG Specification.

Offermann, P., & Bub, A. (2009). A method for information systems development according to SOA. In *Proceedings of the 15th Americas Conference on Information Systems*, San Francisco.

Offermann, P. (2008). SOAM – A method to concept enterprise software with a service-oriented architecture[in German]. *Wirtschaftsinformatik, 6,* 461–471. doi:10.1365/s11576-008-0094-1.

Ogrinz, M. (2009). *Mashup patterns: Designs and examples for the modern enterprise.* Pearson Education.

Oliver, A. (2012). Long live SOA in the cloud era. *InfoWorld.* Retrieved from www.infoworld.com/d/application-development/long-live-soa-in-the-cloud-era-205107

OMG. (2004). Meta-Object Facility (MOF) specification, version 1.4, April 2002. Retrieved from http://www.omg.org/cgi-bin/doc?formal/2002-04-03

Opencloudmanifesto.org. (2013). *Website.* Retrieved from www.opencloudmanifesto.org

Orriëns, B., Yang, J., & Papazoglou, M. P. (2003). Model driven service composition. In *Proceedings in Service-Oriented Computing* (pp. 75–90). Springer-Verlag.

Othman, M. (2009). *Principles of mobile computing and communications.* Auerbach Publication.

Papazoglou, M. P. (2003). Service-oriented computing: Concepts, characteristics and directions. In *Proceedings of the Fourth International Conference on Web Information Systems Engineering* (pp. 3-9). IEEE Computer Society.

Papazoglou, M. P., Traverso, P., Dustdar, S., & Leymann, F. (2008). Service-oriented computing: A research roadmap. *International Journal of Cooperative Information Systems, 17*(2). doi:10.1142/S0218843008001816.

Parr, B. (2009). The evolution of the social media API. Retrieved from http://mashable.com/2009/05/21/social-media-api/

Paton, N. W. (1999). *Active rules in database systems.* New York, NY: Springer Verlag. doi:10.1007/978-1-4419-8656-6.

Paul, S., & Fei, Z. (2001). Distributed caching with centralized control. *Computer Communications, 24*(2), 256–268. doi:10.1016/S0140-3664(00)00322-4.

Pautasso, C., & Wilde, E. (2009). Why is the web loosely coupled? A multi-faceted metric for service design. In *Proceedings of the 18th International World Wide Web Conference*, Madrid, Spain.

Pautasso, C., Zimmermann, O., & Leymann, F. (2008). Restful web services vs. "Big"' web services: Making the right architectural decision. In *Proceedings of the 17th international conference on World Wide Web* (pp. 805-814). ACM.

Phipps, S. (2009). What's the *New York Times* doing with Hadoop? *InfoWorld.* Retrieved from http://www.infoworld.com/d/open-source/whats-the-new-york-times-doing-hadoop-392

Pires, P. F., Benevides, M. R. F., & Mattoso, M. (2003). Building reliable web services compositions. Web Databases and Web Services 2002, LNCS 2593, 59-72. Berlin: Springer-Verlag.

Pistore, M., Marconi, A., Bertoli, P., & Traverso, P. (2005). Automated composition of web services by planning at the knowledge level. In *International Joint Conferences on Artificial Intelligence (IJCAI)* (pp. 1252–1259).

Plummer, C. D., & Smith, M. D. (2009). Three levels of elasticity for cloud computing expand provider options. *Gartner* ID Number G00167400.

Pokraev, S., & Reichert, M. (2006). Mediation patterns for message exchange protocols. In *Open INTEROP-Workshop on Enterprise Modeling and Ontologies for Interoperability* (EMOI), CAiSE (pp. 659-663).

Pokraev, S., Quartel, D., Steen, M., & Reichert, M. (2006). Semantic service modeling - enabling system interoperability. In *International Conference on Interoperability for Enterprise Software and Applications (I-ESA)* (pp. 221-231).

Portio Research. (2012). *Latest mobile state.* Retrieved from http://mobilethinking.com/mobile-marketing-tools/latest-mobile-state

Rahm, E., & Bernstein, P. (2001). A survey of approaches to automatic schema matching. *International Journal on Very Large Databases (VLDB), 10*(4), 334–350. doi:10.1007/s007780100057.

Ramdous, S., & Kannan, G. (2002). Security of mobile code. *Journal of Cryptology, 2*(1), 1–12.

Ranadive, V., & Maney, K. (2011). *The two-second advantage: How to succeed by anticipating the future just enough.* USA: Crown Business.

Raskin, R., & Pan, M. (2003). Semantic web for earth and environmental technology (SWEET). In *Workshop on Semantic Web Technologies for Searching and Retrieving Scientific Data,* ISWC.

Reed, B. (2010). A brief history of smartphones. *Network World.* Retrieved from http://www.networkworld.com/slideshows/2010/061510-smartphone-history.html

Reichert, M., & Dadam, P. (1997). A framework for dynamic changes in workflow management systems. In *DEXA Workshop 1997* (pp. 42-48). IEEE.

Reichert, M., et al. (2009). Enabling poka-yoke workflows with the AristaFlow BPM Suite. In *Proceedings of the BPM'09 Demonstration Track,* Ulm, Germany. CEUR Workshop Proceedings 489.

Reichert, M., & Dadam, P. (1998). ADEPT flex - Supporting dynamic changes of workflows without losing control. *Journal of Intelligent Information Systems, 10,* 93–129. Springer. doi:10.1023/A:1008604709862.

Reichert, M., Dadam, P., & Bauer, T. (2003). Dealing with forward and backward jumps in workflow management systems. *Software & Systems Modeling, 2*(1), 37–58. doi:10.1007/s10270-003-0018-x.

Reichert, M., Rinderle-Ma, S., & Dadam, P. (2009). Flexibility in process-aware information systems. *LNCS Transactions on Petri Nets and Other Models of Concurrency (ToPNoC),* Special Issue on Concurrency in Process-aware Information Systems *LNCS, 5460*(2), 115–135. Springer.

Reichert, M., & Weber, B. (2012). *Enabling flexibility in process-aware information systems: Challenges, methods, technologies.* Springer. doi:10.1007/978-3-642-30409-5.

Reynaert, T., De Groefy, W., Devriesey, D., Desmety, L., & Piessensy, F. (2012). *PESAP: A privacy enhanced social application platform.* Retrieved from https://lirias.kuleuven.be/bitstream/123456789/356922/1/reynaert2012a.pdf

Rinderle, S., & Reichert, M. (2005). On the controlled evolution of access rules in cooperative information systems. In *Proceedings of the 13th International Conference on Cooperative Information Systems (CoopIS'05),* Agia Napa, Cyprus, LNCS 3760 (pp. 238-255). Springer.

Rinderle-Ma, S., & Reichert, M. (2007). A formal framework for adaptive access control models. *Journal on Data Semantics IX Springer.LNCS, 4,* 82–112.

Rinderle-Ma, S., & Reichert, M. (2009). Comprehensive life cycle support for access rules in information systems: The CEOSIS project. *Enterprise Information Systems, 3*(3), 219–251. doi:10.1080/17517570903045609.

Rodríguez, A., Fernández-Medina, E., & Piattini, M. (2007). A BPMN extension for the modeling of security requirements in business processes. *Transactions of the Institute of Electronics, Information and Communication Engineers. E (Norwalk, Conn.), 90-D*(4), 745–752.

Roman, D., Keller, U., Lausen, H., de Bruijn, J., Lara, R., Stollberg, M., & Polleres, A., · , Fensel, D. (2005). Web service modeling ontology. *Applied Ontology, 1*(1), 77–106.

Rosen, M., Lublinsky, B., Smith, K., & Balcer, M. (2008). *Applied SOA: Service-oriented architecture and design strategies.* Indianapolis, IN: John Wiley & Sons.

Russell, N., ter Hofstede, A. H. M., & Mulyar, N. (2006). Workflow control flow patterns: A revised view. *Technical Report BPM-06-22.* BPM Centre.

Russell, N., van der Aalst, W. M. P., & ter Hofstede, A. H. M. (2006). Exception handling patterns in process-aware information systems. *Proceedings of the CAiSE, 06*, 288–302.

Sadiq, S., Sadiq, W., & Orlowska, M. (2005). A framework for constraint specification and validation in flexible workflows. *Information Systems, 30*(5), 349–378. doi:10.1016/j.is.2004.05.002.

Sahu, D., Sharma, S., Dubey, V., & Tripathi, A. (2012). Cloud computing in mobile computing. *International Journal of Scientific and Research Publications, 2*(8).

Salatge, N., & Fabre, J. C. (2007). Fault tolerance connectors for unreliable web services. In DSN (pp. 51–60).

Samarati, P., & di Vimercati, S. D. C. (2000). Access control: Policies, models, and mechanisms. In *Proceedings of Foundations of Security Analysis and Design* (pp. 137–196). Springer-Verlag.

Sandhu, R. S., Coyne, E. J., Feinstein, H. L., & Youman, C. E. (1996). Role-based access control models. *Computer, 29*(2), 38–47. doi:10.1109/2.485845.

Sarmenta, L. F. G. (2001). *Volunteer computing.* (Ph.D. thesis). MIT. Retrieved from http://www.cag.lcs.mit.edu/bayanihan/

Satyanaryanan, M., Noble, B., Kumar, P., & Price, M. (1995). Application-aware adaptation for mobile computing. *ACM SIGOPS Operating Systems Review, 29*(1), 52–55. doi:10.1145/202453.202464.

Scheer, I. D. S. (2005). Business process management: ARIS value engineering – concept. *White Paper.*

Schneider, G., & Vaughan-Brown, J. (2008). The Centra-Site community - Fast-tracking SOA governance using best-of-breed solutions. *White paper.* Software AG.

Schroth, C., & Christ, O. (2007). Brave new web: Emerging design principles and technologies as enablers of a global SOA. In *Proceedings of the IEEE International Conference on Service Computing.*

Schulte, W. (2008). Tutorial for EDA and how it relates to SOA. *Gartner* ID Number G00155163.

Schulte, R. (2004). Event-driven architecture: The next big thing. In *Application integration & web services summit.* Los Angeles, USA: Gartner.

Shankararaman, V., & Lum, K. E. (2011). Integrating a process-based composite application with ERP. *Annual international conference on enterprise resource planning and supply chain management,* Penang, Malaysia.

Shankararaman, V., & Lum, K. E. (2012). Integrating the cloud scenarios and solutions. In Aggarwal, A., & Bento, A. (Eds.), *Cloud computing service and deployment models: Layers and management.* IGI Global. doi:10.4018/978-1-4666-2187-9.ch009.

Shankararaman, V., Tan, W. K., Thonse, S., Gupta, M., & Deshmukh, N. (2007). *Aligning IT solutions with business processes: A methodological approach.* Pearson.

Sharma, D., & Singh, R. K. (2011). QoS and QoE management in wireless communication system. *International Journal of Engineering Science and Technology (IJEST), 3*(3), 2385–2391.

Sheth, A. (1998). Changing focus on interoperability in information systems: From system, syntax, structure to semantics. *Interoperating Geographic Information Systems,* 5-30.

Shirky, C. (2010). *Situated software.* Retrieved from http://www.shirky.com/writings/situated_software.html

Shuster, L. (2008). *Project-oriented SOA. SOA Magazine.* XXI.

Siewe, F., Cau, A., & Zedan, H. (2003). A compositional framework for access control policies enforcement. In FMSE '03 (pp. 32-42). ACM.

Simon, P. (2010). Why new systems fail: Revised edition: An insider's guide to successful IT projects. Boston, MA: Course Technology PTR.

Sirin, E., Parsia, B., Wu, D., Hendler, J. A., & Nau, D. S. (2004). HTN planning for web service composition using shop2. *Journal of Web Semantics, 1*(4), 377–396. doi:10.1016/j.websem.2004.06.005.

Smith, M. A., & Kumar, R. L. (2004). A theory of application service provider use from a client perspective. *Journal of Information and Management.*

Spencer, B., & Liu, Y. (2004). Inferring data transformation rules to integrate semantic web services. In *International Semantic Web Conference (ISWC)* (pp. 456–470).

Srivatsa, M., Iyengar, A., Mikalsen, T. A., Rouvellou, I., & Yin, J. (2007). An access control system for web service compositions. In *Proceedings of the IEEE Conference on Web Services* (pp. 1-8). IEEE.

Stein, S. (2009). *Modelling method extension for service-oriented business process management.* (PhD thesis). University of Kiel, Germany.

Stein, S., Kühne, S., Drawehn, J., Feja, S., & Rotzoll, W. (2008). Evaluation of OrViA framework for model-driven SOA implementations: An industrial case study. In *Proceedings of the 6th International Conference on Business Process Management,* Milan (pp. 310-325).

Sward, R. E., & Boleng, J. (2011). Service-oriented architecture (SOA) concepts and implementations. In SIGAda (pp. 3-4).

Sweeney, L. (2002). k-Anonymity: A model for protecting privacy. *International Journal of Uncertainty. Fuzziness and Knowledge-Based Systems, 10*(5), 557–570. doi:10.1142/S0218488502001648.

Sybase. (2011). *Mobility advantage.* Retrieved from http://www.sybase.com/files/White_Papers/Sybase_SUP_MobilityAdvantagePlatform_wp.pdf

Tan, C., & Goh, A. (1999). Implementing ECA rules in an active database. *Knowledge-Based Systems, 12*(4), 137–144. doi:10.1016/S0950-7051(99)00028-3.

Tang, L., Bastani, F. B., Tsai, W. T., Dong, J., & Zhang, L. J. (2011). Modeling and analyzing enterprise cloud service architecture. *Technical Report UTDCS-26-11.* Dept. of Computer Science, Univ. of Texas at Dallas.

Tang, L., Dong, J., Peng, T., & Tsai, W. T. (2010). Modeling enterprise service-oriented architectural styles. *Service Oriented Computing and Applications (SOCA), 4*, 81–107. doi:10.1007/s11761-010-0059-2.

Tang, L., Dong, J., & Zhao, Y. (2011). SLA-aware enterprise service computing. In Cardellini, V., Casalicchio, E., Branco, K. C., Estrella, J., & Monaco, F. J. (Eds.), *Performance and dependability in service computing: Concepts, techniques and research direction.* IGI Global Publishing. doi:10.4018/978-1-60960-794-4.ch002.

Tang, L., Zhao, Y., & Dong, J. (2009). *Specifying enterprise web-oriented architecture. High Assurance Services Computing* (pp. 241–260). Springer. doi:10.1007/978-0-387-87658-0_12.

Taptu. (2010). The state of the mobile touch web. *Taptu Report, January.* Retrieved from http://robertoigarza.files.wordpress.com/2009/07/rep-the-state-of-the-mobile-touch-web-taptu-2010.pdf

Tartanoglu, I. V., Romanovsky, A., & Levy, N. (2003). Coordinated forward error recovery for composite web services. In *Proceedings of International Symposium. Reliable Distributed Systems (SRDS '03)* (pp. 167-176).

Taylor, R. N., Medvidovic, N., & Dashofy, E. M. (2010). *Software architecture: Foundations, theory, and practices.* Wiley.

The Open Group. (2012). *SOA and enterprise architecture.* Retrieved July 1, 2012, from http://www.opengroup.org/soa/source-book/soa/soa_ea.htm

Themistocleous, M., & Irani, Z. (2001). Benchmarking the benefits and barriers of application integration. *Benchmarking: An International Journal, 8*(4), 317–331. doi:10.1108/14635770110403828.

Thoo, E. (2009). Data in the cloud: The changing nature of managing data accessibility. *Gartner RAS Core Research.* Retrieved from www.gartner.com/id=902416

Tjepkema, J. (2011). Guidelines for a successful mobile customer experience. *Mobile Convention Amsterdam,* 19 April.

Turban, E., McLean, E., & Wetherbe, J. (2006). *Information technology for management* (5th ed.). Wiley & Sons, Inc..

Turner, K. J., Reiff-Marganiec, S., Blair, L., Pang, J., Gray, T., Perry, P., & Ireland, J. (2006). Policy support for call control. *Computer Standards & Interfaces, 28*(6), 635–649. doi:10.1016/j.csi.2005.05.004.

Twitter. (2013). *Website.* Retrieved from https://dev.twitter.com/docs/api

UPnP Forum. (2008). UPnPTM Device Architecture 1.1. Retrieved from http://www.upnp.org/specs/arch/UPnP-arch-DeviceArchitecture-v1.1.pdf

Vallath, M. (2003). *Real application clusters*. Burlington, MA: Digital Press.

Vallecillo, A. (2010). On the combination of domain specific modeling languages. In *Proceedings of The European Conference on Modeling and Applications* (pp. 305-320). Springer-Verlag.

Van der Aalst, W.M.P., Barros, A.P., ter Hofstede, A.H.M., & Kiepuszewski, B. (2000). Advanced workflow patterns. In Proceedings of Cooperative IS 2000 (pp. 18-29). Springer.

Van der Aalst, W. M. P., & ter Hofstede, A. H. M. (2005). Yawl: Yet another workflow language. *Information Systems, 30*(4), 245–275. doi:10.1016/j.is.2004.02.002.

Vaquero, L., Rodero-Merino, L., Caceres, J., & Lindner, M. (2009). A break in the clouds: Towards a cloud definition. *SIGCOMM Computer Communications Review, 39*, 50–55. doi:10.1145/1496091.1496100.

Vembu, N. (2011). *A translator web service for data mediation in web service compositions*. (Master's Thesis). Department of Computer Science, University of Georgia, Athens, USA.

Vizard, M. (2012). *How APIs are fueling the mobile banking wars*. Retrieved from http://blog.programmableweb.com/2012/08/14/how-apis-are-fueling-the-mobile-banking-wars/

Vlissides, J., Brown, K., & Meszaros, G. (2012). *Stove pipe enteprise*. Retrieved July 1, 2012, from http://sourcemaking.com/antipatterns/stovepipe-enterprise

Vlissides, J., Brown, K., & Meszaros, G. (2012). *Vendor lock-in*. Retrieved July 1, 2012, from http://sourcemaking.com/antipatterns/vendor-lock-in

Vogels, W. (2007). *Availability & consistency or how the CAP theorem ruins it all*. Retrieved July 1, 2012, from http://www.infoq.com/presentations/availability-consistency

W3.org. (2013). *Website*. Retrieved from http://www.w3.org/Submission/2003/SUBM-EPAL-20031110/

W3C. (2001). *Web services description language (WSDL 1.1)*. Retrieved from http://www.w3.org/TR/wsdl

W3C. (2001). *XML schema 1.1 recommendation*. Retrieved from http://www.w3.org/XML/Schema.html

W3C. (2007). *Web services description language (WSDL) version 2.0*. Retrieved from http://www.w3.org/TR/wsdl20/

W3C. (2007). *Web services policy 1.5 - Framework*. Retrieved from http://www.w3.org/TR/ws-policy/

W3C. (2012). *HTML5 Editor's Draft 7*. Retrieved from http://dev.w3.org/html5/spec/

Walsh, N. (2005). *Ontology on vCards*. Retrieved October 22, 2012, from http://nwalsh.com/rdf/vCard.ont

Weber, B., Sadiq, S., & Reichert, M. (2009). Beyond rigidity - dynamic process lifecycle support: A survey on dynamic changes in process-aware information systems. *Computer Science - Research & Development, 23*(2), 47-65. Springer.

Weber, I., Hoffmann, J., Mendling, J., & Nitzsche, J. (2007). Towards a methodology for semantic business process modeling and configuration. In *Proceedings of 2nd International Workshop on Business Oriented Aspects concerning Semantics and Methodologies in Service-oriented Computing* (pp. 176-187).

Weber, B., Reichert, M., & Rinderle-Ma, S. (2008). Change patterns and change support features - enhancing flexibility in process-aware information systems. *Data & Knowledge Engineering, 66*(3), 438–466. doi:10.1016/j.datak.2008.05.001.

Weber, B., Reichert, M., Wild, W., & Rinderle-Ma, S. (2009). Providing integrated life cycle support in process-aware information systems. *International Journal of Cooperative Information Systems, 18*(1), 115–165. doi:10.1142/S0218843009001999.

Weber, B., Rinderle, S., & Reichert, M. (2007). Change patterns and change support features in process-aware information systems.[Springer.]. *Proceedings of the CAiSE, 2007*, 574–588.

Weikum, G., & Schek, H.-J. (1992). *Concepts and applications of multilevel transactions and open nested transactions* (pp. 515–553). Morgan Kaufmann Publishers.

Weske, M. (2007). *Business process management - Concepts, languages, architectures*. Springer.

White, S. A. (2004). Business process modeling notation. Object Management Group (OMG) and Business Process Management Initiative.

Widder, A., Ammon, V. R., Schaeffer, P., & Wolff, C. (2007). Identification of suspicious, unknown event patterns in an event cloud. In *Proceedings of the 2007 inaugural international conference on Distributed event-based systems* (pp. 164-170). ACM Press.

Widom, J., & Ceri, S. (1996). *Active database systems: Triggers and rules for advanced database processing.* Morgan Kaufmann.

Wieringa, R. (2003). *Design methods for reactive systems: Yourdon, statemate, and the UML.* Morgan Kaufmann.

Wolter, C., Schaad, A., & Meinel, C. (2007). Deriving XACML policies from business process models. In *Proceedings of Web Information Systems Engineering* (pp. 142–153). Springer-Verlag. doi:10.1007/978-3-540-77010-7_15.

Woods, D. (2010). *Building the enterprise social graph. Forbes.* Retrieved from http://www.forbes.com/2010/09/27/enterprise-social-media-technology-cio-network-woods_print.html

Woods, D., Thurai, A., Dournaee, B., & Musser, J. (2012). *Enterprise-class API patterns for cloud & mobile.* Retrieved from http://www.govhealthit.com/sites/govhealthit.com/files/resource-media/pdf/enterprise-api-patterns-1.pdf

Woods, D. (2003). *Enterprise services architecture.* O'Reilly.

Yahoo. (2013). *Website.* Retrieved from http://pipes.yahoo.com/pipes/

Yan, S., Li, Y., Deng, S., & Wu, Z. (2005). A transaction management framework for service-based workflow. In *Proceedings of the International Conference on Next Generation Web Services Practices* (pp. 377-381).

Yuan, E., & Tong, J. (2005). Attributed Based Access Control (ABAC) for web services. In *Proceedings of the IEEE International Conference on Web Services* (pp. 561-569). IEEE Computer Society.

Yusuf, K. (2004). *Enterprise messaging using JMS and IBM websphere.* Prentice Hall.

ZDNet. (2011). *Fedex CIO carter: Next era of internet is sensor based computing.* Retrieved from http://www.zdnet.com/blog/btl/fedex-cio-carter-next-era-of-internet-is-sensor-based-computing/61315

Zeeb, E., Bobek, A., Bohn, H., & Golatowski, F. (2007). Service-oriented architectures for embedded systems using devices profile for web services. In *AINAW '07 Proceedings of the 21st International Conference on Advanced Information Networking and Applications Workshops* (pp. 956-963). IEEE Computer Society.

Zhang, A., Nodine, M., Bhargava, B., & Bukhres, O. (1994). Ensuring relaxed atomicity for flexible transactions in multi-database systems. In *Proceedings of the ACM SIGMOD* (pp. 67–78).

Zhang, X., Parisi-Presicce, F., Sandhu, R., & Park, J. (2005). Formal model and policy specification of usage control. *ACM Transactions on Information and System Security, 8*(4), 351–387. doi:10.1145/1108906.1108908.

Zhao, H., & Doshi, P. (2009). A hierarchical framework for logical composition of web services. *Journal of Service Oriented Computing and Applications (SOCA), 3*(4), 285–306. doi:10.1007/s11761-009-0052-9.

Zheng, Y., Chan, A., & Ngai, G. (2010). Applying coordination for service adaptation in mobile computing. *IEEE Internet Computing,* 61–67.

Zhu, Y., Hu, H., Ahn, G.-J., Huang, D., & Wang, S.-B. (2012). Towards temporal access control in cloud computing. In *Proceedings of the IEEE INFOCOM* (pp. 2576-2580). IEEE Computer Society.

About the Contributors

Raja Ramanathan is an IT Enterprise Architect and SOA Subject Matter Expert with over 25 years of experience in software architecture and development, enterprise integration, and governance of mission critical systems. The past two decades, Raja has focused on developing strategic enterprise initiatives, providing solutions architecture, and implementing service-oriented and process-centric systems for Fortune 500 companies. He has provided effective technical leadership and evangelism for oil and gas, energy and utilities, software product development, and financial service industries. His current research interests include Service-driven and Cloud Computing. Raja has a M.E.E in Electrical Engineering from the University of Delaware, USA.

Kirtana Raja, an IT Architect, has an S.B in Chemical Engineering from Massachusetts Institute of Technology, S.B in Management Science from MIT Sloan, and MBA from Cornell. Notably, as writer/editor of MIT's *Tech* news journal, Kirtana interviewed Chemistry Nobel Laureate Professor Richard Schrock and Apple's Steve Wozniak on his autobiography *iWoz*. Kirtana has won business and technology awards from Intel, Siemens Westinghouse, Micron, Xerox, Lucent, Society of Plastics Engineers, and Acara Institute. She co-authored a research paper relating to nanotechnology while working in Nobel Laureate Alan MacDiarmid's Laboratory. Kirtana's areas of interest are Cloud, Social Media Analytics, and Storage Solutions.

* * *

Manar Ali has been working as a Lecturer in King Abdulaziz University (KAU), Jeddah, Saudi Arabia since 2004. Manar is currently a full time PhD student at the University of Leicester, UK, and is expected to graduate in 2013. Manar has a B.Sc degree from KAU in Computer Science and obtained her M.Sc in Advanced Computing from Imperial College, London.

Thomas Bauer is a Professor for Business Informatics at the University of Applied Sciences in Neu-Ulm, Germany. Thomas holds a PhD and Diploma in Computer Science. Until 2011, he was a senior researcher at the Daimler Research Centre in Ulm, where he worked on methods for vehicle engineering and business process management. Earlier, Thomas was employed in the Databases and Information Systems Group at the University of Ulm, where he worked on the efficient enactment of enterprise-wide workflows. His current research interests and teaching areas include Business Process Management, Service-oriented Architectures, Database Systems, and Business Intelligence.

Stephan Buchwald is an IT consultant for T-Systems International in the automotive and manufacturing domains. Stephan holds a PhD in Computer Science. Until 2011, he was employed at the Daimler Research Centre in Ulm, where he worked on service-oriented architectures and business process management. He studied computer engineering and applied computer science at the University of Applied Science Ulm.

Stéphanie Chollet is an Associate Professor at the Grenoble Institute of Technology and is member of the LCIS lab. She received her PhD from Grenoble University in 2009 under the direction of Prof. Lalanda. Her research interest is in the design and integration of security properties in complex and heterogeneous systems.

Prashant Doshi is an Associate Professor of Computer Science, Director of the THINC Lab and is a faculty member of the Institute for AI at the University of Georgia, USA. Prashant obtained his PhD from the University of Illinois at Chicago. His current research interests lie in multiagent systems, Web services and the semantic Web. His research has led to approaches for automated and scalable compositions of Web services. Prashant has published numerous papers in the Journal on WSR, IEEE Transactions on Services Computing, Journal of SOCA, ICWS and SCC. He teaches courses on enterprise integration and Web services.

Jing Dong is currently with Hewlett Packard. Previously, he was on the faculty of Computer Science at the University of Texas at Dallas. Jing received his BS in Computer Science from Peking University and PhD in Computer Science from the University of Waterloo. His research interests include cloud computing, software architecture, formal and automated methods for software engineering, software modeling and design, and visualization. He is a senior member of the IEEE and the ACM.

Aurélien Faravelon currently completes his PhD at Grenoble University under the direction of Prof. Christine Verdier and Philippe Saltel. His work focuses on designing and implementing secured heterogeneous and distributed applications by configuring non-functional properties of services.

Alan Megargel is a Senior Lecturer of Information Systems at the Singapore Management University, Singapore. Alan's current areas of specialization include enterprise architecture in banking, service oriented architecture, business process management, and massive-scale in-memory data grid technology. Alan's industry experience includes Chief Technology Officer at TIBCO Software Asia, Vice President and Head of SOA at OCBC Bank, and Senior Enterprise Architect at ANZ Bank. Alan holds an MSc in Software, Systems and Information Engineering from the University of Sheffield.

Lloyd Rebello is an Enterprise Architecture and IT Strategy Advisor to C-Level Executives. Most recently, Lloyd, with the leadership teams of a major public sector organization and a Fortune 100 bank, developed two separate strategies for business enabling technology platforms and IT transformation. Lloyd has also served as the head of product development and chief product architect for two separate consulting companies (CRM & Enterprise Licensing Management) where he helped both transition from being consulting based to becoming product centric. In that most recent product development role, the CRM product made Gartner's Cool Technology list for 2009.

Manfred Reichert is a Professor of Computer Science at the University of Ulm, Germany. Manfred holds a PhD in Computer Science and a Diploma in Mathematics. His major research interests include next generation process management technology, service-oriented computing, and advanced IT applications. Manfred pioneered the work on the ADEPT process management technology and co-founded AristaFlow GmbH which developed the AristaFlow BPM Suite. Manfred has contributed more than 220 papers to several research projects in the BPM area. He was the PC Chair of the BPM'08, CoopIS'11, and EDOC'13 conferences, and General Chair of the BPM'09 Conference in Ulm.

Stephan Reiff-Marganiec has been a Senior Lecturer in the Department of Computer Science at the University of Leicester since 2003. Previously, he worked in the computer industry in Germany and Luxembourg for several years. Stephan was co-chair of several international conferences and the principal investigator of several EU funded projects. Stephan has published over 50 papers in international conferences and journals. Stephan was appointed guest Professor at the China University of Petroleum in 2009 and was elected Member Fellow of the BCS (FBCS) in May 2009. He was visiting Professor at Lamsade at the University of Dauphine, Paris in 2010.

Venky Shankararaman is an Associate Professor of Information Systems at the Singapore Management University, Singapore. Venky has over 20 years of experience in the IT industry as a researcher, faculty member, and industry consultant. He also worked at UK and Singapore universities where he taught and researched in intelligent and distributed systems. His current areas of specialization include business process management, enterprise architecture, and enterprise integration. Venky has designed and delivered professional courses in BPM, enterprise architecture, technical architecture, and enterprise integration in Europe, Asia and USA. He has published over 50 papers in academic journals and conferences.

Leo Shuster is the Director of IT Architecture at Nationwide Insurance. With over 20 years of IT experience, Leo has directed Enterprise Architecture and SOA strategy and execution for Nationwide Insurance, National City Corporation, Ohio Savings Bank and Progressive Insurance. Leo has presented on Enterprise Architecture, SOA, BPM, and related topics in industry events, conferences and blogs. He is a co-author of Thomas Erl's book on *SOA Governance: Governing Shared Services On-Premise and in the Cloud*. Leo holds an MS in Computer Science and Engineering from Case Western Reserve University and an MBA from Cleveland State University.

Longji Tang has served as a Tech Lead, Architect, and Lead Project Manager in FedEx IT since 2000. Longji obtained his PhD in Software Engineering in 2011 at the University of Texas at Dallas. He graduated from Penn State University in 1995 with a Master of Engineering degree in Computer Science & Engineering and a Master of Art degree in Applied Mathematics. Longji has published 30 research papers in computational mathematics and software engineering. His research interests include software architecture, modeling, software design and management, service-oriented architecture, service computing, cloud computing, mobile computing, and applications.

Wei-Tek Tsai is a Professor of Computer Science and Engineering at Arizona State University. Wei-Tek received his M.S. and Ph.D. in Computer Science from University of California at Berkeley, USA, and S.B. from Massachusetts Institute of Technology, USA. He holds visiting professorships in various universities in China and Europe. Wei-Tek has worked on various aspects of software engineering including requirements, design, testing, simulation, maintenance, and metrics. His recent work focuses on SaaS, service-oriented architecture and computing, education on service-oriented computing, and service-oriented robotics. He has written more than 300 papers and four books including books on service-oriented computing.

Nithya Vembu graduated with her M.S. degree in Artificial Intelligence in 2011 from the Institute for AI at the University of Georgia. Prior to this, she was a programmer analyst at Cognizant technology services. Her Master's thesis research was on a principled formulation of the data mediation problem between disparate Web services participating in a composition. Nithya implemented several data mediation approaches within the framework of a translator Web service. This research forms a part of this book chapter.

Keith Worfolk is an innovative IT executive and strategist with 25 years of international experience in leading enterprise architecture, software development, large-scale systems integration, and IT operations in Fortune 500 and Big Five Consulting environments. Keith is a demonstrated problem solver and visionary in leading organizations through change to achieve strategic technology and business advantage via enterprise solutions. He has been involved in building and communicating the IT vision across organizations, ensuring executive alignment. Keith is a prolific thought leader in various publications and events. He has a Masters Degree in Computer Information Systems and an MBA from Duke University.

Index

A

Abstract Process Engine Language (APEL) 175

Access control 132, 141, 163, 165-186, 320, 349, 354-356

Access control policies 163, 165, 167, 169, 171-172, 175, 178

ACID transactions 135, 137-138

actor assignment 106-113, 115, 118, 121-126, 129-130

Agnostic Service 36

Application Programming Interface (API) 1, 3, 5, 8-9, 16, 20-24, 28, 30, 34, 37-42, 62, 64, 68, 82, 202, 278, 282, 287, 336-337, 345, 347, 350, 353, 357-358

Application Service Provider (ASP) 335

Asynchronous Javascript and XML (AJAX) 33

Asynchronous messaging 52, 55, 188, 190, 204-205, 207

Asynchronous Queuing 36

Atomic Service Transaction 36

Atomic Web Service 85, 101

autonomy 2, 6, 14, 37, 135, 162, 188, 208

auto-scaling 352, 358

B

Behavioral Dependency 147

Big Data 53, 65-66, 286

Binding Fault 192

BPaaS 334, 338-339, 345, 353

Broad Reach 299

Business-IT-Mapping Model (BIMM) 107

Business Process Execution Language (BPEL) 13, 28, 97, 140, 166, 172, 186, 206

Business Process Management (BPM) 6, 45, 57, 61, 65-66, 74, 84, 105

business repository 126-127, 129

C

canonical modeling 58-59

Capability Maturity Model (CMM) 226, 243

Center of Excellence (COE) 241, 260, 264-266, 272

change request 110, 112-117, 119-120, 123, 133

channel 9, 22, 53, 64, 70, 72, 140, 275-277, 279-281, 284-285, 287-288, 290, 292, 304, 320

Cloud Auditor 343

Cloud Broker 343

Cloud Carrier 343

cloud computing 3, 9, 23-24, 41, 52, 65-66, 81, 83-84, 186, 213, 238-239, 241-242, 244, 250, 271, 273, 287, 291, 293, 310, 315, 327, 329-330, 332, 334-338, 341-343, 345, 347-349, 354, 357-358

Cloud computing 23

Cloud Consumer 342-343

Cloud Provider 23, 81, 336, 340, 342-343, 345, 348, 350, 354-356

clustering 188, 190, 195-198, 200, 207-208

Code-on-Demand 321, 323

communication constraint 301, 328

Community Cloud 342

compartmentalized role 280

Complex Event Processing (CEP) 56, 61, 66, 78, 84

Component-Based Architecture (CBA) 4

Composites 15-17, 28, 34-35, 38, 195

Composition Fault 192

Comprehensive Compensation 152-153, 156, 158

conflict" 86-87

consumerization 53, 238-239

control flow 90, 105, 107, 137, 139-141, 163

core enterprise asset 283

Created, Read, Updated, or Deleted (CRUD) 72

D

Data confidentiality 165, 168

Data Governance 241, 243, 245, 247, 250-254, 256, 258-260, 262-267, 272-273

Data integrity 35, 136, 165, 168, 200, 202, 206, 209, 352, 355

Dependency 13, 112, 141, 147-148, 154, 159, 200, 233, 246, 278, 348

Design diversity 188, 190, 192-193, 207

design-time mediation 85-86, 95

desktop hosting services 335

Device Profile for Web Services (DPWS) 171

dictatorship 258-260

Discovery Fault 192

Distributed Data Caching 188, 190, 198-199, 207-208

Distributed queues 205

dynamic service composition 26

E

Effective Governance 285, 347

elastic scalability 207, 337, 344, 352

Encapsulation 4, 19, 36, 54, 257-258

Enterprise Application Integration (EAI) 44, 68, 81, 83, 105, 255

Enterprise Data Management (EDM) 241

Enterprise Data Platform Services 255-256, 261

Enterprise Data Services 198, 260-261

Enterprise Information Architecture (EIA 253

Enterprise Integration (EI) 43, 66

Enterprise Mashup 3, 30

Enterprise Metadata Services 260-261

Enterprise mobile security 320

Enterprise Mobile Service Architecture 295, 298, 305, 307-308, 322, 325, 327, 332

Enterprise Mobile Service Architecture Quality Ontology (EMSQ) 298

Enterprise Mobile Service Computing 295-296, 298, 308, 310, 324, 326-327, 332

Enterprise Mobile Service Consumers (MSC) 298

Enterprise Mobile Service Data (EMSD) 298, 307, 311

Enterprise Mobile Service Process (EMSP) 298, 307, 313

Enterprise Mobile SOA Infrastructure (EMSI) 298

Enterprise Mobile SOA Management (EMSM) 298

Enterprise Privacy Authorization Language (EPAL) 174

Enterprise Service Bus (ESB) 8, 34, 45, 60, 66, 72, 84, 115, 119, 133, 190, 240, 255, 257, 274

enterprise social graph 22-23, 41

entity service 7

Event-Driven Architecture (EDA) 55

Event-Driven Process (EDP) 81, 106

Exception 116

eXtensible Access Control Markup Language (XACML) 169

eXtensible Markup Language (XML) 4

Extract-Transform-Load (ETL) 45-46, 56, 61

F

failover 196-199, 208, 343, 345, 352

Failure propagation 140, 148-150

Fault-tolerance 188-195, 198, 201-209, 302-303, 320, 343, 352, 357

federated 13, 37, 49, 63, 86, 245, 258-259, 277, 286, 334-335, 346, 354-356

First-In-First-Out (FIFO) 70

flexibility flag 109-110, 115

Force-fail 135-136, 147-148

front-loading 104-105, 107-111, 113-118, 121-122, 124, 126, 129-130

fulfillment roles 275-276, 279, 281

G

governance 9, 35, 37, 42-43, 48, 50-51, 60, 63, 73-74, 107, 114, 127, 132, 210-218, 220-232, 235-241, 243, 245, 247, 249-254, 256, 258-260, 262-267, 271-273, 277-278, 285, 336, 340, 342, 347-348, 350, 358

Grid Computing 36, 335-336

H

Hardware Constraints 301, 328

High availability 188-190, 192, 196-198, 200, 207, 209, 338, 345, 357

HTML5 298, 310-312, 331-332

hub-and-spoke 54, 56, 67-70, 72, 76-78

hybrid 34, 194-195, 206, 232-234, 258-260, 291, 305, 307, 325-327, 342, 356

hybrid cloud 325, 342, 356

I

IaaS 23-24, 292, 310, 327, 334, 338-340, 344-345, 347-348, 353

Identity Manager 177, 182, 355

implementation policy 18

Infrastructure as a Service (IaaS) 23, 292, 338

In-Memory Data Grid 188, 190, 198, 202-204, 207, 209

interaction policy 18

isolation layer 276, 287

isomorphism 85, 87, 92-94, 96, 98, 102

L

Logical Mobility 321
Long Running Transactions (LRT) 136-138, 140, 142-146, 148-153, 156, 158-161
look-ahead 105-111, 118-122, 126-130
Loose Coupling 2, 13, 211, 245, 283, 289, 337-338, 353, 358

M

MapReduce 336, 353, 356, 358
mashup 1, 3, 8, 28, 30-31, 33-35, 37-41, 314
Master Data Management (MDM) 45, 56, 62, 65-66, 242, 245
Message-Oriented Middleware (MOM) 60, 70, 84
Metadata 18-19, 236-237, 240-241, 243-245, 247-248, 250-254, 256-258, 260-264, 266-267, 272-274
Mobile Adaptability 320, 322, 332
Mobile Agent 321, 324, 328, 332
Mobility, m-Businesses 295
Model-driven Security 172, 174, 183
multi-channel service delivery 285
multi-tenancy 82, 344, 358
Multi-version 193-194

N

Nested Transactions 135, 138, 141, 145, 163-164
Nines availability 188, 190
N-Version Programming 193, 209

O

Object 4-5, 19, 51, 55, 62, 68-70, 73, 83, 92, 95, 112, 114-119, 121-122, 124, 128-129, 133-134, 164, 169, 171, 175-177, 185, 201-204, 209, 258, 332
Object-Oriented Architecture (OOA) 4
Object Relational Mapping 202, 209
Online File Sharing 335
orchestrator 89, 96-97, 175, 177, 180, 182
organizational culture 64
organizational object (OrgObject) 118
Organization for the Advancement of Structured Information Standards (OASIS) 169
Ownership 10, 35, 232-233, 257-258, 272, 275, 277-278, 287-289, 292, 345

P

PaaS 23, 82, 292, 310, 334, 338-340, 344-345, 347-348, 353
Partial Compensation 152, 154, 156, 158
Pervasive computing 165, 167, 171, 185-186
Platform as a Service (PaaS) 23, 292, 338
Platform consolidation 234
Point-to-Point (P2P) 69
Policies 3, 5, 7, 11-12, 17-18, 21-22, 25, 35, 66, 141, 154-155, 158, 161-163, 165, 167, 169, 171-172, 175, 178, 181, 185-186, 208, 211-213, 218, 221, 223, 230-231, 235, 237-238, 244, 253-254, 320, 344, 347-348, 350, 355
Policy Decision Point (PDP) 169
Policy Enforcement Point (PEP) 169
Private Cloud 244, 308, 315, 328, 342, 355-356
Process-Aware Information System (PAIS) 104-105
Process-centric Services 286
Productivity efficiency 234
Public Cloud 308, 315, 342, 346
Publishing Fault 192
publish-subscribe 46, 55, 60, 70-71, 78

Q

quality of service (QoS) 11, 114, 191-192, 303, 326, 351
Quasar Enterprise 109, 131

R

Remote Evaluation 321, 323
REpresentational State Transfer (REST) 1-6, 19-23, 38, 40, 42, 51-52, 61-62, 82, 84, 142, 151, 180, 188-189, 213, 215, 234, 239-240, 276, 293, 308, 311, 328, 333, 355
RESTful Web Service 21, 31, 308, 319, 333
reusability 4-5, 9-10, 14, 18, 118, 245, 318
routing pattern 60
Runtime efficiency 234
Runtime Fault 192
Run-time management 226, 236-238

S

SaaS 23, 81-82, 233, 248, 292, 310, 318, 327, 334, 338-339, 344-345, 347-348, 353, 355
Saga Transactional Model 135, 138
scalability 4-5, 7, 11, 19, 21, 36-37, 52, 54, 182, 188-190, 192, 194, 196, 198-199, 202, 207, 209, 218, 225-226, 298, 303-304, 318, 326-

327, 337-338, 341, 343-344, 350-352, 356-357, 359

Scalability 4-5, 7, 11, 19, 21, 36-37, 52, 54, 182, 188-190, 192, 194, 196, 198-199, 202, 207, 209, 218, 225-226, 298, 303-304, 318, 326-327, 337-338, 341, 343-344, 350-352, 356-357, 359

schema mapping 88

SD 243, 249, 264-272, 274

self-service provisioning 334, 339, 344, 359

service 1-21, 23-31, 33-45, 52, 54-56, 58, 60, 62, 65-70, 72-73, 75, 79, 81-85, 88-91, 97, 99-102, 104-109, 111, 113-116, 119-121, 125-131, 133-134, 139-144, 162-163, 165-168, 170-200, 202-246, 248, 250-267, 271-272, 274-292, 294-296, 298-299, 301, 303-305, 307-322, 324-329, 331-351, 353-358

Service Callback 36

Service Component Architecture (SCA) 3, 15

Service Façade 35

Service Governance 35, 42, 241, 250, 254, 256, 258, 260, 262-263, 265-266

Service lifecycle 210, 212-218, 221-222, 225, 227-231, 235, 237-238, 240

Service Mediation 1, 8, 24, 34, 285

service normalization 241, 257

Service Oriented Architecture 2, 4, 15, 41, 43-44, 66-69, 72, 84, 166, 186, 188, 210, 242, 274-276, 294, 298, 336, 357

Service Pipeline 210, 223-224

service portfolio 8, 222, 226-228, 233, 241, 250

Service Registry 27, 60, 73, 127, 131, 167-168, 179, 182, 187, 218, 220-221, 229-230, 233, 236, 240, 255

Service Repository 109, 236

Service Versioning 1, 3, 13-15, 21, 36, 38, 212, 231, 236, 255

Simple Event Processing (SEP) 77

Simple Object Access Protocol (SOAP) 5, 51, 73, 171

Single-version 193

SOA Governance 50, 60, 73, 132, 210-218, 220-222, 224-228, 230-232, 236-240, 348

social application platform 22, 40

social media 1, 3, 5, 9, 22-24, 38, 40, 64, 82, 296

social network 22, 336

Software as a Service (SaaS) 23, 248, 292, 338

Software Constraints 301, 328

Space-redundancy 188, 193

T

task service 7

Testing efficiency 234

The Stovepipe Enterprise 276

Time-redundancy 188, 193

Time to Live (TTL) 71

transactional pattern 135-137, 140-141, 162

Twitter 9, 22, 40, 42, 280, 284

U

Universal Plug and Play (UPnP) 2, 166, 171, 173, 175, 185-186

utility computing 334-336, 359

utility data center 335

utility service 7-8

V

Vendor Diversification Options 275-278, 287, 292-293

Vendor Lock-in 275-276, 287, 294, 347

virtualization 37, 52, 65, 271, 334, 343-347, 350, 353, 359

vitality attribute 143

Volunteer Computing 335, 358

W

Waterfall methodology 210, 221

Web Hosting 335

Web-oriented architecture (WOA) 3

Web Service Policy (WS-Policy) 11-12, 18, 41, 171

Web Services Modeling Ontology (WSMO) 88

Widget 30-33

Wild West 23, 257, 259-260

Wires 17, 34

WordNet 91-92, 95, 98-100

workflow pattern 136, 141, 162, 164

Y

Yahoo Pipes 33